A TREASURY OF
GREAT PREACHING

VOLUME TWO

LUTHER

to

MASSILLON

1483–1742

A TREASURY OF GREAT PREACHING

VOLUME TWO

LUTHER
to
MASSILLON

1483–1742

CLYDE E. FANT, JR.
WILLIAM M. PINSON, JR.

DONALD E. HAMMER
Research Associate

WORD PUBLISHING
Dallas • London • Vancouver • Melbourne

A TREASURY OF GREAT PREACHING. Volume Two:
Luther to Massillon.

[Formerly, *20 CENTURIES OF GREAT PREACHING*]

Library of Congress Cataloging-in-Publication Data

Fant, Clyde E.
    [20 centuries of great preaching]
    A treasury of great preaching / Clyde E. Fant, Jr., William M.
Pinson, Jr.
    p.   cm.
    Originally published in 1971 under title: 20 centuries of great
preaching.
    Includes bibliographical references and indexes.
    ISBN 0-8499-5121-6
    1. Sermons. 2. Preaching—History.   I. Pinson, William M.
II. Title
BV4241.F34   1995

                            95-16191
                              CIP

Printed in the United States of America
5 6 7 8 9 0 1 2 3 4 QH 9 8 7 6 5 4 3 2 1

Special Thanks:

We are grateful to J. V. Howard, Librarian, New College Library, Edinburgh University, Edinburgh, Scotland, for his search for manuscript sermons of John Knox in New College Library and at the main University Library, and for recommending recent scholarly works on Knox; to Wayne Pipkin for his treatment of Zwingli's preaching and for his translation of Zwingli's sermons; and to the Kunstmuseum Winterthur for the picture of Zwingli's portrait.

Contents

Illustrations

Abbreviations of the Books of the Bible and Apocrypha

Old Testament	Authorized	Douay
Genesis	Gen.	Gen.
Exodus	Exod.	Exod.
Leviticus	Lev.	Lev.
Numbers	Num.	Num.
Deuteronomy	Deut.	Deut.
Joshua	Josh.	Josue
Judges	Judg.	Judges
Ruth	Ruth	Ruth
1 Samuel	1 Sam.	1 Kings
2 Samuel	2 Sam.	2 Kings
1 Kings	1 Kings	3 Kings
2 Kings	2 Kings	4 Kings
1 Chronicles	1 Chron.	1 Par.
2 Chronicles	2 Chron.	2 Par.
Ezra	Ezra	1 Esdras
Nehemiah	Neh.	2 Esdras
Esther	Esther	Esther
Job	Job	Job
Psalms	Ps.	Ps.
Proverbs	Prov.	Prov.
Ecclesiastes	Eccles.	Eccles.
Song of Solomon	Song of Sol.	Cant.
Isaiah	Isa.	Isa.
Jeremiah	Jer.	Jer.
Lamentations	Lam.	Lam.
Ezekiel	Ezek.	Ezech.
Daniel	Dan.	Dan.
Hosea	Hos.	Osee
Joel	Joel	Joel
Amos	Amos	Amos
Obadiah	Obad.	Abdias
Jonah	Jon.	Jon.
Micah	Mic.	Mich.

Old Testament	Authorized	Douay
Nahum	Nah.	Nah.
Habakkuk	Hab.	Hab.
Zephaniah	Zeph.	Soph.
Haggai	Hag.	Aggeus
Zechariah	Zech.	Zach.
Malachi	Mal.	Mal.

New Testament	Authorized and Douay	New Testament	Authorized and Douay
Matthew	Matt.	1 Timothy	1 Tim.
Mark	Mark	2 Timothy	2 Tim.
Luke	Luke	Titus	Titus
John	John	Philemon	Philem.
Acts of the Apostles	Acts	Hebrews	Heb.
Romans	Rom.	James	James
1 Corinthians	1 Cor.	1 Peter	1 Pet.
2 Corinthians	2 Cor.	2 Peter	2 Pet.
Galatians	Gal.	1 John	1 John
Ephesians	Eph.	2 John	2 John
Philippians	Phil.	3 John	3 John
Colossians	Col.	Jude	Jude
1 Thessalonians	1 Thess.	Revelation	Rev. (Apoc.)
2 Thessalonians	2 Thess.		

Apocrypha

The Wisdom of Solomon	Wisd.
Ecclesiasticus	Ecclus.

A TREASURY OF
GREAT PREACHING

VOLUME TWO

LUTHER

to

MASSILLON

1483–1742

MARTIN LUTHER

1483-1546

MARTIN LUTHER, print, courtesy of Augsburg Publishing House.

MARTIN LUTHER

MARTIN LUTHER HAS FEW EQUALS in Christian history. His versatility, devotion to Christian duty, courage, and widespread impact upon the world set him apart from most men. A translator of the Bible, an administrator, a composer of catechisms, a developer of liturgies, a preacher, an author, a family man, a professor, a theologian, a hymn writer, a citizen concerned about public affairs – the list of Luther's activities and achievements is staggering. Above all, he was a devout and pious man, deeply convinced of the truth of his views of the Christian faith.

Life and Times

Martin Luther was born on November 10, 1483, in Eisleben, Germany. His parents were devout peasants; in his home he received his first religious instruction. As a youngster he received his elementary education in the schools at Mansfeld, a town to which his parents had moved. In 1497 he journeyed to Magdeburg where he studied the teachings of the Brethren of the Common Life. After further tutoring and training, he attended the University of Erfurt where he distinguished himself as a scholar.

Luther floundered in determining what vocation to enter. Under some parental pressure, he headed in the direction of law. In 1505 a narrow escape from death caused Luther to change his mind. During a frightening thunderstorm he flung himself down in the road and cried, "St. Anne, help me! I will become a monk!"[1] He entered an Augustinian monastery in Erfurt where he pursued monastic life with vigor and gladly accepted the supervision of his superior, Johann von Staupitz. In 1506 he was consecrated a monk and in 1507 ordained a priest.

A visit to Rome in 1510 in behalf of his order deeply affected the young monk. He journeyed toward the center of the Christian religion with anticipation of the spiritual blessing he would receive there. But he found the city corrupt and the religious life of the people dominated by superstition. The Roman priests privately ridiculed the church and the Mass. He was shocked by priests who tricked the people by saying, "Bread thou art, and bread thou shalt remain. . . ."[2] Deeply troubled, Luther returned to his study and teaching.

He had entered the monastery to find religious peace; he found only further torment. Though he rigorously followed the discipline of the order, he found no satisfaction. His sins troubled him greatly. He thrashed about for answers to his doubt and found none. He came more and more to hate God and to see him only as a vengeful judge. He eagerly pursued his study of the Bible; in his religious life only the Scripture gave him comfort. The Book of Romans and the Book of Galatians particularly impressed and engrossed him. He was finding in-

---

1. Roland Bainton, *Here I Stand: A Life of Martin Luther* (New York: Abingdon Press, 1950), p. 34.
2. Ibid., p. 50.

creasing dissatisfaction with many doctrines of the Roman Catholic church but had no concrete ideas of his own to substitute for them.

In 1512 Luther received the Doctor of Theology degree from the University of Erfurt and began to lecture at the University of Wittenberg. As a professor of theology he continued his diligent biblical studies. Between 1512 and 1517 his fame as a lecturer and preacher spread throughout the area around Wittenberg. He communicated well the truth of the Scripture to the common people and they eagerly gathered to hear him.

During these years of teaching and studying, Luther became convinced of the error of many doctrines and practices of the Roman Catholic church. He was particularly offended by the emphasis upon salvation by sacraments and works. He found support for his views from various sources — Occam's school of theology, Augustine's writings, Paul's letters, and the mysticism of his own country.

By 1517 the basic framework of Protestant theology had been developed by Luther. He was convinced of at least three points: (1) A man is justified by faith alone and not by works. (2) Each believer has access to God directly apart from any human intermediaries. (3) The Bible is the supreme source of authority for both faith and life.

The sale of indulgences by the Roman Catholic church was particularly nauseating to Luther. During this early period of his ministry, funds were being raised to build St. Peter's in Rome; one of the means of fund raising was the selling of indulgences. When the indulgence seller arrived in Wittenberg, Luther was so angry that he felt he could no longer contain his views privately. He therefore posted on the church door at Wittenberg Ninety-five Theses setting forth his position and his objections to certain practices and doctrines of the church. This was not throwing down the gauntlet to the pope: Luther planned no revolt and wanted no fight with the pope. His posting of the theses on the church door was not a particularly dramatic move. It was customary for professors to post theses for debate in the manner which Luther employed.

The impact of his act, however, was dramatic. Like a ricocheting bullet, word of Luther's stand spread throughout Germany. Soon the high ranking officials of the Roman Catholic church had heard of it and were concerned. Some Catholic officials dismissed Luther with the snide remark, "He is merely a drunken German"; others felt that Luther was a brash young theologian who needed only to be shown the truth to alter his position. Luther thoroughly enjoyed his beer, but his theses were not the product of a drunken mind. And though Luther was young (only thirty-four at the time of the posting of the theses), he was no ordinary young professor. He was devout, brilliant, popular, and deeply convinced of his position.

Event succeeded event in dizzying rapidity. Luther was charged with heresy. Debates were held on his position. He was driven further and further away from the Catholic church and there seemed to be no compromise possible. Though he apparently had intended no revolution, he began the most significant revolution in the history of the Christian movement.

In 1520 he acted dramatically to demonstrate his defiance of the pope and burned a papal bull issued against him. Intensifying the situation even further, he did his burning amidst the cheers of the local populace and with the toleration of the local government. In fact, if it had not been for the support of the people and the toleration of his own political rulers, Luther would have been merely another burned heretic smoldering on the landscape of Europe. Fortunately Luther had the backing of his own local prince, Frederick the Wise, Elector of Saxony.

Frederick supported Luther for several reasons. For one thing, he was proud of the fame of his young professor; he was not interested in his being silenced. Further, Luther had appealed not only to religious sentiment but also to political resentment. The Germans resented the power wielded over them by the Italian-dominated Roman Catholic church. They felt that huge sums of money were drained from Germany into Italy. Luther appealed to German pride and nationalism. Because Luther had the backing of Frederick, the pope was reluctant to use extreme measures against him.

That Luther was so long allowed to publicly advocate his position without papal interference can only be understood in the light of the political situation at the time. On January 12, 1519, the Emperor of the Holy Roman Empire, Maximilian, died. The office of the emperor was an elective one; any European prince was eligible. The majority of electors were German princes, but they realized that no German ruler had enough strength to sustain the office of the emperor. The choice, therefore, was between Francis of France and Charles of Spain. The pope was not happy with either of these choices: papal security depended upon a balance of power between France and Spain. Therefore the pope threw his support to Frederick of Saxony. But Frederick defeated himself by voting for Charles of Spain, who became Charles V of the Holy Roman Empire. Even so, the pope could not afford to antagonize Frederick; he still remained the pivotal figure in Germany. And Luther remained under his protection.

Meanwhile, Charles V was in no position to undertake strong measures against Luther. He was involved in Spanish affairs and Germany was a long way from Spain. Further, the religious squabble in Germany interested the new emperor very little.

Yet something had to be done about the German situation. In the Diet of Worms, which met in 1521, Luther was summoned to defend his position. He refused to back down from his stand and was put under the ban of the emperor. Though Luther had the support of the people, Frederick feared for his life. He arranged for Luther to be taken to Wartburg Castle and kept there for security.

In seclusion, Luther maintained his vigorous activity. His most noteworthy accomplishment during his confinement was the translation of the New Testament into German. This translation has been recognized as a classic. It did much to mold the nature of the German language.

When it was safe to come out of hiding, Luther finally returned to Wittenberg and there continued to direct his reform. It became apparent that a new church had to be organized. Luther and his associates developed catechisms, a new form of church government, and revised liturgies.

In the midst of these busy activities he had little time for romance. In fact, as a monk, he felt that it would probably be wrong for him to marry. His position on marriage gradually changed, and in 1525 he married Katherine von Bora. The marriage, which seemed to have so little to commend it in the beginning, developed into a beautiful example of Christian home life. In many ways Luther was a crude and coarse man, but he developed a deep affection for Katherine. His love for his children was profound; the letters from Luther to them are touching in sentiment.

Luther's remaining years were devoted to consolidating the gains of the Reformation. He steered a middle course and refused to be drawn back into the system of the Roman Catholic church. But he also refused to move in radical ways. In many of his attitudes he was quite conservative.

Luther not only spoke and wrote concerning theological issues, but he also gave careful attention to social issues. Because he depended so much on the German princes, political affairs were of great concern to him. Many of his most famous writings deal with the relation of government to church, the responsibility of princes, war, and the duties of citizens. He also wrote volumes of material concerning family life and economic affairs. The titles of the following essays indicate his concern for practical affairs: "Secular Authority: To What Extent It Should Be Obeyed"; "Whether Soldiers, Too, Can Be Saved"; "Address to the German Nobilities"; "On Usury"; "Instructions for the Organization of the Community Chest."

By modern standards Luther was no saint: he was impetuous, rough, and sometimes crude. When his anger was aroused, he issued shockingly harsh statements. Concerning the peasants' revolt, he said, "Therefore, let everyone who can, smite, slay, and stab, secretly or openly, remembering that nothing can be more poisonous, hurtful, or devilish than a rebel."[3] Appalled by the excesses of the Anabaptists, he recommended their execution. Outraged by the lack of response of the Jews to reformed Christianity, he advocated that all the Jews be deported to Palestine; if they could not be driven out of the land, Luther advocated that their synagogues should be burned, their books taken away from them, and the practice of usury denied them so that they would be compelled to earn their living from the land. His attacks on the pope were utterly unrestrained, many of them vulgar and tasteless.

Yet his accomplishments add up to indisputable greatness. He had a profound effect upon his nation, the Christian church, and upon religious life in general. He left a rich heritage of writing and doctrine. His hymns, especially "A Mighty Fortress Is Our God," inspire men today. After hundreds of years Martin Luther still shakes the world.

PREACHING AND SERMONS

The preaching of Martin Luther was like his life — vigorous, blunt, creative. The prodigious courage that challenged both pope and emperor, the crudeness of an earthy age, the stubborn

---

3. Ibid., p. 280.

dogmatisms of a convinced debater, and the warmth of a genuine human being: all of these traits which characterized the life of Martin Luther also appeared in his preaching.

It is hard to imagine the thunderous Luther as ever being afraid, but apparently his first experience at preaching terrified him: "Oh, how I trembled when I was ascending the pulpit for the first time! I would feign have excused myself, but they made me preach." Yet even these early efforts at preaching attracted attention.

While at the University of Wittenberg Luther began to preach on such practical subjects as the Ten Commandments, the Lord's Prayer, repentance, and the true life, but Luther admitted later that he really did not understand the Christian life or the meaning of the cross at that time. Even then, however, his sermons won a good hearing because of the perceptive way in which they treated the spiritual nature of his hearers. Other preachers of the time seemed to deal only with the outward ceremonies and formal doctrines of the church; Luther's sermons, by way of contrast, were directed at the hearts of his hearers, and many of them struck home.

Through his study of the Scripture – probably in the Book of Romans – Luther came to preach more and more on salvation by justification through faith, and less and less on salvation through the works of penance. After the breach with the Roman church became complete, Luther's preaching centered about the doctrine of justification by faith. His plain preaching on this doctrine shook the foundations of the Roman church throughout Germany.

Luther held definite views on the preaching of the Word, which he presented during his talks with young students. He regarded preaching as the central part of public worship and even placed the preaching of the Word above the reading of it. He considered the great subject of preaching to be the "glory of God in Jesus Christ." One question, and one question alone, determined Luther's judgment on a sermon: did it deal with Christ? If it did not, or if it treated him lightly, then the sermon were better not preached. Therefore most of Luther's sermons came from the Gospels; the Epistles occupied far less of his attention and preaching.

In almost every sermon Luther dealt with the moral duty of man to act, but he also laid great stress upon the spiritual nature of man – which nature, as he defined it, was that impulse which led an individual to understand his duty to act in moral ways.

His preaching strongly emphasized the necessity of works growing out of an inner faith. Luther opposed the extreme emphasis
upon works which led to legalism as practiced by the Roman
church; he also opposed the extreme emphasis on the "inner
light" which led some Anabaptists to claim direct communication from God.

Luther's expositions in preaching varied from greatly detailed studies to highly generalized essays, but seldom did he
strain the meaning of a passage or indulge in allegory. He regarded the context of a passage as important to the meaning of
a text and sought to discover the original intent of the biblical
author. Luther never attempted to display his learning. He kept
his sermons as simple as possible. Since he believed that the
preacher should motivate people as well as increase their understanding, he both taught and exhorted in his sermons.

Luther made an issue of simplicity and clearness in sermon
style. He was ultimately concerned with whether or not the
people had understood him and were able to apply to their
lives what they had heard. He spoke all of his sermons in the
language of the common people. In fact, much of his language
was *so* common that it has been regarded by some as crude, not
to say vulgar. But there was never any doubt about what he
meant. Luther never sought pulpit eloquence, which would
have been little appreciated anyhow; instead, he preached to
plain people in plain language:

> When a man comes into the pulpit for the first time, he
> is much perplexed by the number of heads before him.
> When I ascend the pulpit I see no heads, but imagine
> those that are before me to be all blocks. When I preach
> I sink myself deeply down; I regard neither doctors nor
> masters of which there are in the church above forty.
> But I have an eye for the multitude of young people,
> children, and servants, of which there are more than two
> thousand. I preach to them. I direct my discourse to
> those that have need of it.
> A preacher should be a logician and a rhetorician—
> that is, he must be able to teach and admonish. When he
> preaches on any article, he must first distinguish it, then
> define, describe and show what it is; thirdly, he must
> produce sentences from the Scripture to prove and
> strengthen it; fourthly, he must explain it by example;
> fifthly, he must adorn it with similitudes; and lastly, he

must admonish and arouse the indolent, correct the disobedient, and reprove the authors of false doctrine.[4]

In following this method of development, Luther seldom prepared anything like an introduction or conclusion to his sermons — he believed the body of the message to be the only important part of the sermon. He followed the form of a simple homily, interpreting and applying the Scripture as he progressed. Each of his sermons included in this study reveal his careful attention to the text.

Dargan singles out three characteristics which distinguished these sermons from those of Luther's predecessors: they were marked by right interpretation and application of Scripture; they preached Christ alone as Savior; they proclaimed union with him by faith as the only way of salvation.[5] To appreciate these sermons today, they must be read in the context of the Reformation. Compared with other sermons of the period, they are easy to follow and fascinating to read.

The following sermons by Luther display different facets of his personality: his coarseness, his ability as a dogmatic debater, his theological genius, and his rare preaching gifts — including passages of unusual beauty and warmth.

But who would even attempt to summarize Martin Luther? No selection of his sermons could typify Luther any more than a collection of adjectives could define him. Perhaps this group of sermons will at least suggest the versatility and genius of the great reformer.

---

4. Harwood Pattison, *The History of Christian Preaching* (Philadelphia: American Baptist Publication Society, 1903), pp. 136–37.
5. Edwin Charles Dargan, *A History of Preaching*, 2 vols. (Grand Rapids, Mich.: Baker Book House), 1:390.

Sermons

SERMON ON SOBERNESS
AND MODERATION

1 Peter 4:7-11, May 18, 1539

This sermon, preached in the parish church of Wittenberg on the Epistle for Exaudi Sunday, in which Luther deals head-on with a social question of his day, is remarkable for its non-legalistic treatment of the subject. The title given above is that of the printed version which appeared in Augsburg (without date, but not before 1542). Three texts are given in the Weimar edition: Rörer's transcript, Stoltz's transcript, and the printed version which is Aurifaber's based on Rörer's notes. The Rörer transcript forms the basis of this translation, with occasional references to the other two versions.

THIS PART of [the first] Epistle [of Peter] is an exhortation to good conduct. Those who are Christians are to see to it that they are grateful for grace and redemption and conduct themselves modestly, moderately, and soberly, so that one does not go on living the swinish life that goes on in the filthy world. For this Epistle was written to the Greeks, who were great high livers. In those regions there was gluttony just as in Germany today.

Where one can find sermons which will stop the Germans from swilling I do not know. We might just as well have kept silent altogether. Christ says that the coming last day will come upon men unawares and snatch them away (Luke 21 [:35]), and Paul says the same thing in 1 Thess. 5 [:2], and also the prophets likewise. The Italians call us gluttonous, drunken Germans and pigs because they live decently and do not drink until they are drunk. Like the Spaniards, they have escaped this vice. Among the Turks it is really the worst sin for a man to be drunk. So temperate are they that they do not even drink anything which inebriates. That is why they can make war and

Reprinted from Martin Luther, *Sermons I*, Luther's Works, vol. 51, trans. John W. Doberstein (Philadelphia: Fortress Press, 1959), pp. 291–99. Used by permission.

win; while we drunken sows sleep they keep awake, and thus can consider their strategy and then attack and conquer. When the time comes for us to defend ourselves and be prepared, we get drunk. This has become so widespread that there is no help for it; it has become a settled custom.

At first it was the peasants who drank to excess, then it spread to the citizens. In my time it was considered a great shame among the nobility. Now they are worse than the citizens and peasants; now those who are the greatest and best are beginning to fall, indeed, even the princes; and among those who are the ablest it has become a noble and princely virtue. Now the ten-year-old milksops, and the students, too, are beginning, and ruining themselves in their flower; when the corn should be growing and flourishing it is beaten down by a storm. We preach, but who stops it? Those who should stop it do it themselves; the princes even more. Therefore Germany is a land of hogs and a filthy people which debauches its body and its life. If you were going to paint it, you would have to paint a pig.

Some spark of sobriety may remain among young children, virgins, and women, though underneath one finds pigs among them too. However, there remains some bit of decency, for it is still said that it is especially shameful for a woman to be drunken. The Turks have this teaching, which is a fine thing, and the Italians too. Among us it is considered most shameful. But if it ill becomes the children and young women, so that we say that such should be trampled under foot, how much more should not this be so of married women and particularly men, who should be wiser and more virtuous, since the woman is the weaker vessel [1 Pet. 3:7] and the man has more strength and reason? Therefore they should do this even less, and therefore, according to reason, it is a far more shameful thing for men to drink to excess than for women. It might be said in defense of woman that she is foolish and has not such a strong body, and therefore drink affects her more quickly. But this is not so of the man, who is stronger than the woman.

This gluttony and swilling is inundating us like an ocean and among the Spaniards, Italians, and English it is reprehended. We are the laughingstock of all other countries, who look upon us as filthy pigs; and not only upon private persons, but upon nobles and princes also, as if that were the reason why they bear the coat of arms. We would not forbid this; it is possible to tolerate a little elevation, when a man takes a drink or two too much after working hard and when he is feeling low. This must be called a frolic. But to sit day and night, pouring it in and pouring it out again, is piggish. This is not a human way of living, not to say Christian, but rather a pig's life.

What, therefore, shall we do? The secular government does not forbid it, the princes do nothing about it, and the rulers in the cities do nothing at all but wink at it and do the same themselves. We preach and the Holy Scriptures teach us otherwise; but you want to evade what is taught. Eating and drinking are not forbidden, but rather all food is a matter of freedom, even a modest drink for one's pleasure. If you do not wish to conduct yourself this way, if you are going to go beyond this and be a born pig and guzzle beer and wine, then, if this cannot be stopped by the rulers, you must know that you cannot be saved. For God will not admit such piggish drinkers into the kingdom of heaven [cf. Gal. 5:19–21]. It is no wonder that all of you are beggars. How much money might not be saved! Twenty years ago this was considered among the princes to be a shameful vice. If we do not watch out, it will become common among virgins and women. Therefore I am utterly terrified by that word of the Lord concerning gluttony: ["Take heed to yourselves lest your hearts be weighed down with dissipation and drunkenness and cares of this life, and that day come upon you suddenly like a snare" (Luke 21:34)].

Listen to the Word of God, which says, "Keep sane and sober," that it may not be said to you in vain. You must not be pigs; neither do such belong among Christians. So also in 1 Cor. 6 [:9–10]: No drunkard, whoremonger, or adulterer can be saved. Do not think that you are saved if you are a drunken pig day and night. This is a great sin, and everybody should know that this is such a great iniquity, that it makes you guilty and excludes you from eternal life. Everybody should know that such a sin is contrary to his baptism and hinders his faith and his salvation.

Therefore, if you wish to be a Christian, take care that you control yourself. If you do not wish to be saved, go ahead and steal, rob, profiteer as long as you can, but fear Jack Ketch and the magistrates. But if you do want to be saved, then listen to this: just as adultery and idolatry close up heaven, so does gluttony; for Christ says very clearly: Take heed "lest your hearts be weighed down with dissipation and drunkenness and cares of this life, and that day come upon you suddenly" [Luke 21:34], "as the lightning comes from the east and shines as far as the west" [Matt. 24:27]. Therefore be watchful and sober. That is what is preached to us, who want to be Christians.

You parents must help to see to it that your children do not begin too early to fall into this vice. Reason, which God gives to princes and nobles [as an instrument by which to rule, will not accomplish this]; it leads a person downwards; it is a pig. A drunkard is not dissuaded from his drinking by reason any more than a murderer, an adulterer, whoremonger, or usurer; therefore you will not be moved by the reasons that excessive drinking weakens the constitution, consumes money and goods, and causes the Italians, Turks, and the English to spit upon us. What should move you is that God forbids it on pain of damnation and loss of the kingdom of heaven. A ruler cannot punish a greedy-gut, so the whole world is greedy and thus is entangled in the cares of this life [Luke 8:14; 12:34], simply because it goes unpunished; in fact, is even praised. People say it should not be called a sin because it is not punished; they say it is like greed, usury, etc. Very well, go ahead and drink yourself full as a hog, nobody will punish you. If I were not so ill I would like to write a treatise on this matter; perhaps it would move a few people anyhow.

We ought to give thanks to God for providing us with food and drink and then besides, liberating us from the papacy, and feeding us with food and drink. If you are tired and downhearted, take a drink; but this does not mean being a pig and doing nothing but gorging and swilling. It is now becoming a custom even in evangelical cities to establish taprooms; a donkey goes in, pays a penny [*Groschen*], and drinks the whole day long; and the government does nothing about it. These taverns are necessary, of course, even a pious custom. They might better have built money changers' shops. Just because the magistrates and princes do not denounce and punish these vices, we shall not fail to perform our office and remind each one of his office. If we are aware of what is going on we know that such persons should be excluded from all the sacraments and will make it public, just as we would in the case of a murderer. You should be moderate and sober; this means that we should not be drunken, though we may be exhilarated.

Further on in chapter five, Peter states the reason why it is necessary for us to be sober. Why? In order to be able to pray; and this is necessary because we have an adversary, the devil, "who prowls around like a roaring lion, seeking someone to devour" [1 Pet. 5:8]. He seeks, but how does he do so? He is like a wolf circling a sheepfold. What Peter is saying is this: because you are a people who have been called to the post in which you must be on the watch against sin and against the devil and his messengers, who are seeking our souls more greedily than that wolf, therefore you must defend yourself with the Word and with prayer, not only for yourselves but the whole world. You are priests, etc. But when a man is drunk his reason is buried, his tongue and all his members are incapable of praying; he is a drunken pig and the devil has devoured him. Then the devil is occupying his members.

The early Christians went almost too far in this matter of prayer. In the time after the apostles the bishops with great diligence instituted the morning and evening prayers which are called matins and compline. They practiced this custom steadily and rigorously, some of them so strenuously as Augustine says, that they did not eat for three or four days. They were overdoing it. Nevertheless, they went to prayer morning and evening. But later, abuse corrupted this custom; later came the monks, who do not pray but only babble prayers. But we have established the schools in order that morning and evening prayers may be held morning and evening. This we are obliged to do.

God does not forbid you to drink, as do the Turks; he permits you to drink wine and beer; he does not make a law of it. But do not make a pig of yourself; remain a human being. If you are a human being, then keep your human self-control. Even though we do not have a command of God, we should nevertheless be ashamed that we are thus spit upon by other peoples. If you want to be a Christian, do not argue in this way: Nobody reproaches me, therefore God does not reproach me. So it has been from the time of Noah [Gen. 9:21]. And so it was with the Sodomites, who wanted to rape the angels; they were all so drunk they could not find the door [Gen. 19:11]. Sodom and Gomorrah perished because of a flood of drunkenness; this vice was punished. God does not tolerate such confusion and inordinate use of his creatures [i.e., food and drink].

The mind will tolerate a certain degree of elevation, but this must be moderate, not indecent. Here sobriety signifies not merely abstaining from drunkenness, but also moderation in all things, respectability in dress, ornamentation, gait, and conduct in the whole of life in general.

If you have been a pig, then stop being one. Augustine said: I have known many who were drunkards and then ceased being drunkards. But you are today just as you were yesterday and you go on thinking that it is not a sin.

"Sane" means that we should be alert and sensible, in order that we may be enlightened by the Word of God and not be drunken pigs, in order that we may be ready for prayer. "Sober" means that we should not overload the body, and it applies to excess in outward gestures, clothing, ornament, or whatever kind of pomp it may be, such as we have at baptisms and the churching of women. There is no moderation in these things. When there is a wedding or a dance you always have to go to excess. Christmas and Pentecost mean nothing but beer. Christians should not walk around so bedizened that one hardly knows whether one is looking at a man or a beast. We Christians ought to be examples. We Germans are especially swamped in this vice. The Italians and the Turks far surpass us in moderation. The Turk should be put to shame by us and he should be the one to say: They do not overeat, overdrink, and overdress. But actually the tables are turned; they are the ones who give us an example in clothing, etc. They have their peculiar vices, too, of course; and they are really abominable; but in this they are far more temperate than we are. We are a shame to heaven and earth; we do harm to both body and mind.

"Above all." This could well be a sermon in itself. You have been called to love one another. People today, peasants, citizens, and nobles, go on living in hatred and envy, so that none will give another even a piece of bread; they will commit any kind of rascality so long as they can deny it. If you want to be saved, you must possess the red dress which is here described. You have put on the vestment. You are white as snow [Isa. 1:18], pure from all sins. But you must wear this red dress and color now, and remember to love your neighbor. Moreover, it should be a fervent love, not a pale-red love, not the love which is easily provoked to revenge [1 Cor. 13:5]. It should be a strong color, a brown-red love, which is capable not only of doing good toward your neighbor but is also able to bear all malice from him [1 Cor. 13:4, 7]. For this is the way sins are covered, even a multitude, a heap, a sea, a forest of sins. How does it do this? It does not mean my sin in the way the pope interprets this, i.e., whenever I love God and my neighbor then I blot out my sins. No. It is another's love, namely, Christ's love, which has covered my sins, as Peter says in chapter two: He bore them in his body on the cross and erased them completely [1 Pet. 2:24]. This is said with regard to your sins, the sins you commit against me and I against you.

In Christianity it must not happen that one person should hurt another, in the same way that the members of the body, the teeth, tongue, toes, fingers, hands, eyes, touch each other without hurting each other. It is true, of course, that even among Christians life does not go on without offenses being committed. You have only to look at husband and wife in the family. Sometimes a word is uttered or something is done which angers the husband or the wife. But when this is done to a neighbor, then gestures are made which make people angry and the man's relatives come seeking revenge and are not satisfied until the offense has been repaid tenfold. Therefore you must have a strong love, which is best able to cover up sins.

Also consider what Solomon said: "Hatred stirs up strife, but love covers all offenses" [Prov. 10:12]. This is how you should deal with your neighbor. If you do not do this, He will remove his cover. This is what Paul means when he says, "Bear one another's burdens, and so fulfil the law of Christ" [Gal. 6:2]. It is a grievous thing whenever a neighbor has a wife who quarrels. But the Holy Spirit has sanctified you through faith and given you love, in order that you may bear with others. Christ has borne your sins, in order that you may bear with the sins of others.

So in worldly affairs, too; one rubs against the other. Here, too, you must not become angry and be ready to do harm. Rather be content if someone possesses the same thing you have and do not be envious. If anybody speaks against you, you say: May God forgive him. If you do, then there is no love.

The head of a household must punish and should not tolerate evil. But he must not be hateful and vengeful, lest in this way he corrupt the other person. A father does not punish his son in order to make him spiteful and ruin him in body and soul, but rather to ward off his vice; he wants to purify him and wipe away his faults. He hates, not the person, but the vice. This is a wrathful love which is kind and good toward the person; hence it cannot tolerate the nastiness in him. So, too, a woman cannot bear it when there is dirt on her child's nose, but must wipe it away; she does not do this in order to hurt the child.

Magistrates, teachers, and parents must chastise, but this chastisement is fatherly and kindly.

Solomon said, "Faithful are the wounds of a friend; profuse are the kisses of an enemy" [Prov. 27:6]. When an enemy speaks kindly to you, this is not affection, but rather the devil, who is out to destroy you in your sins. Ah, he says, you're doing fine; go ahead! But a friend will be willing to hurt you. This is a rod, but it comes from the heart of a friend.

Up to this point he has been speaking of being patient and bearing with our neighbor. He now goes on to speak of whoever receives a gift. ["As each has received a gift, employ it for one another, as good stewards of God's varied grace" (1 Pet. 4:10)]. If you speak, do so as one who speaks the Word of God. If you have an office, perform it as one who knows that it is of God. There is no nobler work than that of being a parent, a preacher, or a magistrate. If you are a husband, a preacher, or a magistrate, learn not so say: Oh, if I were that fellow; he has the silver chain. Rather look to the station to which you have been called. If you are a preacher, a husband, a magistrate, you do not do what you do as a human work. There Peter has nailed the pope's hands to the cross, so that I need preach nothing but the Word of God. The preacher teaches the church and parents teach their children; they guide the family in upright conduct and command that which is God's commandment. A master does not say: Commit adultery, etc., but rather: Do no injury to me or to others, in order that all things may be governed as of God. Likewise a magistrate does not command stealing, but what is beneficial to the city and the common welfare. Thus we may know with certainty that it is a divine work and that this is God's Word. And nobody should undertake to do anything unless he knows with certainty that he can say: Here is the Word of God. A servant should think in this way: I am not obeying a man, but God. It is not the parents who are honored by their children, but God, Christ. Likewise, if you despise parents, magistrates, preaching, you are really despising God. The pope preached the opposite; he preached that children should leave the parental home and go into the monastery; husbands even deserted their wives. The Anabaptists are also preaching something different and new. Whenever you hear me, you hear not me, but Christ. I do not give you my baptism, my body and blood; I do not absolve you. But he that has an office, let him administer that office in such a way that he is certain that it comes from God and does everything according to the Word of God, not according to our free will. Very much needs to be preached concerning this to check the abuses which the devil has introduced. When everything that is said and done is said and done in accord with God's Word, then the glory of Christ and God will be done to all eternity.

THE THIRD SUNDAY AFTER TRINITY

"Likewise, ye younger submit yourselves unto the elder. Yea, all of you be subject one to another, and be clothed with humility: for God resisteth the proud, and giveth grace to the humble. Humble yourselves therefore under the mighty hand of God, that he may exalt you in due time: Casting all your care upon him; for he careth for you. Be sober, be vigilant; because your adversary the devil, as a roaring lion, walketh about, seeking whom he may devour: Whom resist steadfast in the faith, knowing that the same afflictions are accomplished in your brethren that are in the world. But the God of all grace, who hath called us unto his eternal glory by Christ Jesus, after that ye have suffered a while, make you perfect, establish, strengthen, settle you. To him be glory and dominion for ever and ever. Amen" (1 Peter 5:5–11).

THIS IS THE LAST PART and conclusion of this Epistle of St. Peter. But it is also *an exhortation to good works,* which a Christian or believer must possess and practice; so that it may be seen and known that the doctrine of the Gospel, is not such a doctrine, as has been represented, that it forbids good works, or does not earnestly require and enjoin them; but that this doctrine demands most abundantly the works, which are really good works. And especially are there enumerated in this Epistle; *four* particular points, which also furnish matter for four good sermons.

The first, concerning humility.

The Apostle had immediately before exhorted the elders, that is, the ministers and preachers who are to govern the Church, how with their lives they should be ensamples to the flock, and not elevate themselves above their office, as though they were lords over them, but therewith to serve others. So he now here also exhorts other men, especially the young, that they be subject to the elder; and in general, that all should, among each other, be humble, and, as St. Paul says, "In honor preferring one another." For this is the best and most admirable quality of love, and the most necessary to preserve peace and order among the people; and especially does it adorn, and well become, the young, rendering them beloved and worthy before God and man, bringing many good fruits.

Reprinted from *Dr. Martin Luther's Church-Postil: Sermons on the Epistles* . . . , vol. 2 (New Market, Va.: New Market Evangelical Lutheran Publishing Co., 1869), pp. 29–50.

And if we could prevail with the people to believe this, so that this virtue would prevail, it would go well everywhere, and there would be seen an excellent and beautiful world, full of good works; so that I would rather see a town where the young are brought up in virtue, than one hundred cloisters of mendicant and Carthusian Friars, although they should live in the strictest manner. There is now, alas! everywhere the greatest and most general complaint concerning the disobedience, and violence, and pride of the young, and in general of all conditions; wherefore it were necessary, with all diligence to implant and urge this exhortation particularly among the young, if perhaps, it might do some good.

And in the first place St. Peter places before us the command of God, so that we may know it is not an arbitrary work, which is left to our own choice, but that God positively enjoins it upon us, and that we are to perform it with love and cheerfulness, or else incur his wrath; and no success nor grace shall we enjoy among the people. For pride and haughtiness are hated by every one, denounced by all the world, even by strangers whom it may not concern.

Yea, although a man be engulfed in vice, insensible to his own shame, yet he cannot tolerate this same vice in others, but will hate it and condemn it. And this vice injures no one but yourself. By it you make yourself hostile to God, and contemptible before him and before man; and yet the infamy of being called by every one coarse, proud, impure, contemptible, you must incur; and God will permit such infamy and disgrace to come upon you, in order that you may see that he will not permit such a vice to go unpunished, but will bring it to shame as St. Peter here says: "God resisteth the proud, etc."

And truly, the examples which daily present before our eyes the fulfillment of this passage, should move the people. For should you even disregard your honor and reputation with the world, or, on the other hand, the contempt and execration of all men, which indeed should move you most profoundly, if you had the least spark of Christian principle in you; and should not the glorious example of the exalted being and eternal majesty of the Son of God, our Lord, attract you when you witness his humility, unspeakable and beyond all human thought and understanding, before which a Christian heart should melt, if it would contemplate it adequately: if all this does not move you, then certainly the many terrible examples of the wrath of God, wherewith from the beginning he has overthrown the pride of man and angels, should humble you.

What is more terrible than the eternal and irretrievable fall and banishment of the exalted, angelic nature, when Satan disrobed himself of the honor and glory of pure and blessed spirits, and of the eternal vision of God, and brought upon himself an eternal and insufferable condemnation, because he tried to make himself equal with God, and in the same indulgence of pride brought man also to a miserable fall? But what blind and execrable human beings are ye, who with your odious pride and haughtiness, make yourselves resemble that malignant spirit whereby you incur the enmity of all the world, and presumptuously array yourself against the Divine Majesty itself, before whom even the angels tremble? If you will not be afraid and terrified that you will lose the favor and benevolent prayers of all men, then be afraid that God has placed over your head his lightning and thunder, with which he crushes battlements of iron, the rocks, and the mountains, and that he will hurl you into the abyss forever, just as he cast that proud spirit with his angels.

Therefore, St. Peter exhorts both those who are in the office of the ministry and other Christians, who possess something given them from God, that they abide by their calling and office, and discharge the same in humility, and willingly hear and serve others. For, this vice is most pernicious to Christians; for their entire government, life, and well-being are so ordered of God, that no one is to aspire to be over, and to elevate himself above others, like the Pope as a true Antichrist has done in his government; but there are to be among Christians in all conditions, offices, and services, exclusively humility, and works of Christian love and service.

Pride, in Christian government, is directly and especially contrary to the first Table. It is really the haughtiness of Satan, on the part of such people, against the name and word of God, – people who profess to be wise in matters of faith, and able to master the word of God. They pompously exalt themselves, when they have a gift a little above others, regarding God himself and all men as nothing. For this vice generally belongs to the great, learned, and wise bishops, and to those who learn from them, who adhere to them, especially those who are promoted while still in their novitiate, still untrained and inexperienced, and on this very account, boast and puff themselves up. I am also a learned Doctor, and have the spirit and other gifts, even more than these preachers; and yet we must hear and honor them above all others! Aye, indeed, they know themselves to be so wise, and all others in comparison to them mere geese and fools. – And the greater the talent, the more injurious is this vanity. It often happens in the profession of other arts; when a man knows a little of something, or if he be called a Doctor, he boasts of it, he despises others, as if what he now possesses were not the gift of God, but were inborn with him, and therefore he must be praised and honored by every one; and he has no idea that in this way he acts in opposition to God; and he will more likely plunge himself into the abyss of hell, than fall from heaven.

Look at the examples of our times, how God has overthrown such people! Thomas Munzer with tumultuous prophets, and afterwards the rabble of Anabaptists, were also proud at heart, and would not hear when any thing was said to them; and they were admonished until they were all suddenly ruined, not only with deepest infamy, but also to the extreme and lasting injury of themselves and many people whom they had deceived. Of such haughty spirits there are many at present, and also many who dare not yet manifest themselves. — They have discovered that they are learned, or are otherwise esteemed by the people in points on which they take great pride, and thus remain destitute of the spirit and its fruits, with their skill and learning, if they do not otherwise do great injury, in addition to this, that in this way they condemn themselves.

Thus it happens under various gifts and offices, when there is no humility, no fear of God. Here, those who are to govern as princes, counsellors, and jurists, if they are not also theologians, that is, Christians, and the like, are so proud and insolent, that they imagine themselves to be the only people on earth, and to be esteemed as gods; yet in their pride they despise God and man, and by this presumption they lead the people and the country into misfortune. These have already received their sentence, that they, as enemies of God, must be overthrown; for they have excluded themselves from the kingdom and grace of God, and on them Baptism and Christ, with his sufferings and blood, are lost.

This is the excess of pride against the first Table, when men do not use their spiritual gifts and treasures to the honor of God, and the benefit of their neighbors, and thus become ruined both before God and the people, and in this way fall into the hands of the devil, like unto whom they have now become. In the next place, in reference to the second Table, this vice is equally as prevalent among people in the ordinary condition and concerns of the world, where each man exalts himself and contemns others. Princes and noblemen think that all the world is nothing in comparison to themselves; and then the inhabitants of cities and country gentlemen, who bluster and swell because they have many florins, and think they have a right to defy every body, and do no good to any one, deserve to be despised by every one. And, indeed, such pride becomes them no better than the ornaments of gold and silver become a stone or a wooden block. — And lastly, are the women also, with their foolish pride concerning their raiment, because one perhaps is adorned more beautifully, or more sumptuously than another; what is she but a goose well decorated, who thinks there is no one equal to her? Yea, there is scarcely a hostler, or a maid servant, who does not wish to claim superiority over others.

And in short, it has come to such a pass that each one wishes to move in high distinction, with proud defiance, and no one is willing to humble himself fully before others, claiming full right for himself for this, as if it were not his duty to yield to any one. Thus has civil government become so feeble, that we have no hope of repressing the presumption of all conditions, from the highest to the lowest: So that God must at last interfere with thunder and lightning, and we must be convinced that God resists such people, and will not palliate any form of pride. Therefore we should admonish young people who are still to be reared, and accustom them, as much as possible to guard themselves against this vice.

In reference to this, St. Peter uses a peculiar word, when he says: "Be clothed with humility." This intimates that a society of Christians should so adhere, and be knit to one another, in the strongest ties, like a garment tightly sewed and embroidered throughout its different parts, so that it cannot rend. Thus he implies the great diligence with which Christians should aspire after this virtue, and so manifest and practice it among each other, as if they were bound together in this only. As though he would say, Thus must ye be entwined and tied into each other, with hands interlocked; so that humility may not be renounced, severed, and cast away, even if cause may possibly be given to any one, through the temptation of Satan, or the evil word of another, exciting anger and mutual recrimination, saying, Must I endure this man, being such as I am! But ye must think, as Christians, must endure, and yield to each other as those who exist together as one body; and ye must live among one another on the earth, only that ye may serve one another in love.

And here each one is to learn his own weakness, and reflect that God has conferred gifts upon others, and can confer more liberally than he has; and therefore let every one willingly serve, or yield place to others, whom he also needs at times. For each one is created for the sake of another, so that we all are to serve among one another; and God gives to each a similar portion of grace and salvation, so that no one has any right to exalt himself over another; for if he does, he thereby loses the grace imparted, and falls far below others into condemnation. Therefore, humility must here be strictly observed, in order not to destroy harmony in the church; for Satan seeks to destroy it, and brings forward every cause which will induce one to despise and betray another, and thus strive to outdo each other in insolence and pride, to which flesh and blood are inclined. And in this way humility is speedily banished, if we do not exert ourselves in earnest, and oppose the devil and our own flesh.

This, too, is one of the beautiful garments, one of the ornaments which adorn the Christian before God and the world; as St. Paul, Colossians 3:12, commands us to put on among other things, "humbleness of mind." This is more than all the crowns, all the splendor upon earth, and the true spiritual life that pleases God; so that no one need seek any where else, running into cloisters, into the wilderness, or put on a gray coat, or a monk's cowl. For here all conditions are exhorted to practice this virtue, by St. Peter; and this sermon concerning good works, has reference to all offices in each family, town, village, church, and school, in which children, domestics, subjects, and youths are to be taught humility and obedience towards parents, the aged, and superiors. Again, those who are in superior and more exalted conditions, must serve the lower orders, and even the least. If men would do this we should have abundance of good works; for it is impossible for humility to transgress, but it is obliging, profitable, and acceptable to every one.

By this virtue we can discriminate the truly pious Christian more readily than by all the works of monks and hermits; for it is no great toil or difficulty to wear a gray cowl; nor is it a thing of great self-denial to lie on the ground through the night, and rise at midnight; this is done even by wicked and dishonest men, by thieves, and murderers, and they are compelled to do it. But to wear this angelic garment and to hold it fast, is not quite so compatible with the tastes of the world as it is to fill all the land with monkery. The reason is that flesh and blood do not desire this virtue, and every one desires an easy life, in which he may live for himself, serve no one, and suffer nothing from others, such life as the monks have sought and chosen.

To this exhortation St. Peter now adds the reason: "For God resisteth the proud, and giveth grace to the humble," where, as I said above, he shows the stern command of God, and accompanies it with a severe threat, for he does not say simply, God punishes the proud, or God is their enemy, but that he "resisteth the proud," and opposes them. But what is the pride of all men in comparison to God, but a poor, empty bubble, or anything still more transitory, which exults and swells as though it would storm heaven, and runs headlong against the lightning and thunder which can crush heaven and earth? What can all the power of creation do, when God resists? And how can feeble man, whose life may be destroyed by a slight pestilence, a mere glandulous concretion, provoke that Majesty against himself, which can at any moment plunge him into the abyss? "Why are earth and ashes proud?" says Sirach (Ecclesiasticus 10:9).

Is it not enough, altogether too much, that we have other sins and charges of disobedience upon us, by which we provoke the anger of God, and deserve heavy punishment, that we should yet provoke him by our pride and haughtiness, to such a degree that he must resist us with his Majesty? For, with other sins he may yet have patience, till we are awakened, incited to repentance; but when, in hardened impenitence, we set ourselves in proud defiance against him, he will also rise against us. But who will be able to endure, or stand before him, when he sets his face and power against poor man, who indeed is already subjected to death and the power of Satan?

The experience of innumerable wants from the beginning, has clearly proved this passage, "God resisteth the proud," showing that at all times he has continued to overthrow and reduce the proud world, crushing the arrogant and haughty kings and lords. How was the great king of Babylon, Nebuchadnezzar, humbled, when driven from his royal throne to the beasts of the field, to eat the grass with them! (Dan. 4:30). Again; how quickly was the great King Alexander overthrown, when after the victory and success which God had given him, he became insolent and proud, desiring to be esteemed a god! – Again; King Herod Agrippa, (Acts 12:23). The proud and artful emperor Julian, a virulent scoffer and persecutor of Christ, whom he had denied, – how soon was he drowned in his own blood! And, in a word, what became of all the proud tyrants, who strove to crush and discourage the Christians?

The Pope also in Satanic pride has always exalted himself in the temple of God, like a god, and has continued to domineer over all others in pomp and power, in imitation of heathen emperors, as Diocletian and other tyrants, compelling men to kiss his feet; yea, even forcing this obeisance from kings and emperors. What a notorious and inhuman example of arrogance and pride, did Pope Alexander the third present, who compelled the pious and powerful German emperor, Frederick Barbarossa, by nothing but the vain terrors of his ban, to put himself under the Pope's feet, so that he trod upon him, and said: *Super aspidem et basiliscum ambulabis;* and when, in opposition to his shameful arrogance, the emperor said, *Non tibi, sed Petro,* he again trod upon the emperor, with aggravated insolence, saying, *Et mihi, et Petro.* Such arrogance was truly overdone.

The Turks are also now much prouder than they have ever been; and I hope this pride has now reached its climax, so that he cannot carry it higher, except that he may still continue to ravage and humiliate us; but this also shall have an end, inasmuch as God, in his Divine power, will overthrow both the Pope and the Turks, and, as Daniel says, without human hands. For this text, "God resisteth the proud," will not fail, but must vindicate its truth in actual fact; so that it may be seen what it is to resist God; otherwise no one would believe it. And if the Turks and all the world were even many thousand times as proud and mighty, it will be no protection to them, when he from above, who regards all power of Turkish emperors and Popes, no more than a lifeless insect, will become angry, and begin to lift up his hands.

"It is a fearful thing to fall into the hands of the living God," says the Epistle to the Hebrews, chapter 10:31. But this is nothing less than to run against God with contempt and defiance, and God must also in turn set himself against man, and resist. Therefore, let every one take heed against this, so that he defy not, nor boast against, this Majesty; not only to avoid provoking God, but that he may have grace and encouragement in that which he has to do. For, if you begin anything sustained by your own power, wisdom, and dignity, think not that he will give you success and ability to carry it out. But again, – if you humble yourself, and in the fear of God, and reliance on his grace, begin anything according to his will, it is here promised to you, when he says that "God giveth grace to the humble," that you shall not only have the approbation of men, but in addition to this, prosperity, because you are a useful man both to God and the world, and he will carry out and maintain your enterprise against the opposition of the devil and his followers. For where the grace of God is, there must also follow his blessing, his defence, and protection; and the man enjoying this protection, will not be overthrown, nor have to yield; but even if he be oppressed for a time, he will yet finally come forth triumphant, and be exalted, as St. Peter says, in conclusion, "Humble yourselves therefore, under the mighty hand of God, that he may exalt you in due time."

With these words he shows *what is true humility, and what is called so, and whence it comes;* namely, when, through the knowledge of its sins, the heart, terrified on account of the wrath of God, earnestly seeks grace, and in this way a humility, not only apparently before the people, *but from the heart for God's sake, out of the fear of God, and the knowledge of our own unworthiness and weakness.* For the man who fears God, and, as Isaiah 66:5, says, "Trembles at his word," will certainly not scorn, nor boast against any one; yea, even against enemies will he have a kind and meek heart; therefore he also finds mercy both with God and man.

The cause of all this shall be, as he says: "The mighty hand of God." —As if he would say, Ye are not to do these things—not to do them on account of man—but on account of God, ye are to humble yourselves. This hand is sufficiently strong, mighty, and powerful, in the first place, to thrust down and overthrow the proud and self-confident, however hard and iron-like their hearts may be, so that they will be prostrated in ashes and dust; yea, despair in the anguish and torment of hell, when he lays hold on them but gently with the terrors of his wrath. This the saints also experience; and they complain severely that the hand of God is so heavy to bear. As Psalm 38:2–3: "For thine arrows stick fast in me, and thy hand presseth me sore. There is no soundness in my flesh, because of thine anger." And Psalm 102:9–10: "For I have eaten ashes like bread, and mingled my drink with weeping: because of thine indignation and thy wrath; for thou hast lifted me up, and cast me down." Again Psalm 39:10–11: "I am consumed by the blow of thy hand." And again, "When thou with rebukes dost correct man for iniquity, thou makest his beauty to consume away like a moth."

In the second place, it is also a hand so mighty to raise up, to comfort and strengthen the humble and despairing, and, as St. Peter here says, to exalt again, so that those who are lying prostrate in terror may not therefore despair under it, or flee from God; but that they may arise again, and allow themselves to be comforted on account of God. For, he will also have this shown and preached, that he does not lay hold on us with his hand, in order that we may be ruined, condemned, or lost under it; but that he does it in order to bring us to repentance, otherwise we should never inquire after his word and will; and that when we seek grace, he raises us up, and gives us the remission of sins, the Holy Ghost, and eternal life. Of this the Psalms and Prophets speak in various places; as Psalm 118:18: "The Lord hath chastened me sore: but he hath not given me over unto death." Again, Psalm 146:8: "The Lord raises them that are bowed down."

"That he may exalt you in due time."

For, although this should be delayed, and it should seem to the humble and suffering, that they are pressed under the hand of God, and for an over-long time, so as almost to faint under the weight of it, they nevertheless regret their feelings, when they remember the promise, that he "will not suffer" them "to be tempted above that" which they "are able" to bear, as St. Paul says, 1 Corinthians 10:13; but he will hear their supplication and cry, and will help in due time. On this they may confidently rely. But again, the others who are proud, have reason also to be afraid; for, although he may for awhile let them pass unpunished, and go on with their pride, he is the searcher of them also; and though he awaits his own time, he will yet come upon them so violently that they shall not be able to bear it. For he has already stretched his mighty hand, both to overthrow the ungodly and to exalt the humble.

"Casting all your care upon him, for he careth for you."

He that is to live in his station with piety and humility, and to endure the arrogance, the haughtiness, and malice of the world, what is to become of him among the people? Or where is he to find protection and defence, so that he may continue in his pious efforts? For we see and hear daily how the pious are tormented, and persecuted, and made the mere foot-cloth of the world. Therefore, he says, Because ye Christians have to suffer in the world assaults, opposition, want, and distress, both bodily and spiritual, on account of which your hearts become burdened with cares, and ye think, Oh! what is to become of me? Where shall I maintain myself? Again, What will become of me when I must die? As the world seeks only how it may become rich and luxurious, and anxious, but unbelieving consciences, seek to have, through themselves and their good works, a gracious God, and to die in peace.

He here says, Only hear; I will give you the right counsel and instruction, as to the disposition of your cares. It is a short passage of the fifty-fifth Psalm: "Cast thy burden upon the Lord, and he shall sustain thee: he shall never suffer the righteous to be moved." So do ye also, and let not your burden lie upon yourselves, for ye cannot bear it, and must ultimately sink under it: but cast it from you, and give it to God's disposal, confidently with all joy, saying, Heavenly Father, thou art my Lord and God, who hast created me out of nothing, and besides, hast redeemed me by thy Son. Now in this or that office and work, which thou hast enjoined on, and entrusted to me, things do not proceed as I desire, and there is so much that threatens to press and alarm me, that I find within myself neither counsel nor help; therefore, take thou command of this also, and give me counsel and help, and be thou all thyself in these difficulties.

With this God is well pleased, and says to us, that we shall do what is enjoined on us only, and leave the care to him, as to our success and what we shall accomplish. As other passages also declare, as Psalm 37:5: – "Commit thy way unto the Lord; trust also in him; and he shall bring it to pass." For no heathen philosopher, or jurist, if he have not also the Word of God, can cast his care and burden from himself upon God; but he thinks that all the world, especially the great, the wise, who are to govern, must accomplish every thing themselves, with their own diligence and circumspection; and when it does not succeed, as it has generally failed, even for the very highest and wisest persons, they are ready to become frantic and foolish, and begin to murmur and argue against God and his government, as though he did not govern in a wise manner. But it happens rightly even to them, that he so allows their thoughts and designs to fail, and the contrary to result. For they will not think that they stand in need of him, but think they themselves have wisdom, might, and ability enough, and that God must allow it to proceed as they have determined; and thus they pass away their lives, with many useless and vain designs and cares, and must learn by experience, and confess that the result is often very different.

Therefore, this is called the virtue and the art of Christians, greater than those of all people on earth – that they know where to lay their anxiety, while others torment and afflict themselves therewith, and yet must at last despair. This must necessarily be the consequence of unbelief, which has no God, and would depend upon itself for support. But faith lays hold on this word which St. Peter adduces from the Scriptures, "For he careth for you," and joyfully relies thereon, and performs and suffers whatever is unavoidable, for it knows that it is called to encounter this, but it leaves the care to God, and thus passes vigorously through, against every thing which assails, and calls upon God as a father, and says, I will do what God hath commanded me, but as to how matters may succeed, I will leave to his care.

And this every one must do, if he wishes to proceed secure and safe in the most important matters; namely, in the hour and terror of death, when he cannot perceive nor determine, with the closest scrutiny, what will become of him, or what will be his destiny; but he must close his eyes, his senses, his thoughts, and with faith and confidence cast himself into the hands, the care, and protection of God, and say, God has permitted me, without my care, to live up to the present hour, and has given me his beloved Son as a treasure, a sure pledge of eternal life; therefore, my soul, depart in peace. You have a faithful Father and Redeemer, who has taken you into his hands, and will keep you safe.

Thus, also, the whole Christian Church collectively, in her high spiritual office and government, should do, of which St. Peter here speaks particularly, and which no man nor creature is able by any thought, wisdom, or power possessed by him, to advance and maintain; and there is, therefore, no power, or might, or protection, to be desired from the world, on which one might rely; but it rests entirely in the hands of God alone, who must maintain it through his divine power, as he has also from the beginning preserved her at all times, wonderfully in the world, in the midst of great weakness, divisions arising from sects, and heretics, from persecutions, and tyrants, and the government is his alone, although he enjoins, the office and service upon man, whom he will employ and require to dispense his word and sacrament. Therefore, every Christian should, especially if he be in such office and relation to others, aim at this only, that he may serve God faithfully, in that to which God has called and appointed him, and perform what is commanded him. And the anxiety, as to where and how the church may continue, and may be maintained against the devil and the world, is to be left entirely to the Lord, who has taken it all upon himself, and has thereby entirely divested us of care, so that we may be certain where it shall exist and continue. For if it should depend on the counsel, power, and will of man, the devil, with his power, would soon have it perverted and overthrown.

Likewise should every one, in all offices and conditions, follow this counsel of St. Peter. The prince should seek how he shall protect his country and people, promote the Word of God, maintain peace and good order, secure justice to every one, punish the disobedient. Counsellors, magistrates, and commanders should advise, and faithfully promote the accomplishment of the same. Pastors and preachers should speak faithfully and fearlessly God's word and truth. And each citizen, subject, and private individual should attend his own peculiar vocation, and simply leave to God whatever may in the mean time be accidental. But this the world does not do; but every one thinks, Why should I bring upon myself so much danger, opposition, and ill-will? Also, Why should I have trouble and labor uselessly? I shall, after all, not be able to accomplish it, and in consequence of this fear and solicitude, he either defers the office and duty enjoined on him, or at least becomes negligent.

But these men should know that they are not Christians, nor can they serve, or be useful in his kingdom to God, and in the offices which he has enjoined, and, if they will not do better, should surrender their offices which God has conferred upon them; for, it is not enough that you are in office, and allow yourself to be praised and honored. We all like to hear offices and estates praised and honored; but you should also know, that you are not in office merely to go about in a beautiful garment, occupy an upper seat, and be called a great lord and master; but that you may faithfully execute the office which God has enjoined, and with which he has honored you, not looking upon honor, enjoyment, dishonor, or injury.

But the deficiency on all hands is, that people will not attend to this, and believe and confide in God, that he will take care for us, who has indeed taken it upon himself, and will perform the chief part, which no man is able to perform, who has taken care of us, before we were born, and could very easily do all by himself, dispensing entirely with man's assistance; but he wishes to work by means, and employ, govern, chastise, instruct, and comfort us, in these divine employments.

The world is especially culpable in this, that when it is to perform anything, in great undertakings, upon the command of God, it always presumes beforehand to ascertain all future dangers and accidents, in order to take timely counsel, and anticipate them; it strives to secure human aid, and seeks friendship and assistance wherever it can find them, it forms alliances and other intrigues, upon which it may rely, and believes itself sufficiently strong for its antagonist, and thus tries to feel assured in itself of the result. This is not the exercise of confidence in God, nor submitting to him the undertaking, and the solicitude; but it is to strive, by our own care and foresight, to sustain the whole, not reflecting or believing that, by our care and efforts, we accomplish nothing; and that no human wisdom can foresee what is future, much less control it; whereas the experience of all history should teach us, if we would reflect, how egregiously human wisdom is deceived, when it relies upon itself, and that things do not at all result as we anticipate, but that everything is reversed, and the contrary to what any one would have expected, often happens.

Of this many examples in the Scriptures testify, in the history of the kings, Judah and Israel, whom the Prophets reproved very severely and frequently reproved, because they sought support and assistance from other kings and nations, and the Prophets conjured them not to trust in the help of man, but to act in accordance with the word and command of God, who would not fail to protect and keep them. But they would not hear, but went on contracting friendships and alliances with the kings of Egypt, Syria, Babylon, and Assyria, and thus invited them as guests, and they afterwards came and invaded their country, and led their people into captivity, destroying everything. This was their recompense for refusing to obey the word of God, and for not believing that he would care for, protect, and defend them, if they would confide in him, and be obedient to him.

The wisest and best people among the heathens have also from experience lamented how shamefully they were deceived, in their enterprises which they, too, had maturely deliberated. And yet it is vain to entreat the world to become wiser from the misfortunes of others, even indeed from their own.

Therefore this is preached to none but a few, who are Christians, and who have the Word of God before their eyes, and, being now humbled, have learned not to rely upon their own wisdom, their speculations, or the help and encouragement of man; and have now become a people who believe that God takes care for them, and who perform what they know to be right, and their duty to do, not permitting themselves to be hindered by what gives alarm and agitation to the world, and peril, injury, and opposition, but who commit all this to God, and encouraged by his word, press vigorously through.

What would I have done (to give an example concerning myself), when first I commenced reproving the lies concerning indulgences, and after that the errors of Popery, if I would have listened to and regarded what all the world wrote and said to me, in the most alarming style, as to what danger I was loading upon myself, and what would be my fate on this account. How often did I have to hear, that if I should write against these and other eminent persons, I would provoke such opposition as would be too heavy for me and the whole country of Germany; but inasmuch as I did not begin it myself, but was forced to it on account of my office – I would rather have remained silent – and being led into it and compelled to advance I committed the result to God, and let him take care of both as what it should lead to, and what my fate should be on account of it; and thereby I brought it onward, in spite of the opposition and rage against it, farther than I could at first have dared to think or expect.

O, how much good would not God accomplish through us, if we could persuade the people, especially the great and wise lords and rulers, that it is true, as St. Peter here says, that God careth for us, and if they would not seek, through their own wisdom and counsel, to prepare, sustain, and collect themselves with the power of man, his aid, his friendship, and alliance, to prosper and maintain their affairs. For we see that after all, they fail; and always have failed, and they do nothing more than to hinder and resist the work of God, because they do not trust in him; so that he cannot give any success or grace to that which is begun and founded upon human wisdom and confidence; and we must at last experience and lament it, because we would not believe before.

Let him, therefore, who would be a Christian, by all means learn to believe this, and train and exercise his faith, in the midst of his affairs both bodily and spiritually, in his doings and sufferings, his life and death; so that he may divest himself of anxious thoughts and solicitudes, and vigorously and courageously cast them from himself; not into a corner, as some vainly think to do; for these cares do not, in this manner, suffer themselves to be cast away, when they cleave to the heart; but that he cast both his heart and his cares upon God, for he has abundance of strength, to carry them, and has, moreover, commanded it that we should commit them to him, and you cannot lay and cast so much upon him, but that he is still much more willing to bear it; and he also promises you that he will carry your cares for you, and feel for you your solicitude.

This is truly an excellent promise, and a beautiful, golden sentence, *if we would only believe it.* If some powerful king, or lord, or emperor on earth should make such promise, and would require us to let him provide gold and silver, and the necessaries of this life, how joyfully, and free from all solicitude, would every one depend upon it? Now, this is said by a more excellent lord, who is Almighty and True, and has power over body and life, willing and able to give us every thing we need, both temporal and eternal; and would have by it partially a heaven, nay, a perfect Paradise on earth, if we would believe it. For what is better and nobler than a calm and peaceful heart, for which all men strive and labor? As we, too, have done hitherto, and have run here and there after it, and yet have found it no where but in the Word of God, which tells us to cast peace and our cares and solicitudes on God, and thus seek repose there; so, we must cast on him all that threatens to press and terrify us. For he is unwilling for these cares to be in our hearts, as they really do not belong there, but are thrown there by the devil.

Therefore, a Christian can pass through joyfully, though he may have to endure all kind of hindrance, temptation, and misfortunes, and can say, Gracious Lord God! thou hast enjoined on me to believe, to teach, to govern, to do; this I will venture in thy name, and commit to thy disposal what may befall me on account of it. And thus the Christian is a man qualified for every employment, and he can effect and do much good; for he is divested of the greatest misfortune, and his heaviest burden is cast on God. Whereas, another man may effect nothing, except filling his heart with fear and dejection, attaining no good work, and becoming impotent both to do and to suffer, afraid of every bush, and able to do nothing right, on account of his anxiety and impatience.

As the world now does, inasmuch as princes, lords, counsellors, citizens, and farmers, desire to have only honor and profit, but no one is willing to do any thing; each one fears this or that may befall him, although the world never needed a more stern government than now, and they, therefore, occupy their places, adorned with a beautiful garland, in order to be called lords and princes, and this honor they derive from God, for the purpose also of executing their princely offices and government. For it is still necessary that the world be governed, youth brought up, and the wicked punished. But if you wish to have honor only, and not also to tread in the mire, to endure ill-will, and in it learn to confide in God, and to do everything on account of his will, you are not worthy of the grace which performs anything good and beneficial, and will have to remain to your own punishment, through the wrath of God, unqualified for every good work.

"Be sober, be vigilant; because your adversary the devil, as a

roaring lion, walketh about, seeking whom he may devour: Whom resist steadfast in the faith."

He has taught two articles which are to be the exercise of the whole Christian life; namely, Christian humility, which is piety; and faith and confidence in God. Here also he exhorts to the combat, the struggle, that we may retain the same; for he shows us that we have a foe, an antagonist, who seeks to take from us our treasure, and to deprive us of our happiness and salvation. Therefore, he means to say, Seek not how you may move here on earth in high style, or provide for yourselves; but consider that you humble yourselves before God, and confide in him, and let this be your chief concern, that you abide by this grace, and permit not yourselves to be torn from it. For the devil aims at this, and is the one who excites these forbidden cares, and therefore all disobedience against God, so that he may tear faith and the Word of God out of your hearts.

Therefore, you must not overlook this, and meanwhile seek after other things, or go along thoughtlessly, sleeping, and snoring, as though to you there was no danger; but you must know that you are not placed here in gardens of roses, but in a severe conflict, in which you must be vigilant, and wakeful, and well armed, and place yourselves for defence; for you have a foe, an adversary who is not small, or to be treated with indifference, but is strong and mighty, as well as angry and wrathful, and who fights not with stones and clubs, tearing down rocks and trees; but he aims at you Christians, he is never negligent or weary, but without resting, without ceasing, he follows you up, not only that he may see what you do, perhaps committing some offence or harm which may be overcome, but he desires to swallow you up wholly and entirely.

For his thoughts and designs are bent only on the destruction of man, both spiritually and bodily, as in the beginning when man was created, he led man into the penalty of death. These designs he still carries on in the world to the utmost extremity, with those who do not believe in Christ, and never desists till the last day. Here we see how he rages without intermission, and openly storms against the whole Christian Church, through Turks, and other tyrants, and ungodly people; besides the murder and calamity in general, which in other words he produces, blinding, possessing, and driving the people, so that they injure themselves, or murder others, without any reason, and brings them into ruin by evil and disgraceful deeds.

And in a word, the world is nothing but the devil's den of murder, both in spiritual and physical concerns. And, although God has, in order somewhat to prevent and obstruct literal murder, regulated the world under human governments and parental authority, which should be moderate, diligent, and vigilant in the discharge of their duties, and for which we ought to thank God, and pray that he may help to keep them up, for otherwise there would be no peace at all, and everywhere on earth nothing but murder; nevertheless with this his egregious murders are not yet prevented, which he commits on those who are without the word, and without faith.

Therefore, to this there is needed another defence and protection, another sobriety and vigilance, that we may remain uninjured and undevoured by this blood-thirsty foe, concerning this St. Peter speaks here to the little flock of Christians, and says, you have now, through the blood of Christ, escaped from the devil's lies and murders, and are made alive, and are brought into a heavenly condition, as your beloved fathers, Adam, Abel, etc., who exist no longer under lies and murders, who live in Christ, although their bodies lie in the earth for a time, till life and truth be restored to them, both as to the body and the soul. But because you are yet in the world, you are yet in all manner of danger, therefore you must be diligently on your guard, lest he destroy you again, and murder the souls which dwell in your perishable bodies. It shall do you no harm that the soul was corrupted, and the body is yet subjected to death; "Because I live," says Christ, John 14:19; "Ye shall live also"; only, you are to struggle that you may abide in the life and truth; to this you are appointed, so long as you live on the earth, otherwise you would be in Paradise. But the devil is not yet altogether banished into the punishment of his damnation, and will not be until the last day, when, being thrust from the aerial regions, and from the earth, into the abyss of hell, will no longer be able to assail us; and there will be no cloud or covering between us and God and the angels.

In order now, says he further, that you, being once delivered from his designs, may preserve against him your new life, you must be sober and vigilant, not only with the body, but much more with the soul and spirit. For, although it is true that a Christian, who is to resist the devil, must be sober physically; for an intoxicated man, a drunkard, cannot keep awake, or think about defending himself against the devil, and a Christian must be still more watchful that his soul be not sleepy or drunk. For, as the soul becomes burdened by the body, where it is overloaded with excess, so likewise, when the soul is sober and vigilant, the body will also be temperate and disposed to hear the word of God; but when the body lies in drunkenness, the soul must be drunk beforehand and entirely disregard the word of God, and when it is drunk and drowned in such indifference, it will do no good for the body to afflict itself with great monkish enthusiasm, and with hard, rigorous abstinence and mortification.

Therefore St. Peter here forbids, besides actual drunkenness, also the drunkenness of the soul, when man runs on in carnal indifference, altogether without thought or care how he possess and secure the word of God, and regards neither God's wrath nor grace; moreover permits himself to be filled with the sweet poison of false doctrine, with which the devil and his adherents supply the people, so that they become quite stupefied, and lose their faith, the pure mind and understanding, and afterwards overflow with so much excess and loquacity, pouring it into others.

This happens when we begin to be ingenious and wise in divine things, through the reason of man, which St. Peter calls, in suitable words, *doctas fabulas*, cunningly devised fables, 2 Peter 1:16, when he says, "For we have not followed cunningly devised fables, when we made known unto you the power and coming of our Lord Jesus Christ." These are the beautiful words and declarations which have a great appearance of wisdom and holiness, and naturally are highly pleasing to man. As for instance when we ostentatiously hold forth from philosophy, or the doctrines of the law, which reason can understand, what a fine thing it is that a man live right honorably and chastely, and exercise himself in good works and the virtues! and with such pretensions they seek to establish that proposition, that by these means, and not through faith alone, we become righteous before God; that is, are redeemed from sin and death.

Again, when other factions come with pleasing words, which they have learned from our doctrine, that external things do not aid the soul, the Spirit must do it; they despise holy Baptism and the Sacrament of the Altar. Like Thomas Munzer with his seditious peasants, and the tumultuous Anabaptists, have preached with great ostentation, against the scandalous and wicked life of the world, particularly against lords and princes, that they are ungodly people and tyrants, and have thereby merited the wrath of God, and condign punishment; that, therefore, we should undertake it, and depose, and put them to death, and constitute a new government, in which are to be none but pious and holy people.

This and the like St. Peter calls cunningly devised fables, framed with great wisdom and skill, and applauded and circulated with imposing parade and appearance, and which taste very sweet and agreeable to reason; as from the beginning have sprung all idolatries, heresies, and false doctrines, being framed by fine, learned, and wise people in the world, and decorated in the most beautiful manner.

What an excellent show, what an adventure against the faith in the true Divinity of Christ it was, when Arius and his followers asserted that Christ is to be esteemed above all angels and creatures, and that all honor, dominion, and power, in heaven and on earth, belonged to him; yea, even in all things he is like God; except only that he is not *homousios*, that is, of the same undivided, divine, eternal Essence, which is to be so entirely one, that it cannot be imparted to another; that it would be too much were we to say, that a man is naturally God. With this display, so large a number of Christians was deceived, that even but a few bishops remained by the pure doctrine and faith; and this poison afterwards spread so extensively among the wise in Asia and Greece, until Mahomet with his Saracens and Turks woefully deceived the greater portion of the world.

Even so, too, did the Pope paint and adorn his abominations and idolatry with glorious display, pretending what an exquisitely beautiful thing, his fine, well regulated worship is. Also, what a useful thing the beautiful, orderly government and power of the Church is, being so nicely distributed according to the gradations of office and conditions – there being over the common priest, the bishop, and over him, St. Peter's chair at Rome, which has power, as often as it is necessary, to assemble the general councils, and with them to conclude and decide, in reference to all matters of faith, and whom every one must follow and obey! Also, what a great blessing and comfort to the whole world, is the work, when the priests renew and present before God daily, in the mass, the offering which Christ made on the cross. This is the wine in the golden cup of the scarlet dressed harlot of Babylon, with which she has made drunk all the kings and inhabitants of the earth (Rev. 17:2–4).

Now when the devil finds such people as will turn their ears to such fables, then he carries away, and fills, them so completely, that they neither see nor hear anything on account of these, and their matter must be exclusive, and will not suffer themselves to be shown what is told them in the word of God; and thus they become quite frantic, and deprived of all right understanding in faith, and all the parts of pure doctrine; and they go on merely according to their darkened minds upon their chimerical, lying nonsense, without repentance, or reformation, and have not the grace to teach, or to do any good thing; as the examples of all factions abundantly show.

Therefore, St. Peter now admonishes us to be *sober* and *vigilant*, especially after the spirit, and be on our guard against the sweet poison, and the lies of the devil so beautifully adorned; and he teaches us how we are to arm and defend ourselves against them.

"Whom resist, steadfast in the faith."

This is the true defence and resistance, in order to which we are to be sober and vigilant, *that we be well grounded in the word of God, and hold fast to it*, when the devil seeks to overthrow our faith through his cunningly devised fables, brought faith out of man's understanding and reason, which is the bride of the devil, who always claims to be skillful and wise in divine things, and thinks that what she considers right and good, must also be valid before God. But faith clings to the Word of God, and knows that man's wisdom, great skill, great power, and whatever gifts and virtues man may possess, all avail nothing before God, but his grace only, and the forgiveness of sins in Christ. – Therefore faith can thrust back and beat down all such splendid pretences, and cunningly devised fables.

As when worldly governments, kings, princes, emperors, would boast concerning themselves before God, and arrogantly say, My crown is a crown before God; for I have the sovereignty and power given to me of God; therefore, he must regard, and permit to be valid before him, what I say, and every one, must allow it to be right what I do or require. Or when a wise philosopher or jurist would also boast, and pretend, we are learned, wise rulers of the world, and have rights and laws, excellent and beautiful maxims concerning virtue and good works, therefore, men must heed us, and permit our skill to have the pre-eminence, and avail over all other things; whoever understands or performs these things, is much greater before God, than others.

No, dear man, says faith here, as for me, you may boast of these things, as being also ordained and established of God; but they avail no further than to this earthly government and life. Before the world, a crown shall be a crown, and right and wisdom shall be so called, but before God you must lay down your crown, and yield up your power and might, your right and wisdom, and say, God be merciful to me a sinner! Reason has this on its side, that it is provided and embellished with the declaration of God, that he establishes its government upon earth and is pleased with it; yet so that it must not, on that account, encroach on the government of God, or boast against and defy him, but must know, that what is called prudence and wisdom on earth, is foolishness before God; what is applauded and glorified by the world as beautiful, precious, as honor and virtue, is sin before God, and under his wrath; what is called life on earth, is nothing but death before God.

Now, since all these things, the authority of parents, of government, and of other appointments of God, which he has established by his word, although there be Christians in them, do not secure the life to come, much less will he suffer that to avail before him, which man has conceived and devised in his own heart and head. – If you will be prudent and wise, be so in things which have been commanded you, in your house, your country, and your office; that is, in earthly, material, and temporal things; here rule diligently, and you will find, that with all the books, with reason, and wisdom, you will still be deficient. But if you begin to produce, out of your reason, such arrangements as should avail before God, they may be prudent and wise pretences; but they are nothing else, says St. Peter, than fables and falsehoods.

As, for instance, when a monk comes and says, Whoever puts on a cowl, can lead a reputable, holy life; for he is separated from the world, and can divest himself of all care and trouble, and serve God without hindrance, quite in peace and tranquility. This is indeed wisely said, but at bottom it is nothing but empty, loose, and unprofitable talk. This is found from the word of God, which teaches me, that God has forbidden us to set up a worship of our own; also, that God will have us serve him in common life, and in higher conditions, and not flee from our duty. Therefore, this monkery can be no holy and divine life.

The 119th Psalm, verse 35, says, *Narrauerunt inigui mihi fabulationes:* The proud have digged pits for me, which are not after thy law; that is they preach to me concerning excellent things, and make fine representations with which to ruin me, but when I consider it rightly,

it is not according to thy word and command, which, says he, are altogether truth. For lies always appear beautiful, making a false show
and semblance of truth, having besides the advantage of embellishing
themselves with the Word of God, making this word their pretext,
having perverted it to suit their trifles. On the contrary, truth does
not shine and glitter thus, because it does not put itself on a level with
reason. As, for instance, when common Christians hear the Gospel
with each other, they believe, they receive the Sacrament, and live at
home, in their houses, with their wives and children, in a Christian
manner; this makes no display, like the beautiful, ingenious lies of the
holy Carthusian, or hermit, who being separated from the people,
claims to be a holier servant of God than others, and yet is of no service
to any man, but he leaves others to preach, govern, unrelieved in the
sweat of their labor.

Therefore, we must see to it, in these matters, before all other things,
that we have the Word of God, and judge according to it all doctrines
and pretensions of men, and distinguish, in this way, that the wisdom
and comprehension of reason, is left far and greatly beneath, and that
she avail no further than God has appointed her to govern and judge
the affairs of this temporal life. For he that has faith, can readily see it,
where she is, without the Word of God, or passes beyond it with her
wisdom. As also in worldly things, each one in the condition, office, or
handicraft, which he understands and carries on, readily knows when
another undertakes this, whether he go about it rightly or not; as also
each father of a family readily knows and understands, that he is not
to tolerate it, when the domestics would commit knavery and injustice,
or another, who has no right, would come to his wife and daughters.
Only in these divine things reason can so adorn and attire herself, that
no one perceives it, who has not really by faith apprehended the Word
of God.

For she cannot leave it, but will, and must always, be skillful and
even in things, pertaining to God, where it is not commanded her; and
the devil effects nothing with this, but all manner of calamity, just as
he introduced her into the world, in the beginning, through our
parents, and yet she cannot endure in her own matters and government, that any one should presume to judge of such things, or even
interfere by his actions in other matters and government, not fitting
nor belonging to him.

If, peradventure, a shoemaker would come forward in the Church,
and reprove the people, because they do not all wear such shoes as he
has made, and try to persuade the people that such shoes are necessary
to salvation, such a man we would beat out of the church with shoes
and slippers, and say to him, stay at home in your shop, with your shoes
and lasts, what has this to do with the government of the soul?

But when a factious spirit blusters along out of his wisdom, saying,
I am pious, holy man, and have an especial illumination of the spirit,

therefore it must not be believed, as others say, out of the dead letter, that one person can be God and man; or that a virgin can be a mother; or that man becomes cleansed from sin by the water and oral word. This cannot be gainsayed by any one where the word of God and faith are impure, and reason comes off victorious, if she only bear the honor and name of the spirit, a holy life, etc. Behold what injury the Turks have done, and still do, with their Mahomet, only with the name and honor, that they worship the one God; and that as they alone have the true God, so they and their adherents are alone the people of God on earth, in whose honor they war and fight against Christians. This they carry on so vigorously, having had such great success and victories, that even many Christians, who come among them, fall over to their faith, and become Turks, whereas not one of them becomes a Christian.

Therefore, there is here no other means by which the devil may be resisted, and we may remain undevoured by him, but a steadfast faith, says St. Peter; that is, the heart which firmly cleaves to the Word of God, and embraces the same wholly and entirely, holding it as true. For faith cannot exist or endure without the word; neither can it receive nor embrace anything else; therefore, we must separate, and place all this far above reason, and all human wisdom, so that these powers of man are simply nothing; yea, dead in things pertaining to the government of God; and as to how man is to escape from sin and eternal death, and is only to be silent, and give to the Word of God alone the honor of truth; as St. Paul 2 Corinthians 10:5 says of the office of the preaching of the Gospel: "Bringing into captivity every thought to the obedience of Christ." For if reason is to instruct me in these things what need is there of faith? and why do I not immediately throw away the book of the Gospel, and the entire Scriptures? We Christians, says St. Paul, preach something different and higher than reason understands, and before which the wisdom of the world is nothing but foolishness, 1 Corinthians 1:20-21. If reason would teach me that the mother of Christ is a virgin, the angel Gabriel might indeed have remained in heaven, and been silent about it. But our faith is not "to stand in the wisdom of men, but in the power of God," says St. Paul, again 1 Corinthians 2:5. Yea, those things the devil pretends from reason, against the Word of God, are his real intrigues and artifices, with which he seeks to devour you.

This, now, is the admonition of St. Peter, to all Christians, and especially to preachers, how they are to guard themselves against the deceit of Satan, and the cunning with which he seeks them. And he presents both views; first, that we may know the enemy, and know the quality of his mind, what he intends to do; how we are to be prepared to meet him, and defend ourselves against him, so as to stand and conquer him. He is a terrible enemy, says St. Peter, who is the god of this world, and has wisdom and cunning above all men; he can corrupt and blind reason, so that she willingly believes and follows him.

He is moreover an angry and bitter enemy to you, who have life in Christ. This he cannot endure, and seeks, and meditates only how he may again deprive you of it, and do not, by all means, think that he is far from you, or assails you from a distance; on the contrary, he is encamped as near as possible to you, and round about you; yea, in your own field, that is, in your flesh and blood, where he seeks when he may to reach you, and surprise you when you are unguarded, and tries now this artifice, and then that, when he cannot overthrow you with one; now with false confidence, with doubt; then with anger, impatience, avarice, evil lusts, etc., as he sees his opportunity, and finds you weak.—Therefore, think not that it is a jest, and that he is playing with you, for he is furious, and more hungry than any hungry lions, and aims not only at inflicting wounds upon you, nor giving you a thrust, but at devouring you wholly and entirely, so that there remain not anything of you, either as to the soul or body.

Now, he that would resist such an enemy, must have a different armor and defence, than the wit, understanding, or power, and ability of man; such is no other, as St. Peter says, than *faith* which has the word of God in its behalf, and embraces it.—And while we hold fast to it, he cannot gain any advantage; for it is the truth and power of God, before which he cannot stand, with his lies and designs of murder, but must yield and flee before it; for which reason also, St. Paul, Ephesians 6:16, enjoins: "Above all taking the shield of faith, wherewith ye shall be able to quench all the fiery darts of the wicked"; which are those especially which he infuses into the heart, through beautiful and reasonable thoughts, transforming himself into an angel of light, thereby deranging the true and faithful mind, and leading to false faith and presumption; also into doubt, distrust, hatred, and anger towards God.

So also in other temptations and combats, which concern our life, when he drives man to sin and disobedience against the command of God, to avarice, usury, revenge, lewdness, and other vices. There he also uses the same artifices, in order that he may first tear the word of God out of the heart, and may blind us even with beautiful and sweet thoughts as: It is not so bad; God will not be so angry with you, and can easily have patience with you, you also love the Gospel, etc., and thus he hurries you along with precipitation, under God's dreadful wrath and condemnation.

To stand against this, there is no other way or means, but, through the Word of God, that you fight against such insinuations and enticements, with a steadfast faith; remembering both your former lost condition, and the grace now received,—how you were before under the wrath of God, when you, being without the fear of God, without faith, were the devil's own, and according to all his will you lived, and would have had to perish, if God had not, from unfathomable goodness, forgiven you your sins, and bestowed his grace; now you are to see that you do not again lose this treasure, for which purpose he also promises to give you the Holy Ghost, who will help you to conquer, so that you be not overcome if you continue in faith. Likewise, he also tells you, when you feel weakness, and suffer want, to call upon, and ask of him, and feel assured that he will hear you, as he says, John 16:23: "Whatsoever ye shall ask the Father, in my name, he will give it you." Again, chap. 15:7, "If ye abide in me, and my word abide in you, ye shall ask what ye will, and it shall be done unto you."

For St. Peter designs by this to make Christians fearless and confident, that they may resist the temptations of the devil, and defend themselves, so that they may not become affrighted and discouraged before him, though he should beset them severely, both through the world and their own flesh, and his own importunities, as though he were too strong for them, and they would have to yield themselves his captives; but that, on the contrary, we may take a manly courage, and valiantly fight, through our faith, and know that if only we remain steadfast in it, we have the strength and advantage to prevent him from gaining anything from us, but we shall become conquerors over him.

For to this are we called of God, and placed in this condition, when we become Christians, that we are to renounce the devil, and contend against him, so that we may retain the name, word, and kingdom of God against him. Even so has Christ, our head already in himself, vanquished and subdued for us the devil and his power, and moreover he gives us faith and the Holy Ghost, through which we also can now beat entirely down his remaining malice, anger, and power, which he tries on us.

This I say a Christian has to bear in mind, and thus learn to experience the strength and power of faith, so that he follow not temptations and enticements, nor the gratification of Satan, or the world, to his own eternal injury, and for the sake of a little temporal good, pleasure, or honor, thrust from God's grace, and the Holy Spirit, and place himself again under eternal wrath and condemnation.

"Knowing that the same afflictions are accomplished in your brethren, that are in the world."

This is also a precious and consolatory declaration, which St. Peter did, of course, not only receive by inspiration of the Holy Ghost, but tasted and experienced it himself. As, for instance, when in the house of the high priest he thrice denied his Lord, and immediately fell into such anguish and terror, that he would have followed the traitor, Judas, had not Christ fixed his eyes upon him; — wherefore, after Christ's resurrection, he soon commands the same to be made known to Peter, and, therefore, beforehand tells him himself, Luke 22:32, "But I have prayed for thee that thy faith fail not: and when thou art converted, strengthen thy brethren."

This he does most faithfully by the comforting declaration, that in the world, as he says, ye have to suffer much and heavily, both in spiritual and bodily temptations to sin, against the first and second table; when the devil waylays you with his lies and murders. This is beyond measure painful, according to the flesh and blood, to weak Christians, that they must allow themselves to be continually harassed and tormented by the devil; and the sufferings of each one press him so hard, that he thinks, no one suffers as severely as he; especially in the great spiritual temptations, with which those are assailed, who have great and peculiar talents above others, and who are to oversee others. Just as St. Paul often complains of his great temptations; which the general mass, however, do not understand, nor can they bear them. And God here observes such measure, that he lays upon each one his cross, according to his power of endurance. But these are such sufferings that even great and strong spirits would have to faint and wither under them, if God would not also grant them comfort, for they take hold of the heart in the body, and consume marrow and bone; as the Psalms often sorrowfully complain.

This has also been experienced by several in cloisters, and also occasionally other pious, tender consciences, as to how heavy these are to bear, especially in the blindness and darkness of Popery, when they had but little of true comfort. But there were also some inexperienced, over-curious spirits, who saw this, and did not understand it, and yet pretended to know much about great temptations; but when they experienced them, they could not endure them. As it is said of one who heard others complaining, in fear about their temptations, that he prayed God to let him also taste the same; that God then permitted him to be tempted with fleshly lusts; but when he could not bear them, he again prayed, that God give him another — that of his brother, which he regarded as inferior; but when he had received the same, he prayed much more earnestly that God would again give him the former.

In such temptations, St. Peter now comforts the suffering Christians with the consideration that they are not alone, nor the first who have been thus tempted, as though it were a wonderful, unusual, unexampled cross which they feel, and think they sustain alone; but that they should know that their brother Christians, at all times, scattered every where, have also to suffer the same from the devil and his servants; for it mitigates and comforts beyond measure, when the sufferer sees and knows, that he suffers not alone, but with the multitude.

In external temptations from the world and the devil, of which ordinary Christians have abundance to endure, this comfort, indeed, is easily apprehended, because we see and hear that others endure the same. But when he assails you alone with his poisonous darts, so as to produce doubts about the grace of God, as though you alone were rejected; again, with horribly blasphemous thoughts; to hate God; to judge and condemn his government; and in this way he so torments and terrifies your heart, that you think no man was ever more terribly assailed, then is it necessary to apply this consolation, with which St. Peter comforts you and all Christians; and says, Beloved, only let not the devil and your sufferings terrify and discourage you; for this you must know and not doubt, that you do not suffer it alone; for he cannot assail you so grievously, that he has not done, and still does, the same to others.

For he does not aim at and seek you alone, but all Christians; and yet it always amounts to this, that in their sufferings he tears the Word of God and faith out of their heart, and robs them of their comfort in Christ, and portrays God only in the most terrible and hostile aspect, so that the heart has no grateful affection for him. And he can do this, not only with high, spiritual, and refined thoughts, but also by gross, outward suggestions, before which the man himself has to feel amazed. I have myself seen and heard a maiden complain of an assault, that while she was standing in the church, and saw the elements in the Sacrament lifted up, the thought broke in upon her, Behold, what a great knave does the priest elevate; and that she immediately became affrighted on account of it, so that she sunk to the earth.

Such terror and anguish arise from this, that the individual imagines there is no other person in such horrible temptation as he is, and that he alone has peculiar, unusual, and extraordinary sufferings. Now, although it is true that the temptations of one man may arise from different occasions and circumstances, and in a different manner, from those of another, so that his sufferings seem to him unlike those of others, yet are the sufferings and temptations of all Christians alike and the same in this, that the devil seeks to drive them all from the fear of God, and confidence in him, to contempt, unbelief, hatred, and blasphemy against God. Therefore, do the Apostles call the sufferings of Christians common sufferings and tribulations, and reckon all their sufferings in with the sufferings of Christ our Lord, as those of the head and forerunner, as St. Peter says, 1 Epistle chapter 1:11: "Searching what or what manner of time the spirit of Christ, which was in them, did signify, when it testified beforehand the sufferings of Christ, and the glory that should follow." And St. Paul, Colossians 1:21, says, "Who now rejoice in my sufferings for you, and fill up that which is behind of the affections of Christ, in my flesh for his body's sake, which is the church."

If we speak of sufferings especially heavy, certainly no human heart can conceive or express how great and severe a terror, and overwhelming sorrow our first parents had, on account of their miserable fall. And what misery did Adam afterwards, during nine hundred years of his life, have to experience with his eldest son Cain, and his other children! the like of which no man ever experienced, so that they both went mourning almost one hundred years after the death of Abel, so that these nine hundred years were to them truly a sorrowful and miserable time.

With this our father Adam we may dispute at the Day of Judgment, as to what constitutes great and lonely suffering, of which we know comparatively nothing; and we shall then be ready to confess that in this he is indeed our master and father, and that we are but inferior learners. For truly with him sufferings were heaviest and most dangerous, because he had before him no example of similar sufferings, by which he might comfort himself.

So, if you could rightly consider what the other great and holy Patriarchs, Prophets, Apostles, and especially St. Paul and St. Peter, themselves, and after them all the beloved martyrs and holy ones, suffered, you would readily yourself be compelled to say that all your sufferings and temptations are nothing in comparison to theirs. But before and above all were the temptations and sufferings of Christ the Lord, through whose heart the very fiery darts and bitter stings of the devil penetrate, so that they forced from his body abundantly the bloody sweat of his anguish. He has with his sufferings far exceeded all, so that we with all our sufferings only imitate his example.

Therefore, learn to apprehend well this passage of St. Peter, in order that you may not think that you alone suffer such horrible temptations, and attacks from the devil, but that your brethren, and not only those who are dead, who also have left you a glorious example, but those also who live with you in the world, have suffered, and still suffer such terrors and distress; for they have even the same enemy of Christ and all Christians. So that you may joyfully boast and say, God be praised! I am not alone in these afflictions, but with me there is a noble company of the whole beloved Christian church upon the earth, my beloved brethren and sisters, till to the last day. And here St. Peter comforts and strengthens me, as he was commanded by Christ, who also, indeed, tasted and experienced such sufferings, and surely much more intensely than I and others.

I also sometimes thought in my temptations, I would dispute with St. Peter and Paul, as to whether they could have been tempted more severely than I was. For this the devil does when he can do nothing more that drives a man to look on nothing but his sufferings and misery, and oppresses him with the thought – No man is so entirely rejected of God, or sinks so deep in misery and terror. He has also often made me so weary with such reflections, that I would solve no argument for him, and had simply to refer him from myself to Christ, who can give him enough of disputation. And if we have not Christ with us, the devil much too strong and powerful for us, so that it will be impossible to silence his gainsayings. He will soon have repelled all my skill, and will have conquered me with my own sword.

Alas! the masters of factions, and other less confident spirits, are truly poor, miserable people, who experience nothing at all of this conflict; but become engulfed in their self-conceived and chimerical thoughts, by which they imagine themselves so certain that they cannot fail, and some of them impudently, and without fear, blasphemously say that God himself shall not defeat them; and the devil also strengthens them well in this belief and makes it most agreeable to them, and hardens them more and more. But this is even a sign that they do not yet know the devil, and are already blinded and captured by him, so that he can overthrow them when he will.

For, true Christians are not so confident and insolent, when they are severely assailed; but they exert themselves in great and severe conflicts and terrors, that the devil may not take the word from them. I know that I am also educated for a Doctor, and have tasted a little of what the devil can do; but to this I must bear him witness from daily experience, that he can easily beat me down, if I am not well fortified in faith, and have Christ in the heart. Thomas Munzer was also so firm and confident, as he thought, that he dared to say he looked not upon Christ, if he did himself wish to speak with him; but at last, when the devil commenced laying hands on him, it was soon seen what his insolence and boasting amounted to. No, they are not what they pretend, who do this, who so stoutly boast, as though they had already devoured Satan, and see not that long before this, they have been seven times devoured by him.

The heretic Arius was also self-confident and proud, enough against the pious bishops and Christians; yea, when he was reproved by his bishop, on account of his errors, and exhorted to abstain, he became only the more obstinate, and complained besides of great persecution, and it was quite a calamity to him, that his horrible blasphemies would not be sanctioned; as also, at all times, the factious spirits and all blasphemers, yea, also open murderers and tyrants, wish to be martyrs, if they are not allowed and permitted to rave against the Word of God and pious people. – So quite secure and upright do they consider themselves, that they are not afraid before God, and consider the devil as wholly impotent until at last he suddenly seizes them, and overthrows them in the twinkling of an eye.

And greatly, indeed, do the poor, tempted Christians need the comfort and strength derived from the Word of God. For they have so anxiously to strive and contend for this, that in their temptations they almost lose their God, Christ, faith, and the Lord's prayer. Therefore, the industry enjoined upon Peter is needed here, to strengthen his brethren, just as he had need in his temptations, and was before comforted by Christ, who had prayed for him, that his faith might not entirely fail, and which had nearly been extinguished when he denied his master, until the third day when there remained scarcely the smallest spark.

Therefore, as a faithful Apostle, he now comforts those who experience the like trepidation, terror, and great distress, in consequence of their sinking faith, and says, to all the suffering and comfortless; my dear brother, do not suppose that you alone are plunged into such distress and temptation. There are yet many of your brethren, who have also suffered as severely, if not more severely; and I was as weak as you can ever be. If you will not believe it, then consider what happened to me, at the house of Caiaphas the high priest, whither I had presumed to go with Christ, and to prison, or to death; but soon, when a maid assailed with her inquiry, I fell, denied, and forswore my dear Lord most treacherously; and three whole days did I lie in misery, as I had no one to comfort me, or who had suffered the like with me, except my dear Lord, who gave me with his eyes a friendly look.

Therefore, no one should consider his anguish and distress so great and terrible, as though it were something new, which never happened to others. To you it may seem new and strange; but look around you in the whole company of the beloved Church, from the beginning to this present hour, which has been subjected in the world, to pass continually through the midst of the devil's spears, and permit herself without ceasing to be sifted and winnowed, as Christ himself says, Luke 22:31, as we do with wheat.

Beloved, you have not yet seen or experienced what our first parents suffered and bore as long as they lived; and afterwards all the beloved holy fathers until Christ. St. Peter was also much higher in this experience than I or you; and I would willingly say, that an equal amount of temptation is rarely found. St. Paul also, 1 Corinthians 4:13, says of himself and those Apostles like him, "We are made as the filth of the earth"; and that they are made a spectacle to the angels and the world, so that the devil torments them at his own discretion, and thus takes his pleasure and joy on them. And what is the suffering of all men in comparison to the conflict and anguish of Christ, when he sweated blood for you?

To him refer the devil who torments you with all his temptations, and let them dispute and decide what are the true, real temptations, the death-struggle, the anguish of hell, etc. But comfort yourself with this, that you belong to the rank of those who have been in the community of suffering with yourself, and are still, and will be until the last day. O, this is a glorious company, all under one Lord and head, who is the Lord that has taken the power from the devil and his host. And, in short, your sufferings cannot be so sore, but that those of the beloved Apostles, Prophets, and all the Saints, were equally sore, especially those of Christ himself, with whom, if we suffer with him, we are not to doubt that, as St. Paul says, Romans 8:17, we shall "be also glorified together."

WHITSUNDAY

"And when the day of Pentecost was fully come, they were all with one accord in one place. And suddenly there came a sound from heaven, as of a rushing mighty wind, and it filled all the house where they were sitting. And there appeared unto them cloven tongues like as of fire, and it sat upon each of them. And they were all filled with the Holy Ghost, and began to speak with other tongues, as the Spirit gave them utterance. And there were dwelling at Jerusalem Jews, devout men, out of every nation under heaven. Now when this was noised abroad, the multitude came together, and were confounded, because that every man heard them speak in his own language. And they were all amazed, and marvelled, saying one to another, Behold, are not all these which speak, Galileans? And how hear we every man in our own tongue, wherein we were born? Parthians, and Medes, and Elamites, and the dwellers in Mesopotamia, and in Judea, and Cappadocia, in Pontus, and Asia, Phrygia, and Pamphylia, in Egypt, and in the parts of Libya about Cyrene, and strangers of Rome, Jews and proselytes, Cretes and Arabians, we do hear them speak in our tongues the wonderful works of God. And they were all amazed, and were in doubt, saying one to another, What meaneth this? Others mocking, said, These men are full of new wine" (Acts 2:1–13).

THE HISTORY of this day, as well as the beautiful sermon of the Apostle, St. Peter, delivered through him, by the Holy Ghost, which it would be proper to treat fully at this time, we shall leave for the Special Sermons on all Festivals of the year, and now treat, to a limited extent of the occasion of this festival, and of the office of the Holy Ghost.

This festival, which we call *Pentecost,* has its origin from this fact: – When God led the Children of Israel out of Egypt, he ordered them to celebrate the Feast of the Passover on that very night, and commanded them to celebrate it annually at that season, in memory of their liberation and departure from Egypt. Fifty days from that period, traveling through the wilderness, they arrived at Mount Sinai. There the Law was given to them, by God, through Moses; and they were commanded to celebrate annually, in memory of that event, the fiftieth day after the Feast of the Passover. From this circumstance,

---

Reprinted from *Dr. Martin Luther's Church-Postil: Sermons on the Epistles. . .* , vol. 2 (New Market, Va: New Market Evangelical Lutheran Publishing Co., 1869), pp. 167–71.

the feast, which we call Pentecost, derives its name. For the little word Pentecost comes from the Greek, *Pentecoste,* which means the fiftieth day, which our Saxons, rather more in conformity with the Greek, call *Pingsten.* Hence Luke says here: "When the day of Pentecost was fully come," and they had properly attended to the history relative to the giving of the law of God on Mount Sinai, the Holy Ghost came (as Christ had promised them), and gave them another new law. Thus, we celebrate this feast, not on account of the old, but on account of the new history, namely, in consequence of the *sending of the Holy Ghost.* Hence, we must give some little instruction, and indicate the difference between our Pentecost and the Jewish Pentecost.

The Jews observe this feast, because the law was literally given to them at that time; but we should celebrate it, because the law of God was given to us spiritually. In order to render this clear, it will be necessary first to refer to St. Paul, who makes a distinction, when he speaks of two kinds of declarations, in the second Epistle to the Corinthians 3:6. And as there are two kinds of declarations, there are also two kinds of people.

First, the written law is that which God has commanded, and comprised in writing. It is styled written or letter, because it does not proceed, and penetrate the heart; nor do works result from it, except such as are altogether hypocritical and outwardly extorted. And since it is comprised only in writing and letters, it was entirely dead; it also killed, and ruled a dead people. The heart was dead. It could not cordially observe the commandments of God. For if every one were left to his own choice, to do as he pleases, uninfluenced by fear, we would not find a single one, who would prefer being controlled by the law.

There is no doubt, our nature really feels, that it would prefer acting according to its inclinations, and still it must do otherwise. For it thinks thus: Behold, if I do not observe his commandments, God will punish me, and cast me into hell. Thus our nature feels, that it acts unwillingly and contrary to its own desires. For this reason men soon become enemies to God, on account of punishment, since they feel that they are sinners, and cannot stand justifiable in the sight of God, and, consequently, are not acceptable to him; yes, they would rather God were out of existence. Such enmity against God sticks in the heart, no matter how beautifully nature may adorn itself externally. We perceive, therefore, how the law, whilst it is confined to writing and letters, can make no one pious, or enter his heart. In regard to this, we have elsewhere preached and written much.

The other law is spiritual, not written with pen or ink, nor spoken with lips, like Moses did in regard to the tables of stone; but, as we perceive from the history of this event, the Holy Spirit descended from heaven, and filled them all, so that they appeared with cloven, fiery tongues, and preached so differently from what they did before, that all were filled with wonder and amazement. There he came, pouring through their hearts, and producing different creatures, who now love God, and freely do his will. This is nothing else but the Holy Spirit himself, or his work indeed, wrought in the heart. There he wrote in their hearts, pure, fiery flames, restoring them to life, so as to break forth with flaming tongues and efficient hands, as new creatures, feeling that they have an understanding, disposition, and mind altogether different from that which they before had. Now, all is life, light, understanding, will, and heart, burning and delighting in all that is acceptable to God. This is the true distinction between the written and spiritual law of God, from which we may perceive what the work of the Holy Spirit is.

Hence we should learn what the office of the Holy Spirit is in the Church, and how and through what means he enters and works in the heart. Hitherto, it was maintained relative to him, that he merely makes and imbues what the councils conclude, and the Pope establishes in his spiritless church; when at the same time this is all a mere outward matter, established in reference to external things and regulations. It is, therefore, wholly inconsistent and perverse. Out of the work of the Holy Spirit they make a dead, written law, which at the same time is a living, spiritual law. Thus, they make out of him a Moses, yes, mere human prattle. This results from the want of information in regard to what the Holy Spirit is, the purpose for which he came, and the nature of his office. – Let us, therefore, learn and carefully comprehend these matters, so that we may be able properly to distinguish his office.

Thus you perceive here: He descends and fills the Disciples, who previously sat in fear and sorrow, rendering their tongues fiery and cloven, and so inflaming them that they grew bold, and preached Christ freely, fearing nothing. Here you clearly see, that it is not his office to write books, or to institute laws; but he is such a Spirit as writes in the heart, and produces a new disposition, so that the individual becomes cheerful before God, is filled with love for him, and consequently serves his fellow man with a joyful disposition.

What means and what process does he employ thus to change and renew the heart? This he accomplishes by revealing and preaching Jesus Christ, the Lord, as Christ himself says, "When the comforter is come, whom I will send unto you from the Father, even the Spirit of truth, which proceedeth from the Father, he shall testify of me" (John 15:26). Now, we have frequently heard that the Gospel is God's permission to preach and proclaim to every one in the world, that, whilst no one can become pious through the law, but rather grows worse, he sent down his own beloved Son to die and shed his blood for our sins, from which we could not be released by our own powers and efforts.

But it is not enough simply to preach this, but it is also necessary to believe it. For this reason, God sends the Holy Spirit to impress such preaching in the heart, so that it may inhere and live in it. For, surely there can be no doubt, that Christ accomplished all things, took away our sins, and overcame every obstacle, so that through him we should be lords over all things. Here the treasure lies in a heap; but, it is not, for this reason, distributed and applied every where. If, therefore, we are to enjoy it, the Holy Spirit must come, and communicate it to the heart, so that we may believe and exclaim: I, too, am one of those who have this blessing. Precisely as, to every one, who hears it, such grace is offered through the Gospel, and he is called to it, as it is said, "Come unto me all ye that labor and are heavy laden" (Matthew 11:28).

If, then, we believe that God has thus assisted us, and given us such treasure, it cannot fail, the human heart must be filled with joy towards God, and be so elevated as to exclaim: Beloved Father, if it is thy will to manifest to me love and fidelity so inexpressible, I shall love thee with my heart, and willingly and freely do that which is pleasing to thee.

Here it never beholds God with jealous eyes; it no longer thinks that he will cast it into hell, as it did before the Holy Spirit came, when it felt no love, no good, no fidelity, but God's wrath and displeasure. But when the Holy Spirit impresses the heart with the fact, that God is so friendly and gracious to it, it becomes so joyful and fearless, as to do and suffer for God's sake all that it is necessary to do and suffer.

Thus, you should learn to recognize the Holy Spirit, in order that you may know for what purpose he is given, and what his office is, namely, to present to us the treasure, Christ, and all that he has, and to reveal, apply, and convey these to the heart, through the Gospel, so that they may be our own. Now, when he accomplishes this, and we feel it in our hearts, it is a natural result, we must exclaim: If it is the meaning, that our works avail nothing, but that the Holy Spirit must accomplish it, why shall we burden ourselves with our works and laws? Thus, all human works and laws are excluded; yes, even the law of Moses. For the Holy Spirit gives an individual better instruction than all books do, so that he may understand the Scriptures better than any of those who are occupied simply with the law.

Hence, we have no further use for books, except to strengthen our faith, and to show to others that it is written as the Holy Spirit teaches. For we must not retain our faith simply in ourselves, but we must let it break forth, and to establish and prove it, we must have the Scriptures. Be careful, therefore, not to regard the Holy Ghost as a lawmaker, but as one who proclaims the Gospel of Christ to your heart, and makes you so free, that not a single letter remains, but for the sake of preaching the Gospel.

But here we should know and understand, that every thing is not accomplished in such a manner, that the individual who possesses the Holy Ghost, is at once so entirely perfect, that he is pure in all respects, and no longer feels the law and sin. We do not preach concerning the Holy Spirit and his office, that he has so entirely accomplished and completed every thing; but that he has commenced it, and continually operates and enforces it more and more, without ceasing. Hence, you will find no one that is full of righteousness and joy, and destitute of sin and sorrow, serving every one with pleasure. The Scriptures clearly state what the Holy Ghost does, namely, that his office is to liberate from sins and terrors. But still the object is not thereby entirely completed.

For this reason, a Christian must still feel something of sins in his heart, and the terrors of death; so that he is affected by all that disturbs other sinners. Unbelievers stick so deeply in their sins, that they do not regard them. Believers, however, feel them in deed, but they have a supporter against them, the Holy Spirit, who consoles and strengthens them till he completely accomplishes the object, and terminates it; when they shall no longer feel them.

Hence, I say, we must be prudent here, and careful not to boast of the Holy Spirit too arrogantly and presumptuously, as certain arrogant, presumptuous fanatics do, lest we become too secure, imagining that we are in all respects perfect. For a pious Christian is still flesh and blood, as other persons are; only he strives to resist sins and evil lusts, and feels what he does not wish to feel. But those who are not Christians, rest securely, wholly unconcerned about such things.

It is a matter of no importance, to feel evil lusts, provided we endeavor to resist them. Hence a person who thus feels, must not judge according to his feeling, as if he should be lost on account of it. But with the sins which remain in him, and which he feels, he should contend as long as he lives, sighing without intermission to be relieved of sins, and permitting the Holy Ghost to operate in him. Such sighs never cease in believers; they are so deep that they cannot be expressed, as St. Paul, Romans 8:26, says. But they have a precious hearer, namely, the Holy Spirit himself. He readily perceives such longing, and consoles such conscience with divine consolation.

Consequently there will always be a commingling; we must feel both, the Holy Ghost and our sins and imperfections. We are like a person who is sick and under the hands of a physician, and is to be restored by him. Hence no one should think: This man has the Holy Spirit; therefore he must be altogether strong, performing nothing but precious works, and destitute of imperfections. No, not thus: for whilst we live in the flesh here on earth, we cannot attain such a degree of perfection, as to be free from weakness and imperfection. Hence the holy Apostles themselves often complained of their temptations and sorrows. And consequently the Holy Spirit himself was concealed from them, according to their feelings, except that he strengthened and sustained them through the word and faith, in their temptations.

Therefore the Holy Spirit is given to none, except such as are filled with distress and anxiety. In these the Gospel produces fruits and benefits. The gift is too high and noble. God will not cast it before dogs and swine, which, when they chance to hear it preached, devour it, without knowing what they devour. The heart must see and feel its wretchedness, and its inability to extricate itself. There must be a struggle, if the Holy Spirit is to come and help; and no one should take it in his mind, that it will be effected in any other way.

This we perceive here in this history. The beloved Disciples were filled with fear and terror. They were disconsolate, and destitute of courage. They were sunk in unbelief and despair; so that it was with great difficulty and labor that Christ raised them up again. And still there was no other imperfection in them, but the fainting of their hearts; they were afraid, that the heavens would fall on them. The Lord himself could scarcely console them, until he said to them: The Holy Spirit from heaven shall come down to you, and shall impress me in your hearts, so that you will know me, and also the Father, through me. Then your hearts shall be comforted and strengthened, and filled with joy; as it was fulfilled in them on this day.

THE METHOD AND FRUITS
OF JUSTIFICATION

"Now I say, that the heir, as long as he is a child, differeth nothing from a servant, though he be lord of all; but is under tutors and governors until the time appointed of the father. Even so we, when we were children, were in bondage under the elements of the world: but when the fullness of the time was come, God sent forth His Son, made of a woman, made under the law, to redeem them that were under the law, that we might receive the adoption of sons. And because ye are sons, God hath sent forth the Spirit of His Son into your hearts, crying, Abba, Father. Wherefore thou art no more a servant, but a son; and if a son, then an heir of God through Christ" (Galatians 4:1-7).

Reprinted from *History and Repository of Pulpit Eloquence*, [comp.] Henry C. Fish, vol. 1 (New York: M. W. Dodd, 1857), pp. 458-73.

THIS TEXT TOUCHES THE VERY PITH of Paul's chief doctrine. The cause why it is well understood but by few, is, not that it is so obscure and difficult, but because there is so little knowledge of faith left in the world; without which it is not possible to understand Paul, who every where treats of faith with such earnestness and force. I must therefore speak in such a manner that this text will appear plain; and that I may more conveniently illustrate it, I will speak a few words by way of preface.

First, therefore, we must understand the doctrine in which good works are set forth, far different from that which treats of justification; as there is a great difference between the substance and its working; between man and his work. Justification pertains to man, and not to works; for man is either justified and saved, or judged and condemned, and not works. Neither is it a controversy among the godly, that man is not justified by works, but righteousness must come from some other source than from his own works: for Moses, writing of Abel, says, "The Lord had respect unto Abel, and to his offering." First He had respect to Abel himself, then to his offering; because Abel was first counted righteous and acceptable to God, and then for his sake his offering was accepted also, and not him because of his offering. Again, God had no respect to Cain, and therefore neither to his offering: therefore thou seest that regard is had first to the worker, then to the work.

From this it is plainly gathered that no work can be acceptable to God, unless he which worketh it was first accepted by Him: and again, that no work is disallowed of Him unless the author thereof be disallowed before. I think these remarks will be sufficient concerning this matter at present, by which it is easy to understand that there are two sorts of works, those before justification, and those after it; and that these last are good works indeed, but the former only appear to be good. Hereof cometh such disagreement between God and those counterfeit holy ones; for this cause *nature* and *reason* rise and rage against the Holy Ghost; this is that of which almost the whole Scripture treats. The Lord in His Word defines all works that go before justification to be evil, and of no importance, and requires that man before all things be justified. Again, He pronounces all men which are unregenerate, and have that nature which they received of their parents unchanged, to be unrighteous and wicked, according to that saying "all men are liars," that is, unable to perform their duty, and to do those things which they ought to do; and "Every imagination of the thoughts of his heart are only evil continually"; whereby he is able to do nothing that is good, for the fountain of his actions which is his heart, is corrupted. If he do works which outwardly seem good, they are no better than the offering of Cain.

Here again comes forth *reason*, our reverend mistress, seeming to be marvelously wise, but who indeed is unwise and blind, gainsaying her God, and reproving Him of lying; being furnished with her follies and feeble honor, to wit, the light of nature, free will, the strength of nature; also with the books of the heathen and the doctrines of men, contending that the works of a man not justified, are good works, and not like those of Cain, yea, and so good that he that worketh them is justified by them; that God will have respect, first to the works, then to the worker. Such doctrine now bears the sway every where in schools, colleges, monasteries wherein no other saints than *Cain* was, have rule and authority. Now from this error comes another: they which attribute so much to works, and do not accordingly esteem the worker, and sound justification, go so far that they ascribe all merit and righteousness to works done before justification, making no account of faith, alleging that which James saith, that without works faith is dead. This sentence of the Apostle they do not rightly understand; making but little account of faith, they always stick to works, whereby they think to merit exceedingly, and are persuaded that for their work's sake they shall obtain the favor of God: by this means they continually disagree with God, showing themselves to be the posterity of *Cain*. God hath respect unto man, these unto the works of man; God alloweth the work for the sake of him that worketh, these require that for the work's sake the worker may be crowned.

But here, perhaps, thou wilt say, what is needful to be done? by what means shall I become righteous and acceptable to God? how shall I attain to this perfect justification? The Gospel answers, teaching that it is necessary that thou hear Christ, and repose thyself wholly on Him, denying thyself and distrusting thine own strength; by this means thou shalt be changed from *Cain* to *Abel*, and being thyself acceptable, shalt offer acceptable gifts to the Lord. It is faith that justifies thee, thou being endued therewith, the Lord remitteth all thy sins by the mediation of Christ His Son, in whom this faith believeth and trusteth. Moreover, He giveth unto such a faith His Spirit, which changes the man and makes him anew, giving him another reason and another will. Such a one worketh nothing but good works. Wherefore nothing is required unto justification but to hear Jesus Christ our Saviour, and to believe in Him. Howbeit these are not the works of nature, but of grace.

He, therefore, that endeavors to attain to these things by works, shutteth the way to the Gospel, to faith, grace, Christ, God, and all things that help unto salvation. Again, nothing is necessary in order to accomplish good works but justification; and he that hath attained it performs good works, and not any other. Hereof it sufficiently appears that the beginning, the things following, and the order of man's salvation are after this sort; first of all it is required that thou hear the Word of God; next that thou believe; then that thou work; and so at last become saved and happy. He that changes this order, without doubt is not of God. Paul also describes this, saying "Whosoever shall call upon the name of the Lord shall be saved. How then shall they call on Him in whom they have not believed? and, how shall they believe in Him of whom they have not heard? and, how shall they hear without a preacher? and how shall they preach except they be sent?"

Christ teaches us to pray the Lord of the harvest to send forth laborers into His harvest; that is, sincere preachers. When we hear these preach the true word of God, we may believe; which faith justifies a man, and makes him godly indeed, so that he now calls upon God in the spirit of holiness, and works nothing but that which is good, and thus becomes a saved man. Thus he that believeth shall be saved; but he that worketh without faith is condemned; as Christ saith, he that doth not believe shall be condemned, from which no works shall deliver him. Some say, I will now endeavor to become honest. It is meet surely that we study to lead an honest life, and to do good works. But if one ask them how we may apply ourselves unto honesty, and by what means we may attain it, they answer, that we must fast, pray, frequent temples, avoid sins, etc. Whereby one becomes a Chatterhouse Monk, another chooses some other order of Monks, and another is consecrated a priest: some torment their flesh by wearing hair-cloth, others scourge their bodies with whips, others afflict themselves in a different manner: but these are of *Cain's* progeny, and their works are no better than his; for they continue the same that they were before, ungodly, and without justification: there is a change made of outward works only, of apparel, of place, etc.

They scarce think of faith, they presume only on such works as seem good to themselves, thinking by them to get to heaven. But Christ said, "Enter in at the strait gate, for I say unto you, many seek to enter in, and can not." Why is this? because they know not what this narrow gate is; for it is faith, which altogether annihilates or makes a man appear as nothing in his own eyes, and requires him not to trust in his own works, but to depend upon the grace of God, and be prepared to leave and suffer all things. Those holy ones of Cain's progeny think their good works are the narrow gate; and are not, therefore, extenuated or made less, whereby they might enter.

When we begin to preach of faith to those that believe altogether in works, they laugh and hiss at us, and say, Dost thou count us as Turks and heathens, whom it behooves now first to learn faith? is there such a company of priests, monks, and nuns, and is not faith known? who knoweth not what he ought to believe? even sinners know that. Being after this sort animated and stirred up, they think themselves abundantly endued with faith, and that the rest is now to be finished and made perfect by works. They make so small and slender account of faith, because they are ignorant what faith is, and that it alone doth justify. They call it faith, believing those things which they have heard of Christ; this kind of faith the devils also have, and yet they are not justified. But this ought rather to be called an opinion of men. To believe those things to be true which are preached of Christ, is not sufficient to constitute thee a Christian, but thou must not doubt that thou are of the number of them unto whom all the benefits of Christ are given and exhibited; which he that believes must plainly confess, that he is holy, godly, righteous, the son of God, and certain of salvation; and that by no merit of his own, but by the mere mercy of God poured forth upon him for Christ's sake: which he believes to be so rich and plentiful, as indeed it is, that although he be as it were drowned in sin, he is notwithstanding made holy, and become the son of God.

Wherefore, take heed that thou nothing doubt that thou art the son of God, and therefore made righteous by His grace; let all fear and care be done away. However, thou must fear and tremble that thou mayest persevere in this way unto the end; but thou must not do this as though it consisted in thy own strength, for righteousness and salvation are of grace, whereunto only thou must trust. But when thou knowest that it is of grace alone, and that thy faith also is the gift of God, thou shalt have cause to fear, lest some temptation violently move thee from this faith.

Every one by faith is certain of this salvation; but we ought to have care and fear that we stand and persevere, trusting in the Lord, and not in our own strength. When those of the race of Cain hear faith treated of in this manner, they marvel at our madness, as it seems to them. God turn us from this way, say they, that we should affirm ourselves holy and godly; far be this arrogance and rashness from us: we are miserable sinners; we should be mad, if we should arrogate holiness to ourselves. Thus they mock at true faith, and count such doctrine as this execrable error; and thus try to extinguish the Gospel. These are they that deny the faith of Christ, and persecute it throughout the whole world; of whom Paul speaks: "In the latter times many shall depart from the faith," etc., for we see by these means that true faith lies every where oppressed; it is not preached, but commonly disallowed and condemned.

The pope, bishops, colleges, monasteries, and universities, have more than five hundred years persecuted it with one mind and consent most obstinately, which has been the means of driving many to hell. If any object against the admiration, or rather the mad senselessness of these men, if we count ourselves even holy, trusting the goodness of God to justify us, or as David prayed, "Preserve Thou me, O Lord, for I am holy," or as Paul saith, "The Spirit of God beareth witness with our spirit that we are the children of God"; they answer that the *prophet* and *apostle* would not teach us in these words, or give us an example which we should follow, but that they being particularly and specially enlightened, received such revelation of themselves. In this way they misrepresent the Scripture, which affirms that they are holy, saying that such doctrine is not written for us, but that it is rather peculiar miracles, which do not belong to all. This forged imagination we account of as having come from their sickly brain. Again, they believe that they shall be made righteous and holy by their own works, and that because of them God will give them salvation and eternal blessedness.

In the opinion of these men it is a Christian duty to think that we shall be righteous and sacred because of our works; but to believe that these things are given by the grace of God, they condemn as heretical; attributing that to their own works which they do not attribute to the grace of God. They that are endued with true faith, and rest upon the grace of the Lord, rejoice with holy joy, and apply themselves with pleasure to good works, not such as those of Cain's progeny do, as feigned prayers, fasting, base and filthy apparel, and such like trifles, but to true and good works whereby their neighbors are profited.

Perhaps some godly man may think, If the matter be so, and our works do not save us, to what end are so many precepts given us, and why doth God require that they be obeyed? The present text of the Apostle will give a solution of this question, and upon this occasion we will give an exposition thereof. The Galatians being taught of Paul the faith of Christ, but afterward seduced by false apostles, thought that our salvation must be finished and made perfect by the works of the law; and that faith alone doth not suffice. These Paul calls back again from works unto faith with great diligence; plainly proving that the works of the law, which go before faith, make us only servants, and are of no importance toward godliness and salvation; but that faith makes us the sons of God, and from thence good works without constraint forthwith plentifully flow.

But here we must observe the words of the Apostle; he calls him a *servant* that is occupied in works without faith, of which we have already treated at large: but he calls him a *son* which is righteous by faith alone. The reason is this, although the servant apply himself to good works, yet he does it not with the same mind as doth the son; that is, with a mind free, willing, and certain that the inheritance and all the good things of the Father are his; but does it as he that is hired in another man's house, who hopes not that the inheritance shall come to him. The works indeed of the son and the servant are alike; and almost the same in outward appearance; but their minds differ exceedingly: as Christ saith, "The servant abideth not in the house forever, but the son abideth ever."

Those of Cain's progeny want the faith of sons, which they confess themselves; for they think it most absurd, and wicked arrogancy, to affirm themselves to be the sons of God, and holy; therefore as they believe, even so are they counted before God; they neither become holy nor the sons of God, nevertheless are they exercised with the works of the law; wherefore they are and remain servants forever. They receive no reward except temporal things; such as quietness of life, abundance of goods, dignity, honor, etc., which we see to be common among the followers of *popish* religion. But this is their reward, for they are servants, and not sons; wherefore in death they shall be separated from all good things, neither shall any portion of the eternal inheritance be theirs who in this life would believe nothing thereof. We perceive, therefore, that servants and sons are not unlike in works, but in mind and faith they have no resemblance.

The Apostle endeavors here to prove that the law with all the works thereof makes us but mere servants, if we have not faith in Christ; for this alone makes us sons of God. It is the word of grace followed by the Holy Ghost, as is shown in many places, where we read of the Holy Ghost falling on Cornelius and his family, while hearing the preaching of Peter. Paul teaches that no man is justified before God by the works of the law; for sin only cometh by the law. He that trusts in works, condemns faith as the most pernicious arrogancy and error of all others. Here thou seest plainly that such a man is not righteous, being destitute of that faith and belief which is necessary to make him acceptable before God and His Son; yea, he is an enemy to this faith, and therefore to righteousness also. Thus it is easy to understand that which Paul saith, that no man is justified before God by the works of the law.

The *worker* must be justified before God, before he can work any good thing. Men judge the worker by the works; God judges the works by the worker. The first precept requires us to acknowledge and worship one God, that is, to trust Him alone, which is the true faith whereby we become the sons of God. Thou canst not be delivered from the evil of unbelief by thine own power, nor by the power of the law; wherefore all thy works which thou doest to satisfy the law, can be nothing but works of the law; of far less importance than to be able to justify thee before God, who counteth them righteous only who truly believe in Him; for they that acknowledge Him the true God are His sons, and do truly fulfill the law. If thou shouldst even kill thyself by working, thy heart can not obtain this faith thereby, for thy works are even a hinderance to it, and cause thee to persecute it.

He that studieth to fulfill the law without faith, is afflicted for the devil's sake; and continues a persecutor both of faith and the law, until he come to himself, and cease to trust in his own works; he then gives glory to God who justifies the ungodly, and acknowledges himself to be nothing, and sighs for the grace of God, of which he knows that he has need. Faith and grace now fill his empty mind, and satisfy his hunger; then follow works which are truly good; neither are they works of the law, but of the Spirit, of faith and grace; they are called in the Scripture, the works of God which He worketh in us.

Whatsoever we do of our own power and strength, that which is not wrought in us by His grace, without doubt is a work of the law, and avails nothing toward justification; but is displeasing to God, because of the unbelief wherein it is done. He that trusts in works does nothing freely and with a willing mind; he would do no good work at all if he were not compelled by the fear of hell, or allured by the hope of present good. Whereby it is plainly seen that they strive only for gain, or are moved with fear, showing that they rather hate the law from their hearts, and had rather there were no law at all. An evil heart can do nothing that is good. This evil propensity of the heart, and unwillingness to do good, the law betrays, when it teaches that God does not esteem the works of the hand, but those of the heart.

Thus sin is known by the law, as Paul teaches; for we learn thereby that our affections are not placed on that which is good. This ought to teach us not to trust in ourselves, but to long after the grace of God, whereby the evil of the heart may be taken away, and we become ready to do good works, and love the law voluntarily; not for fear of any punishment, but for the love of righteousness. By this means one is made of a servant, a son; of a slave an heir.[1]

We shall now come to treat more particularly of the text. Verse 1. "The heir, as long as he is a child, differeth nothing from a servant, though he be lord of all." We see that the children unto whom their parents have left some substance, are brought up no otherwise than if they were servants. They are fed and clothed with their goods, but they are not permitted to do with them, nor use them according to their own minds, but are ruled with fear and discipline of manners, so that even in their own inheritance they live no otherwise than as servants. After the same sort it is in spiritual things. God made with his people a covenant, when he promised that in the seed of Abraham, that is in Christ, all nations of the earth should be blessed. That covenant was afterward confirmed by the death of Christ, and revealed and published abroad by the preaching of the Gospel. For the Gospel is an open and general preaching of this grace, that in Christ is laid up a blessing for all men that believe.

Before this covenant is truly opened and made manifest to men, the sons of God live after the manner of servants under the law; and are exercised with the works of the law, although they can not be justified by them; they are true heirs of heavenly things, of this blessing and grace of the covenant; although they do not as yet know or enjoy it. Those that are justified by grace, cease from the works of the law, and come unto the inheritance of justification; they then freely work those things that are good, to the glory of God and benefit of their neighbors. For they have possessed it by the covenant of the Father, confirmed by Christ, revealed, published, and as it were delivered into their hands by the Gospel, through the grace and mercy of God.

---

1. As preached, this was a double discourse, and the division occurs at this place.

This covenant, Abraham, and all the fathers which were endued with true faith, had no otherwise than we have: although before Christ was glorified, this grace was not openly preached and published: they lived in like faith, and therefore obtained the like good things. They had the same grace, blessing, and covenant that we have; for there is one Father and God over all. Thou seest that Paul here, as in almost all other places, treats much of faith; that we are not justified by works, but by faith alone. There is no good thing which is not contained in this covenant of God; it gives righteousness, salvation, and peace. By faith the whole inheritance of God is at once received. From thence good works come; not meritorious, whereby thou mayest seek salvation, but which with a mind already possessing righteousness, thou must do with great pleasure to the profit of thy neighbors.

Verse 2. "But is under tutors and governors until the time appointed of the father." Tutors and governors are they which bring up the heir, and so rule him and order his goods, that he neither waste his inheritance by riotous living, nor his goods perish or be otherwise consumed. They permit him not to use his goods at his own will or pleasure, but suffer him to enjoy them as they shall be needful and profitable to him. They keep him at home, and instruct him whereby he may long and comfortably enjoy his inheritance: but as soon as he arrives to the years of discretion and judgment, it can not but be grievous to him to live in subjection to the commands and will of another.

In the same manner stands the case of the children of God, which are brought up and instructed under the law, as under a master in the liberty of sons. The law profits them in this, that by the fear of it and the punishment which it threatens, they are driven from sin, at least from the outward work: by it they are brought to a knowledge of themselves, and that they do no good at all with a willing and ready mind as becomes sons; whereby they may easily see what is the root of this evil, and what is especially needful unto salvation; to wit, a new and living spirit to that which is good: which neither the law nor the works of the law is able to give; yea, the more they apply themselves to it, the more unwilling they find themselves to work those things which are good.

Here they learn that they do not satisfy the law, although outwardly they live according to its precepts. They pretend to obey it in works, although in mind they hate it; they pretend themselves righteous, but they remain sinners. These are like unto those of Cain's progeny, and hypocrites; whose hands are compelled to do good, but their hearts consent unto sin and are subject thereto. To know this concerning one's self is not the lowest degree toward salvation. Paul calls such constrained works the works of the law; for they flow not from a ready and willing heart; howbeit the law does not require works alone, but the heart itself; wherefore it is said in the first Psalm of the blessed man, "But his delight is in the law of the Lord: and in His law doth he

SERMONS · Method and Fruits　　　　61

meditate day and night." Such a mind the law requires, but it gives it not; neither can it of its own nature: whereby it comes to pass that while the law continues to exact it of a man, and condemns him as long as he hath such a mind, as being disobedient to God, he is in anguish on every side; his conscience being grievously terrified.

Then, indeed, is he most ready to receive the grace of God; this being the time appointed by the Father when his servitude shall end, and he enter into the liberty of the sons of God. For being thus in distress, and terrified, seeing that by no other means he can avoid the condemnation of the law, he prays to the Father for grace; he acknowledges his frailty, he confesses his sin, he ceases to trust in works, and humbles himself, perceiving that between him and a manifest sinner there is no difference at all except of works, that he hath a wicked heart even as every other sinner hath. The condition of man's nature is such that it is able to give to the law, works only, and not the heart; an unequal division, truly, to dedicate the heart, which incomparably excels all other things, to sin, and the hand to the law: which is offering chaff to the law, and the wheat to sin; the shell to God, and the kernel to Satan. Whose ungodliness if one reprove, they become enraged, and would even take the life of innocent Abel, and persecute all those that follow the truth.

Those that trust in works seem to defend them to obtain righteousness; they promise to themselves a great reward for this, by persecuting heretics and blasphemers, as they say, who seduce with error, and entice many from good works. But those that God hath chosen, learn by the law how unwilling the heart is to conform to the works of the law; they fall from their arrogancy, and are by this knowledge of themselves brought to see their own unworthiness. Hereby they receive that covenant of the eternal blessing and the Holy Ghost, which renews the heart: whereby they are delighted with the law, and hate sin; and are willing and ready to do those things which are good. This is the time appointed by the Father, when the heir must no longer remain a servant, but a son; being led by a free spirit, he is no more kept in subjection under tutors and governors after the manner of a servant; which is even that which Paul teaches in the following:

Verse 3. "Even so we, when we were children, were in bondage under the elements of the world." By the world elements, thou mayest here understand the first principles or law written; which is as it were the first exercises and instructions of holy learning; as it is said: "As concerning the time ye ought to be teachers, ye have need that one teach you again which be the first principles of the oracles of God." "Beware lest any man spoil you through philosophy and vain deceit, after the tradition of men, after the rudiments of the world." "How turn ye again to the weak and beggarly elements, whereunto ye desire again to be in bondage."

Here Paul calls the law rudiments; because it is not able to perform that righteousness which it requires. For whereas it earnestly requires a heart and mind given to godliness, nature is not able to satisfy it: herein it makes a man feel his poverty, and acknowledge his infirmity: it requires that of him by right which he has not, neither is able to have. "The letter killeth, but the Spirit giveth life." Paul calls them the rudiments of the world, which, not being renewed by the Spirit, only perform worldly things; to wit, in places, times, apparel, persons, vessels, and such like. But faith rests not in worldly things, but in the grace, word, and mercy of God: counting alike, days, meats, persons, apparel, and all things of this world.

None of these by themselves either help or hinder godliness or salvation. With those of Cain's progeny, faith neither agrees in name or any thing else: one of them eats flesh, another abstains from it; one wears black apparel, another white; one keeps this day holy, and another that: every one has his rudiments, under which he is in bondage: all of them are addicted to the things of the world, which are frail and perishable. Against these Paul speaks, "Wherefore, if ye be dead with Christ from the rudiments of the world, why, as though living in the world, are ye subject to ordinances: touch not, taste not, handle not, which all are to perish with the using, after the commandments and doctrines of men. Which things have indeed a show of wisdom in will-worship and humility, and neglecting of the body; not in any honor to the satisfying of the flesh."

By this and other places above mentioned, it is evident that monasteries and colleges, whereby we measure the state of spiritual men as we call them, plainly disagree with the Gospel and Christian liberty: and therefore it is much more dangerous to live in this kind of life, than among the most profane men. All their works are nothing but rudiments and ordinances of the world; neither are they Christians but in name, wherefore all their life and holiness are sinful and most detestable hypocrisy. The fair show of feigned holiness which is in those ordinances, does, in a marvelous and secret manner, withdraw from faith, more than those manifest and gross sins of which open sinners are guilty. Now this false and servile opinion, faith alone takes away, and teaches us to trust in, and rest upon, the grace of God, whereby is given freely that which is needful to work all things.

Verse 4. "But when the fullness of the time was come, God sent forth His Son, made of a woman, made under the law, to redeem them that were under the law, that we might receive the adoption of sons." After Paul had taught us that righteousness and faith can not come to us by the law, neither can we deserve it by nature, he shows us by whom we obtain it; and who is the author of our justification. The Apostle saith, "When the fullness of the time was come"; here Paul speaks of the time which was appointed by the Father to the son, wherein he should live under tutors, etc. This time being come to the Jews, and ended, Christ came in the flesh; so it is daily fulfilled to others, when they come to the knowledge of Christ, and change the servitude of the law for the faith of sons. Christ for this cause came unto us, that believing in Him, we may be restored to true liberty; by which faith they of ancient times also obtained the liberty of the Spirit.

As soon as thou believest in Christ, He comes to thee, a deliverer and Saviour; and now the time of bondage is ended; as the Apostle saith, the fullness thereof is come.

Verse 6. "And because ye are sons, God hath sent forth the Spirit of His Son into your hearts, crying, Abba, Father." Here we see plainly that the Holy Ghost cometh to the saints, not by works, but by faith alone. Sons believe, while servants only work; sons are free from the law, servants are held under the law, as appears by those things that have been before spoken. But how comes it to pass that he saith "because ye are sons, God hath sent forth the Spirit," etc., seeing it is before said that by the coming of the Spirit we are changed from servants to sons: but here, as though we could be sons before the coming of the Spirit, he saith "because ye are sons," etc. To this question we must answer, that Paul speaks here in the same manner that he did before, that is, before the fullness of the time came, we were in bondage under the rudiments of the world: all that shall become sons are counted in the place of sons with God: therefore he saith rightly, "because ye are sons," that is, because the state of sons is appointed to you from everlasting, "God hath sent forth the Spirit of His Son," to wit, that He might finish it in you, and make you such as He hath long since of His goodness determined that He would make you.

Now if the Father give unto us His Spirit, He will make us His true sons and heirs, that we may with confidence cry with Christ, Abba, Father; being His brethren and fellow heirs. The Apostle has well set forth the goodness of God which makes us partakers with Christ, and causes us to have all things common with Him, so that we live and are led by the same Spirit. These words of the Apostle show that the Holy Ghost proceeds from Christ, as he calls Him his Spirit. So God hath sent forth the Spirit of His Son, that is, of Christ, for He is the Spirit of God, and comes from God to us, and not ours, unless one will say after this manner, "my Holy Spirit," as we say "my God," "my Lord," etc. As He is said to be the Holy Spirit of Christ, it proves Him to be God of whom that Spirit is sent, therefore it is counted His Spirit.

Christians may perceive by this whether they have in themselves the Holy Ghost, to wit, the Spirit of sons; whether they hear His voice in their hearts: for Paul saith, He crieth in the hearts which He possesseth, Abba, Father; he saith also, "We have received the Spirit of adoption, whereby we cry Abba, Father." Thou hearest this voice when thou findest so much faith in thyself that thou dost assuredly without doubting, presume that not only thy sins are forgiven thee, but also that thou art the beloved sons of God, who, being certain of eternal salvation, durst both call Him Father, and be delighted in Him with a joyful and confident heart. To doubt these things brings a reproach upon the death of Christ, as though He had not obtained all things for us.

It may be that thou shalt be so tempted as to fear and doubt, and think plainly that God is not a favorable Father, but a wrathful revenger of sins, as it happened with Job, and many other saints: but in such a conflict, this trust and confidence that thou art a son ought to prevail and overcome. It is said "The Spirit itself maketh intercession for us with groanings which can not be uttered; and that He beareth witness with our spirit that we are the children of God." How can it therefore be that our hearts should not hear this cry and testimony of the Spirit? But if thou dost not feel this cry, take heed that thou be not slothful and secure; pray constantly, for thou art in an evil state.

Cain saith, "My punishment is greater than I can bear. Behold, Thou hast driven me out this day from the face of the earth, and from Thy face shall I be hid; and it shall come to pass that every one that findeth me shall slay me." This is a dreadful and terrible cry, which is heard from all Cain's progeny, all such as trust to themselves and their own works, who put not their trust in the Son of God, neither consider that He was sent from the Father, made of a woman under the law, much less that all these things were done for their salvation. And while their ungodliness is not herewith content, they begin to persecute even the sons of God, and grow so cruel, that, after the example of their father *Cain*, they can not rest until they slay their righteous brother *Abel*, wherefore the blood of Christ continually cries out against them nothing but punishment and vengeance; but for the heirs of salvation it cries by the Spirit of Christ for nothing but grace and reconciliation.

The Apostle here uses a Syrian and Greek word, saying, Abba, Pater. This word Abba, in the Syrian tongue, signifies a father, by which name the chief of monasteries are still called; and by the same name, Heremites in times past, being holy men, called their presidents: at last, by use, it was also made a Latin word. Therefore that which Paul saith is as much as *Father, Father;* or if thou hadst rather, "my Father."

Verse 7. "Wherefore thou art no more a servant, but a son, and if a son, then an heir of God through Christ." He saith, that after the coming of the Spirit, after the knowledge of Christ, "thou art not a servant." A son is free and willing, a servant is compelled and unwilling; a son liveth and resteth in faith, a servant in works. Therefore it appears that we can not obtain salvation of God by works, but before thou workest that which is acceptable to Him, it is necessary that thou receive salvation; then good works will freely flow, to the honor of thy heavenly Father, and to the profit of thy neighbors; without any fear of punishment, or looking for reward.

If this inheritance of the Father be thine by faith, surely thou art rich in all things, before thou hast wrought any thing. It is said "Your salvation is prepared and reserved in heaven, to be showed in the last time," wherefore the works of a Christian ought to have no regard to merit, which is the manner of servants, but only for the use and benefit of our neighbors, whereby we may truly live to the glory of God. Lest that any think that so great an inheritance cometh to us without cost (although it be given to us without *our* cost or merit), yet it cost Christ a dear price, who, that He might purchase it for us, was made under the law, and satisfied it for us, both by life and also by death.

Those benefits which from love we bestow upon our neighbor, come to him freely, without any charges or labor of his, notwithstanding they cost us something, even as Christ hath bestowed those things which are His upon us. Thus hath Paul called back the Galatians from the teachers of works, which preached nothing but the law, perverting the Gospel of Christ. Which things are very necessary to be marked of us also: for the *Pope*, with his prelates and monks hath for a long time intruded, urging his laws, which are foolish and pernicious, disagreeing in every respect with the Word of God, seducing almost the whole world from the Gospel of Christ, and plainly extinguishing the faith of sons, as the Scripture hath in divers places manifestly prophesied of His kingdom. Wherefore let every one that desires salvation, diligently take heed of him and his followers, no otherwise than Satan himself.

EIGHTEENTH SUNDAY AFTER TRINITY

"I thank my God always on your behalf, for the grace of God which is given you by Jesus Christ; That in every thing ye are enriched by him, in all utterance, and in all knowledge; Even as the testimony of Christ was confirmed in you: So that ye come behind in no gift; waiting for the coming of our Lord

Reprinted from *Dr. Martin Luther's Church-Postil: Sermons on the Epistles. . .* , vol. 2 (New Market, Va.: New Market Evangelical Lutheran Publishing Co., 1869), pp. 29–50.

Jesus Christ: Who shall also confirm you unto the end, that ye may be blameless in the day of our Lord Jesus Christ. God is faithful, by whom ye were called unto the fellowship of his Son Jesus Christ our Lord" (1 Corinthians 1:4–9).

THIS IS THE BEGINNING of The Epistle to the Corinthians, which St. Paul was induced to write from the fact, that, after his departure, the condition of things was not so propitious, certain persons having already instigated sects and thrown every thing into confusion, both in regard to doctrine and life; in order that he might censure the evils and remove the factions. Nor is it less necessary at the present period, to read it and enforce it, as the devil never ceases, when the Gospel is preached in its purity, to mingle himself and sow his seed among the children of God.

Now, St. Paul designs to be a little severe, to touch their conscientious sensibilities. But, he commences in a wise manner, showing them what they have received through the Gospel, for the purpose of reminding them that they ought to be thankful to God for it, and that they ought to be harmonious in their teachings and lives, in honor and praise to him, guarding against sects and other offences. Hence, he begins thus:

"I thank my God always on your behalf, for the grace of God which is given you by Jesus Christ," etc.

As if he would say: Dear brethren, only consider the abundant grace and blessings conferred upon you by God, not on account of the law, or your righteousness, merits, and works, of which you have no cause to boast one above another, or to bring about sects and divisions; but, in Christ alone, and on account of his will, has he bestowed all these upon you, through the preaching of the Gospel; that is, such grace as brings with it and presents all manner of gifts, so that you become rich in all things, so much so, that you lack nothing in all that need be given to you of God alone, and that you have still to await the blessed day, when Christ himself with all heavenly blessings, which you now have in faith, will visibly appear.

Here he commends to them the preaching of the Gospel, as he does in many other places, so that they may rightly esteem and appreciate it. He does this, through his own example, in thanking God himself, on their behalf, the more to incite them to gratitude, so that they might remember at least what they had been, and what they have now received through the Gospel, and guard themselves so as not to fall from it into their former blindness, through the forgetfulness of their previous wretchedness and of the grace now received; as was already beginning to be the case among them, in consequence of their factionists, who were weary of the Gospel, and, no longer appreciating the grace so abundant, sought and embraced something different.

Behold here, if the great Apostle, the most eminent teacher among the Gentiles, had to hear of, and see, in his day, the factions and sects which sprang up in his own parish, during his own life, through security, and ingratitude for the Gospel; is it any wonder, if the same thing occurs now, when no such eminent preachers and pious Christians exist, as did at that time? We see the great gifts which were conferred on us; and we also see and feel the factiousness and offences, which the devil has instigated, through our ingratitude, in so easily forgetting the injuries we suffered in our former blindness under Popery, and how shamefully we were deceived, as well as tormented; as it must happen, if we neglect and disregard such blessings, that gratitude and reverence for the Word of God can not follow; for satiated and forgetful Christians go on, and imagine that it was always, and will ever be, as it now is.

For this reason, the people ought to be admonished and incited to consider what they did not possess before, yes, the wretchedness, in which they had been, — a thing, which St. Paul afterwards clearly and plainly portrays to the Corinthians, as we have already heard in several parts of the Epistle to the Corinthians; but here, in the beginning, he gives them to understand, in friendly, courteous terms, that they ought to determine, from that which they have now received through the Gospel, what they lacked before, and of what they might again be deprived.

He, therefore, says: You have now received the grace, by which you are enriched in all things (which you did not possess before, and which you would still not have, had the Gospel not been preached to you); namely, in all that pertains to the life which is to come, — the object of the Gospel is not to make people rich here on earth, — so that you have no lack in any gifts, nor want of any thing, but the coming of the Lord himself; and hence you can live here, by the grace and gifts, with which you have, in every way been enriched, awaiting his coming, until finally you shall be delivered from this sinful, evil life in this world, and all its plagues. This you should know, and thank God, that you need not seek other, or better, or higher gifts or callings, as if you had not all that you should have, as the factionists pretend.

For, determine yourself what any one can have or desire, that is better than that which a Christian has in the Gospel and in his faith, in which he is assured, that in Baptism he has the forgiveness of sins, is cleansed, and pronounced just and holy before God, and thus he is already a child of God and an heir of eternal life; and, even if he afterwards has and feels weakness and sin, yes, even if he is overcome and falls, he can permit himself to be restored, absolved, consoled, and strengthened, by his neighbors, through the Word of God and the service of the Sacrament. He also has the ministration of the Word of God daily, as to how he should believe and live in the various conditions of life. Again, he can entreat and pray in every time of need, having a sure promise, that God will hear and help him.

But what more can a person desire, or what more does he need, than to know, that he is a child of God through Baptism, and has the Word of God as a consolation against sin, and as strength against weakness? Do you regard it as of no importance, as an inferior treasure to know and be assured, that God himself speaks to you, and, through the external office, works in you, teaches, admonishes, consoles, restores; yes, gives you victory and triumph over the devil, death, and all the powers on earth?

What would we not have done or freely given to have had one of these blessings in the distresses and troubles of our consciences. It is true, it was said, when any one was sorrowful, or deeply distressed, that he should seek advice from a discreet, intelligent person, and follow whatever he advised; but such intelligent person could be nowhere found, who could say or advise anything in regard to such matter. For here the counsel of an intelligent person will not accomplish the object; it requires the Word of God. With this you can console yourself, and you should rely upon it as firmly, as if God should reveal himself to you from heaven.

This, St. Paul says here, is a great blessing, a precious treasure, to have the Word of God with certainty, and to have no doubt, that it is his Word. This prevails, this can console and sustain the heart. Such advantages we did not have before, under the restraints and blindness of the Pope. Here we suffered ourselves to be led and driven, by doubtful, human devices, commands, bulls, and falsehoods, the invocation of saints, indulgences, masses, monkeries; and did all that was prescribed to us under the name of the Church, wholly for the purpose of consoling and relieving our minds, so that we might not despair of the grace of God; but these, instead of consoling us, led us to the devil, plunging us still deeper into anguish and terror. For, after all, they were nothing, that could assure us (as they themselves must confess in regard to their own doctrines), that a person could or should be certain, that he is in the grace of God.

Yes, they drive poor, timid, troubled hearts into such straits, that they fear Christ more than the devil, and tremble more at his name, than they do at the name of the devil. This I experienced myself, and in consequence of it took flight to the dead, – St. Barbara, Anna, and other departed saints, – and used them as mediators against the wrath of Christ, and yet I accomplished nothing; nor was I able in that way to redeem myself from the terrors of my timid, fugitive conscience. Here there was none among all of us, who boasted of being highly learned doctors of the holy Scriptures, that could give any proper consolation from the Word of God, saying, This is the Word of God; God desires you to give him the honor, to be comforted, to believe and know, that he has forgiven you your sins, and is not angry with you;

and had there been any one from whom I could have received such information, I would have given all I possessed. Yes, I would have embraced such information or word, and in view of it, would have left all Kings their honor and crowns; for it would have refreshed and preserved my heart, yes, my body and life.

This we should consider, and not forget, so that God may be praised for it; yes, we should count, calculate all that can be calculated, of the preeminently great blessings, in which we have been enriched in every way. For, besides the Word, we also have prayer, the Lord's Prayer, from which we know *how* and *for what we should pray;* — a thing which, God be praised, almost every child knows; whereas, previously, all, especially we monks, tormented themselves with extensive reading and singing, and still prayed for nothing; but chattered like the nuns over the Psalter, or geese, over oat-straw.

I too wanted to be a holy, pious monk; I prepared myself with great devotion for mass and prayer; but even when I was most devout, I approached the altar a doubter, a doubter, I returned. When I said my penance, I still doubted; if I said it not, I doubted again; for we were wholly under the impression, that we could not pray, and that we would not be heard unless we were altogether pure, and without sin, as the saints in heaven are; so that it had been much better, to have neglected prayer entirely, and done something else, than to have used the name of God so vainly. Nevertheless, we monks (yes, all who were styled clerical), thus deceived the people, and promised and sold them our prayers for their gold and property, without knowing whether they were heard, or acceptable to God, or not. Whereas, now we know, thank God, and understand, not only how and for what we should pray and ask, without doubting, but we also are able to add a vigorous Amen, concluding that, according to his promise, he most assuredly hears us.

It is, indeed, also an unspeakable treasure for a Christian to have with perfect certainty the Word of God, which is the word of eternal grace and consolation, Baptism, the Lord's Supper, a knowledge of the Ten Commandments and of the Creed, as well as a sure reliance and confidence, that God will hear us in our necessities, if we call on him; and thus he will have given him, as God promises in the Prophecy of Zechariah, 12:10, both the "Spirit of grace and of supplications."

Besides, he also has information sufficient to determine with certainty the works and conditions, which are really good and acceptable to God. Again, on the other hand, he can distinguish and condemn all useless, vain works and false worship, — things which we could not do before, when we knew not what we believed, or for what we prayed, or lived; we knew nothing but our devised schemes, and sought our consolation and salvation, in our own devised penance, confessions, and satisfactions, through our own works, of monasteries, and obedience of the Pope's commands, presuming that all was accomplished by these means, and regarding these alone as holy works and pious conduct, but the pursuits of common Christians as worldly, dangerous conditions of life.

As, for instance, a picture has been drawn for the people (and the Pope has confirmed it), of a great ship in the wild, broad sea, in which there are none but holy monks, together with the super-holy popes, cardinals, bishops, etc., who throw out their merits to others who are swimming in the water and encountering great perils, or reach out to them their hands, or throw around their bodies their ropes or stoles, and thus draw them up into the ship to themselves.

Observe and consider, on the other hand, whether it is not a great privilege, a rich blessing, worthy of high and honorable estimation, to know from whence consolation is derived for your heart, and help in every time of need, and how to conduct yourself in your station of life, being thus fully provided in every respect; and even if you are not always able to recognize it clearly, you still know that you can continually resort to it, and adhere to it, through the common service and office of the Church and your Christian neighbors; again, that the ordinary works which you perform in the condition, which God ordained, are right, and that, in the performance of these, you do better, and are more acceptable to God, than if you would buy all the works and merits of the monks and hermits.

This St. Paul calls being "enriched," first, in all doctrine or wisdom; that is, high, spiritual understanding of the Word, to which eternal life belongs, that is, the consolation of faith in Christ, and invocation and prayer; and then, in all knowledge, that is, right understanding and discrimination in regard to the whole external, physical life and transactions on earth. For in these is embraced all that a Christian should know and have. These are inexpressibly great treasures and blessings; and he that is able to compare them with the privations and wants which we endured before, cannot be otherwise, than grateful and thankful for them. I myself remember the time, when I used all diligence in studying the Scriptures, what I would have given to have had some one who could explain even a single Psalm correctly, and could I have been able to begin to understand a verse occasionally, I would have thought I was born anew.

For this reason, we should be truly thankful to God for the abundant grace and gifts, which he manifested towards us, in restoring the light, which affords us a correct understanding of the Scriptures, and knowledge in regard to all things. But it goes, and will go, alas! as it did with the Corinthians, who had received most super-abundantly from St. Paul, but wholly misused such bounty, growing most shamefully ungrateful; in consequence of which they were afterwards chastised with false doctrines and deceptions, until ultimately the beautiful church, together with the country and people, was entirely desolated and destroyed.

Much more does similar chastisement threaten us, — it is even at the door, knocking terribly, — through the Turks, and other calamities and plagues; so that we may well pray with thankful hearts and a proper degree of zeal, as St. Paul did here for the Corinthians, that God may finally and irreproachably preserve us in that which he has given us, until the day of our Lord Jesus Christ, etc.

For this reason, he admonishes us to abide by this knowledge, and thankfulness of the favors and gifts of God, and as we are so enriched and blessed by them, as to need nothing more, but to wait henceforth for that which the Lord has promised us, and which is already given us in our faith, until he reveal it openly before our eyes, through his coming.

Hitherto much has been written, and great skill has been displayed in regard to the manner in which we should prepare for death and await the last day; but this tended rather to depress timid consciences the more; as no reference was made to the consolation of the great riches of grace and salvation in Christ, but the people were directed to their own works and pious lives, as a support against death and the judgment of God.

But now, instead of these, we perceive the gracious result, that whoever has the word of the Gospel goes forth, and executes the office and work committed to him, no matter in what condition of life. He consoles himself with the fact, that through Baptism he is incorporated in Christ; he receives the Absolution, and for the strengthening of his faith approaches the Lord's Supper, committing his body and soul to Christ. — Why should such a person fear death? No matter in what hour it may come, whether by pestilence or other sudden calamity, whether awake or asleep, he is always ready and prepared; for he is always found in Christ.

In view of this, a Christian may freely thank and praise God; for he himself perceives that he needs nothing more than he has, and that he cannot obtain anything better than he already has, through the forgiveness of sins, and the gifts of the Holy Spirit, and obedience in his calling, only he should increase daily, and persevere in such faith, and in calling on his Lord. But he cannot have any other or better doctrine, faith, Spirit, Prayer, Sacrament, Salvation, etc., than all the Saints, St. John the Baptist, Peter, Paul, had, and every baptized Christian now has. Therefore, I need not go about with foolish works for the purpose of preparing and encouraging people for death, by reminiscenses and narrations of numerous, daily misfortunes of this life. This will not do it; death will not be terrified by it, nor will its fear be removed.

But the Gospel teaches thus: Believe in Christ, and then pray, and live according to the Word of God; and if, in this condition, death overtake you and seize you, you know that you are Christ's, the Lord's; as St. Paul, Romans 14:8, says: "Whether we live therefore or die, we are the Lord's." For we are Christians, and live on earth, in order that we may have sure consolation and deliverance from and victory over sin, death, hell.

Of this St. Paul reminds us here, and then richly describes it in this Epistle, for the purpose of inducing us to be thankful for this grace, and to live among each other in a brotherly and Christian manner, both in regard to doctrine and life, shunning and avoiding the wickedness and corruptions, intro uced by factionists and other disorderly leaders. For whoever rightly comprehends this grace and these gifts, must in return love and thank God, and conduct himself properly towards his neighbor; and if he finds that he is remiss in this respect, he will endeavor, through the Word of God, and admonition, to make the necessary amends and improvements; but, on the other hand, he that is not thus disposed, most assuredly does not comprehend or appreciate the grace of God; otherwise he would reform and conduct himself properly.

Here you may say: Why does St. Paul boast so gloriously about the Corinthians, as being so rich in all things, as to have no lack in anything; when at the same time, he himself confesses, that they have among them factions and sects, in regard to Baptism, the Sacrament, the faith concerning the resurrection from the dead, and Christian liberty, and that some lived in other respects as they pleased. Is this not having wants and defects? How, then, dare he assert, that they have all things, in spiritual blessings, super-abundantly, so as to lack nothing in the least thing?

Well, here we must know, as I have often said, that the Christian community can never be so pure, that no false and evil persons can be found in it; precisely as in the pure grain, tares, darnel, cockle, and hedge-mustard always exist. For this reason, whoever disregards the Church, because there are still some imperfections and impurities among the masses who are called Christians, will miss the Church, yes, the Gospel and Christ, and never will find or meet a church.

For this reason, it may be said for our comfort: If we have the Gospel in its purity, we have the treasure which God gave to his Church, and which can neither fail nor be defective. But such a degree of perfection has not yet been attained, that all who hear it, fully and completely comprehend it and are pure in their faith and in their course of conduct; but there are always some who do not believe, and others who are still weak and imperfect; nevertheless are the treasure and riches of the doctrine and knowledge truly present, without any defect, producing great results and much fruit. But the fact, that some do not believe, does not impair Baptism or the Gospel, or the Church, but themselves.

In short, where the Word exists, there assuredly the Church also exists. For where the doctrine is pure, there Baptism, the Sacrament, Absolution, the Ten Commandments, the Lord's Prayer, Good Works, all conditions of life, can be kept pure; and wherever there may be any defects, or imperfections, they may be censured, improved, and rectified through the Word.

For there must be some, indeed, who have the Word and Sacraments in their purity and correctness, and believe, pray properly, observe the Commandments of God, etc.; as, God be praised, is the case among us; so that we may conclude with certainty: Were not the true Church here, none of these would exist here. For this reason there must also be true members of the Church and saints among us. And even if children of the world, who neither believe nor lead Christian lives, insinuate themselves among us, as is everywhere and always the case, the faith, Baptism, and the doctrine do not become wrong in consequence of this; neither does the Church cease. But the treasure remains, nevertheless, whole and unimpaired, and God is able to grant his grace, so that some will turn from their unbelief and evil ways, to it, and amend their lives.

On the other hand, those among whom this treasure, namely, the Word or the doctrine and knowledge, does not exist, cannot be the Christian Church, nor members of it; and hence, they neither believe nor pray right, nor perform works acceptable to God. And, consequently, all their lives are condemned and lost before God, even if they boast more about God and the Church, and have in the eyes of the world, greater display and applause of peculiar, holy lives, or greater virtues and honors, than true Christians have. For, it is concluded, that outside of the Church of Christ there is no God, nor grace, nor salvation; as St. Paul, in the Epistle, Ephesians 4:5, next preceding, says: "One Lord, one faith, one baptism, one God," etc.; again, Acts 4:12: "There is none other name under heaven given among men, whereby we must be saved."

Therefore, when he praises the Corinthians, St. Paul does not look upon the factionists, the Epicures, or others who committed open offences among them, as he that had his stepmother; but, he looks upon the fact, that there is still a small number, who have the pure Word of God, Faith, Baptism, the Sacrament (notwithstanding there are some false and wicked ones among them); for the sake of these, no matter how small their number, the inexpressible riches, of which he speaks, still exist there; even as well among three or four, as among hundreds or thousands. For that many do not have it, is not the fault of the Gospel, nor of the minister, nor of the Church, but of those themselves, who close their ears and hearts against it.

Behold, thus St. Paul extolled and described in a most glorious manner the Christian Church, in regard to its existence here on earth, and to the inexpressible blessings and gifts it has from Christ. For this, they should justly thank and praise him, both, by their confession and lives. He now concludes thus, saying:

"God is faithful, by whom ye were called unto the fellowship of his Son Jesus Christ our Lord."

In what Christ has commenced in you, and already given you, he will assuredly preserve you to the end and eternally, if you yourselves only do not fall from it, or reject it, through unbelief. For his word or promise, given you, and his work which he produces in you, are not changeable like the word and work of men, but they are firm, sure, divine, immovable truth. Since, then, you have this divine calling, you should console yourselves with it, and firmly rely on it.

FOR ADDITIONAL INFORMATION ABOUT MARTIN LUTHER:

Bainton, Roland. *Here I Stand.* New York: Abingdon Press, 1950.
Booth, Edwin Prince. *Martin Luther, Oak of Saxony.* New York: Abingdon Press, 1961.
Dillenberger, John, ed. *Martin Luther.* Garden City, New York: Doubleday, 1961.
Howard, Harry C. "Martin Luther." *Princes of the Christian Pulpit and Pastorate.* Nashville: Cokesbury Press, 1928.
Kooiman, Willem Jan. *Luther and the Bible.* Translated by John Schmidt. Philadelphia: Muhlenberg Press, 1961.
Pelikan, Jaroslav, ed. *Interpreters of Luther.* Philadelphia: Fortress Press, 1968.
Ritter, Gerhard. *Luther, His Life and Work.* Translated by John Riches. New York: Harper & Row, 1963.
Todd, John Murray. *Martin Luther.* Westminster, Md.: Newman Press, 1965.

FOR OTHER SERMONS BY MARTIN LUTHER:

Luther's Works. Edited by John W. Doberstein. Vol. 51. Philadelphia: Muhlenberg Press, 1959.
Sermons on the Passion of Christ. Translated by E. Smid and J. T. Isensee. Rock Island, Ill.: Augustana Press, 1956.
Also: *Dr. Martin Luther's Church-Postil: Sermons on the Epistles* (1869), *Sermons on the Gospel of St. John,* chapters 1–4 (1957).

HULDRYCH ZWINGLI

1484–1531

OCCVBVIT ANNO ÆTATIS XLVII
1531

HA

HULDRYCH ZWINGLI, photograph of a painting in the
Kunstmuseum Winterthur.

HULDRYCH ZWINGLI

OF THE MAJOR LEADERS of the Protestant Reformation Huldrych Zwingli is the least famous. Yet some historians have regarded him more highly than Luther, Calvin, or Knox. Archibald Maclaine in his notes to Mosheim's *An Ecclesiastical History, Ancient and Modern* describes Zwingli as "this illustrious reformer, whose learning and fortitude, tempered by the greatest moderation, rendered him, perhaps beyond comparison, the brightest ornament of the protestant cause."[1]

LIFE AND TIMES

At the time of Zwingli's ministry Switzerland was unique among the countries of Europe. Although as divided as Germany or Italy, Switzerland had a degree of unity through a confederation of small republics. The various cantons were strictly independent, but they were related to one another in a common league under a flag bearing the motto, "Each for all, and all for each." The spirit of Swiss independence extended into church affairs. The churches in Switzerland were governed more by civil authority than by the ecclesiastical authority of Rome.

The Roman Catholic church in Switzerland had many problems. Corruption and superstition were common among the clergy. Indulgence sellers, for example, plied their trade throughout Switzerland. Besides being lax in their pastoral duties, numerous priests were also immoral. They took the vow of celibacy but kept mistresses and fathered children. Some of the bishops in Switzerland were noted for their warlike spirit. Matthew Schinner, for example, who became a cardinal, led in efforts to supply Swiss mercenaries to the pope in fighting political wars.

Humanism, particularly as propounded by Erasmus, was widely accepted throughout Switzerland. Humanism, combined with Swiss independence, the condition of the Roman Catholic church, and the mercenary system, had a great influence on the life and ministry of Zwingli.

Huldrych Zwingli was born in the village of Wildhaus, located in eastern Switzerland, on January 1, 1484. He was the third child born into a family of eight sons and two daughters. His father was the chief magistrate of the city, and his uncle Bartholomew was the village priest. His father, a shepherd, provided the family with a comfortable if not luxurious home.

The early childhood of Zwingli was pleasant. During the day he played on the mountain slopes, and at night he enjoyed

---

1. John Laurence Mosheim, *An Ecclesiastical History, Ancient and Modern,* ed. and trans. Archibald Maclaine, 2 vols. (Baltimore: Phoenix N. Wood & Co., 1832), 2:19.

listening to the stories told by his grandmother of the feats of Swiss heroes. When he was about six he went to live with his uncle Bartholomew, who undertook the direction of his education. Zwingli was an exceptional student, and in 1494 his uncle placed him in the School of St. Theodore. Zwingli made rapid progress in Latin, music, and dialectics. In 1496 he moved to a more advanced institution in Bern where he studied under the humanist Heinrich Wölflin. Zwingli was extremely fond of music and in Bern developed his musical talent. Zwingli next studied in the University of Vienna. In 1502 he returned to Switzerland and became a student at the University of Basel and a teacher in St. Martin's School. In 1504 he took the Bachelor of Arts degree and in 1506 the Master of Arts degree.

While in Basel he was influenced strongly by Thomas Wyttenbach, a humanist and biblical scholar. Zwingli remembered Wyttenbach "as having taught him the sole authority of Scripture, the death of Christ as the only price of forgiveness, and the worthlessness of indulgences."[2] Under the humanist influence Zwingli became aware of the need to return to the earlier sources of Christian belief, and he was eager to rid the church of practices he considered superstitious. Unlike Luther, he did not experience a deep spiritual crisis but rather moved in a more intellectual pattern. His entering the priesthood apparently was motivated not so much by a deep spiritual compulsion as by the expectations of his family and his own inclinations.

In December of 1506 he began his duties as priest in Glarus. He endeavored to follow the pattern of ministry advocated by Wyttenbach. Concerning his first experience in the priesthood Zwingli wrote, "Notwithstanding my youth the ecclesiastical functions aroused in me more fear than joy, for I knew, and I remain convinced, that I must give account for the sheep that should perish through my negligence."[3] In Glarus he continued his scholarly work. Particularly important was his interest in learning Greek. Erasmus became the young priest's greatest inspiration in regard to languages. Zwingli also read widely in the patristic literature and probably knew the church fathers better than either Luther or Calvin did.

---

2. Williston Walker, *A History of the Christian Church* (Edinburgh: T. & T. Clark, 1953), p. 360.
3. John T. McNeill, *The History and Character of Calvinism* (New York: Oxford University Press, 1954), p. 23.

During the time Zwingli served in Glarus, he visited Italy twice as a chaplain to mercenary troops from his canton in the service of Pope Julius II against the French. His abhorrence of the practice of foreign governments' recruiting mercenaries in Switzerland began at this time. He did not become an absolute pacifist, but he did take a strong stand against war and severely criticized those he felt to be wanton militarists. His uncompromising opposition to the mercenary system in Switzerland was not a popular position. Many of the Swiss cantons earned vast sums of money by selling their men into military service. Zwingli, however, felt that such a practice was immoral and referred to the mercenary traffic as "that school of blasphemy, that source of a bad conscience."[4]

Zwingli's basic courage and willingness to swim against the stream on controversial issues were further illustrated during his ministry in Einsiedeln. In 1516 he transferred to the famous pilgrim shrine of Einsiedeln. Although his income depended largely on the gifts of the pilgrims, he preached that pilgrimages were not a means of obtaining pardon from sin. Many people traveling to the shrine turned back when they heard what Zwingli was preaching – that Christ alone saves, and that he saves everywhere. His ministry began to attract attention. In 1518 Zwingli received the title of acolyte-chaplain to the pope. He was led to believe that he could expect further honors. Possibly these honors were offered him as a bribe to discourage his making uncomplimentary remarks about the papacy and certain practices in the Roman Catholic church. But Zwingli was not to be bought by gold or by honors. In 1518 when Bernardino Samson, a Franciscan indulgence seller, came to Einsiedeln, Zwingli opposed him. He denounced Samson's traffic in the strongest terms and urged the people to trust the saving merits of Christ alone and to put no faith in indulgences.

It was in Einsiedeln that Zwingli broke his vow of celibacy. Although he was cleared of a charge of having seduced the daughter of a citizen of Einsiedeln, he admitted that "he had been overcome by the blandishments of a woman."[5] Zwingli's behavior was so common among priests that it was not viewed as scandalous. For example, when Zwingli was being con-

---

4. Ibid., p. 25.
5. Ibid., p. 28.

sidered for the post at the Great Minster in Zurich his principal rival for the position was reputed to be the father of six boys.

In 1519, at the age of thirty-five, Zwingli moved to Zurich to assume his new position as people's priest at the Great Minster. Here he began his reform movement in earnest. His great scholarship and oratorical ability were quite effective. His first act was to announce that he would preach on the life of Christ, beginning with a course of sermons interpreting the Gospel of Matthew. This departure from custom was but a foreshadowing of more revolutionary actions to come.

From the beginning Zwingli's preaching in Zurich was electrifying. John T. McNeill describes it as follows:

> It was marked by ample scholarship and the fruits of daily study, and at the same time by simplicity, conviction, and fervor. One hearer said that he felt as if lifted up by the hair and suspended in space. People who had ceased to be churchgoers became constant attendants. Those of the poorer classes were made to feel the preacher's sympathy for them and his understanding of the conditions of their lives, and their marked response was a little disturbing to the more comfortable burghers. In frank language Zwingli examined the motives and exposed the behavior of the citizens and the political and moral faults of their leaders, while he continually summoned them to repentance and a scriptural faith in the Redeemer.[6]

Zwingli's preaching and ministry were based upon a solid foundation of disciplined study and a carefully planned schedule. Oswald Myconius, who wrote the first account of Zwingli's life, described his schedule:

> He carried on all his studies standing up, setting apart certain hours for them, and nothing but dire necessity compelled him to omit them. From early morning to 10 o'clock he gave himself to reading, exegesis, theology, and writing, as time and occasion required. After dinner (the usual hour was 10 A.M.) he attended to those who wished to talk with him or get his advice or he conversed or walked out with his friends till two o'clock; then he

---

6. Ibid., pp. 30–31.

returned to his study. After supper he walked about a little, then generally wrote his letters, which occupation sometimes kept him up till midnight. Moreover, as often as business compelled he was at the command of the Senate.[7]

Significant events followed in rapid succession in Zurich. Zwingli again resisted Samson, the indulgence seller. He fell victim to the plague while ministering to the sick. Facing death he gained a new sense of dependence upon Christ. In 1521 he openly assailed the supporters of mercenary service. Under his influence the magistrates in Zurich resolved to permit no more recruiting for foreign wars. In 1522 he approved the eating of meat during Lent and preached the famous sermon "On the Choice and Free Use of Foods." He indicated that a Christian was free to fast or not to fast according to his conscience, provided he did not scandalize his neighbors. This sermon marked the beginning of Zwingli's vigorous reform effort in Zurich. His movement, like his decision to enter the priesthood, was based not on a crisis religious experience but on a deep conviction that only the Bible is binding on Christians. He attacked all practices of the church which he did not find in the Scripture. Since he did not find celibacy as a scriptural mandate for priesthood, he married Anna Reinhard in 1522. It was not until 1524, however, that he made the marriage public.

In 1523 Zwingli published his Sixty-seven Theses, a summary of his doctrines. He presented his case for reform before the council, people, and town leaders of Zurich in what came to be known as the First Disputation. This disputation, the first of four in the Zurich reformation, was held in the town hall on January 29, 1523, and was attended by more than six hundred persons. In this and the succeeding council meetings Zwingli set forth his opposition to many of the common practices in the church. He repudiated transubstantiation, the authority of the pope, saint worship, pilgrimages, purgatory, fasts, statues and images, and the Mass itself. The magistrates concurred with Zwingli's views, and one by one reforms were instituted. By

---

7. Oswald Myconius, "The Original Life of Zwingli," *The Latin Works and the Correspondence of Huldreich Zwingli Together with Selections from His German Works*, ed. Samuel Macauley Jackson, trans. Henry Preble, Walter Lichtenstein, and Lawrence A. McLouth, 3 vols. (New York: G. P. Putnam's Sons, 1912), 1:11. Used by permission.

1525 most of the reforms had been accomplished. "On April 13, 1525, the first Evangelical communion service took place in the Great Minster, and the mediaeval worship was at an end."[8]

Although the city leaders supported Zwingli, the reform was not effected without opposition. Not only the monks and other clerics whose positions were threatened by the reforms but others as well attempted to silence Zwingli. Some attacked his views in public addresses and in writing; others tried to ruin his reputation by spreading rumors. A number of plots against his life were discovered. Oswald Myconius wrote in 1532, "Zwingli sometimes dined away from home with friends or entertainers. Therefore returning he was almost always escorted, without being aware of it, by good citizens, lest evil should befall him on the way. And the Senate in this perilous time placed watchers around his house at night."[9]

Another intense controversy was created by the claims of the Anabaptists. Regarding the dispute with the Anabaptists McNeill writes:

> Zwingli was caught at a disadvantage. He had some affinity with the Anabaptists, much as he was offended by their separatism. He had suggested that infant baptism is not clearly indicated in the New Testament; he had denied the scriptural basis of tithes, and he had affirmed the paramount authority of Scripture. But the idea of a church of approved saints made sinless by regeneration seemed to him utterly unrealistic as well as unscriptural.[10]

McNeill adds, "The possibility of tolerating a separatist minority seems not to have been considered."[11] On January 17, 1525, a conference was held with the Anabaptists before the town magistrates. The outcome of the conference was that all parents were compelled to have their children baptized by the eighth day of life and that separatist religious meetings were forbidden. A swell of Anabaptist protest against the council's decision developed. In retaliation the state authorities imposed severe penalties. Anabaptists in prison were treated harshly,

8. Thomas M. Lindsay, *A History of the Reformation*, 2 vols. (Edinburgh: T. & T. Clark, 1907), 2:36.
9. Myconius, p. 18.
10. McNeill, pp. 41–42.
11. Ibid., p. 42.

and on March 7 the death penalty by drowning was ordered for those who practiced rebaptism. Felix Manz was drowned on January 5, 1527, while his aged mother, proud of her son, watched from the shore. The Anabaptist movement declined under this onslaught of persecution. Zwingli, like Luther, came to feel that complete religious freedom would lead to anarchy, and he approved restrictive measures which earlier in his career he would have considered tyrannous.

Zwingli carried the reform movement beyond Zurich. Evangelical preachers moved throughout the countryside. Efforts were made to link the Zurich reform with reform in other cities. Zwingli participated in a disputation in Bern which concluded on January 26, 1528, with the initiation of widespread reform in that city. Zwingli's ability as a preacher was evidenced in Bern. Thomas Lindsay describes the event:

> The two sermons which Zwingli preached in the cathedral during the Disputation made a powerful impression on the people of Bern. It was after one of them that M. de Watteville, the Advoyer or President of the Republic, declared himself to be convinced of the truth of the Evangelical faith, and with his whole family accepted the Reformation. His eldest son, a clergyman whose family interest had procured for him no less than thirteen benefices, and who, it was commonly supposed, would be the next Bishop of Lausanne, renounced them all to live the life of a simple country gentleman.[12]

Zurich formed political alliances with other cantons sympathetic with the reformation cause. The Roman Catholic cantons also formed an alliance. As a result Switzerland was divided into two camps. War seemed inevitable. On June 8, 1529, Zurich declared war on the opposing cantons. When the soldiers met, however, they reached a compromise and avoided battle. The terms of the agreement allowed evangelicals to preach in a wider area than previously approved by the Roman Catholic cantons. But the peace was only temporary. Zwingli realized that sooner or later the opposing cantons would go to war.

Zurich was eager to expand its alliances. Furthermore, Zwingli wanted to link the reformation in German-speaking Switzerland to the reformation in Germany under Luther. In

12. Lindsay, pp. 44–45.

October of 1529 Zwingli met with Luther and Melanchthon at
Marburg. Apparently Luther did not want an agreement, for
he arrogantly insisted on submission to his views. On the major
point of disagreement, the nature of the elements in the Eu-
charist, Luther interpreted literally the Scripture which said,
"This is my body." Zwingli, on the other hand, argued for a
symbolic interpretation of "is." The two reformers reached no
agreement. Accounts indicate that Zwingli conducted himself
in a far more scholarly and gentlemanly way than Luther.
Comparing the two, Archibald Maclaine wrote that Zwingli
was much Luther's "superior in learning, capacity, and judgment, and was much fitter to be his master than his disciple."[13]
At the end of the conference, Luther refused to clasp hands
with Zwingli as a brother in Christ.

Zwingli, disappointed by the outcome of the meeting, returned to Zurich, which was becoming increasingly isolated.
Zwingli realized that he could do nothing to prevent a war—a
war which Zurich was not prepared to fight. He endeavored to
arouse the citizens of his city to arms, but he was unsuccessful.
In October Zurich was attacked. The few troops from Zurich
were soon defeated and put to flight. Zwingli was killed, his
last words being, "They may kill the body but not the soul."[14]
His enemies cut his body into four pieces and tossed them into a
fire. Others took up the cause of reform for which Zwingli had
died. But none among the German-speaking Swiss ever attained
the powerful influence that had been exercised by Zwingli.

PREACHING AND SERMONS[15]

There were few days during his ministry in which Zwingli
did not ascend the stairs to the pulpit at least once. Yet for all
this preaching activity—presumably he had more than three
thousand occasions to preach—we have only a handful of his
sermons, a remarkable state of affairs when one realizes that
we have hundreds of sermons by John Calvin.

There are reasons we have so few sermons from Zwingli.
First, he did not preach from a manuscript, and second, he did
not have the stenographers that Calvin had to copy his ser-

---

13. Mosheim, p. 19.
14. McNeill, p. 52.
15. Article by H. Wayne Pipkin, assistant professor of church history, Baylor
University, Waco, Texas.

mons. Zwingli's preaching without a manuscript was an integral part of his preaching style. This is not to say that he did not prepare, but rather that he wanted to be free to maintain an intimate and instant contact with his hearers and free to pursue a line of thought which might only momentarily have called for comment. In essence, preaching without a manuscript was Zwingli's attempt to keep his sermons alive and relevant. Rather than sitting with pen in hand, Zwingli prepared his sermons by spending a good deal of time in thoughtful meditation. The extant sermons of Zwingli were, therefore, written by memory after the event and in most instances were expanded versions of the original. This explains the unwieldy length of most of his published sermons.

Although all of Zwingli's sermons were essentially biblical, they fall into two categories. The characteristic Zwinglian sermon was one of a continuing series of sermons on a book of the Bible. It was his practice to preach straight through one biblical book before going on to the next. Occasionally, however, he either interrupted his series to preach on a particular theme or he accepted an invitation to preach in another pulpit where he chose an appropriate theme for his topic. For example, in the summer of 1522 Zwingli preached two sermons in the Ötenbach convent on the themes of the Word of God and the Virgin Mary. Zwingli's thematic sermons reveal a wealth of classical materials. In addition, numerous biblical citations are the rule rather than the exception.

Zwingli refrained from theatrics and high rhetoric in his sermons.[16] He encouraged his students to avoid flamboyant gestures, to preach neither too fast nor too slow, and to speak neither too loud nor too soft. Zwingli himself had a weak voice, which reportedly he strengthened on Zurich's wine. In his earlier career he was known to have preached too rapidly. The length of his sermons varied somewhat, but generally required a full half hour at the least, and early in his ministry a full hour. But they were never dry expositions or homilies; his personality and humor were very much in evidence. On one occasion Canon Hofman complained that Zwingli's sermons were not

---

16. See Oskar Farner, *Huldrych Zwingli, Seine Verkündigung und ihre ersten Früchte 1520–1525*, vol. 3 of *Huldrych Zwingli* (4 vols.; Zurich: Zwingli-Verlag, 1954), pp. 94–103.

serious enough. Holy laughter was not unknown in the Great Minster. [17]

In the light of the lamentable lack of sermons from Zwingli, it is interesting to note the description of Zwingli's early sermons which Heinrich Bullinger included in his history of the Reformation:

> Soon all kinds of men, especially the common people, were gathering to hear these evangelical sermons of Zwingli. In these sermons he praised God the Father and taught that all men should only trust in the Son of God, Jesus Christ, the unique Savior of all. He attacked disbelief, superstition and hypocritical talk. He vigorously promoted repentance or reformation of life as well as Christian love and trust.[18]

Such a generalized portrayal of Zwingli's preaching cannot provide an authoritative picture of specific content, but this picture is consistent with an understanding of the essential Zwinglian theology. In general, Zwingli's preaching was directed toward the end of freeing his listeners from the world of superstition and counterfeit religion.

Bullinger notes in his description of Zwingli's first sermon at Zurich that he preached "by and with divine truth, and not with human trifles."[19] In a positive sense he urged living the practical Christian life and going beyond appearance to the one and only Savior. This impression is further enhanced by a very brief remark in a letter of Zwingli to Beatus Rhenanus, dated June 7, 1519. He mentions to Rhenanus that he is interested in what Luther's treatment of the adoration of the saints might be in his forthcoming *Exposition of the Lord's Prayer*. Zwingli is concerned with the adoration of the saints because, as he says in passing, "we have forbidden it."[20] At this early date Zwingli confesses that he has forbidden what was certainly in

---

17. Actually Hofman accused Zwingli of including too many "one-liners" (*Spitzlinien*) in his sermons. See Farner, p. 129.
18. Heinrich Bullinger, *Reformationsgeschichte*, ed. J. J. Hottinger and H. H. Voegel, 3 vols. (Frauenfeld: Ch. Beyel, 1838), 1:12.
19. Ibid.
20. Huldrych Zwingli, *Sämtliche Werke*, 14 vols. (Berlin: Schwetschke und Sohn, 1905–), 8:181.

his mind an obvious manifestation of false religion. Adoration was due to God, not creatures.

It is possible to conclude therefore that Zwingli's preaching, even as early as his move to Zurich in 1519, was at once essentially evangelical in character and a powerful force in the development of the Reformation. Whatever the perspective from which one views the preaching of Zwingli in 1519, it must become apparent that the question of reform is involved. Zwingli himself recognized this in a letter to Myconius written December 2, 1518. He first informed Myconius that he had decided to preach through the whole Gospel of Matthew, a type of pulpit practice, he noted, unheard of among the Germans.[21] Zwingli's decision was not unanimously approved in Zurich. Myconius's description of Zwingli's informing the Zurichers indicates the manner in which it was received:

> In the very first meeting with the canons he declared in person what and how he proposed to teach the people, to wit, the history of Christ the Savior as Matthew the Evangelist describes him, nor should his honour be longer obscured, whose excellence had now for a long time been hidden to the detriment of the Divine glory and of souls. The same however, he would expound not according to human reason indeed, seeing that he was sworn to no interpreter, but according to the purpose of the Spirit, which through diligent collating of the Scriptures, and through fervent prayers from the heart, he doubted not that he should be given to understand. On hearing this some mourned, and some rejoiced, just as there had been difference of opinion previously among his electors.[22]

Zwingli's decision could not help but startle his colleagues, for he had indeed determined to make a striking innovation. No longer would he preach merely from the assigned texts for the day, the pericopes, interpreting only in the light of man-made commentaries. Relying upon the inspiration of the Spirit of God he would return to the true source, the Scriptures, and would lay aside the standard commentaries themselves. Whereas formerly the preaching in Zurich followed a predictable and often-trod path of interpretation based on the writings

---

21. Zwingli, 8:106.
22. Myconius, pp. 8–9.

of the Scholastics, Zwingli was proposing a new and more revolutionary method of preaching. The canons were justifiably worried, for they could not tell where this innovative approach would lead them.

Actually he denied that his method of preaching was without precedent. When Canon Conrad Hofman complained that Zwingli used an unprecedented approach to preaching by omitting the pericopes, Zwingli pointed to the custom set centuries before by the Homilies of Chrysostom and Augustine's Homilies on John.[23]

If one considers Zwingli's own understanding of his preaching and the content of his sermons, a clearer picture of his early pulpit activity in Zurich emerges. In the *Archeteles* of 1522 Zwingli had occasion to defend the preaching he had done at Zurich:

> I have never planted any other plant than that which Christ planted at the direction of his Father, which cannot be rooted up. For three years ago [i.e., 1519] now (to give you an account of the preaching I have done at Zurich), I preached the entire Gospel according to Matthew.[24]

He describes his series approach to preaching in this treatise. After finishing Matthew, he preached from the Acts of the Apostles so "that the Church of Zurich might see in what way and with what sponsors the Gospel was carried forth and spread abroad."[25] Following this he preached from 1 Timothy, and then he skipped to Galatians "inasmuch as certain smatterers showed perverted opinions of the faith."[26] Then came 2 Timothy, 1 and 2 Peter, and Hebrews. Zwingli felt that he had preached for three years to his people "that Christ, having been made a sacrifice once for all, has accomplished their salvation forever."[27]

Rilliet has summarized the significance of Zwingli's preach-

23. Bullinger, p. 12.
24. Zwingli, 1:284–85; translated in Samuel Macauley Jackson, ed., *The Latin Works and the Correspondence of Huldreich Zwingli Together with Selections from His German Works*, trans. Henry Preble, Walter Lichtenstein, and Lawrence A. McLouth, 3 vols. (New York: G. P. Putnam's Sons, 1912), 1:238.
25. Zwingli, 1:285; Jackson, 1:238.
26. Ibid.
27. Zwingli, 1:285; Jackson, 1:239.

ing by remarking with regard to his preaching through Matthew that "Scripture now dominates tradition."[28] Zwingli turned from what he thought to be mere human invention and creation to the primary source of true religion. "I have not," he wrote in a significant passage, "used any false nostrums or tricks or exhortations, but in simple words and terms native to the Swiss I have drawn them to the recognition of their trouble, having learned this from Christ himself, who began his own preaching with it."[29] The true standard of his preaching was Christ. It was this norm to which he appealed, in contrast to the "false nostrums or tricks or exhortations" of traditional interpretation. With this true source Zwingli drew his listeners "to the recognition of their trouble," i.e., to the realization of their actual status before God. Zwingli claimed to have patterned his preaching along the lines of Christ's preaching, who began his ministry with a call to repentance.

His commitment to his countrymen was no less evident, for he preached to them "in simple words and terms native to the Swiss." He recognized that his preaching must be at once biblical and personally relevant to the lives of his listeners if it was to be truly effective. His goal was to "call my flock absolutely away, as far as I can, *from hope in any created being to the one true God* and Jesus His only begotten Son, our Lord, he that trusteth in whom shall never die."[30]

Gordon Rupp has noted that when Zwingli announced he would preach straight through the Gospel of Matthew, the Zurich reformation had begun.[31] Indeed, Zwingli's preaching activity was closely tied to the progress of the Reformation. He had made what was tantamount to a rediscovery of the Bible in his preaching. The importance of this event for the Reformation can hardly be overemphasized:

> Shortsighted and with a weak voice, he lacked the gifts
> of the popular orator, but his preaching is the secret
> of his dominance of the great city, and not all his actions

28. Jean Rilliet, *Zwingli*, trans. Harold Knight (Philadelphia: Westminster Press, 1964), p. 57.
29. Zwingli, 1:285–86; Jackson, 1:239.
30. Zwingli, 1:286; Jackson, 1:239. Italics added.
31. E. G. Rupp, "The Reformation in Zürich, Strassburg and Geneva," *The Reformation 1520–59*, vol. 2 of *The New Cambridge Modern History* (14 vols.; Cambridge: Cambridge University Press, 1968), p. 99.

in the small or great council can match it in importance. It is something with few parallels (Calvin, Knox, Latimer?)—this continuous biblical exposition, adjusted to the practical needs of each changing day, in a community small enough for everybody to be known, and where all the effective leadership in the city sat under the Word. The historicity of the mandate of 1520 whereby the council authorized evangelical preaching has been questioned, but of the fact there is no doubt; this scriptural preaching went on here, first of all the cities of Switzerland.[32]

---

32. Ibid.

Sermons

CONCERNING STEADFASTNESS AND PERSEVERANCE IN GOODNESS

Matthew 10:22

SINCE in the midst of the removal of the images, altars, and other things, you are interested in finding that truth which shall be victorious, it seemed profitable to me to speak of steadfastness and perseverance in goodness before our departure. Concerning this matter you should know that steadfastness is the sort of virtue that, without it, nothing just can be achieved. When it is lacking we men are counted as women who are neither pious nor faithful; indeed, no one can be pious or faithful without steadfastness. No fatherland nor home can be preserved without it; in fact, nothing can be preserved from shame and mockery where it is not. As all virtues are hypocrisy without the fear of God and faith, so should we say that we do not see this steadfastness coming from ourselves, but from God, in whom we unflinchingly desire preservation.

Thus we find that our Lord Jesus Christ taught and showed us steadfastness with words and deeds. He remained steadfast even unto the death of the cross, although it is true that his humanity craved somewhat weakly not to die. He neither stopped nor softened his remarks about the obstinacy of his opponents, even though he occasionally restrained himself until his time had come. And thus he taught us: "Whoever is steadfast until the end will be saved" (Matt. 10:22). He meant by such words that one did not need to have doubt; whoever will live, think and confess according to his will and word must suffer persecution, be troubled and brought to grief. However, these things can be overcome with patience that does not despair. The heathen have also said, *"Ferendo vincitur fortuna,"* that

Huldrych Zwingli, "Von Standhafte und Verharren in Guotem," *Der Prediger,* in *Hauptschriften,* ed. Fritz Blanke, Oskar Farner, Rudolf Pfister, 11 vols. (Zurich: Zwingli-Verlag, 1940-), 2:67–78. Translated from the German by H. Wayne Pipkin. The translator wishes to express his appreciation to Jochem F. Burckhardt and Robert C. Walton for their help with some difficult passages.

is, "one must overcome and parry misfortune only with patience and endurance." He teaches us by the prophet Ezekiel that the righteousness of the pious will no longer be considered if he falls (Ezek. 3:20). For it is more disgraceful to desist from work frivolously than never to have begun. He says that no one is wise who does not sit down and figure the cost before he begins to build; so that before the finish of the affair he will not be scoffed at by those who say, "See, the man began to build and cannot complete it." Also, no lord begins a war who does not first consider how many troops he would like to lead out against the enemy (Luke 14:28–32). And whoever sets his hand to the plow and looks back is not fit for the Kingdom of God (Luke 9:62), that is, for the preaching office. Thereby we observe that he wants to have those who move forward.

Who was more steadfast than Moses, whom the children of Israel so often despised, so often undertook to assault? Yet no one could move him from the calm intention of doing good for the people. And as soon as it seemed that God himself was against them, he demanded that God first consume him, then the people (Num. 11:15). For this reason, as Hebrews 3:5 says, he has been justly called the loyal housekeeper of God before all others in the household of God. What kind of a tenacious man was that, who in the fortieth year could be neither broken nor softened so that he would do anything or allow anything to be done for the sake of friends that would be against God and the common well-being; nor despair that God might leave him; or who, in the absence of food and drink, would not run undaunted to God; or that he would ever look back! We live now forty years complaining with afflictions after we have grown up, and he suffered such troubles unweakened for forty years; indeed, he aged and died therein. David traveled about almost fourteen years after he had first been anointed king by Samuel, during which time he did not rule, excepting finally a few years in Hebron. Yet no poverty nor misfortune could bring him to the place that he would not believe God and despise the kingdom or that he would do evil to Saul even though he could do so without danger, but he stuck to the goal of goodness and peace with such piety and integrity until he became a great example of steadfastness for us. The Roman Cornelius Scipio was still so young that he could not be taken into the Council. However, when the battle at Cannae against Hannibal was lost, the nobles who came from there were taking counsel as to how they could leave Italy and take to the sea in flight. Scipio became aware of the suggestion. Unauthorized, he met with several in the Council, took his sword and forced them to swear that they would not leave Italy and Rome, their home, but defend it. He maintained such steadfastness in all things until his death. In short, no virtue is a virtue if it is not executed with steadfastness.

Now when your wisdom and love assail the idolatrous embellishments of the government of the Mass and other things, you need neither counsel nor crowbar more than steadfastness. For first of all, we have several who are untimely clever in the divine Word, who suppose that they act greatly while saying, "One should, in the first place, take the idols out of the heart and then from that place before the eyes." They are half right. Certainly no one removes outwardly what he has not removed from his heart. I grant that to all those who know how they love their little idols: these would not like to suffer their being touched. However, if they are not sad if the idols are cut up into firewood, it is a sign that they are not sorry. Apparently they have already been removed from the heart. Therefore, the clever ones are only talking because they want something special. To say that one should not remove them until no one is offended and they have come out of the hearts of all men is the same as if we were to say that Christ was wrong in overturning the chairs and changing tables, and chasing the changers out with a whip (John 2:14-16). For they were not yet instructed in their hearts that they were wrong. For they said to him, "What sign can you show us that you have the right to do this?" Christ would have had to let the things stand until they had all been instructed.

On the other hand we have many opponents who neither want to hear nor accept the Word of God. These two types will give you much to do, for usually they are not without cunning, and as such they will bring new anxieties and threats every day. However, according to the word of Christ you should not fear them, for he has overcome the world (John 16:33). Therefore we may well observe that they are in his power since he makes us victorious for all time. And no one should get the idea that he himself is not at all times to watch and have care; rather, Christ calls us all to watch. However, I will gladly predict to you that I do not doubt that God will allow such dangers to encounter you and that you will see that he powerfully works for and shelters you. Thus, when the dangers come, do not be frightened! For God will only let you have trials and tribulations so that, confessing the sole honor of God, you may recognize his certain help all the better. For he will lead you into need so that you will not trust yourself to help. He helps you out. For you will see exactly that all things come from him alone, and that he also undoubtedly helps us.

Now, however, some say it will be easy for you to be steadfast, for you have ancestors who will not let you err. For I have never seen a work of God in process which did not come to the point that *"ho theos apo mechanes"* (that is, God) did not have to bring it to a right end with his grace and power. There lie the altars and idols in the temple.[1] Whoever still has a horror of that, though not from con-

---

1. The following marginal note was published with the sermon: "The sermon was held where on the previous evening the images had been thrown on the floor and the altar broken up."

science, must see now whether the idols have mattered for anything or not. The filth and garbage must be gotten out so that the immeasurable amount of money which you have spent for other men on the idolatrous, foolish works, may henceforth be spent on the living image of God.[2] There are those weak and quarrelsome dispositions who complain about the abolition of the idols, even though they now see publicly that they have nothing of the saints – only things decaying and cracking like another piece of wood and stone. Here lies one with its head off, and there is another without its arm. Now if I beheaded or injured the saints who are with God, so that they were injured like the idols are, and had they the power which we (not they themselves) have ascribed to them, then they would allow no man to leave the place alive.

I must also instruct you concerning this matter: disputations will not help the spirit of those who are quarrelsome or weak. For with quarrels it can be no different but that one side must usually be wrong. When now these same ones are as bold as those who actually have the truth, this consoles the ones eager to argue and makes the weak weaker. However, where there is a well-established steadfast spirit, he will accept the truth from wherever it comes. He sees from one hour to the next what colors truth has and which it does not have, and follows happily after truth. Accordingly, he likes to delight and amuse himself in the truth, as if only he or another alone or more could prophesy. Therefore, if anyone has been injured by all this, then he should not be angry. The dispute has happened so that the ones who are eager to argue, although they did not lose heart, lost the boldness to speak against the truth; and the right was given to the Christian community and government to act divinely and honestly, unerring and undaunted. You are provided with God-fearing, pious, learned theologians and preachers. Listen to them in earnest as they expound the divine promises or warnings! Thus will your heart be constantly secured in all deeds and actions with the Word of God, and no error can befall you.

Recognize here the freedom Christ has given you! And stand steadfast therein according to the word of Paul in Galatians 5:1, and do not let yourselves be afflicted any more with the yoke of bondage or servitude. You know how much oppression we have suffered in our consciences since we have been led from one false consolation to another, from one statute to another. These have only loaded down the conscience. They have not comforted it or made it free. However, now you see what freedom and comfort you have in the recognition and confidence you have in the one God through Jesus Christ his only begotten Son. Don't let yourself ever be moved from the freedom and redemption of your heart.

---

2. By this Zwingli means the poor.

More bravery is demanded here than in any other matter. How our forefathers (God be praised!) have always stood bravely and steadfastly in the defense of the physical freedoms. Thus should you much more stand steadfastly in those things which here make us free in conscience and there eternally joyous, without doubting that God who has illumined and drawn you will also draw our dear neighbors, the rest of the confederates, in his time, so that in true friendship God may also allow us to be better enlightened than before. May God who created us and redeemed us all grant this to us and to them! Amen.

ON THE CHOICE AND FREE USE OF FOODS

Mark 7:15

DEARLY BELOVED IN GOD, after you have heard so eagerly the Gospel and the teachings of the holy Apostles, now for the fourth year, teachings which Almighty God has been merciful enough to publish to you through my weak efforts, the majority of you, thank God, have been greatly fired with the love of God and of your neighbor. You have also begun faithfully to embrace and to take unto yourselves the teachings of the Gospel and the liberty which they give, so that after you have tried and tasted the sweetness of the heavenly bread by which man lives, no other food has since been able to please you. And, as when the children of Israel were led out of Egypt, at first impatient and unaccustomed to the hard journey, they sometimes in vexation wished themselves back in Egypt, with the food left there, such as garlic, onions, leeks, and flesh-pots, they still entirely forgot such complaints when they had come into the promised land and had tasted its luscious fruits: thus also some among us leapt and jumped unseemly at the first spurring—as still some do now, who like a horse neither are able nor ought to rid themselves of the spur of the Gospel;

Reprinted from *The Latin Works and the Correspondence of Huldreich Zwingli*, ed. Samuel Macauley Jackson, 3 vols. (New York: G. P. Putnam's Sons, Knickerbocker Press, 1912), 1:70–112.

still, in time they have become so tractable and so accustomed to the salt and good fruit of the Gospel, which they find abundantly in it, that they not only avoid the former darkness, labour, food, and yoke of Egypt, but also are vexed with all brothers, that is, Christians, wherever they do not venture to make free use of Christian liberty. And in order to show this, some have issued German poems, some have entered into friendly talks and discussions in public rooms and at gatherings; some now at last during this fast—and it was their opinion that no one else could be offended by it—at home, and when they were together, have eaten meat, eggs, cheese, and other food hitherto unused in fasts. But this opinion of theirs was wrong; for some were offended, and that, too, from simple good intentions; and others, not from love of God or of his commands (as far as I can judge), but that they might reject that which teaches and warns common men, and they might not agree with their opinions, acted as though they were injured and offended, in order that they might increase the discord. The third part of the hypocrites of a false spirit did the same, and secretly excited the civil authorities, saying that such things neither should nor would be allowed, that it would destroy the fasts, just as though they never could fast, if the poor laborer, at this time of spring, having to bear most heavily the burden and heat of the day, ate such food for the support of his body and on account of his work. Indeed, all these have so troubled the matter and made it worse, that the honorable Council of our city was obliged to attend to the matter. And when the previously mentioned evangelically instructed people found that they were likely to be punished, it was their purpose to protect themselves by means of the Scriptures, which, however, not one of the Council had been wise enough to understand, so that he could accept or reject them. What should I do, as one to whom the care of souls and the Gospel have been entrusted, except search the Scriptures, particularly again, and bring them as a light into this darkness of error, so that no one, from ignorance or lack of recognition, injuring or attacking another come into great regret, especially since those who eat are not triflers or clowns, but honest folk and of good conscience? Wherefore, it would stand· very evil with me, that I, as a careless shepherd and one only for the sake of selfish gain, should treat the sheep entrusted to my care, so that I did not strengthen the weak and protect the strong. I have therefore made a sermon about the choice or difference of food, in which sermon nothing but the Holy Gospels and the teachings of the Apostles have been used, which greatly delighted the majority and emancipated them. But those, whose mind and conscience is defiled, as Paul says (Titus 1:15), it only made mad. But since I have used only the above-mentioned Scriptures, and since those people cry out none the less unfairly, so loud that their cries are heard elsewhere, and since they that hear are vexed on account of their simplicity and ignorance of the matter, it seems to me to be necessary to explain the thing from the Scriptures, so that every one depending on the Divine Scriptures may maintain himself against the enemies of the Scriptures. Wherefore, read and understand; open the eyes and the ears of the heart, and hear and see what the Spirit of God says to us.

First, Christ says, Matthew 15:17, "What goes in at the mouth defileth not the man," etc. From these words anyone can see that no food can defile a man, providing it is taken in moderation and thankfulness. That this is the meaning, is showed by the fact that the Pharisees became vexed and angry at the word as it stands, because according to Jewish law they took great account of the choice of food and abstinence, all of which regulations Christ desired to do away with in the New Testament. These words of Christ, Mark speaks still more clearly, 7:15: "There is nothing from without a man, that entering into him can defile him; but the things which come out from him, those are they that defile the man." So the meaning of Christ is, all foods are alike as far as defilement goes: they cannot defile at all.

Secondly, as it is written in the Acts of the Apostles, 10:10, when Peter was in Joppa (now called Jaffa), he went one day upon the housetop at the sixth hour, and desired to pray. He became hungry and wished to eat; and when the servants were making ready, he fell into a trance and saw heaven opened and a vessel descending as it were a great linen cloth held together by the four corners and let down upon earth, in which cloth were all four-footed animals, wild beasts, and creeping and flying creatures. Then a voice spoke to him, saying: "Arise, Peter, kill and eat." But Peter said, "No, Lord, for I have never eaten forbidden or unclean food." Then again the voice spoke to him, saying: "What God has purified, shalt thou not consider forbidden or unclean." Now, God has made all things clean, and has not forbidden us to eat, as his very next words prove. Why do we burden ourselves wilfully with fasts? Here answer might be made: This miracle, shown to Peter, meant that he should not avoid the heathen, but them also should he call to the grace of the Gospel, and therefore material food should not be understood here. Answer: All miracles that God has performed, although symbolical in meaning, were still real occurrences and events. As when Moses struck the rock with his staff and it gave forth water, it was symbolical of the true Rock of Christ, from which flowed, and ever shall flow for us all, the forgiveness of sins and the blessings of heavenly gifts, but none the less was the rock really smitten and gave forth water. And so here, although this miracle was symbolical, still the words of God's voice are clear: What God hath cleansed, shalt thou not consider unclean. Until I forget these words I shall use them.

Thirdly, Paul writes to the Corinthians (1, 6:12): "All things are lawful unto me, but all things are not expedient: all things are lawful for me, but I will not be brought under the power of any. Meats for the belly and the belly for meats: but God shall destroy both it and them." That is, to me are all things free, although some things are rather to be avoided, in case they offend my neighbor too much. (About the troubling of one's neighbor, I shall speak specially later on.) And therefore no one can take from me my freedom and bring me under his authority. Food is taken into the belly to sustain life. As now the belly and the food are both to be destroyed, it makes no difference what one eats or wherewith one nourishes his mortal body.

Fourthly, Paul says, 1 Corinthians 8:8: "But meat commendeth us not to God: for neither, if we eat, are we the better; nor, if we eat not, are we the worse." This word Paul speaks of the food which was offered to the idols, not now of daily food. Notice this, however, to a clearer understanding. At the time when Paul wrote the epistle, there were still many unbelievers, more indeed, it seems to me, than Christians. These unbelievers offered to their idols, according to custom, animals, such as calves, sheep, and also other forms of food; but at these same offerings, a great part, often all, was given to eat to those that made the offerings. And as unbelievers and Christians lived together, the Christians were often invited to partake of food or meat, that had been sacrificed to the honor of the idols. Then some of the Christians were of the opinion, that it was not proper to eat this food; but others thought that, if they ate the food of the idols, but did not believe in them, such food could not harm them, and thought themselves stronger in their belief, because they had been free to do this thing, than those who from faint-heartedness and hesitation did not venture to eat all kinds of food. To settle this difference, Paul uses the above words: "No kind of food commends us to God." Even if one eats the food of the idols, he is not less worthy before God, nor yet more worthy, than one who does not eat it; and whoever does not eat it is no better. Indeed that will seem very strange to you, not only that meat is not forbidden, but also that even what has been offered to idols a Christian may eat.

Fifthly, Paul says in the First Epistle to the Corinthians, 10:25: "Whatsoever is sold in the shambles, that eat, asking no questions for conscience's sake." These words are clear and need no explanation, except that they are among other words about the offense caused by the food of idols. But do not let yourself err. From the pulpit I shall speak sufficiently of giving offense, and perhaps more clearly than you have ever heard.

Sixthly, Paul also says, Colossians 2:16: "No man shall judge you in meat or in drink, or in respect of a holy day." Again you hear that you are to judge no man either as good or bad from his food or drink; he may eat what he please. If one will, let him eat refuse. Here it should be always understood that we are speaking not of amount but of kind. As far as kind and character of food are concerned, we may eat all foods to satisfy the needs of life, but not with immoderation or greediness.

Seventhly, Paul says again, 1 Timothy 4:1: "Now the Spirit speaketh expressly, that in the latter times some shall depart from the faith, giving heed to seducing spirits, and doctrines of devils; speaking lies in hypocrisy; having their consciences seared with a hot iron; forbidding to marry and commanding to abstain from meats, which God hath created to be received with thanksgiving of them which believe and know the truth. For every creature of God is good, and nothing to be refused, if it be received with thanksgiving: for it is sanctified by the word of God and of prayer." These are all the words of Paul. And what could be more clearly said? He says that God's Spirit spoke this as a warning, that they might withstand this, who had no fixed strong belief, and who did not put trust in God, but in their own works which they themselves chose as good. And that such things are placed in them by seducing spirits and devils, that inspire men with hypocrisy, that is, with the outward form, lead men away from trust in God to confidence in themselves. And yet the same will always surely realise in themselves, that they act dishonorably toward God, and they always feel the pain of it, and know their disgraceful unfaithfulness in that they see only their own advantage or desire and greed of heart. Still they are willing to sell themselves, as though they did it not for their own sakes, but for God's. That is having a conscience branded on the cheek. Then he recounts what they will forbid to do as bad. They shall not enter into marriage or wed. Know too that purity so disgracefully preserved had its original prohibition from the devil, which prohibition has brought more sin into the world than the abstinence from any food. But this is not the place to speak of that. Likewise it is forbidden that one should eat this or that food, which God created for the good and sustenance of men. Look, what does Paul say? Those that take from Christians such freedom by their prohibition are inspired by the devil. "Would I do that?" said the wolf, as the raven sat on the sow's body. Now God placed all things under man at the head of creation, that man might serve him alone. And although certain foods are forbidden in the Old Testament, they are on the contrary made free in the New, as the words of Mark 7:15 clearly show, quoted in the first article above, as also Luke 16:15. "For that which is highly esteemed among men is an abomination in the sight of God." The law and the prophets were only a symbol, or have lasted only to John. Hear now, that which seemed great to men was detested by God (the word is *abominatio*), and as far as the law is ceremonial and to be used at court, it has been superseded. Hear then that whatever a man eats cannot make him evil, if it is eaten in thankfulness. Notice that proper thankfulness consists in this, that a man firmly believe that all our food and living are determined and continued by God alone, and that a man be grateful for it; for we are more worthy in the sight of God than the fowls of the air which he feeds: us then without doubt he will feed. But the greatest thanks is a conscientious recognition that all our necessities are provided by him. Of these words nothing further.

Eighthly, after Paul shows Titus (1:15) that there are many disobedient, many vain talkers and deceivers, which one must overcome, he adds: "Unto the pure all things are pure: but unto them that are defiled and unbelieving is nothing pure; but even their mind and conscience is defiled." Here you see again he did not desire Jewish wiles heeded; this is plainly shown by the words next preceding, where he says: "Wherefore rebuke and punish them sharply (of course with words), that they may be sound in the faith, not listening to Jewish fables and human commandments, that pervert the truth." But they desired to draw the new Christians into abstinence from food, pretending that some food was unclean and improper to eat; but Paul showed that they were wrong, and said: To those of a pure belief, all things are pure, but to the unbelievers nothing is pure. Cause: their hearts and consciences are defiled. They are unbelievers that think the salvation, mercy, and freedom of Christ are not so great and broad as they really are, as Christ chid his disciples, saying that they were of little faith, Matthew 16:8 and 6:30. In these passages we are certainly taught that we are not only fed each day by him, but also controlled and instructed with fatherly fidelity, if we console ourselves confidently alone in his word and commands. Wherefore every Christian should depend alone upon him and believe his words steadfastly. Now if you do that, then you will not believe that any food can defile a man; and if you surely believe it, then it is surely so, for his words cannot deceive. Accordingly all things are pure to you. Why? You believe, therefore all things are pure to you. The unbeliever is impure. Why? He has a doubting heart, which either does not believe the greatness and freedom of God's mercy, or does not believe these to be as great as they are. Therefore he doubts, and as soon as he doubts, he sins, according to Romans 14:23.

Ninthly, Paul says to the Hebrews (8:9): "Be not carried about with divers and strange doctrines. For it is a good thing that the heart be established with grace; not with meats, which have not profited them that have been occupied therein." In these words see first that we should not be carried about with many kinds of doctrines, also that without doubt or suspicion the Holy Gospel is a certain doctrine, with which we can console ourselves and on which we can surely depend. Accordingly it is best to establish the heart with grace. Now the Gospel is nothing but the good news of the grace of God; on this we should rest our hearts—that is, we should know the grace of the Gospel to be so certain and ready, and trust it, so that we may establish our hearts in no other doctrine, and not trust to food, that is, to eating or abstaining from eating (so also Chrysostom takes these words) this or that food; for that such oversight and choice of food was not of profit to those that have clung thereto is clear enough.

These announcements seem to me to be enough to prove that it is proper for a Christian to eat all foods. But a heathen argument I must bring forward for those that are better read in Aristotle than in the Gospels or in Paul. Tell me which you think more necessary to a man, food or money? I think you will say that food is more useful than money, otherwise we should die of hunger with our money, as Midas died, who, according to the poets, desired that everything he touched be turned to gold. And so food is more important to preserve life than money; for man lived on food before money was invented. Now Aristotle says that money is indifferent—that is, it is neither good nor bad in itself, but becomes good or bad according to its use, whether one uses it in a good or bad way. Much more then is food neither good nor bad in itself (which I, however, for the present omit), but it is necessary and therefore more truly good. And it can never become bad, except as it is used immoderately; for a certain time does not make it bad, but rather the abuse of men, when they use it without moderation and belief.

No Christian can deny these arguments, unless he defends himself by denying the Scriptures: He is then, however, no Christian, because he does not believe Christian doctrine. There are nevertheless some who take exception to this, either to the times, or the fasting, or human prohibitions, or giving offense. All these I will answer from the Scriptures later with God's help.

At first then they object to the time: Although all things are pure, still they are not so at all times; and so during the fasts, quarter fasts, Rogation-day week, Shrove Tuesday, Friday, and Saturday, it is improper to eat meat. During fasts also eggs, milk, and milk products are not proper. Answer: I do not say that these are not forbidden by men; we see and hear that daily. But all of my efforts are directed against this assumption, that we are restrained at this and that time by divine law. Let each one fast as often as the spirit of true belief urges him. But in order to see that according to the law of Christ we are free at all times, consider as follows:

First, Mark 2:23, once when Christ was going through the cornfields, his disciples began to pluck the ears (and eat). But the Pharisees said to him: "Lo, what are thy disciples doing that is not proper on the Sabbath day?" And Christ said to them: "Have ye not read what David did when he had need, when he and they with him were hungry; how in the days of Abiathar, the high priest, he went into the house of God and ate the bread that was offered to God, which it was improper for anyone to eat but the priests, and gave also to those with him, saying to them, 'The Sabbath was made for man, and not man for the Sabbath: Therefore the Son of man is also Lord of the Sabbath.'" Notice here that need is superior not only to human but also to divine law; for observing the Sabbath is divine law. And still the hunger of the disciples did not observe the Sabbath. Notice again that no place withstands need, and that David in need might go into the temple. Notice also that the matter of persons is not respected in need; for David and his followers were not priests, but ate the food proper only for priests to eat. This I show you now that you may learn that what is said of one circumstance is said in common of all circumstances in the Scriptures, if anything depends on circumstances or is deduced from circumstances. Circumstances are where, when, how, the person, or about whom. Thus Christ says, Matthew 24:23: "Then if any man shall say unto you, Lo, here is Christ, or there; believe it not." See, this is the circumstance where, or the place. The meaning is that God is not revealed more in one place than in another. Indeed, when the false prophets say that, one is not to believe them. In this way you should understand the circumstance of time, and other circumstances, that not more at one time than at another God is revealed as merciful or as wroth, but at all times alike. Else he would be subject to the times which we had chosen, and he would be changeable who suffers no change. So also of the matter of persons; for God is not more ready or open in mercy and grace to a person of gentle birth than to the base born, as the holy Paul[1] says, Acts 10:34: "Of a truth I perceive that God is no respecter of persons." But we do not need this proof here, where we wish to prove that all time is free to men. For the words of Christ are of themselves clear enough, when he says: the Sabbath is made for man and not man for the Sabbath; the Sabbath is in the power of man, not man in the power of the Sabbath. In a word, the Sabbath and all time are subject to man, not man to the Sabbath. Now if it is true that the Sabbath which God established is to be subject to us, then much more the time which men have imposed upon us. Indeed, not only the time but also the persons, that have thus fixed and established these particular times, are none other than the servants of Christ and co-workers in the secret things of God, not revealed to men. And these same co-workers should not rule Christians, commanding as over-lords, but should be ready only for their service and for their good. Therefore Paul says, 1 Corinthians 7:35: "I say this for your good, not that I would put a noose about your necks" – that is, I would not seize and compel you with a command. Again he speaks, 1 Corinthians 3:21: "All things are yours; whether Paul, or Apollos, or Peter, or the world, or life, or death, or things present, or things to come; all are yours." Here you see that all things are intended for men or for the service of men, not for their oppression, yes, the Apostles themselves are for men, not men for the Apostles.

----

1. It should be Peter, of course.

O overflowing spring of God's mercy! how well Paul speaks when he says, that these things are known but through the Spirit of God. Therefore we have not received the spirit of this world, but the spirit that is from God, because we see what great things are given us by God. You know your liberty too little. Cause: the false prophets have not told you, preferring to lead you about rather as a pig tied with a string; and we poor sinners cannot be led to the love of God any other way but by being taught to summon unto ourselves the Spirit of God, so that we may know the great things which God has given us. For who could but be thankful to God, so kind, and who could but be drawn into a wonderful love of him? Here notice too that it is not the intention of Christ, that man should not keep the Sabbath (for us Christians Sunday is ordained as the Sabbath), but where our use or need requires something else, the Sabbath itself, not only other times, shall be subject to us. Here you are not to understand either the extreme necessity, in which one would be near death, as the mistaken theologists dream, but ordinary daily necessity. For the disciples of Christ were not suffering extreme necessity, when on the Sabbath day they plucked the ears, else they would not have answered Christ as they did, when he asked them, Luke 22:35: "When I sent you without purse and scrip, lacked ye anything?" For the disciples answered: "Nothing." From this we understand that Christ never allowed his disciples to fall into such dire extremity, but that the need, which they felt on Sunday, was nothing but ordinary hunger, as also the word "need" as we use it does not mean the last stages of necessity, but has the usual meaning; as when one says, "I have need," he does not refer to the last or greatest want, but to a sufficiency of that which daily need demands. Then as far as time is concerned, the need and use of all food are free, so that whatever food our daily necessity requires, we may use at all times and on all days, for time shall be subject to us.

Secondly, Christ says, Luke 27:20: "The kingdom of God cometh not with observation: neither shall they say, Lo! here, lo! there." This word observation, Latin *observatio,* has this meaning, as if one carefully watched over something that had its time and moment, and if one did not take it then, it would pass away, as fishermen and fowlers usually watch, because fish and fowl have certain times and are not always to be caught. Not thus the kingdom of God, for it will not come with observation of time or place. Since now the mistaken theologists say that we ourselves deserve the kingdom of God with our works, which we choose of our own free will and complete according to our powers, the words of Christ, who cannot lie, answer: if the kingdom of God cometh not with observation or watching (of time, or place, or of all circumstances, as is proved in the above paragraph), and if at any time the prohibiting of the food which God has left free is nothing else but observation, then the kingdom of God will never be made ready by the prohibition of food. Now it must be that abstinence cannot avail anything as to time, and you are always to understand that it is not our intention to speak here of amount, but only of kind, neither of the times which God hath set, but of those which men have established.

Thirdly, Paul writes to the Galatians (4:9): "But now after ye have known God, how turn ye again to the weak and beggarly elements, whereunto ye deserve to be again in bondage? You have expectation, or you keep day and month, time and year." Here you hear the anger of Paul at the Galatians, because after they had learned and known God (which is nothing else but being known or enlightened of God), they still returned to the elements, which he more closely describes in Colossians 2:20. But since we must use these words later more accurately and must explain them, we shall now pass them over, satisfying ourselves with knowing what the weak elements are. In Latin and Greek the letters were called elements, for the reason that as all things are made up and composed of elements, so also each word was made of letters. Now the Jews and heathen have always clung closely to the letter of the law, which oppresses much, indeed kills, as Paul says. Not only in the Old Testament, but also in the New, it oppresses much. Is that not a severe word which is found in Matthew 5:22? "But I say unto you, that whosoever is angry with his brother shall be in danger of the judgment." So it is, if taken literally, indeed impossible for us weak mortals to keep. And therefore Christ has given it to us that we might recognize our shortcomings therein, and then take refuge alone in him, who mercifully pitied our shortcomings when he said, Matthew 11:28: "Come unto me, all ye that labor and are heavy laden, and I will give you rest."

But whosoever does not know and will not know this narrow way to the mercy of God through Christ, undertakes with his own powers to fulfill the law, sees only the letter of the law and desires with his might to fulfill that, prescribing for himself this and that chastisement and abstinence at certain times, places, and under other circumstances, and after all that he still does not fulfill the law, but the more he prides himself on having fulfilled the law, the less he has fulfilled it, for in his industry he becomes puffed up in himself. As the Pharisee, that boasted of the elements – that is, of the works which he had literally fulfilled – said, "I thank thee, O God, that I am not as other men are; I fast," etc. Consider the over-wise piety that exalts itself at once above other men, from no other reason than that according to his advice or opinion, and powers, he is confident to have fulfilled the law; and, on the other hand, consider the publican hoping for nothing but the rich mercy of God, and counting his own works nothing, but only saying: "O God, be merciful to me, a sinner!" Is not, then, the publican considered more righteous before God than the Pharisee? From all this you see that the weak elements are noth-

ing else than human wisdom and conception of happiness, for man
either purposes to wish and to be able to keep the letter of the law or
else prescribes for himself some work to do, which God has not commanded but left free, and therefore likes to think the works prescribed
by himself to be a sure road to blessedness, and clings to his opinion
to his own injury. And for just this reason Paul complains of the
Galatians, that having been mercifully enlightened of God they turned
again to their own devices, that is, to the weak elements, to which
the Jews and heathen held, and had not so strong a belief in God, that
they trusted alone in him and hoped alone in him, listened alone to
his ordinances and will, but foolishly turned again to the devices of
men, who, as though they desired to improve what had been neglected
by God, said to themselves: "This day, this month, this time wilt thou
abstain from this or that," and make thus ordinances, persuading
themselves that he sins who does not keep them. This abstaining I
do not wish to condemn, if it occurs freely, to put the flesh under
control, and if no self-confidence or vainglory, but rather humility,
results. See, that is branding and injuring one's own conscience
capriciously, and is turning toward true idolatry, and is, as David says,
Psalm 81:12, "walking in one's own counsels." But this God desired
to prevent by the words of David, who says: "Hear, O my people, I
will testify unto thee, Israel (that is, he sees God and trusts him so
thoroughly that he is possessed of him), if thou wilt hearken unto
me; there shall no strange god be in thee; neither shalt thou worship
any strange god. I am the Lord thy God, which brought thee out of the
land of Egypt: open thy mouth, and I will fill or satisfy it. But my
people did not hear my voice, and Israel (that is, that which should
be Israel) did not hearken to me, and I left them to their own desires,
and they will walk in their own counsels." O Christian of right belief,
consider these words well, ponder them carefully, and you will see
that God desires that we hearken to him alone! If now we are thoroughly imbued with him, no new god will be honored within our
hearts, no man instead of God, no feeling of our own instead of God.
But if we do not hear the true warnings of God, he will let us walk
according to the desires and devices of our own hearts. Do we not
see that consolation oftener is sought in human hearts than in God;
that they are more severely punished who transgress human laws than
those who not only transgress but also despise and reject God's laws?
Lo, these are the new idols which we have cast and chiseled in our
hearts. Enough has now been said about these words of Paul, and it
is authority enough to prove that we are as little forbidden by God
to eat at certain times as we are now forbidden by him to eat certain
sorts and kinds of food.

   They will now raise as objections the fasts, or all fast days, saying
that people will never fast if they are allowed to eat meat. Answer:

Have you heretofore fasted because you were not allowed to eat meat, as naughty children that will not eat their broth, because they are not given meat? If any one desires to fast, has he not as much the power to do so, when laborers eat meat, as when they are forced to fast with the idle, and are thus less able to do and to endure their labors? In a word, if you will fast, do so; if you do not wish to eat meat, eat it not; but leave Christians a free choice in the matter. You who are an idler should fast often, should often abstain from foods that make you lustful. But the laborers' lusts pass away at the hoe and plough in the field. You say, the idle will eat meat without need. Answer: The very same fill themselves with still richer foods, that excite more than the highly seasoned and spiced. And if they complain of the breaking up of the custom [of fasting], it is nothing but envy, because they dislike to see that considered proper for common men, for which they can well find a substitute without difficulty and without weakening the body, on the contrary, even with pleasure; for fish eating is surely everywhere a pleasure. You say that many cannot endure this liberty in eating, not from envy, but from fear of God. Answer: O you foolish hypocrites, do you think that there is danger and injury in what God has left free? If there were in it danger to the soul God would not have left it unforbidden. Likewise, if you are so concerned about others, as to what they should not eat, why will you not note their poverty and aid it? If you would have a Christian heart, act to it then. If the spirit of your belief teaches you thus, then fast, but grant also your neighbor the privilege of Christian liberty, and fear God greatly, if you have transgressed his laws, nor make what man has invented greater before God than what God himself hath commanded, or again I will turn out a hypocrite of you, if you are such a knotty block, twisted in yourself and depending upon your own devices.

CONCERNING THE COMMANDMENT OF MEN

Here the first difficulty will occur, when one speaks to those who complaining ask: Is one to let go the ordinances of our pious fathers? Where have the Fathers or the Councils forbidden the use of meat during fasts? They can show no Council, but they come forward with the fasts: referring to canonical law. *De Con. di.*, v., 40.

Is one not to keep the feasts? Answer: Who says or teaches that? If you are not content with the fasts, then fast also Shrovetide. Indeed, I say that it is a good thing for a man to fast, if he fasts as fasts are taught by Christ: Matthew 6:16 and Isaiah 58:6. But show me on the authority of the Scriptures that one cannot fast with meat. Even if it could be shown, as it cannot, still you know very well that laborers are relieved of the burden of fasting, according to your laws. Here I demand of you to show me where meat is forbidden to him not under obligation to fast. Thus they turn away from the observance of the fast, and at last they all come to the canonical law, fourth chapter, "Denique," etc., and when you ask for a wagon, they offer you a chopping-knife. The chapter beginning "Denique" does not command you to forbid laymen to eat meat; it shows that at these same times the laymen fill themselves with meat on the Sundays in the fast more than on other days. You hear, more than on other days: Thus they eat meat on other days, but that they keep it up on Sundays till midnight, troubles Gregory[2]; still he says that they are not to be forced from this custom, lest they do worse. But the priests and the deacons he recommends to abstinence from meat, eggs, and cheese — read this well and with judgment and you will find this rather against you than for you. After that they come with Thomas Aquinas, as though one single mendicant monk had power to prescribe laws for all Christian folk. Finally they must help themselves out with custom, and they consider abstinence from food to be a custom. How old the custom is supposed to be, we cannot really know, especially with regard to meat, but of abstinence from eggs the custom cannot be so very old, for some nations even to-day eat eggs without permission from Rome, as in Austria and elsewhere. Milk food became a sin in the Swiss Confederation in the last century and was again forgiven. And since I have chanced upon this matter, I must show you a pretty piece of business, so that you may protect yourselves thus from the greed of the powerful clergy. Our dear fellow Swiss purchased the privilege of using milk food from the Bishop of Rome in the last century: Proof, the documents about it at Lucerne. Go back now before the time of these letters and think what our forefathers ate before the indulgence, and you cannot say that they ate oil, for in the Bull the complaint was made that people in our country are not accustomed to eat oil, that they ate the foods usual there, milk, whey, cheese, and butter. Now if that was a sin, why did the Roman bishops watch so lazily that they allowed them to eat these fourteen hundred years? If it is not a sin, as it is not, why did they demand money to permit it? Say rather this, I see that it is nothing but air, see that the Roman bishops announced that it was a sin, when it became money to them: Proof, as soon as they announced it as a sin, they immediately sold it for money, and thus abused our simplicity, when we ought fairly to have seen that, if it was sin according to God's law, no man can remit it, any more than that one might murder a man, which is forbidden by divine law, could be permitted by any one, although many distasteful sins of this kind are committed. From all these remarks you notice also that abstinence from meat and drink is an old custom, which however later by the wickedness of some of the clergy came to be viewed as a command. So if the custom is not bad or dishonourable, one is to keep it properly, as long and as thoroughly as the greater

---

2. Gregory the Great, pope, 590-604.

part of men might be offended by its infringement. Answer: This will take a longer time, therefore I shall speak now of offense or vexation.

OF OFFENSE OR VEXATION

Offense or vexation, Greek, *skandalon,* is understood in two ways: first, when one offends others, so that they sin in judgment or decision, and become worse; and of these we desire to speak first; second, offense occurs, although not in the Scriptures, but here as accepted by us, when a man in himself becomes more sinful or worse, or when a whole parish is purposely brought into a worse condition.

First, Christian love demands that every one avoid that which can offend or vex his neighbour, insofar, however, as it does not injure the faith, of course you are to understand. Since the Gospel has been preached frequently in these years, many have therefore become better and more God-fearing, but many on the contrary have become worse. And since there is much opposition to their bad opinion and plans, they attack the Gospel, which attacks the good cannot endure but oppose. From which reason the bad cry out saying: "I wish the Gospel were not preached. It sets us at variance among ourselves." Here one should not yield for that reason, but should keep close before his eyes what Christ says, Matthew 10:32: "Whosoever therefore shall confess me before men, him will I confess also before my Father which is in heaven. Think not that I am come to send peace on earth (understand by this, peace with the godless or sinful): I came not to send peace, but a sword. For I am come to set a man at variance against his father, and the daughter against her mother, and the daughter-in-law against her mother-in-law. And a man's foes shall be they of his own household."

In these words Christ gives us strength not to consider the vexation of those who will not be convinced of the truth; and, even though they are our nearest and dearest, we are not to be worried, if they separate from us, as he says later, Matthew 10:37: "Whosoever loves father and mother more than me, he is not worthy of me; whoever loves his son or daughter better than me, he is not worthy of me, and whoever does not take his cross and follow me, he is not worthy of me." And also Luke 14:26. So wherever it is a matter of God's honor, of the belief or of hope in God, we should suffer all things rather than allow ourselves to be forced from this. But where a thing cannot harm the belief, but offends one's neighbor, although it is not a sin, one should still spare his neighbor in that he should not injure him; as eating meat is not forbidden at any time by divine law; but, where it injures or offends one's neighbour, one should not eat it without cause. One should make those of little faith strong in the faith.

But when one (thirdly) will not be referred to the divine truth and the Scriptures, when one says: "I firmly believe that Christ has never forbidden me any food at any time," and when the one of little faith will not grant it or believe it, although one shows him the Scriptures about it, then the one who believes in liberty shall not yield to him, although he should yield the matter of eating meat in his presence, if it is not necessary; but he should cleave to the Scriptures and not let the sweet yoke of Christ and the light burden become bitter, so that it may not be unpleasant to men or please them less, and thereby show that it is a human and not a divine prohibition. Thus a burgomaster gives an answer, in the name of the Council, and after the answer adds something harsh and hard, which the Council did not command him to say and did not intend. He says: "This I say of myself; the Council has not commanded it." This also, all those that teach in God's name should not sell their commands, ordinances, and burdens as God's, so that the yoke of his mercy should not become unpleasant to anyone, but should leave them free. That I shall prove by the opinion of Christ, Matthew 24:49 and Luke 12:45, where he does not want one to trouble one's fellow servants – that is, one's fellow Christians. "But if that servant say maliciously in his heart, 'My Lord delayeth his coming,' and shall begin to beat his fellow servants and to eat in excess and to drink with drunkards, the Lord of that servant will come on a day when he looketh not for him, and at an hour when he is not watching, and will cut him in sunder, and will appoint the share of the bad servant to the Pharisees." Here open your eyes and see whether the servant, to whom it was given to pasture the sheep of Christ, has not now for a long time beaten his fellow servants – that is, fellow Christians; whether he has not eaten and drunk excessively, and, as though there was no God, run riot, and troubled Christians with great burdens (I speak of bad bishops and priests – take it not of yourself, pious man) so that the sweet yoke of Christ has become to all Christians a bitter herb. On the other hand, see how the Lord has come with his light and illuminated the world with the Gospel, so that Christians, recognizing their liberty, will not let themselves be led any more behind the stove and into the darkness from which a schism has come about, so that we really see that God has uncovered the Pharisees and hypocrites and has made a separate division of them. Yes, in that case I venture to command you to fight against those who prefer to keep the heavy yoke of the hypocrites rather than to take the sweet yoke of Christ upon themselves, and in thus doing to be careful to offend no one, but, as much as is in them, to keep peace with all men, as Paul says. Not every one can do this, or knows how far to yield or to make use of Christian liberty, therefore we will hear the opinion of Paul about offense.

Secondly, Paul teaches in the Epistle to the Romans 14 and 15, how one should avoid giving offense; these words I translate into German and give more according to the sense than the letter. Him, he says, that is weak in the faith, help, but do not lead him into the trouble of still greater doubt. One believes that it is proper for him to eat all things; but the other, weak in faith, eats only herbs. Now the one who is certain that he may eat all things, shall not despise him who does not venture to do such (understand, from little faith); and he who ventures not to eat all things shall not judge the eater, for God has accepted and consoled him. You weak man, who are you that you judge another man's servant? He will stand upright or fall for his own master, still he will be supported or held up, for God can well support or hold him up. One man esteems one day above another, another esteems all days alike. Let every man be fully persuaded in his own mind, that he who regards one day above another may do so to the honor of God, and that he who regards not one day above another does the same to the honor of God (understand that he has so strong a faith that he certainly does not believe himself at any time freed from God's rule, for the greatest honor to God is to recognize him aright and those things which are given us by him: John 17:3 and 1 Corinthians 2:12); also that he who eats all kinds of food, does the same to the honor of the Lord, for he gives the Lord thanks, and he who does not eat, does it also to the honor of God, and is also thankful to God, for no one among us lives for himself or dies for himself. Whether we live, let us live for the Lord, or whether we die, let us die for the Lord; and therefore whether we live or die, we are the Lord's. For to that end Christ died, arose, and lived again, that he might be Lord of the living and the dead. But, you weak man, why do you judge your brother? Or, you stronger man who eat, why do you despise your brother? For we shall all stand before the judgment seat of Christ. For it is written in Isaiah 45:23: "As I live, saith the Lord, to me shall all knees bow, and all tongues shall confess me, who am God." Therefore shall each one of us render God an account. Thus let us not judge one another, but be this our judgment, that no one displease or offend his brother. I know and am taught in Jesus Christ that nothing is unclean of its nature, except that it is unclean to him who considers it unclean. But if your brother is offended or injured on account of food, you do not act according to love (that is, you do not give up the food which injured your brother before he has been correctly instructed). Vex and injure and offend not with food your brother, for whom Christ died, and in return your goodness (that you do all things in your faith, you eat, you keep fast, or not) shall not be despised. For the kingdom of God is not food or drink, but piety, peace, and joy in the Holy Ghost. Whoever serves Christ in these things, is pleasing to God and approved before men. Let us then strive to do the things which lead to peace; and that we may edify one another (that is, properly instruct), do not make God's work (piety, peace, and joy, as is written above) of no avail on account of food. All things are clean, but it is bad that a man eat with vexation and offense as a result. It is proper and good that a man eat no meat and drink no wine, indeed eat nothing, whereby your brother is vexed or offended or whereby he is made ill. You who are stronger, if you have faith, have it in you before God. Happy is he who does not doubt that which he considers certain; but whoever doubts and, in doubt, eats the meat about which he doubts, he is condemned, for the reason that he did not eat from belief; for what is done not in belief, is sin. Also thus should we, who are strong in belief, be patient with the timidity of the weak, and not please ourselves, but each of us please his neighbor by edifying and doing him good; "for even Christ pleased not himself; but, as it is written, 'The reproaches of them that reproached thee fell on me.'" All these are words of Paul, from which you will shortly conclude three things. First, that he who firmly believes that it is proper for him to eat all things, is called strong; and secondly, that one who has no belief is called timid or weak; thirdly, that the strong should not let the weak remain always weak, but should take him and instruct him, that he become also strong, and should yield a point to the weak and not vex him maliciously. How we are to yield a point to the weak, you shall hear.

Thirdly, Paul says of vexation, 1 Corinthians 8:1, to those who were present: They might eat of that which had been offered to the idols, for this reason: they well knew they believed not in the idols, and therefore without soiling their consciences they might eat such food, in spite of those who were badly offended by it; indeed to them he speaks thus: "We know that we all have understanding or knowledge of the food which is offered to the idols. Knowledge puffeth up and maketh conceited, but love edifieth." Here Paul means, that you, although you, a man firm in faith, know you do not sin, when you eat the food of the idols, should, if you love your neighbor, favor him fairly, so that you offend him not; and when in time he is better instructed, he will be greatly edified, when he sees that your Christian love overlooked his ignorance so mercifully. After Paul has said that those well taught in the faith know well there is no idol but only one true God and one Lord Jesus Christ, it is further mentioned that not every one is so well taught as the first mentioned; for some eat the food of the idols in such manner that they still hold to them somewhat, and also that food does not commend us to God (as is shown above in the first part of the fourth division). Indeed after all that he says further: "See that your power or freedom does not vex the weak, for if one of them sees you sitting knowingly at a table where the food of idols is eaten, will not his conscience be strengthened or encouraged to eat the food of idols? And then your weak brother through your knowledge and understanding perishes, for whom Christ died." See how strongly Paul opposes wanton treatment of the weak. It follows further on that when you thus sin against your brethren, frightening and striking their weak consciences, you sin against Christ; therefore, if food offends my brother I will rather never eat meat than that I make my brother offend. Here notice that, although the foregoing words are spoken of

the food of idols, they still show us in a clear way how we should conduct ourselves in this matter of food, namely, that we should abstain
in every way from making to offend, and that he is not without sin,
who acts against his brother, for he acts also against Christ, whose
brother each Christian is. But you say, "What if my brother from
stubbornness will not at all be taught, but always remains weak?"
The answer will follow in the last part.

Fourthly, Paul writes in the above-mentioned epistle, 1 Corinthians
10:23: "All things are lawful for me, but all do not result in usefulness." Let no one seek his own good, let each seek, that is, strive for,
the advantage of the other. Eat all that is sold in the shambles, not
hesitating for conscience's sake; for the earth is the Lord's (as it reads
in Psalm 24:1), and all the fullness of the earth, or all that is in the
earth. If an unbeliever invites you and you want to go with him, eat
all that is placed before you (that is, as far as the kind of food is concerned; otherwise he would be a faithless glutton, if he ate all) not
doubting for conscience's sake. But if one said to you: "That is from
the sacrifice to the idols," eat it not for the sake of him who thus points
it out to you, and for conscience's sake. I say not for *your* conscience's
sake but for the sake of *another's* conscience. For why is my liberty
judged by the conscience of another, if I eat with gratitude? Therefore,
whether you eat or drink or whatever you do, do it to the honor of God;
do not offend Jews or heathen and God's Church, just as I endeavor to
please all men, not regarding myself, but the many, that they be saved;
they are my followers as I am a follower of Christ. Here you see, first,
that we should avoid for the sake of another what otherwise would be
proper; secondly, that all things are proper for us to eat, that are sold
in the shambles, without violence to the conscience; thirdly, how one
should act about eating forbidden food after the manner prescribed
for the food offered to idols; for although our proposition and the one
here in Paul are not wholly alike, still a good rule is to be derived therefrom; fourthly, that although your liberty cannot be judged according
to another's conscience, nor you yourself condemned, still you should
always consider the honor of God, which honor, however, grows the
greater among men, if they see you for the sake of the honor of God
not using your liberty; fifthly, that all things can take place to the
honor of God, indeed the daily custom of eating and drinking, of working, trading, marrying, if a man cleaves to God in all his doings, and
trusts that he is called to, and chosen for, the work by God. And do not
let this idea, which may occur to you, trouble you: "Then I will blaspheme, gamble, commit adultery, do other wrongs, and think I am
called to this by God." For such things do not please the man who
trusts in God. The tree is now good, let it produce only good fruit. And
if one lives not in himself, but Christ lives in him so thoroughly that,
although a mistake escapes him, he suffers from that hour for it, he
is ashamed of his weakness. But those who thus speak are godless,

and with such words insult God and those who have the Spirit of God. Listen to a striking example. No respectable and pious wife, who has a good husband, can allow one to report that which is dishonorable to her husband or let a suspicion arise of a misdeed, which she knows is displeasing to him. So man, in whom God rules, although weak, still cannot endure to be shamefully spoken of against his will. But a wanton likes to hear the disgrace of her husband and what is against him. Thus also those, who speak thus, are godless; otherwise, if they had God in their hearts, they would not willingly hear such disgraceful words.

Fifthly, Paul had Timothy circumcised, although the circumcision was of no service, that he might not offend the Jews, who at that time still believed that one must keep the Old Testament with its ceremonies together with the New Testament; and so he had it done, as it is written in Acts 16:3.

Sixthly, Christ himself did not wish to offend any one; for, when at Capernaum Peter was asked, Matthew 22:24, whether his master paid tribute, Peter answered, "Yes." And after they had entered the house, Christ anticipated Peter (who doubtless was about to ask him something about tribute) and said: "Simon, what thinkest thou? Do the kings of this world take tribute and custom of their children or of strangers?" Peter answered him: "Of strangers." Jesus said to him: "Then are the children free. But lest we should offend them, go to the sea and cast a hook, and the first fish that comes up take; and when thou hast opened his mouth, thou shalt find a coin (it was a penny, that could pay for them both, but was worth much more than the real tax pennies, wherefore I think it was a tribute which they collected from Christ), take it and give it for thee and me." Thus Christ did not desire to vex the authorities, but rather to do what he might otherwise refuse. This paragraph I would not have added, had not my opponents represented it thus: Christ, they said, desired himself to avoid taxation. For this article is more against them than for them; thus, if you spiritual teachers in the flesh are all so inclined to avoid vexation, why do you not then also help to bear the common burden, when you see that the parish is badly vexed about it and cries out: "You go lazily away from our work. Why do you not help us carry the burden?" Hear also that Christ gave the tribute money, in order not to arouse any one to anger. Loose the knot. There are more places still in the Gospel in which the word *skandalon* is written; but it means there either disgrace, or if it means offense, it is used in the following sense: disgrace and contempt, Matthew 23:7. "Woe unto the world because of offenses"—that is, woe unto the world on account of disgrace and contempt, since one despises, refuses, and rejects the simple (who is, however, as much God's as the highest), which the following words mean, when he says: "Take heed lest ye offend one of the least of these." Thus it is also to be understood, Luke 17:1, which also is clear from what precedes about the rich man, who did not let poor Lazarus have the crumbs. Thus also Mark 9:42. But *skandalon* or vexation, so taken, does not fit our purpose, therefore from the first I did not wish to divide it into three parts.

OF AVOIDING VEXATION

From the above-mentioned arguments one can readily learn that one should carefully avoid offense. But still I must think that, as one should forgive the weak, one should also in forgiving teach and strengthen him, and not always feed him with milk, but turn him to heartier food; for Christ says, Matthew 13:41: "The Son of man shall send forth his angels (that is, messengers), and they shall gather out of his kingdom all things that offend and them which are not God-fearing and do iniquity, and shall cast them into a furnace of fire." Are his angels to do that? Yes. Then it is better that we should do it ourselves; then it will not be done by God and punished so severely, as Paul teaches us, 1 Corinthians 11:31: "For if we would judge ourselves, we should not be judged." If we ourselves take the offense, it must not be taken with the judgment of God, to which now St. Paul arouses us.

First, Christ says, Matthew 5:29: "If thy right eye offend thee, pluck it out, and cast it from thee: for it is profitable for thee that one of thy members should perish, and not that thy whole body should be cast into hell. And if thy right hand offend thee, cut it off, and cast it from thee: for it is profitable," etc., as above. The same is also said in Matthew 18:8, except that he adds the foot. Who is now the eye, the hand, the foot, which, offending us, shall be cast away? Every bishop is an eye, every clergyman, every officer, who are nothing more than overseers; and the Greek word *episkopos* is in German an overseer, to which the words of St. Paul refer, Acts 20:28, where he says to the bishops of Ephesus: "Take heed therefore unto yourselves, and to all the flock, over which the Holy Ghost hath made you bishops (that is, overseers or shepherds), to watch and feed the Church of God, which he hath bought with his own blood." Here you see briefly what their duty is: overseeing the sheep, feeding, not flaying and shearing too closely and loading them with unbearable burdens, which is nothing else than giving offense, pointing out sins that are not present, so that weak consciences are troubled and made to despair; this is offending God's little ones: Matthew 18:6. But you see yourself, according to the words of Isaiah 56:10, that his watchmen have become blind, all ignorant, stupid dogs, that cannot bark, taught in loose things, lazily sleeping and dreaming, indeed, preferring dreams to the truth, the most shameless dogs, which cannot be satisfied: shepherds which have no reason, each following his own way or capricious desires, all avaricious, from the highest to the lowest, saying: "Let us drink good wine and become full, and as we do to-day, so shall we do to-morrow, yea, still more." These all are the words of Isaiah, and little is to be added. Do you not see that such eyes offend men much, and, although Christ tells us to pluck them out, we suffer them patiently? Understand also hand and foot which are so nearly related to you, as your own members; indeed, even if they are necessary to you for support and strength as a hand or a foot, still one is to remove them if they abuse their superiority. Now this paragraph is placed here by me to prove that offense should be avoided, and that one should not always endure it, but that everything should take place with timely counsel and reason, not with any one's own assumption and arrogance. If they do not do that, who ought to do it? We should recognize that our sins have deserved of God this, that such blind eyes lead us, the blind, astray and rule us. Nehemiah 9:30: "Thou hast warned them in thy spirit through thy prophets, and they have not followed, and thou hast given them into the hand of the people of the earth" – that is, into the hands of the unbelievers. Also Isaiah 3:4: "And I will give children to be their princes (note this well), and old women shall rule them."

Secondly, the words of Paul are to be considered, Romans 14:1, where it is mentioned above in the second article on giving offense, in which place he says: "Him that is weak in faith receive ye, but not to doubtful disputations." See you, the weak is not to be allowed to remain weak, but is to be instructed in the truth, not with subtle arguments, by which one becomes more doubtful, but with the pure, simple truth, so that all doubt may be removed. Therefore I could well endure that those who are considered steadier and stronger in belief, also understood how to make Christians strong in belief, and gave them really to understand what has been given and left to them by God; but they do exactly the contrary. If anything is strong, they wish to make the same again weak and timid. Woe to them, as Christ spoke to the Pharisees, Matthew 23:13: "For they closed the kingdom of God to men, for they neither go in themselves nor let other people go in." By means of these words of Christ and of Paul, I think I have excused my arrogance, of which certain hypocrites accused me – that is, of having preached upon freedom concerning food on the third Sunday of this fast, when they thought that I ought not to do it. Why? Should I snatch from the hand of those who cling to the Scriptures, which I myself have preached, their means of defense, and contradict the Scriptures and say they lie? And should I have in my hands the key of God's wisdom, as Christ says, Luke 11:52, and not open to the ignorant, but also close it before the eyes of the knowing? Do not deceive yourself that you have persuaded me to this, you vain, loose hypocrite. I will rather take care of my soul, which I have laden with enough other misdeeds, and will not murder it outright with a suppression of the truth.

Thirdly, it is true that Paul had Timothy circumcised, Acts 16:3. But on the other hand, as he says, Galatians 2:3, he did not have Titus circumcised: "Titus, who was with me, did not want to be forced to circumcision. He had this reason: False brethren have slipped unseen among us, who are come into our midst to spy out our liberty, which we have in Jesus Christ, that they might make us again slaves and subjects, to whom we yielded not a moment, that the truth of the Gospel might continue with you." Those who protect the liberty of the Gospel put this up before the ceremonies as a shield and bulwark. If Paul circumcised Timothy, still he did not, on the contrary, have Titus circumcised, although much reproach came to him on that account. What is to be done with him? Is Paul inconsistent with himself? No. If he had Timothy circumcised, it was because he could not keep him from it on account of the great disturbance of the Jews who were Christians. But afterwards, those of the Jews who had become Christians were better taught, so that he was able to spare Titus and protect him without great uproar; and, although some demanded his circumcision, and, when it did not happen, were greatly offended at it, he considered the truth and Christian liberty more than any strife that arose against it from bad feeling. Notice also in these words from Paul how everywhere the false brethren had undertaken to take liberty from Christians.

Fourthly, Paul writes, Galatians 2:12, that Peter ate with the Christians, who had become believers from heathendom; indeed, he ate with the heathen. But when some came from Jerusalem to Antioch who were also Christians but converted from Judaism, he fled from the heathen, so that the Jews might not be offended. Paul did not desire him to do that, but chid him in these words: "You teach the heathen to live as Jews, because you are a Jew by birth"; that is, if you flee from the heathen on account of the Jews, you raise a suspicion against the heathen, that they were not really Christians, or they would have to keep human fasts, as the Jews, or else sin. And about this he said: "When I saw that he did not walk uprightly, I withstood him to his face." At this place you find Paul, who teaches diligently, not offending, not caring if a few want to be offended, providing he could keep the greater multitude unaffected and unsuspicious. For if even the Jews, on whose account Peter fled from the heathen, became offended, still Paul gave them no attention, so that the heathen Christians (thus I call them that were converted from heathendom) could remain free and would not be brought under the oppression of the law by Jewish Christians.

When Christ spoke to the Pharisees, Matthew 15:2, "Not that which goeth into the mouth defileth a man," his disciples said to him: "Knowest thou that the Pharisees who heard these words were offended and angered?" Christ answered them: "Let them go, they be blind leaders of the blind." See that here Christ's meaning is, as it seems to me, that the disciples should let the Pharisees go and should live according to their liberty and custom in spite of them; for they were blind and saw not the truth of liberty; were also leaders of those who erred as they did. Since now in the above two articles, I have spoken enough of offense and of the doing away with offense, it seems to me good to bring together in short statements all that touches upon offense, so that each may know where he shall yield and where not.

I. What clearly affects the divine truth, as the belief and commandments of God, no one shall yield, whether one is offended or not. Psalm 145:18; 1 Corinthians 2:2; Matthew 5:10: "Blessed are they which suffer for righteousness's sake." 2 Corinthians 13:8: "For we can do nothing against the truth, but for the truth."

II. The liberties, which are given to man by God, touching the law of food and other such things, should be considered with regard to God and man.

III. When one speaks of the liberty now under discussion, that we are released by God from all such burdens, one shall not yield in respect to truth and belief, whether one offend or not. For Paul says: "All things are proper for me" (1 Cor. 6:12).

IV. But when the practice of liberty offends your neighbor, you should not offend or vex him without cause; for when he perceives it, he will be offended no more, unless he is angry purposely, as when the Jews became angry at the disciples' eating with unwashed hands and on the Sabbath: Mark 2:24.

V. But you are to instruct him as a friend in the belief, how all things are proper and free for him to eat. Romans 15:1: "We who are stronger in the faith shall receive the weak"—that is, comfort and instruct them.

VI. But when forgiving avails not, do as Christ said, Matthew 15:14: "Let them go."

VII. And use your liberty, wherever you can without public disturbance, just as Paul did not have Titus circumcised: Galatians 2:3.

VIII. But if it causes public uproar, do not use it, just as Paul had Timothy circumcised: Acts 16:3.

IX. Gradually teach the weak with all industry and care, until they are instructed, so that the number of the strong is so large that no one, or still only a few, can be offended; for they will certainly let themselves be taught; so strong is the Word of God, that it will remain not without fruit: Isaiah 55:10.

X. Take this same view in other things, which are only adiaphora: as eating meat, working on holy days after one has heard the Word of God and taken communion, and the like.

Of Being Offended at Innocent Customs

On account of all this they complain very bitterly who have learned the acceptance of virtues rather from Aristotle than from Christ: saying that in this way all good works, as not eating meat, abstaining from labor, and other things which I shall not mention, are done away with. To these I answer as follows: Many mistakes are made as to the choice of good works, although we might well hear what St. James says, 1:17, that all good gifts and presents come from above from the Father of lights. From this we can conclude that all good which pleases God must come from him; for if it came from any other source, there would be two or more sources of good, of which there is however only one; Jeremiah 2:13: "They have forsaken me the fountain of living waters, and hewed them out cisterns, broken cisterns, that can hold no water." Notice the fountain; notice the broken cistern. Thus Christ speaks to the young man who called him good, in order to do him eye-service: "God alone is good." If he alone is good, without doubt no good fruit can come from any source except from the tree which alone is good. Then notice the angels and you will find that, as soon as they depended somewhat upon themselves, they fell. Thus also man, as soon as he depended somewhat upon himself, fell into the trouble that still follows us. See, those are the bad, false, broken cisterns, which are dug and thrown up only by men, not real natural fountains. Thus they thought that that would seem good to God and please Him, which they had attempted and which resulted in great disadvantage to them, from no other reason, as I think, than that they had assumed to know the good or the right, and did not depend alone on God and trust alone in him. Not that I mean to say that abstinence from food is bad; indeed, where it comes from the leading and inspiration of the Divine Spirit, it is without doubt good; but where it comes simply from fear of human command, and is to be considered as a divine command and thus trusted in, and where man begins to please himself thereby, it is not only good but also injurious; unless you show me from the Holy Writ that our inventions must please God. I shall also not be worsted, if you say to me: "Still the assembly of a church may set up ordinances which are kept also in heaven." Matthew 16:19 and 18:18: "Verily I say unto you whatsoever ye shall bind on earth shall be bound in heaven; and whatsoever ye shall loose on earth shall be loosed in heaven." That is true, but the observance is not made by the whole Christian Church, indeed only by certain bishops, who had for a time undertaken to place upon Christians certain laws, without the knowledge of the common people. Also if you should say that silence is a form of consent, I answer: The pious simplicity of Christians has kept silence in many things from fear, and that no one has told them of their liberty coming from the Scriptures. For example, whom did it ever please that the Pope conferred all benefices on his servants? Indeed, every pious man everywhere has said, "I do not believe it is right." But the people kept still about it with much pain, till the Gospel truth gave forth light, when for the first time the mask was taken from it. Thus also here the clergy have taken a hand to control everything, after they have seen Christians willingly following them. Why? They fear us for the reason lest he who transgresses the command be obliged to give us money. Yet it all would have had no success, if such oppressive regulations were not given out as being divine. We sold them for that, and where the agreement was of that kind, after the truth had come to light, you can see what kind of an agreement it was. But we will hear what Paul says of works.

To the Colossians, 2:16 (which passage I have quoted above), he writes: "Let no man judge you in meat, or in drink, or in respect of a holy day, or of the new moon, or of the Sabbath days: which are a shadow of things to come; but the body is of Christ. Let no man beguile you of your reward in a voluntary humility and worshiping of angels, intruding into those things which he hath not seen, vainly puffed up by his fleshly mind, and not holding the Head, from which all the body by joints and bands having nourishment ministered, and knit together, increaseth with the increase of God. Wherefore if ye be dead with Christ from the rudiments of the world, why, as though living in the world, are ye subject to ordinances (touch not, taste not, handle not: which things are all to perish with the using) after the commandments and doctrines of men? Which things indeed have a showing of wisdom in will-worship, humility, and neglecting of the body; not in any honor to the satisfying of the flesh." All these are the words of Paul, which in Latin are not at all intelligible, but in Greek are somewhat clearer. But that each may well understand them, I shall briefly paraphrase them.

No one shall reject you or consider you good on account of any food, or holy day, whether you rest or not (always excepting Sundays, after God's Word has been heard and communion administered). Let the new moon fast and the Sabbath go; for these things have become only symbolical of a Christian holiday, when one is to cease and leave off sinning, also that we, repenting such works, become happy only in the mercy of God; and, as Christ has come, the shadows and symbols are without doubt done away with. One thing more, notice as to the time: It surely seems to me (I cannot help thinking so) that to keep certain times with timidity is an injury and harm to unchanging and everlasting justice, thus: simple people think that everything is right, if only they confess the fasts, fast, enjoy God (i.e., take the sacrament), and let the whole year pass away thus; whereas one should at all times confess God, live piously, and do no more than we think is necessary in the fast. And Christ says again, Matthew 25:13: "Watch therefore, for ye know neither the day nor the hour."

Further, he reminds them that they shall not allow themselves to be beguiled by those who pretend humility. What is beguiling but disregarding the simple meaning of God and wanting to find or show to the simple another shorter way to happiness, and to seek therewith wealth, name, and the reputation of a spiritual man? Therefore Paul advises against this and warns us that we should not allow ourselves to be beguiled—that is, not allow ourselves to be deceived. For the same hypocrites will falsely assert that angels spoke with them and revealed something to them, and will elevate themselves on that account. Listen, how well he paints them in their true colors, and yet we do not want to recognize them. Why do you dream here of the doctrines and ordinances which are chattered out at the pulpit in the cloisters? And why of the crows which nip the ears of some of you? Do you not now hear that all such things are suggested by the flesh, and not by the spirit? For the same depend not on the head of Christ, from which all other members being arranged, co-ordinated, and united, receive their nourishment or support of heavenly life, and progress in a growth that pleases God. Notice here in the spiritual growth and increase a different method than in the bodily. In the body all members grow from the sustenance of the belly, but in the spirit from the head of Christ. Consider now human doctrines: if they are like the opinion of the head, they are sustained by the head; if they are not like it, they come from the belly: O ventres, O ye bellies! But if we are dead with Christ to the rudiments of the world – that is, if Christ by his death made us free from all sins and burdens; then we are also in baptism – that is, in belief, freed from all Jewish or human ceremonies and chosen works, which he calls the rudiments. If we are now dead to the rudiments, why do we burden ourselves with fictitious human ordinances? Just as though God did not consider and think enough, did not give us sufficient instruction and access to blessedness and we make ourselves ordinances, which oppress us saying: "Touch not, taste not, handle not"; which touching or eating does not serve to injure or disturb the soul. For only for this purpose have the false teachers pretended that this was injurious, that with simple-minded people they might have the name of being wise and godly, indeed also with those who prescribe for themselves their own religion, saying: "Is not such abstinence and purification of the body a good thing? Is it not a good thing to prevent sin by good ordinances?" Hear how much weight Paul gives this folly. He says these things have only the form of the good. If they have only the form of the good, they are themselves not good in the sight of God, for they arise from *ethelothriskeia*. It is a Greek word, and means the honor or fear of God, which one has chosen for himself and to which he stubbornly clings: as, for example, many will not cut the beard on Friday and think they greatly honor God thereby; and, when they transgress this, they greatly sin in thus doing, and consider the rule that they themselves have set up so important, that they would three times sooner break their marriage vows, than to do anything against their reputation for wisdom. Indeed, deceive not yourself that things are with God as you have persuaded yourself; that is true superstition, a stubborn self-chosen spirit. Here in the words of Paul consider the greater part of the ordinances and rules, and you will find pretty things. Such are the most of human ordinances, of which Christ says, Matthew 15:9: "But in vain do they worship me, teaching for doctrines the commandments of men." He says *licke*, Greek for impossible, in vain; that tells the very truth. Then this follows: But they are worth nothing, if you consider them according to the need and wants of the body. All food is created for the support of man; as far as it only affects bodily use it is of no moment, whether you eat this or that food. Go rather again to the clearer words of Paul and read them again, and they will be much clearer to you and worthier in your heart.

Pious servants of Christ, these are the opinions, which I have preached from the Holy Writ, and have again collected for no other purpose than that the Scriptures might be forcibly brought to the notice of those ignorant of the same, and as Christ commands that they might rather search them, and that you and your people may be less reviled by them. For as far as I am concerned, it was entirely against my will to write of these things, for the reason that, even if winning by the aid of the Scriptures, as without doubt I shall win with God's help, still I have gained nothing, except that according to divine law no kind of food is forbidden to man at any time; although among the right and humbly thankful this writing of mine causes great joy of conscience, which they rejoice in freedom, even if they never eat meat at forbidden times. And as a result I must have a worse time avoiding offense than if I had left the world in the belief that it was a divine ordinance, which, however, I could not do. You know that the Gospel of Matthew, the Acts of the Apostles, the Epistles to Timothy, to the Galatians, both Epistles of Peter, on which you all heard me preach, are full of such opinions. But one must clear the dear face of Christ of such spots, unseemly things, and of the foulness of human commands; and he will become again dear to us, if we properly feel the sweetness of his yoke, and the lightness of his burden. God bless this his doctrine! Amen.

What has been written above, I am responsible before God and man to account and answer for, and I also desire of all who understand the Scriptures, in case I have misused the same, to inform me of this either orally or by letter, not disgracing the truth by shameless clatter behind one's back, which is dishonorable and unmanly. I desire to be guided everywhere by the New and Old Testaments. But what follows, I only wish to view as submitted, still with proof from the Scriptures, and let each one judge of it in secret for himself.

WHETHER ANYONE HAS POWER TO FORBID FOODS

I. The general gathering of Christians may accept for themselves fasts and abstinence from foods, but not set these up as a common and everlasting law.

II. For God says, Deuteronomy 4:2: "Ye shall not add unto the word which I command you, neither shall ye diminish aught from it."

And also 12:32: "What thing soever I command you, observe to do it: thou shalt not add thereto, nor diminish from it."

III. If one could not and should not add to the Old Testament, then much less to the New.

IV. For the Old Testament has passed away and was not otherwise given except that it should pass away in its time; but the New is everlasting, and can never be done away with.

V. This is shown by the sanctification of both Testaments. The Old is sprinkled and sanctified by the blood of animals, but the New with the blood of the everlasting God, for Christ thus spake: "This is the cup of my blood of a new and everlasting testament," etc.

VI. If now it is a testament, and Paul, Galatians 3:15, says it is: "Though it be but a man's covenant, yet if it be confirmed, no man disannulleth, or addeth thereto,"

VII. How dare a man add to the testament, to the covenant of God, as though he would better it?

VIII. Galatians 1:9, Paul curses what is preached otherwise concerning the Gospel, thus: "If any other gospel is preached to you than ye have heard, let him that preached it be accursed."

IX. Paul says, Romans 8:8: "Owe no man anything, but to love one another."

X. Again, Galatians 5:1: "Stand fast therefore in the freedom wherewith Christ has made us free, and be not entangled again with the yoke of bondage."

XI. If he is to be cursed who preaches beyond what Paul preached, and if Paul nowhere preached the choice of food, then he who dares command this must be worthy of a curse.

XII. If we are not bound by any law but the law of love, and if freedom as to food injures not the love of one's neighbor, in case this freedom is rightly taught and understood, then we are not subject to this commandment or law.

XIII. If Paul commands us to remain in the liberty of Christ, why do you command me to depart from it? Indeed, you would force me from it.

XIV. When Christ said to his disciples, "I have yet much to say to you," he did not say, "I have much yet to teach you how ye shall lay commands on men," but he spake of things which he held up before them and which they, however, scarcely understood. But when the Spirit of Truth shall come, it will teach you all the truth, that they will understand all things according to the light of the Holy Ghost — that is, providing they do not at that time understand, either from ignorance or trouble and fear.

XV. For if such commands are to be understood in this matter, then the disciples have sinned, in not having forbidden labor and the eating of meat, running to the saints, putting on cowls.

XVI. Finally, God spake to Peter, Acts 10:15: "What God hath cleansed, that call thou not common." And the Sabbath is subject to us, not we to the Sabbath, as it is written above.

These points have forced me to think that the church officers have not only no power to command such things, but if they command them, they sin greatly; for whoever is in office and does more than he is commanded, is liable to punishment. How much more then when they transgress that which is forbidden them; and Christ forbade the bishops to beat their fellow servants. Is it not beating, when a command is placed upon a whole people, to which command the general assembly has not consented? Therefore, in these articles I leave to each, free judgment, and still hope I have to those thirsting for Christian freedom made this clear, in spite of the enmity to me that will grow out of it. It is those who fear the spit [on which their meat roasts] will burn off. God be with us all! Amen. I have written all this hastily; therefore may each understand it as best he can. (Given at Zurich, in 1522, on the 16th of April.)

ON MERCENARY SOLDIERS

THE FOREIGN LORDS have so wheedled and enticed us, simple confederates, seeking their own profit, that at length they have brought us into such danger and disagreement between ourselves that we, not regarding our fatherland, have more care how to maintain them in their wealth and power than to defend our own houses, wives, and children. And this were less had we not shame and damage out of this pact. We have at Naples, at Navarre, at Milan, suffered greater loss in the service of these masters than since we have been a Confederacy; in our own wars we have been ever conquerors, in foreign wars often vanquished; such evils, it is to be feared, have been brought about by those who seek more their own private gain than the true interests of their country.

Let each one for himself reflect on the evils of war and think how

Reprinted from *The World's Famous Orations*, ed. William Jennings Bryan, 10 vols. (New York: Funk & Wagnalls Co., 1906), 7:30–37.

it would be with him if he were treated in the manner in which we use our fellow Christians. Think, now, that a foreign mercenary came into thy land with violence; laid waste thy meads, thy fields, thy vineyards; drove off thy cattle; bound thy house furniture together and carted it away; slew thy son in the attack, who would defend himself and thee; violated the chastity of thy daughters; kicked with his feet the dear wife of thy bosom, who went before thee and fell down at the feet of this foreign soldier, begging mercy for thee and herself; dragged out thyself, pious, worthy, old man, even in thine own house and home, from the place where thou wert crouching in fear, knocked thee down in presence of thy wife, despite her cries, and despite thine own trembling, venerable, pleading gray hairs; and then at last set fire to thy dwelling and burned it to the ground — wouldst thou not think within thyself, if the Heaven did not open and spit fire on such villainy, if the earth did not yawn and swallow up such monsters, there were no God? And yet thou doest all this to another and callest it, forsooth, "the right of war"!

Those who, for truth, religion, justice, and native country, venture their lives in war, are true men, and their cause is sacred. But as for those bloodthirsty, mercenary soldiers who take the field for gain, of whom the world is now full, and those wars which princes carry on, from day to day, out of lust of power, filling the earth with bloodshed, I, for my part, not only cannot approve them, but I believe there is nothing more wicked and criminal, and have the opinion that such men deserve to be branded as highway robbers, and that they are unworthy of the name of Christians.

The second danger that threatens us from the foreign lords and their wars is that justice between man and man is stopped; as an old proverb says, "When arms are up in the hands, laws are under the feet." The term "right of war" means nothing but violence, use it as you will, turn it over as you will. Yet it is objected — force must be employed to reduce the disobedient if they refuse to yield obedience to things lawful and right. Yea, verily, it were good it went no farther, and that the thunderbolt of war struck these alone, and that each forced only the disobedient to obedience in things lawful. But what sayest thou of the man who takes money and helps a foreign master to plunder, lay waste, and rob those who have done him no injury whatever; nay, who carries his sword to such masters whom it does not become to go to war at all, bishops, popes, abbots, and this, too, for vile money? Further, the foreign lords do prejudice to the cause of justice insofar that their gifts blind the eyes of every man, be he as wise as you will, and deprive him of his reason as well as of his piety; as Moses teaches, "A gift doth blind the eyes of the wise and pervert the words of the righteous."

The third danger is that with foreign money and foreign wars our manners will become corrupted and debased. This we see very clearly, for our people have never returned from the foreign wars without bringing something new in clothes for themselves and their wives, or without importing home some new extravagance in, eating and drinking, some new oaths; the bad they see and learn with readiness, so that we have reason to fear, if these wars be not desisted from, we shall be inundated with still worse evils.

The morality of the women, too, is corrupted. A woman is a weak creature, and desirous of new, handsome things, ornaments, fine clothes, jewels (as we see in Dinah, who went to Sechem out of curiosity, and was there humbled), and when such like things are made to flash in their eyes and offered to them, think you that they will not be moved by these things, and that the temptation will not be too strong for them? It is to be feared, too, that in time the number of the males will be diminished, although as yet this has been less noticeable. But at least they are unmanned by luxury. Now no one will work to obtain a living, the lands are out of cultivation, and lie waste in many places, because laborers are not to be got, although there be people enough, and a land that could well nourish us all. If it bear not cinnamon, ginger, malmsey, cloves, oranges, silk, and other such dainties for the palate, it bears at least butter, milk, horses, sheep, cattle, lint, wine, and corn, and that to the full, so that we can rear a fine, strong race of men, and as to what we want in our own country we can obtain it elsewhere against our own produce. That we do not hold to this comes from the selfishness that has been introduced among us, and which leads us off from labor to idleness.

And yet to work is noble: it saves from wantonness and vice; it yields good fruit, so that a man can richly nourish his body without care, and without the fear that he sully himself with the blood of the innocent, and live by it. It makes the body, too, hale and strong, dissipates diseases engendered by idleness, and last of all, fruit and increase follow the hand of the worker, as creation itself came from the hand of the all-working God at the beginning, so that, in external things, there is nothing in the universe so like God as the worker.

It is to selfishness we owe it that all our strength and power, which ought to defend our country, are consumed in the service of foreign masters. Behold how unlike we are to our ancestors! These would not suffer foreign masters in their land, but now we lead them in among us by the hand, if they have but money, that some may get hold of the money while many get the stripes. And when a pious man has brought up a well-doing son, then come the captains and steal him away, and he must expose himself to the danger of dying of hunger, disease, murder, shot, or wounds. And if he reckon up his bargained money he will find he could have won more by threshing, without speaking of his being run through the body with a spear ere the account comes to be paid; and last of all, his poor old father that brought him up, and whom he should have maintained in his old age, is reduced to carry the beggar's staff.

But those who get the money want for nothing. They force us into alliances with foreign masters, but only after they themselves have been bought over by heavy bribes. And, when it comes to loss, your neighbor or your neighbor's son must bear it, while they come off scot-free. And although it stands in the conditions that none is to be forced, yet recruiting parties spread themselves over the whole land, and then it is seen what young blood will do when it is up. And with the remuneration it is to be taken into account that those who get the largest bribes conceal them, but, these living in riot and expense, another, who thinks he cannot be less than they, goes to the like expense. And if he cannot afford this, then he is at the mercy of the briber, who at last takes his vineyard, fields, and meadows. Then he helps him to a small pension, on which he cannot live, and so, having lost his all, he must in the end face war and wounds for a wretched pay. In this manner we lose our best sons, who for vile money are consumed in a foreign land. But few, indeed, become rich, but these so rich that they might buy off the rest.

The fourth danger is that the gifts of the foreign lords breed hatred and distrust among us. The Almighty granted to our ancestors grace and favor in his sight, so that they freed themselves from a tyrannous nobility and lived in concord with one another. They prospered; while right and justice were so well administered in this land that all who were oppressed in foreign countries fled hither as to an asylum of safety. Then fear seized the hearts of the princes, who would not themselves act justly, and who yet stood in awe of our bold and un-flinching attitude. But seeing that the Lord was strong on our side, so that they could not overcome us by force, they seduced us by the bait of bribes, and reduced us by enslaving us first to selfishness. They laid their schemes and considered that if one of us were to see a friend or a neighbor suddenly growing rich without any trade or profession, and living at his ease in riches, he, too, would be stirred up, in order that he might dress finely, live in idleness, carousing, and wantonness, like his neighbor; to hunt after riches (for all men incline naturally against work and toward idleness), and that, if the like riches were not vouchsafed to him, he would join himself to the ranks of their opponents; that in this manner disunion would be created, so that father should be against son, brother against brother, friend against friend, neighbor against neighbor, and then that the kingdom, as the Son of God himself says, thus divided against itself, would not stand, and there would be an end of the Confederacy. This was what they calculated upon.

And if anyone should inquire, How are we to deliver ourselves from these evils, and return again to union? — I answer, By abstaining from selfishness. For, if this base passion did not reign among us, the Confederacy were more a union of brothers than of confederates. If one rejoins to this, Selfishness is implanted in the human heart, from whence it cannot be eradicated, for God alone can know and change the heart, then I answer, Do earnestly that which lies in your power. Where you find it punishable, punish it, and let it not grow. And that it may be extirpated out of the very hearts of men, give heed that the divine Word be faithfully preached.

For where God is not in the heart there is nothing but the man himself. Where there is nothing but the man himself, he cares for nothing but that which serves to his interests, pleasures, and lusts. But when God possesses the heart, then man has regard to that which pleases God, seeks the honor of God, and the profit of his fellow man. Now, the knowledge of God can come to us in no way clearer than from the Word of God. Will you, then, have the knowledge of God spread among you, so that you may live in peace and in the fear of God? Then see to it that the Word of God is purely preached, according to its natural sense, unadulterated by the glosses and inventions of man.

FOR ADDITIONAL INFORMATION ON HULDRYCH ZWINGLI:

Courvoisier, Jaques. *Zwingli: A Reformed Theologian.* Richmond, Va.: John Knox Press, 1963.
Farner, Oskar. *Zwingli the Reformer: His Life and Work.* Translated by D. G. Sear. Reprint. Hamden, Conn.: Shoe String Press, 1968.
Garside, Charles, Jr. *Zwingli and the Arts.* New Haven, N.J.: Yale University Press, 1966.
Jackson, Samuel Macauley. *Huldreich Zwingli, the Reformer of German Switzerland.* New York: G. P. Putnam's Sons, 1900.
_____, ed. *The Latin Works and the Correspondence of Huldreich Zwingli Together with Selections from His German Works.* Translated by Henry Preble, Walter Lichtenstein, and Lawrence A. McLouth. 3 vols. New York: G. P. Putnam's Sons, 1912.
Lindsay, Thomas M. "The Reformation in Switzerland under Zwingli." *A History of the Reformation.* Vol. 2. Latest reprint. Edinburgh: T. & T. Clark, 1956.

McNeill, John T. "Huldreich Zwingli and the Reformation in German Switzerland." *The History and Character of Calvinism*. New York: Oxford University Press, 1954.

Rilliet, Jean Horace. *Zwingli, Third Man of the Reformation*. Translated by Harold Knight. Philadelphia: Westminster Press, 1964.

Walton, Robert C. *Zwingli's Theocracy*. Toronto: University of Toronto Press, 1967.

JOHN CALVIN

1509-1564

JOHN CALVIN, from an original painting from *Evangelical Biography* by Erasmus Middleton (London: W. Baynes, 1816).

JOHN CALVIN

FEW PEOPLE have so stamped their names upon the world as Calvin. Not all find his influence a positive one. Will Durant has written, "We shall always find it hard to love the man who darkened the human soul with the most absurd and blasphemous conception of God in all the long and honored history of nonsense."[1] Yet none can deny his influence. In religion,

---

1. Will Durant, *The Reformation* (New York: Simon & Schuster, 1957), pp. 489–90.

theology, politics, sociology, and economics his influence has gone far beyond that of any other reformer.

LIFE AND TIMES

Although John Calvin is often ranked as the most influential reformer, he actually had no hand in initiating the Reformation. The early battles of the Reformation had been won by the time Calvin appeared on the scene. When Calvin was born in 1509, Luther had already spent four years of spiritual anguish searching for a more satisfying interpretation of the Christian faith than the one he knew. While Calvin was still learning to read, Luther was already giving his evangelical lectures on Psalms, Romans, and Galatians at Wittenberg. Calvin was only a schoolboy when Luther began publicly questioning the right of the papacy to levy indulgences. Yet by 1580 – only sixteen years after Calvin's death – the world had already been more deeply influenced by the thought of Calvin than by any other reformer.

In the ancient city of Noyon, almost under the shadow of the cathedral, John Calvin was born on July 10, 1509. His father was a busy notary whose appointments brought him into contact with many prominent families of the city. He was also closely related to the church. Calvin's mother died when he was only three years old, and a stepmother about whom virtually nothing is known soon came into the home. Calvin had a young brother, Antoine, and a half sister, Marie.

Calvin's formal higher education began in 1523 when he entered the University of Paris. At this time Paris was not on the cutting edge of theological thought as it had been in the Middle Ages; it was now largely stuffy and reactionary. From the University of Paris Calvin went to the College de Montaigu – a place noted for strict discipline, conservative theology, and notoriously bad meals. Apparently Calvin's interests changed, and in 1528 he began to study law; for three years he pursued this study at Orleans and Bourges. He was a brilliant student and often filled in for his professors when they were away. Upon the death of his father in 1531, Calvin felt free to follow his own desires in regard to education. He immediately entered eagerly upon the study of ancient languages and literature under the royal lectures established by Francis I at Paris; and by 1532, when he was only twenty-three years old, he had completed his Doctor of Laws degree and had published his first book.

The winds of reformation were beginning to whistle through the academic halls of Paris. Calvin could not escape the influence of the theological revolution: by 1533 he was wholeheartedly on the side of the Reformation. But he was not outspoken at this time. He was looking forward to a life of scholarship and did not want to be troubled with the turmoil that dogged the heels of the reformers.

In 1533 an event occurred which altered his life. Nicholas Cop, the rector of the University of Paris and a close friend of Calvin, preached a university sermon in which he attacked the Paris theologians. The theologians became furious; they retaliated and tried to have Cop arrested for heresy. Apparently Calvin had a hand in the composition of the sermon. He was also forced to flee and escaped Paris just in time to avoid arrest.

Sometime during this period in his life (probably in 1534), John Calvin experienced a significant religious conversion. This was no mere intellectual commitment to the cause of the Reformation—he had already experienced that. It was an encounter with God which completely transformed his life. From that time forward he was fully committed to a ministry of proclaiming the Word of God and purifying the life of the church.

From 1534 until 1536 he traveled throughout France. During this period of his life Calvin studied theology carefully and began to develop his own system of theological thought. By 1535 he had completed the writing of the *Institutes*, and they were published the next year. He was only twenty-six years old when he finished the last chapter of this most famous book of the Reformation: probably it has been the most influential single book on theology in the history of the Christian faith.

In 1536 he was traveling with a friend from Paris to Strassburg when military movements forced them to detour by way of Geneva. There he encountered William Farel, a zealous leader of the first stage of reform in the city. At this time Geneva was a city of approximately 13,000 persons suffering from political and religious tumult. Farel pled with Calvin to remain in Geneva and help establish the city firmly in the Reformation camp.

As Calvin examined the situation, what he found was not to his liking. Farel had initiated primarily a negative reform. The Mass had been abolished and monasteries and nunneries had been closed. Measures had been taken to regulate private morals and to compel attendance at sermons. But the people in general were not in sympathy with the religious emphasis. The city was immoral. Every third house was a tavern, and debauchery was common. A special watch had to be set to prevent the visits of "the religious" to Geneva's red-light district. In short, Geneva had all the vices characteristic of a wealthy, pleasure-loving, medieval town.

Calvin had hoped for a life of contemplative scholarship; he had no taste for public life and all of the controversies attached to it. But Farel's plea was irresistible. Calvin accepted the invitation and began to preach, teach, and organize in Geneva. At first the people responded well to him. But as he became more and more zealous, they increasingly resisted his efforts. Finally, in 1538, Calvin and the people parted ways. Calvin was exiled from Geneva and took up residence in Strassburg where he became a pastor and a lecturer in theology.

While in Strassburg he married Idelette de Bure, a widow who was the mother of a daughter and a son. Calvin and his wife had only one child, a son who died in infancy. The wife herself suffered ill health; in 1549 she died. Unlike Luther, whose family life was a warm and inspiring example of a Christian home, Calvin's home brought little joy to his life. Apparently he was wed more to his work than to his wife.

In 1541 the people of Geneva begged Calvin to return to their town and once again to take up his duties of guiding the church. He returned on September 13, but all of the resistance to his reform plans had not died, and he spent almost fifteen more years of severe struggle against his enemies. Because he had to deal with the councils of the city of Geneva, some of his conflicts were political; most, however, were religious. Since church and state were not separate, often the political and religious controversies merged as one. In any case, by 1555 he had gained the upper hand in Geneva, and after that time he enjoyed less opposition and more influence.

Using police tactics, Calvin set up a system of spies to search out moral breachments of the law. Penalties and fines were meted out for such things as dancing, drinking, criticizing his sermons, saying there was no devil or hell or that the pope was a good man, arguing against capital punishment for heresy, and betrothing one's daughter to a Catholic. Calvin's most serious blunder was to attempt liquor prohibition: this regulation caused such a furor that the law had to be rescinded.

The rest of his life is noted by few headline events. In 1559 he published the final edition of the *Institutes* and helped establish the University of Geneva. He continued to preach and to write. By 1564 he was seriously ill; he died in Geneva on May 27.

The influences on Calvin's life were many. Although he and Luther had few contacts, he benefited by the efforts of Luther to break the power of the Roman church and to open the windows of the church to new theological thought. He was also deeply indebted to the early reformers in Switzerland such as Zwingli and Farel, who in a sense made possible his own ministry; since the Reformation had already begun in Geneva, his task was one of organization and education. This situation directed the course of his life to that of a preacher, church administrator, and teacher.

His law training also had obvious influences upon him. He was a careful and disciplined thinker, able to dispute with the councils in Geneva on political and governmental issues. Some feel that he was too legalistic and lacked compassion, but in the stormy city of Geneva, discipline was needed. And in the providing of a theology for the Reformation, careful development of thought was essential.

His own religious experiences guided his life. He was deeply committed to Jesus Christ and to His cause. Though he was regarded as a cold, calculating man, his relationship to God was alive, dynamic, and warm. He often spoke movingly about his religious experiences and pled with others to experience the joy of doing the will of God. Early in his theological career, he came to the conclusion that the sovereignty of God was the central concept of the faith. This conviction molded almost all of his theology and likely colored his entire theological scheme with a certain formidable grayness.

The influence of his writing has been felt around the world. His theology has been studied, debated, rejected, accepted, and revised for centuries. His teachings concerning civil revolution are often given credit for the revolutions of Scotland, England, and the United States. This is probably an extreme assessment, but his emphasis was certainly influential in the revolutions which spread across Europe in the centuries following his death. Certainly Puritanism, with all of its influences in England and in the United States, largely stems from the thought and writing of John Calvin.

To determine the real character of Calvin is difficult. His contemporaries either cursed or idolized him, probably because most of the persons related to him were either staunch friends or avowed enemies. Certain characteristics, however, are evident.

He was a disciplined and hard-working man. He labored twelve to eighteen hours a day as preacher, administrator, professor of theology, superintendent of churches and schools, advisor to municipal councils, and regulator of public morals and church liturgy. Meanwhile he kept enlarging the *Institutes*, wrote commentaries on the Bible, and maintained correspondence second in extent only to that of Erasmus. He slept little, ate sparingly, fasted frequently, and amazed his friends that one man could carry so heavy and varied a burden.

He was also courageously committed to his task as a preacher. Personally he longed for a life of contemplation and scholarship, but this was denied him. Instead he faced the disorder and debauchery of Geneva, rolled up his sleeves, and went to work to set things right. During the end of his first stay in Geneva, the town grew increasingly hostile to him. He was insulted in the streets, town thugs threatened to throw him in the river, and crowds gathered outside of his house and sang obscene songs. Shots were fired in the night around his home, more than fifty in one night—"more than enough to astonish the poor scholar, timid as I am, and as I confess I have always been," Calvin admitted.

In the quiet and pleasant work of Strassburg, he found great contentment. When the call came for him to return to Geneva, he was loathe to accept it; he wept as he pondered the choice. Church leaders urged him to return while his own personal desires pled with him to remain in Strassburg. Finally he agreed to return and face a trying and difficult job.

Once committed to a task, Calvin attacked it ferociously. He was a terrifying opponent. He may have thought of himself as a quiet scholar, but he was a man of vigorous verbal combat. He described his opponents as riffraff, idiots, dogs, asses, pigs, and stinking beasts. His opponents found themselves humiliated, exiled – and sometimes even burned at the stake.

Calvin was no secluded saint, concerned only about matters of spiritual well-being; he was deeply concerned about the total life of his flock in Geneva. He has been ridiculed for his efforts to curtail immorality in Geneva. It is true that he did strive to curtail bawdiness, gambling, and frivolity, but he also worked diligently for broader reforms for the community good. He was influential in the adoption of statutes providing for sanitary reforms, protection from fires, balcony railings to keep children from falling, and the introduction of manufacturing to provide employment for the people.

In his writing and in his life he displayed a genuine concern for family life, economics, politics, and all aspects of human relations. Though basically he was committed to organizing and developing the church in Geneva, he also had plenty of energy to expend on social issues. Much of his time was spent in dealing with the city council and politicians; sometimes he met defeat at their hands, but he triumphed more often than not.

Calvin advocated a partnership of church and state; both were to function for the good of the people, yet each had its own distinctive role. Calvin was very sensitive to any encroachment on the freedom of the pulpit. He believed that there were some matters in church life into which the state had no right to interfere; on the other hand, he denied that church and state should go completely separate ways. He believed that the state should enforce the laws of God upon the people.

Calvin's role in economics is often judged by historians as more significant than his role in politics. Some have attributed the rise of capitalism to Calvin. This is an overstatement of the case, although Calvin's economic emphasis certainly bolstered the position of capitalism and stimulated its advance, and as Calvinism was expressed in Puritanism, it most certainly helped expand the growing middle class of England and of the United States.

Not many preachers have had sermons and writings analyzed by historians to determine their teachings about government, economics, and social theory. But Calvin was no ordinary preacher. He deserves careful study by an age confronted with similar problems.

Preaching and Sermons

It would be easy enough to picture John Calvin seated at his writing desk, meticulously preparing his next sermon. Studiously he adds and amends, crossing out unsuitable words and adding more polished phrases. Argument piles upon argument, rhetorical expression upon expression: slowly the sermon takes shape. At last the great theologian and intellectual enters the pulpit and carefully reads each polished word.

Such a description might seem in keeping with Calvin's character, but it is absolutely untrue. Somehow that's how Calvin has been pictured, a meticulous scholar—and a meticulous manuscript writer. The truth is, Calvin was an excellent preacher who spoke entirely without manuscript and frequently without specific preparation. The very criticisms we might imagine of Calvin—cold, dull, lost-in-his-manuscript, pedantic—are entirely unjustified. He did speak slowly and deliberately, but always extemporaneously and directly. His preaching was logical, but never without underlying power and confidence. On the other hand, the virtues we imagine—the careful study, the meticulous argument—are the very points at which he has been most severely criticized. Many of his sermons were delivered entirely without preparation—and they reflect it. But we must remember that Calvin preached almost daily over a number of years; and although his general study continued without interruption, specific preparation on any one sermon was frequently absent.

Calvin was an autocrat with an autocrat's personality. He was practically destitute of humor and imagination, although he could be a warm friend. (He could be an even warmer enemy, as Servetus found out.) But it would be a mistake to believe that Calvin was a weak and forceless preacher. Beza, who knew him well, said of his preaching, "Every word weighed a pound." His sermons were filled with strong expressions, sometimes as crude as those of Luther himself. Calvin was very much involved with practical affairs, and his preaching showed it. He was not lost in philosophical speculations as were the mystics; his words were suited to the common hearers who listened to his daily preaching.

In spite of the absence of specific sermon study, Calvin's exegesis of Scripture has been described by Broadus as the ablest, soundest, clearest expositions of Scripture that had been seen in a thousand years. Since he took nothing but the Scriptures with him into the pulpit, Calvin must have had a prodigious memory; Beza states that Calvin preached two hundred eighty-six sermons and delivered one hundred eighty-six lectures on theology in one year.

Calvin generally spoke with great simplicity and brevity, avoiding rhetorical elegance. His delivery was quiet and slow – which was a good thing, since most of his sermons were preserved by auditors who took notes from his oral delivery which Calvin afterwards prepared for printing.

Calvin kept long hours in his study. From this continuous study he was able to preach without additional preparation. By five or six in the morning his books were brought to him in bed and his secretary stood ready to take notes. He spent most of the day on his couch – no doubt due to his weakness because of asthma – but he continued to work steadily. Late in his life Calvin ate only one meal a day, after which he would walk for a half hour, then return to his study. Recreation was almost unknown to him. His sermons bear evidence of his studious life and his lack of recreation.

Calvin's style was clear, vigorous, and pointed, but severe. Bossuet called Calvin's style *triste* (sad, gloomy), but his sermons showed an intensity of conviction that did not need flowery oratory.

One of the greatest classical students of John Calvin was Emile Doumergue. On July 2, 1909, at St. Peter's Church in Geneva where Calvin had preached, Doumergue delivered a lecture in commemoration of the four hundredth anniversary of the birth of Calvin. From Calvin's own pulpit he described the setting of one of Calvin's sermons:

> The bell . . . rings for the sermon at six o'clock in the morning or three o'clock in the afternoon. Calvin makes his way to the cathedral, leaning perhaps on his cane or on the arm of a friend, for often he is sick and weariness oppresses him. The crowd has gathered: some benches, many chairs; and to the rear, standing, the listeners in spite of themselves, who came in order not to be criticized by the Consistory, and in order to criticize hearers and preacher.
>
> But as soon as the latter appears in the place, silence reigns. His great forehead, his regular and distinguished

features, his eyes sunken in a perfect oval draw everyone's attention. And soon his look scintillates like a
flame. His narrow lips, which in intimacy, express gentleness and something like the sadness of physical and
moral suffering that is without repose, move fluently.
And from his entire person there frees itself an impression of authority that is for the time being irresistible.

He speaks slowly, with the short breath of the con-
sumptive, but all his faith, all his energy and all his
passion escape from this mighty head from which one
cannot turn away one's eyes, from this feeble breath
that is so distinctly apparent.[2]

Doumergue refused to describe Calvin as a man of action,
though there was much of action about him; nor as a man of
thought, though he presented a system of theology with profound influence: Doumergue insisted on painting him as a man
of words—a preacher:

That is the Calvin who seems to me the real and authentic Calvin, the one who explains all the others: Calvin,
the preacher of Geneva, moulding by his words the spirit
of the Reformed of the sixteenth century.

By his word!—evidently by a certain word. Which one?
Let us listen to Calvin himself as he speaks.

"We saw yesterday"; "we have seen this morning":
that is all to start the sermon. "Therefore we see now, in
summary, what Moses means. We will have to save the
rest until tomorrow": that is all to finish. As for divisions, transitions, and other homiletic artifices, there
is no more of them than there is of exordiums or perora-
tions: "that is the second thing we must note"; "so much
for one item"; "this is what we must conclude from this
passage," and the paraphrase goes on to the next one.
Nothing for appearance or filling-in: everything for application, edification, for substantial reality.[3]

Surprisingly enough, Calvin was a colorful preacher—at least
more than he has been pictured. Calvin used illustrations from
the farm, from wine making, from cooking, from city life. He
complained of the "mists," the morning frosts, and of the

---

2. Leroy Nixon, *John Calvin: Expository Preacher* (Grand Rapids, Mich.:
Wm. B. Eerdmans Pub. Co., 1950), p. 36. Used by permission.
3. Ibid., p. 38.

"borers," those insects "which ate the inside of the wheat." His expressions were vigorous.

Doumergue graphically described the language of Calvin, and in so doing, he had to apologize for the crudeness of some of Calvin's words. Doumergue reminded his audience that he did not bring those words into that pulpit—he found them there:

> Besides we see here a really astonishing number of proverbs, several to a sermon, sometimes several in a single phrase: "Without wings, they want to take the moon in their teeth, as they say." "Sicknesses come by horse and go away on foot." Some greedy ones "would drink the sea and the fishes." . . . It is the tone, the real tone of the people, restored, recalled; and Calvin sticks to it. . . .
>
> Instead of: "I blame," he would say: "I spit in his face." Instead of "I am wrong," he would say: "I deserve to have my face spit upon." Instead of: "the Lord spurns those ceremonies," he would say: "It it as though He spat upon all those services." Instead of: "perverse, human nature," he would say: "each one would scratch out his neighbor's eyes if there were not some restraints."[4]

But Calvin was not all coarseness: Doumergue pictured him as one who often spoke in tender tones. He compared God to a hen who "gathers us and draws us under his wing like little chicks" (one of his favorite expressions). He depicted God as "alluring us"; he spoke of God as a parent speaking to a child: "I will give you a lovely hat; I will buy you a pretty dress." Calvin made himself heard by his vigorous expressions and realistic dialogue.

The sermons of John Calvin that remain are largely due to a poor French refugee called Denis Reguenier, who accepted the office of secretary to Calvin in 1549 and worked until his death in 1560. He was competent enough as a shorthand writer to take down Calvin's sermons; he was helped in his work by Calvin's asthma which made him speak slowly and deliberately. Reguenier gave all of his time to this occupation. He carefully took down Calvin's sermons in shorthand and afterwards wrote out a copy in full, then bound the whole series in folio volumes and gave them into the care of the deacons. Anyone who wished

---

4. Ibid., p. 38.

to read these manuscripts was allowed to, if he had Reguenier's permission.[5]

We can be thankful for the careful work of such a copyist because of the abundance of Calvin's sermon materials which remain. When we attempt to study the preaching of John Knox, who had no such secretary, it is even easier to be grateful for Calvin's secretary. One listing of Calvin's preaching reveals two thousand twenty-three manuscript sermons in Geneva; only two sermons by John Knox have survived.

Calvin's philosophy of preaching was simple: he regarded the Bible as the Word of God; Calvin strongly believed that the preacher entered the pulpit only to proclaim God's Word and not his own ideas: "So when we enter the pulpit, it is not to bring there our dreams and fancies. . . ." But what the preacher has received he must pass on faithfully without any addition. That which was not discussed in Scripture should not be discussed in the pulpit: the spoken word in the pulpit should be a sermon from the written word in the Book. (Calvin's influence on Karl Barth at this point is evident.) Calvin said: "In short, St. Paul informs us that we must not pick and cull Scripture to please our own fancy, but must receive the whole without exception." Calvin believed that a preacher "must attempt nothing with his brain."

To be a good corrector of men, the preacher must first correct himself. He must "ratify and seal in effect the doctrine he bears," and show that what he says "he has so conceived in his heart, and has it so printed and engraved in him, that it is as though he spoke before God." Calvin believed that preachers should be sufficiently impressed with the importance of their task, if not with the importance of themselves:

> Let them argue with the mountains, let them rise up against the hills; in other words let them not be dazzled by men, but let them show that the word that they carry, that is committed to them, is like the royal scepter of God under which all creatures bow their heads and bend their knees. . . .
> Let them boldly dare all things, and constrain all the glory, highness, and power of this world to obey and to yield to the divine majesties; let them by this same Word

5. T. H. L. Parker, *The Oracles of God* (London: Lutterworth Press, 1947), pp. 39–40.

have command over everyone; let them edify the house of Christ, overthrowing the reign of Satan; let them lead the flock to pasture and kill the wolves; let them bind and let loose thunder and lightning, if that is their calling —but all in God's Name.[6]

With those words Calvin described the calling of every minister: better yet, with those words he described his own preaching more succinctly than any of the scholars who have studied him in the centuries since his day. As usual, Calvin has the last word.

---

6. Nixon, p. 58.

Sermons

THE WORD OUR ONLY RULE

"Unto the pure all things are pure; but unto them that are defiled and unbelieving is nothing pure; but even their mind and conscience is defiled. They profess that they know God; but in works they deny him: being abominable and disobedient, and unto every good work reprobate" (Titus 1:15–16).

ST. PAUL HATH SHOWN US that we must be ruled by the Word of God, and hold the commandments of men as vain and foolish; for holiness and perfection of life belongeth not to them. He condemneth some of their commandments, as when they forbid certain meats, and will not suffer us to use that liberty which God giveth the faithful. Those who troubled the church in St. Paul's time, by setting forth such traditions, used the commandments of the law as a shield. These were but men's inventions: because the temple was to be abolished at the coming of our Lord Jesus Christ. Those in the church of Christ, who hold this superstition, to have certain meats forbidden, have not the authority of God, for it was against His mind and purpose that the Christian should be subject to such ceremonies.

To be short, St. Paul informs us in this place that in these days we have liberty to eat of all kinds of meat without exception. As for the health of the body, that is not here spoken of; but the matter here set forth is that men shall not set themselves up as masters, to make laws for us contrary to the Word of God. Seeing it is so, that God putteth no difference between meats, let us so use them; and never inquire what men like, or what they think good. Notwithstanding, we must use the benefits that God hath granted us, soberly and moderately. We must remember that God hath made meats for us, not that we should fill ourselves like swine, but that we should use them for the sustenance of life: therefore, let us content ourselves with this measure, which God hath shown us by His Word.

If we have not such a store of nourishment as we would wish, let

Reprinted from John Calvin, *The Mystery of Godliness* (Grand Rapids, Mich.: Wm. B. Eerdmans Pub. Co., 1950), pp. 69–80. Used by permission.

us bear our poverty patiently, and practice the doctrine of St. Paul; and know as well how to bear poverty as riches. If our Lord give us more than we could have wished for, yet must we bridle our appetites. On the other side, if it please Him to cut off our morsel, and feed us but poorly, we must be content with it, and pray Him to give us patience when we have not what our appetites crave. To be short, we must have recourse to what is said in Romans 13: "But put ye on the Lord Jesus Christ, and make not provision for the flesh, to fulfill the lusts thereof." Let us content ourselves to have what we need, and that which God knoweth to be proper for us; thus shall all things be clean to us, if we be thus cleansed.

Yet it is true that although we were ever so unclean, the meats which God hath made are good; but the matter we have to consider is the use of them. When St. Paul saith *all things are clean,* he meaneth not that they are so of themselves, but as relateth to those that receive them; as we have noticed before, where he saith to Timothy, all things are sanctified to us by faith and giving of thanks. God hath filled the world with such abundance that we may marvel to see what a fatherly care He hath over us: for to what end or purpose are all the riches here on earth, only to show how liberal He is toward man!

If we know not that He is our Father, and acteth the part of a nurse toward us, if we receive not at His hand that which He giveth us, insomuch that when we eat, we are convinced that it is God that nourisheth us, He cannot be glorified as He deserveth; neither can we eat one morsel of bread without committing sacrilege; for which we must give an account. That we may lawfully enjoy these benefits, which have been bestowed upon us, we must be resolved upon this point (as I said before), that it is God that nourisheth and feedeth us.

This is the cleanness spoken of here by the apostle; when he saith, all things are clean, especially when we have such an uprightness in us that we despise not the benefits bestowed upon another, but crave our daily bread at the hand of God, being persuaded that we have no right to it, only to receive it as the mercy of God. Now let us see from whence this cleanness cometh. We shall not find it in ourselves, for it is given us by faith. St. Peter saith, the hearts of the old fathers were cleansed by this means; to wit, when God gave them *faith* (Acts 15).

It is true that he here hath regard to the everlasting salvation; because we were utterly unclean until God made Himself known to us in the name of our Lord Jesus Christ; who, being made our Redeemer, bought the price and ransom of our souls. But this doctrine may, and ought to be applied to what concerneth this present life; for until we know that, being adopted in Jesus Christ, we are God's children, and consequently that the inheritance of this world is ours, if we touch one morsel of meat, we are thieves; for we are deprived of, and banished from all the blessings that God made, by reason of Adam's sin until we get possession of them in our Lord Jesus Christ.

Therefore, it is faith that must cleanse us. Then will all meats be clean to us: that is, we may use them freely without wavering. If men enjoin spiritual laws upon us, we need not observe them, being assured that such obedience cannot please God, for in so doing, we set up rulers to govern us, making them equal with God, who reserveth all power to Himself. Thus, the government of the soul must be kept safe and sound in the hands of God. Therefore, if we allow so much superiority to men that we suffer them to inwrap our souls with their own bands, we so much lessen and diminish the power and empire that God hath over us.

And thus the humbleness that we might have in obeying the traditions of men would be worse than all the rebellion in the world; because it is robbing God of His honor, and giving it, as a spoil, to mortal men. St. Paul speaketh of the superstition of some of the Jews, who would have men still observe the shadows and figures of the law; but the Holy Ghost hath pronounced a sentence which must be observed to the end of the world: that God hath not bound us at this day to such a burden as was borne by the old fathers; but hath cut off that part which He had commanded, relative to the abstaining from meats; for it was a law but for a season.

Seeing God hath thus set us at liberty, what rashness it is for worms of the earth to make new laws; as though God had not been wise enough. When we allege this to the papists, they answer that St. Paul spake of the Jews, and of meats that were forbidden by the law. This is true, but let us see whether this answer be to any purpose, or worth receiving. St. Paul not only saith that it is lawful for us to use that which was forbidden, but he speaketh in general terms, saying, *all things are clean.* Thus we see that God hath here given us liberty, concerning the use of meats; so that He will not hold us in subjection, as were the old fathers.

Therefore, seeing God hath abrogated that law which was made by Him, and will not have it in force any longer, what shall we think when we see men inventing traditions of their own; and not content themselves with what God hath shown them? In the first place, they still endeavor to hold the church of Christ under the restrictions of the Old Testament. But God will have us governed as men of years and discretion, which have no need of instruction suitable for children. They set up man's devices, and say we must keep them under pain of deadly sin; whereas God will not have His own law to be observed among us at this day, relative to types and shadows, because it was all ended at the coming of our Lord Jesus Christ.

Shall it then be lawful to observe what men have framed in their own wisdom? Do we not see that it is a matter which goeth directly against God? St. Paul setteth himself against such deceivers: against such as would bind Christians to abstain from meats as God had commanded in His law. If a man say, it is but a small matter to abstain from flesh on Friday, or in Lent, let us consider whether it be a small

matter to corrupt and bastardize the service of God! For surely those
that go about to set forth and establish the tradition of men, set themselves against that which God hath appointed in His Word, and thus
commit sacrilege.

Seeing God will be served with obedience, let us beware and keep
ourselves within those bounds which God hath set; and not suffer
men to add any thing to it of their own. There is something worse in
it than all this: for they think it a service that deserveth something
from God to abstain from eating flesh. They think it a great holiness:
and thus the service of God, which should be spiritual, is banished, as
it were, while men busy themselves about foolish trifles. As the common saying is, they leave the apple for the paring.

We must be faithful, and stand fast in our liberty; we must follow
the rule which is given us in the Word of God, and not suffer our souls
to be brought into slavery by new laws, forged by men. For it is a hellish tyranny, which lesseneth God's authority and mixeth the truth of
the gospel with figures of the law; and perverteth and corrupteth the
true service of God, which ought to be spiritual. Therefore, let us consider how precious a privilege it is to give thanks to God with quietness
of conscience, being assured it is His will and pleasure that we should
enjoy His blessings: and that we may do so, let us not entangle ourselves with the superstitions of men, but be content with what is contained in the pure simplicity of the gospel. Then, as we have shown
concerning the first part of our text, *unto them that are pure, all
things will be pure.*

When we have received the Lord Jesus Christ, we know that we
shall be cleansed from our filthiness and blemishes; for by His grace
we are made partakers of God's benefits, and are taken for His children, although there be nothing but vanity in us. "But unto them
that are defiled and unbelieving, is nothing pure." By this St. Paul
meaneth that whatsoever proceedeth from those that are defiled and
unbelieving is not acceptable to God but is full of infection. While
they are unbelieving, they are foul and unclean; and while they
have such filthiness in them, whatsoever they touch becomes polluted with their infamy.

Therefore, all the rules and laws they can make shall be nothing but
vanity: for God disliketh whatsoever they do; yea, He utterly abhorreth
it. Although men may torment themselves with ceremonies and outward performances, yet all these things are vain until they become
upright in heart: for in this the true service of God commenceth. So
long then as we are faithless, we are filthy before God. These things
ought to be evident to us; but hypocrisy is so rooted within us that we
are apt to neglect them. It will readily be confessed that we cannot
please God by serving Him until our hearts be rid of wickedness.

God strove with the people of old time about the same doctrine; as
we see especially in the second chapter of the prophet Haggai: where

he asketh the priests, if a man touch a holy thing, whether he shall be made holy or not, the priests answered, no. On the contrary, if an unclean man touch a thing, whether it shall become unclean or no, the priests answered and said, it shall be unclean: so is this nation, saith the Lord, and so are the works of their hands. Now let us notice what is contained in the figures and shadows of the law. If an unclean man had handled any thing, it became unclean, and therefore must be cleansed. Our Lord saith, consider what ye be: for ye have nothing but uncleanness and filth; yet notwithstanding, ye would content Me with your sacrifices, offerings, and such like things. But He saith, as long as your minds are entangled with wicked lusts, as long as some of ye are whoremongers, adulterers, blasphemers, and perjurers, as long as ye are full of guile, cruelty, and spitefulness, your lives are utterly lawless, and full of all uncleanness; I cannot abide it, how fair soever it may seem before men.

We see then that all the services we can perform, until we are truly reformed in our hearts, are but mockeries; and God condemneth and rejecteth every whit of them. But who believeth these things to be so? When the wicked, who are taken in their wickedness, feel any remorse of conscience, they will endeavor by some means or other to compound with God by performing some ceremonies: they think it sufficient to satisfy the minds of men, believing that God ought likewise to be satisfied therewith. This is a custom which has prevailed in all ages.

It is not only in this text of the prophet Haggai that God rebuketh men for their hypocrisy, and for thinking that they may obtain His favor with trifles, but it was a continual strife which all the prophets had with the Jews. It is said in Isaiah 1:13, 14, 15: "Bring no more vain oblations; incense is an abomination unto me; the new moons and sabbaths, the calling of assemblies, I cannot away with: it is iniquity, even the solemn meeting, your new moons and your appointed feasts my soul hateth: they are a trouble unto me; I am weary to bear them. And when ye spread forth your hands, I will hide mine eyes from you; yea, when ye make many prayers, I will not hear: your hands are full of blood."

And again it is said, "Though ye offer me burnt offerings, and your meat offerings, I will not accept them; neither will I regard the peace offerings of your fat beasts" (Amos 5:22). God here showeth us that the things which He Himself had commanded were filthy and unclean when they were observed and abused by hypocrites. Therefore, let us learn that when men serve God after their own fashion, they beguile and deceive themselves. It is said in another text of Isaiah, "Who hath required these things at your hands?" Wherein it is made manifest that if we will have God approve our works, they must be according to His divine Word.

Thus we see what St. Paul's meaning is when he saith there is nothing *clean* to them that are *unclean*. And why? *For even their mind and conscience are defiled.* By this he showeth (as I before observed) that until such times as we have learned to serve God aright, in a proper manner, we shall do no good at all by our own works; although we may flatter ourselves that they are of great importance, and by this means rock ourselves to sleep.

Let us now see what the traditions of *popery* are. The chief ends of them is to make an agreement with God, by their works of supererogation, as they term them; that is, their surplus works; which are, when they do more than God commandeth them. According to their own notions, they discharge their duty towards Him and content Him with such payment as they render by their works, and thereof make their account. When they have fasted their *saints* evenings, when they have refrained from eating flesh upon Fridays, when they have attended mass devoutly, when they have taken holy water, they think that God ought not to demand any thing more of them and that there is nothing amiss in them.

But in the meantime, they cease not to indulge themselves in lewdness, whoredom, perjury, blasphemy, etc.: every one of them giving himself to those vices; yet notwithstanding, they think God ought to hold Himself well paid with the works they offer Him; as for example, when they have taken holy water, worshipped images, rambled from altar to altar, and other like things, they imagine that they have made sufficient payment and recompense for their sins. But we hear the doctrine of the Holy Ghost concerning such as are defiled; which is, there is nothing pure nor clean in all their doings.

But we will put the case, by supposing that all the abominations of the papists were not evil in their own nature; yet notwithstanding, according to this doctrine of St. Paul, there can be nothing but uncleanness in them, for they themselves are sinful and unclean. The holiness of these men consists in gewgaws and trifles. They endeavor to serve God in the things that He doth not require, and at the same time leave undone things that He hath commanded in His law.

It has been the case in all ages that men have despised God's law for the sake of their own traditions. Our Lord Jesus Christ upbraided the Pharisees, when He saith, "Why do ye also trangress the commandment of God by your tradition?" (Matt. 15:3). Thus it was in former times, in the days of the prophets. Isaiah crieth out, "Wherefore the Lord said, forasmuch as this people draw near me with their mouth, and with their lips do honor me, but have removed their heart far from me, and their fear toward me is taught by the precept of men: therefore, behold, I will proceed to do a marvelous work and wonder; for the wisdom of their wise men shall perish, and the understanding of their prudent men shall be hid" (Isa. 25:13). While men occupy themselves about traditions, they pass over the things that God hath commanded in His Word.

This it is that caused Isaiah to cry out against such as set forth men's traditions; telling them plainly that God threatened to blind the wisest of them, because they turned away from the pure rule of His Word to follow their own foolish inventions. St. Paul likewise alludes to the same thing, when he saith they have no fear of God before their eyes. Let us not deceive ourselves; for we know that God requireth men to live uprightly, and to abstain from all violence, cruelty, malice, and deceit; that none of these things should appear in our life. But those that have no fear of God before their eyes, it is apparent that they are out of order, and that there is nothing but uncleanness in their whole life.

If we wish to know how our life should be regulated, let us examine the contents of the Word of God; for we cannot be sanctified by outward show and pomp, although they are so highly esteemed among men. We must call upon God in sincerity, and put our whole trust in Him; we must give up pride and presumption, and resort to Him with true lowliness of mind that we be not given to fleshly affections. We must endeavor to hold ourselves in awe, under subjection to God, and flee from gluttony, whoredom, excess, robbery, blasphemy, and other evils. Thus we see what God would have us do, in order to have our life well regulated.

When men would justify themselves by outward works, it is like covering a heap of filth with a clean linen cloth. Therefore, let us put away the filthiness that is hidden in our hearts; I say, let us drive the evil from us, and then the Lord will accept of our life: thus we may see wherein consists the true knowledge of God! When we understand this aright, it will lead us to live in obedience to His will. Men have not become so beastly, as to have no understanding that there is a God who created them. But this knowledge, if they do not submit to His requirements, serves as a condemnation to them: because their eyes are blindfolded by Satan; insomuch, that although the gospel may be preached to them, they do not understand it; in this situation we see many at the present day. How many there are in the world that have been taught by the doctrine of the gospel, and yet continue in brutish ignorance!

This happeneth because Satan hath so prepossessed the minds of men with wicked affections that although the light may shine ever so bright, they still remain blind, and see nothing at all. Let us learn, then, that the true knowledge of God is of such a nature that it showeth itself, and yieldeth fruit through our whole life. Therefore to know God, as St. Paul said to the Corinthians, we must be transformed into His image. For if we pretend to know Him, and in the meantime our life be loose and wicked, it needeth no witness to prove us liars; our own life beareth sufficient record that we are mockers and falsifiers, and that we abuse the name of God.

St. Paul saith in another place, if ye know Jesus Christ, ye must put off the old man: as if he should say, we cannot declare that we know Jesus Christ, only by acknowledging Him for our head, and by His receiving us as His members; which cannot be done until we have cast off the old man, and become new creatures. The world hath at all times abused God's name wickedly, as it doth still at this day; therefore, let us have an eye to the true knowledge of the Word of God, whereof St. Paul speaketh.

Finally, let us not put our own works into the balance, and say they are good, and that we think well of them; but let us understand that the good works are those which God hath commanded in His law and that all we can do beside these, are nothing. Therefore, let us learn to shape our lives according to what God hath commanded: to put our trust in Him, to call upon Him, to give Him thanks, to bear patiently whatsoever it pleaseth Him to send us; to deal uprightly with our neighbors, and to live honestly before all men. These are the works which God requireth at our hands.

If we were not so perverse in our nature, there would be none of us but what might discern these things: even children would have skill enough to discern them. The works which God hath not commanded are but foolishness and an abomination; whereby God's pure service is marred. If we wish to know what constitutes the good works spoken of by St. Paul, we must lay aside all the inventions of men, and simply follow the instructions contained in the Word of God; for we have no other rule than that which is given by Him; which is such as He will accept, when we yield up our accounts at the last day, when He alone shall be the judge of all mankind.

Now let us fall down before the face of our good God, acknowledging our faults, praying Him to make us perceive them more clearly: and to give us such trust in the name of our Lord Jesus Christ that we may come to Him and be assured of the forgiveness of our sins; and that He will make us partakers of sound faith, whereby all our filthiness may be washed away.

BEHAVIOR IN THE CHURCH

"These things write I unto thee, hoping to come unto thee shortly: But if I tarry long, that thou mayest know how thou

---

Reprinted from John Calvin, *The Mystery of Godliness* (Grand Rapids, Mich.: Wm. B. Eerdmans Pub. Co., 1950), pp. 113–25. Used by permission.

oughtest to behave thyself in the house of God, which is the
church of the living God, the pillar and ground of the truth"
(1 Timothy 3:14–15).

WE SEE WHAT HOLINESS AND PERFECTION St. Paul required in all those
that had any public charge in the church of God; we see also how he
concluded that those who behaved themselves well and faithfully in
office, "purchased to themselves a good degree, and great boldness in
the faith which is in Jesus Christ." When there is good order in the
church, and the children of God do their duty faithfully, it is an honor
to them; and men think them worthy of reverence. This is not to puff
them up, and make them proud, but that they may be more and more
enabled to serve God; and that men may more willingly hear them,
and receive counsel and advice from them: this is the meaning of
St. Paul.

Those that do not their duty as they ought have their mouths stopped;
they can do nothing with the people, but are worthily mocked; although they are bold, yet they have no gravity; therefore their doctrine
cannot be received. Those that are called to fill offices in the church of
God must strive so much the more to do well, and endeavor to serve
God, and the people of God, faithfully. But now-a-days, the wicked
seem to bear the sway, before whom, the world, as it were, trembles.

Thus we see that things are much out of order among us. Where is
our liberty at the present day? Not in the faith, but in all wickedness;
among those that are hardened and past all shame. We see good men
oppressed, who dare not speak in their own defence. If a man reprove
sin, and go about to redress matters, and set them in order, he is beset
on all sides by the wicked. We see not many that trouble themselves
to maintain a good cause, for every man betrayeth the truth. We suffer
things to go as evil as they can; these are the days spoken of by the
prophet Isaiah; righteousness and justice are hunted out from among
us; and there is no man that hath zeal enough to set himself against
wickedness. It may well seem that we have conspired to foster wickedness, and bring it to full maturity.

The wrath of God is kindled against us; all things are out of order.
Those that walk as becometh Christians, and labor to serve God purely,
are marked out as enemies, and men seek to trample them under foot.
On the other hand, we see the wicked do what they list; they act as
wild beasts; yet men stand in fear of them; and this liberty that is
given them maketh them the more hardened. When we see such disorder, have we not reason to sigh and be ashamed of ourselves, knowing that God doth not rule at all among us, but that the devil hath full
possession? Shall we boast that we have the gospel? It is true, His
Word is preached among us, but do we not see that it is contemned,
and that men make a mock of it? But let them flatter themselves in

hardening their hearts against God; yet notwithstanding, this doctrine will continue, and will be preached for a witness against us in
the latter day, unless the Lord come speedily and reform us.

St. Paul writeth these things to Timothy, that if he tarry long, before
he come, he may know how to behave himself in the house of God.
Here St. Paul exhorteth Timothy, and in his person all the faithful,
to walk warily and carefully in conformity to the spiritual government
of the church. For the house of God, if He dwell therein, is the upholder of the truth. Therefore it is no trifling matter to be called of
the Lord, to serve Him in the office spoken of by St. Paul. We must beware and fail not, seeing God bestoweth upon us the honor of govern-
ing His house: yea, that house wherein He hath His abode and will
make known His majesty: which is, as it were, a closet where His
truth is kept, that it may be maintained and preserved in the world. If
the matter stand thus, have not those whom God hath thus honored
great occasion to be watchful, and to endeavor to execute the charge
committed to them? Thus we see St. Paul's meaning.

But before we go any farther, it will be necessary to put aside the
impudency of the *papists*, who abuse this text, in order to establish
their own tyranny. For if they can once set up the church of God, they
think they have won the field. But they should first prove that theirs is
the church of God; which is so difficult a matter for them to do, that
the contrary is evident. And why so? Because St. Paul saith the church
is the house of God. They have driven our Lord Jesus Christ out of
doors, so that He reigneth no more among them as ruler, whereto He
was appointed by the Father; who requireth that we should do Him
homage, submitting ourselves wholly to His doctrine.

Do the papists suffer Jesus Christ to govern them purely and peace-
ably? Nay, I am sure they do not. They coin and stamp whatever they
think proper; and whatsoever they decree is taken for articles of belief.
They mingle and confound the doctrine of the gospel with notions devised by themselves; so that we may easily see it is not God's house:
otherwise Jesus Christ would not be banished therefrom. Moreover,
St. Paul addeth, the church must uphold the truth. But we see in these
times that it is oppressed by the tyranny of the *pope;* where there
remaineth nothing but lies, errors, corruption, and idolatry. Seeing
this is the case, we may well conclude that theirs is not the true church
of God.

But we will go farther. It was not the meaning of St. Paul (as the papists imagine) that the church cannot err because it is governed by the
Holy Ghost, and that whatsoever they think good, must be received.
But on the contrary, St. Paul observes that the church is the upholder
of the truth; because God will have His truth preached by the mouth of
men; therefore He hath appointed the ministration of His Word that
we might know His will; for God useth this means, that men may

know His truth, and reverence it from age to age. This is the reason why the church is called a pillar.

The papists endeavor to bury the doctrine of the gospel when they say the church cannot err. Let us consider, say they, that God will inspire us; yet in the mean time they leave the Word of God, thinking they may wander here and there, without committing evil. And why? Oh, the church cannot err. But on the other hand, let us see upon what condition our Lord hath honored His church. St. Paul informeth us that He doth not bind us to devise what we think good, but He holdeth us tied and bound to His Word; as it is said, "I have put my words in thy mouth, and have covered thee in the shadow of mine hand, that I may plant the heavens, and lay the foundations of the earth, and say unto Zion, Thou art my people" (Isa. 51:16).

How is it that God promiseth that He will reign in the midst of His people? He doth not say, because He inspireth them, that they have leave to coin new articles of faith! No, no: but He saith He will put the words of our Lord Jesus Christ into the mouths of such as must preach His name. For that promise was not made for the time of the law only, but is proper for the church of Christ, and shall continue to the end of the world. Thus we see how the church must be the pillar to bear up the truth of God.

God will not come down from heaven, neither will He send His angels to bring us revelations from above; but He will be made known to us by His Word. Therefore, He will have ministers of the church preach His truth, and instruct us therein. If we attend not to these things, we are not the church of God; but are guilty, as much as lieth in us, of abolishing His truth; we are traitors and murderers. And why so? Because God could maintain His truth otherwise if He would: He is not bound to these means, neither hath He any need of the help of men. But He will have His truth made known by such preaching as He hath commanded. What then would become of us, if we should leave off this preaching? Should we not thereby endeavor to bring this truth to nought? It is said, the gospel (as it is preached) "is the power of God unto salvation to every one that believeth" (Rom. 1:16).

And how so? Is it because God hath no other means, but by the voice of men? in this sound that vanisheth away in the air? No, no; but yet He hath appointed this means, to the end that when we are restored by His grace, we may attend to the hearing of His Word with all reverence: then shall we feel that His doctrine is not vain and unprofitable but hath its effect, and is of such efficacy as to call us to eternal life. For St. Paul saith, "Faith cometh by hearing" (Rom. 10:17) and we know it is faith that quickeneth our souls, which otherwise would be helpless and lost. Thus let us mark well St. Paul's meaning, whereby we may know how impudent and beastly the papists are to claim this text in order to establish their tyranny, which is entirely contrary to the meaning of the apostle.

But it is not enough to reprove the papists; *we also* must be edified by the doctrine contained in the text. Therefore, first of all, those that have charge to preach the doctrine of the gospel, must take heed to themselves. And why so? Because they are set in God's house to govern it. If a man do any one the honor to put the rule and government of his house and goods in his hands, ought he not to conduct himself in such a manner, as to please the one who committed this trust to him? If a prince make a man overseer of his household, is he not bound to do his duty faithfully? So the living God appointeth those that must preach His Word in His house and temple: He will have them govern His people in His name, and bear the message of salvation. Seeing they are called to this high station, what carefulness and humility ought there to be in them!

Therefore, let those that are appointed ministers of the Word of God know that they have not only to do with men, but that they are accountable to Him who hath called them to this high office: let them not be pulled up with the honor and dignity of their station, but know that they shall be so much the less able to excuse themselves if they walk not uprightly; and that they commit horrible sacrilege, and shall have a fearful vengeance of God prepared for them, if they labor not to serve Him as they ought.

First of all, we are exhorted to do our duty; God having honored us who were so unworthy, we ought to labor on our part to fill the office whereunto we are called. When the church is called the house of the living God, it ought to awaken us to walk otherwise than we do. Why do we sleep in our sins? Why do we run into wickedness? Do we think that God doth not see us? that we are far out of His sight, and from the presence of our Lord Jesus Christ? Let us remember that the Word of God is preached to us, that God dwelleth among us, and is present with us; as our Lord Jesus Christ saith, "Where two or three are gathered together in my name, there am I in the midst of them" (Matt. 18:20). And we know, as it is said, that "In him dwelleth all the fulness of the Godhead bodily" (Col. 2:9).

So then, how oft soever the devil attempts to rock us to sleep, and tie us to the vanities of this world, or tempt us with wicked lusts, we ought to remember this sentence, and set it before our eyes; *that God dwelleth in the midst of us, and that we are His house.* Now we must consider that God cannot dwell in a foul place: He must have a holy house and temple. And how? Oh, there is no difficulty in setting out ourselves finely that all the world may gaze at us; but God taketh no pleasure in all these vanities of the world. Our beautifying must be spiritual: we must be clad with the graces of the Holy Ghost: this is the gold and silver, these are the precious stones spoken of by the prophet Isaiah, when he describeth the temple of God (Isa. 60:6).

Seeing God is so gracious as to have His Word preached among us, let us live in obedience to His divine commands, that He may reside with us, and we be His temple. For this cause, let us see that we cleanse ourselves from all our filthiness, and renounce it, that we may be a fit place for God's holiness to dwell in. If we attend to these things, we shall reap great joy, seeing our Lord joineth Himself to us, and maketh His residence in our souls and bodies. What are we? There is nothing but rottenness in us: I speak not of the body only, but more particularly of the soul, which is still more infected; and yet we see the Lord will build us up, that we may be fit temples for His majesty to reside in. We have great occasion to rejoice by reason of this text; and ought to strive to obtain the pureness which is required by the gospel, because God will have us joined to Him, and sanctified by His Holy Spirit.

Our text says *the church of God is the pillar and ground of the truth*. God is not under the necessity of borrowing any thing from man, as we before observed; He can cause His truth to reign without our help: but He doth us this honor, and is so gracious as to employ us in this worthy and precious calling. He could instruct us without our hearing the voice of man; He could also send His angels, as He did to His servants in ancient times: but He calleth and gathereth us together in His church; there is His banner which He will set up among His flock; this is the kingly sceptre whereby He will have us ruled.

Therefore God hath shut up His truth in the Scriptures, and will have it preached and expounded to us daily. For when St. Paul speaketh of the truth, he meaneth the doctrine of salvation, which God hath revealed to us in His Word. The apostle saith the doctrine of God (which is the incorruptible seed, whereby we are born anew to everlasting life) is the truth. This is set forth in Colossians 1:5, John 16:13, and 17:17. St. John often speaketh of the gospel by calling it the truth: as if He should say, without it we know nothing, and whatsoever we can comprehend, is vain: so that this is the only sure foundation upon which we can rest.

And indeed, what would it profit us if we knew all other things, and were destitute of the knowledge of our God? If we know not God, I say, alas, are we not more than miserable? But as God hath imprinted His image in His Word, it is there He presenteth Himself to us, and will have us to behold Him, as it were, face to face (2 Cor. 3 and 4). Therefore it is not in vain that St. Paul giveth this title to the preaching of the Word of God: namely, *that it is the truth*. By this means He maketh Himself known to us; it is also the means of our salvation; it is our life, our riches, and the seed whereby we become the children of God: in short, it is the nourishment of our souls, by which we are quickened.

Therefore let us remember that St. Paul saith the truth is maintained among us by the preaching of the gospel, and men are appointed thereunto. First of all, we are miserable (as I before observed) if we know not God. And how shall we know Him, unless we suffer ourselves to be taught by His Word? We must learn to seek for this treasure, and apply all our labor to find it: and when God is so gracious, as to offer it to us, let us receive it as poor beggars starved with hunger. When it pleaseth Him to bestow such a benefit upon us, let us withdraw ourselves from worldly matters, that we may not despise His inestimable blessings.

Seeing the truth of God cannot reign among us, unless the gospel be preached, we ought to esteem it highly, knowing that He otherwise holdeth Himself afar off. If these things were observed as they ought to be, we should see more reverence for the doctrine of the Word of God. In these days we can hardly tell what the word *church* meaneth. It is true, men boast that the gospel is preached, and that there is a reformation according to the Word of God; but while they use this word *church,* they know not what it means.

Some say they believe there is a universal church; but they speak in language which they do not understand. Such are the papists, who are so ignorant of the word *church,* being bewitched after the traditions of men, and bound by their tyranny, that they cannot understand it; neither dare they inquire what the church of God is. They have their foolish devotions, to which they are so much given, that they cannot be brought from them to the right way of salvation. As for us, we have the Word of God, but we hardly know how to maintain it. We see what contempt there is cast upon it, when it is preached among us, and how it is set at nought, every man being his own teacher.

Many are glutted, as it were, with the gospel; and think they know more than is necessary: they know so much that they become sensible of their own condemnation. Thus they shall be twice guilty; because they have once tasted the heavenly gifts, and are now such contemners of the Word of God: we plainly perceive that they cast off all honesty, reverence, and religion and would be content to have God unknown among them. We ought to be greatly ashamed, seeing God hath so enlightened us, that we give ourselves to such wickedness; and cause the gospel to be evil spoken of among the ignorant and unbelievers.

If we knew how to profit by what is contained in this place, we should have great reason to rejoice; seeing God will have His truth maintained by the means of preaching. There is nothing in men but wickedness; and yet God will use them for witnesses of His truth, having committed it to their keeping. Although there are few that preach the Word of God, yet notwithstanding, this treasure is common to the whole church. Therefore we are keepers of the truth of God; that is to say, of His precious image, of that which concerneth the majesty of the doctrine of our salvation, and the life of the world.

When God calleth us to so honorable a charge, have we not great reason to rejoice and praise His holy name? Let us remember to keep this treasure safe, that it be not profaned among us. St. Paul speaketh not only to instruct those that are called to preach the gospel, but that we may all know what blessings God hath bestowed upon us, when His word is preached in its purity. Our salvation is a matter of great importance; and we must come to it by means of the gospel. For faith is the life of our souls: as the body is quickened by the soul, so is the soul by faith. So then we are dead, until God calleth us to the knowledge of His truth. Therefore we need not fear, for God will adopt us for His children, if we receive the doctrine of the gospel.

We need not soar above the clouds, we need not travel up and down the earth, we need not go beyond the seas, nor to the bottomless pit, to seek God; for we have His Word in our hearts, and in our mouths. God openeth to us the door of paradise when we hear the promises that are made to us in His name. It is as much as if He reached out His hand visibly, and received us for His children. God sealeth this doctrine by the signs which are annexed to it: for it is certain that the sacraments have a tendency to this end, that we may know that the church is the house of God, in which He is resident, and that His truth is maintained thereby.

When we are baptized in the name of our Lord Jesus Christ, we are brought into God's household: it is the mark of our adoption. Now, He cannot be our Father, unless we are under His divine protection, and governed by His Holy Spirit: as we have an evident witness in baptism, and a greater in the Lord's Supper: that is, we have a plain declaration that we are joined to God, and made one with Him. For our Lord Jesus Christ showeth us that we are His body; that every one is a member; that He is the head whereby we are nourished with His substance and virtue. As the body is not separate from the head, so Jesus Christ showeth us that His life is common with ours, and that we are partakers of all His benefits.

When we behold this, is it not enough to make the truth of God precious to us? Is it not a looking-glass, in which we may see that God not only dwelleth among us, but that He also dwelleth in every one of us? God, having made us one with our Lord Jesus Christ, will not suffer us to be separated from Him in any way whatsoever. Therefore, when we have this inestimable honor conferred upon us, should we not be ravished, as it were, and learn more and more to withdraw ourselves from the corruptions of this world, and truly show that it is not in vain that the Son of God will have us belong to Him? How are we made one with our Lord Jesus Christ? By being pilgrims in this world, passing through it as true citizens of heaven. St. Paul saith, "Ye are no more strangers and foreigners, but fellow-citizens with the saints, and of the household of God" (Eph. 2:19).

When He exhorteth us to withdraw from all wicked affections, He calleth us to our Savior Jesus Christ, who is our life, who is in heaven: must we not then take pains to come unto Him? Now let us meditate upon this subject with solemnity, seeing we are to celebrate the Lord's

Supper next sabbath. Let us see how we are disposed: for God will not have us come to Him as liars and deceivers. Therefore, let us see if we are disposed to receive God, not as a guest that travelleth by the way, but as Him that hath chosen us for His dwelling place forever: yea, as Him that hath dedicated us to Himself, as His temples; that we may be as a house built upon a rock. We must receive God by faith, and be made truly one with our Lord Jesus Christ, as I have already shown.

And are these things practised among us? Nay; on the contrary, we seem to despise God, and as it were, put Jesus Christ to flight, that He may no more be acquainted with us. Observe the disorder that is among us; should I enumerate the difficulties, where should I make an end? Let every one open his eyes! It is impossible for us to think of the confusion that reigns among us now-a-days, without being amazed, if we have any fear of God before us. Men flatter and please themselves in their sins, and have become as stocks and stones; so that in us is fulfilled that which was spoken by the prophet: namely, that we have a spirit of drunkenness, and a spirit of slumber, and can discern nothing.

As I have already observed, if we had any fear of God before our eyes, we should be cast down in ourselves, and not only be ashamed, but detest such confusion as is seen among us both in public and private. We see men so far out of the way that one would think they were disposed to lift up themselves against God, and do contrary to His will. Thus, it seemeth that the Word of God serveth to harden men in wickedness; for they seem to be at defiance with Him both in public and private, as I have already observed. We daily hear blasphemies, perjuries, and other contempts of God's name: we see that there is disorder among us, that we are so far from honoring God, that many act as hypocrites, while others withdraw themselves from all order of the church, and are worse than the Turks and Heathens.

As for my part, I may say, that I am ashamed to preach the Word of God among you, seeing there is so much confusion and disorder manifested. And could I have my wish, I would desire God to take me out of this world. We may boast that we have a reformation among us, and that the gospel is preached to us; but all this is against us, unless we attend to the duty which God hath enjoined upon us. It is long ago that God warned us, and it is to be feared He will speak no more in mercy, but will raise His mighty arm against us in judgment.

Therefore, let us take heed to ourselves; for these things are not spoken to stir us up against God, but that we may know our faults, and learn to be more and more displeased with ourselves, that we may not become hardened against God. For He calleth us to repentance, and showeth that He is ready to receive us to mercy, if we return and embrace the promises, and fear the threatenings, contained in His gospel. Those that are in public office ought to be diligent in their duty, that justice may not be violated. Those that are appointed ministers of the Word, should have a zeal to purge out all filthiness and pollution from among the people.

We should so examine and cleanse ourselves that when we receive the supper of our Lord Jesus Christ, we may be more and more confirmed in His grace; that we may be ingrafted into His body, and be truly made one with Him; that all the promises we perceive in the gospel may be better confirmed in us. We must know that He is our life, and that we live in Him, as He dwelleth in us: and thus we know that God owneth and taketh us for His children. Therefore, we should be the more earnest to call upon Him, and trust in His goodness, that He may so govern us by His Holy Spirit, that poor ignorant creatures may through our example be brought into the right way. For we see many at this day who are in the way to destruction. May we attend to what God hath enjoined upon us, that He would be pleased to show His grace, not only to one city or a little handful of people, but that He would reign over all the world; that every one may serve and worship Him in spirit and in truth.

THE DOCTRINE OF ELECTION

"Who hath saved us, and called us with an holy calling, not according to our works, but according to his own purpose and grace, which was given us in Christ Jesus before the world began; But is now made manifest by the appearing of our Saviour Jesus Christ, who hath abolished death, and hath brought life and immortality to light through the gospel" (2 Timothy 1:9–10).

WE HAVE SHOWN THIS MORNING, according to the text of St. Paul, that if we will know the free mercy of our God in saving us, we must come to His everlasting counsel: whereby He chose us before the world began. For there we see, He had no regard to our persons, neither to our worthiness, nor to any deserts that we could possibly

Reprinted from John Calvin, *The Mystery of Godliness* (Grand Rapids, Mich.: Wm. B. Eerdmans Pub. Co., 1950), pp. 39–51. Used by permission.

bring. Before we were born, we were enrolled in His register; He had already adopted us for His children. Therefore let us yield the whole to His mercy, knowing that we cannot boast of ourselves, unless we rob Him of the honor which belongs to Him.

Men have endeavored to invent cavils, to darken the grace of God. For they have said, although God chose men before the world began, yet it was according as He foresaw that one would be diverse from another. The Scripture showeth plainly that God did not wait to see whether men were worthy or not when He chose them: but the sophisters thought they might darken the grace of God by saying, though He regarded not the deserts that were passed, He had an eye to those that were to come. For, say they, though Jacob and his brother Esau had done neither good nor evil, and God chose one and refused the other, yet notwithstanding He foresaw (as all things are present with Him), that Esau would be a vicious man, and that Jacob would be as he afterwards showed himself.

But these are foolish speculations: for they plainly make St. Paul a liar who saith, God rendered no reward to our works when He chose us, because He did it before the world began. But though the authority of St. Paul were abolished, yet the matter is very plain and open, not only in the Holy Scripture, but in reason; insomuch that those who would make an escape after this sort, show themselves to be men void of all skill. For if we search ourselves to the bottom, what good can we find? Are not all mankind cursed? What do we bring from our mother's womb, except sin?

Therefore we differ not one whit, one from another; but it pleaseth God to take those to Himself whom He would. And for this cause, St. Paul useth these words in another place, when he saith, men have not whereof to rejoice, for no man finds himself better than his fellows, unless it be because God discerneth him. So then, if we confess that God chose us before the world began, it necessarily follows, that God prepared us to receive His grace; that He bestowed upon us that goodness, which was not in us before; that He not only chose us to be heirs of the kingdom of heaven, but He likewise justifies us, and governs us by His Holy Spirit. The Christian ought to be so well resolved in this doctrine, that he is beyond doubt.

There are some men at this day, that would be glad if the truth of God were destroyed. Such men fight against the Holy Ghost, like mad beasts, and endeavor to abolish the Holy Scripture. There is more honesty in the papists, than in these men: for the doctrine of the papists is a great deal better, more holy, and more agreeable to the sacred Scripture, than the doctrine of those vile and wicked men, who cast down God's holy election; these dogs that bark at it, and swine that root it up.

However, let us hold fast that which is here taught us: God having chosen us before the world had its course, we must attribute the cause of our salvation to His free goodness; we must confess that He did not take us to be His children, for any deserts of our own; for we had nothing to recommend ourselves into His favor. Therefore, we must put the cause and fountain of our salvation in Him only, and ground ourselves upon it: otherwise, whatsoever and howsoever we build, it will come to nought.

We must here notice what St. Paul joineth together; to wit, the grace of Jesus Christ, with the everlasting counsel of God the Father: and then he bringeth us to our calling, that we may be assured of God's goodness, and of His will, that would have remained hid from us, unless we had a witness of it. St. Paul saith in the first place, that the grace which hangeth upon the purpose of God, and is comprehended in it, is given in our Lord Jesus Christ. As if he said, seeing we deserve to be cast away, and hated as God's mortal enemies, it was needful for us to be grafted, as it were, into Jesus Christ; that God might acknowledge, and allow us for His children. Otherwise, God could not look upon us, only to hate us; because there is nothing but wretchedness in us; we are full of sin, and stuffed up as it were with all kinds of iniquity.

God, who is justice itself, can have no agreement with us, while He considereth our sinful nature. Therefore, when He would adopt us before the world began, it was requisite that Jesus Christ should stand between us and Him; that we should be chosen in His person, for He is the well beloved Son: when God joineth us to Him, He maketh us such as pleaseth Him. Let us learn to come directly to Jesus Christ, if we will not doubt God's election: for He is the true looking glass, wherein we must behold our adoption.

If Jesus Christ be taken from us, then is God a judge of sinners; so that we cannot hope for any goodness or favor at His hands, but look rather for vengeance: for without Jesus Christ, His majesty will always be terrible and fearful to us. If we hear mention made of His everlasting purpose, we cannot but be afraid, as though He were already armed to plunge us into misery. But when we know that all grace resteth in Jesus Christ, then we may be assured that God loved us, although we were unworthy.

In the second place, we must notice that St. Paul speaketh not simply of God's election, for that would not put us beyond doubt; but we should rather remain in perplexity and anguish; but he adds, *the calling;* whereby God hath opened His counsel, which before was unknown to us, and which we could not reach. How shall we know then that God hath chosen us, that we may rejoice in Him, and boast of the goodness that He hath bestowed upon us? They that speak against God's election, leave the gospel alone; they leave all that God layeth before us, to bring us to Him; all the means that He hath appointed for us, and knoweth to be fit and proper for our use. We must not go on so; but according to St. Paul's rule, we must join the calling with God's everlasting election.

It is said, we are called; and thus we have this second word, calling. Therefore God calleth us: and how? Surely, when it pleaseth Him to certify us of our election; which we could by no other means attain unto. For who can enter into God's counsel? as saith the prophet Isaiah; and also the apostle Paul. But when it pleaseth God to communicate Himself to us familiarly, then we receive that which surmounteth the knowledge of all men: for we have a good and faithful witness, which is the Holy Ghost; that raiseth us above the world, and bringeth us even into the wonderful secrets of God.

We must not speak rashly of God's election, and say, we are predestinate; but if we will be thoroughly assured of our salvation, we must not speak lightly of it; whether God hath taken us to be His children or not. What then? Let us look at what is set forth in the gospel. There God showeth us that He is our Father; and that He will bring us to the inheritance of life, having marked us with the seal of the Holy Ghost in our hearts, which is an undoubted witness of our salvation, if we receive it by faith.

The gospel is preached to a great number, which notwithstanding, are reprobate; yea, and God discovereth and showeth that He hath cursed them: that they have no part nor portion in His kingdom, because they resist the gospel, and cast away the grace that is offered them. But when we receive the doctrine of God with obedience and faith, and rest ourselves upon His promises, and accept this offer that He maketh us, to take us for His children, this, I say, is a certainty of our election. But we must here remark, that when we have knowledge of our salvation, when God hath called us and enlightened us in the faith of His gospel, it is not to bring to nought the everlasting predestination that went before.

There are a great many in these days that will say, who are they whom God hath chosen, but only the faithful? I grant it; but they make an evil consequence of it; and say faith is the cause, yea, and the first cause of our salvation. If they called it a middle cause, it would indeed be true; for the Scripture saith, "By grace are ye saved through faith" (Eph. 2:8). But we must go up higher; for if they attribute faith to men's free will, they blaspheme wickedly against God, and commit sacrilege. We must come to that which the Scripture showeth; to wit, when God giveth us faith, we must know that we are not capable of receiving the gospel, only as He hath framed us by the Holy Ghost.

It is not enough for us to hear the voice of man, unless God work within, and speak to us in a secret manner by the Holy Ghost; and from hence cometh faith. But what is the cause of it? Why is faith given to one and not to another? St. Luke showeth us: saying, "As many as were ordained to eternal life believed" (Acts 13:48). There were a great number of hearers, and yet but few of them received the promise of salvation. And what few were they? Those that were appointed to salvation. Again, St. Paul speaketh so largely upon this subject, in his epistle to the Ephesians, that it cannot be but the enemies of God's predestination are stupid and ignorant, and that the devil hath plucked out their eyes; and that they have become void of all reason, if they cannot see a thing so plain and evident.

St. Paul saith, God hath called us, and made us partakers of His treasures and infinite riches, which were given us through our Lord Jesus Christ: according as He had chosen us before the world began. When we say that we are called to salvation because God hath given us faith, it is not because there is no higher cause; and whosoever cannot come to the everlasting election of God, taketh somewhat from Him, and lesseneth His honor. This is found in almost every part of the Holy Scripture.

That we may make a short conclusion of this matter, let us see in what manner we ought to keep ourselves. When we inquire about our salvation, we must not begin to say, Are we chosen? No, we can never climb so high; we shall be confounded a thousand times, and have our eyes dazzled, before we can come to God's counsel. What then shall we do? Let us hear what is said in the gospel: when God hath been so gracious, as to make us receive the promise offered, know we not that it is as much as if He had opened His whole heart to us, and had registered our election in our consciences!

We must be certified that God hath taken us for His children, and that the kingdom of heaven is ours; because we are called in Jesus Christ. How may we know this? How shall we stay ourselves upon the doctrine that God hath set before us? We must magnify the grace of God, and know that we can bring nothing to recommend ourselves to His favor; we must become nothing in our own eyes, that we may not claim any praise; but know that God hath called us to the gospel, having chosen us before the world began. This election of God is, as it were, a sealed letter; because it consisteth in itself, and in its own nature: but we may read it, for God giveth a witness of it, when He called us to Himself by the gospel and by faith.

For even as the original or first copy taketh nothing from the letter or writing that is read, even so must we be out of doubt of our salvation. When God certifieth us by the gospel that He taketh us for His children, this testimony carries peace with it; being signed by the blood of our Lord Jesus Christ, and sealed by the Holy Ghost. When we have this witness, have we not enough to content our minds? Therefore, God's election is so far from being against this, that it confirmeth the witness which we have in the gospel. We must not doubt but what God hath registered our names before the world was made, among His chosen children: but the knowledge thereof He reserved to Himself.

We must always come to our Lord Jesus Christ, when we talk of our election; for without Him (as we have already shown), we cannot come nigh to God. When we talk of His decree, well may we be astonished, as men worthy of death. But if Jesus Christ be our guide, we

may with cheerfulness depend upon Him; knowing that He hath worthiness enough in Him to make all His members beloved of God the
Father; it being sufficient for us that we are grafted into His body,
and made one with Him. Thus we must muse upon this doctrine, if
we will profit by it aright: as it is set forth by St. Paul; when he saith,
this grace of salvation was given us *before the world began*. We must
go beyond the order of nature, if we will know how we are saved, and
by what cause, and from whence our salvation cometh.

God would not leave us in doubt, neither would He hide His counsel,
that we might not know how our salvation was secured; but hath
called us to Him by His gospel, and hath sealed the witness of His
goodness and fatherly love in our hearts. So then, having such a certainty, let us glorify God, that He hath called us of His free mercy. Let
us rest ourselves upon our Lord Jesus Christ, knowing that He hath
not deceived us, when He caused it to be preached that He gave Himself for us, and witnessed it by the Holy Ghost. For faith is an undoubted token that God taketh us for His children; and thereby we
are led to the everlasting election, according as He had chosen us
before.

He saith not that God hath chosen us because we have heard the
gospel, but on the other hand, he attributes the faith that is given us
to the highest cause; to wit, because God hath fore-ordained that He
would save us; seeing we were lost and cast away in Adam. There are
certain dolts, who, to blind the eyes of the simple and such as are like
themselves, say, the grace of salvation was given us because God
ordained that His Son should redeem mankind, and therefore this is
common to all.

But St. Paul spake after another sort; and men cannot by such
childish arguments mar the doctrine of the gospel: for it is said plainly,
that God hath saved us. Does this refer to all without exception? No;
he speaketh only of the faithful. Again, does St. Paul include all the
world? Some were called by preaching, and yet they made themselves
unworthy of the salvation which was offered them: therefore they
were reprobate. God left others in their unbelief, who never heard
the gospel preached.

Therefore St. Paul directed himself plainly and precisely to those
whom God had chosen and reserved to Himself. God's goodness will
never be viewed in its true light, nor honored as it deserveth, unless
we know that He would not have us remain in the general destruction
of mankind; wherein He hath left those that were like unto us: from
whom we do not differ; for we are no better than they: but so it pleased
God. Therefore all mouths must be stopped; men must presume to
take nothing upon themselves, except to praise God, confessing themselves debtors to Him for all their salvation.

We shall now make some remarks upon the other words used by
St. Paul in this place. It is true that God's election could never be

profitable to us, neither could it come to us, unless we knew it by means of the gospel; for this cause it pleased God to reveal that which He had kept secret before all ages. But to declare His meaning more plainly, he adds, that this grace is revealed to us now. And how? "By the appearing of our Savior Jesus Christ." When he saith that this grace is revealed to us by the appearing of Jesus Christ, he showeth that we should be too unthankful, if we could not content and rest ourselves upon the grace of the Son of God. What can we look for more? If we could climb up beyond the clouds, and search out the secrets of God, what would be the result of it? Would it not be to ascertain that we are His children and heirs?

Now we know these things, for they are clearly set forth in Jesus Christ. For it is said, that all who believe in Him shall enjoy the privilege of being God's children. Therefore we must not swerve from these things one jot, if we will be certified of our election. St. Paul hath already shown us, that God never loved us, nor chose us, only in the person of His beloved Son. When Jesus Christ appeared He revealed life to us, otherwise we should never have been the partakers of it. He hath made us acquainted with the everlasting counsel of God. But it is presumption for men to attempt to know more than God would have them know.

If we walk soberly and reverently in obedience to God, hearing and receiving what He saith in the Holy Scripture, the way will be made plain before us. St. Paul saith, when the Son of God appeared in the world, He opened our eyes, that we might know that He was gracious to us before the world was made. We were received as His children, and accounted just; so that we need not doubt but that the kingdom of heaven is prepared for us. Not that we have it by our deserts, but because it belongs to Jesus Christ, who makes us partakers with Himself.

When St. Paul speaketh of the appearing of Jesus Christ, he saith, "He hath brought life and immortality to light through the gospel." It is not only said that Jesus Christ is our Savior, but that He is sent to be a mediator, to reconcile us by the sacrifice of His death; He is sent to us as a lamb without blemish; to purge us and make satisfaction for all our trespasses; He is our pledge, to deliver us from the condemnation of death; He is our righteousness; He is our advocate, who maketh intercession with God that He would hear our prayers.

We must allow all these qualities to belong to Jesus Christ, if we will know aright how He appeared. We must look at the substance contained in the gospel. We must know that Jesus Christ appeared as our Savior, and that He suffered for our salvation; and that we were reconciled to God the Father through His means; that we have been cleansed from all our blemishes, and freed from everlasting death. If we know not that He is our advocate, that He heareth us when we pray to God, to the end that our prayers may be answered, what will become of us;

what confidence can we have to call upon God's name, who is the fountain of our salvation? But St. Paul saith, Jesus Christ hath fulfilled all things that were requisite for the redemption of mankind.

If the gospel were taken away, of what advantage would it be to us that the Son of God had suffered death, and risen again the third day for our justification? All this would be unprofitable to us. So then, the gospel putteth us in possession of the benefits that Jesus Christ hath purchased for us. And therefore, though He be absent from us in body, and is not conversant with us here on earth, it is not that He hath withdrawn Himself, as though we could not find Him; for the sun that shineth doth no more enlighten the world, than Jesus Christ showeth Himself openly to those that have the eyes of faith to look upon Him, when the gospel is preached. Therefore St. Paul saith, Jesus Christ hath brought *life to light*, yea, everlasting life.

He saith, the Son of God hath abolished death. And how did He abolish it? If He had not offered an everlasting sacrifice to appease the wrath of God, if He had not entered even to the bottomless pit to draw us from thence; if He had not taken our curse upon Himself, if He had not taken away the burden wherewith we were crushed down, where should we have been? Would death have been destroyed? Nay, sin would reign in us, and death likewise. And indeed, let every one examine himself, and we shall find that we are slaves to Satan, who is the prince of death. So that we are shut up in this miserable slavery, unless God destroy the devil, sin, and death. And this is done: but how? He hath taken away our sins by the blood of our Lord Jesus Christ.

Therefore, though we be poor sinners, and in danger of God's judgment, yet sin cannot hurt us; the sting, which is venomous, is so blunted that it cannot wound us, because Jesus Christ has gained the victory over it. He suffered not the shedding of His blood in vain; but it was a washing wherewith we were washed through the Holy Ghost, as is shown by St. Peter. And thus we see plainly that when St. Paul speaketh of the gospel, wherein Jesus Christ appeared, and appeareth daily to us, he forgetteth not His death and passion, nor the things that pertain to the salvation of mankind.

We may be certified that in the person of our Lord Jesus Christ we have all that we can desire; we have full and perfect trust in the goodness of God, and the love He beareth us. But we see that our sins separate us from God, and cause a warfare in our members; yet we have an atonement through our Lord Jesus Christ. And why so? Because He hath shed His blood to wash away our sins; He hath offered a sacrifice whereby God hath become reconciled to us; to be short, He hath taken away the curse, that we may be blessed of God. Moreover, He hath conquered death, and triumphed over it; that He might deliver us from the tyranny thereof; which otherwise would entirely overwhelm us.

Thus we see that all things that belong to our salvation are accomplished in our Lord Jesus Christ. And that we may enter into full possession of all these benefits we most know that He appeareth to us daily by His gospel. Although He dwelleth in His heavenly glory, if we open the eyes of our faith we shall behold Him. We must learn not to separate that which the Holy Ghost hath joined together. Let us observe what St. Paul meant by a comparison to amplify the grace that God showed to the world after the coming of our Lord Jesus Christ; as if he said, the old fathers had not this advantage, to have Jesus Christ appear to them, as He appeared to us.

It is true, they had the self-same faith; and the inheritance of heaven is theirs, as well as ours; God having revealed His grace to them as well as us, but not in like measure, for they saw Jesus Christ afar off, under the figures of the law, as St. Paul saith to the Corinthians. The veil of the temple was as yet stretched out, that the Jews could not come near the sanctuary, that is, the material sanctuary. But now, the veil of the temple being removed, we draw nigh to the majesty of our God: we come most familiarly to Him, in whom dwelleth all perfection and glory. In short, we have the body, whereas they had but the shadow (Col. 2:17).

The ancient fathers submitted themselves wholly to bear the affliction of Jesus Christ; as it is said in the 11th chapter of the Hebrews; for it is not said, Moses bore the shame of Abraham, but of Jesus Christ. Thus the ancient fathers, though they lived under the law, offered themselves to God in sacrifices, to bear most patiently the afflictions of Christ. And now, Jesus Christ having risen from the dead, hath brought *life to light*. If we are so delicate that we cannot bear the afflictions of the gospel, are we not worthy to be blotted from the book of God, and cast off? Therefore, we must be constant in the faith, and ready to suffer for the name of Jesus Christ, whatsoever God will; because life is set before us, and we have a more familiar knowledge of it than the ancient fathers had.

We know how the ancient fathers were tormented by tyrants, and enemies of the truth, and how they suffered constantly. The condition of the church is not more grievous in these days, than it was then. For now hath Jesus Christ brought life and immortality to light through the gospel. As often as the grace of God is preached to us, it is as much as if the kingdom of heaven were opened to us; as if God reached out His hand, and certified us that life was nigh; and that He will make us partakers of His heavenly inheritance. But when we look to this life, which was purchased for us by our Lord Jesus Christ, we should not hesitate to forsake all that we have in this world, to come to the treasure above, which is in heaven.

Therefore, let us not be willingly blind; seeing Jesus Christ layeth daily before us the life and immortality here spoken of. When St. Paul speaketh of life, and addeth immortality, it is as much as if he said, we already enter into the kingdom of heaven by faith. Though we be as strangers here below, the life and grace of which we are made partakers through our Lord Jesus Christ shall bring its fruit in convenient time; to wit, when He shall be sent of God the Father to show us the effect of things that are daily preached, which were fulfilled in His person when He was clad in humanity.

ON THE FINAL ADVENT OF OUR LORD JESUS CHRIST

"God is just in giving affliction to those who afflict you, and rest with us to you who are afflicted, on that day when the Lord Jesus will manifest Himself from heaven with the Angels of his power, and in flame of fire, working vengeance against those who know not God, and do not obey the Gospel of our Lord Jesus Christ, who will suffer punishment: namely, eternal perdition before the face of the Lord, and by the glory of His power, when He shall come to be glorified in His saints and to be admired by all believers, because our testimony to you was believed" (2 Thessalonians 1:6–10).

OUR LORD JESUS CHRIST must appear from heaven. It is one of the principle articles of our faith. His coming must not be useless. Then, we should look for it, waiting for our redemption and salvation. We need not doubt it. For that would violate all that our Lord Jesus Christ did and suffered. For why did He descend into this world? Why was He clothed in human flesh? Why was He exposed to death? Why was He raised from the dead and lifted into heaven? It was to gather us into His Kingdom when He shall appear. Thus this coming of our Lord is to seal and ratify everything He did and endured for our salvation. Now that should fully suffice to brace us up to resist all the temptations of this world.

But since we are so frail that we cannot place faith in what God says to us, St. Paul now uses a new argument to better confirm us in this

Reprinted from John Calvin, *The Deity of Christ*, trans. Leroy Nixon (Grand Rapids, Mich.: Wm. B. Eerdmans Pub. Co., 1950), pp. 290–302. Used by permission.

hope, to which he had exhorted us in the person of the Thessalonians. God will not allow Himself to be thus despised by those who hold the Gospel in contempt, who do not take account of His celestial majesty. He is not willing to permit His creatures to rise against Him and to resist Him. That is why we ought to be all the more confirmed in the hope of our salvation, since God is interested in it as His own cause. This point we should note well.

Although God amply assures us of His concern for our salvation, our nature is so full of distrust that we are always in doubt. But when the teaching is set before us that God will maintain His right and that He will not permit His majesty to be trodden underfoot by men, it should fill us with assurance. Then it is certain that God gives us this grace of joining His glory with our salvation so that there is an inseparable bond between the two. Since God cannot do otherwise than maintain His majesty against the pride and rebellion of men, is it not infallibly certain that our Lord Jesus will come to give us release and rest?

Let us note, then, that Jesus Christ cannot maintain the glory of His Father unless He declares Himself to be our Redeemer. These things cannot be separated. We see the infinite love of God for His faithful ones, when He joins Himself in such a way to them that, just as He cannot forget His glory, so He cannot forget our salvation. When He employs His power to take vengeance on those who resist Him, He will all the more punish those who have afflicted unjustly His own. That is the intention of St. Paul when he brings out here that Jesus Christ will come even to take vengeance upon those who have not known God and obeyed His Gospel. It is as if he said, "Here are your enemies who persecute you. Now will you question whether God regards your afflictions to pity you and apply the remedy? Do you think that God does not take account of His glory and that He is not willing to maintain it? Although adversaries afflict you because you adhere to the Gospel, God also in maintaining His cause will show Himself to be your protector."

However, St. Paul here gives us other admonitions which are very useful to us. For when he speaks of the vengeance which is prepared for our enemies, he says, "Jesus Christ will come, even with the Angels of His power and in flame of fire." And to what purpose? It is to confirm what he goes on to say: namely, that the enemies of the truth will suffer their punishment before God and before the face of His majesty. It is as if he said that we can never understand what will be the torment of unbelievers, just as also we do not see the glory of God, for when we speak of the glory of God we know that it is infinite. We cannot measure it, but we must be rapt in astonishment. Such is the horrible punishment prepared for all unbelievers, since God unleashes His power against them. For since His majesty is inestimable, their torment must also be incomprehensible to us. So much for item one.

Besides, when St. Paul speaks of infidels and enemies of God, he says, "They have not known Him," and that they have not obeyed the Gospel, or that they have been rebels. This manner of speaking implies a very useful doctrine. For when one asks men, although they may be very wicked, if they wish to wage war against God they will say no. However, they do everything contrary to what they profess, since they are not willing to be fully subject to the Gospel. How can that be? It is said that we cannot obey God except by faith. So says St. Paul in both the Epistle to the Romans and in the book of Acts. Since faith is true obedience and such as God requires and approves, it follows that all those who do not wish to believe the Gospel are rebels against Him and as much as they are able they rise against Him. If they protest that such is not their intention, the deed is such, all the same. By this we are taught that we cannot serve God acceptably unless in the first place we believe the Gospel and accept all that is contained there to humble us. In short, faith is the principal service which God asks of men. It is true, however, that we must note that faith is not simple assent of the mind to what we are taught, but also we must bring the heart and the affections. For not only by mouth or by imagination must we accept what is said to us, but it must be impressed upon the heart and we must know that we are not permitted to set ourselves against our God. But with true desire we ask to adhere to the doctrine offered to us. Faith, then, is from the heart where it has its root and is not knowledge pure and simple. For if we were only convinced that the Gospel is a reasonable doctrine and meanwhile we did not at all relish it and perhaps it even displeased and angered us, would that be obedience? Certainly not.

Let us learn, then, in order to obey God, not only to regard the doctrine of the Gospel as good and holy, but to love it, and also to join reverence with love according to what David says of the Law, that he finds it more sweet than honey and more precious than gold or silver. We must, then, prize and hold in high esteem and take the doctrine of the Gospel above all that may be sweet and lovable to us. When we do that, then God will approve our obedience. That is the peculiar service He asks of us. On the contrary it will be in vain for us to do this or that, everything that we can attempt will be an abomination before God, until we have believed the Gospel.

In that see how miserable is the condition of the Papists. They torment themselves more and more with their so-called devotions. It seems to them as if they have a good grip on God. When they joke as they do, when they babble their paternosters, hear many masses, trot on pilgrimage, pay their money to do their abomination, it seems to them that God must allow that much good to their credit. And why then? They lack the principal thing, which is faith. For even if those things were not evil, nor against God, yet they will become frivolous before God when they are offered without faith on the part of men.

Then we see that although the Papists work confidently to serve God, they only add to their condemnation and bring down His wrath still more upon their heads. So much so that they are here named rebels against God, since they do not wish to be subject to the doctrine of the Gospel. To be sure they will say, "Look, our intention is to serve God, and we do this and that to this end."

Very well. But here is God who invites you to Himself. He shows you that your only good rests in His pure grace and mercy, that you must look for salvation only in Jesus Christ. He declares to you that He has sent His Son so that you might experience the result of His passion, that in His Name and through Him all your debts will be receipted and remitted, that you ought not to seek any other advocate than Him to find access to His majesty, that you should ask to be renewed by His Holy Spirit. Behold our Lord, Who speaks in this way. You Papists, what are you doing? There is nothing but pride and presumption in you. You charge like a bull against all the promises God gives you and claim to have gotten by yourselves what only Christ can give you. You place confidence in your works and in your merits. You go to seek such patrons and advocates as seem good to you. Meanwhile Jesus Christ is left behind. There is no faith in you. What is worse, you are rebels against God, you wage mortal war against Him instead of serving and honoring Him, as you think you do.

So then we surely have to magnify our God, because He has drawn us out of such depths and has shown us what is the true entrance into His service: namely, that He joins us purely to the doctrine of the Gospel and that we receive the promises He gives us. Besides, if we perceive that men are humbled, that is a true preparation to bring them to the service of God, even the full and perfect obedience which God approves. That then is a point, that all unbelief is rebellion against God, since there is no obedience unless it begins by faith.

St. Paul says that those who do not obey the Gospel do not know God at all. By which we see that ignorance is no excuse for men, as much as they trust in it as a shield. It seems to them enough if they are not openly convicted of having sinned knowingly. They reckon that God must forgive them everything. Really? But St. Paul says particularly that Jesus Christ will come to destroy those who have not known God. Let us realize then, that we are bewildered and lost unless we know Him Who has created us and Him Who has redeemed us. In fact, that is very reasonable. For why has God given us sense and spirit, unless that knowing Him we may adore Him, and that we may render to Him the honor which belongs to Him? Men would like to be highly esteemed and honored, no matter what becomes of their Creator. Is that proper? Is it not against nature?

However, note that the ignorance of unbelievers does not proceed from pure simplicity, but there are malice, pride, and hypocrisy, which cause them not to have discretion and sense. How so? For if we could know God, it is certain that we would come to humble ourselves before Him. For it is impossible for men to think of what God really is, without being touched to the quick by some fear so as to bow under Him. Thus, when we are rebels against Him, it is a sign that we have never known Him. For this knowledge of God is a thing too much alive for us to say we see it and then be obstinate and rebels like unbelievers.

If one alleges that they are ignorant, it is true. But so are they also evil-doers and hypocrites. For have we not all of us enough things to render us inexcusable? Even though there were only the seed that God put in us by nature, that contemplating the sky and the earth we ought to think there is a Creator from which everything proceeds, God reveals to us as in a mirror His majesty and His glory, and there is no one who is not convinced by that. The most wicked, even though they have mocked God, if they find themselves in any distress, will have recourse to Him without thinking of it. For God drives them to it in order to take away from them every excuse so that unbelievers are not so ignorant that they have no hypocrisy in them. They wish to cover themselves, but they close their eyes knowingly. There is also pride and malice in it. For if we would bring honor to God such as belongs to Him, we should have a great anxiety to inquire about Him and His will. When, then, we are so cowardly and cold it is a sign that we scorn Him. Then we do not ask for anything but to be left in darkness. How can that be? For when we approach God and He reprimands us for our faults, we ought to learn to be grieved for our vices and to correct ourselves. We are content to be asleep in our rags. That is how we avoid the piercing rays of God.

Note well, then, that not without cause men are punished, notwithstanding their ignorance. For they cannot allege that it was simple ignorance, but rather hypocrisy, pride and malice are mixed up in it. That is why St. Paul, when he says that those who have sinned without the Law (that is, those who have no knowledge of the Word of God) shall be lost nevertheless, he adds that God has engraved a law upon the hearts of all. While we may not have Scripture nor preaching, yet we have our conscience which ought to serve us as a law, and that will be enough to condemn in the last day. We may well have many subterfuges before men, and we will think that we ought to be acquitted, but our accounting will be found to be very faulty when we appear before the celestial Judge. There we shall find that all our excuses are frivolous. Let us note well this passage where it is said that our Lord will come to execute His vengeance upon all those who have not known God and who have not obeyed the Gospel, that is, all unbelievers. Thereby we see that faith is the only door to salvation and life, since Jesus Christ must come to confuse those who have not believed.

Besides, let us observe that until God has enlightened men they are entirely ignorant and blind. And why so? For we may well comprehend everything in heaven or upon earth, but until we have known God, what is all the rest worth? We shall not know Him until He enlightens us by His Holy Spirit. So we see that we shall not be excused on account of our ignorance, so let no one flatter himself or go to sleep. However, let us note also that when we have known God it is only reasonable that we should be subject to Him, and that He should hold us in check, and that His will should guide our thoughts and affections, and that we should have such faith in the Gospel that we can profess like David that this doctrine is sweeter to us than honey and more precious than gold or silver. So much for this point.

Besides, we see here how God wishes to assure us of our salvation. For if Jesus Christ is to come to take vengeance upon all those who have not believed the Gospel, but have resisted it, we can and we must conclude that the world will be judged only according to the Gospel. Now it is said to us that when we have received in true faith the promises of God we must not doubt His goodness nor His love toward us, nor doubt that Jesus Christ will make good what He has offered for us and our redemption. All those, then, who believe in the Gospel can pride themselves without any doubt, that Jesus Christ will come as their Redeemer. God gives us this certainty, provided we do not refuse such a gift.

As for what St. Paul here says of the power and glory of Jesus Christ, it is so that His coming may be more terrible to all unbelievers and rebels. Is it a small thing when it is said that Jesus Christ will come in the company of Angels, that He will come with flame of fire, that He will come with an incomprehensible majesty, indeed to strike down with lightening against all His enemies? So, we see that St. Paul here wished to admonish unbelievers, in case there was any remedy for them, that they be warned not to remain always incorrigible. However, when we see that all those who are drawn by Satan and hardened only mock all the threats of God, may we take a lesson from that. And when we hear that Jesus Christ will come in such a terrible fashion, may we be held in fear and in check in such a way that, when Satan comes to sting or tickle us to turn away from obeying the Gospel, we may think to say to ourselves, "Where are we going? into what perdition? are we provoking against ourselves Him to Whom all majesty, dominion and glory is given so as to cast into the abyss those who oppose Him?" If we thought of this, certainly we would be held back in such a way that all the lusts of our flesh and all the temptations of the world could do nothing against us.

Now, however, St. Paul has also wished to compare the first coming of our Lord Jesus Christ with the second. Why do the wicked and the despisers of the Gospel rise so boldly so that we see them enraged and uncontrolled? It is because they hear that Jesus, while here in this world, took the condition of a servant, even that He emptied Himself of everything, as St. Paul says, even to this death which was shameful and full of disgrace. Although the enemies of God do not know Jesus

Christ apart from this weakness, they take it as an opportunity to blaspheme against Him with such fury. To be sure, but they do not consider that, as He suffered according to the weakness of the flesh, so also He was raised by the power of His Spirit. He unfolded, then, a glory under which we all, both great and small, should tremble. But again, if unbelievers do not know what the Power was that appeared in the resurrection of our Lord Jesus Christ, may they listen to what is here said: namely, that He is not coming to be held in contempt.

He appeared thus, then, to be made obedient in our name, as was necessary to satisfy for our sins. But now He will come to be Judge. He has been judged and condemned so that we might be delivered before the judgment seat of God, and that we might be absolved of all our sins. It will no longer be a matter of coming in such humility. He will come then with the Angels of His glory. That is what St. Paul meant by saying that the coming of our Lord Jesus Christ will be dreadful.

Further, let us note that he adds still more. "He will come to be admired in His saints" and to be glorified in them. Not without cause St. Paul adds this sentence. For who are we to endure the presence of the Son of God, when He comes in burning fire and flames? When He comes with strength beyond understanding, alas! shall we not melt before Him like snow in the sun, and shall we not be reduced to nothing? Even the mention of this Divine glory of Jesus Christ would be enough to sink us into the depths. But St. Paul shows us that if we are of the number of the faithful, and we believe today the Gospel, we need not fear when Jesus Christ appears, nor be frightened by the majesty that will then be shining in Him. And how is this?

For He will come (says he) to be glorified in His saints and to be admired in them. As if he said that, what he said above of fire and flame, what he spoke of terror and dread, is not to discourage believers, that they should not desire the coming of our Lord Jesus Christ and raise their heads every time it is spoken to them. For He will come for their redemption. The doctrine that our Lord joins together these two things is common enough in Holy Scripture. He will come to take vengeance on His enemies, and He will come to deliver His own. He will come to be Savior of those who have served and honored Him, and to cast down and confound those who have hardened themselves against Him and His Word. Let us remember well then that this terrible description which is put here is not to frighten us but rather to make us glad that such is the love and grace of God toward us. Our Lord Jesus will come, indeed, with a dreadful power. And what for? To cast into the abyss all His enemies, to avenge the injuries, insults, and afflictions that we shall have endured.

How are we worthy that the Son of God should thus unfold His majesty and show Himself with such terror against those who are His creatures? We certainly are not, but He wills to do it because He loves us. As I have already mentioned, we should be consoled when he says that the Son of God will come, even with such a fright and such dreadful majesty. For in this He effectively declares the infinite love which He bears and shows toward us, since He spares not His power and His majesty to do vengeance for all the injuries which we have endured. But we would not be able to take any pleasure in it unless what St. Paul says here is observed: namely, that our Lord Jesus Christ will come not only for revenge against His enemies and those who have been rebels against His Gospel, but also to be glorified and to be admired in His saints and those who have believed.

When St. Paul adds this, it is as if he said, "He will come to make us sharers in His glory, that everything worthy to be honored and revered in Him will then be communicated to us." Briefly, St. Paul declares that our Lord Jesus is not coming to keep His glory to Himself alone, but that it may be poured out upon all the members of His body. This is why he says to the Colossians, "Now our life is hidden, but it will be shown at the coming of our Lord Jesus Christ." He is not coming, then, to have anything peculiar to Himself and of which we are deprived, but rather that His glory may be communicated to us, not that He had not always preeminence over His own, which is the reason why He is the Head of His Church. In fact, the glory which He has communicated to us is neither to detract from nor obscure His own but rather that we must be transformed, as says St. Paul to the Philippians. Instead of being pitiably full of infirmities as we are now, we must be conformed to the heavenly life of our Lord Jesus Christ.

So St. Paul in speaking thus has paid special attention to the condition of believers as it is in this life. For we are marked men, they point fingers at us; they shoot out the tongue: we see the evil-doers mock the children of God. We must be thus rendered contemptible so that we may learn not to seek our glory in this world. God could surely make us to be esteemed by all if it pleased Him, but He wills that we bear such infamies so that we may look on high to seek our triumph there. And besides, would it be proper that we should be glorified and applauded here while God were dishonored? Evil-doers fully mock God and if it were possible they would even spit in His face. Would we still wish to be honored by them? If we desire it, must it not be said that we are too cowardly? Continuing what I began to say, although the faithful are now despised and rejected, some mock them, others oppress them, they are eaten out of house and home, and they are trodden under foot; for this reason the Apostle reminds us of the last day, saying that then we shall be admired, even as the Son of God is. However, let us not fear that the glory which He places upon us will fail to frighten our enemies, so they will be made our footstool, as Scripture says.

But St. Paul shows here especially who ought to hope to share the glory of the Son of God, and he describes the character of those who have believed when he calls them "the Saints." For he shows (1) that those who are given to the pollutions of this world must not expect to have any part or portion in this inheritance, nor to have anything in common with the Son of God. However when he adds "those who have believed" he shows (2) that faith is the true source and origin of all holiness. And thirdly he shows (3) that if we have pure and upright faith we cannot help becoming more and more sanctified. Those are the three points we have to remember.

The first is that if now we are going to defile ourselves and wallow in our filthiness and pollutions we are cut off from the Son of God and we need not expect that His coming will be of any profit to us, but let us remember what the Prophet said, "Desire not that the Day of the Lord come, for it will be to us (sic) a day of terror and astonishment and not a day of salvation and joy. It will be a day of cruelty and confusion. It will be a day of darkness and shadows." Since at that time there were many hypocrites who shielded themselves with the Name of God, the Prophet shows them that it will cost them very dear. Likewise today we see the most wicked people making confession with full mouth and voice. How is that? Do they think we do not fear God and we do not also wish to be as good Christians as others? True enough. Yet they are people debauched and full of all impiety who have as much religion as dogs and swine. When they are finally examined on their life, it will be seen that they are full of disloyalty, that they have no more faith or loyalty in them than foxes; that they are full of treachery and perjuries, full of cruelty, full of bitterness against their neighbors; that they are given to every nuisance and outrage, that whoever will offer them the most will win their vote; they open a shop to grab with both hands so that they sell not only their faith but their honor before men; they open a fair and a market to lay themselves open to every evil. In short, they are seen to be extremely impudent and contemptible, although they never stop boasting that they are some of the most advanced in the Church of God, and God will help them, so it seems to them, as if He were most obliged to them. As we see today, the Prophet speaking to those of his own time says, "How is that? Why do you boast? of the Day of the Lord? Do you think His coming will get you anything? No, not at all. But it will be to you an appalling day, a terrible and fearful day. There will be nothing but fright and astonishment for you." So we must remember from this passage of St. Paul that if we wish that the coming of our Lord Jesus Christ may profit us, and that He may appear to us as Redeemer for our salvation, we must learn well to dedicate ourselves to holiness and we must be separated from the pollutions of this world and of the flesh. So much for the first point.

But to succeed in it let us note that we must begin by faith, which also follows what we have already discussed considerably. In fact, faith is the source of all holiness, as is mentioned in Acts 15, where

St. Peter says that God purifies the hearts of men by faith. That is said to show that, however beautiful men may appear, they will always be polluted and infected before God until He purifies them by faith.

Now by the third proposition we are admonished that, if we have true faith, we cannot help becoming more and more sanctified. That is, *we are reformed for the service of God only* and we are dedicated *to honor Him alone.* How is that? As soon as by faith we embrace Jesus Christ, He will dwell in us, as all the Scripture says, as St. Paul especially says. Jesus Christ (says he) dwells in your hearts by faith. I pray you is it not incompatible that Jesus Christ dwells in us and we are still given to all villainies and filthy things? Do we think that He wishes to dwell in a pig-sty? We must, then, be consecrated to Him.

Besides, He cannot be with us except by His Spirit. And is He not the Spirit of holiness, justice and uprightness? Would it not, then, be a strange mixture if men were to boast of having faith in Jesus and at the same time lived lives dissolute, wicked, and polluted by all the infections of the world? That would be to say "I accept the sun, but not its brightness." That would reverse the whole order of nature. For the sun without its brightness would come sooner than Jesus Christ without His justice. Note well, then, we must not take this covering of hypocrisy to say that we have faith in the Gospel and believe it with a sure knowledge, unless our life corresponds, we show that we have received Jesus Christ, and by the grace of His Spirit He dedicates and sanctifies us to the obedience of God His Father.

Thus we shall not rely upon false tokens to usurp this title of faith, as it is such a sacred thing. Let us beware then, lest we profane it. But if we believe in the Son of God, let us show by the result that we have believed in Him. It is also certain that He will cause us to experience His power. He will give us grace to wait with patience for His coming. Although we must suffer in this world many injuries for His Name, in the end we shall be reclothed with His glory and His righteousness. He has given us the promise, the force of which He will cause us to feel provided we receive it without any doubt.

Let us bow in humble reverence before our God.

FOR ADDITIONAL INFORMATION ABOUT JOHN CALVIN:

Breen, Quirinus. *John Calvin: A Study in French Humanism.* Grand Rapids: Wm. B. Eerdmans Pub. Co., 1931.

Cadier, Jean. *The Man God Mastered.* Translated by O. R. Johnston. London: Inter-varsity Fellowship, 1960.

Calvin, Jean. *A Calvin Treasury.* Edited by William F. Keesecker. New York: Harper, 1961.

Harkness, Georgia E. *John Calvin: The Man and His Ethics.* New York: Abingdon Press, 1958.

Kerr, Hugh T., ed. *By John Calvin.* New York: Association Press, 1960.

Mackinnon, James. *Calvin and the Reformation.* New York: Russell & Russell, 1962.

Murray, John. *Calvin on Scripture and Divine Sovereignty.* Grand Rapids: Baker Book House, 1960.

Nixon, Leroy. *John Calvin, Expository Preacher.* Grand Rapids: Wm. B. Eerdmans Pub. Co., 1950.

Walker, Williston. *John Calvin: The Organizer of Reformed Protestantism.* New York: Schocken Books, 1969.

FOR OTHER SERMONS BY JOHN CALVIN:

The Deity of Christ and Other Sermons. Grand Rapids, Mich.: Wm. B. Eerdmans Pub. Co., 1950.

The Gospel According to Isaiah. Translated by Leroy Nixon. Grand Rapids: Wm. B. Eerdmans Pub. Co., 1953.

Also: *Sermons from Job* (1952), *The Mystery of Godliness, and Other Selected Sermons* (1950).

JOHN KNOX

1513-1572

JOHN KNOX, The Mansell Collection

JOHN KNOX

1513	Born near Edinburgh, Scotland (some scholars assign his birth to 1505)
1540	Ordained to priesthood
1543	Experienced spiritual awakening
1547	Joined rebel group of Protestants in Castle of St. Andrew's, captured by French
1549	Released from prison and became pastor at Berwick on Tweed, England
1554	Fled England for the Continent and Geneva; later became pastor of English exiles in Frankfort, Germany
1555	Returned to Geneva and then to Scotland; married Marjorie Bowes (probable date)
1556	Went again to Geneva to pastor an English-speaking congregation
1558	Published First Blast of the Trumpet Against the Monstrous Regiment of Women
1559	Returned to Scotland amidst political turmoil
1560	Led Protestant forces to victory in Scotland
1561	Entered severe conflict with Queen Mary, who returned to Scotland
1567	Supported forced abdication of Mary
1570	Suffered a paralytic stroke
1572	Died November 24, in Edinburgh

THE FIERY REFORMER of Scotland combined preaching and political revolution in such an effective way that Scotland underwent the most thorough reformation of any nation in Europe. His success came in spite of the combined forces of a Roman Catholic queen, a corrupt court, and a greedy nobility.

LIFE AND TIMES

The date of Knox's birth is unknown. Some scholars place it as early as 1505; most assign his birth to 1513. He was born near Edinburgh, Scotland. As a youth he gained an excellent education in the grammar schools and universities of Scotland. In the schools he received mostly Catholic teaching, although some of his professors had been affected by Reformation thought.

About 1543 he experienced a spiritual awakening. Though he had been ordained to the priesthood a few years earlier, he became convinced that the teachings of the Roman Catholic church were in error. He became associated with Protestant leaders such as George Wishart. In 1546 Wishart was tried for heresy and burned at the stake. The Protestant rebels retaliated by assassinating a leading Catholic churchman. When some of the rebels took refuge in the Castle of St. Andrew's, Knox joined them. He acted as chaplain for the group and administered the first Protestant version of the Lord's Supper. In 1547 the Catholic forces, aided by the French, captured the castle, and Knox and his companions were imprisoned.

Knox was placed on a French warship, chained as a galley slave and forced to pull oars. In the midst of these horrible conditions, he kept his hope alive. He never doubted that one day he would preach the gospel in Scotland.

Released from enslavement in 1549, he journeyed to England and became pastor of an English congregation at Berwick on Tweed. He proved to be a successful minister and occupied a number of important positions in England. When the Protestant government in England was replaced by a government with Catholic sentiment, he fled to the Continent and ultimately to Geneva. For the next five years Knox journeyed about Europe. For a time he pastored an English-speaking congregation in Frankfort, Germany; he spent time in Geneva with Calvin; he made at least one trip to Scotland to encourage the Protestant cause there; and he wrote an elaborate statement on predestination and his notorious *First Blast of the Trumpet Against the Monstrous Regiment of Women,* a denunciation of women rulers.

Meanwhile, back in Scotland and England, women rulers were in control. The conflict among them was to pave the way for the Reformation in Scotland. In 1558, Elizabeth became queen of England. The Roman party in England claimed that she was not a legitimate ruler; she was the daughter of Anne Boleyn, whose marriage to Henry VIII the Roman Catholic church had never recognized. Instead of Elizabeth, the Roman Catholic party insisted that Mary was the legitimate ruler. Also in 1558, Mary married the heir to the French throne. In the next year he became Francis II of France. Protestants in both England and Scotland feared the union of France, England, and Scotland under the reign of Francis II and Mary, both of whom were committed Catholics.

In 1559 Knox arrived at Edinburgh. In order to unite the Protestants against the Catholic queen, he utilized their fears to the fullest. The Scottish regent, Mary of Guise, declared Knox an outlaw. He retaliated by denouncing the Mass. The people arose in a demonstration of violence, sacking monasteries and destroying images in churches. Armies took to the field; the forces led by Knox were backed by the English. In 1560 the regent died, and within a month the French and English forces were withdrawn by treaty. While Mary, the queen, was absent in France, it was agreed that the Scottish government would be run by a council of Scots.

When the council met, it was radically Protestant. It overthrew completely the Roman Catholic church in Scotland. A confession of faith drafted by Knox and others was adopted. In December, 1560, Francis II died. Mary, now widowed, returned to Scotland determined to bring the country back under the Roman Catholic faith. She also had plans to gain the English throne.

Knox and Mary were on a collision course. They clashed in a battle of words and political ploys. Mary had Knox arrested for treason, but the court acquitted him. Knox thundered against Mary again and again. Ultimately the position of Knox prevailed, and in 1567 Mary was forced to abdicate. She was imprisoned, but escaped in 1568 – only to be imprisoned by Elizabeth in England. In the place of Mary, James VI, her infant son, became king. Since the government was placed in the hands of a regency administered by a Protestant, the political structure in Scotland backed the Protestant cause. Knox and the forces of Protestantism had gained almost total victory.

In 1570 Knox suffered a paralytic stroke and he never regained full strength. On November 4, 1572, he died in Edinburgh. His last years had been devoted primarily to preaching and counseling in Edinburgh and St. Andrew's. Many historians regard John Knox as the most significant man in Scottish history. He influenced not only the character of religious life in Scotland but also the political destiny of the country.

When Knox was born, Scotland was a poor and backward country. The corrupt nobility, always at each other's throats, kept the monarch weak. Though the church owned half of the lands, it was also weakened by corruption. Education was not up to the continental standard, and poverty was widespread.

During most of Knox's lifetime the situation was little changed; the political revolutions which swept the little country blocked progress. The people were seriously divided between Protestant and Catholic factions. Since both England and France endeavored either to dominate or to win an alliance from Scotland, the nation was torn between the French and English parties.

Knox was so successful in his reform that he finally established both religious and political unity. After the final overthrow of Mary, Scotland became firmly established in the Protestant camp. The little nation was also able to win independence without becoming dependent upon either France or England. Much of the internal squabbling ceased.

With relative peace at home, many strides forward were made. Education was stressed: the universities of Scotland came to be among the finest in the world; her scholars dominated many fields. Authors, poets, mathematicians, and scientists abounded in the land. Religiously, Scotland came to the forefront: her preachers became world-renowned for their ability. Missionary zeal flowered: in later years, the name of David Livingston became a household word throughout the Christian world. Scottish theologians were recognized as second to none. Scottish piety became famous.

Not all of these advances can be attributed to Knox, of course. But without him and without the change in national life which he made possible, no doubt Scotland would never have achieved the greatness which she did. It is probably accurate to say that never in history has one man so altered the life of a nation as did John Knox in Scotland.

PREACHING AND SERMONS

Fewer sermons by Knox remain than by any other famous Reformation preacher. Some writers mention three extant sermons, but modern collections indicate that only two sermons remain: one on Isaiah 26:13-21 and one on Matthew 4:1. Both of these were printed in *The Select Practical Writings of John Knox*, issued by a Committee of the General Assembly of the Free Church of Scotland, published in Edinburgh in 1845. Only the first of these sermons was reproduced in *The Works of John Knox*, collected and edited by David Laing, a six-volume work published in Edinburgh between 1846 and 1864; this set was based upon the McCrie manuscripts of Knox's works, now deposited in the Main University Library in Edinburgh. Apparently none of the other sermons of Knox have survived. In 1968 the librarian of New College Library, Edinburgh, reported no additional manuscript sermons of Knox in their collection, nor has further research discovered any other sermons by him anywhere.

This absence of sermons is all the more unusual because of the lengthy ministry of Knox in Edinburgh as well as the eminence Knox attained in his lifetime. We might expect that some reporter would have at least taken notes on the extensive preaching of the famous reformer, but apparently no one did.

What little we do know about the preaching of Knox comes from those sermons that exist and the preface Knox wrote for one of them. In this preface, written for the sermon on Isaiah 26:13-21 which he preached at St. Giles Church in Edinburgh, Knox explained the absence of written material from him:

> Wonder not, Christian Reader, that of all my study and travail within the scriptures of God these twenty years, I have set forth nothing in expounding any portion of scripture, except this only rude and indigest sermon preached by me in the public audience of the Church in Edinburgh, the day and year above mentioned. That I did not in writing communicate my judgment from the scriptures, I have ever thought and yet think myself to have most just reason.
>
> For considering myself rather called of my God to instruct the ignorant, comfort the sorrowful, confirm the weak, and rebuke the proud by tongue and lively voice in these most corrupt days than to compose books for the age to come, seeing that so much is written (and that by men of most singular condition), and yet so little well observed; I decreed to contain myself within the bonds of that vocation whereunto I find myself especially called.

I dare not deny (less than in so doing I should be injurious to the giver), but that God hath revealed unto me secrets unknown to the world; and also that he made my tongue a trumpet to forewarn realms and nations, yea, certain great personages, of translations and changes, when no such things were feared, nor yet was appearing; a portion whereof can not the world deny (be it ever so blind) to be fulfilled; and the rest, alas! I fear shall follow with great expedition and in more perfection than my sorrowful heart desireth.

These revelations and assurances not withstanding, I did ever abstain to commit anything to writing, contented only to have obeyed the charge of Him who commanded me to cry.

Knox plainly declared himself to be a preacher first and foremost; he refused to direct his energies in any other direction. Like Luther, Knox was a man of many talents, but always and preeminently a preacher. Nevertheless, it is regretable that no more manuscripts remain of Knox's fiery sermons.

Strangely enough, the preaching career of Knox began in timidity. Because of his religious and political views, Knox joined a small band of reformers in hiding at the Castle of St. Andrew's. One of these reformers was an eloquent preacher named John Rough, who directly addressed Knox at the close of one of his sermons:

Brother, you shall not be offended, although I speak unto you that which I have in charge, even from all those that are here present, which is this: In the name of God, and His Son, Jesus Christ, and in the name of all that presently call you by my mouth, I charge you that you refuse not this holy vocation; but, as you tender the glory of God, the increase of Christ's kingdom, the edification of your brethren, and the comfort of me, whom you understand well enough to be oppressed by the multitude of labours, that you take the public office and charge of preaching, even as you look to avoid God's heavy displeasure, and desire that He shall multiply His graces unto you.[1]

Overwhelmed by this unexpected and solemn charge, Knox

1. G. Barnett Smith, *John Knox and the Scottish Reformation* (Edinburgh: The Religious Tract and Book Society of Scotland, 1905), p. 17.

attempted to address the audience, then burst into tears and rushed out of the assembly and shut himself in his chamber. When he finally came forth he accepted the charge of the group and began to preach. Even with all of his courage, made famous by the statement that "he never feared man"—a statement which the writings of Knox reveal to be untrue—there were many occasions during his ministry when the fear of preaching came upon him.

Nevertheless, fear was the exception in the career of John Knox. Even while confined to the French galleys, Knox showed his indomitable spirit. As the vessel lay off the coast of Scotland between Dundee and St. Andrew's, James Balfore, who was confined in the same ship with him, pointed to the spires of St. Andrew's and asked Knox if he knew the place. "Yes," replied the sickly Knox, "I know it well; for I see the steeple of that place where God first opened my mouth in public to his glory; and I am now fully persuaded, how weak soever I now appear, that I shall not depart this life, till that my tongue shall glorify His godly name and in the same place."[2] Balfore repeated this statement before a number of witnesses many years before Knox returned to Scotland, when it seemed certain that it would never be fulfilled.

Others may have doubted that these prophetic words would be fulfilled; Knox did not. After release from imprisonment, he went to England. For five years he made his influence felt by his sermons in London and his ministry in Berwick. But when Mary Tudor's reign began, Knox had to flee to Frankfort— where he promptly called the emperor a "Nero" and was obliged to leave the city. After a temporary exile in Geneva, Knox intended to return to England on the death of Mary Tudor; but his tract, *The First Blast of the Trumpet Against the Monstrous Regiment of Women*, offended Elizabeth and he was forced to sail directly to Edinburgh—where his vision of preaching at St. Andrew's was fulfilled.

When he reached Scotland, the preaching of Knox created a sensation at both Dundee and Perth, and Perth became the scene of a riot. On the ninth of June, 1559, the archbishop assembled an armed force and told Knox that if he attempted to preach in the cathedral, he would give orders to the soldiers to fire upon him. The noblemen advised Knox to submit. Nothing was further from Knox's mind.

2. Ibid., p. 20.

McCrie reports that Knox resisted all the entreaties of his friends:

> He could take God to witness, he said that he never preached in contempt of any man, nor with the design of hurting any earthly creature; but to delay to preach next day (unless forcibly hindered), he could not in conscience agree. In that town, and in that church, had God first raised him to the dignity of a preacher, and from it he had been "reft" by French tyranny. . . . The length of his imprisonment, and the tortures which he had endured, he would not at present recite; but one thing he could not conceal, that, in the hearing of many yet alive, he had expressed his confident hope of again preaching in St. Andrews. Now, therefore, when Providence, beyond all men's expectation, had brought him to that place, he besought them not to hinder him. "As for the fear of danger that may come to me," continued he, "let no man be solicitous for my life is in the custody of Him whose glory I seek. I desire the hand nor weapon of no man to defend me. I only crave audience; which, if it be denied here unto me at this time, I must seek where I may have it."[3]

His reply silenced all opposition, and the next day Knox appeared in the pulpit and preached to a great crowd without experiencing any interruption. He took for his subject the casting out of the money changers by Christ; he applied this text to the corruptions which had been introduced into the church under the papacy, and he urged Christians to remove them. For three days following he preached in the same place, and his influence was such that the magistrates and inhabitants agreed to establish reformed worship in the town. The church was stripped of its images and the monasteries were pulled down.

Knox undertook a lengthy preaching tour through Scotland and visited many of the cities. Everywhere his preaching had sensational effects. Thomas Randolph, Elizabeth's ambassador, reported that Knox's voice would "put life into them more than 500 trumpets."

Another view of the preaching of Knox was given by his repeated conflicts with the young queen, Mary Stuart. On the Sunday following her return to Scotland in August of 1561,

---

3. Ibid., pp. 53–54.

she had the Mass said in Holyrood Castle. Knox was alarmed and thundered against her from his pulpit in St. Giles; he said that "one Mass was more fearfull to him, than if ten thousand armed enemies was landed in any part of the realme, of purpose to suppress the whole religion." The battle between the reformer and the queen began.

Much of the style of Knox can be seen in the reports of these controversies with the queen. He was fearless, stubborn, and brilliant. His replies to the queen were apt, quick as lightning, and exceptionally sharp. One of these incidents, as detailed in Knox's *History of the Reformation*, will suggest the nature of their exchange:

The queen, in a vehement fume, began to cry out that never prince was handled as she was. "I have," said she, "borne with you in all your rigorous manner of speaking, both against myself and against my uncles; yea, I have sought your favor by all possible means; I have offered unto you presents and audience whence wherever it pleased you to admonish me, and yet I can not be quit of you. I vow to God I shall be once revenged."

And with these words scarcely did Marnock, her secret chamber-boy, get napkins to hold her eyes dry for the tears. And the howling, besides womanly weeping, stayed her speech. . . .

True it is, Madam, your grace and I have been in divers controversies, into the which I never perceived your grace to be offended at me. But when it shall please God to deliver you from that bondage of darkness and error in the which ye have been nourished, for the lack of true doctrine, your Majesty will find in the liberty of my tongue nothing offensive. Without the preaching place, Madam, I think few have occasion to be offended at me; and there, Madam, I am not master of myself, but must obey Him who commands me to speak plain, and to flatter no flesh upon the face of the earth. . . .

I am sent to preach the Evangel of Jesus Christ to such as please to hear it; and it hath two parts, Repentance and Faith. Now, Madam, in preaching repentance, of necessity it is that the sins of man be so noted, that they may know wherein they offend; but so it is, that the most part of your nobility are so addicted to your affections, that neither God's Word, nor yet their commonwealth, are rightly regarded; and therefore, it becomes me so to speak, that they may know their duty.

This passage reveals much about Knox's philosophy of preaching as well as his style of speaking.

The preaching of Knox kept the nobility in a constant uproar. On the 19th of August, 1565, the weak King Henry—formerly Lord Darnley—made the mistake of attending one of Knox's sermons. He made a solemn appearance in St. Giles Church and sat on a throne prepared for his reception. Whether by accident or on purpose, Knox quoted the words of Scripture, "I will give children to be their princes, and babes shall rule over them, children of their oppressors, and women rule over them." He also mentioned that God punished Ahab for not correcting his idolatrous wife, Jezebel.

Darnley was infuriated. He returned to the palace in steaming anger, pouting like a child, refusing all of his food, and complaining to the queen about the insolence of Knox. Late in the day Knox was taken from his bed and carried before the Privy Council. He was told he had offended the king and must refrain from preaching so long "as their majesties were in Edinburgh." Knox replied that "he had spoken nothing but according to his text; and that the Church had commanded him to speak or abstain, he would obey, so far as the Word of God would permit him." He not only stood by what he had said in the pulpit but added, "that as the king, for the queen's pleasure, had gone to Mass . . . so should she, in her justice, be the instrument of his overthrow." The queen was enraged at this answer, and as usual burst into tears.

Knox judged it necessary for his own exoneration to write out the sermon in full as he had spoken it, "so far as memory would serve"; and if he had not, virtually nothing of his preaching would remain. In the preface of the sermon Knox explained his method of sermon preparation. According to that source, he prepared himself by careful study to expound the passage of Scripture selected for his text, then trusted to his feelings at the time for the mode of expression which he might use in delivery. No doubt this freedom accounts in part for the great power he exercised over his hearers:

> . . . in the public place I consult not with flesh and blood what I shall propound to the people, but as the spirit of my God who hath sent me, and to whom I must answer, moveth me, so I speak; and when I have once pronounced threatenings in His Name (however unpleasant they may be to the world), I dare no more deny them than

I dare deny that God hath made me His messenger to forewarn the disobedient of their assured destruction.[4]

In such remains of his sermons as we have, Knox displays careful organization. Though he may have expounded upon the divisions of his text in an extemporaneous fashion, the form of the sermon reveals careful study and organization. Yet the casual nature of his discourse, which at times approximates discursive rambling, suggests that Knox allowed the body of the sermon to turn in whatever direction he felt led at the moment. He seemed particularly fond of biblical illustrations, if the sermons that remain are any fair example of his work.

Toward the end of his life Knox visibly declined in strength; he found it impossible to enter the pulpit without help. In 1571, only a year before his death, a student at St. Andrew's wrote an account of Knox's preaching in his last days. James Melville, one of his constant hearers, wrote in his diary:

> Of all the benefits that I have had in that year (1571), was the coming of that most notable prophet and apostle of our nation, Mr. John Knox, to St. Andrews, who because the faction of the Queen occupied the castle and town of Edinburgh, was compelled to remove therefrom with a number of the best, and chose to come to St. Andrews. I heard him teach there the prophecies of Daniel, that summer and the winter following.
>
> I had my pen and my little book and took away such things as I could comprehend. In the opening up of his text he was moderate to space of half an hour; but when he entered to application, he made me so to thrill and tremble, I could not hold a pen to write.
>
> He was very weak. I saw him every day of his doctrine, going slowly and wearily, with a furring of marticks about his neck, a staff in the one hand and good, godly Richard Ballend, his servant, holding him up by the other armpit, from the Abbey to the parish Church; and, by the said Richard and another servant, lifted up to the pulpit, where he found it necessary to lean at his first entry; but before he had done with his sermon, he was so active and vigorous, that he was like to ding the pulpit in blads [beat the pulpit into pieces], and fly out of it![5]

---

4. David Laing, ed., *The Works of John Knox* (Edinburgh: Thomas George Stevenson, 1865), pp. 230–31. Spelling modernized.
5. Smith, pp. 147–48. Spelling modernized.

So the fiery Knox came to the end of his labors. The famous eulogy delivered by Regent Morton at the burial of Knox has been often quoted, "Here lies one who never feared the face of man." Perhaps a better one was written by Knox himself in a letter he sent to England in the year 1568:

> I would most gladly pass through the course that God hath appointed to my labors . . . giving thanks to His Holy Name; for that it hath pleased His mercy to make me not a Lord-like Bishop, but a painful preacher of His blessed Evangel.[6]

6. Laing, p. 559. Spelling modernized.

Sermons

THE FIRST TEMPTATION OF CHRIST

"Then was Jesus led up of the Spirit into the wilderness, to be tempted of the devil" (Matthew 4:1).

THE CAUSE MOVING ME TO TREAT of this place of Scripture is, that such as by the inscrutable providence of God fall into divers temptations, judge not themselves by reason thereof to be less acceptable in God's presence. But, on the contrary, having the way prepared to victory by Jesus Christ, they shall not fear above measure the crafty assaults of that subtle serpent Satan; but with joy and bold courage, having such a guide as here is pointed forth, such a champion, and such weapons as here are to be found (if with obedience we will hear, and unfeigned faith believe), we may assure ourselves of God's present favor, and of final victory, by the means of Him, who, for our safeguard and deliverance, entered in the battle, and triumphed over His adversary, and all his raging fury.

And that this being heard and understood, may the better be kept in memory; this order, by God's grace, we propose to observe in treating the matter: First, What this word temptation meaneth, and how it is used within the Scriptures. Secondly, Who is here tempted and at what time this temptation happened. Thirdly, How and by what means He was tempted. Fourthly, Why He should suffer these temptations, and what fruits ensue to us from the same.

First, Temptation, or to tempt, in the Scriptures of God, is called to try, to prove, or to assault the valor, the power, the will, the pleasure, or the wisdom — whether it be of God, or of creatures. And it is taken sometimes in good part, as when it is said that God tempted Abraham; God tempted the people of Israel; that is, God did try and examine them, not for His own knowledge, to whom nothing is hid, but to certify others how obedient Abraham was to God's commandment and how weak and inferior the Israelites were in their journey toward the promised land. And this temptation is always good, because it proceeds immediately from God, to open and make manifest the secret

Reprinted from *The World's Great Sermons*, comp. Grenville Kleiser, vol. 1 (New York: Funk & Wagnalls Co., 1909), pp. 173–201.

motions of men's hearts, the puissance and power of God's word, and the great lenity and gentleness of God toward the iniquities (yea, horrible sins and rebellions) of those whom He hath received into His regimen and care. For who could have believed that the bare word of God could so have moved the heart and affections of Abraham, that to obey God's commandment he determined to kill, with his own hand, his best-beloved son Isaac? Who could have trusted that, so many torments as Job suffered, he should not speak in all his great temptation one foolish word against God? Or who could have thought that God so mercifully should have pardoned so many and so manifest transgressions committed by His people in the desert, and yet that His mercy never utterly left them, but still continued with them, till at length he performed His promise made to Abraham? Who, I say, would have been persuaded of these things, unless by trials and temptations taken of His creatures by God, they had come by revelation made in His holy Scriptures to our knowledge?

And so this kind of temptation is profitable, good, and necessary, as a thing proceeding from God, who is the fountain of all goodness, to the manifestation of His own glory, and to the profit of the suffered, however the flesh may judge in the hour of temptation. Otherwise temptation, or to tempt, is taken in evil part; that is, he that assaults or assails intends destruction and confusion to him that is assaulted. As when Satan tempted the women in the garden, Job by divers tribulations, and David by adultery. The scribes and Pharisees tempted Christ by divers means, questions, and subtleties. And of this matter, saith St. James, "God tempteth no man"; that is, by temptation proceeding immediately from Him He intends no man's destruction. And here you shall note, that although Satan appears sometimes to prevail against God's elect, yet he is ever frustrated of his final purpose. By temptation He led Eve and David from the obedience of God, but He could not retain them forever under His thraldom. Power was granted to Him to spoil Job of his substance and children, and to strike his body with a plague and sickness most vile and fearful, but He could not compel his mouth to blaspheme God's majesty; and, therefore, although we are laid open sometimes, as it were, to tribulation for a time, it is that when He has poured forth the venom of His malice against God's elect it may return to His own confusion, and that the deliverance of God's children may be more to His glory, and the comfort of the afflicted: knowing that His hand is so powerful, His mercy and good-will so prompt, that He delivers His little ones from their cruel enemy, even as David did his sheep and lambs from the mouth of the lion. For a little benefit received in extreme danger more moves us than the preservation from ten thousand perils, so that we fall not into them. And yet to preserve from dangers and perils so that we fall not into them, whether they are of body or spirit, is no less the work of God than to deliver from them; but the weakness of our faith does not perceive it: this I leave at the present.

Also, to tempt means simply to prove or try without any determinate purpose or profit or damage to ensue; as when the mind doubteth of anything, and therein desires to be satisfied, without great love or extreme hatred of the thing that is tempted or tried. David tempted; that is, tried himself if he could go in harness (1 Sam. 17). And Gideon said, "Let not thine anger kindle against me, if I tempt thee once again." So the Queen of Sheba came to tempt Solomon in subtle questions. This famous queen, not fully trusting the report and fame that was spread of Solomon, by subtle questions desired to prove his wisdom; at the first, neither extremely hating nor fervently loving the person of the king. And David, as a man not accustomed to harness, would try how he was able to go, and behave and fashion himself therein, before he would hazard battle with Goliath so armed. And Gideon, not satisfied in his conscience by the first that he received, desired, without contempt or hatred of God, a second time to be certified of his vocation. In this sense must the apostle be expounded when he commands us to tempt; that is, to try and examine ourselves, if we stand in the faith. Thus much for the term.

Now to the person tempted, and to the time and place of his temptation. The person tempted is the only well-beloved Son of God; the time was immediately after His baptism; and the place was the desert or wilderness. But that we derive advantage from what is related, we must consider the same more profoundly. That the Son of God was thus tempted gives instructions to us, that temptations, although they be ever so grievous and fearful, do not separate us from God's favor and mercy, but rather declare the great graces of God to appertain to us, which makes Satan to rage as a roaring lion; for against none does He so fiercely fight as against those of whose hearts Christ has taken possession.

The time of Christ's temptation is here most diligently to be noted. And that was, as Mark and Luke witness, immediately after the voice of God the Father had commended His Son to the world, and had visibly pointed to Him by the sign of the Holy Ghost; He was led or moved by the Spirit to go to a wilderness, where forty days he remained fasting among the wild beasts. This Spirit which led Christ into the wilderness was not the devil, but the holy Spirit of God the Father, by whom Christ, as touching His human and manly nature, was conducted and led; likewise by the same Spirit He was strengthened and made strong, and, finally, raised up from the dead. The Spirit of God, I say, led Christ to the place of His battle, where He endured the combat for the whole forty days and nights. As Luke saith, "He was tempted," but in the end most vehemently, after His continual fasting, and that He began to be hungry. Upon this forty days and this fasting of Christ do our Papists found and build their Lent; for, say they, all the actions of Christ are our instructions; what He did we ought to follow. But He fasted forty days, therefore we ought to do the like. I answer, that if we ought to follow all Christ's actions, then ought we neither to eat nor drink for the space of forty days, for so fasted Christ; we ought to go upon the waters with our feet; to cast out devils by our word; to heal and cure all sorts of maladies; to call again the dead to life; for so did Christ. This I write only that men may see the vanity of those who, boasting themselves of wisdom, have become fools.

Did Christ fast those forty days to teach us superstitious fasting? Can the Papists assure me, or any other man, which were the forty days that Christ fasted? plain it is he fasted the forty days and nights that immediately followed His baptism, but which they were, or in what month was the day of His baptism, Scripture does not express; and although the day were expressed, am I or any Christian bound to counterfeit Christ's actions as the ape counterfeits the act or work of man? He Himself requires no such obedience of His true followers, but saith to the apostles, "Go and preach the gospel to all nations, baptizing them in the name of the Father, the Son, and the Holy Ghost; commanding them to observe and keep all that I have commanded you." Here Christ Jesus requires the observance of His precepts and commandments, not of His actions, except in so far as He had also commanded them; and so must the apostle be understood when he saith, "Be followers of Christ, for Christ hath suffered for us, that we should follow His footsteps," which can not be understood of every action of Christ, either in the mystery of our redemption, or in His actions and marvelous works, but only of those which He hath commanded us to observe. But where the Papists are so diligent in establishing their dreams and fantasies, they lose the profit that here is to be gathered; that is, why Christ fasted those forty days; which were a doctrine more necessary for Christians than to corrupt the simple hearts with superstition, as though the wisdom of God, Christ Jesus, had taught us no other mystery by His fasting than the abstinence from flesh, or once on the day to eat flesh, for the space of forty days. God hath taken a just vengeance upon the pride of such men, while He thus confounds the wisdom of those that do most glory in wisdom, and strikes with blindness such as will be guides and lanterns to the feet of others, and yet refuse themselves to hear or follow the light of God's word. From such deliver thy poor flock, O Lord!

The uses of Christ's fasting these forty days I find chiefly to be two: The first, to witness to the world the dignity and excellence of His vocation, which Christ, after His baptism, was to take upon Him openly; the other, to declare that he entered into battle willingly for our cause, and does, as it were, provoke his adversary to assault Him: although Christ Jesus, in the eternal counsel of His Father, was appointed to be the Prince of Peace, the angel (that is, the messenger) of His testament, and He alone that could fight our battles for us, yet He did not enter in execution of it, in the sight of men, till He was commended to mankind by the voice of His heavenly Father; and as He was placed and anointed by the Holy Ghost by a visible sign given to the eyes of men. After which time He was led to the desert, and fasted, as before is said; and this He did to teach us with what fear, carefulness, and reverence the messengers of the Word ought to enter on their vocation, which is not only most excellent (for who is worthy to be God's ambassador?) but also subject to most extreme troubles and dangers. For he that is appointed pastor, watchman, or preacher, if he feed not with his whole power, if he warn and admonish not when he sees the snare come, and if, in doctrine, he divide not the Word righteously, the blood and souls of those that perish for lack of food, admonition, and doctrine shall be required of his hand.

But to our purpose; that Christ exceeded not the space of forty days in His fasting, He did it to the imitation of Moses and Elias; of whom, the one before the receiving of the law, and the other before the communication and reasoning which he had with God in Mount Horeb, in which He was commanded to anoint Hazael king over Syria, and Jehu king over Israel, and Elisha to be prophet, fasted the same number of days. The events that ensued and followed this supernatural fasting of these two servants of God, Moses and Elias, impaired and diminished the tyranny of the kingdom of Satan. For by the law came the knowledge of sin, the damnation of such impieties, specially of idolatry, and such as the devil had invented; and, finally, by the law came such a revelation of God's will that no man could justly afterward excuse his sin by ignorance, by which the devil before had blinded many. So that the law, although it might not renew and purge the heart, for that the Spirit of Christ Jesus worketh by faith only, yet it was a bridle that did hinder and stay the rage of external wickedness in many, and was a schoolmaster that led unto Christ. For when man can find no power in himself to do that which is commanded, and perfectly understands, and when he believes that the curse of God is pronounced against those that abide not in everything that is commanded in God's law to do them—the man, I say, that understands and knows his own corrupt nature and God's severe judgment, most gladly will receive the free redemption offered by Christ Jesus, which is the only victory that overthrows Satan and his power. And so by the giving of the law God greatly weakened, impaired, and made frail the tyranny and kingdom of the devil. In the days of Elias, the devil had so prevailed that kings and rulers made open war against God, killing His prophets, destroying His ordinances, and building up idolatry, which did so prevail that the prophet complained that of all the true fearers and worshipers of God he was left alone, and wicked Jezebel sought His life also. After this, his fasting and complaint, he was sent by God to anoint the persons aforenamed, who took such vengeance upon the wicked and obstinate idolaters that he who escaped the sword of Hazael fell into the hands of Jehu, and those whom Jehu left escaped not God's vengeance under Elisha.

The remembrance of this was fearful to Satan, for, at the coming of

Christ Jesus, impiety was in the highest degree among those that pretended most knowledge of God's will; and Satan was at such rest in his kingdom that the priests, scribes and Pharisees had taken away the key of knowledge; that is, they had so obscured and darkened God's Holy Scriptures, by false glosses and vain traditions, that neither would they themselves enter into the kingdom of God, nor suffer and permit others to enter; but with violence restrained, and with tyranny struck back from the right way, that is, from Christ Jesus Himself, such as would have entered into the possession of life everlasting by Him. Satan, I say, having such dominion over the chief rulers of the visible Church, and espying in Christ, such graces as before he had not seen in man, and considering Him to follow in fasting the footsteps of Moses and Elias, no doubt greatly feared that the quietness and rest of his most obedient servants, the priests, and their adherents, would be troubled by Christ. And, therefore, by all engines and craft, he assaults Him to see what advantage he could have of Him. And Christ did not repel him, as by the power of His Godhead He might have done, that he should not tempt Him, but permitted him to spend all his artillery, and received the strokes and assaults of Satan's temptations in His own body, to the end He might weaken and enfeeble the strength and tyrannous power of our adversary by His long suffering. For thus, methinks, our Master and Champion, Jesus Christ, provoked our enemy to battle: "Satan, thou gloriest of thy power and victories over mankind, that there is none able to withstand thy assaults, nor escape thy darts, but at one time or other thou givest him a wound: lo! I am a man like to my brethren, having flesh and blood, and all properties of man's nature (sin, which is thy venom, excepted); tempt, try, and assault me; I offer you here a place most convenient—the wilderness. There shall be no mortal to comfort me against thy assaults; thou shalt have time sufficient; do what thou canst, I shall not fly the place of battle. If thou become victor, thou shalt still continue in possession of thy kingdom in this wretched world; but if thou canst not prevail against me, then must thy prey and unjust spoil be taken from thee; thou must grant thyself vanquished and confounded, and must be compelled to leave off from all accusation of the members of my body; for to them appertains the fruit of my battle, my victory is theirs, as I am appointed to take the punishment of their sins in my body."

What comfort ought the remembrance of these signs to be to our hearts! Christ Jesus hath fought our battle; He Himself hath taken us into His care and protection; however the devil may rage by temptations, be they spiritual or corporeal, he is not able to bereave us out of the hand of the almighty Son of God. To Him be all glory for His mercies most abundantly poured upon us!

There remains yet to be spoken of the time when our Lord was tempted, which began immediately after His baptism. Whereupon we have to note the mark, that although the malice of Satan never ceases, but always seeks for means to trouble the godly, yet sometimes he rages more fiercely than others, and that is commonly when God begins to manifest His love and favor to any of His children, and at the end of their battle, when they are nearest to obtain final victory. The devil, no doubt, did at all times envy the humble spirit that was in Abel, but he did not stir up the cruel heart of Cain against him till God declared His favor toward him by accepting his sacrifice. The same we find in Jacob, Joseph, David, and most evidently in Christ Jesus.

How Satan raged at the tidings of Christ's nativity! what blood he caused to be shed on purpose to have murdered Christ in His infancy! The evangelist St. Matthew witnesses that in all the coasts and borders of Bethlehem the children of two years old and less age were murdered without mercy. A fearful spectacle and horrid example of insolent and unaccustomed tyranny! And what is the cause moving Satan thus to rage against innocents, considering that by reason of their imperfections they could not hurt his kingdom at that instant? Oh, the crafty eye of Satan looked farther than to the present time; he heard reports by the three wise men, that they had learned by the appearance of a star that the King of the Jews was born; and he was not ignorant that the time prophesied of Christ's coming was then instant; for a stranger was clad with the crown and scepter of Judah. The angel had declared the glad tidings to the shepherds, that a Savior, which was Christ the Lord, was born in the city of David. All these tidings inflamed the wrath and malice of Satan, for he perfectly understood that the coming of the promised Seed was appointed to his confusion, and to the breaking down of his head and tyranny; and therefore he raged most cruelly, even at the first hearing of Christ's birth, thinking that although he could not hinder nor withstand His coming, yet he could shorten his days upon earth, lest by long life and peaceable quietness in it, the number of good men, by Christ's doctrine and virtuous life, should be multiplied; and so he strove to cut Him away among the other children before He could open His mouth on His Father's message. Oh, cruel serpent! in vain dost thou spend thy venom, for the days of God's elect thou canst not shorten! And when the wheat is fallen on the ground, then doth it most multiply.

But from these things mark, what hath been the practise of the devil from the beginning—most cruelly to rage against God's children when God begins to show them His mercy. And, therefore, marvel not, dearly beloved, although the like come unto you. If Satan fume or roar against you, whether it be against your bodies by persecution, or inwardly in your conscience by a spiritual battle, be not discouraged, as though you were less acceptable in God's presence, or as if Satan might at any time prevail against you. No; your temptations and storms, that arise so suddenly, argue and witness that the seed which is sown is fallen on good ground, begins to take root and shall, by God's grace, bring forth fruit abundantly in due season and convenient time. That is it which Satan fears, and therefore thus he rages, and shall rage against you, thinking that if he can repulse you now suddenly in the beginning, that then you shall be at all times an easy prey, never able to resist his assaults. But as my hope is good, so shall my prayer be, that so you may be strengthened, that the world and Satan himself may perceive or understand that God fights your battle.

For you remember that being present with you and treating of the same place, I admonished you that Satan could not long sleep when his kingdom was threatened. And therefore I willed you, if you were in mind to continue with Christ, to prepare yourselves for the day of temptation. The person of the speaker is wretched, miserable, and nothing to be regarded, but the things that were spoken are the infallible and eternal truth of God; without observation of which, life neither can or shall come to mankind. God grant you continuance to the end.

This much have I briefly spoken of the temptation of Christ Jesus, who was tempted; and of the time and place of His temptation. Now remains to be spoken how He was tempted, and by what means. The most part of expositors think that all this temptation was in spirit and in imagination only, the corporeal senses being nothing moved. I will contend with no man in such cases, but patiently will I suffer every man to abound in his own knowledge; and without prejudice of any man's estimation, I offer my judgment to be weighed and considered by Christian charity.

It appears to me by the plain text that Christ suffered this temptation in body and spirit. Likewise, as the hunger which Christ suffered, and the desert in which He remained, were not things offered to the imagination, but that the body did verily remain in the wilderness among beasts, and after forty days did hunger and faint for lack of food; so the external ear did hear the tempting words of Satan, which entered into the knowledge of the soul, and which, repelling the venom of such temptations, caused the tongue to speak and confute Satan, to our unspeakable comfort and consolation. It appears also that the body of Christ Jesus was carried by Satan from the wilderness unto the temple of Jerusalem, and that it was placed upon the pinnacle of the same temple, from whence it was carried to a high mountain and there tempted. If any man can show to the contrary hereof by the plain Scriptures of God, with all submission and thanksgiving I will prefer his judgment to my own; but if the matter stand only in probability and opinion of men, then it is lawful for me to believe as the Scripture here speaks; that is, that Satan spake and Christ answered, and Satan took Him and carried Him from one place to another.

Besides the evidence of the text affirming that Satan was permitted to carry the body of Christ from place to place, and yet was not permitted to execute any further tyranny against it, is most singular comfort to such as are afflicted or troubled in body or spirit. The weak and feeble conscience of man under such temptations, commonly gathers and collects a false consequence. For man reasons thus: The body or the spirit is vexed by assaults and temptations of Satan, and he troubles or molests it, therefore God is angry with it, and takes no care of it. I answer, tribulations or grievous vexations of body or of mind are never signs of God's displeasure against the sufferer, neither yet does it follow that God has cast away the care of His creatures because He permits them to be molested and vexed for a time. For if any sort of tribulation were the infallible sign of God's displeasure, then should we condemn the best beloved children of God. But of this we may speak hereafter. Now to the temptation.

Verse 2. "And when he fasteth forty days and forty nights, He was afterwards an hungered." Verse 3. "Then came to Him the tempter," and said, "If you be the Son of God, command that these stones be made bread," etc. Why Christ fasted forty days and would not exceed the same, without sense and feeling of hunger, is before touched upon, that is, He would provoke the devil to battle by the wilderness and long abstinence, but He would not usurp or arrogate any more to Himself in that case than God had wrought with others, His servants and messengers before. But Christ Jesus (as St. Augustine more amply declares), without feeling of hunger, might have endured the whole year, or to time without end, as well as He did endure the space of forty days. For the nature of mankind was sustained those forty days by the invisible power of God, which is at all times of equal power. But Christ, willing to offer further occasion to Satan to proceed in tempting of Him, permitted the human nature to crave earnestly that which it lacked, that is to say, refreshing of meat; which Satan perceiving took occasion, as before, to tempt and assault. Some judge that Satan tempted Christ to gluttony, but this appears little to agree with the purpose of the Holy Ghost; who shows us this history to let us understand that Satan never ceases to oppugn the children of God, but continually, by one mean or other, drives or provokes them to some wicked opinions of their God; and to have them desire stones to be converted into bread, or to desire hunger to be satisfied, has never been sin, nor yet a wicked opinion of God. And therefore I doubt not but the temptation was more spiritual, more subtle, and more dangerous.

Satan had respect to the voice of God, which had pronounced Christ to be His well-beloved Son, etc. Against this voice he fights, as his nature is ever to do against the assured and immutable Word of God; for such is his malice against God, and against His chosen children, that where and to whom God pronounces love and mercy, to these he threatens displeasures and damnation; and where God threatens death, there is he bold to pronounce life; and for this course is Satan called a liar from the beginning.

And so the purpose of Satan was to drive Christ into desperation, that he should not believe the former voice of God His Father; which appears to be the meaning of this temptation: "Thou hast heard," would Satan say, "a voice proclaimed in the air, that Thou wast the beloved Son of God, in whom His soul was pleased; but mayst Thou not be judged more than mad, and weaker than the brainless fool if Thou believest any such promise? Where are the signs of His love? Art Thou not cast out from comfort of all creatures? Thou art in worse case than the brute beasts, for every day they hunt for their prey, and the earth produces grass and herbs for their sustenance, so that none of them are pined and consumed away by hunger; but Thou hast fasted forty days and nights, ever waiting for some relief and comfort from above, but Thy best provision is hard stones! If Thou dost glory in thy God, and dost verily believe the promise that is made, command that these stones be bread. But evident it is that so Thou canst not do; for if Thou couldst, or if Thy God would have showed Thee any such pleasure, Thou mightest long ago have removed Thy hunger, and needest not have endured this languishing for lack of food. But seeing Thou hast long continued thus, and no provision is made for Thee, it is vanity longer to believe any such promise, and therefore despair of any help from God's hand, and provide for Thyself by some other means!"

Many words have I used here, dearly beloved, but I can not express the thousandth part of the malicious despite which lurked in this one temptation of Satan. It was a mocking of Christ and of His obedience. It was a plain denial of God's promise. It was the triumphing voice of him that appeared to have gotten victory. Oh, how bitter this temptation was no creature can understand but such as feel the grief of such darts as Satan casts at the tender conscience of those that gladly would rest and repose in God, and in the promises of His mercy. But here is to be noted the ground and foundation. The conclusion of Satan is this: Thou art none of God's elect, much less His well-beloved Son. His reason is this: Thou art in trouble and findest no relief. There the foundation of the temptation was Christ's poverty, and the lack of food without hope of remedy to be sent from God. And it is the same temptation which the devil objected to Him by the princes of the priests in His grievous torments upon the cross; for thus they cried, "If he be the Son of God, let him come down from the cross and we will believe in him; he trusted in God, let him deliver him, if he have the pleasure in him."

As though they would say, God is the deliverer of His servants from troubles; God never permits those that fear Him to come to confusion; this man we see in extreme trouble; if He be the Son of God, or even a true worshiper of His name, He will deliver Him from this calamity. If He deliver Him not, but suffer Him to perish in these anguishes, then it is an assured sign that God has rejected Him as a hypocrite, that shall have no portion of His glory. Thus, I say, Satan takes occasion to tempt, and moves also others to judge and condemn God's elect and chosen children, by reason that troubles are multiplied upon them.

But with what weapons we ought to fight against such enemies and assaults we shall learn in the answer of Christ Jesus, which follows: But He, answering, said "It is written, man shall not live by bread alone, but by every word which proceedeth out of the mouth of God." This answer of Christ proves the sentence which we have brought of the aforesaid temptation to be the very meaning of the Holy Ghost; for unless the purpose of Satan has been to have removed Christ from all hope of God's merciful providence toward Him in that His necessity, Christ had not answered directly to his words, saying, "Command that these stones be made bread." But Christ Jesus, perceiving his art and malicious subtility, answered directly to his meaning, His words nothing regarded; by which Satan was so confounded that he was ashamed to reply any further.

But that you may the better understand the meaning of Christ's answer, we will express and repeat it over in more words. "Thou laborest, Satan," would Christ say, "to bring into my heart a doubt and suspicion of My Father's promise, which was openly proclaimed in My baptism, by reason of My hunger, and that I lack all carnal provision. Thou art bold to affirm that God takes no care for Me, but thou art a deceitful and false corrupt sophister, and thy argument, too, is vain, and full of blasphemies; for thou bindest God's love, mercy, and providence to the having or wanting of bodily provision, which no part of God's Scriptures teach us, but rather the express contrary. As it is written, 'Man doth not live by bread alone, but by every word that proceedeth out of the mouth of God,' that is, the very life and felicity of man consists not in the abundance of bodily things, or the possession and having of them makes no man blest or happy; neither shall the lack of them be the cause of his final misery; but the very life of man consists in God, and in His promises pronounced by His own mouth, unto which whoso cleaves unfeignedly shall live the life everlasting. And although all creatures in earth forsake him, yet shall not his bodily life perish till the time appointed by God approach.

"For God has means to feed, preserve, and maintain, unknown to man's reason, and contrary to the common course of nature. He fed His people Israel in the desert forty years without the provision of man. He preserved Jonah in the whale's belly; and maintained and kept the bodies of the three children in the furnace of fire. Reason and the natural man could have seen nothing in these cases but destruction and death, and could have judged nothing but that God had cast away the care of these, His creatures, and yet His providence was most vigilant toward them in the extremity of their dangers, from which He did so deliver them, and in the midst of them did so assist them, that His glory, which is His mercy and goodness, did more appear and shine after their troubles than it could have done if they had fallen in them. And therefore I measure not the truth and favor of

God by having or by lacking of bodily necessities, but by the promise which He has made to me. As He Himself is immutable, so is His word and promise constant, which I believe, and to which I will adhere, and so cleave, whatever can come to the body outwardly."

In this answer of Christ we may perceive what weapons are to be used against our adversary the devil, and how we may confute his arguments, which craftily, and of malice, he makes against God's elect. Christ might have repulsed Satan with a word, or by commanding him to silence, as He to whom all power was given in heaven and earth; but it pleased His mercy to teach us how to use the sword of the Holy Ghost, which is the word of God, in battle against our spiritual enemy. The Scripture which Christ brings is written in the eighth chapter of Deuteronomy. It was spoken by Moses a little before His death, to establish the people in God's merciful providence. For in the same chapter, and in certain others that go before, He reckons the great travail and divers dangers with the extreme necessities that they had sustained in the desert the space of forty years, and yet, notwithstanding how constant God had been in keeping and performing His promise, for throughout all perils He had conducted them to the sight and borders of the promised land. And so this Scripture more directly answers to the temptation of Satan; for thus does Satan reason, as before is said, "Thou art in poverty and hast no provision to sustain thy life. Therefore God takes no regard nor care of Thee, as He doth over His chosen children."

Christ Jesus answered: "Thy argument is false and vain; for poverty or necessity precludes not the providence or care of God; which is easy to be proved by the people of God, Israel, who, in the desert, oftentimes lacked things necessary to the sustenance of life, and for lack of the same they grudged and murmured; yet the Lord never cast away the providence and care of them, but according to the word that He had once pronounced, to wit, that they were His peculiar people; and according to the promise made to Abraham, and to them before their departure from Egypt, He still remained their conductor and guide, till He placed them in peaceable possession of the land of Canaan, their great infirmities and manifold transgressions notwithstanding."

Thus are we taught, I say, by Christ Jesus, to repulse Satan and his assaults by the Word of God, and to apply the examples of His mercies, which He has shown to others before us, to our own souls in the hour of temptation, and in the time of our trouble. For what God doth to one at any time, the same appertains to all that depend upon God and His promises. And, therefore, however we are assaulted by Satan, our adversary, within the Word of God is armor and weapons sufficient. The chief craft of Satan is to trouble those that begin to decline from his obedience, and to declare themselves enemies to iniquity, with divers assaults, the design whereof is always the same; that is, to put variance betwixt them and God into their conscience, that they should not repose and rest themselves in His assured promises.

And to persuade this, he uses and invents divers arguments. Sometimes he calls the sins of their youth, and which they have committed in the time of blindness, to their remembrance; very often he objects their unthankfulness toward God and present imperfections. By sickness, poverty, tribulations in their household, or by persecution, he can allege that God is angry, and regard them not. Or by the spiritual cross which few feel and fewer understand the utility and profit of, he would drive God's children to desperation, and by infinite means more, he goeth about seeking, like a roaring lion, to undermine and destroy our faith. But it is impossible for him to prevail against us unless we obstinately refuse to use the defense and weapons that God has offered.

Yea, I say, that God's elect can not refuse it, but seek for their Defender when the battle is most strong; for the sobs, groans, and lamentations of such as fight, yea, the fear they have lest they be vanquished, the calling and prayer for continuance, are the undoubted and right seeking of Christ our champion. We refuse not the weapon, although sometimes, by infirmity, we can not use it as we would. It suffices that your hearts unfeignedly sob for greater strength, for continuance, and for final deliverance by Christ Jesus; that which is wanting in us, His sufficiency doth supply; for it is He that fighteth and overcometh for us. But for bringing of the examples of the Scriptures, if God permit, in the end we shall speak more largely when it shall be treated why Christ permitted Himself thus to be tempted.

Sundry impediments now call me from writing in this matter, but, by God's grace, at convenient leisure I purpose to finish, and to send it to you. I grant the matter that proceeds from me is not worthy of your pain and labor to read it; yet, seeing it is a testimony of my good mind toward you, I doubt not but you will accept it in good part. God, the Father of our Lord Jesus Christ, grant unto you to find favor and mercy of the Judge, whose eyes and knowledge pierce through the secret cogitations of the heart, in the day of temptation, which shall come upon all flesh, according to that mercy which you (illuminated and directed by His Holy Spirit) have showed to the afflicted. Now the God of all comfort and consolation confirm and strengthen you in His power unto the end. Amen.

THE SOURCE AND BOUNDS OF
KINGLY POWER

"O Lord our God, other lords besides Thee have had dominion over us; but by Thee only will we make mention of Thy name. They are dead, they shall not live; they are deceased, they shall not rise: therefore hast Thou visited and destroyed them, and made all their memory to perish. Thou hast increased the nation, O Lord, Thou hast increased the nation, Thou art glorified; Thou hast removed it far unto the ends of the earth. Lord, in trouble have they visited Thee, they poured out a prayer when Thy chastening was upon them" (Isaiah 26: 13–16).

As THE SKILLFUL MARINER (being master), having his ship tossed with a vehement tempest, and contrary winds, is compelled oft to traverse, lest that, either by too much resisting to the violence of the waves, his vessel might be overwhelmed; or by too much liberty granted, might be carried whither the fury of the tempest would, so that his ship should be driven upon the shore, and make shipwreck; even so doth our prophet Isaiah in this text, which now you have heard read. For he, foreseeing the great desolation that was decreed in the council of the Eternal, against Jerusalem and Judah, namely, that the whole people that bare the name of God should be dispersed; that the holy city should be destroyed; the temple wherein was the ark of the covenant, and where God had promised to give His own presence, should be burned with fire; and the king taken, his sons in his own presence murdered, his own eyes immediately after be put out; the nobility, some cruelly murdered, some shamefully led away captives; and finally the whole seed of Abraham razed, as it were, from the face of the earth — the prophet, I say, fearing these horrible calamities, doth, as it were, sometimes suffer himself, and the people committed to his charge to be carried away with the violence of the tempest, without further resistance than by pouring forth his and their dolorous complaints before the majesty of God, as in the thirteenth, seventeenth, and eighteenth verses of this present text we may read. At other times he valiantly resists the desperate tempest, and pronounces the fearful destruction of all such as trouble the Church of God; which he pronounces that God will multiply, even when it appears utterly to be exterminated. But because there is no final rest to the whole body till the Head return to judgment, He exhorts the afflicted to patience, and promises a visitation whereby the wicked-

Reprinted from *Masterpieces of Pulpit Eloquence* [comp.] Henry C. Fish, Pulpit Eloquence Library, vol. 1, pt. 2 (Cleveland: F. M. Barton, 1907), pp. 130–51.

ness of the wicked shall be disclosed, and finally recompensed in their own bosoms.

These are the chief points of which, by the grace of God, we intend more largely at this present to speak:

First, The prophet saith, "O Lord our God, other lords besides Thee have ruled us."

This, no doubt, is the beginning of the dolorous complaint, in which he complains of the unjust tyranny that the poor afflicted Israelites sustained during the time of their captivity. True it is that the prophet was gathered to his fathers in peace, before this came upon the people: for a hundred years after his decease the people were not led away captive; yet he, foreseeing the assurance of the calamity, did beforehand indite and dictate unto them the complaint, which afterward they should make. But at the first sight it appears that the complaint has but small weight; for what new thing was it that other lords than God in His own person ruled them, seeing that such had been their government from the beginning? For who knows not that Moses, Aaron, and Joshua, the judges, Samuel, David, and other godly rulers, were men, and not God; and so other lords than God ruled them in their greatest prosperity?

For the better understanding of this complaint, and of the mind of the prophet, we must, *first,* observe from whence all authority flows; and *secondly,* to what end powers are appointed by God: which two points being discussed, we shall better understand what lords and what authority rule beside God, and who they are in whom God and His merciful presence rules.

The *first* is resolved to us by the words of the Apostle, saying, "There is no power but of God." David brings in the eternal God speaking to judges and rulers, saying, "I have said, ye are gods, and sons of the Most High." And Solomon, in the person of God, affirmeth the name, saying, "By Me kings reign, and princes discern the things that are just." From which place it is evident that it is neither birth, influence of stars, election of people, force of arms, nor, finally, whatsoever can be comprehended under the power of nature, that makes the distinction betwixt the superior power and the inferior, or that establishes the royal throne of kings; but it is the only and perfect ordinance of God, who willeth His terror, power, and majesty, partly to shine in the thrones of kings, and in the faces of judges, and that for the profit and comfort of man. So that whosoever would study to deface the order of government that God has established, and allowed by His holy word, and bring in such a confusion that no difference should be betwixt the upper powers and the subjects, does nothing but avert and turn upside down the very throne of God, which He wills to be fixed here upon earth; as in the end and cause of this ordinance more plainly shall appear: which is the *second* point we have to observe, for the better understanding of the prophet's words and mind.

The end and cause then, why God imprints in the weak and feeble flesh of man this image of His own power and majesty, is not, to puff up flesh in opinion of itself; neither yet that the heart of him that is exalted above others should be lifted up by presumption and pride, and so despise others; but that he should consider he is appointed lieutenant to One, whose eyes continually watch upon him, to see and examine how he behaves himself in his office. St. Paul, in few words, declares the end wherefore the sword is committed to the powers, saying, "It is to the punishment of the wicked doers, and unto the praise of such as do well."

Of which words it is evident that the sword of God is not committed to the hand of man to use as it pleases him, but only to punish vice and maintain virtue, that men may live in such society as is acceptable before God. And this is the true and only cause why God has appointed powers in this earth.

For such is the furious rage of man's corrupt nature that, unless severe punishment were appointed and put in execution upon male-factors, better it were that man should live among brutes and wild beasts than among men. But at this present I dare not enter into the descriptions of this common-place; for so should I not satisfy the text, which by God's grace I purpose to explain. This only by the way—I would that such as are placed in authority should consider whether they reign and rule by God, so that God rules them; or if they rule without, besides, and against God, of whom our prophet here com-plains.

If any desire to take trial of this point, it is not hard; for Moses, in the election of judges, and of a king, describes not only what per-sons shall be chosen to that honor, but also gives to him that is elected and chosen the rule by which he shall try himself, whether God reign in him or not, saying, "When he shall sit upon the throne of his king-dom, he shall write to himself an exemplar of this law, in a book by the priests and Levites; it shall be with him, and he shall read therein, all the days of his life: that he may learn to fear the Lord his God, and to keep all the words of His law, and these statutes, that he may do them; that his heart be not lifted up above his brethren, and that he turn not from the commandment, to the right hand, or to the left."

The same is repeated to Joshua, in his inauguration to the govern-ment of the people, by God Himself, saying, "Let not the book of this law depart from thy mouth, but meditate in it day and night, that thou mayest keep it, and do according to all that which is written in it. For then shall thy way be prosperous, and thou shall do prudently."

The *first* thing then that God requires of him who is called to the honor of a king, is, The knowledge of His will revealed in His word.

The *second* is, An upright and willing mind, to put in execution such things as God commands in His law, without declining to the right, or to the left hand.

Kings, then, have not an absolute power to do in their government what pleases them, but their power is limited by God's word; so that if they strike where God has not commanded, they are but murderers; and if they spare where God has commanded to strike, they and their throne are criminal and guilty of the wickedness which abounds upon the face of the earth, for lack of punishment.

O that kings and princes would consider what account shall be craved of them, as well of their ignorance and misknowledge of God's will as for the neglecting of their office! But now to return to the words of the prophet. In the person of the whole people he complains unto God that the Babylonians (whom he calls "other lords besides God," both because of their ignorance of God and by reason of their cruelty and inhumanity) had long ruled over them in great rigor, without pity or compassion upon the ancient men and famous matrons; for they, being mortal enemies to the people of God, sought by all means to aggravate their yoke, yea, utterly to exterminate the memory of them, and of their religion, from the face of the earth.

Hereof it is evident that their disobedience unto God and unto the voices of the prophets was the source of their destruction. Now have we to take heed how we should use the good laws of God, that is, His will revealed unto us in His Word; and that order of justice which, by Him, for the comfort of man, is established among men. There is no doubt but that obedience is the most acceptable sacrifice unto God, and that which above all things He requires; so that when He manifests Himself by His Word, men should follow according to their vocation and commandment. Now so it is that God, by that great Pastor our Lord Jesus, now manifestly in His Word calls us from all impiety, as well of body as of mind, to holiness of life, and to His spiritual service; and for this purpose He has erected the throne of His mercy among us, the true preaching of His word, together with the right administration of His sacraments; but what our obedience is, let every man examine his own conscience, and consider what statutes and laws we would have to be given unto her.

Wouldst thou, O Scotland! have a king to reign over thee in justice, equity, and mercy? Subject thou thyself to the Lord thy God, obey His commandments, and magnify thou the Word that calleth unto thee, "This is the way, walk in it": and if thou wilt not, flatter not thyself; the same justice remains this day in God to punish thee, Scotland, and thee Edinburg especially, which before punished the land of Judah and the city of Jerusalem. Every realm or nation, saith the prophet Jeremiah, that likewise offendeth, shall be likewise punished, but if thou shalt see impiety placed in the seat of justice above thee, so that in the throne of God (as Solomon complains) reigns nothing but fraud and violence, accuse thine own ingratitude and rebellion against God; for that is the only cause why God takes away "the strong man and the man of war, the judge and the prophet, the prudent and the aged, the captain and the honorable, the counselor and the cunning artificer;

and I will appoint, saith the Lord, children to be their princes, and babes shall rule over them. Children are extortioners of my people, and women have rule over them."

If these calamities, I say, apprehend us, so that we see nothing but the oppression of good men and of all godliness, and that wicked men without God reign above us; let us accuse and condemn ourselves, as the only cause of our own miseries. For if we had heard the voice of the Lord our God, and given upright obedience unto the same, God would have multiplied our peace, and would have rewarded our obedience before the eyes of the world. But now let us hear what the prophet saith further: "The dead shall not live," saith he, "neither shall the tyrants, nor the dead arise, because Thou hast visited and scattered them, and destroyed all their memory."

From this fourteenth verse unto the end of the nineteenth, it appears that the prophet observes no order; yea, that he speaks things directly repugning one to another; for, *first,* he saith, "The dead shall not live"; afterward he affirms, "Thy dead men shall live." *Secondly,* he saith, "Thou hast visited and scattered them, and destroyed all their memory." Immediately after, he saith, "Thou hast increased Thy nation, O Lord, Thou hast increased Thy nation. They have visited Thee, and have poured forth a prayer before Thee."

Who, I say, would not think that these are things not only spoken without good order and purpose, but also manifestly repugning one to another? For to live, and not to live, to be so destroyed that no memorial remains, and to be so increased that the coasts of the earth shall be replenished, seems to impart plain contradiction. For removing of this doubt, and for better understanding the prophet's mind, we must observe, that the prophet had to do with divers sorts of men; he had to do with the conjured and manifest enemies of God's people, the Chaldeans or Babylonians; even so, such as profess Christ Jesus have to do with the Turks and Saracens. He had to do with the seed of Abraham, whereof there were three sorts. The ten tribes were all degenerated from the true worshiping of God and corrupted with idolatry, as this day are our pestilent papists in all realms and nations; there rested only the tribe of Judah at Jerusalem, where the form of true religion was observed, the law taught, and the ordinances of God outwardly kept. But yet there were in that body, I mean in the body of the visible Church, a great number that were hypocrites, as this day yet are among us that profess the Lord Jesus, and have refused papistry; also not a few that were licentious livers; some that turned their back to God, that is, had forsaken all true religion; and some that lived a most abominable life, as Ezekiel saith in his vision; and yet there were some godly, as a few wheat-corns oppressed and hid among the multitude of chaff: now, according to this diversity, the prophet keeps divers purposes, and yet in most perfect order.

And first, after the first part of the complaint of the afflicted as we have heard, in vehemency of spirit he bursts forth against all the proud enemies of God's people, against all such as trouble them, and against all such as mock and forsake God, and saith, "The dead shall not live, the proud giants shall not rise; Thou hast scattered them, and destroyed their memorial." In which words he contends against the present temptation and dolorous state of God's people, and against the insolent pride of such as oppressed them; as if the prophet should say, O ye troublers of God's people! howsoever it appears to you in this your bloody rage, that God regards not your cruelty, nor considers what violence you do to His poor afflicted, yet shall you be visited, yea, your carcasses shall fall and lie as stinking carrion upon the face of the earth, you shall fall without hope of life, or of a blessed resurrection; yea, howsoever you gather your substance and augment your families, you shall be so scattered that you shall leave no memorial of you to the posterities to come, but that which shall be execrable and odious.

Hereof the tyrants have their admonition, and the afflicted Church inestimable comfort: the tyrants that oppress shall receive the same end which they did who have passed before: that is, they shall die and fall with shame, without hope of resurrection, as is aforesaid. Not that they shall not arise to their own confusion and just condemnation; but that they shall not recover power to trouble the servants of God; neither yet shall the wicked arise, as David saith, in the counsel of the just. Now the wicked have their counsels, their thrones, and finally handle (for the most part) all things that are upon the face of the earth; but the poor servants of God are reputed unworthy of men's presence, envied and mocked; yea, they are more vile before these proud tyrants than is the very dirt and mire which is trodden under foot. But in that glorious resurrection this state shall be changed; for then shall such as now, by their abominable living and cruelty, destroy the earth and molest God's children, see Him whom they have pierced; they shall see the glory of such as now they persecute, to their terror and everlasting confusion. The remembrance hereof ought to make us patient in the days of affliction, and so to comfort us that when we see tyrants in their blind rage tread under foot the saints of God, we despair not utterly, as if there were neither wisdom, justice, nor power above in the heavens to repress such tyrants, and to redress the dolors of the unjustly afflicted. No, brethren, let us be assured that the right hand of the Lord will change the state of things that are most desperate. In our God there is wisdom and power, in a moment to change the joy and mirth of our enemies into everlasting mourning, and our sorrows into joy and gladness that shall have no end.

Therefore, in these apparent calamities (and marvel not that I say *apparent* calamities for he that sees not a fire is begun, that shall burn more than we look for, unless God of His mercy quench it, is more than blind), let us not be discouraged, but with unfeigned repentance let us return to the Lord our God; let us accuse and condemn our former negligence, and steadfastly depend upon his promised deliverance; so shall our temporal sorrows be converted into everlasting joy. The doubt that might be moved concerning the destruction of those whom God exalteth, shall be discussed, if time will suffer, after we have passed throughout the text. The prophet now proceeds and saith, "Thou hast increased the nations, O Lord, Thou hast increased the nations; Thou art made glorious, Thou hast enlarged all the coasts of the earth. Lord, in trouble," etc.

In these words the prophet gives consolation to the afflicted, assuring them that how horrible soever the desolation should be, yet should the seed of Abraham be so multiplied, that it should replenish the coasts of the earth; yea, that God should be more glorified in their affliction than He was during the time of their prosperity. This promise, no doubt, was incredible when it was made; for who could have been persuaded that the destruction of Jerusalem should have been the means whereby the nation of the Jews should have been increased? seeing that much rather it appeared, that the overthrow of Jerusalem should have been the very abolishing of the seed of Abraham: but we must consider, to what end it was that God revealed Himself to Abraham, and what is contained in the promise of the multiplication of his seed, and the benediction promised thereto.

[Instances are here adduced in which God has "notified His name" in the history of the Jews.]

Wherefore, dear brethren, we have no small consolation, if the state of all things be rightly considered. We see in what fury and rage the world, for the most part, is now raised, against the poor Church of Jesus Christ, unto which He has proclaimed liberty, after the fearful bondage of that spiritual Babylon, in which we have been holden captives longer space than Israel was prisoner in Babylon itself: for if we shall consider, upon the one part, the multitude of those that live wholly without Christ; and, upon the other part, the blind rage of the pestilent papists; what shall we think of the small number of them that profess Christ Jesus, but that they are as a poor sheep, already seized in the claws of the lion; yea, that they, and the true religion which they profess, shall in a moment be utterly consumed?

But against this fearful temptation, let us be armed with the promise of God, namely, that He will be the protector of His Church; yea, that He will multiply it, even when to man's judgment it appears utterly to be exterminated. This promise has our God performed, in the multiplication of Abraham's seed, in the preservation of it when Satan labored utterly to have destroyed it, and in deliverance of the same, as we have heard, from Babylon. He hath sent His Son Christ Jesus, clad in our flesh, who hath tasted of all our infirmities (sin excepted), who hath promised to be with us to the end of the world; He hath further kept promise in the publication, yea, in the restitution of His glorious Gospel. Shall we then think that He will leave His Church destitute in this most dangerous age? Only let us cleave to His truth, and study to conform our lives to the same, and He shall multiply His knowledge, and increase His people. But now let us hear what the prophet saith more:

"Lord, in trouble have they visited Thee, they poured out a prayer when Thy chastening was upon them."

The prophet means that such as in the time of quietness did not rightly regard God nor His judgments, were compelled, by sharp corrections, to seek God; yea, by cries and dolorous complaints to visit Him. True it is, that such obedience deserves small praise before men; for who can praise, or accept that in good part, which comes as it were of mere compulsion? And yet it is rare that any of God's children do give unfeigned obedience, until the hand of God turn them. For if quietness and prosperity make them not utterly to forget their duty, both toward God and man, as David for a season, yet it makes them careless, insolent, and in many things unmindful of those things that God chiefly craves of them; which imperfections being espied, and the danger that thereof might ensue, our heavenly Father visits the sins of His children, but with the rod of His mercy, by which they are moved to return to their God, to accuse their former negligence, and to promise better obedience in all times hereafter; as David confessed, saying, "Before I fell in affliction I went astray, but now will I keep Thy statutes."

But yet, for the better understanding of the prophet's mind, we may consider how God doth visit man, and how man doth visit God; and what difference there is betwixt the visitation of God upon the reprobate, and His visitation upon the chosen.

God sometimes visits the reprobate in His hot displeasure, pouring upon them His plagues for their long rebellion; as we have heard before that He visited the proud, and destroyed their memory. At other times God is said to visit His people, being in affliction, to whom He sends comfort or promise of deliverance, as He visited the seed of Abraham, when oppressed in Egypt. And Zacharias said that "God had visited His people, and sent unto them hope of deliverance," when John the Baptist was born. But of none of these visitations our prophet here speaks, but of that only which we have already touched; namely, when God layeth His correction upon His own children, to call them from the venomous breasts of this corrupt world, that they suck not in over great abundance the poison thereof; and He doth, as it were, wean them from their mother's breasts, that they may learn to receive other nourishment. True it is, that this weaning (or speaning, as we term it) from worldly pleasure, is a thing strange to the flesh. And yet it is a thing so necessary to God's children, that, unless they are weaned from the pleasures of the world, they can never feed upon that delectable milk of God's eternal verity; for the corruption of the one either hinders the other from being received, or else so troubles the whole powers of man, that the soul can never so digest the truth of God as he ought to do.

Although this appears hard, yet it is most evident; for what can we receive from the world, but that which is in the world? What that is, the apostle John teaches; saying, "Whatsoever is in the world, is either the lust of the eyes, the lust of the flesh, or the pride of life." Now, seeing that these are not of the Father, but of the world, how can it be, that our souls can feed upon chastity, temperance, and humility, so long as our stomachs are replenished with the corruption of these vices?

Now so it is, that flesh can never willingly refuse these forenamed, but rather still delights itself in every one of them; yea, in them all, as the examples are but too evident.

It behooves, therefore, that God Himself shall violently pull His children from these venomous breasts, that when they lack the liquor and poison of the world, they may visit Him, and learn to be nourished of Him. Oh if the eyes of worldly princes should be opened, that they might see with what humor and liquor their souls are fed, while their whole delight consists in pride, ambition, and the lusts of the corrupt flesh! We understand then how God doth visit men, as well by His severe judgments as by His merciful visitation of deliverance from trouble, or by bringing trouble upon His chosen for their humiliation; and now it remains to understand how man visits God. Man doth visit God when he appears in His presence, be it for the hearing of His word, or for the participation of His sacraments; as the people of Israel, besides the observation of their sabbaths and daily oblations, were commanded thrice a year to present themselves before the presence of the tabernacle; and as we do, and as often as we present ourselves to the hearing of the word. For there is the footstool, yea, there is the face and throne of God Himself, wheresoever the Gospel of Jesus Christ is truly preached, and His sacraments rightly ministered.

But men may on this sort visit God hypocritically; for they may come for the fashion; they may hear with deaf ears; yea, they may understand, and yet never determine with themselves to obey that which God requires: and let such men be assured, that He who searches the secrets of hearts will be avenged of all such; for nothing can be more odious to God, than to mock Him in His own presence. Let every man therefore examine himself, with what mind, and what purpose, he comes to hear the word of God; yea, with what ear he hears it, and what testimony his heart gives unto Him, when God commands virtue, and forbids impiety.

Repinest thou when God requires obedience? Thou hearest to thine own condemnation. Mockest thou at God's threatenings? Thou shalt feel the weight and truth of them, albeit too late, when flesh and blood can not deliver thee from His hand! But the visitation, whereof our prophet speaks, is only proper to the sons of God, who, in the time when God takes from them the pleasures of the world or shows His angry countenance unto them, have recourse unto Him, and confessing their former negligence, with troubled hearts, cry for His mercy. This visitation is not proper to all the afflicted, but appertains only to God's children: for the reprobates can never have access to God's mercy in time of their tribulation, and that because they abuse His long patience, as well as the manifold benefits they receive from His hands; for as the same prophet heretofore saith, "Let the wicked obtain mercy, yet shall he never learn wisdom, but in the land of righteousness"; that is, where the true knowledge of God abounds, "he will do wickedly." Which is a crime above all others abominable; for to what end is it that God erects His throne among us, but that we should fear Him? Why does He reveal His holy will unto us, but that we should obey it? Why does He deliver us from trouble, but that we should be witnesses unto the world, that He is gracious and merciful?

Now, when men, hearing their duty, and knowing what God requires of them, do malapertly fight against all equity and justice, what, I pray you, do they else but make manifest war against God? Yea, when they have received from God such deliverance, that they can not deny but that God Himself hath in His great mercy visited them, and yet they continue wicked as before; what deserve they but effectually to be given over unto a reprobate sense, that they may headlong run to ruin, both of body and soul? It is almost incredible that a man should be so enraged against God, that neither His plagues, nor yet His mercy showed, should move him to repentance; but because the Scriptures bear witness of the one and the other, let us cease to marvel, and let us firmly believe, that such things as have been, are even at present before our eyes, albeit many, blinded by affection, can not see them.

[The case of Ahab is instanced as an illustration.]

"Like as a woman with child, that draweth near her travail, is in sorrow, and crieth in her pains, so have we been in Thy sight, O Lord; we have conceived, we have borne in vain, as though we should have brought forth the wind. Salvations were not made to the earth, neither did the inhabitants of the earth fall."

This is the second part of the prophet's complaint, in which he, in the person of God's people, complains, that of their great affliction there appeared no end. This same similitude is used by our Master Jesus Christ; for when He speaks of the troubles of His Church, He compares them to the pains of a woman travailing in child-birth. But it is to another end; for there He promises exceeding and permanent joy after a sort, though it appear trouble. But here is the trouble long and vehement, albeit the fruit of it was not suddenly espied. He speaks no doubt of that long and dolorous time of their captivity, in which they continually labored for deliverance, but obtained it not before the complete end of seventy years. During which time the earth, that is, the land of Judah, which sometimes was sanctified unto God, but was then given to be profaned by wicked people, got no help, nor perceived any deliverance: for the inhabitants of the world fell not; that is, the tyrants and oppressors of God's people were not taken away, but still remained and continued blasphemers of God, and troublers of His Church. But because I perceive the hours to pass more swiftly than they have seemed at other times, I must contract that which remains of this text into certain points.

The prophet first contends against the present despair; afterward he introduces God Himself calling upon His people; and, last of all, he assures His afflicted that God will come, and require account of all the blood-thirsty tyrants of the earth.

First, Fighting against the present despair, he saith, "Thy dead shall live, even my body (or with my body) shall they arise; awake and sing, ye that dwell in the dust; for thy dew is as the dew of herbs."

The prophet here pierces through all impediments that nature could object; and, by the victory of faith, he overcomes not only the common enemies, but the great and last enemy of all, death itself; for this would he say, Lord, I see nothing for Thy chosen, but misery to follow misery, and one affliction to succeed another; yea, in the end I see that death shall devour Thy dearest children. But yet, O Lord! I see Thy promise to be true, and Thy love to remain toward Thy chosen, even when death appears to have devoured them: "For Thy dead shall live; yea, not only shall they live, but my very dead carcase shall arise"; and so I see honor and glory to succeed this temporal shame; I see permanent joy to come after trouble, order to spring out of this terrible confusion; and, finally, I see that life shall devour death, so that death shall be destroyed, and so Thy servants shall have life. This, I say, is the victory of faith, when to the midst of death, through the light of God's word, the afflicted see life. Hypocrites, in the time of quietness and prosperity, can generally confess that God is true to His promises; but bring them to the extremity, and there the hypocrite ceases further to trust in God, than he seeth natural means, whereby God useth to work. But the true faithful, when all hope of natural means fail, flee to God Himself and to the truth of His promise, who is above nature; yea, whose works are not so subject to the ordinary course of nature, that when nature fails, His power and promise fail also therewith. [The text is here further explained.]

This vision, I say, given to the prophet, and by the prophet preached to the people, when they thought that God had utterly forgotten them, compelled them more diligently to advert to what the former prophets had spoken. It is no doubt but that they carried with them both the prophecy of Isaiah and Jeremiah, so that the prophet Ezekiel is a commentary to these words of Isaiah, where he saith, "Thy dead, O Lord, shall live, with my body they shall arise." The prophet brings in this similitude of the dew, to answer unto that part of their fidelity, who can believe no further of God's promises than they are able to apprehend by natural judgment; as if he would say, Think ye this impossible that God should give life unto you, and bring you to an estate of a commonwealth again, after that ye are dead, and, as it were, razed from the face of the earth? But why do you not consider what God worketh from year to year in the order of nature? Sometimes you see the face of the earth decked and beautified with herbs, flowers, grass, and fruits: again you see the same utterly taken away by storms and the vehemence of the winter: what does God to replenish the earth again, and to restore the beauty thereof? He sends down his small and soft dew, the drops whereof, in their descending, are neither great nor visible, and yet thereby are the pores and secret veins of the earth, which before, by vehemence of frost and cold were shut up, opened again, and so does the earth produce again the like herbs, flowers and fruits. Shall you then think that the dew of God's heavenly grace will not be as effectual in you, to whom He hath made His promise, as it is in the herbs and fruits which, from year to year bud forth and decay? If you do so, the prophet would say your incredibility is inexcusable; because you neither rightly weigh the power nor the promises of your God.

The like similitude the Apostle Paul uses against such as called the resurrection in doubt, because by natural judgment they could not apprehend that flesh once putrified, and dissolved as it were into other substances, should rise again, and return again to the same substance and nature: "O fool," saith he, "that which thou sowest is not quickened, except it die; and that which thou sowest, thou sowest not that body that shall be, but bare corn, as it falleth, of wheat, or some other, but God giveth it a body as it pleaseth Him, even to every seed His own body." In which words and sentence the Apostle sharply rebukes the gross ignorance of the Corinthians, who began to call in doubt the chief article of our faith, the resurrection of the flesh after it was once dissolved, because that natural judgment, as he said, reclaimed thereto. He reproves, I say, their gross ignorance, because they might have seen and considered some proof and document thereof in the very order of nature; for albeit the wheat or other corn, cast in the earth, appears to die or putrify, and so to be lost, yet we see that it is not perished, but that it fructifies according to God's will and ordinance.

Now, if the power of God be so manifest in raising up of the fruits of the earth, unto which no particular promise is made by God, what shall be His power and virtue in raising up our bodies, seeing that thereto He is bound by the solemn promise of Jesus Christ, His Eternal Wisdom, and the Verity itself that can not lie? Yea, seeing that the members must once communicate with the glory of the Head, how shall our bodies, which are flesh of His flesh, and bone of His bones, lie still forever in corruption, seeing that our Head, Jesus Christ, is now exalted in His glory? Neither yet is this power and good-will of God to be restrained unto the last and general resurrection only, but we ought to consider it in the marvelous preservation of His Church, and in the raising up of the same from the very bottom of death, when by tyrants it has been oppressed from age to age.

Now, of the former words of the prophet, we have to gather this comfort; that if at any time we see the face of the Church within this realm so defaced, as I think it shall be sooner than we look for—when we shall see, I say, virtue to be despised, vice to be maintained, the verity of God to be impugned, lies and men's inventions holden in authority—and finally, when we see the true religion of our God, and the zealous observers of the same, trodden under the feet of such as in their heart say, that "There is no God," let us then call to mind what have been the wondrous works of our God from the beginning—that it is His proper office to bring light out of darkness, order out of confusion, life out of death; and finally, that this is He that calleth things that are not even as if they were, as before we have heard. And if in the day of our temptation, which in my judgment approaches fast, we are thus armed, if our incredulity can not utterly be removed, yet shall it be so corrected, that damnable despair oppress us not. But now let us hear how the prophet proceeds: —

"Come, thou My people, enter within thy chamber, shut thy door after thee, hide thyself a very little while, until the indignation pass over."

Here the prophet brings in God amiably, calling upon His people to come to Himself, and to rest with Him, until such time as the fury and sharp plagues should be executed upon the wicked and disobedient. It may appear at the first sight, that all these words of the prophet, in the person of God, calling the people unto rest, are spoken in vain; for we neither find chambers nor rest, more prepared for the dearest children of God, so far as man's judgment can discern, than for the rebellious and disobedient; for such as fell not by the edge of the sword, or died not of pestilence, or by hunger, were either carried captives unto Babylon, or else departed afterward into Egypt, so that none of Abraham's seed had either chamber or quiet place to remain in within the land of Canaan. For the resolution hereof, we must understand, That albeit the chambers whereunto God has called His chosen be not visible, yet notwithstanding they are certain, and offer unto God's children a quiet habitation in spirit, howsoever the flesh be travailed and tormented.

The chambers, then, are God's sure promises, unto which God's people are commanded to resort; yea, within which they are commanded to close themselves in the time of greatest adversity. The manner of speaking is borrowed from that judgment and foresight which God has printed in this our nature; for when men espy great tempests appearing to come, they will not willingly remain uncovered in the fields, but straightway they will draw them to their houses or holds, that they may escape the vehemence of the same; and if they fear any enemy pursues them, they will shut their doors, to the end that the enemy should not suddenly have entry.

After this manner God speaks to His people; as if He should say, The tempest that shall come upon this whole nation shall be so terrible, that nothing but extermination shall appear to come upon the whole body. But thou My people, that hearest My word, believest the same, and tremblest at the threatenings of My prophets, now, when the world does insolently resist—let such, I say, enter within the secret chamber of My promises, let them contain themselves quietly there; yea, let them shut the door upon them, and suffer not infidelity, the mortal enemy of My truth and of My people that depend thereupon, to have free entry to trouble them, yea, further to murder, in My promise; and so shall they perceive that My indignation shall pass, and that such as depend upon Me shall be saved.

Thus we may perceive the meaning of the prophet; whereof we have first to observe that God acknowledges them for His people who are in the greatest affliction; yea, such as are reputed unworthy of men's presence are yet admitted within the secret chamber of God. Let no man think that flesh and blood can suddenly attain to that comfort; and therefore most expedient it is, that we be frequently exercised in meditation of the same. Easy it is, I grant, in time of prosperity, to say and to think that God is our God, and that we are His people; but when He has given us over into the hands of our enemies, and turned, as it were, His back unto us, then, I say, still to reclaim Him to be our God, and to have this assurance, that we are His people, proceeds wholly from the Holy Spirit of God, as it is the greatest victory of faith, which overcomes the world; for increase whereof we ought continually to pray.

This doctrine we shall not think strange, if we consider how suddenly our spirits are carried away from our God, and from believing His promise. So soon as any great temptation apprehends us, then we begin to doubt if ever we believed God's promises, if God will fulfill them to us, if we abide in His favor, if He regards and looks upon the violence and injury that is done unto us; and a multitude of such cogitations which before lurked quietly in our corrupted hearts, burst violently forth when we are oppressed with any desperate calamity. Against which this is the remedy—once to apprehend, and still to retain God to be our God, and firmly to believe, that we are His people whom He loves, and will defend, not only in affliction, but even in the midst of death itself.

Again, Let us observe, That the judgments of our God never were, nor yet shall be so vehement upon the face of the earth, but that there has been, and shall be, some secret habitation prepared in the sanctuary of God, for some of His chosen, where they shall be preserved until the indignation pass by; and that God prepares a time, that they may glorify Him again, before the face of the world, which once despised them. And this ought to be unto us no small comfort in these appearing dangers, namely, that we are surely persuaded, that how vehement soever the tempest shall be it yet shall pass over, and some of us shall be preserved to glorify the name of our God, as is aforesaid.

Two vices lurk in this our nature: the one is, that we can not tremble at God's threatenings, before the plagues apprehend us, albeit we see cause most just why His fierce wrath should burn as a devouring fire; the other is, that when calamities before pronounced, fall upon us, then we begin to sink down in despair, so that we never look for any comfortable end of the same.

To correct this our mortal infirmity, in time of quietness we ought to consider what is the justice of our God, and how odious sin is; and, above all, how odious idolatry is in His presence, who has forbidden it, and who has so severely punished it in all ages from the beginning: and in the time of our affliction we ought to consider, what have been the wondrous works of our God, in the preservation of His Church when it hath been in uttermost extremity. For never shall we find the Church humbled under the hands of traitors, and cruelly tormented by them, but we shall find God's just vengeance full upon the cruel persecutors, and His merciful deliverance showed to the afflicted. And, in talking of this trial, we should not only call to mind the histories of ancient times, but also we should diligently mark what notable works God hath wrought, even in this our age, as well upon the one as upon the other. We ought not to think that our God bears less love to His Church this day, than what He has done from the beginning; for as our God in His own nature is immutable, so His love toward His elect remains always unchangeable. For as in Christ Jesus He hath chosen His Church, before the beginning of all ages; so by Him will He maintain and preserve the same unto the end. Yea, He will quiet the storms and cause the earth to open her mouth, and receive the raging floods of violent waters, cast out by the dragon, to drown and carry away the woman, which is the spouse of Jesus Christ, unto whom God for His own name's sake will be the perpetual Protector.

This saw that notable servant of Jesus Christ, Athanasius, who being exiled from Alexandria by that blasphemous, apostate, Julian the emperor, said unto his flock, who bitterly wept for his envious banishment, "Weep not, but be of good comfort, for this little cloud will suddenly vanish." He called both the emperor himself and his cruel tyranny a little cloud; and albeit there was small appearance of any deliverance to the Church of God, or of any punishment to have apprehended the proud tyrants, when the man of God pronounced these words, yet shortly after God did give witness that those words did not proceed from flesh nor blood, but from God's very Spirit. For not long after, being in warfare, Julian received a deadly wound, whether by his own hand, or by one of his own soldiers, the writers clearly conclude not; but casting his own blood against the heaven, he said, "At last Thou hast overcome, thou Galilean": so in despite he termed the Lord Jesus. And so perished that tyrant in his own iniquity; the storm ceased, and the Church of God received new comfort.

Such shall be the end of all cruel persecutors, their reign shall be short, their end miserable, and their name shall be left in execrations to God's people; and yet shall the Church of God remain to God's glory, after all storms. But now shortly, let us come to the last point:

"For behold," saith the prophet, "the Lord will come out of His place, to visit the iniquity of the inhabitants of the earth upon them; and the earth shall disclose her blood, and shall no more hide her slain." Because that the final end of the troubles of God's chosen shall not be, before the Lord Jesus shall return to restore all things to their full perfection.

The prophet brings forth the eternal God, as it were, from his own place and habitation, and therewith shows the cause of His coming to be, that He might take account of all such as have wrought wickedly; for that he means, where he saith, "He will visit the iniquity of the inhabitants of the earth upon them." And lest any should think the wrong doers are so many, that they can not be called to an account, he gives unto the earth as it were an office and charge, to bear witness against all those that have wrought wickedly, and chiefly against those that have shed innocent blood from the beginning; and saith, "That the earth shall disclose her blood, and shall no more hide her slain men."

If tyrants of the earth, and such as delight in the shedding of blood, should be persuaded that this sentence is true, they would not so furiously come to their own destruction; for what man can be so enraged that he would willingly do, even before the eyes of God, that which might provoke His Majesty to anger, yea, provoke Him to become his enemy forever, if he understood how fearful a thing it is to fall into the hands of the living God?

The cause, then, of this blind fury of the world is the ignorance of God, and that men think that God is but an idol; and that there is no knowledge above that beholds their tyranny; nor yet justice that will, nor power that can, repress their impiety. But the Spirit of truth witnesses the contrary, affirming, that as the eyes of the Lord are upon the just, and as His ears are ready to receive their sobbing and prayers, so is His visage angry against such as work iniquity; He hateth and holdeth in abomination every deceitful and blood-thirsty man, whereof He has given sufficient document from age to age, in preserving the one, or at least in avenging their cause, and in punishing the other.

Where it is said, "That the Lord will come from His place, and that He will visit the iniquity of the inhabitants of the earth upon them, and that the earth shall disclose her blood"; we have to consider, what most commonly has been, and what shall be, the condition of the Church of God, namely, that it is not only hated, mocked, and despised, but that it is exposed as a prey unto the fury of the wicked; so that the blood of the children of God is spilled like unto water upon the face of the earth.

The understanding whereof, albeit it is unpleasant to the flesh, yet to us it is most profitable, lest that we, seeing the cruel treatment of God's servants, begin to forsake the spouse of Jesus Christ, because she is not to be dealt with in this unthankful world, as the just and upright dealings of God's children do deserve. But contrariwise, for mercy they receive cruelty, for doing good to many, of all the reprobate they receive evil; and this is decreed in God's eternal counsel, that the members may follow the trace of the Head; to the end that God in His just judgment should finally condemn the wicked. For how should He punish the inhabitants of the earth, if their iniquity deserved it not? How should the earth disclose our blood, if it should not be unjustly spilled? We must then commit ourselves into the hands of our God, and lay down our necks; yea, and patiently suffer our blood to be shed, that the righteous Judge may require account, as most assuredly He will, of all the blood that hath been shed, from the blood of Abel the just, till the day that the earth shall disclose the same. I say, every one that sheds, or consents to shed the blood of God's children, shall be guilty of the whole; so that all the blood of God's children shall cry vengeance, not only in general, but also in particular, upon every one that has shed the blood of any that unjustly suffered.

And if any think it strange that such as live this day can be guilty of the blood that was shed in the days of the Apostles, let them consider that the Verity itself pronounced, That all the blood that was shed from the days of Abel, unto the days of Zacharias, should come upon the unthankful generation that heard His doctrine and refused it.

The reason is evident; for as there are two heads and captains that rule over the whole world, namely, Jesus Christ, the Prince of justice and peace, and Satan, called the prince of the world; so there are but two armies that have continued battle from the beginning, and shall fight unto the end. The quarrel which the army of Jesus Christ sustains, and which the reprobate persecute, is the same, namely, The eternal truth of the eternal God, and the image of Jesus Christ printed in his elect — so that whosoever, in any age, persecutes any one member of Jesus Christ for his truth's sake, subscribes, as it were with his hand, to the persecution of all that have passed before him.

And this ought the tyrants of this age deeply to consider; for they shall be guilty, not only of the blood shed by themselves, but of all, as is said, that has been shed for the cause of Jesus Christ from the beginning of the world.

Let the faithful not be discouraged, although they be appointed as sheep to the slaughter-house; for He, for whose sake they suffer, shall not forget to avenge their cause. I am not ignorant that flesh and blood will think that kind of support too late; for we had rather be preserved still alive, than have our blood avenged after our death.

And truly, if our felicity stood in this life, or if temporal death should bring unto us any damage, our desire in that behalf were not to be disallowed or condemned: but seeing that death is common to all, and that this temporal life is nothing but misery, and that death fully joins us with our God, and gives unto us the possession of our inheritance, why should we think it strange to leave this world, and go to our Head and sovereign Captain, Jesus Christ?

Lastly, We have to observe this manner of speaking, where the prophet saith that "the earth shall disclose her blood": in which words the prophet would accuse the cruelty of those that dare so unmercifully and violently force, from the breasts of the earth, the dearest children of God, and cruelly cut their throats in her bosom, who is by God appointed the common mother of mankind, so that she unwillingly is compelled to open her mouth and receive their blood.

If such tyranny were used against any woman, as violently to pull her infant from her breasts, cut the throat of it in her own bosom, and compel her to receive the blood of her dear child in her own mouth, all nations would hold the act so abominable that the like had never been done in the course of nature. No less wickedness commit they that shed the blood of God's children upon the face of their common mother, the earth, as I said before. But be of good courage, O little and despised flock of Christ Jesus! for He that seeth your grief, hath power to revenge it; He will not suffer one tear of yours to fall, but it shall be kept and reserved in His bottle, till the fullness thereof be poured down from heaven, upon those that caused you to weep and mourn. This your merciful God, I say, will not suffer your blood forever to be covered with the earth; nay, the flaming fires that have licked up the blood of any of our brethren; the earth that has been defiled with it, I say, with the blood of God's children (for otherwise, to shed the blood of the cruel bloodshedders, is to purge the land from blood, and as it were to sanctify it), the earth, I say, shall purge herself of it, and show it before the face of God. Yea, the beasts, fowls, and other creatures whatsoever, shall be compelled to render that which they have received, be it flesh, blood, or bones, that appertained to Thy children, O Lord! which altogether Thou shalt glorify, according to Thy promise, made to us in our Lord and Saviour Jesus Christ, Thy well-beloved Son; to whom, with Thee, and the Holy Ghost, be honor, praise, and glory forever and ever. Amen.

Let us now humble ourselves in the presence of our God, and from the bottom of our hearts let us desire Him to assist us with the power of His Holy Spirit; that albeit, for our former negligence, God gives us over into the hands of others than such as rule in His fear; that yet He let us not forget His mercy, and the glorious name that hath been proclaimed among us; but that we may look through the dolorous storm of His present displeasure, and see as well what punishment He has appointed for the cruel tyrants, as what reward He has laid in store for such as continue in His fear to the end. That it would further please Him to assist, that albeit we see His Church so diminished, that it appears to be brought, as it were, to utter extermination, we may be assured that in our God there is great power and will, to increase the number of His chosen, until they are enlarged to the uttermost parts of the earth. Give us, O Lord! hearts to visit Thee in time of affliction; and albeit we see no end of our dolors, yet our faith and hope may conduct us to the assured hope of that joyful resurrection, in which we shall possess the fruit of that for which we now labor. In the mean time, grant unto us, O Lord! to repose ourselves in the sanctuary of Thy promise, that in Thee we may find comfort, till this Thy great indignation, begun among us, may pass over, and Thou Thyself appear to the comfort of Thine afflicted, and to the terror of Thine and our enemies.

Let us pray with heart and mouth,

Almighty God, and merciful ·Father, etc. Lord, unto Thy hands I commend my spirit; for the terrible roaring of guns,[1] and the noise of armor, do so pierce my heart, that my soul thirsteth to depart.

For ADDITIONAL INFORMATION ABOUT JOHN KNOX:

Howard, Harry Clay. "John Knox." *Princes of the Christian Pulpit and Pastorate.* Nashville: Cokesbury Press, 1927.

Laing, David, ed. *The Works of John Knox.* Vols. 1–5, Edinburgh: Johnstone and Hunter; vol. 6, Edinburgh: Thomas George Stevenson, 1914.

Lang, Andrew. *John Knox and the Reformation.* Port Washington, N.Y.: Kennikat Press, 1967.

McEwen, James S. *The Faith of John Knox.* Richmond: John Knox Press, 1961.

MacGregor, Geddes. *The Thundering Scot, a Portrait of John Knox.* Philadelphia: WestminsterPress, 1957.

Ridley, Jasper G. *John Knox.* New York: Oxford University Press, 1968.

Walker, Williston. "John Knox." *Great Men of the Christian Church.* Chicago: University of Chicago Press, 1908.

Whitley, Elizabeth. *Plain Mr. Knox.* Richmond: John Knox Press, 1960.

---

1. The Castle of Edinburgh was shooting against the exiled for Christ Jesus' sake.

RICHARD BAXTER

1615-1691

RICHARD BAXTER, National Portrait Gallery, London.

RICHARD BAXTER

1615	*Born November 12 at Rowton, near Shrewsbury, Shropshire, England*
1630	*Converted*
1634	*Decided to enter ministry*
1637	*Ordained in Worcester Cathedral*
1640	*Became pastor at Kidderminster*
1646	*Returned to Kidderminster after serving as chaplain in Cromwell's army*
1660	*Denied pastorate*
1662	*Deprived of place in church by Act of Uniformity*
1685	*Brought to trial and imprisoned*
1691	*Died December 8 in London*

NEVER IN THE HISTORY of England were times more chaotic than during the lifetime of Richard Baxter. Yet in spite of war, division, persecution, and ill health, Baxter became one of history's most memorable preachers. His biographer said of him, "Of all the admirable preachers who have influenced the religious life of the English people, Baxter unquestionably has the pre-eminence."[1]

LIFE AND TIMES

During Baxter's lifetime (from 1615 to 1691), the religious and political life of England fragmented into scores of warring camps. In 1603 James Stewart—James VI of Scotland and James I of England—ascended the English throne. James, a devout believer in the divine right of kings, committed himself to the establishment of an absolute government. One of his

---

1. Albert H. Currier, *Nine Great Preachers* (Boston: The Pilgrim Press, 1912), p. 125.

first acts was to announce a policy of opposition to Puritanism—
that movement within the Church of England that was devoted
to eradicating from the church the remains of Catholic ritual
and practice. The Church of England then was composed of
two highly different groups: high church Anglicans, who
leaned toward formality and ritual; and the Puritans, who
craved a simpler service.

James' opposition to the Puritans was based on several facts
and fears. James feared that the Puritans wanted to adopt a
democratic form of church government like that in Scotland.
He believed that absolute government was impossible apart
from a state church ruled from the top through bishops; he
shouted to the Puritan clergy, "No bishop, no king." Furthermore, the Puritans were disturbing the tranquility of the church
and thereby the peace of the land. By his opposition to them,
James won the bitter enmity of the Puritan faction in England.
Meanwhile, he managed to alienate the Catholics also; he had
both ends of the religious spectrum turned against him. Next
he alienated Parliament: he lectured the members of Parliament on the divine right of kings, and they retaliated by stating
the power of Parliament in a way he could understand. Parliament controlled the purse strings in England and James lived
beyond his means. When he attempted to gain more money,
Parliament refused to increase taxes. Again and again the king
dismissed Parliament, recalled a new one, found his efforts
blocked, and repeated the process all over again. When he died,
he left a discredited monarchy to his son, Charles I.

Charles almost immediately ran into conflict with the Parliament, and so from 1629 to 1640 he attempted to rule without
Parliament. Meanwhile, he alienated the common people by
throwing his support to high church Anglicans, who promptly
attempted to smother Puritanism. He angered the wealthier
members of society by imposing upon them higher and higher
taxes.

In 1637 Charles made a fatal mistake: he determined to extend Anglican service to Scotland. His English subjects had
been reluctant to rebel, but the Scots knew no such reluctance
and met Charles' efforts with armed force. Because Charles
had little financial resources—only Parliament could have
raised taxes, and he refused to call a Parliament—he had an
inadequate army. The Scots beat back the English army and
demanded a large indemnity as the price of withdrawal from

English land. Charles was forced to call a Parliament into session to raise money to pay the indemnity.

Through law and execution the Parliament destroyed absolutism in England forever in the years 1640 to 1646. When Parliament met in 1640, almost to a man the members were determined to curb the absolute powers of Charles I. Some members of Parliament wanted to go even further; they intended to transfer the powers of the king to Parliament. But they were divided over how far Parliament should go in taking power to itself. The issue was divided along both religious and political grounds: on one side were the Puritans and Parliamentarians; on the other side were the moderate Anglicans and the Royalists.

In 1642 this tension erupted in civil war. Charles made an attempt to arrest those members of Parliament who were the recognized leaders of opposition to him. In self-defense the House of Commons raised an army, whereupon the king fled to Oxford and took with him the Royalist minority in the Commons and a majority of the House of Lords.

From 1642 until 1646 civil war raged in England. The leader of the king's opposition was Oliver Cromwell, who gathered a well-armed and thoroughly disciplined group of men. He subjected them to military and moral requirements which were harsh but effective. Cromwell's men finally defeated the forces of the king, and Charles surrendered in 1646.

The victorious forces faced a decision as to what to do next: some wanted to continue as a limited monarchy, with Charles as monarch; others did not trust him. Succeeding events led the revolution to more and more radical measures. Finally, to the shock of the world and most of England, Charles was executed.

Cromwell took control of the government as the lord protector and ruled with the backing of the army. Evidence indicates that this is not what Cromwell wanted and certainly not what most of the people wanted, but it seemed to Cromwell the best means to prevent the nation from falling into further war. Under Cromwell the nation pulled itself together and regained both its prosperity and its prestige.

After Cromwell's death, the English turned again to a monarch. They restored the monarchy to Charles II after providing guarantees that the powers of Parliament would be recognized as fixed by the Act of 1640–41. In 1660 the new king took the throne.

The Anglican church, suppressed under Cromwell, regained power. The austere rule of Cromwell and the Puritans made the English hungry for merrier times, and a severe reaction against Puritanism broke out. For a time dissenters were persecuted, but generally peaceful conditions prevailed.

Charles II was a popular ruler at first: he was charming and witty, and he brought a glitter to the English court. But Charles immediately began to plot to gain absolute rule once again for English monarchs. By bribery and by almost every other possible means, he manipulated for more and more power. He played the various parties and factions in England against one another in order to divide the people so that he could gain absolute power.

Charles became particularly unpopular with the dissenting faction within the church because of various acts passed under his rule. The Cooperation Act of 1661 prevented anyone who was not an Anglican from sharing in municipal government. The Act of Conformity in 1662 resulted in the expulsion of 2,000 Puritan clergymen from the Church of England because they refused to assent to the prescribed prayer book. By 1664 those who persisted in attending nonconformist services were subject to imprisonment. In 1670, by secret treaty with Louis XIV in France, Charles II promised to restore Catholicism to England in return for a huge financial subsidy.

The dissenters agitated for assurance of protection from Catholicism. Fear of a Roman Catholic takeover resulted in the death of many innocent Catholics. Two main parties began to take shape: one was nicknamed the Tories, the other the Whigs. The Tories were supporters of the king and of the Anglican church. The Whigs argued for a constitutional monarchy with a Protestant king and toleration for dissenters. Charles managed to balance the two factions carefully enough to avoid war; he also managed to rule without Parliament.

The death of Charles in 1685 brought to the throne James II, a Roman Catholic, who moved immediately to improve the place of Catholics in England. In 1687 he issued a Declaration of Indulgence which provided for the free exercise of religion to every person regardless of his faith. The high church Tories objected, and even the dissenters objected because they feared Catholics as much as they craved the freedom to worship. By 1688 the policies of James II had united both Whig and Tory against him. Both parties sent a message to William of Orange in Holland to come and take the throne. William agreed, landed on November 5, 1688, and found that the English welcomed him as a deliverer. James II was allowed to escape to France.

Under William, great strides were taken toward religious freedom and the settling of disputes between factions within England. The Toleration Act of 1689 did not establish total religious freedom; it granted freedom of worship to everyone *except* Unitarians and Roman Catholics. The Church of England remained the state church. But harsh persecution, imprisonment, and violence on religious issues ceased.

Richard Baxter lived during all of this turmoil. His life spanned the reigns of James I, Charles I, Oliver Cromwell, Charles II, James II, and the coming of William of Orange. Baxter was born November 12, 1615 at Rowton, near Shrewsbury, Shropshire, England. His parents were pious, middle-class people who gave him careful religious training. He experienced a religious conversion during his fifteenth year and decided to enter the ministry when he was nineteen.

Baxter received no university training – he was self-educated. He read widely in all fields and was better educated than many who went through the formal disciplines of academic life. When he was in his twenty-third year he was ordained in Worcester Cathedral. After two years of preaching in various places without holding a settled pastorate, he went to Kidderminster in 1640 as pastor.

When civil war broke out between the king and Parliament, Baxter was suspected of sympathizing with the Puritan party. Actually he seems to have been a believer in monarchy and originally was loyal to the king. Yet he was publicly denounced as a traitor in Kidderminster, and his friends urged him to leave town. He took refuge in Coventry where he ministered to the people and to the soldiers. Ultimately Baxter became a chaplain in the Parliamentary Army and was involved in a number of battles in which he displayed extraordinary courage.

In the midst of the troops he was always alert for anything he considered to be heresy; yet he never attempted to counter heresy with force, but rather with words. He also expressed his opposition to Cromwell: he insisted that Cromwell was wrong in taking the monarchy away from England, and Cromwell heard him tolerantly.

A serious illness, coupled with his disgust for many of Cromwell's actions, led him to leave the army and return to Kidderminster where he was welcomed by the people. The end of the war brought some relief to the tension between conflicting parties and Baxter enjoyed a fruitful ministry.

In addition to his preaching, visiting, and conferences, he developed other approaches to ministry and evangelism. He utilized laymen extensively in his ministry. He believed that laymen should visit those around them and share the Christian faith with them. He began prayer meetings throughout the area and used these prayer meetings for evangelism. The results of his efforts were impressive. Baxter says:

> When I first came there, there was about one family in a street that worshipped God; when I came away there were some streets where there was not one family that did not so, and that did not by professing serious godliness give any hopes of their sincerity.[2]

Baxter worked hard at writing; scores of volumes resulted from his efforts. Some of these survive as classic readings in Christian literature. His published works numbered more than 170 volumes before the end of his life. Many of these were highly controversial; others were devotional.

Things went well in Kidderminster until 1660 when Charles II took the English throne. Immediately the high Anglicans exerted their power and dissenters were expelled from pulpits. Because of his views, Baxter was denied his pastorate at Kidderminster. Two years later, under the Act of Uniformity, he was expelled from the Church of England. Baxter urged the church to adopt religious liberty; he pled for the right of dissenters to hold church positions and to preach. But he was refused the right to speak. Nevertheless, he continued to express his views through writing. In the midst of the loss of his pastorate, he found some comfort in marriage. Earlier in his ministry he had been harsh in his criticism of others. Age brought a mellowing to his personality, and he became less cutting and more effective.

In 1685 he was brought to trial for sedition; the trial was a mockery. When Baxter attempted to defend himself, the judge silenced him and reprimanded him: "Richard, Richard, dost thou think we'll hear thee poison the court? Richard, thou art an old fellow, an old knave; thou hast written books enough to

---

2. Ibid., pp. 128-29.

load a cart, every one as full of sedition – I might say treason –
as an egg is full of meat."[3] Baxter was convicted of sedition
and sentenced to a heavy fine, and imprisonment until the fine
was paid. He spent two years in prison before the fine was
remitted by the king.

After his release Baxter lived in London, preached occasionally, and continued to write. His last few years were lived in the
peace and religious toleration brought by the reign of William of
Orange. He lived to see what he had long advocated – that different religious groups could live together in reasonable peace
and harmony.

In London, on December 8, 1691, he died. He had been a
man ahead of his times. In his concept of ministry, in his insights on personal evangelism, in his utilization of the laity, in
his concepts of religious liberty and toleration, Baxter was by
no means a man of his age. He displayed courage in the face of
king and protector, bravery in battle, compassion for his flock,
and brilliance in his writing. He wrote some of the most soothing and comforting devotional literature in the English language, yet lived a life of stormy controversy. A study in contrasts
and convictions, the life of Richard Baxter was eloquent testimony to the power of God.

PREACHING AND SERMONS

Baxter was one of the first preachers to emphasize an oral
style in preaching – a *talking* style – though he usually read his
sermons. Many of the passages in his published works, such as
"The Call to the Unconverted," are transcripts of those sermons
which preserve for us his characteristic style. These sermons
give evidence of a natural, conversational manner of delivery.
Baxter believed in using only the plainest words:

> The plainest words are the most profitable oratory in
> the weightiest matters. Fineness is for ornament and
> delicacy for delight, but they answer not necessity. Yea,
> it is hard for the hearer to observe the matter of orna-
> ment and delicacy, and not be carried from the matter
> of necessity; for it usually hinders the due operation of
> the matter, keeps it from the heart, stops it in the fancy
> and makes it seem light as the style. . . .
> All our teaching must be as plain and evident as we

---

3. Ibid., p. 160.

can make it. If you would not teach men, what are you doing in the pulpit? If you would, why do you not speak so as to be understood?[4]

Baxter strove for plainness and achieved eloquence. Even his printed sermons give evidence of the eloquence which attracted and impressed all classes of men, educated and uneducated, rich and poor. Baxter said of his success:

My pulpit preaching met with an attentive, diligent hearing. The congregation was usually full so that we were forced to build five galleries after my coming; the church being the most commodious that ever I was in.[5]

Nor was his success limited to the confines of the church walls: the whole community of Kidderminster felt the effect of his fervent preaching, and soon a different atmosphere marked the town. Baxter wrote, "On the Lord's Days there was no disorder to be seen in the streets, but you might hear a hundred families singing songs and repeating sermons as you passed them."

Baxter's preaching was characterized from the beginning by evangelistic earnestness; neither Whitefield nor Wesley surpassed Baxter in this quality. It was his chief distinction as a preacher and affected all of his methods. McBates said of him, "It was Baxter's meat and drink, the life and joy of his life, to do good for souls." Nothing else occupied the thinking of Baxter as much as the importance of the soul's salvation and the adequacy of the gospel in effecting conversion; he thought that "if men only heard this as they ought, they could scarcely be able to withstand it."

There is not much doubt of his "convincing force." He had all the fervor and intensity of Whitefield but excelled him in logical thought. Baxter was possessed with "a familiar moving voice"—his own term for it—marked by "the accent of conviction." His personal appearance in the pulpit complemented his voice. Baxter had an unmistakable sincerity and earnestness about him, and his delicate health that often brought him near to death added a profound note to his words. He said in a famous phrase that "he preached as a dying man to dying men." He

4. Ibid., p. 118.
5. Ibid., p. 119.

regarded himself as "a man who was betwixt living and dead."

Whatever feebleness there was in his body did not appear in his speaking; in fact, he gave the impression that he could preach forever without fatigue. He spoke with zeal and animated gestures. Archdeacon Trench said that he was marked "by a robust and masculine eloquence."

Baxter took great care in the preparation and delivery of his sermons. He made a careful study of the art of preaching and gave detailed attention to the construction of his sermons:

> In the study of our sermons we are too negligent. We must study how to convince, and *get within men*, and how to bring each truth to the quick, and not leave all this to our extemporary promptitude. . . . How few ministers preach with all their might! There is nothing more unsuitable to such a business than to be slight and dull. What! Speak boldly for God and for men's salvation! Let the people see that you are in earnest. Men will not cast away their dearest pleasures upon a drowsy request.
>
> A great matter lies in the very pronunciation and tone of speech. The best matter will scarcely move men if it be not movingly delivered. See that there be no affectation, but let us speak as familiarly to our people as we would do if we were talking to any of them personally. We must lay siege to the souls of sinners. In preaching there is intended a communion of souls and the communication from ours unto theirs. I have observed that God seldom blesses any man's works so much as his whose heart is set upon success.[6]

Even recent works on homiletics have not improved upon that definition of the preacher's task. Baxter clearly understood the need for careful preparation of a sermon suited to the needs of his hearers; more important, he was one of the first in Christian history to define conversational preaching: "Let us speak as familiarly to our people as we would do if we were talking to any of them personally."

In the midst of the long ages of superficial elegance that followed him, Baxter stands as a monument to that true preaching of the gospel which seeks nothing more than communication of the truth to the needs of men.

---

6. Harry C. Howard, *Princes of the Christian Pulpit and Pastorate* (Nashville: Cokesbury Press, 1928), p. 111.

These gifts would have been enough for success, but to them must be added one other quality: flexibility of thought. Baxter was forever changing in his thinking. He refused to become the slave of the thoughts of yesterday and maintained an eagerness for learning to the end of his life. He wrote:

> Formerly I knew much less than now, and yet was not half so much acquainted with my ignorance. I had a great delight in the daily new discoveries which I made in the light which shined upon me, like a man that cometh into a country where he never was before; but I little knew either how imperfectly I understood those very points whose discovery so much delighted me, or how many things I was yet a stranger to. . . . I have, therefore, far meaner thoughts of my own understanding though I know that it is better finished than it was then.[7]

In another place Baxter revealed his changing thoughts about men:

> And now I see that good men are not so good as I once thought they were . . . that nearer approach and fuller trial make the best appear more weak and faulty than their admirers at a distance think; and I find that few were so bad as either malicious enemies or sensorious professors do imagine. In some, indeed, I find that human nature is corrupted into a greater likeness to devils than I once thought; but even in the wicked, usually, there is more for grace to take advantage of than I once believed.[8]

Early in his ministry Baxter was given to sharp and cutting argument and lived to regret many of the things that he said:

> I cannot forgive myself for rash words or deeds by which I have seemed less tender and kind than I should have been to my near and dear relations. When such are dead, every sour or cross provoking word which I gave them may get me almost unreconcilable with myself; and tells me how repentance brought some of old in the hurry of their passion to pray to the dead whom they had wronged to forgive them.[9]

---

7. Currier, p. 151.
8. Ibid.
9. Ibid., p. 148.

This remark was no doubt prompted because of Baxter's famous controversy with Edward Bagshaw, a former friend who had taken offense at a book he had published; Baxter and Bagshaw then exchanged a series of particularly bitter and foolish articles against one another. Baxter said of his last reply: "About the day that it came out, Mr. Bagshaw died a prisoner, which made it grievous to me to think that I must seem to write against the dead to the world that will decide all our controversies. . . ."

After that bitter controversy, Baxter was a changed man; for the remainder of his life he was marked by kindness and sympathetic understanding in his preaching and writing. He wrote:

> I have perceived that nothing so much hinders the reception of the truth as urging it on men with too harsh importunity and falling too heavily on their errors; for hereby you engage their honor in the business and they defend their errors as themselves, and stir up all their wit and ability to oppose you. In a learning way men are ready to receive the truth, but in a disputing way, they come armed against it with prejudice and animosity.[10]

Perhaps the summation of Baxter's life can best be stated in these words he discovered in a Latin treatise of Rupertus Meldenius, obscure German writer and conciliatory theologian of the seventeenth century, words which became the motto of his life: *"In necessary things unity, in unnecessary things liberty, in all things charity."*

---

10. Ibid., p. 142.

Sermons

MAKING LIGHT OF CHRIST
AND SALVATION

"But they made light of it" (Matthew 22:5).

BELOVED HEARERS; the office that God hath called us to is, by declaring the glory of His grace, to help under Christ to the saving of men's souls. I hope you think not that I come hither to-day on another errand. The Lord knows I had not set a foot out-of-doors but in hope to succeed in this work for your souls. I have considered, and often considered, what is the matter that so many thousands should perish when God hath done so much for their salvation; and I find this that is mentioned in my text is the cause.

It is one of the wonders of the world, that when God hath so loved the world as to send His Son, and Christ hath made a satisfaction by His death sufficient for them all, and offereth the benefits of it so freely to them, even without money or price, that yet the most of the world should perish; yea, the most of those that are thus called by His Word! Why, here is the reason—when Christ hath done all this, men make light of it. God hath showed that He is not unwilling; and Christ hath showed that He is not unwilling that men should be restored to God's favor and be saved; but men are actually unwilling themselves. God takes not pleasure in the death of sinners, but rather that they return and live. But men take such pleasure in sin that they will die before they will return. The Lord Jesus was content to be their physician, and hath provided them a sufficient plaster of His own blood; but if men make light of it, and will not apply it, what wonder if they perish after all? This Scripture giveth us the reason of their perdition.

This, sad experience tells us, the most of the world is guilty of. It is a most lamentable thing to see how most men do spend their care, their time, their pains, for known vanities, while God and glory are cast aside; that He who is all should seem to them as nothing, and that which is nothing should seem to them as good as all; that God should

Reprinted from *The World's Great Sermons*, comp. Grenville Kleiser, vol. 2 (New York: Funk & Wagnalls Co., 1908), pp. 59–81.

set mankind in such a race where heaven or hell is their certain end, and that they should sit down, and loiter, or run after the childish toys of the world, and so much forget the prize that they should run for. Were it but possible for one of us to see the whole of this business as the all-seeing God doth; to see at one view both heaven and hell, which men are so near; and see what most men in the world are minding, and what they are doing every day, it would be the saddest sight that could be imagined. Oh, how should we marvel at their madness, and lament their self-delusion! O poor distracted world! what is it you run after? and what is it that you neglect? If God had never told them what they were sent into the world to do, or whither they were going, or what was before them in another world, then they had been excusable; but He hath told them over and over, till they were weary of it. Had He left it doubtful, there had been some excuse; but it is His sealed word, and they profess to believe it, and would take it ill of us if we should question whether they do believe it or not.

Beloved, I come not to accuse any of you particularly of this crime; but seeing it is the commonest cause of men's destruction, I suppose you will judge it the fittest matter for our inquiry, and deserving our greatest care for the cure. To which end I shall, (1) endeavor the conviction of the guilty; (2) shall give them such considerations as may tend to humble and reform them; (3) I shall conclude with such direction as may help them that are willing to escape the destroying power of this sin.

And for the first, consider: It is the case of most sinners to think themselves freest from those sins that they are most enslaved to; and one reason why we can not reform them is because we can not convince them of their guilt. It is the nature of sin so far to blind and befool the sinner, that he knoweth not what he doth, but thinketh he is free from it when it reigneth in him, or when he is committing it: it bringeth men to be so much unacquainted with themselves that they know not what they think, or what they mean and intend, nor what they love or hate, much less what they are habituated and disposed to. They are alive to sin, and dead to all the reason, consideration, and resolution that should recover them, as if it were only by their sinning that we must know that they are alive. May I hope that you that hear me to-day are but willing to know the truth of your case, and then I shall be encouraged to proceed to an inquiry. God will judge impartially; why should not we do so? Let me, therefore, by these following questions, try whether none of you are slighters of Christ and your own salvation. And follow me, I beseech you, by putting them close to your own hearts, and faithfully answering them.

Things that men highly value will be remembered; they will be matter of their freest and sweetest thoughts. This is a known case.

Do not those then make light of Christ and salvation that think of them so seldom and coldly in comparison of other things? Follow thy own heart, man, and observe what it daily runneth after; and then judge whether it make not light of Christ.

We can not persuade men to one hour's sober consideration what they should do for an interest in Christ, or in thankfulness for His love, and yet they will not believe that they make light of Him.

Things that we highly value will be matter of our discourse; the judgment and heart will command the tongue. Freely and delightfully will our speech run after them. This also is a known case.

Do not those men make light of Christ and salvation that shun the mention of His name, unless it be in a vain or sinful use? Those that love not the company where Christ and salvation is much talked of, but think it troublesome, precise discourse: that had rather hear some merry jests, or idle tales, or talk of their riches or business in the world; when you may follow them from morning to night, and scarce have a savory word of Christ; but perhaps some slight and weary mention of Him sometimes; judge whether these make not light of Christ and salvation. How seriously do they talk of the world and speak of vanity! but how heartlessly do they make mention of Christ and salvation!

The things that we highly value we would secure the possession of, and therefore would take any convenient course to have all doubts and fears about them well resolved. Do not those men then make light of Christ and salvation that have lived twenty or thirty years in uncertainty whether they have any part in these or not, and yet never seek out for the right resolution of their doubts? Are all that hear me this day certain they shall be saved? Oh, that they were! Oh, had you not made light of salvation, you could not so easily bear such doubting of it; you could not rest till you had made it sure, or done your best to make it sure. Have you nobody to inquire of, that might help you in such a work? Why, you have ministers that are purposely appointed to that office. Have you gone to them, and told them the doubtfulness of your case, and asked their help in the judging of your condition? Alas! ministers may sit in their studies from one year to another, before ten persons among a thousand will come to them on such an errand! Do not these make light of Christ and salvation? When the gospel pierceth the heart indeed, they cry out, "Men and brethren, what shall we do to be saved?" Trembling and astonished, Paul cries out, "Lord, what wilt Thou have me to do?" And so did the convinced Jews to Peter. But when hear we such questions?

The things that we value do deeply affect us, and some motions will be in the heart according to our estimation of them. O sirs, if men made not light of these things, what working would there be in the hearts of all our hearers! What strange affections would it raise in them to hear of the matters of the world to come! How would their hearts melt before the power of the gospel! What sorrow would be wrought in the discovery of their sins! What astonishment at the consideration of their misery! What unspeakable joy at the glad tidings of salvation by the blood of Christ! What resolution would be raised in them upon the discovery of their duty! Oh, what hearers should we have, if it were not for this sin! Whereas now we are liker to weary them, or preach them asleep with matters of this unspeakable moment. We talk to them of Christ and salvation till we make their heads ache: little would one think by their careless carriage that they heard and regarded what we said, or though we spoke at all to them.

Our estimation of things will be seen in the diligence of our endeavors. That which we highliest value, we shall think no pains too great to obtain. Do not those men then make light of Christ and salvation that think all too much that they do for them; that murmur at His service, and think it too grievous for them to endure? that ask His service as Judas of the ointment. What need this waste? Can not men be saved without so much ado? This is more ado than needs. For the world they will labor all the day, and all their lives; but for Christ and salvation they are afraid of doing too much. Let us preach to them as long as we will, we can not bring them to relish or resolve upon a life of holiness. Follow them to their houses, and you shall not hear them read a chapter, nor call upon God with their families once a day; nor will they allow Him that one day in seven which He hath separated to His service. But pleasure, or worldly business, or idleness, must have a part. And many of them are so far hardened as to reproach them that will not be as mad as themselves. And is not Christ worth the seeking? Is not everlasting salvation worth more than all this? Doth not that soul make light of all these that thinks his ease more worth than they? Let but common sense judge.

That which we most highly value, we think we can not buy too dear. Christ and salvation are freely given, and yet the most of men go without them because they can not enjoy the world and them together. They are called but to part with that which would hinder them Christ, and they will not do it. They are called but to give God His own, and to resign all to His will, and let go the profits and pleasures of this world, when they must let go either Christ or them, and they will not. They think this too dear a bargain, and say they can not spare these things: they must hold their credit with men; they must look to their estates: how shall they live else? They must have their pleasure, whatsoever becomes of Christ and salvation: as if they could live without Christ better than without these; as if they were afraid of being losers by Christ, or could make a saving match by losing their souls to gain the world. Christ hath told us over and over that if we will not forsake all for Him we can not be His disciples. Far are these men from forsaking all, and yet will needs think that they are His disciples indeed.

That which men highly esteem, they would help their friends to as well as themselves. Do not those men make light of Christ and salvation that can take so much care to leave their children portions in the world, and do so little to help them to heaven? that provide outward necessaries so carefully for their families, but do so little to the saving of their souls? Their neglected children and friends will witness that either Christ, or their children's souls, or both, were made light of.

That which men highly esteem, they will so diligently seek after that you may see it in the success, if it be a matter within their reach. You may see how many make light of Christ, by the little knowledge they have of Him, and the little communion with Him, and the communication from Him; and the little, yea, none, of His special grace in them. Alas! how many ministers can speak it to the sorrow of their hearts, that many of their people know almost nothing of Christ, though they hear of Him daily! Nor know they what they must do to be saved: if we ask them an account of these things, they answer as if they understood not what we say to them, and tell us they are no scholars, and therefore think they are excusable for their ignorance. Oh, if these men had not made light of Christ and their salvation, but had bestowed but half as much pains to know and enjoy Him as they have done to understand the matters of their trades and callings in the world, they would not have been so ignorant as they are: they make light of these things, and therefore will not be at the pains to study or learn them. When men that can learn the hardest trade in a few years have not learned a catechism, nor how to understand their creed, under twenty or thirty years' preaching, nor can abide to be questioned about such things, doth not this show that they have slighted them in their hearts? How will these despisers of Christ and salvation be able one day to look Him in the face, and to give an account of these neglects?

Thus much I have spoken in order to your conviction. Do not some of your consciences by this time smite you, and say, I am the man that have made light of my salvation? If they do not, it is because you make light of it still, for all that is said to you. But because, if it be the will of the Lord, I would fain have this damning distemper cured, and am loath to leave you in such a desperate condition, if I knew how to remedy it, I will give you some considerations, which may move you, if you be men of reason and understanding, to look better about you; and I beseech you to weigh them, and make use of them as we go, and lay open your hearts to the work of grace, and sadly bethink you what a case you are in, if you prove such as make light of Christ.

Consider, 1. Thou makest light of Him that made not light of thee who deserve it. Thou wast worthy of nothing but contempt. As a man, what art thou but a worm to God? As a sinner, thou art far viler than a toad: yet Christ was so far from making light of thee and thy happiness, that He came down into the flesh, and lived a life of suffering, and offered Himself a sacrifice to the justice which thou hadst provoked, that thy miserable soul might have a remedy. It is no less than miracles of love and mercy that He hath showed to us; and yet shall we slight them after all?

Angels admire them, whom they less concern, and shall redeemed sinners make light of them? What barbarous, yea, devilish – yea, worse than devilish – ingratitude is this! The devils never had a savior offered to them; but thou hast, and dost thou yet make light of Him?

2. Consider, the work of man's salvation by Jesus Christ is the masterpiece of all the works of God, wherein He would have His love and mercy to be magnified. As the creation declareth His goodness and power, so doth redemption His goodness and mercy; He hath contrived the very frame of His worship so that it shall much consist in the magnifying of this work; and, after all this, will you make light of it? "His name is wonderful." "He did the work that none could do." "Greater love could none show than His." How great was the evil and misery that He delivered us from! the good procured from us! All are wonders, from His birth to His ascension; from our new birth to our glorification, all are wonders of matchless mercy – and yet do you make light of them?

3. You make light of matters of greatest excellency and moment in the world: you know not what it is that you slight: had you well known, you would not have done it. As Christ said to the woman of Samaria, "Hadst thou known who it is that speaketh to thee, thou wouldst have asked of Him the waters of life"; had they known they would not have crucified the Lord of Glory. So, had you known what Christ is, you would not have made light of Him; had you been one day in heaven, and but seen what they possess, and seen also what miserable souls must endure that are shut out, you would never sure have made so light of Christ.

O sirs, it is no trifles or jesting matters that the gospel speaks of. I must needs profess to you that when I have the most serious thoughts of these things myself, I am ready to marvel that such amazing matters do not overwhelm the souls of men; that the greatness of the subject doth not so overmatch our understandings and affections as even to drive men besides themselves, but that God hath always somewhat allayed it by the distance; much more that men should be so blockish as to make light of them. O Lord, that men did but know what everlasting glory and everlasting torments are: would they then hear us as they do? would they read and think of these things as they do? I profess I have been ready to wonder, when I have heard such weighty things delivered, how people can forbear crying out in the congregation; much more how they can rest till they have gone to their ministers, and learned what they should do to be saved, that this great business might be put out of doubt. Oh, that heaven and hell should work no more on men! Oh, that everlastingness work no more! Oh, how can you forbear when you are alone to think with yourselves what it is to be everlastingly in joy or in torment! I wonder that such thoughts do not break your sleep, and that they come not in your mind when you are about your labor! I wonder how you can almost do anything else! how you can have any quietness in your minds! How you can eat, or drink, or rest, till you have got some ground of everlasting consolations! Is that a man or a corpse that is not affected with matters of this moment? that can be readier to sleep than to tremble when he heareth how he must stand at the bar of God? Is that a man or a clod of clay that can rise or lie down without being deeply affected with his everlasting estate? that can follow his worldly business and make nothing of the great business of salvation or damnation; and that when they know it is hard at hand?

Truly, sirs, when I think of the weight of the matter, I wonder at the very best of God's saints upon the earth that they are no better, and do no more in so weighty a case. I wonder at those whom the world accounteth more holy than needs, and scorns for making too much ado, that they can put off Christ and their souls with so little; that they pour not out their souls in every supplication; that they are not more taken up with God; that their thoughts be more serious in preparation for their account. I wonder that they be not a hundred times more strict in their lives, and more laborious and unwearied in striving for the crown, than they are. And for myself, as I am ashamed of my dull and careless heart, and of my slow and unprofitable course of life, so the Lord knows I am ashamed of every sermon that I preach: when I think what I have been speaking of, and who sent me, and that men's salvation or damnation is so much concerned in it, I am ready to tremble lest God should judge me as a slighter of His truth and the souls of men, and lest in the best sermon I should be guilty of their blood. Methinks we should not speak a word to men in matters of such consequence without tears, or the greatest earnestness that possibly we can: were not we too much guilty of the sin which we reprove, it would be so. Whether we are alone, or in company, methinks our end, and such an end, should still be in our mind, and before our eyes; and we should sooner forget anything, and set light by anything, or by all things, than by this.

Consider, 4. Who is it that sends this weighty message to you? Is it not God Himself? Shall the God of heaven speak and man make light of it? You would not slight the voice of an angel or a prince.

5. Whose salvation is it that you make light of? Is it not your own? Are you no more near or dear to yourselves than to make light of your own happiness or misery? Why, sirs, do you not care whether you be saved or damned? Is self-love lost? are you turned your own enemies? As he that slighteth his meat doth slight his life, so if you slight Christ, whatsoever you may think, you will find it was your own salvation that you slighted. Hear what He saith, "All they that hate me love death."

6. Your sin is greater, in that you profess to believe the gospel

which you make so light of. For a professed infidel to do it that believes not that ever Christ died, or rose again, or doth not believe that there is a heaven or hell, this were no such marvel – but for you, that make it your creed, and your very religion, and call yourselves Christians, and have been baptized into this faith, and seemed to stand to it, this is the wonder, and hath no excuse. What! believe that you shall live in endless joy or torment, and yet make no more of it to escape torment, and obtain that joy! What! believe that God will shortly judge you, and yet make no preparation for it! Either say plainly, I am no Christian, I do not believe these wonderful things, I will believe nothing but what I see, or else let your hearts be affected with your belief, and live as you say you do believe. What do you think when you repeat the creed, and mention Christ's judgment and everlasting life?

7. What are these things you set so much by as to prefer them before Christ and the saving of your soul? Have you found a better friend, a greater and a surer happiness than this? Good Lord! what dung is it that men make so much of, while they set so light by everlasting glory? What toys are they that are daily taken up with, while matters of life and death are neglected? Why, sirs, if you had every one a kingdom in your hopes, what were it in comparison of the everlasting kingdom? I can not but look upon all the glory and dignity of this world, lands and lordships, crowns and kingdoms, even as on some brain-sick, beggarly fellow, that borroweth fine clothes, and plays the part of a king or a lord for an hour on a stage, and then comes down, and the sport is ended, and they are beggars again. Were it not for God's interest in the authority of magistrates, or for the service they might do Him, I should judge no better of them. For, as to their own glory, it is but a smoke: what matter is it whether you live poor or rich, unless it were a greater matter to die rich than it is? You know well enough that death levels all. What matter is it at judgment, whether you be to answer for the life of a rich man or a poor man? Is Dives, then, any better than Lazarus? Oh, that men knew what poor, deceiving shadow they grasp at while they let go the everlasting substance! The strongest, and richest, and most voluptuous sinners do but lay in fuel for their sorrows, while they think they are gathering together a treasure. Alas! they are asleep, and dream that they are happy; but when they awake, what a change will they find! Their crown is made of thorns; their pleasure hath such a sting as will stick in the heart through all eternity, except unfeigned repentance do prevent it. Oh, how sadly will these wretches be convinced ere long, what a foolish bargain they made in selling Christ and their salvation for these trifles! Let your farms and merchandise, then, save you, if they can, and do that for you that Christ would have done. Cry then to Baal, to save thee! Oh, what thoughts have drunkards and adulterers, etc., of Christ, that will not part with the basest lust for Him? "For a piece of bread," saith Solomon, "such men do transgress."

8. To set so light by Christ and salvation is a certain mark that thou hast no part in them, and if thou so continue, that Christ will set as light by thee: "Those that honor him he will honor, and those that despise him shall be lightly esteemed." Thou wilt feel one day that thou canst not live without Him; thou wilt confess then thy need of Him; and then thou mayest go look for a savior where thou wilt; for He will be no Savior for thee hereafter, that wouldst not value Him, and submit to Him here. Then who will prove the loser by thy contempt? Oh, what a thing will it be for a poor miserable soul to cry to Christ for help in the day of extremity, and to hear so sad an answer as this! Thou didst set lightly by Me and My law in the day of thy prosperity, and I will now set as light by thee in the day of thy adversity. Read Proverbs 1:24, to the end. Thou that, as Esau, didst sell thy birthright for a mess of pottage, shalt then find no place for repentance, though thou seek it with tears. Do you think that Christ shed His blood to save them that continue to make light of it? and to save them that value a cup of drink or a lust before His salvation? I tell you, sirs, though you set so light by Christ and salvation, God doth not so: He will not give them on such terms as these: He valueth the blood of His Son, and the everlasting glory, and He will make you value them if ever you have them. Nay, this will be thy condemnation, and leaveth no remedy. All the world can not save him that sets lightly by Christ. None of them shall taste of His supper. Nor can you blame Him to deny you what you made light of yourselves. Can you find fault if you miss of the salvation which you slighted?

9. The time is near when Christ and salvation will not be made light of as now they are. When God hath shaken those careless souls out of their bodies, and you must answer for all your sins in your own name, oh, then, what would you not give for a Savior! When a thousand bills shall be brought in against you, and none to relieve you, then you will consider, Oh! Christ would now have stood between me and the wrath of God; had I not despised Him, He would have answered all. When you see the world hath left you, and your companions in sin have deceived themselves and you, and all your merry days are gone, then what would you not give for that Christ and salvation that now you account not worth your labor! Do you think that when you see the judgment seat, and you are doomed to everlasting perdition for your wickedness, that you should then make as light of Christ as now? Why will you not judge now as you know you shall judge then? Will He then be worth ten thousand worlds? And is He not now worth your highest estimation and dearest affection?

10. God will not only deny thee that salvation thou madest light of, but He will take from thee all that which thou didst value before it: he that most highly esteems Christ shall have Him, and the creatures, so far as they are good here, and Him without the creature hereafter, because the creature is not useful; and he that sets more by the crea-

ture than by Christ, shall have some of the creature without Christ here, and neither Christ nor it hereafter.

So much of these considerations, which may show the true face of this heinous sin.

What think you now, friends, of this business? Do you not see by this time what a case that soul is in that maketh light of Christ and salvation? What need then is there that you should take heed lest this should prove your own case! The Lord knows it is too common a case. Whoever is found guilty at the last of this sin, it were better for that man he had never been born. It were better for him he had been a Turk or Indian, that never had heard the name of a Savior, and that never had salvation offered to him: for such men "have no cloak for their sin." Besides all the rest of their sins, they have this killing sin to answer for, which will undo them. And this will aggravate their misery, that Christ whom they set light by must be their Judge, and for this sin will He judge them. Oh, that such would now consider how they will answer that question that Christ put to their predecessors: "How will ye escape the damnation of hell?" or, "How shall we escape if we neglect so great salvation?" Can you escape without a Christ? or will a despised Christ save you then? If he be accurst that sets light by father or mother, what then is he that sets light by Christ? It was the heinous sin of the Jews, that among them were found such as set light by father and mother. But among us, men slight the Father of Spirits! In the name of God, brethren, I beseech you to consider how you will then bear this anger which you now make light of! You that can not make light of a little sickness or want, or of natural death, no, not of a toothache, but groan as if you were undone; how will you then make light of the fury of the Lord, which will burn against the contemners of His grace! Doth it not behoove you beforehand to think of these things?

Dearly beloved in the Lord, I have now done that work which I came upon; what effect it hath, or will have, upon your hearts, I know not, nor is it any further in my power to accomplish that which my soul desireth for you. Were it the Lord's will that I might have my wish herein, the words that you have this day heard should so stick by you that the secure should be awakened by them, and none of you should perish by the slighting of your salvation. I can not follow you to your several habitations to apply this word to your particular necessities; but oh, that I could make every man's conscience a preacher to himself that it might do it, which is ever with you! That the next time you go prayerless to bed, or about your business, conscience might cry out, Dost thou set no more by Christ and thy salvation? That the next time you are tempted to think hardly of a holy and diligent life (I will not say to deride it as more ado than needs), conscience might cry out to thee, Dost thou set so light by Christ and thy salvation? That the next time you are ready to rush upon unknown sin, and to please your fleshly desires against the command of God, conscience might cry out, Is Christ and salvation no more worth than to cast them away, or venture them for thy lust? That when you are following the world with your most eager desires, forgetting the world to come, and the change that is a little before you, conscience might cry out to you, Is Christ and salvation no more worth than so? That when you are next spending the Lord's day in idleness or vain sports, conscience might tell you what you are doing. In a word, that in all your neglects of duty, your sticking at the supposed labor or cost of a godly life, yea, in all your cold and lazy prayers and performances, conscience might tell you how unsuitable such endeavors are to the reward; and that Christ and salvation should not be so slighted. I will say no more but this at this time, it is a thousand pities that when God hath provided a Savior for the world, and when Christ hath suffered so much for their sins, and made so full a satisfaction to justice, and purchased so glorious a kingdom for His saints, and all this is offered so freely to sinners, to lost, unworthy sinners, even for nothing, that yet so many millions should everlastingly perish because they make light of their Savior and salvation, and prefer the vain world and their lusts before them. I have delivered my message, the Lord open your hearts to receive it. I have persuaded you with the word of truth and soberness; the Lord persuade you more effectually, or else all this is lost. Amen.

A SERMON OF REPENTANCE

"Then shall ye remember your own evil ways, and your doings that were not good, and shall loathe yourselves in your own sight, for your iniquities, and for your abominations" (Ezekiel 36:31).

THE WORDS are a part of God's prognostics of the Jews' restoration, whose dejection he had before described. Their disease began within, and there God promiseth to work the cure. Their captivity was but the fruit of their voluntary captivity to sin, and their grief of heart was but

Reprinted from *Select Practical Writings of Richard Baxter*, 2nd. ed., [ed.] Leonard Bacon, vol. 2 (New Haven: Durrie & Peck, 1835), pp. 328–52.

the fruit of their hardness of heart, and their sharpest suffering of their foul pollutions; and, therefore, God promiseth a methodical cure, even to take away their old and stony heart, and cleanse them from their filthiness, and so to ease them by the removing of the cause. How far, and when, this promise was to be made good to the Jews, as nationally considered, is a matter that requires a longer disposition than my limited hour will allow; and the decision of that case is needless, as to my present end and work. That this is part of the gospel covenant, and applicable to us believers now, the Holy Ghost, in the Epistle to the Hebrews, hath assured us.

The text is the description of the repentance of the people, in which the beginning of their recovery doth consist, and by which the rest must be attained. The evil which they repent of is, in general, all their iniquities, but especially their idolatry, called their abominations. Their repentance is foretold, as it is in the understanding and thoughts, and as in the will and affections. In the former, it is called "remembering their own evil ways." In the latter, it is called "loathing themselves in their own sight, for their iniquities and abominations." When the Septuagint translates it by displeasure, and the Chaldee by groaning, and the Syriac by the wrinkling of the face, and the Septuagint in chapter 22:43, by smiting on the face, the Arabic here perverts the sense by turning all to negatives ye shall not, he turns it by the tearing of the face. I have purposely chosen a text that needs no long explication, that, in obedience to the foreseen straits of time, I may be excused from that part, and be more on the more necessary. This observation contains the meaning of the text, which, by God's assistance, I shall now insist on, viz.

The remembering of their own iniquities, and loathing themselves for them, is the sign of a repenting people and the prognostic of their restoration, so far as deliverance may be here expected.

For the opening of which, observe these things following: —

2. It is not all kind of remembering that will prove you penitent. The impenitent remember their sin, that they may commit it; they remember it with love, desire, and delight: the heart of the worldling goeth after his airy or earthen idol. The heart of the ambitious feedeth on his vain glory, and the people's breath; and the filthy fornicator is delighted in the thoughts of the object and exercise of his lust. But it is a remembering, (1.) from a deep conviction of the evil and odiousness of sin. (2.) And with abhorrence and self-loathing. (3.) That leadeth to a resolved and vigilant forsaking, that is the proof of true repentance, and the prognostic of a people's restoration.

3. And it is not all self-loathing that will signify true repenting, for there is a self-loathing of the desperate, and the damned soul that abhorreth itself, and teareth and tormenteth itself, and cannot be restrained from self-revenge, when it finds that it hath willfully, foolishly, and obstinately, been its own destroyer. But the self-loathing of the truly penitent hath these following properties: —

(1.) It proceedeth from the predominant love of God, whom we have abused and offended. The more we love him, the more we loathe what is contrary to him.

(2.) It is much excited by the observation and sense of his exceeding mercies, and is conjunct with gratitude.

(3.) It continueth and increaseth under the greatest assurance of forgiveness, and sense of love, and dieth not when we think we are out of danger.

(4.) It containeth a loathing of sin as sin, and a love of holiness as such, and not only a love of ease and peace, and a loathing of sin, as the cause of suffering.

(5.) It resolveth the soul against returning to its former course, and resolveth it for an entire devotedness to God for the time to come.

(6.) It deeply engageth the penitent in a conflict against the flesh, and maketh him victorious, and setteth him to work in a life of holiness, as his trade and principal business in the world.

(7.) It bringeth him to a delight in God and holiness, and a delight in himself, so far as he findeth God and heaven, and holiness within him. He can, with some comfort and content, own himself and his conversation, so far as God (victorious against his carnal self) appeareth in him. For, as he loveth Christ in the rest of his members, so must he in himself. And this is it that self-loathing doth prepare for.

This must be the self-loathing that must afford you comfort, as a penitent people in the way to restoration.

1. Where you see it is implied that, materially, it containeth these common acts. (1.) Accusing and condemning thoughts against ourselves. It is a judging of ourselves, and makes us call ourselves, with Paul, foolish, disobedient, deceived; yea, mad; (as Acts 26:11) and with David to say, I have done foolishly (2 Sam. 24:10). (2.) It containeth a deep distaste and displeasure with ourselves, and a heart rising against ourselves. (3.) As also a holy indignation against ourselves, as apprehending that we have played the enemies to ourselves and God. (4.) And it possesseth us with grief and trouble at our miscarriages. So that a soul, in this condition, is sick of itself, and vexed with its self-procured woe.

2. Note, also, that when self-loathing proceedeth from mere conviction, and is without the love of God and holiness, it is but the tormentor of the soul, and runs it deeper into sin, provoking men here to destroy their lives; and in hell it is the never-dying worm.

3. Note, also, that it is themselves that they are said to loathe, because it is ourselves that conscience hath to do with, as witness, and as judge; it is ourselves that are naturally nearest to ourselves, and our own affairs that we are most concerned in. It is ourselves that must have the joy or torment, and, therefore, it is our own actions and estate that we have first to mind. Though yet, as magistrates,

ministers, and neighbors, we must next mind others, and must loathe iniquity wherever we meet it, and a vile person must be condemned in our eyes, while we honor them that fear the Lord (Ps. 15:4).

And as by nature, so in the commandment, God hath given to every man the first and principal care and charge of himself, and his own salvation, and consequently of his own ways, so that we may with less suspicion loathe ourselves than others, and are more obliged to do it.

4. Note, also, that it is not for our troubles, or our disgrace, or our bodily deformities, or infirmities, or for our poverty and want, that penitents are said to loathe themselves, but for their iniquities and abominations. For, (1.) This loathing is a kind of justice done upon ourselves, and therefore is exercised, not for mere infelicities, but for crimes. Conscience keepeth in its own court, and meddleth but with moral evils, which we are conscious of. (2.) And also it is sin that is loathed by God, and makes the creature loathsome in his eyes; and repentance conformeth the soul to God, and therefore causeth us to loathe as he doth, and on his grounds. And, (3.) There is no evil but sin, and that which sin procureth; and therefore it is for sin that the penitent loathes himself.

5. Note, also, that it is here implied, that, till repentance, there was none of this remembering of sin, and loathing of themselves. They begin with our conversion, and, as before described, are proper to the truly penitent. For, to consider them distinctly, (1.) The deluded soul that is bewitched by his own concupiscence is so taken up with remembering of his fleshly pleasures, and his alluring objects, and his honors, and his earthly businesses and store, that he hath no mind or room for the remembering of his foolish, odious sin, and the wrong that he is doing to God, and to himself. Death is oblivious, and sleep hath but a distracted, ineffectual memory, that stirreth not the busy dreamer from his pillow, nor despatcheth any of the work he dreams of. And the unconverted are asleep, and dead in sin. The crowd of cares and worldly businesses, and the tumultuous noise of foolish sports, and other sensual passions and delights, do take up the minds of the unconverted, and turn them from the observation of the things of greatest everlasting consequence. They have a memory for sin and the flesh, to which they are alive, but not for things spiritual and eternal, to which they are dead. They remember not God himself as God, with any effectual remembrance. God is not in all their thoughts (Ps. 10:4). They live as without him in the world (Eph. 2:12). And if they remember not God, they cannot remember sin as sin, whose malignity lieth in its opposition to the will and holiness of God. They forget themselves, and therefore must needs forget their sinfulness.

Alas! they remember not effectually and savingly what they are, and why they were made, and what they are daily nourished and preserved for, and what business they have to do here in the world.

They forget that they have souls to save or lose, that must live in end-less joy or torment. You may see by their careless and ungodly lives that they forget it. You may hear by their carnal, frothy speech that they forget it. And he that remembereth not himself, remembereth not his own concernments. They forget the end to which they tend; the life which they must live forever; the matters everlasting, whose greatness and duration, one would think, should so command the mind of man, and take up all his thoughts and cares, in despite of all the little trifling matters that would avert them, that we should think almost of nothing else. Yet these, even these, that nothing but dead-ness or madness should make a reasonable creature to forget, are daily forgotten by the unconverted soul, or ineffectually remembered. Many a time have I admired that men of reason who are here to-day, and in endless joy or misery to-morrow, should be able to forget such inexpressible concernments! Methinks they should easier forget to rise, or dress themselves, or to eat, or drink, or any thing, than forget an endless life, which is so undoubtedly certain, and so near. A man that hath a cause to be heard to-morrow, in which his life or honor is concerned, cannot forget it; a wretch that is condemned to die to-morrow, cannot forget it. And yet poor sinners, that are continually uncertain to live an hour, and certain speedily to see the majesty of the Lord, to their unconceivable joy or terror, as sure as now they live on earth, can forget these things for which they have their memory; and which, one would think, should drown the matters of this world, as the report of a cannon doth a whisper, or as the sun obscureth the poorest glow-worm.

O wonderful stupidity of an unrenewed soul! O wonderful folly and distractedness of the ungodly! That ever man can forget, I say again, that they can forget, eternal joy, eternal woe, and the Eternal God, and the place of their eternal, unchangeable abode, when they stand even at the door, and are passing in, and there is but the thin veil of flesh between them and that amazing sight, that eternal gulf; and they are daily dying, and even stepping in. O, could you keep your honors here forever; could you ever wear that gay attire, and gratify your flesh with meats, and drinks, and sports, and lusts; could you ever keep your rule and dignity, or your earthly life in any state, you had some little poor excuse for not remembering the eternal things (as a man hath that preferreth his candle before the sun); but when death is near and inexorable, and you are sure to die as you are sure to live; when every man of you that sitteth in these seats to-day can say, "I must shortly be in another world, where all the pomp and pleasure of this world will be forgotten, or remembered but as my sin and folly," one would think it were impossible for any of you to be ungodly, and to remember the trifles and nothings of the world, while you forget that everlasting all, whose reality, necessity, magnitude, excel-lency, concernment, and duration, are such as should take up all the powers of your souls, and continually command the service and attendance of your thoughts against all seekers, and contemptible competitors whatsoever. But, alas! though you have the greatest helps (in subservience to these commanding objects), yet will you not remember the matters which alone deserve remembrance. Sometimes the preachers of the gospel do call on you to remember; to remember your God, your souls, your Savior, your ends, and everlasting state, and to remember your misdoings, that you may loathe yourselves, and in returning may find life; but some either scorn them, or quarrel with them, or sleep under their most serious and importunate solicitations, or carelessly and stupidly give them the hearing, as if they spoke but words of course, or treated about uncertain things, and spoke not to them from the God of heaven, and about the things that every man of you shall very shortly see or feel.

Sometimes you are called on by the voice of conscience within, to remember the unreasonableness and evil of your ways; but conscience is silenced, because it will not be conformable to your lusts. But little do you think what a part your too late awakened conscience hath yet to play, if you give it not a more sober hearing in time. Sometimes the voice of common calamities, and national or local judgments, call on you to remember the evil of your ways; but that which is spoken to all, or many, doth seem to most of them as spoken unto none. Sometimes the voice of particular judgments, seizing upon your families, persons or estates, doth call on you to remember the evil of your ways; and one would think the rod should make you hear. And yet you most disregardfully go on, or are only frightened into a few good purposes and promises, that die when health and prosperity revive. Sometimes God joineth all these together, and pleadeth both by word and rod, and addeth also the inward pleadings of his Spirit; he sets your sins in order before you (Ps. 1:21), and expostulateth with you the cause of his abused love, despised sovereignty, and provoked justice; and asketh the poor sinner, "Hast thou done well to waste thy life in vanity, to serve thy flesh, to forget thy God, thy soul, thy happiness; and to thrust his services into corners, and give him but the odious leavings of the flesh?" But these pleas of God cannot be heard.

O horrible impiety! By his own creatures; by reasonable creatures (that would scorn to be called fools or madmen) the God of heaven cannot be heard! The brutish, passionate, furious sinners will not remember. They will not remember what they have done, and with whom it is that they have to do, and what God thinks and saith of men in their condition; and whither it is that the flesh will lead them; and what will be the fruit and end of all their lusts and vanities; and how they will look back on all at last; and whether an holy or a sensual life will be sweetest to a dying man; and what judgment it is that they will all be of, in the controversy between the flesh and Spirit, at the latter end. Though they have life and time, and reason for their uses, we cannot entreat them to consider of these things in time. If our lives lay on it, as their salvation, which is more, lieth on it, we cannot entreat them. If we should kneel to them, and with tears beseech them, but once a day, or once a week, to bestow one hour in serious consideration of their latter end, and the everlasting state of saints and sinners, and of the equity of the holy ways of God, and the iniquity of their own, we cannot prevail with them. Till the God of heaven doth overrule them, we cannot prevail. The witness that we are forced to bear is sad: it is sad to us; but it will be sadder to these rebels, that shall one day know that God will not be outfaced; and that they may sooner shake the stable earth, and darken the sun by their reproaches, than outbrave the Judge of all the world, or by all their cavils, wranglings, or scorns, escape the hands of his revenging justice.

But if ever the Lord will save these souls, he will bring their misdoings to their remembrance. He will make them think of that which they were so loath to think on. You cannot now abide these troubling and severe meditations; the thoughts of God, and heaven, and hell; the thoughts of your sins, and of your duties, are melancholy, unwelcome thoughts to you; but O, that you could foreknow the thoughts that you shall have of all these things! even the proudest, scornful, hardened sinner, that heareth me this day, shall shortly have such a remembrance as will make him wonder at his present blockishness. O, when the irresistible power of Heaven shall open all your sins before you, and command you to remember them, and to remember the time, and place, and persons, and all the circumstances of them; what a change will it make upon the most stout or stubborn of the sons of men; what a difference will there then be between that trembling, self-tormenting soul, and the same that now, in his gallantry, can make light of all these things, and call the messenger of Christ, who warneth him, a Puritan, or a doting fool!

Your memories now are somewhat subject to your wills; and if you will not think of your own, your chief, your everlasting concernments, you may choose. If you will choose rather to employ your noble souls on beastly lusts, and waste your thoughts on things of nought, you may take your course, and chase a feather with a childish world, till, overtaking it, you see you have lost your labor. But when justice takes the work in hand, your thoughts shall be no more subject to your wills; you shall then remember that which you are full loath to remember, and would give a world that you could forget. O, then one cup of the waters of oblivion would be of inestimable value to the damned! O, what would they not give that they could but forget the time they had lost, the mercy they abused, the grace which they refused, the holy servants of Christ whom they despised, the willful sins which they committed, and the many duties which they willfully omitted! I have often thought of their case when I have dealt with melancholy or despairing persons. If I advised them to cast away such thoughts, and turn their minds to other things, they tell me they cannot; it is not in their power; and I have long found that I may almost as well persuade a broken head to give over aching. But when the holy God shall purposely pour out the vials of his wrath on the consciences of the ungodly, and open the books, and show them all that ever they have done, with all the aggravations, how, then, shall these worms be able to resist?

And now, I beseech you all, consider, is it not better to remember your sins on earth, than in hell? before your Physician, than before your Judge? for your cure, than for your torment? Give me leave, then, before I go any further, to address myself to you as the messenger of the Lord, with this importunate request, both as you stand here in your private and your public capacities. In the name of the God of heaven, I charge you, remember the lives that you have led! remember what you have been doing in the world! remember how you have spent your time! and whether, indeed, it is God that you have been serving, and heaven that you have been seeking, and holiness and righteousness that you have been practicing in the world till now! Are your sins so small, so venial, so few, that you can find no employment on them for your memories? Or is the offending of the Eternal God so slight and safe a thing as not to need your consideration? God forbid you should have such atheistical conceits! Surely God made not his laws for nought; nor doth he make such a stir by his word, and messengers, and providences, against an harmless thing; nor doth he threaten hell to men for small, indifferent matters; nor did Christ need to have died, and done all that he hath done, to cure a small and safe disease. Surely that which the God of heaven is pleased to threaten with everlasting punishment, the greatest of you all should vouchsafe to think on, and with greatest fear and soberness to remember.

It is a pitiful thing, that with men, with gentlemen, with professed Christians, God's matters, and their own matters, their greatest matters, should seem unworthy to be thought on; when they have thoughts for their honors, and their lands, and friends; and thoughts for their children, their servants, and provision; and thoughts for their horses, and their dogs, and sports. Is God and heaven less worthy than these? are death and judgment matters of less moment? Gentlemen, you would take it ill to have your wisdom undervalued, and your reason questioned; for your honor's sake do not make it contemptible yourselves in the eyes of all that are truly wise. It is the nobleness of objects that most ennobles your faculties, and the baseness of objects doth abase them. If brutish objects be your employment and delight, do I need to tell you what you make yourselves? If you would be noble indeed, let God and everlasting glory be the object of your faculties; if you would be great, then dwell on greatest things: if you would be high, then seek the things that are above, and not the sordid things of earth (Col. 3:1–3), and if you would be safe, look after the enemies of your peace; and, as you had thoughts of sin that led you to commit it, entertain the thoughts that would lead you to abhor it. O that I might have but the grant of this reasonable request from you, that, among all your thoughts, you would bestow now and then an hour in the serious thoughts of your misdoings, and soberly, in your retirement between God and your souls, remember the paths that you have trod; and whether you have lived for the work for which you were created. One sober hour of such employment might be the happiest hour that ever you spent, and give you more comfort at your final hour than all the former hours of your life; and might lead you into that new and holy life, which you may review with everlasting comfort.

Truly, gentlemen, I have long observed that Satan's advantage lieth so much on the brutish side, that the work of man's conversion is so much carried on by God's exciting of our reason, and that the misery of the ungodly is, that they have reason in faculty, and not in use, in the greatest thing, that I persuade you to this duty with the greater hopes; if the Lord will but persuade you to retire from vanity, and soberly exercise your reason, and consider your ways, and say, What have we done? And what is it that God would have us do? And what shall we wish we had done at last? I say, could you now be but prevailed with to bestow as many hours on this work, as you have cast away in idleness, or worse, I should not doubt but I should shortly see the faces of many of you in heaven that have been recovered by the use of this advice. It is a thousand pities, that men are thought wise enough to be intrusted with the public safety, and to be the physicians of a broken state, should have any among them that are untrusty to their God, and have not the reason to remember their misdoings, and prevent the danger of their immortal souls. Will you sit all day here to find out the remedy of a diseased land; and will you not be entreated by God or man to sit down one hour, and find out the disease of, and remedy for, your own souls? Are those men likely to take care of the happiness of so many thousands, that will still be so careless of themselves? Once more, therefore, I entreat you, remember your misdoings, lest God remember them; and bless the Lord that called you this day, by the voice of mercy, to remember them upon terms of faith and hope. Remembered they must be, first or last. And believe it, this is far unlike the sad remembrance at judgment, and in the place of woe and desperation.

And I beseech you observe here, that it is your own misdoings that you must remember. Had it been only the sins of other men, especially those that differ from you, or have wronged you, or stand against your interest, how easily would the duty have been performed! How little need should I have had to press it with all this importunity! How confident should I be that I could convert the most, if this were the conversion! It grieves my soul to hear how quick and constant, high and low, learned and unlearned, are at this uncharitable, contumelious remembering of the faults of others; how cunningly they can bring in their insinuated accusations; how odiously they can aggravate the smallest faults, where difference causeth them to distaste the person; how ordinarily they judge of actions by the persons, as if any thing were a crime that is done by such as they dislike, and all were virtue that is done by those that fit their humors; how commonly brethren have made it a part of their service of God to speak or write uncharitably of his servants, laboring to destroy the hearer's charity, which had more need, in this unhappy time, of the bellows than the water; how usual it is with the ignorant that cannot reach the truth, and the impious that cannot bear it, to call such heretics that know more than themselves, and to call such precisians, Puritans (or some such name which hell invents as there is occasion), who dare not be so bad as they; how odious, men pretending to much gravity, learning, and moderation, do labor to make those that are dearer to God; and what a heart they have to widen differences, and make a sea of every lake; and that, perhaps, under pretense of blaming the uncharitableness of others; how far the very sermons and discourses of some learned men are from the common rule of doing as we would be done by; and how loudly they proclaim that such men love not their neighbors as themselves; the most uncharitable words seeming moderate, which they give; and all called intemperate that savoreth not of flattery, which they receive! Were I calling the several exasperated factions, now in England, to remember the misdoings of their supposed adversaries, what fullmouthed and debasing confessions would they make! What monsters of heresy, and schism, of impiety, treason, and rebellion, of perjury and perfidiousness, would too many make of the faults of others, while they extenuate their own to almost nothing! It is a wonder to observe how the case doth alter with the most, when that which was their adversary's case becomes their own. The very prayers of the godly, and their care of their salvation, and their fear of sinning, doth seem their crime in the eyes of some that easily bear the guilt of swearing, drunkenness, sensuality, filthiness, and neglect of duty in themselves, as a tolerable burden.

But if ever God indeed convert you (though you will pity others, yet), he will teach you to begin at home, and take the beam out of your own eyes, and to cry out, "I am the miserable sinner."

And lest these generals seem insufficient for us to confess on such a day as this, and lest yet your memories should need more help, is it not my duty to remind you of some particulars? which yet I shall not do by way of accusation, but of inquiry. Far be it from me to judge so hardly of you, that when you come hither to lament your sins, you cannot with patience endure to be told of them.

1. Inquire, then, whether there be none among you that live a sensual, careless life, clothed with the best, and faring deliciously every day! In rioting and drunkenness, chambering and wantonness,

strife and envying, not putting on Christ, nor walking in the Spirit, but making provision for the flesh, to satisfy the lusts thereof (Rom. 13-14). Is there none among you that spend your precious time in vanities, that is allowed you to prepare for life eternal? That have time to waste in compliments, and fruitless talk, and visits; in gaming, and unnecessary recreations; in excessive feasting and entertainments, while God is neglected, and your souls forgotten, and you can never find an hour in a day to make ready for the life which you must live forever? Is there none among you that would take the man for a Puritan, or fanatic, that should employ but half so much time for his soul, and in the services of the Lord, as you do in unnecessary sports and pleasures, and pampering your flesh? Gentlemen, if there be any such among you, as you love your souls, remember your misdoings, and bewail these abominations before the Lord, in this day of your professed humiliation.

2. Inquire whether there be none among you, that, being strangers to the new birth, and to the inward workings of the Spirit of Christ upon the soul, do also distaste a holy life, and make it the matter of your reproach, and pacify your accusing consciences with a religion made up of mere words, and heartless outside, and so much obedience as your fleshly pleasures will admit, accounting those that go beyond you, especially if they differ from you in your modes and circumstances, to be but a company of proud, Pharisaical, self-conceited hypocrites, and those whom you desire to suppress. If there be one such person here, I would entreat him to remember that it is the solemn asseveration of our Judge, that, "except a man be converted, and be born again, of water and the Spirit, he cannot enter into the kingdom of heaven" (John 3:3-5; Matt. 18:3); that "if any man have not the Spirit of Christ, he is none of his" (Rom. 8:9); that "if any man be in Christ, he is a new creature; old things are passed away, and all things are become new" (2 Cor. 5:17); that "without holiness none shall see God" (Heb. 12:14); that "the wisdom that is from above is first pure, and then peaceable" (James 3:17); that "God is a Spirit, and they that worship him must worship him in spirit and in truth" (John 4:23, 24); that "they worship in vain that teach for doctrines the commandments of men" (Matt. 15:8, 9); and that "except your righteousness shall exceed that of the Scribes and Pharisees ye shall in no wise enter into the kingdom of heaven" (Matt. 5:20). And I desire you to remember that "it is hard to kick against the pricks, and to prosper in rage against the Lord; and that it is better for that man that offendeth one of his little ones to have a millstone fastened to his neck, and to have been cast into the bottom of the sea" (Matt. 18:6). It is a sure and grevious condemnation that waiteth for all that are themselves unholy; but to the haters or despisers of the holy laws and servants of the Lord how much more grievous a punishment is reserved!

3. Inquire also whether there be none among you that let loose your passions on your inferiors, and oppress your poor tenants, and make them groan under the task, or at least do little to relieve the needy, nor study not to serve the Lord with your estates, but sacrifice all to the pleasing of your flesh, unless it be some inconsiderable pittance, or fruitless drops, that are unproportionable to your receivings. If there be any such, let them remember their iniquities, and cry for mercy before the cry of the poor to heaven do bring down vengeance from him that hath promised to hear their cry, and speedily to avenge them (Luke 18:7, 8).

4. Inquire whether there be none that live the life of Sodom, in pride, fullness of bread, and idleness (Ezek. 16:49); and that are puffed up with their estates and dignities, and are strangers to the humility, meekness, patience, and self-denial of the saints; that ruffle in bravery, and contend more zealously for their honor and preëminence than for the honor and interest of the Lord. For pride of apparel, it was wont to be taken for a childish or womanish kind of vice, below a man; but it is now observed among the gallants, that (except in spots) the notes of vanity are more legibly written on the hair and dress of a multitude of effeminate males than on the females; proclaiming to the world that pride, which, one would think, even pride itself should have concealed; and calling by these signs to the beholders to observe the emptiness of their minds, and how void they are of that inward worth which is the honor of a Christian and of a man. It being a marvel to see a man of learning, gravity, wisdom, and the fear of God, appear in such antic dress.

I have done with the first part, "the remembering of your own evil ways and doings." I beseech you practically go along with me to the next; "The loathing of yourselves in your own eyes, for all your iniquities and abominations."

Every true convert doth thus loathe himself for his iniquities; and when God will restore a punished people upon their repentance, he bringeth them to this loathing of themselves.

1. A converted soul hath a new and heavenly light to help him to see those matters of humbling use which others see not.

2. More particularly, he hath the knowledge of sin and of himself. He seeth the odious face of sin, and seeth how much his heart and life, in his sinful days, abounded with it, and how great a measure yet remains.

3. He hath seen by faith the Lord himself; the majesty, the holiness, the jealousy, the goodness of the eternal God whom he hath offended, and therefore must needs abhor himself (Job 42:6).

4. He hath tasted of God's displeasure against him for his sin, already. God himself hath set it home, and awakened his conscience, and held it on, till he hath made him understand that the consuming fire is not to be jested with.

5. He hath seen Christ crucified, and mourned over him. This is the glass that doth most clearly show the ugliness of sin; and here he hath learned to abhor himself.

6. He hath foreseen, by faith, the end of sin, and the doleful recompense of the ungodly: his faith beholdeth the misery of damned souls, and the glory which sinners cast away. He heareth them beforehand, repenting, and lamenting, and crying out of their former folly, and wishing in vain that all this were to do again, and that they might once more be tried with another life, and resolving then how holily, how self-denyingly they would live! He knows that if sin had had its way, he had been plunged into this hellish misery himself; and therefore he must needs loathe himself for his iniquities.

7. Moreover, the true convert hath had the liveliest taste of mercy, of the blood of Christ, of the offers and covenant of grace, of reprieving mercy, of pardoning mercy, of healing and preserving mercy, and of the unspeakable mercy contained in the promise of everlasting life; and to find that he hath sinned against all this mercy, doth constrain him to abhor himself.

8. And it is only the true convert that hath a new and holy nature, contrary to sin; and, therefore, as a man that hath the leprosy doth loathe himself because his nature is contrary to his disease, so is it (though operating in a freer way) with a converted soul as to the leprosy of sin. O, how he loathes the remnants of his pride and passion; his excessive cares, desires, and fears; the backwardness of his soul to God and heaven! Sin is to the new nature of every true believer as the food of a swine to a stomach of a man; if he have eaten it, he hath no rest until he hath vomited it up; and then, when he looketh on his vomit, he loatheth himself to think how long he kept such filth within him; and that yet in the bottom there is some remains.

9. The true convert is one that is much at home; his heart is the vineyard which he is daily dressing; his work is ordinarily about it; and, therefore, he is acquainted with those secret sins, and daily failings, which ungodly men, that are strangers to themselves, do not observe, though they have them in dominion.

10. Lastly, a serious Christian is a workman of the Lord's, and daily busy at the exercise of his graces, and, therefore, hath occasion to observe his weaknesses, and failings, and from sad experience is forced to abhor himself.

But with careless, unrenewed souls, it is not so: some of them may have a mild, ingenuous disposition, and the knowledge of their unworthiness; and customarily they will confess such sins as are small disgrace to them, or cannot be hid; or under the terrible gripes of conscience in the hour of distress, and at the approach of death, they will do more; and abhor themselves, perhaps, as Judas did; or make a constrained confession through the power of fear; but so far are they from this loathing of themselves for all their iniquities, that sin is to them as their element, their food, their nature, and their friend.

And now, honorable, worthy, and beloved auditors, it is my duty to inquire, and to provoke you to inquire, whether the representative body of the commons of England, and each man of you in particular, be thus affected to yourselves or not. It concerns you to inquire of it, as you love your souls, and love not to see the death marks of impenitency on them. It concerneth us to inquire of it, as we love you and the nation, and would fain see the marks of God's return in mercy to us, in your self-loathing and return to God. Let conscience speak as before the Lord that sees your hearts, and will shortly judge you: have you had such a sight of your natural and actual sin and misery, of your neglect of God, your contempt of heaven, your loss of precious, hasty time, your worldly, fleshly, sensual lives, and your omission of the great and holy works which you were made for? Have you had such a sight and sense of these as hath filled your souls with shame and sorrow, and caused you, in tears, or hearty grief, to lament your sinful, careless lives, before the Lord? Do you loathe yourselves for all this, as being vile in your own eyes, and each man say, "What a wretch was I! what an unreasonable, self-hating wretch, to do all this against myself! what an unnatural wretch! what a monster of rebellion and ingratitude, to do all this against the Lord of love and mercy! what a deceived, foolish wretch, to prefer the pleasing of my lusts and senses, a pleasure that perisheth in the fruition, and is past as soon as it is received, before the manly pleasures of the saints, and before the soul's delight in God, and before the unspeakable, everlasting pleasures! Was there any comparison between the brutish pleasures of the flesh, and the spiritual delights of a believing soul, in looking to the endless pleasure which we shall have with all the saints and angels in the glorious presence of the Lord? Was God and glory worth no more than to be cast aside for satiating of an unsatisfiable flesh and fancy, and to be sold for a harlot, for a forbidden cup, for a little air of popular applause, or for a burdensome load of wealth and power, for so short a time? Where is now the gain and pleasure of all my former sins? What have they left but a sting behind them? How near is the time when my departing soul must look back on all the pleasures and profits that ever I enjoyed, as a dream when one awaketh; as delusory vanities, that have done all for me that ever they will do, and all is but to bring my flesh unto corruption (Gal. 6:8), and my soul to this distressing grief and fear! and then I must sing and laugh no more! I must brave it out in pride no more! I must know the pleasures of the flesh no more! but be leveled with the poorest, and my body laid in loathsome darkness, and my soul appear before that God whom I so willfully refused to obey and honor.

"O, wretch that I am! where was my understanding, when I played so boldly with the flames of hell, the wrath of God, the poison of sin! when God stood by, and yet I sinned! when conscience did rebuke me, and yet I sinned! when heaven or hell were hard at hand, and yet I sinned! when, to please my God and save my soul, I would not forbear a filthy lust, or forbidden vanity of no worth! when I would not be persuaded to a holy, heavenly, watchful life, though all my hopes of heaven lay on it! I am ashamed of myself; I am confounded in the remembrance of my willful, self-destroying folly! I loathe myself for all my abominations! O that I had lived in beggary and rags when I lived in sin! And O that I had lived with God in a prison, or in a wilderness, when I refused a holy, heavenly life, for the love of a deceitful world! Will the Lord pardon what is past, I am resolved through his grace to do so no more, but to loathe that filth that I took for pleasure, and to abhor that sin that I made my sport, and to die to the glory and riches of the world, which I made my idol; and to live entirely to that God that I did so long ago and so unworthily neglect; and to seek that treasure, that kingdom, that delight, that will fully satisfy my expectation, and answer all my care and labor, with such infinite advantage. Holiness or nothing shall be my work and life, and heaven or nothing shall be my portion and felicity."

These are the thoughts, the affections, the breathing of every regenerate, gracious soul. For your souls' sake inquire now, is it thus with you. Or have you thus returned with self-loathing to the Lord, and firmly engaged your souls to him at your entrance into a holy life? I must be plain with you, gentlemen, or I shall be unfaithful; and I must deal closely with you, or I cannot deal honestly and truly with you. As sure as you live, yea, as sure as the word of God is true, you must all be such converted men, and loathe yourselves for your iniquities, or be condemned as impenitent to everlasting fire. To hide this from you, is but to deceive you, and that in a matter of a thousand times greater moment than your lives. Perhaps I could have made shift, instead of such serious admonitions, to have wasted this hour in flashy oratory, and neat expressions, and ornaments of reading, and other things that are the too common matters of ostentation with men that preach God's word in jest, and believe not what they are persuading others to believe. Or, if you think I could not, I am indifferent, as not much affecting the honor of being able to offend the Lord, and wrong your souls, by dallying with holy things. Flattery in these things of soul concernment is a selfish villany, that hath but a very short reward; and those that are pleased with it to-day may curse the flatterer forever. Again, therefore, let me tell you that which I think you will confess, that it is not your greatness, nor your high looks, nor the gallantry of your spirits, that scorns to be thus humbled, that will serve your turn when God shall deal with you, or save your carcasses from rottenness and dust, or your guilty souls from the wrath of the Almighty.

Nor is it your contempt of the threatenings of the Lord, and your stupid neglect, or scorning at the message, that will endure when the sudden, irresistible light shall come in upon you, and convince you, or you shall see and feel what now you refuse to believe! Nor is it your outside, hypocritical religion, made up of mere words, or ceremonies, and giving your souls but the leavings of the flesh, and making God an underling to the world, that will do any more to save your souls than the picture of a feast to feed your bodies. Nor is it the stiffest conceits that you shall be saved in an unconverted state, or that you are sanctified when you are not, that will do any more to keep you from damnation than a conceit, that you shall never die, will do to keep you here forever. Gentlemen, though you are all here in health, and dignity, and honor, to-day, how little a while is it, alas! how little, until you shall be every man in heaven or hell! Unless you are infidels, you dare not deny it. And it is only Christ and a holy life that is your way to heaven; and only sin, and the neglect of Christ and holiness, that can undo you. Look, therefore, upon sin as you should look upon that which would cast you into hell, and is daily undermining all your hopes. O, that this honorable assembly could know it in some measure as it shall be shortly known; and judge of it as men do, when time is past, and delusions vanished, and all men are awakened from their fleshly dreams, and their naked souls have seen the Lord! O, then, what laws would you make against sin! How speedily would you join your strength against it as against the only enemy of your peace, and as against a fire in your houses, or a plague that were broken out upon the city where you are! O, then, how zealously would you all concur to promote the interest of holiness in the land, and studiously encourage the servants of the Lord! How severely would you deal with those that, by making a mock of godliness, do hinder the salvation of the people's souls! How carefully would you help the laborers that are sent to guide men in the holy path! and yourselves would go before the nation as an example of penitent self-loathing for your sins, and hearty conversion to the Lord! Is this your duty now? or is it not? If you cannot deny it, I warn you from the Lord, do not neglect it; and do not, by your disobedience to a convinced conscience, prepare for a tormenting conscience. If you know your Master's will, and do it not, you shall be beaten with many stripes.

And your public capacity and work doth make your repentance and holiness needful to others as well as to yourselves. Had we none to govern us, but such as entirely subject themselves to the government of Christ; and none to make us laws, but such as have his law transcribed upon their hearts, O, what a happy people should we be! Men are unlikely to make strict laws against the vices which they love and live in; or if they make them, they are more unlikely to execute them. We can expect no great help against drunkenness, swearing, gaming, filthiness, and profaneness, from men that love these abominations so well, as that they will rather part with God and their salvation than they will let them go. All men are born with a serpentine malice and enmity against the seed of Christ, which is rooted in their very natures. Custom in sin increaseth this to malignity; and it is only renewed grace that doth overcome it. If, therefore, there should be any among our rulers that are not cured of this mortal malady, what friendship can be expected from them to the cause and servants of the Lord? If you are all the children of God yourselves, and heaven be your end, and holiness your delight and business, it will then be your principal care to encourage it, and help the people to the happiness that you have found yourselves. But if in any the original (increased) enmity to God and godliness prevail, we can expect no better (ordinarily) from such, than that they oppose the holiness which they hate, and do their worst to make us miserable. But woe to him that striveth against his Maker. Shall the thorns and briers be set in battle against the consuming fire and prevail? (Isa. 27:4).

O, therefore, for the nation's sake, begin at home and cast away the sins which you would have the nation cast away! All men can say, that ministers must teach by their lives, as well as by their doctrines (and woe to them that do not); and must not magistrates as well govern by their lives, as by their laws? Will you make laws which you would not have men obey? Or would you have the people to be better than yourselves? Or can you expect to be obeyed by others, when you will not obey the God of heaven and earth yourselves? We beseech you, therefore, for the sake of a poor, distressed land, let our recovery begin with you. God looks so much at the rulers of a nation in his dealings with them, that ordinarily it goes with the people as their rulers are. Until David had numbered the people, God would not let out his wrath upon them, though it was they that were the great offenders. If we see our representative body begin in loathing themselves for all their iniquities, and turning to the Lord with all their hearts, we should yet believe that he is returning to us, and will do us good, after all our provocations. Truly, gentlemen, it is much from you that we must fetch our comfortable or sad prognostics of the life or death of this diseased land. Whatever you do, I know that it shall go well with the righteous; but for the happiness or misery of the nation, in general it is you that are our best prognostication. If you repent yourselves, and become a holy people to the Lord, it promiseth us deliverance; but if you harden your hearts, and prove despisers of God and holiness, it is like to be our temporal, and sure to be your eternal undoing, if saving grace do not prevent it.

And I must needs tell you that, if you be not brought to loathe yourselves, it is not because there is no loathsome matter in you. Did you see your inside, you could not forbear it. As I think it would somewhat abate the pride of the most curious gallants, if they did but see what a heap of phlegm, and filth, and dung (and perhaps crawling worms), there is within them; much more should it make you loathe yourselves if you saw those sins that are a thousand times more odious. And to instigate you hereunto, let me further reason with you.

1. You can easily loathe an enemy; and who hath been a greater enemy to any of you than yourselves? Another may injure you; but no man can everlastingly undo you, but yourselves.

2. You abhor him that kills your dearest friends; and it is you by your sins that have put to death the Lord of life.

3. Who is it but yourselves that have robbed you of so much precious time, and so much precious fruit of ordinances, and of all the mercies of the Lord?

4. Who is it but yourselves that hath brought you under God's displeasure? Poverty could not have made him loathe you, nor any thing besides your sins.

5. Who wounded conscience, and hath raised all your doubts and fears? Was it not your sinful selves?

6. Who is it but yourselves that hath brought you so near the gulf of misery, and endangered your eternal peace?

7. Consider the loathsome nature of your sins; and how, then, can you choose but loathe yourselves?

(1.) It is the creature's rebellion or disobedience against the Absolute Universal Sovereign.

(2.) It is the deformity of God's noblest creature here on earth, and the abusing of the most noble faculties.

(3.) It is a stain so deep that nothing can wash out but the blood of Christ. The flood that drowned a world of sinners did not wash away their sins. The fire that consumed the Sodomites did not consume their sins. Hell itself can never end it, and, therefore, shall have no end itself. It dieth not with you when you die: though churchyards are the guiltiest spots of ground, they do not bury and hide our sin.

(4.) The church must loathe it, and must cast out the sinner as loathsome, if he remain impenitent; and none of the servants of the Lord must have any friendship with the unfruitful works of darkness.

(5.) God himself doth loathe the creature for sin, and for nothing else but sin. "My soul loathed them" (Zech. 11:8); "When the Lord saw it, he abhorred them, because of the provoking of his sons and daughters" (Deut. 32:19); "My soul shall abhor you" (Lev. 26:30); "When God heard this, he was wroth, and greatly abhorred Israel" (Ps. 78:59); "He abhorred his very sanctuary" (Lam. 2:7); "For he is of purer eyes than to behold iniquity" (Hab. 1:13). In a word, it is the sentence of God himself, that a "wicked man is loathsome and cometh to shame" (Prov. 13:5), so that you see what abundant cause of self-abhorrence is among us.

But we are much afraid of God's departure, when we see how common self-love is in the world, and how rare this penitent self-loathing is.

1. Do they loathe themselves that on every occasion are contending for their honor, and exalting themselves, and venturing their very souls, to be highest in the world, for a little while?

2. Do they loathe themselves that are readier to justify all their sins, or at least to extenuate them, than humbly confess them?

3. Do they loathe themselves for all their sins that cannot endure to be reproved, but loathe their friends and the ministers of Christ that tell them of their loathsomeness?

4. Do they loathe themselves that take their pride itself for manhood, and Christian humility for baseness, and brokenness of heart for whining hypocrisy or folly, and call them a company of priest-ridden fools that lament their sin, and ease their souls by free confession? Is the ruffling bravery of this city, and the strange attire, the haughty carriage, the feasting, idleness, and pomp, the marks of such as loathe themselves for all their abominations? Why, then, was fasting, and sackcloth, and ashes, the badge of such in ancient times?

5. Do they loathe themselves for all their sins, who loathe those that will not do as they, and speak reproachfully of such as run not with them to the same excess of riot (1 Pet. 4:4); and count them precisians that dare not spit in the face of Christ, by willful sinning as venturously and madly as themselves?

6. Or, do they loathe themselves for all their sins, that love their sins even better than their God, and will not, by all the obtestations, and commands, and entreaties of the Lord, be persuaded to forsake them? How far all these are from this self-loathing, and how far that nation is from happiness, where the rulers or inhabitants are such, is easy to conjecture.

I should have minded you what sins of the land must be remembered, and loathed, if we would have peace and healing. But as the glass forbids me, so, alas! as the sins of Sodom, they declare themselves. Though, through the great mercy of the Lord, the body of this nation, and the sober part, have not been guilty of that covenant-breaking, perfidiousness, treason, sedition, disobedience, self-exalting, and turbulency, as some have been, and as ignorant foreigners, through the calumnies of malicious adversaries, may possibly believe; yet must it be for a lamentation through all generations, that any of those who went out from us have contracted the guilt of such abominations, and occasioned the enemies of the Lord to blaspheme; and that any, in the pride or simplicity of their hearts, have followed the conduct of Jesuitical seducers, they knew not whither or to what.

That profaneness aboundeth on the other side, and drunkenness, swearing, fornication, lasciviousness, idleness, pride, and covetousness, doth still survive the ministers that have wasted themselves against them, and the labors of faithful magistrates, to this day! And that the two extremes of heresy and profaneness do increase each other; and while they talk against each other, they harden one another, and both afflict the church of Christ. But especially woe to England for that crying sin, *the scorning of a holy life,* if a wonder of mercy do not save us. That people, professing the Christian religion, should scorn the diligent practice of that religion which themselves profess! That obedience to the God of heaven, that imitation of the example of our Savior, who came from heaven to teach us holiness, should not only be neglected, unreasonably and impiously neglected, but also by a transcendent impious madness should be made a matter of reproach! That the Holy Ghost, into whose name, as the Sanctifier, these men were themselves baptized, should not only be resisted, but his sanctifying work be made a scorn! That it should be made a matter of derision for a man to prefer his soul before his body, and heaven before earth, and God before a transitory world, and to use his reason in that for which it was principally given him, and not to be willfully mad in a case where madness will undo him unto all eternity! Judge, as you are men, whether hell itself is like much to exceed such horrid wickedness! And whether it be not an astonishing wonder that ever a reasonable soul should be brought to such a height of abomination! That they that profess to believe the holy catholic church, and the communion of saints, should deride the holiness of the church, and the saints, and their communion! That they that pray for the hallowing of God's name, the coming of his kingdom, and the doing of his will, even as it is done in heaven, should make a mock at all this that they pray for!

How much further, think you, is it possible for wicked souls to go on sinning? Is it not the God of heaven himself that they make a scorn of? Is not holiness his image? Did not he make the law that doth command it; professing that none shall see his face without it (Heb. 12:14)? O sinful nation! O people laden with iniquity! Repent, repent speedily, and with self-loathing; repent of this inhuman crime, lest God should take away your glory, and enter himself into judgment with you, and plead against you the scorn that you have cast upon the Creator, the Savior, the Sanctifier, to whom you were engaged in your baptismal vows! Lest, when he plagueth and condemneth you, he say, "Why persecuted you me?" (Acts 9:4). "Inasmuch as ye did it to one of the least of these my brethren, ye did it unto me." Read Prov. 20 to the end. When Israel mocked the messengers of the Lord, and despised his words, and misused his prophets, his wrath arose against his people till there was no remedy (2 Chron. 26:16); and O that you, who are the physicians of this diseased land, would specially call them to repentance for this, and help them against it for the time to come!

Having called you first to remember your misdoings, and secondly to loathe yourselves in your own eyes for them, I must add a third, that you stop not here, but proceed to reformation, or else all the rest is but hypocrisy. And here it is that I most earnestly entreat this honorable assembly for their best assistance. O make not the forementioned sins your own, lest you hear from God, "Quod minus crimine, quam absolutione peccatum est." Though England hath been used to cry loud for liberty, let them not have liberty to abuse their Maker, and to damn their souls, if you can hinder it. "Optimus est reipublicae status, ubi nulla libertas deest, nisi licentia pereundi," as Nero was once told by his unsuccessful tutor. Use not men to a liberty of scorning the laws of God, lest you teach them to scorn yours; for can you expect to be better used than God? And "Cui plus licet quan par est, plus vult quam licet." We have all seen the evils of liberty to be wanton in religion. Is it not worse to have liberty to deride religion? If men shall have leave to go quietly to hell themselves, let them not have leave to mock poor souls from heaven. The suffering to the sound in faith is as nothing; for what is the foaming rage of madmen to be regarded? But that, in England, God should be so provoked, and souls so hindered from the paths of life, that whoever will be converted and saved must be made a laughing-stock, which carnal minds cannot endure; this is the mischief which we deprecate.

The eyes of the nation, and of the Christian world, are much upon you, some high in hopes, some deep in fears, some waiting in dubious expectations for the issue of your counsels. Great expectations, in deep necessities, should awake you to the greatest care and diligence. Though I would not, by omitting any necessary directions or admonitions to you, invite the world to think that I speak to such as cannot endure to hear, and that so honorable an assembly doth call the ministers of Christ to do those works of their proper office, which yet they will be offended if they do, yet had I rather err in the defective part than by excess, and therefore shall not presume to be too particular. Only in general, in the name of Christ, and on the behalf of a trembling, yet hoping nation, I most earnestly beseech and warn you, that you own and promote the power and practice of godliness in the land, and that as God, whose ministers you are (Rom. 13:4), is a rewarder of them that diligently seek him (Heb. 11:6), and hath made this a principal article of our faith, so you would imitate your absolute Lord, and honor them that fear the Lord, and encourage them that diligently seek him.

And may I not freely tell you that God should have the precedency? And that you must first seek his kingdom and the righteousness thereof, and he will facilitate all the rest of your work? Surely no powers on earth should be offended, that the God from whom, and for whom, and through whom, they have what they have, is preferred before them, when they should own no interest but his, and what is subservient to it. I have long thought that pretenses of a necessity of beginning with our own affairs, hath frustrated our hopes from many parliaments already; and I am sure that by delays, the enemies of our peace have got advantage to cross our ends, and attain their own. Our calamities began in differences about religion, and still that is the wound that most needs closing. And if that were done, how easily, I dare confidently speak it, would the generality of sober, godly people be agreed in things civil, and become the strength and glory of the sovereign under God! And though, with grief and shame, we see this work so long undone (may we hope that God hath reserved it to this season), yet I have the confidence to profess, that, as the exalting of one party, by the ejection and persecuting of the rest, is the sinful way to your dishonor and our ruin so the terms on which the differing parties most considerable among us may safely, easily, and suddenly unite, are very obvious, and our concord a very easy thing, if the prudent and moderate might be the guides, and selfish interests and passion did not set us at a further distance than our principles hath done. And to show you the facility of such an agreement, were it not that such personal matters are much liable to misinterpretations, I should tell you, that the late reverend Primate of Ireland consented, in less than half an hour's debate, to five or six propositions which I offered him, as sufficient for the concord of the moderate Episcopal and Presbyterians, without forsaking the principles of their parties.

O that the Lord would yet show so much mercy to a sinful nation, as to put it into your hearts to promote but the practice of those Christian principles which we are all agreed in! I hope there is no controversy among us whether God should be obeyed, and hell avoided, and heaven first sought, and Scripture be the rule and test of our religion, and sin abhorred and cast out. O that you would but further the practice of this with all your might! We crave not of you any lordship or dominion, nor riches, nor interest in your temporal affairs; we had rather see a law to exclude all ecclesiastics from all power of force. The God of heaven, that will judge you and us, will be a righteous judge betwixt us, whether we crave any thing unreasonable at your hands. These are the sum of our requests – 1. That holiness may be encouraged, and the overspreading profaneness of this nation effectually kept down. 2. That an able, diligent ministry may be encouraged, and not corrupted by temporal power. 3. That discipline may be seriously promoted, and ministers no more hindered by magistrates in the exercise of their office than physicians and schoolmasters are in theirs, seeing it is but a government like theirs, consisting in the liberty of conscionably managing the works of our own office, that we expect. Give us but leave to labor in Christ's vineyard with such encouragements as the necessity of obstinate souls requireth, and we will ask no more. You have less cause to restrain us from discipline than from preaching. For it is a more flesh-displeasing work that we are hardlier brought to. I foretell you that you shut out me, and all that are of my mind, if you would force us to administer sacraments, without discipline, and without the conduct of our own discretion, to whom the magistrate appoints it, as if a physician must give no physic but by your prescript. The antidisciplinarian magistrate I could as resolutely suffer under as the superstitious, it being worse to cast out discipline than to err in the circumstances of it. The question is not, whether bishops or no, but whether discipline or none. And whether enough to use it. 4. We earnestly request that Scripture sufficiency, as the test of our religion and only universal law of Christ, may be maintained, and that nothing unnecessary may be imposed as necessary, nor the church's unity laid on that which will not bear it, nor ever did. O that we might but have leave to serve God only as Christ hath commanded us, and to go to heaven in the same way as the apostles did! These are our desires; and whether they are reasonable, God will judge.

Give first to God the things that are God's, and then give to Caesar the things that are Caesar's. Let your wisdom be first pure, and then peaceable. Not but that we are resolved to be loyal to sovereignty, though you deny us all these. Whatever malicious men pretend, that is not, nor shall not, be our difference. I have proved more publicly, when it was more dangerous to publish it, that the generality of the orthodox, sober ministers, and godly people of this nation, did never consent to king-killing, and resisting sovereign power, nor the change of the ancient government of this land, but abhorred the pride and ambition that attempted it. I again repeat it, the blood of some, the imprisonment and displacing of others, the banishment or flight of others, and the detestations and public protestations of more; the oft-declared sense of England, and the wars and sad estate of Scotland, have all declared before the world, to the shame of calumniators, that the generality of the orthodox, sober Protestants of these nations, have been true to their allegiance, and detesters of unfaithfulness and ambition in subjects and resisters of heresy and schism in the church, and of anarchy and democratical confusions in the commonwealth.

And though the land hath ringed with complaints and threatenings against myself, for publishing a little of the mixture of Jesuitical and Familistical contrivances, for taking down together our government and religion, and setting up new ones for the introduction of Popery, infidelity, and heresy, yet I am assured that there is much more of this confederacy for the all-seeing God to discover in time, to the shame of Papists, that cannot be content to write themselves for the killing of kings when the pope hath once excommunicated them, and by the decrees of a general council at the Lateran, to depose princes that will not extirpate such as the pope calls heretics, and absolve all their subjects from their fidelity and allegiance, but they must also creep into the councils and armies of Protestants, and, taking the advantage of successes and ambition, withdraw men at once from their religion and allegiance, that they may cheat the world into a belief that treasons are the fruits of the Protestant profession, when these masked jugglers have come by night, and sown and cherished these Romish tares. As a Papist must cease to be a Papist if he will be truly and fully loyal to his sovereign (as I am ready to prove against any adversary), so a Protestant must so far cease to be a Protestant, before he can be disloyal. For Romans 13 is part of the rule of his religion. Unhappily there hath been a difference among us which is the higher power, when those that have their shares in the sovereignty are divided; but whether we should be subject to the higher power, is no question with us.

Gentlemen, I have nothing to ask of you for myself, nor any of my brethren, as for themselves, but that you will be friends to serious preaching and holy living, and will not ensnare our consciences with any unscriptural inventions of men. This I would beg of you as on my knees: 1. As for the sake of Christ, whose cause and people it is that I am pleading for. 2. For the sake of thousands of poor souls in this land, whose salvation or damnation will be much promoted by you. 3. For the sake of thousands of the dear servants of the Lord, whose eyes are waiting to see what God will do by your hands. 4. For your own sakes, who are undone if you dash yourselves on the rock you should build on, and set against the holy God, and turn the cries of his servants to heaven for deliverance from you (Luke 18:8). If you stumble on Christ, he will break you in pieces; but if he fall upon you, he will grind you to powder. 5. For the sake of your posterity, that they may not be bred up in ignorance or ungodliness. 6. For the honor of the nation and yourselves, that you turn by all the suspicions and fears that are raised in the land. 7. For the honor of sound doctrine and church-government, that you may not bring schism into greater credit than now you have brought it to deserve shame. For if you frown on godliness under pretense of uniformity in unnecessary things, and make times worse than when libertinism and schism so prevailed, the people will look back with groans and say, "What happy times did we once see!" And so will honor schism, and libertinism, and usurpation, through your oppression. 8. Lastly, I beg this of you, for the honor of sovereignty, and the nation's peace. A prince of a holy people is most honorable. The interest of holiness is Christ's own. Happy is that prince that espouseth this, and subjecteth all his own unto it (see Ps. 1:1–2 and 15:4). It is the conscionable, prudent, godly people of the land, that must be the glory and strength of their lawful sovereign. Their prayers will serve him better than the hideous oaths and curses of the profane. Woe to the rulers that set themselves against the interest of Christ and holiness! (read Ps. 2) or that make snares for their consciences, that they may persecute them as disobedients, who are desirous to obey their rulers in subordination to the Lord (see Dan. 3 and 6:5, 10, 13).

I have dealt plainly with you, and told you the very truth. If God have now a blessing for you and us, you will obey it; but if you refuse, then look to yourselves, and answer it if you can. I am sure, in spite of earth and hell, it shall go well with them that live by faith.

FOR ADDITIONAL INFORMATION ABOUT RICHARD BAXTER:

Baxter, Richard. *The Autobiography of Richard Baxter*. New York: E. P. Dutton and Co., 1931.

————. *The Reformed Pastor*. Edited by Hugh Martin. Richmond: John Knox Press, 1956.

Carter, Sydney Charles. *Richard Baxter*. London: Church Book Room Press, n.d.

Currier, Albert H. "Richard Baxter." *Nine Great Preachers*. New York: Pilgrim Press, 1912.

Howard, Harry C. "Richard Baxter." *Princes of the Christian Pulpit and Pastorate*. Nashville: Cokesbury Press, 1928.

Kemp, Charles F. *A Pastoral Triumph: The Story of Richard Baxter and His Ministry at Kidderminster*. New York: Macmillan Co., 1948.

Loane, Marcus L. "Richard Baxter." *Makers of Religious Freedom in the Seventeenth Century*. Grand Rapids: Wm. B. Eerdmans Pub. Co., 1961.

Martin, Hugh. *Puritanism and Richard Baxter*. London: SCM Press, 1954.

FOR OTHER SERMONS BY RICHARD BAXTER:

Making Light of Christ and Salvation Too Oft the Issue of Gospel-Invitations. London: R. White, 1658.

Select Practical Writings of Richard Baxter. Vol. 2. 2nd ed. New Haven: Durrie & Peck, 1835.

JACQUES BÉNIGNE BOSSUET

1627-1704

BOSSUET, Rigaud portrait, used by permission of National Museum, Paris.

JACQUES BÉNIGNE BOSSUET

1627	*Born September 27, Dijon, France*
1644	*Master of Arts, College of Navarre, Paris*
1652	*Doctor of Divinity, College of Navarre, Paris;*
	appointed archdeacon of Metz
1659	*Became court preacher in Paris*
1669	*Appointed bishop of Condom*
1670	*Appointed instructor of the Dauphin*
1671	*Elected to the French Academy*
1681	*Appointed bishop of Meaux*
1704	*Died April 12*

IN HIS PREACHING to the court of Louis XIV, Jacques Bénigne Bossuet earned the reputation as one of the most eloquent preachers ever to come from the French Catholic church. He was not a mere flatterer of the king in his sermons, as the former court preachers were. Though he could never quite free himself from his age, he honestly preached to effect a change of life in his hearers through sermons saturated with Scripture.

LIFE AND TIMES

Bossuet's love for the Bible began early. As a boy he discovered a copy of the Bible in an uncle's room. He opened it and began to read in Isaiah, and was fascinated and excited by what he read. He interrupted a conversation between his father and his uncle, who were talking politics, to beg them to listen as he read from the Scriptures. He read to them chapter after chapter.

His ability as an orator was also discovered early in childhood. While Bossuet was a student in a Jesuit college, his eloquence attracted the attention of many. Whenever he spoke, his fellow students listened in rapt attention.

These two factors—eloquence and the love for the Scriptures—characterized his life. After finishing the Jesuit college, Bossuet entered the College of Navarre in Paris. There he gained a thorough education, receiving both master's and doctor's degrees. Upon completion of his academic training, he entered the active service of his church and was appointed to a number of significant posts.

Probably the most determinative influence in the career of Bossuet was the reign of Louis XIV. Louis began his seventy-two-year reign in 1643 when Bossuet was sixteen years old. As a boy king, Louis XIV's affairs were mainly in the hands of others. As he grew older and took control of the monarchy, he guided the destiny of France. He built the huge palace at Versailles and gathered around him an extensive court. His way of life became the pattern for all the monarchs of Europe.

Into this materialistic and corrupt court came Bossuet. He was involved with Louis XIV in two ways. First, he was the court preacher; he preached often to the king and to his retinue. Court preachers were chosen for their ability as orators and for their loyalty to the crown. Bossuet qualified in both regards: he was an extremely gifted preacher, and he was totally loyal to Louis XIV. His second contact with Louis began with his appointment as the instructor of the Dauphin, heir apparent to the throne. In this position the preacher served as tutor to the young monarch-to-be in the matter of spiritual devotion. For nearly eleven years he labored at this task.

Another significant influence in the life of Bossuet was the changing Roman Catholic church, to which he gave unfaltering loyalty. He lived during the day of the Catholic Counter Reformation. The unity of European religious life had been shattered by the Protestant Reformation. The Catholic church had responded with vigor to try to regain lost ground. In France, Protestantism was gaining converts on every hand. Bossuet felt that his duty was to stem the tide of Protestantism. At every opportunity he preached against the Protestant teachings. Yet he also displayed a willingness to try to understand and to relate to the "separated brethren." For his day, he demonstrated an amazing temperance toward his ecclesiastical enemies.

His dual devotion to sovereign and to church caused Bossuet moments of agony when the two devotions came in conflict, and he tried desperately to resolve those differences. He felt that the emphasis of the French church must be orthodox.

Bossuet was thoroughly French: he was swept along with the tide of French nationalism. Though he tried often to understand other points of view, he saw almost everything through French-colored glasses. He was also affected by the rising tide of French materialism. Early in his youth he seemed to be aware of the dangers of materialism, but later he was so much a part of the splendor of the French court that he was blinded to its evils. He did display some concern for the plight of the poor in France, but this was only a minor part of his preaching emphasis. He never seemed to understand the horrible circumstances of the French peasant – which circumstances in only a few years were to lead to the French Revolution and the overthrow of the monarchy.

French society during this time was also marked by the moral corruption of the nobility and the court at Versailles. For the most part the courtiers who surrounded the king were corrupt. Bossuet seemed to close his eyes to much of this corruption. In the church, however, Bossuet saw more clearly. Corruption in the monasteries under his jurisdiction occupied a great deal of his time during the last portion of his life; he tried to clean up life in these monasteries. Certain laxities and even immoralities in the monasteries were the object of open warfare on his part. He eventually won over most of those who had been opposed to him and at the same time corrected their ways – which, in itself, is a testimony to his genius.

Bossuet was a practical man. He really never understood the mysticism of some of those around him. Another of the French court preachers, Fénelon, was far more turned toward mysticism than was Bossuet. One of the last and bitterest controversies that Bossuet faced involved a conflict with Fénelon over mysticism. Bossuet also became deeply involved in the significant national issues of France. His life touched the lives of the leaders of the nation – the king and his court. With all of his opportunity, however, Bossuet apparently had little effect in the court.

His ineffectiveness cannot be attributed to his lack of eloquence – he was an eloquent orator. Perhaps he was ineffective because corruption was too far advanced for any man to do much to correct it. But no doubt Bossuet could have accomplished more, had his life been more in keeping with his preaching. Many who have studied his life carefully admit that he preached a better life than he lived. In his writing and speaking

Bossuet was an idealist: he wrote of the glorious visions of man's possibilities of holiness. But when he left his sermons and his writings, his interests became submerged in worldly affairs; and he never seemed to be able to bring together the realities of the world in which he lived and the aspirations of his heart.[1]

Nevertheless, remember that Bossuet had a formidable challenge. The hearers of his sermons were surrounded by numerous hardening influences; the men were vain, corrupt, and often perverted. Intrigue abounded. The style of powdered wig, high-heeled shoes, and gaudy costume was indicative of the total situation. The ladies of the court were no better than the men. With mounds of hair piled on their heads, yards of silk wrapped around wire net draped on their bodies, and a willingness to sell themselves to the highest bidder, they were not given to listening carefully to the words of a preacher. Often Bossuet reduced his court audience to tears, but the weeping seemed to be more a part of the whole dramatic pattern of French court life than an intention to change a pattern of living.

In short, Bossuet was not prophetic enough to bring change: he was trapped by his own culture. In the beginning of an age of revolution, he was one of the defenders of the *status quo.* The divine right of kings, the entire structure of the Roman Catholic church, the interest of the nobility—all of these he defended with passion. The common people saw in him no advocate of their cause; the court and nobility saw in him one of their own. Such a man, no matter how eloquent, has little impact upon his age.

Preaching and Sermons

It may be surprising to discover how scriptural the sermons of Bossuet really are. Protestant readers somehow never expect to find biblical material in Catholic sermons. But it would be hard to find a man who involved the Scripture more in his preaching than did Bossuet. To be sure, his use of the Bible would not satisfy the modern definition of "biblical"; but then, neither would the preaching of anybody who lived in his time, Protestant or Catholic.

---

1. E. K. Sanders, *Jacques Bénigne Bossuet: A Study* (London: SPCK, 1921), p. 2.

No one can take up Bossuet's sermons without being struck by the extent to which he cited both the Old and New Testaments in striking applications. In his memoirs we are told that he knew the Bible almost by heart, and yet read and reread it every day. More often than not he quoted from his own original translation of the text for his sermon. Bossuet's sermon manuscripts were freely written over with Greek footnotes; Abbe le Dieu reported that he wrote Greek freely and rapidly, but not always legibly.

Naturally his sermons also cited the Church Fathers: St. Augustine was Bossuet's favorite author; Tertullian is next in the number of citations. A long list could be given of other Church Fathers who find their way into Bossuet's sermons at one time or another. There is considerable philosophical speculation and reliance upon tradition in the preaching of Bossuet; nevertheless, the allegorical speculations of Bossuet seem comparatively restrained and sane, given the circumstances of his times. His reliance on tradition was based on a deep study of that tradition itself, particularly the writings of the Church Fathers.

His genuine desire to see unity between the church of Rome and the "separated brethren" was another significant factor in his ministry. He did his best to portray the Roman church as attractively as possible to those who had left it. Evidently on the personal level he was friendly to the Huguenots – as friendly as the times would permit him to be.

Bossuet's desire to occupy a mediating position is evident in his polemical preaching; that is, he always wanted to win the other to his point of view, whether "the other" was a Huguenot or a Jew or a Jansenist. But his presentation of the question usually revealed an attempt to understand the contrary opinion. Though we might congratulate Bossuet for any attempt to be conciliatory toward the opposition in his time, we must not think that Bossuet was all sweetness and light toward his opponents. In his sermons he treated the Huguenots with abusive expressions: he called the Calvinist communion "a church of darkness" and their pastor "a minister of iniquity." Such expressions can scarcely be regarded as the new wave of ecumenicity. For his own time, however, he does show surprising openness and genuine concern for reconciliation.

It is hard to resist the temptation to play the game called "putting the preacher in another century": Bossuet is one who is tempting indeed. With his embryonic interest in church unity among the brethren and his early concern with inequality as it applied to the economic realm, we wonder what Bossuet might have said if he had lived a century and a half later when Christian socialism was on the rise. We must recognize that each of these early influences from men such as Bossuet, however dim and unformed, played their own role in forming those Christian opinions which would later emerge.

As is often true among opponents, Bossuet demonstrated more concern for reconciliation with the "separated brethren" than he did in disputes involving his own fellow priests. His conflict with Fénelon was absurd and unjustified. In his later years Bossuet seemed to mistake his own voice and opinions with that of divinity itself. He could tolerate no opposition. His little understanding or information toward mysticism led to estrangement with Fénelon and condemnation of another mystic, Madame de Guyon. The church supported him at that time, but history has been less sympathetic; and even in his own time, his reputation was not helped by the controversy.

Nevertheless, he was universally admired as a classic orator. Colbert, one of Bossuet's contemporaries, wrote of his preaching style:

> His preaching is austere but it is very Christian, and those who know him personally say that his life accords with his preaching. He always seems to me to be very clever and I know that he is good. His appearance is not deceptive, for it is charming. He gives the impression of being modest, contented and thoughtful. I know nothing of him that is not excellent.[2]

These remarks which bear on his character were written in 1662 when Bossuet was thirty-five; thirty years later, it would be impossible to find such an estimate. In fact, there is a second report on Bossuet in Colbert's *Confidential Correspondence* which shows him in a different light:

> . . . keen-witted, sympathetic, eager to please everyone with whom he came in contact and to agree with everyone's opinion, and most unwilling to take any side lest by so doing he should hinder the attainment of his real

---

2. Ibid., p. 38.

object. . . . When he sees the part that will bring him the highest fortune he will accept it whatever it may be, and it is likely that he will play it very well.

His ambition, however, was not self-directed, as the authentic records of his life show; but rather Bossuet was overeager to win agreement and a ready hearing. And whatever his personal faults, they evidently did not hinder his splendid oratory, as Colbert himself attests.[3]

Others spoke of his persuasive force and authority of language as "unexcelled upon earth." Sainte-Beuve said that "Bossuet is the most powerful, the most truly eloquent speaker and writer that our language has ever known." These flowery opinions are no doubt overstated. He most certainly is not the "most eloquent speaker and writer" that the French language ever had. But for his day – and even for a great many other days – it would be hard to find many who were superior to him in classical elegance.

His preaching is chiefly distinguished for its depth of scholarship. His language today seems stilted, but in the days of Louis XIV there was a splendor and a grandeur, even a nobility about it.

We know little of Bossuet's techniques. Apparently he often spoke with scant preparation, so that few of his sermons were put on paper before being delivered. Bossuet was not alone in that: one of the most surprising conclusions from a careful study of the notable preachers from every century is that many of them did only oral or mental composition before they spoke.

Overall, Bossuet was noted for direct speech in an era of flattery. It cannot be truthfully said that he avoided the role of court flatterer, but at least he modified the extravagant eulogy which was expected of the court preacher. Many court preachers portrayed the kings as if they could do no wrong. Bossuet was certainly indulgent of the faults of the French nobility – a nobility noted for anything but its piety – but his sermons emphasized the truths of the gospel more than the virtues of the sovereign. His main contribution was that of a leavening influence in the corrupt court that surrounded Louis XIV. His own personal loyalty to the king was never in question; in fact, that personal loyalty judiciously ignored many of the faults of

---

3. Ibid., p. 39.

the king himself, even if it did not blind him to the faults of the king's followers.

Bossuet, like many others before and after him, was faced with the cruel dilemma of either speaking softly concerning really crucial issues, or else speaking plainly and eventually having no opportunity to exercise influence. Had he chosen the latter course he would be remembered as a prophet; as it was, he chose the former course, and is remembered today only as a court preacher to Louis XIV.

Sermons

ON THE EMINENT DIGNITY OF THE POOR
IN THE CHURCH

"The last shall be first, and the first last" (Matthew 20:16).
"He shall spare the poor and needy, and save the souls of the
poor" (Psalm 72:13).

THE FIRST SHALL BE LAST, and the last first." These words of our Saviour Christ will not fully be accomplished until the general resurrection, when the just whom the world despised will hold the highest
place, and the wicked and impious who possessed their kingdom on
earth will be banished in shame to the outer darkness. Nevertheless,
this great reversal of human stations has already begun in this life,
and we see the first tokens of it in the institution of the Church. The
ineffable city whose foundations were laid by God himself has her own
laws, her own manner of government. But because Christ her Founder
came into the world to reverse the order pride had set there, it
must needs be that the Church's polity is directly opposed to the
world's; and I find that opposition chiefly in three things. First, in
the world, the rich are everywhere at advantage and are given the
first place; in the kingdom of Christ the primacy is with the poor, who
are the Church's first-born and her true children. Secondly, in the
world, the poor are subject to the rich and seem born only to serve
them; whereas in Holy Church, there is no entrance for the rich except on condition they serve the poor. Thirdly, in the world, favours
and privileges are for the rich and powerful, and the poor have no
share unless through their protection; but in Christ's Church, favours
and blessings are for the poor, and the rich have no privilege unless
by their means. Thus the words of my text have some fulfilment in
this life also. The last are the first, and the first last: since the poor, the
world's last, are the Church's first; since the rich, who claim everything for themselves and trample upon the poor, are only within the

Reprinted from *Rich and Poor in the Christian Tradition*, trans. Walter Shew-
ring (London: Burns & Oates Ltd., 1948), pp. 179–92. Preached on behalf of a
house of the poor. Used by permission.

Church at all in order to serve the poor; since the graces of the New
Covenant are the poor's by right, and the rich receive them only at
their hands. These are weighty truths, you rich of the world; they
should teach you how to act by the poor; that is, to honour their station,
relieve their needs, share their privileges; all which, by God's grace,
I mean to show you.

I

The learned and eloquent doctor, St. John Chrysostom, has a notable
parable to teach us how poverty may have the better of wealth. He puts
before us two cities, one with none but rich men, the other with none
but poor men within its walls; and he then considers which is the
stronger. In most men's opinion, doubtless the rich would win the day;
yet the great Chrysostom gives judgment for the poor. His reason is
this. The rich men's city would have much pomp and magnificence,
but it would lack strength and firm foundations. Plenty – the enemy
of labour – without self-restraint and always hastening in quest of
pleasures, would debauch men's minds and unman their spirits with
luxury, pride and idleness. Thus the arts would be neglected, the land
untilled; the laborious tasks which preserve the race would be utterly
abandoned; and the splendid city, with no enemies from without,
would fall of itself at last, ruined by its opulence. In the city of the
poor, industrious necessity, fertile in inventions and mother of useful
arts, would direct men's wits by need, whet them by study, inspire
them with manly vigour by the practice of patience; sparing no sweat,
it would execute the great works which call for great labour. . . .

But to speak of things as they are, we know that this distinction of
the two cities is no more than a pleasant fancy. Cities, bodies politic,
no less than men's temperaments, have need of blending and leavening; and therefore, in human polity, St. Chrysostom's city of the poor
is a parable only. It was left to our Saviour and to the polity of heaven
to build us a city which should be truly the city of the poor. This city
is Holy Church; and if you question the name, I give you my reason
thus. The Church in its first planning was built for the poor alone; they
are the true citizens of the blessed city which Scripture calls the City
of God. Strange as you may think this doctrine, it is none the less true.
To convince you of it, I would have you observe that there is this difference between the Synagogue and the Church; to the Synagogue
God promised temporal blessings, but the Church's glory, as the inspired Psalmist says, is all hidden and from within. "God give thee,
said Isaac to his son Jacob, the dew of heaven and the fat of the earth."
There is the blessing of the Synagogue. And in the Old Testament
God always promises his servants to lengthen their days, enrich their
families, multiply their herds, bless their land and inheritance. Such
being the promises, it is clear that riches and plenty were the portion

of the Synagogue and that hence in its institution it could not but have men of power and houses of abundance. But with the Church it is not so. In the promises of the Gospel we hear no more of temporal blessings, the lure of the gross, the playthings of children. Christ set in place of them crosses and afflictions; and by this great change the last have become first and the first last; for the rich, the first in the Synagogue, have no rank in the Church, whose true citizens are the poor and needy. . . .

In the Old Dispensation, God was pleased to show himself in splendour and majesty, and hence it was fit that the Synagogue his bride should have marks of outward greatness; in the New, God hid his infinite power under the form of a servant; hence the Church, his mystical body, must be an image of his lowliness and bear about her the marks of his free abasement. And therefore the same God in the form of his humility, desiring, as he says, that "his house should be filled," commands his servants to seek out all the distressed. "Go, he says, to the street corners, and bring me quickly" – whom? – "the poor and the feeble." Whom else? "The blind and the lame." With such he will fill his house; he will see nothing there that is not weak, for he will see nothing that does not bear his sign, weakness and the cross. The Church of Christ, therefore, is truly the city of the poor. The rich, I make bold to say, or more strictly the rich in so far as they are rich, being of the world's following, stamped with its sign, are suffered within the Church only by tolerance; it is to the poor and needy, who bear the sign of God's Son, that it properly belongs to be welcomed there. And hence it is that the inspired Psalmist calls them "God's poor." Why "God's poor"? He thus names them in prophecy because in the New Covenant God was pleased to adopt the poor with a special prerogative.

For consider: was it not to them that our Saviour was sent? *The Lord has sent me* – these are his words – *to preach the Gospel to the poor.* Again, is it not to them he speaks when in his Sermon upon the Mount, not deigning to speak to the rich except to confound their pride, he brings his words to the poor as to the appointed receivers of his Gospel? *Blessed are you poor; for yours is the kingdom of heaven.* If theirs is heaven, the kingdom of God in eternity, theirs too is the Church, the kingdom of God in time.

And as the Church is theirs, so also they are the first to enter it. "You see," said the inspired Apostle, "that there are not in the Church many wise men according to the world, not many mighty, not many noble; but God has willed to choose that which was most despised"; whence we may see plainly that Christ's Church was an assembly of the poor. And at its first founding, if the rich were received into it, at the very entrance they stripped themselves of their goods and cast them at the Aspotles' feet, coming thus with the mark of poverty to the Church, the city of the poor. So truly the Holy Ghost had willed, in that beginning of Christianity, to assert the special prerogative of the poor members of Jesus Christ! . . .

This salutary doctrine must teach us to honour the poor and needy as our elders in Christ's family, as those chosen by his Father to be the citizens of his Church, who, bearing the clearest marks of him, are also his most precious members. The Apostle St. James is my master here. "Listen," he says, "my dearest brothers"; surely he means to put before us something of note and weight. What soul so hardened as not to heed when the voice is an Apostle's – that Apostle's whom Scripture glorifies by the title of brother of our Lord. But come, here are his words: "Has not God chosen the poor to be rich in faith, and heirs of the kingdom God has promised to those who love him?" "And then," he goes on, "and then you dare to despise the poor!" The Apostle, as you see, wishes us here to consider the eminent dignity of the poor, and that prerogative of their vocation which I have sought to expound. God, he says, has chosen them in a special manner to be rich in faith, and the heirs of his kingdom. Is not this what I have said – that they are called to the Church with the honour and preference of a special choice? And must we not conclude, as St. James concludes, that it is lamentable blindness not to honour the poor, whom God himself has so honoured by the grace of pre-eminence he gives them in his Church? Christian men, pay them respect, honour their station.

St. Paul gives us example. Writing to the Romans of alms he was taking to the faithful at Jerusalem, he speaks thus: "I beseech you, my brothers, by our Lord Jesus Christ and the charity of the Holy Ghost, to help me in your prayers before God, that the service I offer may be acceptable to the saints who are in Jerusalem." Who would not be amazed at the honour he gives the poor? He does not say "the alms I am to give them," nor "the help I am to bestow on them"; he says *the offering up of my service (obsequii oblatio)*. He goes further; and I beg you to meditate his words. "Pray God," he says, "my dear brethren, that my service be acceptable to them." What does the Apostle mean? So many precautions to make an alms acceptable? What moves him to such words is the lofty dignity of the poor. A man may give for two motives: to win affection or to relieve necessity; through esteem or through pity; there you have a gift, here an alms. With an alms, men commonly think that the giving is enough; with a gift, they take more care, and there is an innocent art in setting off the gift by the manner and circumstances of its offering. It is thus that St. Paul assists the poor. He does not see them as so many unfortunates to be relieved; he sees that in their wretchedness they are the chief members of Christ and the first-born of the Church. He considers them, so ennobled, as persons to be courted; and therefore he does not rest content with relieving them by his gift, but hopes that his service may be acceptable; and to win this grace he sets the whole Church to praying. . . .

And you, ladies, clothe yourselves with the mind of St. Paul; and in your care for this house, look with respect on the poor who are its members. Consider gravely in the charity of our Lord that if the honours of the world set you above them, the seal of Christ, which they have the honour to wear, raises them above you. Honour, while you serve them, the mysterious ways of God's providence, which gives them the first rank in the Church, and that too with such a prerogative that the rich may only enter there in order to serve the poor.

II

I turn to the second truth. Christ, who in his Gospel promises only crosses and afflictions, has plainly no need of rich men in his holy Church; their grandeur has nothing in common with his deep abasement, with God's humbling himself even to the cross. We may judge, therefore, that he does not seek the rich for their own sake. For to what use can he put them in his kingdom? To build him grand temples, to enrich his altars with gold and precious stones? Do not suppose that he takes pleasure in such adornments. He accepts them from men's hands as marks of their piety, as the homage of their devotion; but so far from his asking for such costliness, is it not manifest that there is nothing more cheap and common than the necessities of his worship? He asks only the simplest water for the regeneration of his children, a little bread and wine for the celebration of his mysteries, spring of all graces. Never has he held himself better served than when men sacrificed to him in dungeons, and when faith and humility were the only adornment of his temples. Before, in the ancient law, he required pomp for his service; but in the worship of the New Covenant his way is simplicity, and this is to show the rich of the world that he needs neither them nor their treasures except for the service of the poor.

But for the poor's sake he does confess that he needs the rich; he begs their aid. *See, I tell you a mystery.* Christ needs nothing, and Christ needs all; nothing, according to his power; all, according to his compassion. This is the mystery of the New Covenant. The same mercy which once constrained him, Christ the sinless, to bear the burden of every guilt, constrains him now, Christ the blessed, to bear the burden of every wretchedness. For as the most sinless is he who bore most of sin, so the richest is he who bears most of need. Here he is hungry, there thirsty; there he groans in chains, here is racked by diseases; he suffers at once both heat and cold. Poor indeed, and poorest of the poor; for all other poor suffer for themselves only; "Christ alone suffers in the universal body of all the poor." And thus through the besetting needs of his poor members he is forced to relent in favour of the rich.

He would be well content to see in his Church those only who bear his mark — only the poor, only the needy, only the afflicted, only the distressed. But if there are none but unfortunates there, who will relieve them? What will become of the poor in whom he suffers and all whose needs he feels? He might send them his holy angels; but it is more equitable that they should be helped by their fellow-men. Come then, you rich, enter his Church; her door is opened for you at last, but opened in favour of the poor, and on condition you serve them. It is for the children's sake that strangers may come in. See then the miracle of poverty! Yes, the rich were aliens, but they are naturalised by service of the poor and helped to wash away the defilement taken from their riches. Therefore, you rich of this world, take what proud titles you will; you may bear them in the world; in the Church of Christ you are only the servants of the poor. . . .

But what service are we to pay them? In what are we bound to help them? You have already the example of Abraham. But the glorious St. Augustine will give you more particular counsel. "The service you owe the needy is to join in bearing some part of the burden that oppresses them." St. Paul commands the faithful to *bear one another's burdens*. The poor have their burden, the rich have theirs. The poor have their burden; we all know it. When we see them sweating and groaning, we cannot but know that such wretchedness is a burden which lies on their shoulders heavily indeed. The rich walk at ease; on them nothing seems to weigh; yet they have their burden too. What then is the burden of the rich? Will you believe me, Christian men? It is their own riches. The poor man's burden is need; the rich man's is abundance. . . . What then? Is it a grave burden to have excess of goods? How many a worldling do I hear wishing in his heart for such a burden! But let such men check their hasty wishes. The false presumptions of the world may forbid their understanding here how heavy abundance weighs; but when they come to that country where over much wealth will go against them, when they appear before that judgment-seat where they must render account not only of talents used but of talents buried, when they must answer before that inexorable Judge not only for their spending but for their saving and husbanding—then they will know that riches are heavy indeed, and repent in vain that they did not unburden them.

Let us not wait for that hour of doom; rather, while time is ours, let us practise the counsel of St. Paul and bear one another's burdens. Man of riches, bear the poor man's burden, relieve his necessity, help him to sustain the distress he groans under; and know that in unburdening him you unburden yourself; when you give to him, you lessen his burden, and he yours; you carry the need that weighs on him, he carries the superfluity that oppresses you. . . . For what injustice it is, my brothers, that the poor should carry the burden whole, that all the weight of distress should crush their shoulders! If they complain at it, if they murmur against God's providence—Lord, suffer me to speak so—it is with some colour of justice. For since we are all kneaded of one mass, and since there can be no great differences between clay here and clay there, why should we see, on the one side, joyfulness, favour, affluence; on the other, sadness, despair, utter need, and contempt and servitude besides? Why should one favoured man live in such abundance, able to gratify the idlest desires of a studied fastidiousness, while this other in distress – as much a man as he – cannot keep his poor family or relieve the hunger which besets him? With inequality so bewildering, could one defend divine providence for such ill apportioning of common treasures if it had not taken another means to provide for the poor's necessity and to set some equality among men again? God's means, Christian men, was the founding of his Church, where the rich may indeed enter, but on condition they serve the poor. . . . Understand this, my brothers: unless you carry the burden of the poor, you will be overwhelmed by your own, and the weight of your ill-dispensed riches will pull you down to perdition. Share with the poor the burden of poverty; take your portion of their distress, and you will earn thereby a share in their privileges.

III

Unless they so share in the privileges of the poor, there is no salvation for the rich. I can prove this to you easily, keeping still to the same principles. For if it is true, as I have said, that the Church is the city of the poor; if they hold first place there; if it was chiefly for their sake that the blessed city was built – then it follows clearly that the privileges are theirs.

In every kingdom, in every empire, there are privileged men; that is to say, eminent persons with rights beyond the ordinary; and the source of these privileges is that by birth or by office they are closer the person of the prince. It belongs to the sovereign's greatness and majesty that the lustre of his crown should be in some sort reflected on those who approach him near. Now we know from Holy Writ that the Church is a kingdom well-ordered; do not doubt then that it too has its privileged men. And whence will they gain their privileges but from fellowship with its prince, Jesus Christ? But if we would be united with Christ, let us not look among the rich for the privileges of Holy Church. Our monarch's crown is a crown of thorns, its lustre is suffering and affliction. In the poor, in those who suffer – there dwells the majesty of the spiritual kingdom. Christ himself being poor and needy, it was right that he should enter into fellowship with those like him, and shed his favours on those who share his lot.

You must not despise poverty now; you must not call it base. True, it belonged once to the dregs of the people; but the King of Glory has wedded it, he has ennobled it as his bride, and hence he bestows on the poor all the privileges of his empire. To the poor, he promises his kingdom; to the mourners, comfort; to the hungry, food; to the suffering, eternal joy. If every right, every favour, every privilege of the Gospel belongs to Christ's poor, what is left for you rich? What part

will be yours in his kingdom? He speaks of you in his Gospel only
to shiver your pride. *Woe to you that are rich!* Who would not tremble
at such a sentence? Who would not be struck with fear? Against that
terrible curse, your one hope is this. True, those privileges are the
poor's; but you may win them from them, you may gain them at their
hands; to them the Holy Ghost sends you to find heaven's favours.
Would you have your iniquities pardoned? *Redeem them,* he says, *by
alms.* Do you ask God for mercy? Seek it at the hands of the poor by
showing mercy towards them. *Blessed are the merciful.* Last, would
you enter the kingdom? The doors, says Christ, will be opened to you
if the poor will usher you in. "Make for yourselves friends who shall
receive you into everlasting dwellings." Thus, then, grace, mercy,
remission of sins, the very kingdom itself, is in their hands; and the
rich may not go in unless the poor receive them.

So, then, you poor, what wealth is yours! But you rich, what poverty
is yours! If you cling to your own goods, you will be deprived for ever
of the goods of the New Covenant, and the only portion left you will
be the terrible *Woe!* of the Gospel. *Woe to you rich, for you have received your consolation!* If you would avert that thunder, if you would
be safely sheltered from that inescapable curse, take refuge under the
wing of poverty: make exchange with the poor; give temporal goods
and reap spiritual blessings; share the distress of the afflicted, and
God will grant you to share in their privileges.

Thus much on the primacy of poverty and the need of serving it.
After which there remains nothing but to exclaim with the prophet
David: *Blessed is he that is understanding concerning the needy
and the poor.* It is not enough, Christian men, to open your bodily eyes
on the poor; you must consider them too with the eyes of understanding. Those who look on them with the outward eye see nothing in them
but what is base; they despise them. But those who open the inward
eye – understanding guided by faith – these see in them Jesus Christ;
they discern in the poor the likenesses of his poverty, the citizens of
his kingdom, the heirs of his promises, the dispensers of his graces,
the true children of his Church, the first members of his mystical
body. They hasten to aid them therefore with all the zeal of charity.
Yet it is not enough to assist them in their needs. There are those who
help the poor, yet are not understanding concerning the poor. A man
may apportion them some alms, constrained by their importunity or
touched by natural compassion; he relieves the poor man's distress,
yet he is not understanding concerning the poor. But the man who
sees the poor as the Church's first children, who honours that rank
in them and holds himself bound to serve them, who hopes for no
share in the Gospel's blessings except through brotherly love and
fellowship – that man, and he alone, understands in truth the mystery
of charity. . . .

THE HONOUR OF THE WORLD

Daniel 3:11

THE HONOUR OF THE WORLD is that great golden statue which Nabuchodonosor set up in the plain of Dura (Dan. 3:1), commanding all men to fall down and adore it. It is of prodigious height, "sixty cubits" (says Holy Scripture), for nothing appears more lofty and elevated than the honour of the world. It is of "pure gold," for nothing seems richer or more precious than this same honour. "All peoples and languages adored the golden statue," they offered sacrifices in its honour; the trumpet, lute, and harp rang out its praises. And are not these a true figure of renown, of the applause and acclamations which go to make up what men call glory? Well, it is this great and splendid idol which I want to-day to cast down at the feet of the Saviour. I am not content, with the three holy children of Babylon, to refuse to burn incense to it, and to deny it that adoration which the multitude are paying to it. No, that will not satisfy me; I want to hurl the thunderbolt of Gospel truth at this idol; I want to cast it down full length before the Cross of my Saviour; I want to crush it, to reduce it to atoms, and then to offer it in sacrifice to Christ Crucified.

Come forth, then, honour of the world, vain phantom deluding the ambitious and the proud; I summon you before a tribunal at which your condemnation is inevitable. It is not before Caesars and princes, it is not before heroes and great generals, that I force you to appear; as they were all your adorers, they would give sentence in your favour. No, I call you to a bar of judgment at which presides a King crowned with thorns. They have mockingly robed Him in purple, they have nailed Him to a Cross, that He may offer to the whole world a spectacle of ignominy. It is to this tribunal that I remand you; it is before this King that I accuse you. And of what crimes, do you ask – you who are listening to me? I will tell you. There are three capital crimes of which I accuse the honour of the world.

In the first place, I accuse it of flattering and of corrupting virtue; secondly, of disguising vice and of lending credence to its professions; finally, to fill up the measure of its presumption, of ascribing to men what belongs to God alone, and of enriching them, where it is possible, with those things of which it has robbed His Divine Majesty.

In the first place, then, before the Cross of Jesus Christ I accuse the honour of the world of being the corrupter of virtue and innocence.

Reprinted from *Great French Sermons from Bossuet, Bourdaloue, and Massillon*, ed. D. O'Mahony (London: Sands and Co., 1917), pp. 238–53. Used by permission.

And it is not I alone who bring this accusation, I have St. John Chrysostom to support me in it. In his 17th Homily upon the Epistle to the Romans, the great preacher tells us that virtue which loves praise and vainglory is like a woman who gives herself up to a life of sin and shame. Indeed it is a remarkable fact that purity and modesty not only shrink from every act and word that is contrary to decency and propriety, but also from every kind of vainglorious display and from extravagant praise and admiration. This is so with both men and women who have been brought up from their childhood in well-regulated homes, in an atmosphere of purity and delicacy. And assuredly this is because reason itself as well as a God-given instinct teaches us that just as the body has its purity which immodesty corrupts, so the soul has a certain integrity which may be violated by praise.

We must, however, go further and penetrate into the origin of that shame which a soul, well-nurtured and in the grace of God, feels in receiving the praises of the world. This shame is natural to virtue, to Christian virtue of which alone I take any cognizance. It is, I say, in the very nature of such virtue to dread praise; how can it be otherwise when we remember our Divine Lord's warnings and commands on this subject? He says: "Take heed that you do not your justice before men to be seen by them" (Matt. 6:1). Again, as regards prayer: "When thou shalt pray, enter into thy chamber and having shut thy door pray to thy Father in secret" (Matt. 6:6). Again, respecting almsgiving: "When thou dost an almsdeed, sound not a trumpet before thee; let not thy left hand know what they right hand doeth" (Matt. 6:3, 6).

Following out this teaching of the Gospel, this insistence upon the retiring nature of Christian virtue, its beauty and sweetness which it loves to keep hidden from the eyes of the world, I find an exact prototype in the character of a modest, pure-minded young girl brought up under the parental roof in extreme quietness and seclusion. She is not taken to theatres or public assemblies of any sort. She stays at home, busy with her simple daily occupations, under the watchful eyes of God her Father. This Heavenly Father loves to see her thus modest, self-restrained, retiring; He destines for her a Bridegroom, Jesus Christ Himself; He desires that she should give to this Divine Spouse a pure heart which has never been corrupted by any other affection. He prepares for her, in the happy future, honour and praise such as is alone worth having; and meantime until that joyful day comes He will not let her be spoilt by the praises of men. This is why she shuns society, this is why she loves her secrecy and her solitude. If indeed occasionally the world catches a glimpse of her marvellous loveliness—for it is too radiant to be always entirely hidden—her perfect simplicity shields her from that notice which she never wishes to attract; all those who admire her beauty are warned by her modesty "to glorify her Father Who is in Heaven" (Matt. 5:16). This is a perfect picture of Christian virtue. Is there anything more admirable than its discreet and modest loveliness?

But now how does vainglory act towards this beautiful creature, so pleasing in God's sight? St. John Chrysostom tells us that it lays traps for her innocence, enters like a thief into the quiet household, poisons the wells of pure and wholesome teaching; then it entices her from her modest retirement, persuades her to court the admiration of men, though hitherto she had believed that she was (as she truly is) made only for God; and then it leads her, step by step, along that broad road that seems to her so smooth and bordered with such gay flowers, on and on, a little further and a little further, then down a steeper way that loses itself in a deep gulf where innocence is lost; and this creature, once so pure and lovely, now lies tangled in the brambles, soiled with the mud of that bottomless pit of shame. Ah! my Crucified Jesus, this is the crime of which I accuse the honour of the world, which undertakes first to corrupt virtue and then to sell it at so vile a price, to sell it for the praise of men. Do Thou, O holiest Lord, judge and condemn this most vile crime!

My second ground of accusation against the honour of the world is its desire to accredit vice by making it appear wholly different, in the eyes of men, from what it really is. In justification of this accusation, I assert in the first place that all those who are dominated by the honour of the world are invariably and inevitably vicious. *"Vice,"* says St. Thomas Aquinas, *"comes from an ill-regulated judgment."* Now I maintain that there is nothing more ill-regulated than the judgment of those of whom we are speaking; since, making (as they do) honour to be their sole end and aim, it follows naturally that they prefer it even to virtue; and such being the case, you may imagine how far astray they are certain to wander, how ill-regulated their conduct and whole life are sure to be! Virtue is one of God's many gifts to man, and the most precious of them all; honour is a gift bestowed by men upon one another, and not even the greatest of those gifts which it is in their limited power to give. And yet, in your pride and blindness, you are actually foolish enough to prefer this almost contemptible human gift to that Divine one which the Eternal Father produces from His treasury of precious things for your acceptance! Is not this a proof that your judgment is worse than ill-regulated? that it is upset, distorted, absolutely overthrown? You must then, honour of the world, in the first place admit being actually confounded and struck dumb by my demonstration that nothing originating from you, claiming you as its author and producer, can be otherwise than vicious.

In the second place, however, we must notice that vicious as this brood is and must be, it does not include those who are the most deeply degraded, the most steeped in infamy of every sort and kind. To attempt to glorify the Achabs and Jezabels of Sacred Scripture, the Neros, Domitians and Heliogabaluses of profane history, even to wish to do it, would be mere absurdity. To honour vice which is nothing but vice, which shows itself in all its hideous deformity, without one sheltering rag of decency, is a thing impossible; matters are not yet so desperate even in this poor world. No, the vices which the honour of the world crowns are more decent vices; or to speak more correctly — for what decency can there be in vices? — they are more specious ones; there is about them some semblance of virtue. Honour which was intended like a faithful handmaid to wait upon virtue, knows exactly how she clothes and adorns herself, and cunningly steals from the beautiful creature some of her ornaments with which to deck and disguise the monster vice which it desires to set up in the world in her stead. That this is done we know too well by sad experience; how it is done it is now my business to discover, and to expose this mystery of iniquity in all its breadth and length.

In order to do this I must first remind you that there are two classes of virtues. One is the true and the Christian sort, severe, constant, inflexible, always keeping closely and steadily to its rules of conduct, incapable of being turned aside from them by any influence however powerful. This is not the world's virtue; that world does indeed give it some slight recognition as it passes it, some scant and grudging praise for form's sake, but never advances it to posts of distinction; it is not thought capable of dealing with business matters; something more yielding and accommodating is wanted to win the favour of the public. It is, moreover, far too serious and too retiring; and if it is unwilling to take part in the intrigues and schemes of society, does it expect to be sought out in its retirement and privacy? No, no, the world will hear nothing of this sort of virtue.

There is quite another kind which the world fashions for itself, much more accommodating and plastic; a virtue adjusted, not to rules that would be too austere, but to the opinion, to the varying humours of men. This is a commercial virtue; it will take great care not always to break its word, but on certain occasions it will not be in the least degree scrupulous, and it will manage to keep up a good appearance at the expense of others. This is the virtue of the worldly-wise; that is to say, of those who really have no virtue at all; or rather it is the specious mask beneath which they hide their vices. Saul gives his daughter Michol to David, he has promised her to the slayer of the giant Goliath; he must satisfy the people and keep his word, but when the opportunity presents itself he will find a pretext for taking her away from him. Jehu, having destroyed the house of Achab, according to the command of the Lord, offers in sacrifice to the living God the idol of Baal, his temples, his priests, his prophets; he does not, says Holy Scripture, leave a single one of them alive (4 Kings [2 Kings] 10:17, 25-27).

This in itself is a good action; but, says the Scripture, "he departed not from the ways of Jeroboam, who made Israel to sin, nor did he forsake the golden calves of Bethel and Dan" (4 Kings 10:29). Why did he not destroy them as well as Baal and his temple? Because that would have injured his own prospects, interfered with his own plans. Because he remembered the miserable policy of Jeroboam: "If I suffer these people to go up to Jerusalem to offer sacrifices to God in His Temple, they will return to the House of Judah," to those kings who are their lawful sovereigns (3 Kings [1 Kings] 12:26); I will build an altar for them here; I will give them gods whom they may worship without leaving my kingdom and putting my throne in peril.

Such is in truth the virtue of the world, a deceitful, fictitious virtue which has only the semblance of the reality. Why was it ever invented, since that same world wishes to be vicious without hindrance or restraint? "Because," says St. Chrysostom, "evil cannot stand quite alone, it is either too malignant or too weak, it must be supported by some kind of good, even it be only the shadow of virtue or some one of its many ornaments." Let a man profess himself openly to be a cheat and a swindler, and no one will be taken in by him; let a thief take the life of a comrade in order to rob him, and he will be shunned as you would shun a poisonous reptile. Men so absolutely vicious as that are at a discount with everyone. But it is very easy for them to change this. There is no need for them to put on the mask of virtue or the gilded trappings of hypocrisy; vice may still appear as vice, and, provided there is just a little suspicion of something better in their character and dealings with one another, that is quite enough to gain for them the world's honour.

Take for instance a man who has grown rich by tremendous frauds, his life is one long course of sordid avarice, everyone despises him; still he always keeps a good table and makes a show of liberality, spending for his own purposes what is really other people's money, and is, on the whole, considered to be a very respectable member of society. Take another instance; two men quarrel, and settle their dispute by a duel, in which one is killed. It is a very disgraceful affair; still there was some show of courage in it, both men (says the world) made a brave fight; and the survivor, although the laws condemn him and the Church excommunicates him, is applauded by that world in spite of laws and Church. Is there in fact any one vice which the honour of the world does not accredit, however little it may try to disguise itself? Even the vilest and most shameful of sins, which when openly practised is called debauchery, if it puts on ever so flimsy a disguise, a little show of fidelity, discretion, perseverance, does it not at once find that it can show a bold front and seem worthy of the noblest and the most exalted in the land? Why, it actually loses its odious name and is called gallantry, courtesy, a suitable characteristic of a man of the world! It is marvellous that such things can be. And yet if we remember that those who know nothing about precious stones are easily taken in by a little glitter and colour, so as to be satisfied to spend their money on a mere counterfeit bauble, and if we also consider how very little the world knows about real virtue, it may seem less surprising that it should be dazzled by the faintest semblance of it, and that the honour of the world should find it very easy to accredit vice.

Therefore the sinner lives at his ease, in a sort of triumph, enjoying more or less a public reputation for every kind of excellence. If from time to time his conscience is troubled, if there are moments when it denies him that honour which the world is always eager to give him, there is a remedy soon found for his ill.

Here are flatterers, numerous and busy enough for the purpose, thronging his doorsteps, his antechamber, nay, his very banqueting hall, even sitting down at his table, so intimate are they with him. Let him listen to their whispers, so softly and insidiously breathed into his ear. They tell him that he has a name in the world, that his reputation is an established fact. They know well enough that there is always lurking within his breast a secret flatterer, which will chime in with all that these outsiders may suggest or assert, and which has the power of making itself heard at all moments. They make a careful study of his character and get such a clever hold of his weak points, that he falls in at once with all that they suggest to him. He quite gives up the task of looking into his own conscience, which shows him his own ugly deformity too plainly; he will use no mirror but this one which flatters him; and, in the words of St. Gregory, "forgetting entirely what he really is, he goes about always on the lookout for what others may be saying of him, and fancies himself just what flattery represents him to be." Assuredly God will revenge Himself upon him; and this will be His vengeance: He will silence at last all flatterers and will abandon the proud sinner to the reproaches of his own conscience.

O Lord, I beseech Thee, judge the honour of the world, which makes vice not only pleasing to others but even to itself. Thou wilt do this, I know. Yes, the day of His Judgment will come, and then will the prophecy of Isaias be fulfilled: "The mirth of the timbrels hath ceased, the noise of them that rejoice is ended, the melody of the harp is silent" (Isa. 24:8). At last this tumult of applause has ceased to deafen the ears of the sinner; all is silent; his flatterers seem to be struck dumb, the music of their praises no longer soothes and delights him. What a change this will be! what a day of sudden amazement for all, both the wise and the foolish! The Bridegroom will come at an hour when none look for Him, when none expect Him. The Wise Virgins will go forth to meet Him with their lamps burning; their good works are the oil which feed them; now they shine brightly before God and men in that night of darkness and distress; now Jesus Himself, in Whom alone they gloried, will praise them in the presence of His Eternal Father. But as for you, O Foolish Virgins, what will you do? You who have no oil in your lamps, and who are vainly imploring others to give you of theirs? You to whom no praises are due, and who long so passionately and so hopelessly for a little borrowed glory? In vain will you cry: "Give us of your oil! we too desire praise, we too would fain hear from those lips Divine one word of that approval which is so lavishly bestowed upon others!" Alas! for those foolish virgins there can be no such word. Across the solemn darkness comes this stern demand: "Who are you?" and then, "I know you not" (Matt. 25:9–12). Like those foolish virgins, the sinner, self-deceived and blinded by the false glare of the world's honour, will in that dreadful day cry out for light, marvelling that he should be thus abandoned, forsaken, overtaken by such horrible darkness and despair. Where are his flatterers now? They are taking part against him. Their own damnation is certain, it is a just reward of their crime in leading him into sin; therefore they desire to drag him down with them into the lowest depths of everlasting misery.

Yes, sinful and degraded soul, now when it is too late you will see that you were yourself the chief of all your flatterers. Now you will detest your life, now you will curse all your actions; and the shame of your perfidies, the injustice of your frauds, the infamy of your adulterous conduct, will be eternally before your eyes. What has become of that honour of the world which palliated all your sins? It has vanished into smoke. Oh, honour of the world, how short was your reign? how I laugh to scorn all your vain triumph and pompous show which lasted only for a day! how flimsy and poor was the disguise in which you managed to cloak vice! so flimsy that you cannot prevent the monster from being recognized by that tribunal before which I am accusing you! Having summed up my evidence and finished my accusation, I now demand sentence to be pronounced. You will have no favour shown you in this judgment; because, besides the fact that your own crimes are inexcusable, you have infringed upon the rights of Him Who presides at the tribunal, and you have done this that you might invest His creatures with them. This is the crowning point of my indictment.

Since all good belongs to God, and man is of himself nothing, it is clear that nothing can be attributed to man without encroaching upon the rights of God and His sovereign dominion. This proposition, the truth of which is so well known, is of itself sufficient to justify what I assert, namely, that the most serious of all the charges brought against the honour of the world is that of desiring to deprive God of what is His due in order to invest His creatures with it. In fact if the honour of the world contented itself with representing our advantages to us so that we might give thanks and praise to our Lord for them, we should not call it by such a name, but should without a moment's hesitation rank it among the Christian virtues. Man, however, who desires to be flattered, cannot enter into this feeling; if you compel him to attribute his possession of any sort of good, wealth, talents, no matter what it may be, to any source except himself, he thinks that you are robbing him of it, and no praise is really acceptable to him unless he can with the most intense self-satisfaction say in his heart, *"I did it all myself!"*

Although it may not be possible to express in words the audacity of this conduct, we may yet form some idea of it from the reasoning of St. Fulgentius. That great bishop tells us that men set themselves up above God in two different ways: either by doing what He condemns, or by attributing to themselves what is His gift. You do what God condemns, when you make a bad use of His creatures; you attribute to yourselves what God gives you, when you presume upon yourselves. Doubtless these two modes of behaviour are very criminal, but we can easily understand that the latter is by far the most insolent; and although we can never sufficiently blame the audacity of a man who, whatever may be his way of doing so, abuses the gifts of His Creator, yet that audacity is unquestionably more outrageous when he appropriates these gifts to himself than when he simply makes a perverted use of them. And why? Because the first is the action of a rebellious subject who disobeys his Sovereign, whereas the second is an attempt against the person of that Sovereign, and an attack upon His throne; and if by the first crime the rebel repudiates the authority of the Prince, by the second he attempts in some sort to make himself that Prince's equal by attributing His power to himself.

You may perhaps think that so insane an attempt is rarely to be met with among men, that they are not yet so outrageous as to wish to make themselves equal with God; but I must disabuse you to such an idea. I must, alas! tell you that this crime is, to our shame, only too common among us; yes, ever since our first parents lent an ear to that most dangerous flattery: "You shall be as gods" (Gen. 3:5). Since then we all really wish to be little gods, we are all striving and struggling for independence. Listen to what the Holy Ghost says to the King of Tyre, addressing in the person of that haughty sovereign all the proud of the earth: "Thy heart is lifted up, and thou hast said: I am God" (Ezech. 28:2).

Is it possible that a man can so absolutely forget what he really is as to say: "I am God?" No, that is not said so openly; we should like to be able to do so, but the consciousness of our mortal, our finite nature forbids it. How then does a man say: "I am God?" The words following the passage which I have just quoted, give the explanation: "Thou hast set thy heart as if it were the heart of God" (Ezech. 28:2). What is the exact meaning of these most significant words?

In the first place, we must remember that as God is the universal principle and the common centre of all things; as He is, in the words of an ancient writer, the treasury of being, and possesses all things in Himself in the infinity of His nature, He must of necessity be filled with Himself, He must think only of Himself, He must be occupied only with Himself. It is fitting, indeed, that Thou, O King of Ages, shouldst have a heart filled only with Thyself! O Source of all things! Centre of the Universe! . . . But the heart of the creature is fashioned, ah! how differently. It is but a little brook which must flow back to its source; it possesses nothing in itself, it is rich only in its origin; it is nothing in itself, and must only seek itself in that essence from which it came forth. Proud man, this thought is beyond you; you are but a vile creature, and yet "you have set your heart as if it were the heart of God"; you seek for honour in yourself, you are full of nothing but yourself.

Let us, then, judge ourselves, and not in our pride and self-complacency flatter ourselves. Here is a man of rare eloquence, holding a prominent position in council, swaying the minds of his audience by his powerful language and carefully thought-out arguments; well, this man, this gifted orator, if he does not go back to the fountain-head, if he believes that it is his own eloquence and not the resistless power of God which is touching the hearts of his hearers, is tacitly saying to himself: "Our lips are our own" (Ps. 11:5). Again, the great statesman who has brought the most complicated and troublesome affairs to a successful issue and is dizzy with the applause of his fellow politicians, if he fails to render to God the honours due to Him, is assuredly saying in his heart: "Our mighty hand, and not the Lord, hath done all these things" (Deut. 32:27). Or the clever business man, who by lucky investments and every kind of crafty financial scheme has made his fortune without one thought of God Who gave him all his power of mind and action; is he not saying with Pharaoh: "The river is mine, and I made myself" (Ezech. 29:3)? Yes, thus it is that the honour of the world makes us attribute to ourselves all that we do, and ends by setting us upon pedestals like little gods.

Well, proud and self-complacent soul, thus deified by the honour of the world, see how the eternal, the living God abases Himself in order to confound you! Man makes himself God through pride, God makes Himself man through humility! Man falsely attributes to himself what belongs to God; and God, in order to teach him to humble himself, takes truly what belongs to man. This is the remedy for insolence; this alone has power to confound the honour of the world. I have arraigned it before this God-Man, before this humbled God; you have heard this accusation, now hear the sentence. Yet it will not be spoken by word of mouth; it is enough for you to see it written as it is in letters of blood. You will need nothing more to convince you that the honour of the world has lost its suit. This sentence condemns the judgment of men by an entirely new method of judgment. Jesus Christ only condemns them by allowing Himself to be judged by them and to receive from them on His own Person the most unjust sentence ever known; the excess of this injustice makes all their other judgments henceforth discredited. At that supreme moment, at that awful Trial, all who took part in it, whether as judges, accusers, witnesses, or mere onlookers, with scarcely an exception, judged wrongly; Jews and Romans, high and low, rich and poor, the chosen of God and the pagans, the learned and the ignorant, priests and people, our Lord's friends and His enemies, His persecutors and His disciples. Yes, on that Hill of Calvary, on that Cross of shame, Jesus Christ the Incarnate God, our Pattern, our Master, our King, deigned in His own sacred Person to undergo a sentence than which nothing so malicious and corrupt, nothing so blindly extravagant, nothing so lawless, so varying, so precipitate, so impious, has ever been known or ever will be known in the world's history; and this He did to disabuse our minds for ever of any confidence in, any esteem for, that shifty, many-sided, dishonoured thing which we call the Honour of the World.

FOR ADDITIONAL INFORMATION ABOUT JACQUES BOSSUET:

Calvet, Jean. *Bossuet: L'Homme et L'Oeuvre.* Paris: Boivin & Co., 1941.
Currier, Albert H. "Bossuet." *Nine Great Preachers.* New York: Pilgrim Press, 1912.
Lear, Henrietta Louisa. *Bossuet and His Contemporaries.* New York: Pott, Young & Co., 1875.
Sanders, Ella K. *Jacques Bénigne Bossuet: A Study.* London: SPCK, 1921.
Simpson, William J. Sparrow. *A Study of Bossuet.* New York: Macmillan Co., 1937.

FOR OTHER SERMONS BY JACQUES BOSSUET:

Sermons. 4 vols. Nouv. éd. complète. Suivant le texte de l'éd. de Versailles. Paris: Garnier, 1873.
Great French Preachers. Vols. 1 and 2. London: Grant Richards, 1904.

O'Mahony, D., ed. *Great French Sermons from Bossuet, Bourdaloue and Massillon.* London: Sands & Co., 1917.
Also: *Select Sermons and Funeral Orations* (1803).

JOHN BUNYAN

1628-1688

JOHN BUNYAN

1628	*Born in Elstow, Bedfordshire, England*
1644	*Joined the army*
1646	*Left the army and married*
1653	*Baptized by John Gifford, Bedford Baptist Church*
1655	*Began to preach*
1659	*Married second wife after death of first*
1660	*Forbidden by the government to preach, arrested for disobeying and placed in jail*
1672	*Released from prison and became pastor of Bedford Baptist Church*
1675	*Placed in jail for another six months*
1688	*Died in August while visiting a friend in London*

HE SPENT HIS LIFE within five miles of his birthplace, except for a few trips to London; but today his name is known throughout the world. As a young adult, he could neither read nor write; yet by the end of his life he ranked among the most famous of Christian authors—his imaginative writing has been ranked with that of Dante and Milton. He was not converted until he was in his late twenties, nor did he begin to preach until he was almost thirty; yet he is known as one of the greatest Christians and most significant preachers of his day. John Bunyan was an amazing man.

He is better known for his writing than for his preaching—his sermons are unknown, while *Pilgrim's Progress* is perhaps the best known book in all Christian literature apart from the Bible. Nevertheless he was an active preacher; he could move men to God by the preached word as well as by the written word.

LIFE AND TIMES

Bunyan lived in one of the most significant periods in English history. His was an age of famous men: when Bunyan was born, Richard Baxter was thirteen years of age; George Fox, the founder of Friends, was four; John Milton was twenty; Oliver Cromwell was twenty-eight; Shakespeare had been dead for only twelve years. The colonists in New England had suffered through eight winters; those in Virginia had moved toward the building of a permanent colony after twenty-one years of labor.

During Bunyan's life a number of monarchs were to seriously affect his destiny. Charles I was on the throne when he was born, and he lived under the reigns of Charles II and of James II. Bunyan died shortly before the coming of William and Mary to the throne of England and the dawn of religious liberty. In France, Louis XIV was monarch. In his court the famous French preachers were sounding forth their messages. But the old monarchies were growing shaky; it was a revolutionary age. Two revolutions in England had special meaning for Bunyan: the political revolution which caused him to spend many years in prison, and the religious revolution which significantly affected his religious concepts and experiences.

In a sense the political revolution in England had been brewing for years and years, but the immediate conflict which affected Bunyan began in the year of his birth. In 1628 Parliament had passed the Petition of Rights as an effort to limit the monarchy in England. It represented the effort of the people to gain more rights and liberties. Charles I, the reigning monarch, responded by dismissing Parliament. For eleven years he attempted to rule without Parliament. In desperate need of funds, Charles finally recalled Parliament in 1640. Parliament responded by bringing to trial and punishment a number of the king's allies in high places of government. Charles responded with a show of military force, and by 1642 civil war had broken out in England.

The forces of Parliament and king faced one another in battle. Neither side had the ability to gain total victory. The war seesawed back and forth across the land with no apparent end in sight. Finally, under the leadership of Oliver Cromwell, a group of men fighting under the banner of Parliament slowly began to be effective in battle. They were devout, disciplined, and committed to basic democratic concepts; they refused to allow class structure to interfere with military efficiency. The king's army fell back in confusion and defeat before the troops of Cromwell.

In 1649 Charles I was beheaded. Cromwell led republican England to great power throughout the world. He also established some degree of religious liberty, particularly in regard to Protestant groups and sects. Many Puritan emphases were implemented by law under Cromwell, but the people grew weary of his strict and somber rule, and when he died in 1658 the nation moved back toward monarchy. In 1660 Charles II was welcomed to the throne of England. Whereas England had been in the sober confines of Puritanism, Charles II brought in an era of extravagant sensual display. Under Charles II, the Act of Uniformity was revived—an act which required all pastors to register with the state church. It was designed to curtail the growth of groups such as Baptists and other dissenters.

In 1685 James II became king. He tried to return England to the Catholic church but the people rebelled; soon he was removed from power and fled England. In 1688 William and Mary came to the throne and the day of enlightenment dawned for England.

In the midst of political upheaval, England was also being shaken by religious revolution. The Protestant Reformation had never been as thorough in England as it had been in other parts of Europe, and much business remained unsettled. Catholics and Protestants struggled with one another for power and control, while in the Protestant camp itself there was much division between the Episcopalians, the Presbyterians, and the various dissenter groups.

Religious life in the established church had become sterile and worldly. Those who objected to this deadness in the church appealed for a purer form of church life; these people became the "Puritans" of Cromwell's day. Puritanism took on many forms in England, but in general there was agreement among Puritans that there should be sobriety and godliness in life and in the church. Some of the Puritans endeavored to purify the church from within, but others were not members of the established church and believed in a reform from without. Bunyan was deeply influenced by the Puritan concepts of his day. He was not a member of the established church, and therefore was subject to persecution both by Puritans within the church and by those who did not agree with Puritan views at all.

Into this tumultuous seventeenth century English world, John Bunyan was born. His family was poor—his father was a tinker by trade. He taught his son how to repair pots and pans but had little else to give him. When Bunyan was sixteen years old his mother and sister died; his father remarried almost immediately, and Bunyan went into a period of rebellion.

He joined the army, fighting in the forces of the Parliament against Charles I. The religious fervor of the army under the leadership of Cromwell influenced almost all the troops. Though Bunyan was not converted at this time, he could not help but be affected by the Puritan zeal of Cromwell's forces.

Returning home to Elstow, Bunyan married. He was extremely poor and so was his new wife: all she brought into their marriage were two books, *The Plain Man's Pathway to Heaven* and *The Practice of Piety*. But this young woman powerfully influenced his life. Up until Bunyan's marriage he had been in total spiritual rebellion; his life had been shallow and worldly. Under the guidance of his wife, other Christians in the community, and John Gifford, pastor of the Baptist Church at Bedford, Bunyan began to think seriously about the Christian faith.

After a long struggle and great consideration, he professed faith in Jesus Christ and was baptized by John Gifford. Bunyan became a member of the Baptist Church at Bedford in 1653. To Bunyan's great sorrow, his wife died in 1655. Her Christian influence continued through him: in that same year he began to preach. People responded enthusiastically to him and to his message. He continued to follow his trade as a tinker, preaching as he moved from house to house and village to village. During this time Bunyan also began to do some writing; his first writing was directed against the Quakers. In 1659 he married his second wife, Elizabeth, who was to be an effective helpmate in the troubled years ahead.

In 1660 Charles II took the throne of England. By the restoration of the Act of Uniformity, Bunyan was forbidden by the government to preach. He refused to obey the government order, was arrested, and thrown in jail.

The authorities urged him to fulfill the simple request of the law—to register with the state church. He refused. He told them that if he were released he would immediately begin to preach again. For six years he remained in jail. He supported himself and helped support his family by making lace. His wife and blind daughter suffered greatly in his absence.

Even while in prison Bunyan preached. He won the confidence of the jailers, who released him to go into the woods to proclaim a sermon to his congregation and then return to prison. He also preached through the bars of his cell and often talked to his jailers about the truth of the gospel.

In 1666 he was released from prison. He immediately began to preach, was promptly rearrested and returned to jail. He spent another six years in Bedford jail. His twelve years' imprisonment might be attributed to mere stubbornness; it should more properly be attributed to his deep commitment to religious liberty and his refusal to acknowledge the supremacy of secular government over the church.

Released from prison in 1672, Bunyan became pastor of the Bedford Baptist Church where he served as a distinguished pastor. He not only preached in his own church but also in the surrounding territory; he made trips to London to visit with friends and to proclaim the gospel. Often, with only one day's notice, his crowds would be so huge that the places of worship could not hold them.

John Bunyan was a preacher who dealt forthrightly with the issues of his day. He thundered against the vice and corruption creeping across the nation as a shadow cast by the degenerate court of Charles II. He also grappled with the problem of government and its relation to churches. By his life, his writing, and his preaching, Bunyan pled for the cause of religious liberty. Others may have argued more brilliantly, but none were more persuasive in the cause for freedom of religion.

Some pastors are remembered most for their preaching; this is not the case with John Bunyan. Bunyan is remembered for the courage he displayed in dealing with the issues of his revolutionary period and for the brilliant and inspiring writing which has become part of the great heritage of English literature rather than for his sermons. In fact, his sermons are not read today except by those interested in the specialized study of the history of preaching; his great literary works have overshadowed his splendid sermons. But we must not let Bunyan the brilliant political reformer, nor Bunyan the masterful writer, cause us to forget Bunyan the excellent preacher; to him preaching was the great task to which God had led him.

PREACHING AND SERMONS

After reading *Pilgrim's Progress*, Bunyan's sermons are a little disappointing. We expect the same imaginative style, and it is not there: we look for the same dramatic flair, the imaginative use of description. Only occasionally do these qualities of his sublime allegory find their way into Bunyan's preaching. On the other hand, he was no Jekyll-and-Hyde preacher whose writings rank among the classics and whose sermons sound very much like a Bedford tinker. Even if Bunyan had never written *Pilgrim's Progress*, he might still be remembered as one of the greatest preachers of the Christian church.

In spite of the faults of his sermons which were quite typical for his day—such as extreme length, digression, tedious divisions—Bunyan's sermons had many strengths: they are picturesque and lively, even if not as colorful as *Pilgrim's Progress*; each has a thorough explanation of the text in simple, vigorous language; and every one shows a masterful use of dialogue in answering objections or supporting arguments. To these qualities must be added Bunyan's earnest conviction and powers of personal appeal.

Bunyan was unmistakably a Puritan preacher, but he was not a *typical* Puritan preacher: in Froude's history of the Puritan period he said of Bunyan, "No such preacher to the uneducated English masses was to be found within the four seas. . . . With the thing which these people meant by inspiration he was abundantly supplied."[1] This evaluation is all the more remarkable since Froude took great pains in the same history to exonerate those who imprisoned Bunyan.

Bunyan's fame as a preacher was not confined to the limits of Bedfordshire although most of his ministry was spent there; it also extended to London, where on various occasions he preached to great crowds. A contemporary admirer and citizen of London wrote:

> When Mr. Bunyan preached in London, if there was one day's notice given there would be more people come together to hear him preach than the meetinghouse could hold. I have been to hear him preach by my computation to about 1200 at a morning sermon by 7:00 o'clock on a working day in the dark winter time. I also computed about 3000 that came to hear him one Lord's day in London at a town's end meetinghouse so that half were compelled to go away again for want of room, and then himself had to enter a back door and be pulled almost over people to get up stairs to his pulpit.[2]

1. Albert H. Currier, *Nine Great Preachers* (Boston: The Pilgrim Press, 1912), p. 208.
2. Ibid., p. 209.

Bunyan appealed not only "to the uneducated English masses" but also to the noblemen and scholars: the learned Dr. John Owen was one of his frequent hearers in London and invited him to preach to his own select congregation in Moorefields. King Charles II reportedly asked Owen how he could go to hear that tinker preach. Owen replied that he would willingly exchange his learning for the ability to preach as well as the tinker.

Bunyan continued to live in Bedford, preaching for short periods in London once or twice a year. His little Baptist chapel became too small and a larger one was built. In Bedford he offended many of his own denomination by exchanging pulpits with Presbyterians and Independents – apparently Bunyan both preached and practiced an unusual ecumenicity for his age. But he had some preferences at that point – one phrase in his sermon, "The Heavenly Footman," is particularly interesting:

> Mistrust thy own strength, and throw it away; down on thine knees in prayer to the Lord for the spirit of truth; search His word for direction; flee seducers' company; keep company with the soundest Christians, that have most experience of Christ; and be sure thou have a care of Quakers, Ranters, Freewillers: also do not have too much company with some Anabaptists, though I go under that name myself.

The various sermons chosen as representative of the preaching of Bunyan are among his best. Each is different, but all of them have certain strengths in common. The style of these sermons, even if inferior to *Pilgrim's Progress*, is excellent. His words are simple and well-chosen, his sentences brief. Bunyan practiced his own rule for good style: "to be plain and simple, and lay down the things as it was." He was successful on both counts. Macaulay said of his style:

> The vocabulary is the vocabulary of the common people. Yet no writer (or speaker as well) has said more exactly what he meant to say. For magnificence, for pathos, for vehement exhortation, for every purpose of the poet, the orator and the divine, this homely dialect – the dialect of plain working men, is sufficient.[3]

---

3. Ibid., p. 211.

John Brown, biographer of Bunyan said, "Let him write on what subject he may, he writes not long before he melts with tenderness or closes with fire."

As for his intention to "lay down the things as it was," no one could doubt he succeeded; his sermons are marked by enthusiasm and earnestness. Bunyan never lost himself in his literary gifts — he struck straight to the heart of the issue, urging his hearers to repent and be converted. Few preachers knew how to conclude more forcefully than Bunyan:

> Well, then, sinner, what sayest thou? Where is thy heart? . . . Think quickly, man; have no dallying in this matter. Confer not with flesh and blood; look up to heaven, and see how thou likest it; also to hell, and accordingly devote thyself. If thou dost not know the way, inquire at the Word of God; if thou wantest company, cry for God's Spirit; if thou wantest encouragement, entertain the promises. But be sure thou begin betimes; get into the way, run apace, and hold out to the end; and the Lord give thee a prosperous journey. Farewell.

Bunyan said of his preaching, "I did labor so to speak the Word that, if it were possible, the sin and the person guilty be particularized by it." His applications show his attempt to be specific in his preaching. With such pointed preaching Bunyan sometimes condemned himself by his own words, but he never allowed the thought of his own sin to weaken his preaching:

> When, sometimes, I have been about to preach upon some smart and searching portion of the word, I have found the tempter suggest, "This condemns yourself; of this your own soul is guilty. Wherefore preach not of it at all; or if you do, you so mince it as to make way for your own escape, lest instead of awakening others, you lay such guilt upon your own soul as you will never get from under."
>
> But I thank the Lord I have been kept from consenting to these horrid suggestions, and have rather, as Samson, bowed myself with all my might, to condemn sin and transgression wherever I found it, though therein I did bring guilt upon my own conscience. Let me die, thought I, with the Philistines, rather than deal corruptly with the blessed word of God.[4]

---

4. Ibid.

As a reading of *Pilgrim's Progress* might suggest, Bunyan's sermons are filled with scriptural allusions; most of his illustrations and descriptive imagery come from biblical themes. Few men ever studied the Bible harder than he did; "I never was out of the Bible, either by reading or meditation. . . . I have not fished in other men's waters: my Bible and concordance are my only library." Bunyan gained his own personal strength from the Bible, and this faith was shared with others through his preaching.

Even with all of his genius, John Bunyan best represents that great number of uneducated men whose dedicated talents and simple trust in the Bible have made them effective preachers of the Word of God.

Sermons

THE HEAVENLY FOOTMAN

"So run that ye may obtain" (1 Corinthians 9:24).

HEAVEN AND HAPPINESS is that which every one desireth, insomuch that wicked Balaam could say, "Let me die the death of the righteous, and let my last end be like his." Yet, for all this, there are but very few that do obtain that ever-to-be-desired glory, insomuch that many eminent professors drop short of a welcome from God into this pleasant place. The apostle, therefore, because he did desire the salvation of the souls of the Corinthians, to whom he writes this epistle, layeth them down in these words such counsel, which if taken, would be for their help and advantage.

First, Not to be wicked, and sit still, and wish for heaven; but to run for it.

Secondly, Not to content themselves with every kind of running, but, saith he, "So run that ye may obtain." As if he should say, some, because they would not lose their souls, begin to run betimes, they run apace, they run with patience, they run the right way. Do you so run. Some run from both father and mother, friends and companions, and thus, they may have the crown. Do you so run. Some run through temptations, afflictions, good report, evil report, that they may win the pearl. Do you so run. "So run that ye may obtain."

These words were taken from men's running for a wager; a very apt similitude to set before the eyes of the saints of the Lord. "Know you that they which run in a race run all, but one obtaineth the prize? So run that ye may obtain." That is, do not only run, but be sure you win as well as run. "So run that ye may obtain."

I shall not need to make any great ado in opening the words at this time, but shall rather lay down one doctrine that I do find in them; and in prosecuting that, I shall show you, in some measure, the scope of the words.

The doctrine is this: They that will have heaven, must run for it; I

Reprinted from *The World's Great Sermons*, comp. Grenville Kleiser, vol. 2 (New York: Funk & Wagnalls Co., 1908), pp. 105–32.

say, they that will have heaven, they must run for it. I beseech you to heed it well. "Know ye not, that they which run in a race run all, but one obtaineth the prize? So run ye." The prize is heaven, and if you will have it, you must run for it. You have another scripture for this in Hebrews 12:1-3: "Wherefore seeing also," saith the apostle, "that we are compassed about with so great a cloud of witnesses, let us lay aside every weight, and the sin which doth so easily beset us, and let us run with patience the race that is set before us." And let us run, saith he. Again, saith Paul, "I so run, not as uncertainly: so fight I," etc.

But before I go any farther:

1. Fleeing. Observe, that this running is not an ordinary, or any sort of running, but it is to be understood of the swiftest sort of running; and therefore, in Hebrews 6:18 it is called a fleeing: "That we might have strong consolation, who have fled for refuge, to lay hold on the hope set before us." Mark, who have fled. It is taken from Joshua 20, concerning the man that was to flee to the city of refuge, when the avenger of blood was hard at his heels, to take vengeance on him for the offense he had committed; therefore it is a running or fleeing for one's life: a running with all might and main, as we use to say. So run.

2. Pressing. Secondly, this running in another place is called a pressing. "I press toward the mark"; which signifieth, that they that will have heaven, they must not stick at any difficulties they meet with; but press, crowd, and thrust through all that may stand between heaven and their souls. So run.

3. Continuing. Thirdly, this running is called in another place, a continuing in the way of life. "If you continue in the faith grounded, and settled, and be not moved away from the hope of the gospel of Christ." Not to run a little now and then, by fits and starts, or half-way, or almost thither, but to run for my life, to run through all difficulties, and to continue therein to the end of the race, which must be to the end of my life. "So run that ye may obtain." And the reasons are:

(1.) Because all or every one that runneth doth not obtain the prize; there may be many that do run, yea, and run far too, who yet miss of the crown that standeth at the end of the race. You know all that run in a race do not obtain the victory; they all run, but one wins. And so it is here; it is not every one that runneth, nor every one that seeketh, nor every one that striveth for the mastery that hath it. "Though a man do strive for the mastery," saith Paul, "yet he is not crowned, unless he strive lawfully"; that is, unless he so run, and so strive, as to have God's approbation. What, do you think that every heavy-heeled professor will have heaven? What, every lazy one? every wanton and foolish professor, that will be stopt by anything, kept back by anything, that scarce runneth so fast heavenward as a snail creepeth on the ground? Nay, there are some professors that do not go on so fast in the way of God as a snail doth go on the wall; and yet these think that heaven and happiness is for them. But stay, there are many more that run than there be that obtain; therefore he that will have heaven must run for it.

(2.) Because you know, that though a man do run, yet if he do not overcome, or win, as well as run, what will they be the better for their running? They will get nothing. You know the man that runneth, he doth do it to win the prize; but if he doth not obtain it, he doth lose his labor, spend his pains and time, and that to no purpose; I say, he getteth nothing. And ah! how many such runners will there be found in the day of judgment? Even multitudes, multitudes that have run, yea, run so far as to come to heaven-gates, and not able to get any farther, but there stand knocking when it is too late, crying, Lord! Lord! when they have nothing but rebukes for their pains. Depart from Me, you come not here, you come too late, you run too lazily; the door is shut. "When once the master of the house is risen up," saith Christ, "and hath shut to the door, and ye begin to stand without, and to knock, saying, Lord, Lord, open to us, I will say, I know you not, depart," etc. Oh, sad will the state of those be that run and miss; therefore, if you will have heaven, you must run for it; and "so run that ye may obtain."

(3.) Because the way is long (I speak metaphorically), and there is many a dirty step, many a high hill, much work to do, a wicked heart, world, and devil to overcome; I say, there are many steps to be taken by those that intend to be saved, by running or walking in the steps of that faith of our father Abraham. Out of Egypt thou must go through the Red Sea; thou must run a long and tedious journey, through the vast howling wilderness, before thou come to the land of promise.

(4.) They that will go to heaven they must run for it; because, as the way is long, so the time in which they are to get to the end of it is very uncertain; the time present is the only time; thou hast no more time allotted thee than thou now enjoyest: "Boast not thyself of to-morrow, for thou knowest not what a day may bring forth." Do not say, I have time enough to get to heaven seven years hence; for I tell thee, the bell may toll for thee before seven days more be ended; and when death comes, away thou must go, whether thou art provided or not; and therefore look to it; make no delays; it is not good dallying with things of so great concernment as the salvation or damnation of thy soul. You know he that hath a great way to go in a little time, and less by half than he thinks of, he had need to run for it.

(5.) They that will have heaven, they must run for it; because the devil, the law, sin, death, and hell follow them. There is never a poor soul that is going to heaven, but the devil, the law, sin, death, and hell, make after the soul. "The devil, your adversary, as a roaring lion, goeth about, seeking whom he may devour." And I will assure you, the devil is nimble, he can run apace, he is light of foot, he hath over-taken many, he hath turned up their heels, and hath given them an everlasting fall. Also the law, that can shoot a great way, have a care thou keep out of the reach of those great guns, the Ten Command-ments. Hell also hath a wide mouth; it can stretch itself farther than you are aware of. And as the angel said to Lot, "Take heed, look not behind thee, neither tarry thou in all the plain" (that is, anywhere between this and heaven), "lest thou be consumed"; so I say to thee, Take heed, tarry not, lest either the devil, hell or the fearful curses of the law of God do overtake thee, and throw thee down in the midst of thy sins, so as never to rise and recover again. If this were all considered, then thou, as well as I, wouldst say, They that will have heaven must run for it.

(6.) They that go to heaven must run for it; because perchance the gates of heaven may be shut shortly. Sometimes sinners have not heaven-gates open to them so long as they suppose; and if they be once shut against a man, they are so heavy that all the men in the world, nor all the angels in heaven, are not able to open them. "I shut, and no man can open," saith Christ. And how if thou shouldst come but one quarter of an hour too late? I tell thee, it will cost thee an eternity to bewail thy misery in. Francis Spira can tell thee what it is to stay till the gate of mercy be quite shut; or to run so lazily that they be shut before you get within them. What, to be shut out! what, out of heaven! Sinner, rather than lose it, run for it; yea, "and so run that thou mayst obtain."

(7.) Lastly, because if thou lose, thou losest all, thou losest soul, God, Christ, heaven, ease, peace, etc. Besides, thou layest thyself open to all the shame, contempt, and reproach, that either God, Christ, saints, the world, sin, the devil, and all can lay upon thee. As Christ saith of the foolish builder, so I will say of thee, if thou be such a one who runs and misses; I say, even all that go by will begin to mock at thee, saying, This man began to run well, but was not able to finish. But more of this anon.

Question. But how should a poor soul do to run? For this very thing is that which afflicteth me sore (as you say), to think that I may run, and yet fall short. Methinks to fall short at last, oh, it fears me greatly. Pray tell me, therefore, how I should run.

Answer. That thou mayst indeed be satisfied in this particular, consider these following things.

The first direction: If thou wouldst so run as to obtain the kingdom of heaven, then be sure that thou get into the way that leadeth thither: For it is a vain thing to think that ever thou shalt have the prize, though thou runnest never so fast, unless thou art in the way that leads to it. Set the case, that there should be a man in London that was to run to York for a wager; now, though he run never so swiftly, yet if he run full south, he might run himself quickly out of breath, and be never nearer the prize, but rather the farther off. Just so is it here; it is not simply the runner, nor yet the hasty runner, that winneth the crown, unless he be in the way that leadeth thereto. I have observed, that little time which I have been a professor, that there is a great running to and fro, some this way, and some that way, yet it is to be feared most of them are out of the way, and then, though they run as swift as the eagle can fly, they are benefited nothing at all.

Here is one runs a-quaking, another a-ranting; one again runs after the baptism, and another after the Independency: here is one for Free-will, and another for Presbytery; and yet possibly most of all these sects run quite the wrong way, and yet every one is for his life, his soul, either for heaven or hell.

If thou now say, Which is the way? I tell thee it is Christ, the Son of Mary, the Son of God. Jesus saith, "I am the way, the truth, and the life; no man cometh to the Father but by me." So then thy business is (if thou wouldst have salvation), to see if Christ be thine, with all His benefits; whether He hath covered thee with His righteousness, whether He hath showed thee that thy sins are washed away with His heart-blood, whether thou art planted into Him, and whether you have faith in Him, so as to make a life out of Him, and to conform thee to Him; that is, such faith as to conclude that thou art righteous, because Christ is thy righteousness, and so constrained to walk with Him as the joy of thy heart, because he saveth thy soul. And for the Lord's sake take heed, and do not deceive thyself, and think thou art in the way upon too slight grounds; for if thou miss of the way, thou wilt miss of the prize, and if thou miss of that I am sure thou wilt lose thy soul, even that soul which is worth more than the whole world.

Mistrust thy own strength, and throw it away; down on thy knees in prayer to the Lord for the spirit of truth; search His word for direction; flee seducers' company; keep company with the soundest Christians, that have most experience of Christ; and be sure thou have a care of Quakers, Ranters, Freewillers: also do not have too much company with some Anabaptists, though I go under that name myself. I will tell thee this is such a serious matter, and I fear thou wilt so little regard it, that the thought of the worth of the thing, and of thy too light regarding of it, doth even make my heart ache whilst I am writing to thee. The Lord teach thee the way by His Spirit, and then I am sure thou wilt know it. So run.

The second direction: As thou shouldst get into the way, so thou shouldst also be much in studying and musing on the way. You know men that would be expert in anything, they are usually much in studying of that thing, and so likewise is it with those that quickly grow expert in any way. This therefore thou shouldst do; let thy study be much exercised about Christ, which is the way, what He is, what He hath done, and why He is what He is, and why He hath done what is done; as why "He took upon Him the form of a servant" (Phil. 2); why He was "made in the likeness of man"; why He cried; why He died; why He "bare the sin of the world"; why He was made sin, and why He was made righteousness; why He is in heaven in the nature of man, and what He doth there. Be much in musing and considering of these things; be thinking also enough of those places which thou must not come near, but leave some on this hand, and some on that hand; as it is with those that travel into other countries; they must leave such a gate on this hand, and such a bush on that hand, and go by such a place, where standeth such a thing. Thus therefore you must do: "Avoid such things, which are expressly forbidden in the Word of God." Withdraw thy foot far from her, "and come not nigh the door of her house, for her steps take hold of hell, going down to the chambers of death." And so of everything that is not in the way, have a care of it, that thou go not by it; come not near it, have nothing to do with it. So run.

The third direction: Not only thus, but in the next place, thou must strip thyself of those things that may hang upon thee, to the hindering of thee in the way to the kingdom of heaven, as covetousness, pride, lust, or whatever else thy heart may be inclining unto, which may hinder thee in this heavenly race. Men that run for a wager, if they intend to win as well as run, they do not use to encumber themselves, or carry those things about them that may be a hindrance to them in their running. "Every man that striveth for the mastery is temperate in all things"; that is, he layeth aside everything that would be anywise a disadvantage to him; as saith the apostle, "Let us lay aside every weight, and the sin that doth so easily beset us, and let us run with patience the race that is set before us." It is but a vain thing to talk of going to heaven, if thou let thy heart be encumbered with those things that would hinder. Would you not say that such a man would be in danger of losing, though he run, if he fill his pockets with stones, hang heavy garments on his shoulders, and get lumpish shoes on his feet? So it is here; thou talkest of going to heaven, and yet fillest thy pockets with stones—i e fillest thy heart with this world, lettest that hang on thy shoulders, with its profits and pleasures. Alas! alas! thou art widely mistaken: if thou intendest to win, thou must strip, thou must lay aside every weight, thou must be temperate in all things. Thou must so run.

The fourth direction: Beware of by-paths; take heed thou dost not turn into those lanes which lead out of the way. There are crooked paths, paths in which men go astray, paths that lead to death and damnation, but take heed of all those. Some of them are dangerous because of practise, some because of opinion, but mind them not; mind the path before thee, look right before thee, turn neither to the right hand nor to the left, but let thine eyes look right on, even right before thee; "Ponder the path of thy feet, and let all thy ways be established." Turn not to the right hand nor to the left. "Remove thy foot far from evil." This counsel being not so seriously taken as given, is the reason of that starting from opinion to opinion, reeling this way and that way, out of this lane into that lane, and so missing the way to the kingdom. Though the way to heaven be but one, yet there are many crooked lanes and by-paths that shoot down upon it, as I may say. And again, notwithstanding the kingdom of heaven be the biggest city, yet usually those by-paths are most beaten, most travelers go those ways; and therefore the way to heaven is hard to be found, and as hard to be kept in, by reason of these. Yet, nevertheless, it is in this case as it was with the harlot of Jericho; she had one scarlet thread tied in her window, by which her house was known: so it is here, the scarlet streams of Christ's blood run throughout the way to the kingdom of heaven; therefore mind that, see if thou do not find the besprinkling of the blood of Christ in the way, and if thou do, be of good cheer, thou art in the right way; but have a care thou beguile not thyself with a fancy; for then thou mayst light into any lane or way; but that thou mayst not be mistaken, consider, though it seem never so pleasant, yet if thou do not find that in the very middle of the road there is written with the heart-blood of Christ, that he came into the world to save sinners, and that we are justified, though we are ungodly, shun that way; for this it is which the apostle meaneth when he saith, "We have boldness to enter into the holiest by the blood of Jesus, by a new and living way which He hath consecrated for us, through the vail—that is to say, His flesh." How easy a matter it is in this our day, for the devil to be too cunning for poor souls, by calling his by-paths the way to the kingdom. If such an opinion or fancy be but cried up by one or more, this inscription being set upon it by the devil, "This is the way of God," how speedily, greedily, and by heaps, do poor simple souls throw away themselves upon it; especially if it be daubed over with a few external acts of morality, if so good. But it is because men do not know painted by-paths from the plain way to the kingdom of heaven. They have not yet learned the true Christ, and what His righteousness is, neither have they a sense of their own insufficiency; but are bold, proud, presumptuous, self-conceited. And therefore,

The fifth direction: Do not thou be too much in looking too high in thy journey heavenward. You know men that run a race do not use to stare and gaze this way and that, neither do they use to cast up their eyes too high, lest haply, through their too much gazing with their eyes after other things, they in the meantime stumble and catch a fall. The very same case is this: if thou gaze and stare after every opinion and way that comes into the world, also if thou be prying overmuch into God's secret decrees, or let thy heart too much entertain questions about some nice foolish curiosities, thou mayst stumble and fall, as many hundreds in England have done, both in ranting and quakery, to their own eternal overthrow, without the marvelous operation of

God's grace be suddenly stretched forth to bring them back again. Take heed, therefore; follow not that proud, lofty spirit, that, devil-like, can not be content with his own station. David was of an excellent spirit, where he saith, "Lord, my heart is not haughty, nor mine eyes lofty, neither do I exercise myself in great matters, or things too high for me. Surely I have behaved and quieted myself as a child that is weaned of his mother: My soul is even as a weaned child." Do thou so run.

The sixth direction: Take heed that you have not an ear open to every one that calleth after you as you are in your journey. Men that run, you know, if any do call after them, saying, I would speak with you, or go not too fast and you shall have my company with you, if they run for some great matter, they use to say, Alas! I can not stay, I am in haste, pray talk not to me now; neither can I stay for you, I am running for a wager: if I win I am made; if I lose I am undone, and therefore hinder me not. Thus wise are men when they run for corruptible things, and thus shouldst thou do, and thou hast more cause to do so than they, forasmuch as they run for things that last not, but thou for an incorruptible glory. I give thee notice of this betimes, knowing that thou shalt have enough call after thee, even the devil, sin, this world, vain company, pleasures, profits, esteem among men, ease, pomp, pride, together with an innumerable company of such companions; one crying, Stay for me; the other saying, Do not leave me behind; a third saying, And take me along with you. What, will you go, saith the devil, without your sins, pleasures, and profits? Are you so hasty? Can you not stay and take these along with you? Will you leave your friends and companions behind you? Can you not do as your neighbors do, carry the world, sin, lust, pleasure, profit, esteem among men, along with you? Have a care thou do not let thine ear open to the tempting, enticing, alluring, and soul-entangling flatteries of such sink-souls as these are. "My son," saith Solomon, "if sinners entice thee, consent thou not."

You know what it cost the young man whom Solomon speaks of in Proverbs 6 that was enticed by a harlot: "With much fair speech she won him, and caused him to yield, with the flattering of her lips she forced him, till he went after her as an ox to the slaughter, or as a fool to the correction of the stocks"; even so far, "till the dart struck through his liver," and he knew not "that it was for his life." "Hearken unto me now therefore," saith he, "O ye children, and attend to the words of my mouth, let not thine heart incline to her ways, go not astray in her paths, for she hast cast down many wounded, yea, many strong men have been slain (that is, kept out of heaven); by her house is the way to hell, going down to the chambers of death." Soul, take this counsel, and say, Satan, sin, lust, pleasure, profit, pride, friends, companions, and everything else, let me alone, stand off, come not nigh me, for I am running for heaven, for my soul, for God, for Christ, from hell and everlasting damnation; if I win, I win all; and if I lose, I lose all; let me alone, for I will not hear. So run.

The seventh direction: In the next place, be not daunted though thou meetest with never so many discouragements in thy journey thither. That man that is resolved for heaven, if Satan cannot win him by flatteries, he will endeavor to weaken him by discouragements; saying, Thou art a sinner, thou hath broken God's law, thou art not elected, thou comest too late, the day of grace is passed, God doth not care for thee, thy heart is naught, thou art lazy, with a hundred other discouraging suggestions. And thus it was with David, where he saith, "I had fainted, unless I had believed to see the loving-kindness of the Lord in the land of the living." As if he should say, the devil do so rage, and my heart was so base, that had I judged according to my own sense and feeling, I had been absolutely distracted; but I trusted to Christ in the promise, and looked that God would be as good as his promise, in having mercy upon me, an unworthy sinner; and this is that which encouraged me, and kept me from fainting. And thus must thou do when Satan, or the law, or thy own conscience, do go about to dishearten thee, either by the greatness of thy sins, the wickedness of thy heart, the tediousness of the way, the loss of outward enjoyments, the hatred that thou wilt procure from the world or the like; then thou must encourage thyself with the freeness of the promises, the tenderheartedness of Christ, the merits of His blood, the freeness of His invitations to come in, the greatness of the sin of others that have been pardoned, and that the same God, through the same Christ, holdeth forth the same grace as free as ever. If these be not thy meditations, thou wilt draw very heavily in the way of heaven, if thou do not give up all for lost, and so knock off from following any farther; therefore, I say, take heart in thy journey, and say to them that seek thy destruction, "Rejoice not against me, O my enemy, for when I fall I shall arise, when I sit in darkness the Lord shall be a light unto me." So run.

The eighth direction: Take heed of being offended at the cross that thou must go by before thou come to heaven. You must understand (as I have already touched) that there is no man that goeth to heaven but he must go by the cross. The cross is the standing way-mark by which all they that go to glory must pass.

"We must through much tribulation enter into the kingdom of heaven." "Yea, and all that will live godly in Christ Jesus shall suffer persecution." If thou art in thy way to the kingdom, my life for thine thou wilt come at the cross shortly (the Lord grant thou dost not shrink at it, so as to turn thee back again). "If any man will come after me," saith Christ, "let him deny himself, and take up his cross daily, and follow me." The cross it stands, and hath stood, from the beginning, as a way-mark to the kingdom of heaven. You know, if one ask you the way to such and such a place, you, for the better direction, do not only say, This is the way, but then also say, You must go by such a gate, by such a stile, such a bush, tree, bridge, or such like. Why, so it is here; art thou inquiring the way to heaven? Why, I tell thee, Christ is the way; into Him thou must get, into His righteousness, to be justified; and if thou art in Him, thou wilt presently see the cross, thou must go close by it, thou must touch it, nay, thou must take it up, or else thou wilt quickly go out of the way that leads to heaven, and turn up some of those crooked lanes that lead down to the chambers of death.

It is the cross which keepeth those that are kept from heaven. I am persuaded, were it not for the cross, where we have one professor we should have twenty; but this cross, that is it which spoileth all.

The ninth direction: Beg of God that He would do these two things for thee: First, enlighten thine understanding: And, secondly, inflame thy will. If these two be but effectually done, there is no fear but thou wilt go safe to heaven.

One of the great reasons why men and women do so little regard the other world is because they see so little of it: And the reason why they see so little of it is because they have their understanding darkened: And therefore, saith Paul, "Do not you believers walk as do other Gentiles, even in the vanity of their minds, having their understanding darkened, being alienated from the life of God through the ignorance (or foolishness) that is in them, because of the blindness of their heart." Walk not as those, run not with them: alas! poor souls, they have their understandings darkened, their hearts blinded, and that is the reason they have such undervaluing thoughts of the Lord Jesus Christ, and the salvation of their souls. For when men do come to see the things of another world, what a God, what a Christ, what a heaven, and what an eternal glory there is to be enjoyed; also when they see that it is possible for them to have a share in it, I tell you it will make them run through thick and thin to enjoy it. Moses, having a sight of this, because his understanding was enlightened, "He feared not the wrath of the king, but chose rather to suffer afflictions with the people of God than to enjoy the pleasures of sin for a season. He refused to be called the son of the king's daughter"; accounting it wonderful riches to be accounted worthy of so much as to suffer for Christ with the poor despised saints; and that was because he saw Him who was invisible, and had respect unto the recompense of reward. And this is that which the apostle usually prayeth for in his epistles for the saints, namely, "That they might know what is the hope of God's calling, and the riches of the glory of his inheritance in the saints; and that they might be able to comprehend with all saints, what is the breadth, and length, and depth, and height, and know the love of Christ, which passeth knowledge."

The tenth direction: Cry to God that He would inflame thy will also with the things of the other world. For when a man's will is fully set to do such or such a thing, then it must be a very hard matter that shall hinder that man from bringing about his end. When Paul's will was set resolvedly to go up to Jerusalem (though it was signified to him before what he should there suffer), he was not daunted at all; nay, saith he, "I am ready (or willing) not only to be bound, but also to die at Jerusalem for the name of the Lord Jesus." His will was inflamed with love to Chirst; and therefore all the persuasions that could be used wrought nothing at all.

Your self-willed people, nobody knows what to do with them: we use to say, he will have his own will, do all what you can. Indeed, to have such a will for heaven, is an admirable advantage to a man that undertaketh a race thither; a man that is resolved, and hath his will fixed, saith he, I will do my best to advantage myself; I will do my worst to hinder my enemies; I will not give out as long as I can stand; I will have it or I will lose my life; "though he slay me, yet will I trust in him. I will not let thee go except thou bless me." I will, I will, I will, oh this blest inflamed will for heaven! What is it like? If a man be willing, then any argument shall be a matter of encouragement; but if unwilling, then any argument shall give discouragement; this is seen both in saints and sinners; in them that are the children of God, and also those that are the children of the devil. As,

1. The saints of old, they being willing and resolved for heaven, what could stop them? Could fire and fagot, sword or halter, stinking dungeons, whips, bears, bulls, lions, cruel rackings, stoning, starving, nakedness, etc., "and in all these things they were more than conquerors, through him that loved them"; who had also made them "willing in the day of his power."

2. See again, on the other side, the children of the devil, because they are not willing, how many shifts and starting-holes they will have. I have a married wife, I have a farm, I shall offend my landlord, I shall offend my master, I shall lose my trading, I shall lose my pride, my pleasures, I shall be mocked and scoffed, therefore I dare not come. I, saith another, will stay till I am older, till my children are out, till I am got a little aforehand in the world, till I have done this and that and the other business; but, alas! the thing is, they are not willing; for, were they but soundly willing, these, and a thousand such as these, would hold them no faster than the cords held Samson, when he broke them like burnt flax. I tell you the will is all: that is one of the chief things which turns the wheel either backward or forward; and God knoweth that full well, and so likewise doth the devil; and therefore they both endeavor very much to strengthen the will of their servants; God, He is for making of His a willing people to serve Him; and the devil, he doth what he can to possess the will and affection of those that are his with love to sin; and therefore when Christ comes closer to the matter, indeed, saith He, "You will not come to me. How often would I have gathered you as a hen doth her chickens, but you would not." The devil had possessed their wills, and so long he was

sure enough of them. Oh, therefore cry hard to God to inflame thy will for heaven and Christ: thy will, I say, if that be rightly set for heaven, thou wilt not be beat off with discouragements; and this was the reason that when Jacob wrestled with the angel, though he lost a limb, as it were, and the hollow of his thigh was put out of joint as he wrestled with him, yet saith he, "I will not," mark, "I will not let thee go except thou bless me." Get thy will tipped with the heavenly grace, and resolution against all discouragements, and then thou goest full speed for heaven; but if thou falter in thy will, and be not found there, thou wilt run hobbling and halting all the way thou runnest, and also to be sure thou wilt fall short at last. The Lord give thee a will and courage.

Thus I have done with directing thee how to run to the kingdom; be sure thou keep in memory what I have said unto thee, lest thou lose thy way. But because I would have thee think of them, take all in short in this little bit of paper.

1. Get into the way. 2. Then study on it. 3. Then strip, and lay aside everything that would hinder. 4. Beware of by-paths. 5. Do not gaze and stare too much about thee, but be sure to ponder the path of thy feet. 6. Do not stop for any that call after thee, whether it be the world, the flesh, or the devil: for all these will hinder thy journey, if possible. 7. Be not daunted with any discouragements thou meetest with as thou goest. 8. Take heed of stumbling at the cross. 9. Cry hard to God for an enlightened heart, and a willing mind, and God give thee a prosperous journey.

Provocation: Now that you may be provoked to run with the foremost, take notice of this. When Lot and his wife were running from curst Sodom to the mountains, to save their lives, it is said, that his wife looked back from behind him, and she became a pillar of salt; and yet you see that neither her example, nor the judgment of God that fell upon her for the same, would cause Lot to look behind him. I have sometimes wondered at Lot in this particular; his wife looked behind her, and died immediately, but let what would become of her, Lot would not so much as once look behind him to see her. We do not read that he did so much as once look where she was, or what was become of her; his heart was indeed upon his journey, and well it might: there was the mountain before him, and the fire and brimstone behind him; his life lay at stake, and he had lost it if he had looked behind. Do thou so run and in thy race remember Lot's wife, and remember her doom; and remember for what that doom did overtake her; and remember that God made her an example for all lazy runners, to the end of the world; and take heed thou fall not after the same example. But,

If this will not provoke thee, consider thus, 1. Thy soul is thine own soul, that is either to be saved or lost; thou shalt not lose my soul by thy laziness. It is thine own soul, thine own ease, thine own peace, thine own advantage or disadvantage. If it were my own that thou art desired to be good unto, methinks reason should move thee somewhat to pity it. But, alas! it is thine own, thine own soul. "What shall it profit a man if he shall gain the whole world, and lose his own soul?" God's people wish well to the souls of others, and wilt not thou wish well to thine own? And if this will not provoke thee, then think.

Again, 2. If thou lose thy soul, it is thou also that must bear the blame. It made Cain stark mad to consider that he had not looked to his brother Abel's soul. How much more will it perplex thee to think that thou hadst not a care of thine own? And if this will not provoke thee to bestir thyself, think again.

3. That, if thou wilt not run, the people of God are resolved to deal with thee even as Lot dealt with his wife — that is, leave thee behind them. It may be thou hast a father, mother, brother, etc., going post-haste to heaven, wouldst thou be willing to be left behind them? Surely no.

Again, 4. Will it not be a dishonor to thee to see the very boys and girls in the country to have more with them than thyself? It may be the servants of some men, as the housekeeper, plowman, scullion, etc., are more looking after heaven than their masters. I am apt to think, sometimes, that more servants than masters, that more tenants than landlords, will inherit the kingdom of heaven. But is not this a shame for them that are such? I am persuaded you scorn that your servants should say that they are wiser than you in the things of this world; and yet I am bold to say that many of them are wiser than you in the things of the world to come, which are of greater concernment.

Well, then, sinner, what sayest thou? Where is thy heart? Wilt thou run? Art thou resolved to strip? Or art thou not? Think quickly, man; have no dallying in this matter. Confer not with flesh and blood; look up to heaven, and see how thou likest it; also to hell, and accordingly devote thyself. If thou dost not know the way, inquire at the Word of God; if thou wantest company, cry for God's Spirit; if thou wantest encouragement, entertain the promises. But be sure thou begin betimes; get into the way, run apace, and hold out to the end; and the Lord give thee a prosperous journey. Farewell.

THE BARREN FIG-TREE

"And he answering, said unto him, Lord let it alone this year also, till I shall dig about it, and dung it; and if it bear fruit, well; and if not, then after that, thou shalt cut it down" (Luke 13:8–9).

THESE ARE THE WORDS of the Dresser of the vineyard, who, I told you, is Jesus Christ. (For "He made intercession for the transgressors.") And they contain a petition presented to offended justice, praying, that a little more time and patience might be exercised toward the barren cumber-ground fig-tree.

In this petition there are six things considerable. 1. That justice might be deferred. "O that justice might be deferred! Lord, let it alone, etc., a while longer." 2. Here is time prefixed, as a space to try if more means will cure a barren fig-tree. "Lord, let it alone this year also." 3. The means to help it are propounded; "till I shall dig about it, and dung it." 4. Here is also an insinuation of a supposition that by thus doing God's expectation may be answered: "and if it bear fruit, well." 5. Here is a supposition that the barren fig-tree may yet abide barren, when Christ has done what he will unto it: "and if it bear fruit," etc. 6. Here is at last a resolution, that if thou continue barren, hewing days will come upon thee: "and if it bear fruit, well; and if not, then after that, thou shalt cut it down."

But to proceed according to my former method, by way of exposition. *Lord, let it alone this year also.* Here is astonishing grace indeed! Astonishing grace, I say, that the Lord Jesus should concern Himself with a barren fig-tree; that He should step in to stop the blow from a barren fig-tree! True He stopped the blow but for a time: but why did He stop it at all? Why did He not fetch out the ax? Why did He not do execution? Why did He not cut it down? Barren fig-tree, it is well for thee that there is a Jesus at God's right hand, a Jesus of that largeness of bowels as to have compassion for a barren fig-tree; else justice had never let thee alone to cumber the ground as thou hast done. When Israel also had sinned against God, down they had gone, but that Moses stood in the breach. "Let Me alone," said God to him, "that I may consume them in a moment, and I will make of thee a great nation." Barren fig-tree! dost thou hear? Thou knowest not how oft the hand of divine justice hath been up to strike, and how many years since thou hadst been cut down, had not Jesus caught hold of his Father's ax. "Let Me alone, let Me fetch My blow," or, "Cut it

Reprinted from *Masterpieces of Pulpit Eloquence,* [comp.] Henry C. Fish, Pulpit Eloquence Library, vol. 1 (Cleveland: F. M. Barton, 1907), pp. 225–36.

down! why cumbereth it the ground?" Wilt thou not hear yet, barren fig-tree? Wilt thou provoke still? Thou hast wearied men, and provoked the justice of God: and wilt thou weary my God, also?

Lord, let it alone this year. "Lord, a little longer! Let us not lose a soul for want of means. I will try. I will see if I can make it fruitful. I will not beg a long life, nor that it might still be barren, and so provoke Thee. I beg, for the sake of the soul, the immortal soul, Lord, spare it one year only, one year longer, this year also. If I do any good to it, it will be in little time. Thou shalt not be overwearied with waiting; one year, and then!"

Barren fig-tree! dost thou hear what a striving there is between the vine-dresser and the husbandman for thy life? "Cut it down," says one; "Lord, spare it," saith the other. "It is a cumber-ground," saith the Father. "One year longer," prays the Son. "Let it alone this year also."

Till I shall dig about it, and dung it. The Lord Jesus, by these words, supposeth two things as causes of the want of fruit in a barren fig-tree; and two things He proposeth as a remedy. The things that are a cause of the want of fruit, are, 1. It is earth-bound. "Lord, the fig-tree is earth-bound." 2. A want of warmer means, or fatter means.

Wherefore accordingly He propoundeth, 1. To loosen the earth, to dig about it. 2. And then to supply it with manure: to "dig about it, and dung it."

Lord, let it alone this year also, until I shall dig about it. I doubt it is too much earth-bound. The love of this world, and the deceitfulness of riches lie too close to the roots of the heart of this professor. The love of riches, the love of honors, the love of pleasures, are the thorns that choke the word. "For all that is in the world, the lust of the flesh, and the lust of the eyes, and the pride of life, is not of the Father, but of the world." How then (where these things bind up the heart) can there be fruit brought forth to God?

Barren fig-tree! see how the Lord Jesus, by these very words, suggesteth the cause of thy fruitlessness of soul. The things of this world lie too close to thy heart; the earth with its things has bound up thy roots; thou art an earth-bound soul, thou art wrapped up in thick clay. "If any man love the world, the love of the Father is not in him"; how then can he be fruitful in the vineyard? This kept Judas from the fruit of caring for the poor. This kept Demas from the fruit of self-denial. And this kept Ananias and Sapphira his wife from the goodly fruit of sincerity and truth. What shall I say? These are "foolish and hurtful lusts, which drown men in destruction and perdition; for the love of money is the root of all evil." How then can good fruit grow from such a root, the root of all evil, "which, while some coveted after, they have erred from the faith, and pierced themselves through with many sorrows"? It is an evil root, nay, it is the root of all evil. How then can the professor that hath such a root, or a root wrapped up in such earthly things, as the lusts, and pleasures, and vanities of this world, bring forth fruit to God?

Till I shall dig about it. — "Lord, I will loosen his roots; I will dig up this earth, I will lay his roots bare. My hand shall be upon him by sickness, by disappointments, by cross providences. I will dig about him until he stands shaking and tottering, until he be ready to fall; then, if ever, he will seek to take faster hold." Thus, I say, deals the Lord Jesus ofttimes with the barren professor; He diggeth about him, He smiteth one blow at his heart, another blow at his lusts, a third at his pleasures, a fourth at his comforts, another at his self-conceitedness: thus He diggeth about him. This is the way to take bad earth from the roots, and to loosen his roots from the earth. Barren fig-tree! see here the care, the love, the labor, and way, which the Lord Jesus, the Dresser of the vineyard, is fair to take with thee, if haply thou mayest be made fruitful.

2. *Till I shall dig about it, and dung it.* — As the earth, by binding the roots too closely, may hinder the tree's being fruitful, so the want of better means may also be a cause thereof. And this is more than intimated by the Dresser of the vineyard; "till I shall dig about it and dung it." "I will supply it with a more fruitful ministry, with a warmer word. I will give them pastors after Mine own heart. I will dung them." You know dung is a more warm, more fat, more hearty and succoring matter, than is commonly the place in which trees are planted.

I will "dig about it, and dung it." That is, "I will bring it under a heart-awakening ministry; the means of grace shall be fat and good. I will also visit it with heart-awakening, heart-warming, heart-encouraging considerations. I will apply warm dung to its roots. I will strive with him by My Spirit, and give him some tastes of the heavenly gift, and the power of the world to come. I am loath to lose him for want of digging." "Lord, let it alone this year also, until I shall dig about it and dung it."

And if it bear fruit, well. — "And if the fruit of all My labor doth make this fig-tree fruitful, I shall count My time, My labor, and means, well bestowed upon it. And Thou also, O My God, shalt be therewith much delighted. For Thou art gracious and merciful, and repentest Thee of the evil which Thou threatenest to bring upon a people."

These words, therefore, inform us that if a barren fig-tree, a barren professor, shall now at last bring forth fruit to God, it shall go well with that professor, it shall go well with that poor soul. His former barrenness, his former tempting of God, his abuse of God's patience and long suffering, his misspending year after year, shall now be all forgiven him. Yea, God the Father, and our Lord Jesus Christ, will now pass by, and forget all, and say, Well done, at the last. "When I say to the wicked, O wicked man thou shalt surely die; if he then do that which is lawful and right, if he walk in the statutes of life, without committing iniquity, he shall surely live, he shall not die."

Barren fig-tree! dost thou hear? The ax is laid to thy roots; the Lord Jesus prays God to spare thee. Hath He been digging about thee? Hath He been manuring thee? O barren fig-tree? now thou art come to the point. If thou shalt now become good; if thou shalt, after a gracious manner, suck in the Gospel, and if thou shalt bring forth fruit unto God, well; but if not, the fire is the last. Fruit, or the fire; fruit or the fire, barren fig-tree! "If it bear fruit, well!"

And if not, then after that Thou shalt cut it down. — "And if not," etc. The Lord Jesus, by this *if,* giveth us to understand that there is a generation of professors in the world that are incurable, that will not, that can not repent, nor be profited by the means of grace. A generation, I say, that will retain a profession, but will not bring forth fruit; a generation that will wear out the patience of God, time and tide, threatenings and intercessions, judgments and mercies, and after all will be unfruitful.

O the desperate wickedness that is in thy heart! Barren professor, dost thou hear? The Lord Jesus stands yet in doubt about thee; there is an *if* stands yet in the way. I say, the Lord Jesus stands yet in doubt about thee, whether or no at last thou wilt be good; whether He may not labor in vain; whether His digging and dunging will come to more than lost labor. "I gave her space to repent, and she repented not." "I digged about it, I dunged it; I granted time, and supplied it with means; but I labored here in vain, and spent My strength for naught and in vain." Dost thou hear, barren fig-tree? There is yet a question whether it will be well with thy soul at last?

And if not, after that Thou shalt cut it down. There is nothing more exasperating to the mind of a man than to find all his kindness and favor slighted. Neither is the Lord Jesus so provoked with any thing, as when sinners abuse His means of grace. "If it be barren and fruitless under My Gospel; if it turn My grace into wantonness; if after digging and dunging, and waiting, it yet remain unfruitful, I will let thee cut it down."

Gospel-means applied, is the last remedy for a barren professor. If the Gospel, if the grace of the Gospel will not do, there can be nothing expected, but "cut it down." "Then after that thou shalt cut it down." "O Jerusalem, Jerusalem, thou that killest the prophets, and stonest them that are sent unto thee, how often would I have gathered thy children together, as a hen gathereth her chickens under her wings, and ye would not! Behold your house is left unto you desolate." Yet it can not be but that this Lord Jesus who at first did put a stop to the execution of His Father's justice, because He desired to try more means with the fig-tree; I say it can not be but that a heart so full of compassion as His is, should be touched to behold this professor must now be cut down. "And when He was come near, He beheld the city, and wept over it, saying, If thou hadst known, *even thou,* at least in this thy day, the things which belong unto thy peace! But now they are hid from thine eyes."

After that Thou shalt cut it down. When Christ giveth thee over, there is no intercessor or mediator, no more sacrifice for sin. All is gone but judgment, but the ax, but "a certain fearful looking-for of judgment, and fiery indignation, which shall devour the adversaries."

Barren fig-tree! take heed that thou comest not to these last words, for these words are a give-up, a cast-up, a cast-up of a castaway. "After that thou shalt cut it down." They are as much as if Christ had said, "Father, I begged for more time for this barren professor; I begged until I should dig about it, and dung it; but now, Father, the time is out, the year is ended, the summer is ended, and no good done. I have also tried with My means, with the Gospel; I have digged about it; I have laid also the fat and hearty dung of the Gospel to it, but all comes to nothing. Father, I deliver up this professor to Thee again; I have done. I have done all, I have done praying and endeavoring, I will hold the head of Thine ax no longer: take him into the hands of justice. Do justice! Do the law! I will never beg for him more." "After that Thou shalt cut it down." "Woe unto them when I depart from them!"

Now then, I will show you, by some signs, how you may know that the day of grace is ended, or near to ending with the barren professor. "And after that, thou shalt cut it down."

He that hath stood it out against God, and that hath withstood all those means for fruit that God hath used for the making of him (if it might have been) a fruitful tree in His garden, is in this danger. And this, indeed, is the sum of the parable. The fig-tree here mentioned was blessed with the application of means, had time allowed it to receive the nourishment; but it outstood, withstood, overstood, all — all that the husbandman did, all that the vine-dresser did.

But a little distinctly to particularize as to the signs of being past grace.

The day of grace is like to be past, *when a professor hath withstood, abused, and worn out God's patience.* Then he is in danger; this is a provocation; then God cries, "Cut it down." There are some men that steal into a profession, nobody knows how, even as this fig-tree was brought into the vineyard, by other hands than God's — and there they abide lifeless, graceless, careless, and without any good conscience to God at all. Perhaps they came in for the loaves, for a trade, for credit, for a blind; or it may be to stifle and choke the shocks and grinding pangs of an awakened and disquieted conscience. Now having obtained their purpose, like the sinners of Zion, they are at ease, secure; saying, like Agag, "Surely the bitterness of death is past"; in other words, "I am well, I shall be saved, and go to heaven." Thus in these vain conceits they spend a year, two or three; not remembering that at every season of grace, and at every opportunity of the Gospel, the Lord comes seeking fruit. Well, sinner! well, barren fig-tree! this is but a coarse beginning: God comes for fruit.

"What have I here?" saith God. "What fig-tree is this, that hath stood this year in My vineyard, and brought Me forth no fruit? I will cry unto him, 'Professor, barren fig-tree, be fruitful! I look for fruit!' I expect fruit; I must have fruit; therefore bethink thyself." At this the professor pauses; but these are words, not blows; therefore off goes this consideration from the heart. When God comes the next year, He finds him still as he was, a barren fruitless cumber-ground. And now again He complains. "Here are two years gone, and no fruit appears! Well, I will defer Mine anger for My name's sake; I will defer Mine anger for My praise; I will refrain from thee, that I cut thee not off, as yet. I will wait, I will yet wait to be gracious." But this helps not. This hath not the least influence upon the barren fig-tree. "Tush!" saith he, "here is no threatening. God is merciful. He will defer His anger, He waits to be gracious; I am not yet afraid." O! how ungodly men, that are unawares crept into the vineyard—how do they turn the grace of our God into lasciviousness! Well, He comes the third year for fruit, as He did before, but still He finds but a barren fig tree; not fruit! Now, He cries out again, "O thou dresser of My vineyard, come hither; here is a fig-tree hath stood these three years in My vineyard, and hath at every season disappointed My expectations, for I have looked for fruit in vain. Cut it down; My patience is worn out. I shall wait on this fig-tree no longer."

2. And now He begins to shake the fig-tree with His threatenings. "Fetch out the ax." Now the ax is death. Death, therefore, is called for. "Death, come, smite Me this fig-tree." And withal the Lord shakes this sinner, and whirls him upon a sick bed, saying, "Take him, Death. He hath abused My patience and forbearance, not remembering that it should have led him to repentance, and to the fruits thereof. Death, fetch away this fig-tree to the fire, fetch away this fig-tree to the fire, fetch this barren professor to hell!" At this Death comes, with grim looks into the chamber, yea, and Hell follows with him to the bed-side, and both stare this professor in the face, yea, begin to lay hands upon him, one smiting him with pains in his body, with head-ache, heart-ache, back-ache, shortness of breath, fainting qualms, trembling of joints, stopping at the chest, and almost all the symptoms of a man past all recovery. Now, while Death is thus tormenting the body, Hell is doing with the mind and conscience, striking them with its pains, casting sparks of fire in thither, wounding with sorrows and fears of everlasting damnation, the spirit of this poor creature.

And now he begins to bethink himself, and to cry to God for mercy, "Lord, spare me! Lord, spare me!" "Nay," saith God, "you have been a provocation to Me these three years. How many times have you disappointed Me? How many seasons have you spent in vain? How many sermons and other mercies did I or My patience afford you, but to no purpose at all? Take him, Death." "O! good Lord," saith the sinner; "spare me but this once. Indeed I have been a barren professor, and have stood to no purpose at all in Thy vineyard; but spare! O spare this one time, I beseech Thee, and I will be better." "Away, away! you will not; I have tried you these three years already; you are naught; if I should recover you again, you would be as bad as you were before." (And all this talk is while Death stands by.) The sinner cries again. "Good Lord, try me this once; let me get up again this once, and see if I do not mend." "But will you promise Me to mend?" "Yes, indeed, Lord, and I vow it too. I will never be so bad again, I will be better." "Well," saith God, "Death, let this professor alone for this time; I will try him a while longer. He hath promised, he hath vowed that he will amend his ways. It may be he will mind to keep his promises. Vows are solemn things; it may be he may fear to break his vows. Arise from off thy bed."

And now God lays down his ax. At this the poor creature is very thankful, praises God, and fawns upon Him, shows as if he did it heartily, and calls to others to thank Him too. He, therefore, riseth, as one would think, to be a new creature indeed. But by that time he hath put on his clothes, is come down from his bed, and ventured into the yard or shop, and there sees how all things are gone to sixes and sevens, he begins to have second thoughts, and says to his folks, "What have you all been doing? How are all things out of order? I am, I can not tell what, behindhand: one may see if a man be but a little to aside, that you have neither wisdom nor prudence to order things." And now, instead of seeking to spend the rest of his time to God, he doubleth his diligence after this world. "Alas!" he says, "all must not be lost; we must have provident care." And thus, quite forgetting the sorrows of death, the pains of hell, the promises and vows which he made to God to be better because judgment was not (now) speedily executed, therefore the heart of this poor creature is fully set in him to do evil.

3. These things proving ineffectual, God takes hold of His ax again, sends death to a wife, to a child, to his cattle. "Your young men have I slain, and taken away your horses." "I will blast him, cross him, disappoint him, and cast him down, and will set Myself against him in all that he putteth his hand unto." At this the poor barren professor cries out again, "Lord, I have sinned; spare me once more, I beseech thee. O take not away the desire of mine eyes; spare my children, bless me in my labors, and I will mend and be better." "No," saith God, "you lied to me last time; I will trust you in this no longer." And withal He tumbleth his wife, the child, the estate, into a grave, and then returneth to His place, till this professor, more unfeignedly acknowledgeth his offense.

At this the poor creature is afflicted and distressed, rends his clothes, and begins to call the breaking of his promise and vows to mind. He mourns and prays, and, like Ahab, a while walks softly at the remembrance of the justness of the hand of God upon him. And now he renews his promise, "Lord, try me this one time more; take off Thy hand and see; they go far that never turn." Well, God spareth him again, sets down His ax again. "Many times He did deliver them, but they provoked Him with their counsel, and were brought low for their iniquity." Now they seem to be thankful again, and are as if they were resolved to be godly indeed. Now they read, they pray, they go to meetings, and seem to be serious a pretty while. But at last they forget. Their lusts prick them; suitable temptations present themselves, wherefore they turn to their crooked ways again. "When He slew them, then they sought Him, and they returned and inquired early after God; nevertheless they did flatter Him with their mouth, and lied unto Him with their tongue."

4. Yet again, the Lord will not leave this professor, but will take up His ax again, and will put him under a more heart-searching ministry; a ministry that shall search him and turn him over and over; a ministry that shall meet with him, as Elijah met with Ahab, in all his acts of wickedness. And now the ax is laid to the roots of the tree. Besides, this ministry doth not only search the heart, but presenteth the sinner with the golden rays of the glorious Gospel. Now is Christ Jesus set forth evidently; now is grace displayed sweetly; now, now are the promises broken like boxes of ointment, to the perfuming of the whole room. But, alas! there is yet no fruit on this fig-tree. While his heart is searching, he wrangles; while the glorious grace of the Gospel is unvailing, this professor wags and is wanton; gathers up some scraps thereof; tastes the good word of God, and the powers of the world to come; drinketh in the rain that comes oft upon him, but bringeth not forth fruit meet for Him, whose Gospel it is, takes no heed to walk in the law of the Lord God of Israel with all his heart, but counteth that the glory of the Gospel consisteth in talk and show, and that our obedience thereto is a matter of speculation; that good works lie in good words; and if they can finely talk, they think they bravely please God. They think the kingdom of God consisteth only in word, not in power. And thus proveth ineffectual this fourth means also.

5. Well, now the ax begins to be heaved higher. For now, indeed, God is ready to smite the sinner; yet before He will strike the stroke, He will try one way more at last, and if that misseth, down goes the fig-tree. Now this last way is to tug and strive with this professor by the Spirit. Wherefore the Spirit of the Lord is now come to him, but not always to strive with man. Yet awhile He will strive with him; He will awaken, He will convince, He will call to remembrance former sins, former judgments, the breach of former vows and promises, the misspending of former days; He will also present persuasive arguments, encouraging promises, dreadful judgments, the shortness of

time to repent in, and that there is hope if He come. Further, He will show him the certainty of death, and of the judgment to come; yea, He will pull and strive with this sinner. And behold, the mischief now lies here; here is tugging and striving on both sides! The Spirit convinces, the man turns a deaf ear to God; the Spirit saith, Receive My instruction and live, but the man pulls away his shoulder; the Spirit shows him whither he is going, but the man closeth his eyes against it; the Spirit offereth violence, the man strives and resists. They have "done despite unto the Spirit of grace." The Spirit parlieth a second time, and urgeth reasons of a new nature; but the sinner answereth, "No, I have loved strangers, and after them I will go." At this God's fury comes up into His face; now He comes out of His holy place, and is terrible; now He sweareth in His wrath, they shall never enter into His rest. "I exercised toward you My patience, yet you have not turned unto Me," saith the Lord. "I smote you in your person, in your relations, in your estate, yet you have not returned unto Me," saith the Lord. "In thy filthiness is lewdness. Because I have purged thee, and thou wast not purged, thou shalt not be purged from thy filthiness any more, till I have caused My fury to rest upon thee." Cut it down; why doth it cumber the ground?

But to give you, in a few particulars, the manner of this man's dying:

1. Now he hath his fruitless fruit beleaguer him round his bed, together with all the bands and legions of his other wickedness. "His own iniquities shall take the wicked himself, and he shall be holden with the cords of his sins."

2. Now some terrible discovery of God is made out unto him, to the perplexing and terrifying of his guilty conscience. "God shall cast upon him, and not spare; he would fain flee out of His hand."

3. The dark entry he is to go through will be a sore amazement to him, for "fears shall be in the way." Yea, terrors will take hold on him, when he shall see the yawning jaws of death to gape upon him, and the doors of the shadow of death open to give him passage out of the world. "Now, who will meet me in this dark entry? how shall I pass through this entry into another world?"

4. For by reason of guilt, and a shaking conscience, his life will hang in continual doubt before him, and he shall be afraid day and night, and shall have no assurance of his life.

5. Now also, Want will come up against him; it will come up like an armed man. This is a terrible enemy to him that is graceless in heart, and fruitless in life. This Want will continually cry in thine ears, "Here is a new birth wanting! a new heart, and a new spirit wanting! here is faith wanting! here are love and repentance wanting! here is the fear of God wanting! and a good conversation wanting!" "Thou art weighed in the balances, and art found wanting."

6. Together with these standeth by the companions of death; death and hell, death and devils, death and endless torment in the everlasting flames of devouring fire. "When God shall come up unto the people, He will invade them with His troops."

But how will this man die? Can his heart now endure, or can his hands be strong?

1. God, and Christ, and pity, have left him. Sin against light, against mercy, and the long-suffering of God, is come up against him; his hope and confidence are now dying by him, and his conscience totters and shakes continually within him.

2. Death is at work, cutting him down; hewing both bark and heart, both body and soul asunder. The man groans, but Death hears him not; he looks ghastly, carefully, dejectedly; he sighs, he sweats, he trembles — Death matters nothing.

3. Fearful cogitations haunt him; misgivings, direful apprehensions of God terrify him. Now he hath time to think what the loss of heaven will be, and what the torments of hell will be; now he looks no way but he is frighted.

4. Now would he live, but may not; he would live though it were but the life of a bed-rid man, but must not. He that cuts him down, sways him, as the feller of woods sways the tottering tree; now this way, then that; at last a root breaks, a heart-string, an eyestring snaps asunder!

5. And now, could the soul be annihilated, or brought to nothing, how happy would it count itself! But it sees that may not be. Wherefore it is put to a wonderful strait. Stay in the body it may not; go out of the body it dares not! Life is going; the blood settles in the flesh, and the lungs being no more able to draw breath through the nostrils, at last out goes the weary trembling soul, and is immediately seized by devils, who lie lurking in every hole in the chamber for that very purpose. His friends take care of the body, and wrap it up in the sheet or coffin; but the soul is out of their thought and reach, going down to the chambers of death!

I had thought to have enlarged, but I forbear. God, who teaches man to profit, bless this brief and plain discourse to thy soul, who yet standest a professor in the land of the living, among the trees of His garden! Amen.

THE NEW BIRTH

(Bunyan's last sermon: Preached in London, July 1688)

"Which were born, not of blood, nor of the will of the flesh, nor of the will of man, but of God" (John 1:13).

THESE WORDS have a dependence on what goes before, and therefore I must direct you to it for the right understanding of them. You have it thus: "He (Christ) came unto his own, and his own received him not. But as many as received him, to them gave he power to become the sons of God, even to them that believe on his name: which were born, not of blood, nor of the will of the flesh, nor of the will of man, but of God."

In the words before us, you have two things. 1. Some of Christ's own nation rejecting him when he offered himself to them. 2. Others of his own receiving him, and making him welcome. Those that reject him, he also passes by; but those "that receive him, he gives them power to become the sons of God." Now, lest any one should look upon it as good luck or fortune, he says, "They were born, not of blood, nor of the will of the flesh, nor of the will of man, but of God." They that did not receive him, were only born of flesh and blood; but those that did receive him, they that receive the doctrine of Christ with a vehement desire, they have God to their father.

I. The Origin of the New Birth. "Not of blood," etc.

1. I'll show you what he means by blood. They that believe are born to it, as an heir is to an inheritance; they are born of God, not of flesh, nor of the will of man, but of God. Not of blood, that is, not by generation, not born to the kingdom of heaven by the flesh; not because I am the son of a godly man or woman. That is meant by blood (Acts 17:26). "He hath made of one blood all nations." But when he says here, "Not of blood," he also rejects all carnal privileges they did boast of. They boasted they were Abraham's seed: "No, no," says he, "it is not of blood. 'Think not to say you have Abraham to your father,'" You must be born of God, if you go to the kingdom of heaven.

2. "Nor of the will of the flesh": What must we understand by that? It is taken often for those vehement inclinations that are in man, to all manner of looseness; "fulfilling the desires of the flesh." But that must not be understood here. Men are not made the children of God by fulfilling their lustful desires. It must be understood here in the best sense. There is not only in carnal men a will to be vile, but there

Reprinted from *The Practical Works of John Bunyan*, [ed] J. Newton Brown, vol. 2 (Philadelphia: American Baptist Publication Society, 1852), pp. 399–406.

is in them a will to be saved also, a will to go to heaven also. But this will not do: it will not privilege a man in the things of the kingdom of God. Natural desires after the things of another world, are not an argument to prove a man shall go to heaven whenever he dies. I am not a free-willer, I do abhor it, yet there is not the wickedest man, but he desires some time or other to be saved; he will read some time or other, or it may be, pray; but this will not do. "It is not in him that wills, nor in him that runs, but in God that shows mercy"; there is willing and running, and yet to no purpose (Rom. 9:16). "Israel which followed after the law of righteousness have not obtained it." Here I do not understand, as if the apostle had denied a virtuous course of life to be the way to heaven; but that a man without grace, though he have natural gifts, yet he shall not obtain privilege to go to heaven, and be a son of God. Though a man without grace may have a will to be saved, yet he cannot have that will in God's way; nature cannot know any thing but the things of nature; the things of God knows no man, but by the Spirit of God. Unless the Spirit of God be in you, it will leave you on this side the gates of heaven.

3. "Not of blood, nor of the will of the flesh, nor of the will of *man*, but of God." It may be some may have a will, a desire that Ishmael may be saved; know this, it will not save thy child. If it was of our will, I would have you all go to heaven. How many are there in the world that pray for their children, and cry, and are ready to die for them, and all this will not do? God's will is the rule of all. It is only through Jesus Christ. "Which were born not of flesh, nor of the will of man, but of God." Now I come to the doctrine.

Men that believe in Jesus Christ to the effectual receiving of Jesus Christ, are born to it. He does not say they shall be born to it, but they are born to it. A man is born of God unto God, and the things of God, before he receives Christ to eternal salvation. "Except a man be born again he cannot see the kingdom of God." Now unless he be born of God he cannot see it. Suppose the kingdom of God be what it will, he cannot see it before he be begotten of God; suppose it be the gospel, he cannot see it before he be brought into a state of regeneration; believing is the consequence of the new birth: "Not of blood, nor of the will of man, but of God."

II. I will give you a clear description of this New Birth under a similitude or two: A child before it be born into the world is in the dark dungeon of its mother's womb; so a child of God before he be born again is in the dark dungeon of sin, and sees nothing of the kingdom of God. Therefore it is called a new birth. The same soul has love one way in its carnal condition, another way when it is born again.

As it is compared to a birth, resembling a child in his mother's womb; so it is compared to a man being raised out of the grave; and to be born again, is the same as to be raised out of the grave of sin —

"Awake thou that sleepest, and arise from the dead, and Christ shall give thee light." To be raised from the grave of sin, is by a figure to be begotten and born. There is a famous instance of Christ: He is "the first-begotten from the dead" (Rev. 1:5), he is "the first-born from the dead," unto which our regeneration alludeth, that is, if you be born again by seeing those things that are above. Then there is a similitude betwixt Christ's resurrection and the new birth. "Which were born," which were restored out of this dark world, and translated out of the kingdom of this dark world into the kingdom of his dear Son. This makes us live a new life; this is to be born again. As he that is delivered from the mother's womb, it is by the help of the mother; so he that is born of God, it is by the Spirit of God.

III. I must give you a few consequences of a New Birth.

1. A child you know is incident to cry as soon as it comes into the world; for if there be no noise, they say it is dead. You that are called born of God, and Christians, if you be not criers, there is no spiritual life in you; if you be born of God, you are crying ones; as soon as he has raised you out of the dark dungeon of sin, you cannot but cry to God, "What must I do to be saved?" As soon as ever God had touched the jailer he cries out, "Men and brethren what must I do to be saved?" Oh! how many prayerless professors are there in London, that never pray? Coffee-houses will not let you pray, trades will not let you pray, looking-glasses will not let you pray; but if you were born of God, you would.

2. It is not only natural for a child to cry, but it must crave the breast, it cannot live without the breast. Therefore Peter makes it the true trial of a new-born babe. The new-born babe desires the sincere milk of the word, that he may grow thereby; if you be born of God, make it manifest by desiring the breast of God. Do you long for the milk of the promises? A man lives one way when he is in the world, another way when he is brought unto Jesus Christ. So Isaiah: "They shall suck and be satisfied, with the breasts of consolation." If you be born again, there is no satisfaction until you get the milk of God's word into your souls (Isa. 66:11). O what is a promise of God to a carnal man! a harlot's song, it may be, is more sweet to him. But if you be born again you cannot live without the milk of God's word. What is a woman's breast to a horse? But what is it to a child? there is its comfort night and day. O how loath are they it should be taken from them! Minding heavenly things, says a carnal man, is but vanity, but to a child of God, there is his comfort.

3. A child that is newly born, if it have not other comforts to keep it warm, than it had in its mother's womb, dies; it must have something got for its succor. So at his birth Christ had swaddling clothes prepared for him. So those that are born again, must have some promise of Christ to keep them alive. Those that are in a carnal state, warm them-

selves with other things; but those that are born again, cannot live without some promise of Christ to keep them alive, as he did the poor infant in Ezekiel 16. "I have covered thee with embroidered gold." When women are with child, what fine things will they prepare for their child! O but what fine things has Christ prepared to wrap all in that are born again! O what wrappings of gold has Christ prepared for all that are born again! Women will dress their children, that every one may see them, how fine they are. So he says in Ezekiel 16:11, "I decked thee also with ornaments, and I put bracelets upon thine hands, and a chain on thy neck, and I put a jewel on thy forehead, and earrings in thine ears, and a beautiful crown upon thine head"; and he adds in the 13th verse, "Thou didst prosper to a kingdom." This is to set out nothing in the world; but the righteousness of Christ and the graces of the Spirit, without which a new born babe cannot live. They perish unless they have the golden righteousness of Christ.

4. A child when it is born, is nursed in its mother's lap. The mother takes great delight to have that which will be for its comfort. So it is with God's children; they shall be kept on his knee (Isa. 66:11), they shall "suck and be satisfied with the breasts of consolations." Again, verse 13, "As one whom his mother comforteth, so will I comfort you." There is a similitude in these things that nobody knows of, but those that are born again.

5. There is usually some similitude betwixt the father and the child; it may be the child looks like its father. So those that are born again have a new similitude, they have the image of Jesus Christ (Gal. 4). Every one that is born of God, has something of the features of heaven upon him. Men love those children that are likest them, most usually; so does God his children, therefore they are called the children of God: but others do not look like him; therefore they are called Sodomites. Christ describes children of the devil by their features; the children of the devil, his works they will do. All works of unrighteousness, are the devil's works. If you are earthly, you have borne the image of the earthly, if heavenly, you have borne the image of the heavenly.

6. When a man has a child, he trains him up to his own liking; "they have learned the custom of their father's house." So those that are born of God, have learned the custom of the true church of God; there they learn to cry, "My Father and my God." They are brought up in God's house; they learn the method and form of God's house, for regulating their lives in this world.

7. Children! it is natural for them to depend upon their father for what they want. If they want a pair of shoes, they go and tell him; if they want bread, they go and tell him. So should the children of God do. Do you want spiritual bread? go tell God of it. Do you want strength of grace? ask it of God. Do you want strength against Satan's temptations? go and tell God of it. When the devil tempts you, run home and

tell your heavenly Father; go pour out your complaints to God. This also is natural to children; if any wrong them, they go and tell their father; so do those that are born of God, when they meet with temptations, go and tell God of them.

The *first* use of the subject is this; to make a strict inquiry, whether you be born of God or not. Examine by those things I laid down before, of a child of nature, and a child of grace. Are you brought out of the dark dungeon of this world into Christ? Have you learned to cry "My Father"? "And I said, thou shalt call me thy Father" (Jer. 3:19). All God's children are criers. Cannot you be quiet without you have your fill of the milk of God's word? Cannot you be satisfied without you have peace with God? Pray you consider it, and be serious with yourselves. If you have not these marks, you will fall short of the kingdom of God, you shall never have an interest there; there is no intruding: they will say, "Lord, Lord, open to us"; and he will say, "I know you not."

2. No child of God, no heavenly inheritance. We sometimes give something to those that are not our children, but not our lands. O do not flatter yourselves with a portion among the sons, unless you live like sons. When we see a king's son play with a beggar, this is unbecoming. So if you be the king's children, live like the king's children; if you be risen with Christ, set your affections on things above, and not on things below. When you come together, talk of what your Father has promised you. You should all love your Father's will, and be content, and be pleased with the exercises you meet with in the world.

3. If you are children of God, live together lovingly; if the world quarrel with you, it is no matter; but it is sad if you quarrel together. If this be amongst you, it's a sign of ill breeding; it is not according to rules you have in the word of God. Dost thou see a soul that has the image of God in him? love him, love him; say, "this man and I must go to heaven one day." Serve one another, do good for one another, and if any wrong you, pray to God to right you; and love the brotherhood.

Lastly, If you be the children of God, learn that lesson, "Gird up the loins of your mind as obedient children, not fashioning yourselves according to your former conversation, but be ye holy in all manner of conversation." Consider that the holy God is your Father, and let this oblige you to live like the children of God, that you may look your Father in the face with comfort another day.

FOR ADDITIONAL INFORMATION ABOUT JOHN BUNYAN:

Barr, Gladys H. *The Tinker's Armor: The Story of John Bunyan.* Nashville: Broadman Press, 1961.

Bunyan, John. *The Practical Works of John Bunyan.* 8 vols. Philadelphia: American Baptist Publication Society, 1852.

Currier, Albert H. "John Bunyan." *Nine Great Preachers.* New York: Pilgrim Press, 1912.

Fullerton, W. Y. *The Legacy of Bunyan.* London: Ernut Benn Ltd., 1928.

Loane, Marcus L. "John Bunyan." *Makers of Religious Freedom in the Seventeenth Century.* Grand Rapids: Wm. B. Eerdmans Pub. Co., 1961.

Sharrock, Roger. *John Bunyan.* New York: St. Martin's Press, 1968.

Talon, Henri A. *John Bunyan.* London: Longmans, Green, & Co., 1956.

Tindall, William York. *John Bunyan, Mechanick Preacher.* New York: Russell & Russell, 1934.

LOUIS BOURDALOUE

1632-1704

BOURDALOUE, *Bourdaloue at Prayer* engraved by Rossler after Jouveret, Radio Times Hulton Picture Library.

LOUIS BOURDALOUE

1632   *Born August 20 in Bourges, France*
1640   *Entered Jesuit College in Bourges*
1647   *Completed education in the Jesuit College*
1648   *Entered the Society of Jesus*
1661   *Began to preach extensively*
1670   *Began ministry as court preacher*
1704   *Died May 13 in Paris*

THE PREACHER TO KINGS, and the king of preachers—that is the title most often given to Louis Bourdaloue. He earned it for serving thirty-four years as court preacher to Louis XIV of France, where he extended the improvement in court preachers begun by Bossuet. He was respected by his own countrymen and has been idolized by preachers from all nations.

LIFE AND TIMES

The family of Bourdaloue prepared him well for his life's task. Born into a home of both piety and intellect, he received gifts which were to be valuable in his ministry. His father was a lawyer and an eloquent speaker. His mother was both intelligent and devoted, and she cared well for the moral and religious training of the young boy.

Early in his life Bourdaloue felt the leadership of God into the ministry; perhaps his education in the Jesuit College in his hometown of Bourges had something to do with this impression. In his studies he showed a special talent for mathematics and philosophy, but his real interest was in proclaiming the Christian faith. When he was sixteen years old he ran away to Paris to enter the Jesuit order.

His father came after him and brought him back home. As an only son, Bourdaloue was encouraged by his father to follow in his footsteps and become a lawyer. Bourdaloue, displaying the persuasive ability for which he was later to become famous, convinced his father that he should become a Jesuit. The father returned his son to Paris and himself entered him in the order of the Society of Jesus.

Bourdaloue was a gifted student, and following his graduation he spent several years in teaching grammar, literature, rhetoric, philosophy, and theology. All of this experience provided him with an excellent background for preaching in the most difficult pulpit of Europe – the court of Louis XIV.

For ten years, including the later years of his teaching, he was something of a home missionary: he roamed the countryside, preaching to the people. His sermons drew great crowds. Soon the Jesuit authorities began to recognize his great ability as a preacher. A Jesuit associate describing the effect of Bourdaloue's preaching at Rouen said: "All the mechanics left their shops, and the merchants their business, lawyers left the palace and the doctors their patients." The Jesuit reporter good-humoredly adds, "For my part, when I preached there the next year, I put everything straight again; nobody left his business anymore."

At the age of thirty-seven Bourdaloue was brought to Paris. His preaching there caused a sensation; great crowds heard him. In 1670 he first preached before the French monarch and soon he became a preacher in the court. For thirty-four years Bourdaloue was the leading court preacher.

But even during his court ministry he continued to preach in the parish churches where he attracted crowds from all of the surrounding areas. It is to his credit that he was heard as eagerly by the common crowd as he was by the king and the court. After one sermon in a parish pulpit the crowd showed astonishment at his simplicity: they asked, "Is this the famous Paris preacher? Why, we understood all he said."

In the French court he was known as much for his character as for his pulpit ability. He was a sincere man with a clean and upright life. Unlike others in the court, he was not concerned with matters of state or intrigue. He was less of an orator and more of a prophet than other preachers of his day.

One of the marks of character displayed most conspicuously

by Bourdaloue was courage. He did not fawn over the court nor flatter the king; instead, he was a sharp critic. He pointed out the sins and the corruption of the nobility. He even challenged the king. Once after having preached on the adultery of David and the rebuke by Nathan, he turned to King Louis XIV and said, "Thou art the man!" As the story goes, the unnerved monarch called in the preacher for a private hearing, but he was able to convince the king of his loyalty. Bourdaloue insisted that he wanted to see Louis as the greatest of monarchs and the holiest of kings.

Because of the condition of the court, Bourdaloue's primary concerns in preaching were ethical. His approach was to assault the conscience of his hearers through reason. He was considerably effective in getting his point across; nevertheless, the lives of most of his hearers changed little.

The court was well aware of his ability. On one occasion as Bourdaloue entered the pulpit, one of the famous generals of France was heard to mutter, "Silence, here comes the enemy." On another occasion a less cultured member of the military interrupted one of his sermons with an exclamation, "Zounds, he's right!" King Louis XIV enjoyed listening to sermons—in that day, sermons were one form of entertainment. The theater was beginning to rival preaching, but men such as Bourdaloue could still gather a crowd simply by the effect of their words.

But Bourdaloue was not content to merely entertain Louis XIV. He tried to convert him. He spent his life in an effort to bring the king into the fold of the Christian faith in a genuine way rather than a formal allegiance. There is evidence that he had some effect: the king did become more of an orthodox, practicing Catholic. But there is little to indicate that the basic nature and quality of his life was altered much by the preaching of Bourdaloue.

Working in the midst of great corruption, Bourdaloue stood as a pillar of both righteousness and sympathy. He understood the plight in which the courtiers were caught; he did not condone their ways but he tried to understand their needs. He worked to move them to holier and better lives as best he could. He courageously stood his ground and worked at his task even though he must have been disappointed with the results.

There is much in the life of this famous Frenchman to inspire preachers of any day: his quality of life; his determination to stay at the task to which God had assigned him; and his courage to face and to condemn sin, while displaying sympathy for the sinner – all of these are worthy of duplication in any life.

PREACHING AND SERMONS

Even the careful student of preaching finds it nearly impossible to separate the French Catholic preachers: Bossuet, Bourdaloue, Fénelon, Massillon. They all preached at the French court of Louis XIV; what is the difference among them?

Actually, a great deal. Bossuet was an eloquent orator, but too indulgent of the faults of the court; his oratory often degenerated into flattery. Fénelon was saintly and mystical; but his sermons do not show the logic or eloquence of the others. Massillon had polish and fire; the literary style of his sermons brought even Voltaire's praise.

The sermons of Bourdaloue, in contrast to those of the other court preachers, seem bony and overly worked. He lacks the eloquence of Bossuet; he lacks the zeal of Massillon; he is not a mystical saint like Fénelon. It is true that Bourdaloue was hampered in his preaching by his relationship to the French court even as his predecessor, Bossuet. It is true that he was a strong and rigid Jesuit; it is true that his sermons have extreme length, as do all of the sermons of his contemporaries; it is true that his interpretation of Scripture was frequently quite weak. Where, then, is his merit?

Notice the compliment that Voltaire paid him: "Bourdaloue seeks rather to convince than to persuade; the idea of pleasing his hearers never for a moment enters his mind. He was the first model of the good preachers in Europe."

That is the key: Bourdaloue did not seek to please. Perhaps Fénelon did not either, but Fénelon does not approach the preaching gifts of Bourdaloue, even with all of his flaws. Fénelon and La Breuyere criticized Bourdaloue's sermon organization as rigid and arbitrarily mechanical, and they were right; on the other hand, they did admit that his repetitious method was useful as a memory aid for the speaker and listeners. But it is not the organization of a sermon that finally marks its greatness or its failure, but the content of it. Bourdaloue was honest – at least as much as his position and age would permit. His predecessor, Bossuet, vacillated between flattery and arbitrariness: when he was eloquent, he grossly exaggerated;

when he was honest, he was frequently arbitrary and unfair.

That is Bourdaloue's surpassing ability among his contemporaries, his honesty and ethical relevance. He was cautious, to be sure, in his sermons to the monarchy; nevertheless, his condemnation of the faults of nobility rings throughout his sermons. He concerned himself with the problems of wealth in the midst of poverty. He denounced the sins of the court hangers-on who imitated the vices of their monarch and possessed none of his strengths.

The methodical, intricately logical mind of a highly trained Jesuit is evident in all of the sermons of Bourdaloue. His technique was complex: all of his sermons were divided into two parts. The first part, the more general of the two, discussed the theme of the sermon and ended with a "Hail Mary." The second part of the sermon developed this theme in three parts: exposition of the Scripture with opinions from the Church Fathers; a lesson to be learned from the exposition; and a discussion of the deviations from these principles, which he observed in the lives of the worldly people about him. These three points were further divided into sub-points.

Needless to say, oratory does not appear at its best in such a corset; the interruptions from such extensive dividing and re-dividing are considerable. But his basic honesty, as well as the highly logical structure of his sermons – even if tedious – still provides considerable impact today.

Nor was Bourdaloue's homiletical scholasticism his only fault. His delivery suffered from another problem: he scarcely ever lifted his eyes from the page. That is not too surprising, really, considering the intricate nature of his material. If he had lifted his eyes he would not have known if he were in "exordium the first" or "exordium the second," or in sub-point seven or sub-point eight. At other times he even closed his eyes and preached entire sermons with his eyes shut to keep the audience from distracting him. What a contrast to Augustine, who changed his sermon in midstream depending upon the reaction of the audience!

Yet given all of his faults, the sermons of Bourdaloue are remarkably good. The one included in this study has notable passages of power and eloquence. His descriptive powers are fine; there are moments of illustrative truth that are still instructive. Bourdaloue shows a remarkable use of indirect discourse or *prosopopoeia* (imaginary discourse) throughout the sermon. He asks rhetorical questions of himself as though they were being spoken by the audience; these he proceeds to answer. Even today there are few devices which are more useful for engaging the mind of an audience in dialogue.

This sermon, the second part of "Divine Judgment," shows vigor and power. After a rather weak beginning the sermon becomes easy to read, even by modern standards. And Bourdaloue's remarks to men and women who "love the flesh" show brilliant insight; he displays his incisive logic and true understanding of human nature as he exhorts these sinners "to love their flesh if they must," but to love it with an eternally useful love through obedience to Christ. This sermon by Bourdaloue is even more impressive if you read others from the same period along with it.

Sermons

THE JUDGMENT: ITS INFLEXIBLE
IMPARTIALITY

Matthew 24:30

SOMEWHERE there is bound to exist rigorous and flawless Equity.
It is difficult for us to doubt, moreover, that such Equity is to be
found enshrined in God; or that it *is* there enshrined in order that it
may one day serve to make good and to correct the innumerable shortcomings and abuses proceeding from our love of self.

No matter what amount of light we may enjoy for the purpose of
conducting this process of introspection, yet we very seldom possess
the necessary courage to proceed against ourselves and to treat ourselves with a severity proportioned to the fulness and accuracy of our
self-knowledge.

We *do* condemn ourselves — pay attention, if you please, to these
Three Thoughts, to which I reduce all that I have to say in this Second
Part — we do condemn ourselves; but at the same time we (*a*) give the
condemned self a good deal of grace, and we are anxious, too, that
others should treat it tenderly likewise; aye, even in that most Holy
Place whither we repair to receive *present* judgment: I mean where
we make confession of our sins.

We acknowledge ourselves to be sinners in the sight of God, but at
the same time we (*b*) take into account our position in society, expecting to reap some secret advantage from our social standing and from
conventional class-distinctions.

We acknowledge ourselves to be guilty and deserving of punishment;
but in the same breath we whisper to ourselves (*c*) that we are weak,
or to put it more euphemistically, nervous and highly strung, and
ought therefore to be let off; demanding at the hands of others, and
for the same reason, the like consideration and leniency of treatment.

Three forms of Self-Love: three mistakes which often keep worldly-
minded people in a state of impenitence for a life-time together. Three

Reprinted from *Advent and Christmas*, tr. and ed. Charles Hyde Brooke,
Great French Preachers, vol. 2 (London: Grant Richards, 1904), pp. 101–18.

symptoms of flagging spiritual vitality, for which the inflexible justice of God must supply the remedy, and in the following way: —

God, My Dear Hearers, will judge us without any reference or deference to our social distinctions whatsoever; all of which will, on the contrary, tell against us. He will judge us without considering the tension of our nerves or the state of our feelings; indeed, this overwrought sensibility of ours will offer the chief point of incidence for the onslaught of His formidable indictment.

One moment more! before abandoning these reflections.

In passing sentence upon ourselves we always make allowances. God will make none; and here we have the most fearful of all the facts presented to us by our Religion; but which is at the same time one of the best established; for we possess the following definition of the Divine Judgment enunciated by the Holy Spirit Himself: *Judicium sine misericordiâ.* "For he shall have judgment without mercy."

Judgment without Mercy! And why must it be so? In order that it may neutralize the noxious leniency shown by us in dealing with Ourselves.

The misconception we labour under is this: we think that the case in question being our own we have as a natural consequence the right to pronounce judgment in our own favour: whereas, on the contrary, that is the very reason why it is impossible for us to bring to bear upon it a severity too uncompromising. If it were a question of judging some other person, that would be the time for allowing the quality of mercy its freest play; when, indeed, it could hardly be pushed too far, or run much risk of being misdirected.

But the moment we become our own judges, then the chief snare to be avoided is the tendency to be over-indulgent, and to show a too great considerateness, entirely self-begotten, and which is therefore never at a loss to invent hundreds of excuses for the defence of its prolific parent. Yet that is always what happens. We demand that our very priests; they who in God's stead preside at the secret judgment of souls in the Sacrament of Penance; should so far become our accomplices as to give their sanction to this self-indulgent treatment.

By being indulgent towards ourselves in the matter, we oblige *them* also to a certain extent, and after a sort, to become so too: granting us, that is, whatever our convenience demands and dispensing us from everything that might cause us pain, or involve our mortification.

Whence it daily comes to pass that while (with an inconsistency as unbecoming as it is, at the same time, thoroughly characteristic of our day) we, as a *community,* are scandalized at the too great indulgence shown generally by the Church's Ministers, yet as *individuals* we are privy to it; using all sorts of artifices whereby to induce her ministers to adopt our views or further our interests; being at a loss to find Confessors severe enough to deal with *other* people's sins, but securing the most indulgent and accommodating ones we can find when we have to confess our own!

It is owing to this, moreover, that they feel themselves placed by us under a kind of obligation to provide excuses and to hunt up extenuating circumstances; and all to their own hindrance in the discharge of the Holy Function entrusted to them; but which they lack the courage duly to perform, simply because *our* courage is so conspicuous in trying to abate their earnestness and to weaken their authority.

But God, Christian People, who is the Supreme Judge; at whose Bar not only our misdoings but the estimate we have formed of our misdoings shall be dealt with, will then upset all those arguments and arrangements with His Great Final Verdict which He has declared shall be without mercy: *Judicium sine misericordiâ!*

The reason, as Saint Augustine tells us, is that Justice will then be acting *alone*. It does act now, of course, but not alone; or, rather it is Mercy acting *in* and *through* Justice; for this very Justice which God sets in motion against us here in this life is often nothing less than some special exhibition of His Mercy; since it is certain that God never punishes us in this world merely for the sake of punishing us. His punishments, on the contrary, are means employed for our *Conversion*, our *Sanctification*, and our *Instruction;* so that according to the Rudiments of the Faith, His chastisements are just so many benefits, just so many tokens of His good will toward us.

But at that Great and Final Judgment He will listen to nothing but Justice; He will execute nothing but Justice; He will consider exclusively the claims of Justice; for the largesse of His Mercy will have been already offered and neglected or rejected. Its resources will have been at length exhausted.

Worse still! That Mercy which was offered to us all in vain, that Mercy which we treated with contempt and scorn, that Mercy which we trampled underfoot, will serve only to aggravate the rigour of the Justice. And if you ask me in what manner—I answer: "by turning into an Accusing Witness, that Mercy which might have served us as a Zealous Advocate": *Judicium sine misericordiâ*. Judgment without mercy!

Ah! Christian People! What will that unwarrantable leniency extorted by us from the Vicars of Jesus Christ avail us *then*? Will those allowances they used to make for us be accepted in our favour?

Will God admit them? Will He conform *His* judgment to *theirs*? What they loosed on earth will He loose in Heaven? Does the Power-of-the-Keys with which He invested them go that length?

No! No! Dear Hearers, that can never be! God would have them by all means show themselves Ministers of Mercy, but of a Mercy firm and wise; not of a mere indiscriminate, spongelike good nature; a Mercy, rather, which deals with vicious propensities and bad habits

as a pruning-knife, not one that fosters and flatters them; a Mercy
that protects the honour and credit of His Name, not such as sullies
and dishonours it. For any such Mercy as that – weak, timid, ready to
give way at every point – will damn the Priest while it can never save
the Sinner! So much so, that neither the one nor the other of them can
look for anything at the Hands of God save Judgment without Mercy:
Judicium sine misericordiâ!

(*b*) And now for a *second* abuse, which follows as a natural consequence of the first.

We presume upon our Social Distinction; so that finding ourselves
highly placed among the well-born and the well-to-do whom the world
looks up to with abject awe, we expect that God will feel equally impressed and overcome. So very seriously, in fact, do we take ourselves,
that when those Ministers of His Justice, the Priests of the Dispensation of Grace, proceed to deal with us according to the commonly
accepted and universal rules of the Christian Religion of which we
make profession – then we take it amiss: begging that they will use
some discretion and not confound us with the common herd.

In fact we measure their claim to the qualification "discreet and
learned" by their quickness of discernment as to "Who is Who."

Is not this just what does pass between those who minister the
"benefit of absolution" and ourselves?

Now let us see what passes at God's Judgment Seat.

Were I to tell you, that the distinction most affected by God in Holy
Scripture is that He should be regarded as "No Respecter of Persons"
– the Pharisees themselves giving Jesus Christ this much credit
even to His face, that His opinions and decisions were formed and
arrived at without regard to the Persons of Men: *non enim respicis
personam hominum;* and that even in the case of His Mother, the
most exalted, that is, of all His creatures; this God-Man acted with
the like exclusive impartiality, neither exalting her in this world, nor
assigning her a place in the Glory of that which is to come, in consequence of her particular importance or dignity, but solely with regard to her *character* and personal merit: *Laudent eam opera ejus* –
Were I to tell you all that; I should simply be telling you what you
have heard a hundred times already, and what ought to have upset
your absurd pretensions, based as they are upon the artificial inequalities of Social Precedence.

To-day, however, I have something more startling to tell you.

"And what might that be?"

This: that your Rank and Quality, very far from turning to your advantage, will make God more severe and implacable in dealing with
you than ever.

"Who says so?"

Himself – in the following judgment pronounced by Wisdom in

Person; each word of which should sound like a thunder-clap in your ears; words, moreover, which have already proved the conversion of so many among the Leaders of Society: *Audite ergo vos qui continetis multitudines et placetis vobis in turbis nationum. Quia horrende et cito apparebit vobis; quoniam judicium durissimum his qui praesunt.*

"Take notice, you who rule nations, and who have pleasure in the multitude of peoples by whom you are looked up to! Take notice that this God of Majesty shall suddenly come upon you in a manner that shall fill you with fear. For a sharp judgment shall be to them that be in high places: *quoniam judicium durissimum his qui praesunt.*"

To attempt to show you the reasons for such a declaration would be to impose upon myself a useless task; since your own melancholy experience has made you but too familiar with them, namely: the disregard of God in which those live who are accounted Great upon earth: their forgetfulness of their dependent condition: the display they make of their power: and — not to enter into any further particulars — the want of feeling shown to those who are placed under them: these supply an ample justification of the severity with which God in His Providence shall judge them.

There, any way, stands the decree uttered by Eternal Wisdom: "For Wisdom will soon pardon the meanest: but mighty men shall be mightily tormented."

If there must mingle with God's Justice some strain of Mercy, it will be for the feeble and the insignificant; but as for the Great and Powerful of the day — the grander their position, the heavier the stroke!

I was mistaken therefore, when I said that God would take no account of your Social Rank and Quality.

Yes, My Dear Hearers! you shall appear once more, and that before His Judgment Seat, just as you are here, decked with all the gold and tinsel you are wearing now. But that is just what will kindle God's anger against you and bring his most scathing anathemas about your head!

Your wish, *then,* will be that God had been kind enough to make no difference or distinction at all in your favour, and that He had classed you in the very last and lowest rank of those before Him; but that is precisely what the rules of His inviolable Justice would never have permitted Him to do.

You must be judged, whether you like it or not, as Important Personages, since it is as such that you will have to be punished. Thus fared the Pharaohs, the Belshazzars, and the Antiochuses. They were Princes, and that is why God in Holy Scripture fulminates against them decrees which make us quake even at this day!

You may safely take it for granted that their fate will be your own; and that living as they lived, what happened to them will surely happen to you. If you demand why; I answer: because to this rule there is no exception: *Quoniam judicium durissimum his qui praesunt.* "The Mighty Men shall be mightily tormented."

(*c*) I now come to the third and last abuse, which is this:

We imagine that we are nervous and sensitive, and because it is our good pleasure so to be, we establish the right, nay we impose upon ourselves the obligation of sparing our feelings. Thus, what God looks at as self-indulgence and impenitence, that we enthrone as a duty!

When it is a matter of sparing ourselves we have no scruples at all; but when, on the other hand, it is a case of self not getting let off, then we should be very glad of a few.

Though Scripture speaks to us, moreover, of the indispensable necessity of crucifying the flesh with its sinful lusts, yet we seize the first pretext for escape offered by the smallest inconvenience, or the slightest want, felt or fancied as the case may be.

Again: If this over-sensitiveness affected merely certain self-imposed exercises suggested by Christian Penitence, certain acts of voluntary self-discipline less explicitly enjoined — *well*. But what is most to be deplored is that people make use of it as a plea for wholesale dispensation from rules and observances, even of the strictest, most universal, and most formal kind.

As for fasting and abstinence they are looked upon as part of an unworkable system. Should the Church's Ministers, depositories as they are of her laws, and charged with their execution, enter seriously upon the consideration of these injunctions without first of all consulting *us* on the matter, they are held to be Ministers of the *in*discreetest kind, and but little versed in the ordinary affairs of life.

But what affords them a still more legitimate ground of complaint is the fact that the rich and well-to-do of our day are they who make the most fuss about their pretended weaknesses and their delicate health; just because the abundance amid which they live has sapped their strength, and that surrounded by all that can please and pamper their fleshly nature they find themselves quite worn out and unable to undergo what others living under hard conditions both bravely and consistently face!

Hence, no care on their part to give satisfaction to God.

Yet there is satisfaction owing to God, and God will have His due. "How will He get it?"

Well, since our delicate condition hinders us from giving Him satisfaction, He will take it of His own accord, and by means of the inflexible impartiality of His Judgment.

"But in a Court of such rigorous equity, should not this alleged impotence avail us as a legitimate plea?"

Strange, My Dear Hearers, that man should be seeking to justify himself before God by pleading the very circumstance on account of which God is about to condemn him! Strange that presumption should be pushed to the point of screening ourselves with our own failings in order to avoid paying the penalty which is due!

For we base our procedure on this squeamishness of ours in order that we may muster up some courage and assurance in prospect of Divine Judgment; yet it is because of this same squeamishness that God will condemn us.

"How can He do that?" Why, by reminding us of what is only too patent and too true; by making us see that that delicacy was all affectation, as unreasonable as it was exaggerated and carried to extremes; and that therefore in allowing that we are weak we acknowledge that we are wicked. So that, far from calling for any modification of our sentence, it should make it all the heavier, in proportion to its responsibility for our having gone from bad to worse, and for having furnished us with a means of ridding our minds from all anticipation of any penalty or pain whatever.

Listen, further, Christian People, to the formidable decree which the Lord has already promulgated in the Scriptures, and which He will pronounce with His own lips and with all the pomp and circumstance of His Heavenly Assize: *Quantum in deliciis, tantum date illi tormentum et luctum.* "How much she hath glorified herself, and lived deliciously, so much torment and sorrow give her."

Her sloth, her indolence, her ease, and her life of luxury shall be the gauge and measure of her damnation and her torment. Thus did He exterminate of old, and thus will He exterminate at the last, but more effectually, Effeminacy together with the Effeminate.

Thus will He round on them, recouping Himself with interest for the voluntary satisfaction He awaited at their hands, but which they declined to offer Him.

Abstulit effeminos de terra.

I conclude what I have to say on this point, My Dear Hearers, with some important advice I have to give you; but at which possible you may take offence, should you fail to understand it in the sense intended.

For I say: Love yourselves, Brethren! Love your flesh too, if you like! I am quite agreeable. It is not precisely the love of yourselves or the love of your bodies that God condemns; since no one, according to the Holy Spirit's statement, ever yet hated his own flesh. *Nemo enim umquam carnem suam odio habuit.*

Therefore, once more I say, Love! Love that flesh of yours! But love it with a Christian Love, not with an unwholesome affection, an affection that is of the earth, earthy. Love it I say for the next world, and not for this. Of all the ills that flesh is heir to, spare it the greatest: namely, that of everlasting pain with which it is already threatened and towards which it is being driven by self-indulgence!

Nor can you ever be said to love it with that wise and genuine love, until you have come to hate it – to hate it, I mean, for the present, by afflicting it, by renouncing it, by keeping it under, by making a victim of it, and by offering it as a living sacrifice.

Such language sounds harsh, I know; and the flesh of course will resent the proposed treatment, but that does not cause me the least surprise; since it involves the mastery of it, its own crucifixion and that of all its sinful lusts. Yet a thousand times more harshly will ring the sentence which God shall finally pronounce against it, saying: "Get thee to thy burning! Depart into everlasting fire!" *Discedite in ignem aeternum!*

What! You a pleasure-seeking man of the world! And you a woman of the world of fashion who worship your fleshly nature! You love that flesh, and yet you expose it to the most stinging and crushing blow that it can possibly encounter! You love it! And yet you risk its being flung into the flames kindled by the hot breath of God's displeasure, and fanned by the whirlwind of his wrath! You love it! And yet you render it liable to an Eternity of suffering – and such suffering!

Well, if that be love, I call it love not only of the blindest but of the maddest sort! My very heart is moved with pity for you, pity which becomes all the keener as I watch you ever more and more in love with yourselves, and yet shrinking and wincing at the slightest pin prick!

Let us, My Dear Hearers, let us treat ourselves here in this life with all Gospel-hardness; if we would have God treat us at the Day of Judgment with the fulness of His Father's love.

Let us give ourselves no quarter in anything; that He may overlook much and make allowance for more.

Let us arm ourselves *against* ourselves with the Lord's implacable justice, that He may look upon us with the eyes of His pardoning mercy.

Let us avoid His Judgment by pronouncing our own; or since we must of necessity present ourselves for sentence at God's Bar, let us by the rigour of our own judgment win for ourselves that favourable verdict which shall place the Elect of God in full possession of their Eternal Happiness!

And that is my wish, my earnest prayer to God for you all: through JESUS CHRIST. Amen.

FOR ADDITIONAL INFORMATION ABOUT LOUIS BOURDALOUE:

Belin, Ferdinand. *La Société française au XVIIe siècle d'après les sermons de Bourdaloue.* Paris, 1875.

Bourdaloue, Louis. *Oeuvres.* Paris, 1837.

Bungener, Laurence L. *Bourdaloue in the Court of Louis XIV.* Boston: Gould and Lincoln, 1853.

Reville, John C. *Herald of Christ, Louis Bourdaloue, S. J.: King of Preachers and Preacher of Kings.* New York: Schwartz, Kirwin & Fauss, 1922.

FOR OTHER SERMONS BY LOUIS BOURDALOUE:

Sermons of John Baptist Massillon and Lewis Bourdaloue. Translated by Flint Abel. Hartford: Lincoln & Gleason, 1805.

O'Mahony, D., ed. *Great French Sermons from Bossuet, Bourdaloue and Massillon.* London: Sands & Co., 1917.

Also: *Eight Sermons for Holy Week and Easter* (1884), *Home-Thrusts* (1899).

FRANÇOIS DE SALIGNAC DE LA MOTHE FÉNELON

1651-1715

FÉNELON, The Mansell Collection

FRANÇOIS DE SALIGNAC DE LA MOTHE FÉNELON

1651	*Born at the castle of Fénelon in Perigord, France*
1663	*Entered Jesuit College in Cahors*
1666	*Entered Jesuit College du Plessis, Paris*
1668	*Continued theological studies at the Seminary of St. Sulpice and began services in the parish of St. Sulpice*
1675	*Ordained to the priesthood*
1678	*Appointed supervisor of a women's association designed to educate and train young Protestant women inclined to the Catholic faith*
1685	*Preached in a mission in Saintonge*
1687	*Preached in a mission in Aunis*
1689	*Appointed preceptor to Duke of Burgundy, the grandson of Louis XIV*
1695	*Consecrated to the archbishopric of Cambrai*
1715	*Died at Cambrai January 7*

"I WOULD BURN MY FRIEND with my own hands, and with joy I would burn myself, to save the church." Thus spoke François de Salignac de la Mothe Fénelon, emotional, impetuous, single-minded priest, devoted to the order, authority, and preservation of the Roman Catholic church.

An educator, a writer, a church administrator, a court preacher, a persecutor of the Huguenots—Fenélon's life was packed with ardent activity; yet strangely enough he was a fanatical proponent of mysticism. It is difficult to determine whether he was a mystical activist or an activistic mystic.

Fénelon was born in Perigord, France, at the castle of Féne-lon. He was the offspring of an elderly father who had married a young wife; and early in his life he was adopted by an uncle. Though often sick as a child, he was quick to learn and zeal-ously studied Greek and Latin classics. His uncle introduced Fénelon to Bossuet, the famous preacher who was to be a close friend of his for ten years. Later Bossuet was to figure in the most serious conflict of Fénelon's life.

Fénelon received a splendid education. In 1663, on the brink of his teen-age years, he entered the Jesuit College at Cahors. Journeying to Paris in 1666, he entered the Jesuit College du Plessis, and then continued his theological studies at the Semi-nary of St. Sulpice. When he was twenty-four years old, he was ordained to the priesthood. He served effectively in the parish of St. Sulpice.

In 1678 while still in his twenties, he was appointed as super-visor of an association formed to educate young Protestant women who were inclined toward the Catholic faith. He was an able educator and served his church well in this super-visory capacity, in an age in which the Roman church was trying desperately to win back to her fold those who had entered the Protestant camp. Education was one of the means used, and education of the young was a particularly important tactic.

In 1689 he was appointed preceptor to the duke of Burgundy, the young grandson of Louis XIV. At the time it appeared that this boy would one day rule France. Fénelon accepted the task with a determination to turn the little duke into superb king-material. He held a concept of education which insisted that enthusiasm was one of the primary ingredients for learning. Therefore as an instructor he enthusiastically presented the material that he felt the child should learn—but the education of the young duke was no easy task. The boy was spoiled and given to temper tantrums: he would frequently break the clocks which struck an hour calling him to a task he did not like; he would rage at the rain when it interfered with planned activity. Yet Fénelon was able to mold him toward manhood in a creative way. His success must have impressed the king: in 1695 he was consecrated to the archbishopric of Cambrai and occupied this position until his death.

The character of Fénelon's work was largely influenced by

his social awareness. He was a member of the aristocratic class of French society—a loyal supporter of the royalty, distrustful of democracy, suspicious of any effort to give the people more voice, fearful of anarchy, and disdainful of those who had less training and education than he. Yet he was not a typical member of the French aristocracy; he recognized the plight of the poor and did much to alleviate their suffering through his work as a churchman. He was not as harsh in his tactics as many were. And his life was impeccable in regard to morality.

Fénelon was a devoted son of the Catholic church; he loved the order and the doctrine of the church. Throughout his entire life he threw himself vigorously into defending the church and strengthening its hold on France. Later in life he came into conflict with the authority of the church in France; nevertheless, he was never opposed to the Catholic church as such. Whenever he came into conflict with higher authority, he always submitted. Strongly opposed to revolution and anarchy, he willingly yielded to the dictates of others. Whenever an issue or dispute was settled against him, he accepted the verdict. He did not continue the struggle openly nor try to overthrow those in higher positions.

Volatile issues abounded in his day. One of these issues centered in the corruption of the church leadership in France. Not all of the clergy were corrupt and immoral, but many were; particularly was there corruption among those closely associated with the nobility. Fénelon did not oppose the church, but he did oppose the corruption within it. Because of his attitude toward corruption, he gained many enemies in high positions, both civil and ecclesiastical.

The persecution of Protestants was another significant issue that involved Fénelon. The Huguenots were the largest group of Protestants in France; Fénelon believed that they must be won back to the Catholic church. At times he advocated using any means necessary to effect their conversion, but in other instances he recognized that the wayward must be won back through persuasion. He argued that forced conversion was no real conversion.

He wrote to the secretary of state in 1687:

> In the present condition of men's minds we could easily bring them all to confession and communion if we chose to use a little pressure and so glorify our mission.

> But what is the good of bringing men to confession who do not yet recognize the Church? How can we give Jesus Christ to those who do not believe they are receiving Him? We should expect to bring a terrible curse upon us if we were satisfied with hasty, superficial work, all meant for show. We can but multiply our instructions, invite the people to come heartily to sacraments, but give them only to those who come of their own accord to seek them in unreserved submission.[1]

Although he was a member of the aristocracy, Fénelon recognized the corruption of French nobility. It was a period of extravagance, worldly display, and of unconcern for the poor. Fénelon was a social reformer who advocated many changes in the political and economic order. He was also a reformer in education and argued for changes in educational methods. His most famous writing, *Télémaque*, bears evidence of his concern for educational and social reform. The book primarily discusses education, but it also contains a fearless portrayal of some of the king's weaknesses. The book was received with great displeasure by the French court and cost Fénelon his position there.

This was not the only occasion on which Fénelon exposed the faults of the nobility. One day Louis XIV was astonished to find only Fénelon and the priest at the chapel; the usual large congregation was absent. The king asked, "What is the reason of all this?" Fénelon answered, "Why, I caused it to be given out, Sire, that Your Majesty did not attend chapel today, so that you might know who came to worship God and who to flatter the king."

Fénelon's most serious controversy arose over a theological issue. Madame Guyon's writings on mysticism were creating great unrest within the Catholic church. Her writings were opposed by Bossuet as well as by most of the clergy of the church in France. Bossuet won the support of the court of France and the teachings of Madame Guyon were vigorously suppressed. Fénelon, himself committed to mysticism, had championed her cause; he was bitterly rebuked and lost all of his favor with the French court.

The controversy between Fénelon and Bossuet was both

---

1. James Mudge, *Fénelon: The Mystic* (Cincinnati: Jennings and Graham, 1906), p. 69.

fierce and lengthy. In many ways Fénelon displayed a gentle and loving spirit, even if Bossuet did not; he showed considerable self-restraint and dignity. Nevertheless, this entire affair, like his persecution of the Huguenots, is a blot upon his life. Yet we must remember his times; in the light of his day he displayed a rare spirit of kindness and of grace.

When the pope formally disapproved of Fénelon's position, he submitted to the will of the pope at once and gave his writings to be burned. Fénelon was allowed to continue in his church position, but he was ordered to remain within his diocese. All correspondence with his former pupil, the duke of Burgundy, was terminated. During the rest of his life he tended to his duties in Cambrai. He directed most of his revenues to the care of the poor; he served effectively and won the devotion of the people in his area. His later life was not devoid of significant activity: he continued to write; he founded a seminary; he took an active interest in practical affairs. In 1715 Fénelon died in Cambrai.

Of the various French Catholic preachers, Fénelon evidently was the most saintly. His life bears testimony that spirituality and active participation in significant public affairs are not mutually exclusive. His life is also evidence that faithfulness to one's convictions as a follower of Christ is more important than maintaining station and position. In the face of obvious corruption, Fénelon would not keep silent even though it cost him a position of fame, power, and prestige. He incurred the wrath of Louis XIV, but he won the admiration of the ages.

PREACHING AND SERMONS

Among the quartet of French preachers—Bossuet, Bourdaloue, Massillon, and Fénelon—Fénelon is by far the hardest to characterize. Part of this is due to the scarcity of his sermonic material. He did not customarily write his sermons; only ten complete sermons remain, along with eighteen sermon plans or outlines.

Nor are the comments from history in agreement with reference to him. Some say that his preaching showed sympathetic understanding of the Protestant heretics and that he refused to use force against them in his position as bishop of Cambrai. Yet his personal statements do not sound like the words of a man noted for toleration. He called tolerance "that cowardly indulgence, that false compassion, which could let the gangrene of disobedience creep over the whole body of the people, rather than nerve itself to sever the festering limb at one blow." He did not understand Protestantism and believed it to be essentially wicked; neither did he understand the ways of providence in allowing it to continue, especially among the young:

> Trembling we must adore that inscrutable counsel, that unfathomable judgment of God, which delivers over to heresy so many young children, who, at an age so tender, suck in poison with their mother's milk, whose misfortune is brought about by the blind tenderness of the parents whom God hath appointed for them, so that their very docility leads them astray.[2]

Perhaps the confusion concerning Fénelon's attitude toward Protestants is due in part to confusing his administrative methods with his personal concepts. In administrative methodology he did not believe that mere force would gain the objectives which the Catholic church desired, but in his personal opinions he regarded Protestants and heretics as those who had no right to exist.

In 1678 Fénelon was appointed superior of the New Catholics. These "New Catholics" were supposedly Protestant converts to Catholicism. His appointment to this position would indicate that Fénelon seemed to have some success at winning the Huguenots back to the Catholic fold. In reality, however, these New Catholics were likely children who had been forcibly taken from their Protestant parents in order to be raised as Catholics in Catholic children's homes. And if these children were indeed taken forcibly from their homes to be raised as Catholics, Fénelon can scarcely be described as an example of toleration. Although Fénelon held this office, it is questionable how much actual contact he had with this practice or with the homes of these people. In any event, the issue is uncertain.

About the only indisputable fact concerning Fénelon's preaching was his attraction toward mysticism: his preaching was filled with the devotional interests of the pious mystic. Interestingly enough, he never practiced the allegorical method in his preaching, as did other mystics, and flatly rejected it. He

---

2. Viscount St. Cyres, *François de Fénelon* (London: Methuen and Co., 1901), p. 19.

was convinced that scriptural objectives could not best be obtained by such devious interpretation.

In Fénelon's day mysticism was a definite science of spiritual perfection, a means of supernatural approach to God. Madame Guyon, who profoundly influenced him, practiced a particular brand of mysticism which contained a twofold principle: self-renunciation and perfect union with the divine will. In retrospect it appears that Fénelon was trying to preserve the best in mysticism without subscribing to its gross errors. But his involvement with Madame Guyon brought him into conflict with Bossuet, who had already repudiated her, and neither would back down. The result was the ridiculous conflict between the two court preachers.

As usual, Bossuet overstated everything; his attacks upon Fénelon were immoderate and caused the pope to rebuke him for his intemperate statements. Bossuet's reputation suffered because of the ill-chosen wording of his attacks; Fénelon was widely regarded as "saintly" and pious.

But Fénelon by no means escaped unscathed from the controversy: Rome forced him to withdraw part of his previous opinions, and he stood corrected for his involvement with the mystical thinkers. Intellectually, then, Bossuet won out; but personally, Fénelon's reputation increased even during the controversy while the reputation of Bossuet was seriously injured.

Fénelon was really not as capable in his preaching as he was in his writing. Yet his sermons are notable for the clarity of their development; no one in his time outlined a sermon as well as Fénelon. In the sermon included in this collection, "The Saints Converse with God," Fénelon presents the following outline of 1 Thessalonians 5:17:

    I. The general necessity of prayer

   II. The peculiar duty of prayer

  III. The manner in which we ought to pray

This outline is not exactly a model of homiletical creativity or skill, but it is worlds apart from the usually confusing and intricate reasonings of his contemporaries.

Fénelon was concerned more with the emotion of his hearers than with their reason; he was reputed to be a preacher who spoke from the heart as well as from the head, and that kind of preaching met the needs of the people who heard him. Apparently he first learned to speak with great emotional fervor at Cambrai: at the beginning of his ministry he preached from detailed notes; at Cambrai he no longer carried notes to his pulpit but spoke freely from his previous preparation.

Probably Fénelon never was an orator like Bossuet; his preaching is characterized more by simplicity and depth of spiritual insight than by powerful oratory. Nevertheless, the French had an expression, "To think like Pascal, to write like Bossuet, and to speak like Fénelon"; which supposedly expressed the apex of human skills. Frankly, while "thinking like Pascal" might be a worthy challenge for anyone, it seems that the expression should have been, "to speak like Bossuet and write like Fénelon," if anything, since Fénelon was a gifted writer and Bossuet a notable orator. On the other hand, as erratic as Fénelon was, and as given to flattery and exaggeration as Bossuet was, perhaps neither would be ideal.

The truth is, for all of his mystical devotion, Fénelon's personality was a mass of contradictions. On the one hand he seemed to desire the quietistic, mystical life of contemplation and self-renunciation. On the other hand he was a driving bundle of self-assertiveness. Perhaps his mysticism reflected the yearning of his personality for balance, a devout seeking after spiritual gifts which were not easily or naturally his. It must be admitted that he was at least partly successful in these objectives, for his sermons indicate many clear spiritual insights.

Yet without his writings, Fénelon would never have attracted the attention which he has enjoyed: his sermonic works are simply not superior enough in themselves, even though they are clearly organized and spiritually helpful. Neither the delivery of his sermons, nor his treatises on education or history or politics or the art of ruling, have preserved the reputation of Fénelon. Only his devotional writings remain of general interest. Perhaps his mystical inclinations, after all, secured Fénelon's place in history.

Sermons

THE SAINTS CONVERSE WITH GOD

"Pray without ceasing" (1 Thessalonians 5:17).

OF ALL THE DUTIES enjoined by Christianity none is more essential, and yet more neglected, than prayer. Most people consider this exercise a wearisome ceremony, which they are justified in abridging as much as possible. Even those whose profession or fears lead them to pray, do it with such languor and wanderings of mind that their prayers, far from drawing down blessings, only increase their condemnation. I wish to demonstrate, in this discourse, first, the general necessity of prayer; secondly, its peculiar duty; thirdly, the manner in which we ought to pray.

First. God alone can instruct us in our duty. The teachings of men, however wise and well disposed they may be, are still ineffectual, if God do not shed on the soul that light which opens the mind to truth. The imperfections of our fellow creatures cast a shade over the truths that we learn from them. Such is our weakness that we do not receive, with sufficient docility, the instructions of those who are as imperfect as ourselves. A thousand suspicions, jealousies, fears, and prejudices prevent us from profiting, as we might, by what we hear from men; and though they announce the most serious truths, yet what they do weakens the effect of what they say. In a word, it is God alone who can perfectly teach us.

St. Bernard said, in writing to a pious friend—If you are seeking less to satisfy a vain curiosity than to get true wisdom, you will sooner find it in deserts than in books. The silence of the rocks and the pathless forests will teach you better than the eloquence of the most gifted men. "All," says St. Augustine, "that we possess of truth and wisdom is a borrowed good flowing from that fountain for which we ought to thirst in the fearful desert of this world, that, being refreshed and invigorated by these dews from heaven, we may not faint upon the road that conducts us to a better country. Every attempt to satisfy the cravings of our hearts at other sources only increases the void. You

Reprinted from *The World's Great Sermons*, comp. Grenville Kleiser, vol. 2 (New York: Funk & Wagnalls Co., 1908), pp. 203–17.

will be always poor if you do not possess the only true riches." All light that does not proceed from God is false; it only dazzles us; it sheds no illumination upon the difficult paths in which we must walk, along the precipices that are about us.

Our experience and our reflections cannot, on all occasions, give us just and certain rules of conduct. The advice of our wisest and most sincere friends is not always sufficient; many things escape their observation, and many that do not are too painful to be spoken. They suppress much from delicacy, or sometimes from a fear of transgressing the bounds that our friendship and confidence in them will allow. The animadversions of our enemies, however severe or vigilant they may be, fail to enlighten us with regard to ourselves. Their malignity furnishes our self-love with a pretext for the indulgence of the greatest faults. The blindness of our self-love is so great that we find reasons for being satisfied with ourselves, while all the world condemn us. What must we learn from all this darkness? That it is God alone who can dissipate it; that it is He alone whom we can never doubt; that He alone is true, and knoweth all things; that if we go to Him in sincerity, He will teach us what men dare not tell us, what books cannot – all that is essential for us to know.

Be assured that the greatest obstacle to true wisdom is the self-confidence inspired by that which is false. The first step toward this precious knowledge is earnestly to desire it, to feel the want of it, and to be convinced that they who seek it must address themselves to the Father of lights, who freely gives to him who asks in faith. But if it be true that God alone can enlighten us, it is not the less true that He will do this simply in answer to our prayers. Are we not happy, indeed, in being able to obtain so great a blessing by only asking for it? No part of the effort that we make to acquire the transient enjoyments of this life is necessary to obtain these heavenly blessings. What will we not do, what are we not willing to suffer, to possess dangerous and contemptible things, and often without any success? It is not thus with heavenly things. God is always ready to grant them to those who make the request in sincerity and truth. The Christian life is a long and continual tendency of our hearts toward that eternal goodness which we desire on earth. All our happiness consists in thirsting for it. Now this thirst is prayer. Ever desire to approach your Creator and you will never cease to pray.

Do not think that it is necessary to pronounce many words. To pray is to say, Let Thy will be done. It is to form a good purpose; to raise your heart to God; to lament your weakness; to sigh at the recollection of your frequent disobedience. This prayer demands neither method, nor science, nor reasoning; it is not essential to quit one's employment; it is a simple movement of the heart toward its Creator, and a desire that whatever you are doing you may do it to His glory. The best of all prayers is to act with a pure intention, and with a continual reference to the will of God. It depends much upon ourselves whether our prayers be efficacious. It is not by a miracle, but by a movement of the heart that we are benefited; by a submissive spirit. Let us believe, let us trust, let us hope, and God never will reject our prayer. Yet how many Christians do we see strangers to the privilege, aliens from God, who seldom think of Him, who never open their hearts to Him; who seek elsewhere the counsels of a false wisdom, and vain and dangerous consolations, who cannot resolve to seek, in humble, fervent prayer to God, a remedy for their griefs and a true knowledge of their defects, the necessary power to conquer their vicious and perverse inclinations, and the consolations and assistance they require, that they may not be discouraged in a virtuous life.

But some will say, "I have no interest in prayer; it wearies me; my imagination is excited by sensible and more agreeable objects, and wanders in spite of me."

If neither your reverence for the great truths of religion, nor the majesty of the ever-present Deity, nor the interest of your eternal salvation, have power to arrest your mind and engage it in prayer, at least mourn with me for your infidelity; be ashamed of your weakness, and wish that your thoughts were more under your control; and desire to become less frivolous and inconstant. Make an effort to subject your mind to this discipline. You will gradually acquire habit and facility. What is now tedious will become delightful; and you will then feel, with a peace that the world cannot give nor take away, that God is good. Make a courageous effort to overcome yourself. There can be no occasion that more demands it.

Secondly. The peculiar obligation of prayer. Were I to give all the proofs that the subject affords, I should describe every condition of life, that I might point out its dangers, and the necessity of recourse to God in prayer. But I will simply state that under all circumstances we have need of prayer. There is no situation in which it is possible to be placed where we have not many virtues to acquire and many faults to correct. We find in our temperament, or in our habits, or in the peculiar character of our minds, qualities that do not suit our occupations, and that oppose our duties. One person is connected by marriage to another whose temper is so unequal that life becomes a perpetual warfare. Some, who are exposed to the contagious atmosphere of the world, find themselves so susceptible to the vanity which they inhale that all their pure desires vanish. Others have solemnly promised to renounce their resentments, to conquer their aversions, to suffer with patience certain crosses, and to repress their eagerness for wealth; but nature prevails, and they are vindictive, violent, impatient, and avaricious.

Whence comes it that these resolutions are so frail? That all these people wish to improve, desire to perform their duty toward God and man better, and yet fail? It is because our own strength and wisdom, alone, are not enough. We undertake to do everything without God; therefore we do not succeed. It is at the foot of the altar that we must seek for counsel which will aid us. It is with God that we must lay our plans of virtue and usefulness; it is He alone that can render them successful. Without Him, all our designs, however good they may appear, are only temerity and delusion. Let us then pray that we may learn what we are and what we ought to be. By this means we shall not only learn the number and the evil effects of our peculiar faults, but we shall also learn to what virtues we are called, and the way to practise them. The rays of that pure and heavenly light that visit the humble soul will beam on us and we shall feel and understand that everything is possible to those who put their whole trust in God. Thus, not only to those who live in retirement, but to those who are exposed to the agitations of the world and the excitements of business, it is peculiarly necessary, by contemplation and fervent prayer, to restore their souls to that serenity which the dissipations of life and commerce with men have disturbed. To those who are engaged in business, contemplation and prayer are much more difficult than to those who live in retirement; but it is far more necessary for them to have frequent recourse to God in fervent prayer. In the most holy occupation a certain degree of precaution is necessary.

Do not devote all your time to action, but reserve a certain portion of it for meditation upon eternity. We see Jesus Christ inviting His disciples to go apart, in a desert place, and rest awhile, after their return from the cities, where they had been to announce His religion. How much more necessary is it for us to approach the source of all virtue, that we may revive our declining faith and charity, when we return from the busy scenes of life, where men speak and act as if they had never known that there is a God! We should look upon prayer as the remedy for our weakness, the rectifier of our own faults. He who was without sin prayed constantly; how much more ought we, who are sinners, to be faithful in prayer!

Even the exercise of charity is often a snare to us. It calls us to certain occupations that dissipate the mind, and that may degenerate into mere amusement. It is for this reason that St. Chrysostom says that nothing is so important as to keep an exact proportion between the interior source of virtue and the external practise of it; else, like the foolish virgins, we shall find that the oil in our lamp is exhausted when the bridegroom comes.

The necessity we feel that God should bless our labors is another powerful motive to prayer. It often happens that all human help is vain. It is God alone that can aid us, and it does not require much faith to believe that it is less our exertions, our foresight, and our industry than the blessing of the Almighty that can give success to our wishes.

Thirdly. Of the manner in which we ought to pray. 1. We must pray with attention. God listens to the voice of the heart, not to that of the lips. Our whole heart must be engaged in prayer. It must fasten upon what it prays for; and every human object must disappear from our minds. To whom should we speak with attention if not to God? Can He demand less of us than that we should think of what we say to Him? Dare we hope that He will listen to us, and think of us, when we forget ourselves in the midst of our prayers? This attention to prayer, which it is so just to exact from Christians, may be practised with less difficulty than we imagine. It is true that the most faithful souls suffer from occasional involuntary distractions. They cannot always control their imaginations, and, in the silence of their spirits, enter into the presence of God. But these unbidden wanderings of the mind ought not to trouble us; and they may conduce to our perfection even more than the most sublime and affecting prayers if we earnestly strive to overcome them, and submit with humility to this experience of our infirmity. But to dwell willingly on frivolous and worldly things during prayer, to make no effort to check the vain thoughts that intrude upon this sacred employment and come between us and the Father of our spirits – is not this choosing to live the sport of our senses, and separated from God?

2. We must also ask with faith; a faith so firm that it never falters. He who prays without confidence cannot hope that his prayer will be granted. Will not God love the heart that trusts in Him? Will He reject those who bring all their treasures to Him, and repose everything upon His goodness? When we pray to God, says St. Cyprian, with entire assurance, it is Himself who has given us the spirit of our prayer. Then it is the Father listening to the words of His child; it is He who dwells in our hearts, teaching us to pray. But must we confess that this filial confidence is wanting in all our prayers? Is not prayer our resource only when all others have failed us? If we look into hearts, shall we not find that we ask of God as if we had never before received benefits from Him? Shall we not discover there a secret infidelity that renders us unworthy of His goodness? Let us tremble, lest, when Jesus Christ shall judge us, He pronounce the same reproach that He did to Peter, "O thou of little faith, wherefore didst thou doubt?"

3. We must join humility with trust. Great God, said Daniel, when we prostrate ourselves at Thy feet, we do not place our hopes for the success of our prayers upon our righteousness, but upon Thy mercy. Without this disposition in our hearts, all others, however pious they may be, cannot please God. St. Augustine observes that the failure of Peter should not be attributed to insincerity in his zeal for Jesus Christ. He loved his Master in good faith; in good faith he would rather have died than have forsaken Him; but his fault lay in trusting to his own strength, to do what his own heart dictated.

It is not enough to possess a right spirit, an exact knowledge of duty, a sincere desire to perform it. We must continually renew this desire, and enkindle this flame within us, at the fountain of pure and eternal light.

It is the humble and contrite heart that God will not despise. Remark the difference which the evangelist has pointed out between the prayer of the proud and presumptuous Pharisee and the humble and penitent publican. The one relates his virtues, the other deplores his sins. The good works of the one shall be set aside, while the penitence of the other shall be accepted. It will be thus with many Christians. Sinners, vile in their own eyes, will be objects of the mercy of God; while some, who have made professions of piety, will be condemned on account of the pride and arrogance that have contaminated their good works. It will be so because these have said in their hearts, "Lord, I thank thee that I am not as other men are." They imagine themselves privileged; they pretend that they alone have penetrated the mysteries of the kingdom of God; they have a language and science of their own; they believe that their zeal can accomplish everything. Their regular lives favor their vanity; but in truth they are incapable of self-sacrifice, and they go to their devotions with their hearts full of pride and presumption. Unhappy are those who pray in this manner! Unhappy are those whose prayers do not render them more humble, more submissive, more watchful over their faults, and more willing to live in obscurity!

4. We must pray with love. It is love says St. Augustine, that asks, that seeks, that knocks, that finds, and that is faithful to what it finds. We cease to pray to God as soon as we cease to love Him, as soon as we cease to thirst for His perfections. The coldness of our love is the silence of our hearts toward God. Without this we may pronounce prayers, but we do not pray; for what shall lead us to meditate upon the laws of God if it be not the love of Him who has made these laws? Let our hearts be full of love, then, and they will pray. Happy are they who think seriously of the truths of religion; but far more happy are they who feel and love them! We must ardently desire that God will grant us spiritual blessings; and the ardor of our wishes must render us fit to receive the blessings. For if we pray only from custom, from fear, in the time of tribulation—if we honor God only with our lips, while our hearts are far from Him—if we do not feel a strong desire for the success of our prayers—if we feel a chilling indifference in approaching Him who is a consuming fire—if we have no zeal for His glory—if we do not feel hatred for sin, and a thirst for perfection, we cannot hope for a blessing upon such heartless prayers.

5. We must pray with perseverance. The perfect heart is never weary of seeking God. Ought we to complain if God sometimes leaves us to obscurity, and doubt, and temptation? Trials purify humble souls, and they serve to expiate the faults of the unfaithful. They confound those who, even in their prayers, have flattered their cowardice

and pride. If an innocent soul, devoted to God, suffer from any secret disturbance, it should be humble, adore the designs of God, and redouble its prayers and its fervor. How often do we hear those who every day have to reproach themselves with unfaithfulness toward God complain that He refuses to answer their prayers! Ought they not to acknowledge that it is their sins which have formed a thick cloud between Heaven and them, and that God has justly hidden Himself from them? How often has He recalled us from our wanderings! How often, ungrateful as we are, have we been deaf to His voice and insensible to His goodness! He would make us feel that we are blind and miserable when we forsake Him. He would teach us, by privation, the value of the blessings that we have slighted. And shall we not bear our punishment with patience? Who can boast of having done all that he ought to have done; of having repaired all his past errors; of having purified his heart, so that he may claim as a right that God should listen to his prayer? Most truly, all our pride, great as it is, would not be sufficient to inspire such presumption! If then, the Almightly do not grant our petitions, let us adore His justice, let us be silent, let us humble ourselves, and let us pray without ceasing. This humble perseverance will obtain from Him what we should never obtain by our own merit. It will make us pass happily from darkness to light; for know, says St. Augustine that God is near to us even when He appears far from us.

6. We should pray with a pure intention. We should not mingle in our prayers what is false with what is real; what is perishable with what is eternal; low and temporal interests with that which concerns our salvation. Do not seek to render God the protector of your self-love and ambition, but the promoter of your good desires. You ask for the gratification of your passions, or to be delivered from the cross, of which He knows you have need. Carry not to the foot of the altar irregular desires and indiscreet prayers. Sigh not for vain and fleeting pleasures. Open your heart to your Father in heaven, that His Spirit may enable you to ask for the true riches.

How can He grant you, says St. Augustine, what you do not yourself desire to receive? You pray every day that His will may be done, and that His kingdom may come. How can you utter this prayer with sincerity when you prefer your own will to His, and make His law yield to the vain pretexts with which your self-love seeks to elude it? Can you make this prayer – you who disturb His reign in your heart by so many impure and vain desires? You, in short, who fear the coming of His reign, and do not desire that God should grant what you seem to pray for? No! If He, at this moment, were to offer to give you a new heart, and render you humble, and willing to bear the cross, your pride would revolt, and you would not accept the offer; or you would make a reservation in favor of your ruling passion, and try to accommodate your piety to your humor and fancies!

FOR ADDITIONAL INFORMATION ABOUT FÉNELON:

De la Bedoyere, Michael. *The Archbishop and the Lady: The Story of Fénelon and Madame Guyon.* New York: Pantheon, 1956.
Fénelon, François de Salignac de La Mothe. *Dialogues on Eloquence.* Edited by William S. Howell. Princeton: Princeton University Press, 1951.
Little, Katharine Day. *François de Fénelon.* New York: Harper & Bro., 1951.
Merton, Thomas. *Letter of Love and Counsel.* Selected and translated by John McEwen. New York: Harcourt, Brace & World, 1964.
Spiritual Letters of François de Salignac de la Mothe-Fénelon. Cornwall-on-the-Hudson, New York: Idlewild Press, 1945.
Upham, Thomas C. *Life, Religious Opinions and Experience of Madame de la Mothe Guyon, together with Some Account of the Personal History and Religious Opinions of Fénelon, Archbishop of Cambray.* London: Sampson, Low, Marston, Searle, & Rivington, 1877.
Whiston, Charles F., ed. *Christian Perfection.* Translated by Mildred Whitney Stillman. New York: Harper, 1947.

FOR OTHER SERMONS BY FÉNELON:

Sermons Choisis sur Divers Sujets. Nouvelle édition sur l'original de l'auteur. Paris, 1744.

JEAN BAPTISTE MASSILLON

1663-1742

MASSILLON, engraving from *Oeuvres de Massillon*
(Paris: Chez Firmin Ditot Frères, Libraires, 1838),
frontispiece.

JEAN BAPTISTE MASSILLON

1663	*Born June 24 at Hyères, France*
1689	*Taught philosophy and theology in Vienne*
1691	*Entered the priesthood*
1696	*Became director of seminary of Saint-Magloire*
1699	*Appointed to preach before King Louis XIV*
1717	*Appointed bishop of Clermont*
1719	*Made a member of the French Academy*
1742	*Died on September 20*

THE MINISTRY OF MASSILLON began as the glory of France declined. At first the decline was imperceptible to the average eye; Massillon may not have been fully aware of what was happening. Yet he spoke so clearly to the ills which were ultimately to destroy France that he must be placed among the great prophetic preachers. When Massillon was appointed to preach before King Louis XIV in 1699, his text for his first sermon was "Blessed are they that mourn."

LIFE AND TIMES

Unlike most of the other great French preachers of his day, Massillon came from a humble home. Like Bossuet and Bourdaloue, his father was a lawyer; but his family had neither the wealth nor the connections of the families of these other men. Massillon was born on June 24, 1663, at Hyères, France. He studied in the colleges of Hyères and Marseilles. When eighteen, he entered the Congregation of the Oratory, and in 1691 he was ordained a priest.

Although he had natural gifts for oratory, Massillon shrank from preaching; he felt inadequate for the task and desired a quieter life. He spent several years in teaching at Montbrison,

Vienne, and Paris before his superiors persuaded him that he should preach. He first gained widespread attention by his delivery of funeral orations.

In 1696 he became head of one of the schools of his order, the Oratorians. In this position he preached often; crowds flocked to hear him, and his fame reached the court of Louis XIV.

The king summoned him to preach before the court in 1699. Thereafter he preached numerous sermons before the king and court. From 1701 to 1704 he preached the Lenten sermons before the king. In the last years of Louis XIV's life he no longer summoned Massillon to preach in the court. His disfavor was based partly on suspected theological leanings of Massillon to Jansenism. Probably more important was Massillon's direct attack upon the worldliness, corruption, and spiritual blandness of the court; too, Massillon kept waving before the nobility the suffering and hunger of the masses of people. Such subjects made him extremely unpopular. Though he was an exceptionally effective preacher, his hearers could not tolerate his plain attack upon the indifference of the nobility to the ills of French society. Nevertheless, Massillon was so respected as a funeral orator that he was asked to preach the funeral of Louis XIV.

In 1717 Massillon was appointed bishop of Clermont, one of the largest dioceses in France; two years later he was made a member of the French Academy. Other honors and offers came his way, but he determined to give his time to his church responsibilities. He labored among his people to make the Christian faith real for them. With charity and gentleness he worked among all classes. He kept his own life pure and expected the clergy working under him to do likewise. Whenever he discovered corruption and immorality, he demanded reform. He sought to maintain discipline among the clergy and good morals among all the people.

After the death of Louis XIV, he maintained some contact with the French court. In 1718 he was called to preach the Lenten sermons before Louis XV, great-grandson of Louis XIV; addressed primarily to a child, these discourses are intriguingly unique. Massillon preached to the boy king Louis XV, to the aging Louis XIV, to the hierarchy of his church, and to the common people – and all were moved by his message. He had a rare ability to communicate with persons from all ranks and walks of life.

Even more significant, Massillon set an example in his life for others to follow. In many ways, he was a model as a preacher. He was courageous and cared more for proclaiming the truth of the gospel than for maintaining his position in society; he refused to be the kept preacher of the French court. Devout and pure, his personal life was above reproach. He was sensitive to the great social issues around him and applied the message of Christ to those issues; he particularly lashed out at the insensitivity of the nobility to the suffering of the poor. He pled for reform in French society. He warned that if reform did not come, the whole of the French national fabric would be torn to shreds. As a prophet he was startlingly accurate: only a few years after his death the rumblings of the French Revolution shook the world.

Preaching and Sermons

With all of their virtues, the sermons of the other famous French court preachers are not exciting reading; in fact, it is hard to find a sermon from them that has kept much of its interest at all. But Massillon is exciting: he may well be one of the most undervalued preachers who ever lived.

In all of the classic comparisons among Bourdaloue, Bossuet, Fénelon, and Massillon, Massillon is usually left to the also-ran position. He is said not to have the oratorical genius of Bossuet or Bourdaloue, nor the saintly mysticism of Fénelon. Perhaps not. Perhaps his only ability was his incredible gift of preaching.

To be sure, the sermons of Massillon do not read like a contemporary sermon, particularly in style; they have suffered in translation, and in places they bear the marks of an older style of composition. Sometimes the language is obscure, largely due to a translation which itself is now obsolete. In spite of these handicaps, the sermons of Massillon are stirring, vigorous, powerful. At times he preaches with such thunder that for a moment you forget that you are reading Massillon and think instead of Jonathan Edwards or Dwight L. Moody. At times Massillon spoke with a social passion which has never been equaled even in the modern age of social interest.

For an example of his skills as an evangelist, read "On the Small Number of the Saved." When Massillon spoke these words his audience broke forth with groaning and weeping, and Massillon himself was forced to turn aside in tears:

I confine myself to you, my brethren, who are gathered here. I speak no longer to the rest of mankind. I look at you as if you were the only ones on the earth; and here is the thought that seizes me, and that terrifies me. I make the supposition that this is your last hour, and the end of the world; that the heavens are about to open above your heads, that Jesus Christ is to appear in his glory in the midst of this sanctuary, and that you are gathered here only to wait for him, and his trembling criminals on whom is to be pronounced either a sentence of grace or a decree of eternal death.

For vainly do you flatter yourselves; you will die such in character as you are today. All those impulses toward change with which you amuse yourselves, you will amuse yourselves with them down to the bed of death. Such is the experience of all generations. The only thing new you will then find in yourselves will be, perhaps, a reckoning a trifle larger than that which you would today have to render; and according to what you would be if you were at this moment to be judged, you may almost determine what will befall you at the termination of your life.

Now I ask you—and I ask it smitten with terror, not separating in this matter my lot from yours, and putting myself in the same frame of mind into which I desire you to come—I ask you, then, if Jesus Christ were to appear in this sanctuary, in the midst of this assembly, the most illustrious in the world, to pass judgment on us, to draw the dread line of distinction between the goats and the sheep, do you believe that the majority of all of us who are here would be set on his right hand? Do you believe that all things would even be equal? Nay, do you believe that there would be found so many as the ten righteous men whom anciently the Lord could not find in whole cities? I put the question to you, but I know not; I know not myself. Thou only, oh my God, knowest those that belong to thee!

But if we know not those who belong to Him, at least we know that sinners do not belong to Him. Now of what classes of persons do the professing Christians in this assembly consist? Titles and dignities must be counted for naught; of these you shall be stripped before Jesus Christ. Who make up this assembly? Sinners in great number, who do not wish to be converted; and still greater number, sinners who would like it, but who put off their conversion; many others who would be converted, only to relapse into sin; finally, a multitude who think they have no need of conversion. You have thus made up the company of the reprobate.

Cut off these four classes of sinners from the sacred assembly, for they will be cut off from it at the great day! Stand forth now, ye righteous! Where are you? Remnant of Israel, pass to the right hand! True wheat of Jesus Christ, disengage yourselves from this chaff, doomed to the fire! Oh, God! Where are thine elect? In what remains there for Thy portion?

When Massillon was asked to preach the same sermon on a second occasion, the assembled nobles again broke into groaning and weeping—even though they knew what was coming! Perhaps we do not flatter Massillon when we compare him favorably with Jonathan Edwards and Dwight L. Moody. Did Dwight L. Moody or Jonathan Edwards ever deliver such an exhortation? Even "Sinners in the Hands of an Angry God" does not exceed it in force.

Likewise, Massillon's ability to describe the plight of the poor and the neglect of the rich was superb. In his sermon, "On Charity," he reminded the wealthy of their duties and warned them of the impending disaster that would fall upon them if they did not heed the cries of the poor:

What do your passions suffer from the public calamities? If the misfortune of the times forces you to retrench from your expenses, begin with those of which religion condemns the use; regulate your tables, your apparel, your amusements, your followers, and your edifices according to the gospel; let your retrenchings in charity at least only follow the others. Lessen your triumphs before you begin to diminish from your duties. . . .

But that the public misfortunes should be discernible neither in the splendor and pride of your clothing, nor in the sensuality of your feasts, nor in the magnificence of your palaces, nor in your rage for gaming and every criminal pleasure, but solely in your inhumanity toward the poor; that everything abroad, the theaters, the profane assemblies of every description, the public festivals, should continue with the same vigor and animation, while charity alone should be chilled; that luxury should every day increase, while compassion alone shall diminish; that the world and Satan should lose nothing through the misery of the times, while Jesus Christ alone shall suffer in his afflicted member; that the rich, sheltered in their opulence, should see only from afar the anger of heaven, while the poor and the innocent shall become its melancholy victims: Great God! Thou wouldst then overwhelm only the unfortunate in sending these scourges upon the earth!

Even Dickens did not call up so melancholy a ghost to haunt Scrooge as Massillon summoned from the grave to rebuke the rich:

Alas! we are sometimes astonished to see fortunes apparently the best established, go to wreck in an instant; those ancient, and formerly so illustrious names fallen into obscurity, no longer to offer to our view but the melancholy wrecks of their ancient splendor; and their estates become the property of their rivals, or perhaps of their own servants.

Ah! could we investigate the source of their misfortunes; if their ashes, and the pompous wrecks, which in the pride of their monuments remain to us of their glory, could speak,—they would say to us, these sad marks of our grandeur? "It is the tears of the poor, whom we neglected, whom we oppressed, which have gradually sapped, and at last have totally overthrown them: their cries have drawn down the thunder of Heaven upon our palaces. The Lord hath blown upon our superb edifices, and upon our fortune, and hath dissipated them like dust. Let the name of the poor be honorable in your sight, if you wish that your names may never perish in the memory of men. Let compassion sustain your houses, if you wish that your posterity be not buried under their ruins. Become wise at our cost; and let our misfortunes, in teaching you our faults, teach you also to shun them.

Remember that this sermon was written in 1709, six years before the death of Louis XIV and eighty years before the storming of the Bastille by the peasants. Remember that these solemn warnings called France to a repentance she would not heed, yet warned her of a disaster that most certainly befell her.

But Massillon was not a preacher who contented himself

with accusations and rebukes and never offered any positive suggestions. Some of the social visions of Washington Gladden or Walter Rauschenbusch seem dimly foreshadowed in this remarkable passage from the same sermon, written centuries before the graduated income tax:

> If each of you were, according to the advice of the apostle, to appropriate a certain portion of your wealth toward the subsistence of the poor; if, in the computation of your expenses and of your revenues, this item were to be always regarded as the most sacred and the most inviolable one, then we should quickly see the number of the afflicted to diminish: we should soon see renewed in the church that peace, that happiness, and that cheerful equality which reigned among the first Christians; we should no longer behold with sorrow that monstrous disproportion, which, elevating the one, places him on the pinnacle of prosperity and opulence, while the other crawls on the ground, and groans in the gulf of poverty and affliction.
>
> No longer should there be any unhappy except the impious among us; no secret miseries except those which sin operates in the soul; no tears except those of penitence; no sighs but for heaven; no poor, but those blessed disciples of the gospel, who renounce all to follow their master.
>
> Our cities would be the abode of innocence and compassion; religion, a commerce of charity; the earth the image of heaven, where, in different degrees of glory, each is equally happy; and the enemies of faith would again, as formerly, be forced to render glory to God, and to confess that there is something of divine in a religion which is capable of uniting men together in a manner so new.

Rather than suggesting that the visions of this sermon foreshadow later ideas, it might be better to say that social prophets like Rauschenbusch and Massillon both drew their visions from the same source, the inspired revelation of a compassionate God.

The other sermons of Massillon are less notable, but nonetheless are fine examples of his work. In every sermon Massillon displays an earnest desire to appeal to the whole man, both in intellect and emotion.

After examining these sermons by Massillon, we may not be

surprised to read the striking compliment Louis XIV paid him: "Father, I have heard in this chapel many great orators, and have been much pleased with them, but whenever I have heard you, I have been displeased with myself." Needless to say, that kind of preacher was not often invited to speak before the court – compliment or not – and Massillon never attained the favor at court his predecessors enjoyed.

Nor was that an accident. Massillon resolved not to preach like his predecessors; "I feel their intellectual force, I recognize their great talents, but if I preach, I shall not preach like them." By avoiding the oratorical art of Bossuet with his flatteries, and the tedious though sometimes powerful analytical style of Bourdaloue, and by speaking more directly and plainly than Fénelon, though not with his mystical charm – Massillon excelled them all.

The most famous moment in the preaching career of Massillon came at the funeral oration on Louis XIV. Notre Dame Cathedral was filled to overflowing; it was a spectacular moment in a spectacular age, a moment that many preachers might envy but few could meet. The lengthy reign of the glorious Louis XIV had ended; the new age of the decadent Louis XV was about to begin. And beyond that, there loomed a catastrophic day which only the prophetic Massillon had dared to imagine.

The audience fell silent. Massillon announced his text from the Vulgate, Ecclesiastes 1:16: "I spoke in my heart, saying, Behold, I have become great, and have advanced in wisdom beyond all who were before me in Jerusalem."

Massillon paused for a moment to let the solemn text take effect, and a profound silence filled the great cathedral. Massillon said:

> God only is great, my brethren; and above all in those last moments when he presides at the death of the kings of the earth. The more their glory and their power have shown forth, the more in vanishing: then do they render homage to his supreme greatness; God then appears all that He is, and man is no more at all that which he believed himself to be.[1]

1. Edwin Charles Dargan, *A History of Preaching*, 2 vols. (Grand Rapids: Baker Book House, 1954), 2:115.

The effect was electrifying. Even in such a moment, Massillon had glorified God.

Never did a Christian preacher stand in a more difficult place than did Massillon; never did a preacher have more temptations to compromise with the wealthy or flatter the powerful. He would neither compromise nor flatter. He spoke the truth about the king, about the wealthy, about the poor. He spoke with the powerful urgings of an evangelist and the social conscience of a reformer—in short, he was a truly Christian preacher.

Sermons

ON THE SMALL NUMBER OF THE SAVED

"And many lepers were in Israel in the time of Eliseus the prophet; and none of them was cleansed, saving Naaman the Syrian" (Luke 4:27).

EVERY DAY, my brethren, you continue to demand of us, if the road to heaven is really so difficult, and the number of the saved is indeed so small, as we say? To a question so often proposed, and still oftener resolved, our Savior answers you at present, that there were many widows in Israel afflicted with famine; but the widow of Sarepta was alone found worthy the succor of the prophet Elias: that the number of lepers was great in Israel in the time of the prophet Eliseus; and that Naaman was only cured by the man of God.

Were I here, my brethren, for the purpose of alarming, rather than instructing you, I needed only to recapitulate what in the holy writings we find dreadful with regard to this great truth; and running over the history of the just, from age to age, to show you that, in all times, the number of the saved has been very small. The family of Noah alone saved from the general flood; Abraham chosen from amongst men to be the sole depositary of the covenant with God; Joshua and Caleb the only two of six hundred thousand Hebrews who saw the Land of Promise; Job the only upright man in the Land of Uz – Lot, in Sodom. To representations so alarming would have succeeded the sayings of the prophets. In Isaiah you would see the elect as rare as the grapes which are found after the vintage, and have escaped the search of the gatherer; as rare as the blades which remain by chance in the field, and have escaped the scythe of the mower. The Evangelist would still have added new traits to the terrors of these images. I might have spoken to you of two roads – of which one is narrow, rugged, and the path of a very small number; the other broad, open, and strewed with flowers, and almost the general path of men: that every where, in the holy writings, the multitude is always spoken of as forming the party

Reprinted from John-Baptist Massillon, *Sermons*, last London ed. (Boston: Waite, Peirce & Co., 1845), pp. 38–53.

of the reprobate; while the saved, compared with the rest of mankind, form only a small flock, scarcely perceptible to the sight. I would have left you in fears with regard to your salvation; always cruel to those who have not renounced faith and every hope of being amongst the saved. But what would it serve to limit the fruits of this instruction to the single point of proving how few persons are saved? Alas! I would make the danger known, without instructing you how to avoid it; I would show you, with the prophet, the sword of the wrath of God suspended over your heads, without assisting you to escape the threatened blow; I would alarm the conscience without instructing the sinner.

My intention is, therefore, to-day, in our morals and manner of life, to search for the cause of this number being so small. As every one flatters himself he will not be excluded, it is of importance to examine if his confidence be well founded. I wish not, in marking to you the causes which render salvation so rare, to make you generally conclude, that few will be saved; but to bring you to ask of yourselves, if, living as you live, can you hope to be so? Who am I? What is it I do for heaven; and what can be my hopes in eternity? I propose no other order, in a matter of such importance. What are the causes which render salvation so rare? I mean to point out three principal ones, which is the only arrangement of this discourse. Art and far-sought reasonings would here be ill-timed. O attend, therefore, be whom you may! No subject can be more worthy your attention, since it goes to inform you what may be the hopes of your eternal destiny.

Part I.—Few are saved; because in that number we can only comprehend two descriptions of persons;—either those who have been so happy as to preserve their innocence pure and undefiled; or those who, after having lost, have regained it by penitence:—first cause. There are only these two ways of salvation; and heaven is only open to the innocent or the penitent. Now, of which party are you? Are you innocent? Are you penitent?

Nothing unclean shall enter the kingdom of God. We must consequently carry there, either an innocence unsullied, or an innocence regained. Now, to die innocent, is a grace to which few souls can aspire; and to live penitent, is a mercy, which the relaxed state of our morals renders equally rare. Who indeed will pretend to salvation, by the claim of innocence? Where are the pure souls in whom sin has never dwelt; and who have preserved to the end the sacred treasure of grace confided to them by baptism, and which our Savior will redemand at the awful day of punishment?

In those happy days, when the whole church was still but an assembly of saints, it was very uncommon to find an instance of a believer, who, after having received the gifts of the Holy Spirit, and acknowledged Jesus Christ in the sacrament, which regenerates us, fell back to his former irregularities of life. Ananias and Sapphira were the only prevaricators in the church of Jerusalem; that of Corinth had only one incestuous sinner. Church-penitence was then a remedy almost unknown; and scarcely was there found among these true Israelites one single leper, whom they were obliged to drive from the holy altar, and separate from communion with his brethren. But, since that time, the number of the upright diminishes, in proportion as that of believers increases. It would appear, that the world, pretending now to have become almost generally Christian, has brought with it into the church its corruptions and its maxims. Alas! we all go astray, almost from the breast of our mothers! The first use which we make of our heart is a crime; our first desires are passions; and our reason only expands and increases on the wrecks of our innocence. The earth, says a prophet, is infected by the corruption of those who inhabit it: all have violated the laws, changed the ordinances, and broken the alliance which should have endured for ever: all commit sin; and scarcely is there one to be found who does the work of the Lord. Injustice, calumny, lying, treachery, adultery, and the blackest crimes have deluged the earth. The brother lays snares for his brother; the father is divided from his children; the husband from his wife: there is no tie which a vile interest does not dissolve. Good faith and probity are no longer virtues but among the simple people; animosities are endless; reconciliations feints; and never is a former enemy regarded as a brother: they tear, they devour each other. Assemblies are no longer but for the purpose of public and general censure. The purest virtue is no longer a protection from the malignity of tongues. Gaming is become either a trade, a fraud, or a fury. Repasts, those innocent ties of society, degenerate into excesses, of which we dare not speak. Our age witnesses horrors, with which our forefathers were unacquainted. Behold, then, already one path of salvation shut to the generality of men. All have erred. Be whom you may, who listen to me at present, the time has been, when sin reigned over you. Age may perhaps have calmed your passions; but what was your youth? Long and habitual infirmities may perhaps have disgusted you with the world; but what use did you formerly make of the vigor of health? A sudden inspiration of grace may have turned your heart; but do you not most fervently entreat, that every moment prior to that inspiration may be effaced from the remembrance of the Lord?

But with what am I taking up my time? We are all sinners, O my God! and thou knowest our hearts. What we know of our errors, is perhaps in thy sight the most pardonable; and we all allow, that by innocence we have no claim to salvation. There remains, therefore, only one resource, which is penitence. After our shipwreck, say the saints, it is the happy plank which alone can conduct us into port;

there is no other mean of salvation for us. Be whom you may, prince
or subject, great or low, penitence alone can save you. Now, permit
me to ask—Where are the penitent? You will find more, says a holy
father, who have never fallen, than who, after their fall, have raised
themselves by true repentance. This is a terrible saying; but do not
let us carry things too far: the truth is sufficiently dreadful, without
adding new terrors to it by vain declamation.

Let us only examine if the majority of us have a right, through penitence, to salvation. What is a penitent? According to Tertullian, a
penitent is a believer, who feels every moment the unhappiness which
he formerly had, to forget and lose his God: who has his guilt incessantly before his eyes; who finds every where the traces and remembrance of it.

A penitent is a man, intrusted by God with judgment against himself; who refuses himself the most innocent pleasures, because he
had formerly indulged in the most criminal; who puts up with the
most necessary ones with pain; who now regards his body as an enemy,
whom it is necessary to conquer—as an unclean vessel which must be
purified—as an unfaithful debtor, of whom it is proper to exact to the
last farthing. A penitent regards himself as a criminal condemned to
death, because he no longer is worthy of life. In the loss of riches or
health, he sees only a privation of favors that he had formerly abused;
in the humiliations which happen to him, but the pains of his guilt;
in the agonies with which he is racked, but the commencement of
those punishments he has justly merited: such is a penitent. But I
again ask you—Where amongst us are penitents of this description?
Now, look around you. I do not tell you to judge your brethren, but to
examine what are the manners and morals of those who surround
you; nor do I speak of those open and avowed sinners, who have
thrown off even the appearance of virtue; I speak only of those who,
like yourselves, live like the generality, and whose actions present
nothing to the public view particularly shameful or depraved. They
are sinners, and they admit of it: you are not innocent, and you confess
it yourselves. Now, are they penitent; or are you? Age, avocations,
more serious employments, may perhaps have checked the sallies of
youth: even the bitterness which the Almighty has made attendant
on our passions: the deceits, the treacheries of the world; an injured
fortune, with ruined constitution, may have cooled the ardor, and confined the irregular desires of your heart: crimes may have disgusted
you even with crimes; for passions gradually extinguish themselves.
Time, and the natural inconstancy of the heart, will bring these about;
yet nevertheless, though detached from sin by incapability, you are
no nearer your God. According to the world you are become more prudent, more regular, more what it calls men of probity; more exact in
fulfilling your public or private duties; but you are not penitent. You

have ceased from your disorders, but you have not expiated them: you are not converted; this great stroke, this grand change of the heart, which regenerates man, has not yet been felt by you. Nevertheless, this situation, so truly dangerous, does not alarm you: sins, which have never been washed away by sincere repentance, and consequently never obliterated from the book of life, appear in your eyes as no longer existing; and you will tranquilly leave this world in a state of impenitence, so much the more dangerous, as you will die without being sensible of your danger. What I say here, is not merely a rash expression, or an emotion of zeal; nothing is more real, or more exactly true: it is the situation of almost all men, even the wisest and most esteemed of the world.

The morality of the younger stages in life is always lax, if not licentious. Age, disgust, and establishment for life, fix the heart, and withdraw it from debauchery: but where are those who are converted? Where are those who expiate their crimes by tears of sorrow and true repentance? Where are those who, having begun as sinners, end as penitents? Show me, in your manner of living, the smallest trace of penitence. Are your graspings at wealth and power, your anxieties to attain the favor of the great (and by these means an increase of employments and influence)—are these proofs of it? Would you wish to reckon even your crimes as virtues?—that the sufferings of your ambition, pride, and avarice, should discharge you from an obligation which they themselves have imposed? You are penitent to the world, but are you so to Jesus Christ? The infirmities with which God afflicts you; the enemies he raised up against you; the disgraces and losses with which he tries you; do you receive them all as you ought, with humble submission to his will, and, far from finding in them occasions of penitence, do you not turn them into the objects of new crimes? It is the duty of an innocent soul to receive with submission the chastisements of the Almighty; to discharge, with courage, the painful duties of the station allotted to him, and to be faithful to the laws of the gospel; but do sinners owe nothing beyond this? And yet they pretend to salvation; but upon what claim? To say that you are innocent before God, your own conscience will bear testimony against you. To endeavor to persuade yourselves that you are penitent, you dare not; and you would condemn yourselves through your own mouths. Upon what, then, dost thou depend, O man! who thus livest so tranquil?

And what renders it still more dreadful is, that, acting in this manner, you only follow the torrent: your morals are the morals of almost all men. You may, perhaps, be acquainted with some still more guilty (for I suppose you have still remaining some sentiments of religion, and regard for your salvation); but do you know any real penitents? I am afraid we must search the deserts and solitudes for them. You can scarcely particularize, among persons of rank and usage of the world, a small number whose morals and mode of life, more austere and more guarded than the generality, attract the attention, and very like the censure of the public: all the rest walk in the same path. I see clearly that every one comforts himself by the example of his neighbor: that, in that point, children succeed to the false security of their fathers; that none live innocent; that none die penitent; I see it, and I cry, O God! if thou have not deceived us; if all thou hast told us with regard to the road to eternal life, shall be fulfilled to the point; if the number of those who must perish shall not influence Thee to abate from the severity of thy laws, what will become of that immense multitude of creatures which every hour disappears from the face of the earth? Where are our friends, our relations, who have gone before us, and what is their lot in the eternal regions of death? What shall we ourselves be one day? When formerly a prophet complained to the Lord, that all Israel had forsaken his protection, he replied, that seven thousand still remained who had not bowed the knee to Baal: behold the number of pure and faithful souls which a whole kingdom then contained? But couldst thou still, O my God! comfort the anguish of thy servants to-day by the same assurance? I know that thine eye discerns still some upright amongst us; that the priesthood has still its Phineases; the magistracy its Samuels; the sword its Joshuas; the court its Daniels, its Esthers, and its Davids: for the world only exists for thy chosen, and all would perish were the number accomplished. But those happy remains of the children of Israel who shall inherit salvation, what are they, compared to the grains of sand in the sea; I mean, to that number of sinners who combat for their own destruction? You come after this, my brethren, to inquire if it be true, that few shall be saved? Thou hast said it, O my God! and consequently it is a truth which shall endure for ever.

But, even admitting that the Almighty had not spoken thus, I would wish, in the second place, to review, for an instant, what passes among men: – the laws by which they are governed; the maxims by which the multitude is regulated: this is the second cause of the paucity of the saved; and, properly speaking, is only a development of the first – the force of habit and customs.

Part II. – Few people are saved, because the maxims most universally received in all countries, and upon which depend, in general, the morals of the multitude, are incompatible with salvation. The rules laid down, approved, and authorized by the world, with regard to the application of wealth, the love of glory, Christian moderation, and the duties of offices and conditions, are diametrically opposite to those of the evangelists, and consequently can lead only to death. I shall not, at present, enter into a detail too extended for a discourse, and too little serious, perhaps, for Christians.

I need not tell you, that this is an established custom in the world, to allow the liberty of proportioning expenses to rank and wealth; and, provided it is a patrimony we inherit from our ancestors, we may distinguish ourselves by the use of it, without restraint to our luxury, or without regard, in our profusion, to anything but our pride and caprice.

But Christian moderation has its rules. We are not the absolute masters of our riches; nor are we entitled to abuse what the Almighty has bestowed upon us for better purposes. Above all, while thousands of unfortunate wretches languish in poverty, whatever we make use of beyond the wants and necessary expenses of our station, is an inhumanity to, and a theft from, the poor. These are refinements of devotion, say they; and, in matters of expense and profusion, nothing is excessive or blamable, according to the world, but what may tend to derange the fortune. I need not tell you that it is an approved custom, to decide our lots, and to regulate our choice of professions and situations in life, by the order of our birth, or the interests of fortune. But, O my God! does the ministry of thy gospel derive its source from the worldly considerations of a carnal birth? We cannot establish all, says the world, and it would be melancholy to see persons of rank and birth in avocations unworthy of their dignity. If born to a name distinguished in the world, you must get forward by dint of intrigue, meanness and expense. Make fortune your idol. That ambition, however much condemned by the laws of the gospel, is only a sentiment worthy your name and birth.

You are of a sex and rank which introduce you to the gayeties of the world: you cannot but do as others do; you must frequent all the public places where those of your age and rank assemble; enter into the same pleasures; pass your days in the same frivolities; and expose yourself to the same dangers: these are the received maxims, and you are not made to reform them. Such is the doctrine of the world.

Now, permit me to ask you here, who conforms you in these ways? By what rule are they justified to your mind? Who authorizes you in this dissipation, which is neither agreeable to the title you have received by baptism, nor perhaps to those you hold from your ancestors? Who authorizes those public pleasures, which you only think innocent, because your soul, already too familiarized with sin, feels no longer the dangerous impressions or tendency of them? Who authorizes you to lead an effeminate and sensual life, without virtue, sufferance, or any religious exercise? – to live like a stranger in the midst of your own family, disdaining to inform yourself with regard to the morals of those dependent upon you? – through an affected state, to be ignorant whether they believe in the same God; whether they fulfil the duties of the religion you profess? Who authorizes you in maxims so little Christian? Is it the gospel of Jesus Christ? Is it the doctrine of the apostles and saints? For surely some rule is necessary to assure us that we are in safety. What is yours? Custom: that is the only reply you can make. We see none around us but what conduct themselves in the same way, and by the same rule. Entering into the world, we find the manners already established: our fathers lived thus, and from them we copy our customs: the wisest conform to them: an individual cannot be wiser than the whole world, and must not pretend to make himself singular, by acting contrary to the general voice. Such, my brethren, are your only comforters against all the terrors of religion. None act up to the law. The public example is the only guaranty of our morals. We never reflect, that, as the Holy Spirit says, the laws of the people are vain: that our Savior has left us rules, in which neither times, ages, nor customs, can ever authorize the smallest change; that the heavens and the earth shall pass away; that customs and manners shall change; but that the divine laws will everlastingly be the same.

We content ourselves with looking around us. We do not reflect that what, at present, we call custom, would, in former times, before the morals of Christians became degenerated, have been regarded as monstrous singularities; and, if corruption has gained since that period, these vices, though they have lost their singularity, have not lost their guilt. We do not reflect, that we shall be judged by the gospel, and not by custom: by the examples of the holy, and not by men's opinions – that the habits, which are only established among believers by the relaxation of faith, are abuses we are to lament, not examples we are to follow – that, in changing the manners, they have not changed our duties – that the common and general example which authorizes them, only proves that virtue is rare, but not that profligacy is permitted – in a word, that piety and a real Christian life are too unpalatable to our depraved nature ever to be practised by the majority of men. Come now, and say that you only do as others do. It is exactly by that you condemn yourselves. What! the most terrible certainty of your condemnation shall become the only motive for your confidence! Which, according to the Scriptures, is the road that conducts to death? Is it not that which the majority pursues? Which is the party of the reprobate? Is it not the multitude? You do nothing but what others do. But thus, in the time of Noah, perished all who were buried under the waters of the deluge: all who, in the time of Nebuchadnezzar, prostrated themselves before the golden calf: all who, in the time of Elijah, bowed the knee to Baal: all who, in the time of Eleazer, abandoned the law of their fathers. You only do what others do, but that is exactly what the Scriptures forbid: Do not, say they, conform yourselves to this corrupted age. Now, the corrupted age means not the small number of the just, whom you endeavor not to imitate; it means the multitude whom you follow. You only do what others do; you will consequently experience the same lot. Now, "Misery to thee" (cried formerly St. Augustine), "fatal torrent of human customs; wilt thou never suspend thy course? To the end wilt thou drag in the children of Adam to thine immense and terrible abyss?"

In place of saying to ourselves, "What are my hopes? In the church of Jesus Christ there are two roads; one broad and open, by which almost the whole world passes, and which leads to death: the other narrow, where few indeed enter, and which conducts to life eternal; in which of these am I? Are my morals the usual ones of persons of my rank, age, and situation in life? Am I with the great number? Then I am not in the right path. I am losing myself. The great number in every station is not the party saved." Far from reasoning in this manner, we say to ourselves, "I am not in a worse state than others. Those of my age and rank live as I do: why should I not live like them?" Why, my dear hearers? For that very reason: the general mode of living cannot be that of a Christian life. In all ages, the holy have been remarkable and singular men. Their manners were always different from those of the world; and they have only been saints, because their lives had no similarity to those of the rest of mankind.

In the time of Esdras, in spite of the defence against it, the custom prevailed of intermarrying with stranger women: this abuse became general: the priests and the people no longer made any scruple of it. But what did this holy restorer of the law: did he follow the example of his brethren? Did he believe that guilt, in becoming general, became more legitimate? No: he recalled the people to a sense of the abuse. He took the book of the law in his hand, and explained it to the affrighted people – corrected the custom by the truth. Follow, from age to age, the history of the just; and see if Lot conformed himself to the habits of Sodom, or if nothing distinguished him from the other inhabitants; if Abraham lived like the rest of his age; if Job resembled the other princes of his nation; if Esther conducted herself, in the court of Ahasuerus, like the other women of that prince; if many widows in Israel resembled Judith; if, among the children of the captivity, it is not said of Tobias alone that he copied not the conduct of his brethren, and that he even fled from the danger of their commerce and society. See, if in those happy ages, when Christians were all saints, they did not shine like stars in the midst of the corrupted nations; and if they served not as a spectacle to angels and men, by the singularity of their lives and manners: if the pagans did not reproach them for their retirement, and shunning of all public theatres, places, and pleasures: if they did not complain that the Christians affected to distinguish themselves in every thing from their fellow citizens; to form a separate people in the midst of the people; to have their particular laws and customs; and if a man from their side embraced the party of the Christians, they did not consider him as for ever lost to their pleasures, assemblies and customs; in a word, see, if in all ages the saints whose lives and actions have been transmitted down to us, have resembled the rest of mankind.

You will perhaps tell us, that all these are singularities and exceptions, rather than rules which the world is obliged to follow. They are exceptions, it is true: but the reason is, that the general rule is to throw away salvation; that a religious and pious soul in the midst of the world, is always a singularity approaching to a miracle. The whole world, you say, is not obliged to follow these examples; but is not piety the general duty of all? To be saved, must we not be holy? Must heaven with difficulty and sufferance be gained by some, while with ease by others? Have you any other gospel to follow; other duties to fulfil; other promises to hope for, than those of the Holy Bible? Ah! since there was another way more easy to arrive at salvation, wherefore, ye pious Christians, who at this moment enjoy in heaven, that kingdom, gained with toil, and at the expense of your blood, did ye leave us examples so dangerous and useless?

Wherefore have ye opened for us a road, rugged, disagreeable and calculated to repress our ardor, seeing there was another you could have pointed out, more easy, and more likely to attract us, by facilitating our progress? Great God! how little does mankind consult reason in the point of eternal salvation!

Will you console yourselves, after this, with the multitude, as if the greatness of the number could render the guilt unpunished, and the Almighty durst not condemn all those who live like you? But what are all creatures in the sight of God? Did the multitude of the guilty prevent him from destroying all flesh at the deluge? from making fire from heaven descend upon the five iniquitous cities? from burying, in the waters of the Red Sea, Pharaoh and all his army? from striking with death all who murmured in the desert? Ah! the kings of the earth may have regard to the number of the guilty, because the punishment becomes impossible, or at least dangerous, when the fault is become general. But God, who wipes the impious, says Job, from off the face of the earth, as one wipes the dust from off a garment; God, in whose sight all people and nations are as if they were not, numbers not the guilty: he has regard only to the crimes; and all that the weak and miserable sinner can expect from his unhappy accomplices, is to have them as companions in his misery. So few are saved, because the maxims most universally adopted are maxims of sin: so few are saved, because the maxims and duties most universally unknown, or rejected, are those most indispensable to salvation. Last reflection, which is indeed nothing more than the proof and the explanation of the former ones.

What are the engagements of the holy vocation to which we have all been called? The solemn promises of baptism. What have we promised at baptism? To renounce the world, the devil, and the flesh: these are our vows: this is the situation of the Christian: these are the essential conditions of our covenant with God, by which eternal life has been promised to us. These truths appear familiar, and destined for the common people; but it is a mistake. Nothing can be more sublime; and, alas! nothing is more generally unknown. It is at the courts of kings, and to the princes of the earth, that without ceasing we ought to announce them. Alas! they are well instructed in all the affairs of the world, while the first principles of Christian morality are frequently more unknown to them than to humble and simple hearts. At your baptism, you have then renounced the world. It is a promise you have made to God, before the holy altar; the church has been the guarantee and depository of it; and you have only been admitted into the number of believers, and marked with the indefeasible seal of salvation, upon the faith that you have sworn to the Lord, to love neither the world, nor what the world loves. Had you then answered, what you now repeat every day, that you find not the world so black and pernicious as we say; that, after all, it may innocently be loved; and that we only decry it so much, because we do not know it; and since you are to live in the world, you wish to live like those who are in it: had you answered thus, the church would not have received you into its bosom; would not have connected you with the hope of Christians, nor joined you in communion with those who have overcome the world. She would have advised you to go and live with those infidels who know not our Savior. For this reason it was, that in former ages, those of the Catechumen, who could not prevail upon themselves to renounce the world and its pleasures, put off their baptism till death; and durst not approach the holy altar, to contract, by the sacrament, which regenerates us, engagements of which they knew the importance and sanctity; and to fulfil which they felt themselves still unqualified. You are therefore required, by the most sacred of all vows, to hate the world; that is to say, not to conform yourselves to it. If you love it, if you follow its pleasures and customs, you are not only, as St. John says, the enemy of God, but you likewise renounce the faith given in baptism; you abjure the gospel of Jesus Christ; you are an apostate from religion, and trample under foot the most sacred and irrevocable vows that man can make. Now, what is this world which you ought to hate? I have only to answer that it is the one you love. You will never mistake it by this mark. This world is a society of sinners, whose desires, fears, hopes, cares, projects, joys and chagrins, no longer turn but upon the successes or misfortunes of this life. This world is an assemblage of people who look upon the earth as their country; the time to come as an exilement; the promises of faith as a dream; and death as the greatest of all misfortunes. This world is a temporal kingdom, where our Savior is unknown; where those acquainted with his name, glorify him not as their Lord, hate his maxims, despise his followers, and neglect or insult him in his sacraments and worship. In a word, to give a proper idea at once of this world, it is the great number: behold the world which you ought to shun, hate, and combat against by your example!

Now, is this your situation in regard to the world? Are its pleasures a fatigue to you; do its excesses afflict you; do you regret the length of your pilgrimage here? Are not its laws your laws; its maxims your maxims? What it condemns, do you not condemn? Do you not approve what it approves? And should it happen, that you alone were left upon the earth, may we not say, that the corrupt world would be revived in you; and that you would leave an exact model of it to your posterity? When I say you, I mean, and I address myself to almost all men.

Where are those who sincerely renounce the pleasures, habits, maxims and hopes of this world? We find many who complain of it, and accuse it of injustice, ingratitude and caprice, who speak warmly of its abuses and errors; but in decrying, they continue to love, to follow it; they cannot bring themselves to do without it; in complaining of its injustice, they are only piqued at it, they are not undeceived; they feel its hard treatment, but they are unacquainted with its dangers; they censure, but where are those who hate it? And now, my brethren, you may judge if many can have a claim to salvation.

In the second place, you have renounced the flesh at your baptism; that is to say, you are engaged not to live according to the sensual appetites; to regard even indolence and effeminacy as crimes; not to flatter the corrupt desires of the flesh: but to chastise, crush and crucify it. This is not an acquired perfection; it is a vow: it is the first of all duties, the character of a true Christian, and inseparable from faith. In a word you have anathematized Satan and all his works. And what are his works? That which composes almost the thread and end of your life; pomp, pleasure, luxury and dissipation; lying, of which he is the father; pride, of which he is the model; jealousy and contention, of which he is the artisan. But I ask you, where are those who have not withdrawn the anathema they had pronounced against Satan? Now, consequently (to mention it as we go along), behold many of the questions answered.

You continually demand of us, if theatres, and other public places of amusement, be innocent recreations for Christians? In return, I have only one question to ask you: Are they the works of Satan or of Jesus Christ? for there can be no medium in religion. I mean not to say, but that many recreations and amusements may be termed indifferent. But the most indifferent pleasures which religion allows, and which the weakness of our nature renders even necessary, belong, in one sense, to Jesus Christ, by the facility with which they ought to enable us to apply ourselves to more holy and more serious duties. Every thing we do, every thing we rejoice or weep at, ought to be of such a nature as to have a connection with Jesus Christ, and to be done for his glory. Now, upon this principle, the most incontestable, and most universally allowed in Christian morality, you have only to decide whether you can connect the glory of Jesus Christ with the pleasures of a theatre. Can our Savior have any part in such a species of recreation? And before you enter them, can you, with confidence, declare to him, that, in so doing, you only propose his glory, and to enjoy the satisfaction of pleasing him! What! the theatres, such as they are at present, still more criminal by the public licentiousness of those unfortunate creatures who appear on them, than by the impure and passionate scenes they represent,—the theatres are works of Jesus Christ? Jesus Christ would animate a mouth, from whence are to proceed sounds lascivious, and calculated to corrupt the heart? But these blasphemies strike me with horror. Jesus Christ would preside in assemblies of sin, where every thing we hear weakens his doctrines; where the poison enters into the soul by all the senses; where every art is employed to inspire, awaken and justify the passions he condemns? Now, says Tertullian, if they are not the works of Jesus Christ, they must be the works of Satan. Every Christian, therefore, ought to abstain from them. When he partakes of them, he violates the vows of baptism. However innocent he may flatter himself to be, in bringing from these places an untainted heart, it is sullied by being there; since by his presence alone he has participated in the works of Satan, which he had renounced at baptism, and violated the most sacred promises he had made to Jesus Christ and to his church.

These, my brethren, as I have already told you, are not merely advices and pious arts; they are the most essential of our obligations. But, alas! who fulfils them? Who even knows them? Ah! my brethren, did you know how far the title you bear, of Christian, engages you; could you comprehend the sanctity of your state; the hatred of the world, of yourself, and of every thing which is not of God, that it ordains you; that life according to the gospel, that continual watching, that guard over the passions; in a word, that conformity with Jesus Christ crucified, which it exacts of you; could you comprehend it, could you remember, that as you ought to love God with all your heart, and all your strength, a single desire that has not connection with him defiles you, you would appear a monster in your own sight. How! would you say to yourself, duties so holy, and morals so profane! A vigilance so continual, and a life so careless and dissipated! A love of God so pure, so complete, so universal, and a heart the continual prey of a thousand impulses, either foreign or criminal! If thus it is, who, O my God! will be entitled to salvation?

Few indeed, I am afraid, my dear hearers; at least it will not be you (unless a change takes place), nor those who resemble you; it will not be the multitude. Who shall be saved? Those who work out their salvation with fear and trembling; who live in the world without indulging in its vices. Who shall be saved? That Christian woman, who, shut up in the circle of her domestic duties, rears up her children in faith and in piety; divides her heart only between her Savior and her husband; is adorned with delicacy and modesty; sits not down in the assemblies of vanity; makes not a law of the ridiculous customs of the world, but regulates those customs by the law of God; and makes virtue appear more amiable by her rank and example. Who shall be saved? That believer, who, in the relaxation of modern times, imitates the manners of the first Christians; whose hands are clean, and his heart pure; watchful, "who hath not lifted up his soul to vanity"; but who, in the midst of the dangers of the great world, continually applies himself to purify it; just, who swears not deceitfully against his neighbor, nor is indebted to fraudulent ways for the innocent aggrandisement of his fortune; generous, who with benefits repays the enemy who sought his ruin; sincere, who sacrifices not the truth to a vile interest, and knows not the part of rendering himself agreeable, by betraying his conscience; charitable, who makes his house and interest the refuge of his fellow creatures, and himself the consolation of the afflicted; regards his wealth as the property of the poor; humble in affliction, Christian under injuries, and penitent even in prosperity. Who will merit salvation? You, my dear hearer, if you will follow these examples; for such are the souls to be saved. Now these assuredly do not form the greatest number. While you continue, therefore, to live like the multitude, it is a striking proof that you disregard your salvation.

These, my brethren, are truths which should make us tremble; nor are they those vague ones which are told to all men, and which none apply to themselves. Perhaps there is not in this assembly an individual, who may not say of himself, "I live like the great number; like those of my rank, age, and situation; I am lost, should I die in this path." Now, can any thing be more capable of alarming a soul, in whom some remains of care for his salvation still exist? It is the multitude nevertheless, who tremble not. There is only a small number of just, which operates apart its salvation, with fear and trembling; all the rest are tranquil. After having lived with the multitude, they flatter themselves they shall be particularized at death; every one augurs favorably for himself, and chimerically thinks he shall be an exception.

On this account it is, my brethren, that I confine myself to you who, at present, are assembled here: I include not the rest of men: but consider you alone existing on the earth. The idea which occupies and frightens me, is this—I figure to myself the present, as your last hour, and the end of the world; that the heavens are going to open above your heads; our Savior in all his glory to appear, in the midst of this temple; and that you are only assembled here to wait his coming, like trembling criminals, on whom the sentence is to be pronounced, either of life eternal, or of everlasting death; for it is vain to flatter yourselves that you shall die more innocent than you are at this hour. All those desires change with which you are amused, will continue to amuse you till death arrives; the experience of all ages proves it; the only difference you have to expect, will most likely be only a larger balance against you than what you would have to answer for at present; and from what would be your destiny, were you to be judged this moment, you may almost decide upon what will take place at your departure from life. Now, I ask you (and, connecting my own lot with yours, I ask it with dread), were Jesus Christ to appear in this temple, in the midst of this assembly, to judge us, to make the dreadful separation between the goats and sheep, do you believe that the greatest number of us would be placed at his right hand? Do you believe that the number would at least be equal? Do you believe there would even be found ten upright and faithful servants of the Lord, when formerly five cities could not furnish so many? I ask you. You know not; and I know it not. Thou alone, O my God! knowest who belong to thee.

But if we know not who belong to him, at least we know that sinners do not. Now, who are the just and faithful assembled here at present? Titles and dignities avail nothing; you are stripped of all these in the presence of your Savior. Who are they? Many sinners who wish not to be converted; many more who wish, but always put it off: many others, who are only converted in appearance, and again fall back to their former courses; in a word, a great number, who flatter themselves they have no occasion for conversion. This is the party of the reprobate. Ah! my brethren, cut off from this assembly these four classes of sinners, for they will be cut off at the great day. And now appear, ye just: where are ye? O God! where are thy chosen? And what a portion remains to thy share!

My brethren, our ruin is almost certain; yet we think not of it. When, even in this terrible separation which will one day take place, there should be only one sinner in this assembly on the side of the reprobate, and that a voice from heaven should assure us of it, without particularizing him, who of us would not tremble, lest he should be the unfortunate and devoted wretch? Who of us would not immediately apply to his conscience, to examine if its crimes merited not this punishment? Who of us seized with dread, would not demand of our Savior, as the apostles formerly did, and say, "Lord, is it I?" And should a small respite be allowed to our prayers, who of us would not use every effort, by tears, supplications, and sincere repentance, to avert the misfortune? Are we in our senses, my dear hearers? Perhaps, among all who listen to me, ten just would not be found, perhaps fewer. What do I know, O my God? I dare not with a fixed eye regard the depths of thy judgments and justice. More than one, perhaps, would not be found amongst us all. And this danger affects you not, my dear hearer? You persuade yourself, that in this great number who shall perish, you will be the happy individual; you, who have less reason, perhaps, than any other to believe it; you, upon whom alone the sentence of death should fall, were only one of all who hear me to suffer. Great God! how little are the terrors of thy law known to the world! In all ages, the just have shuddered with dread, in reflecting on the severity and extent of thy judgments upon the destinies of men. Alas! what do they prepare for the children of Adam?

But what are we to conclude from these grand truths? That all must despair of salvation? God forbid! The impious alone, to quiet his own feelings in his debaucheries, endeavors to persuade himself that all men shall perish as well as he.

This idea ought not to be the fruit of the present discourse, it is meant to undeceive you with regard to the general error, that any one may do whatever others do; to convince you, that, in order to merit salvation, you must distinguish yourself from the rest; in the midst of the world, lead a life to the glory of God, and resemble not the multitude.

When the Jews were led in captivity from Judea to Babylon, a little before they quitted their own country, the prophet Jeremiah, whom the Lord had forbid to leave Jerusalem, spoke thus to them: "Children of Israel, when you shall arrive at Babylon, you will behold the inhabitants of that country, who carry upon their shoulders gods of silver and gold. All the people will prostrate themselves, and adore them. But you, far from allowing yourselves, by these examples, to be led to impiety, say to yourselves in secret, It is thou, O Lord! whom we ought to adore."

Let me now finish, by addressing to you the same words.

At your departure from this temple, you go to enter into another Babylon; you go to see idols of gold and silver, before which all men prostrate themselves; you go to regain the vain objects of human passions, wealth, glory, and pleasure, which are the gods of this world, and which almost all men adore; you will see those abuses which all the world permits, those errors which custom authorizes, and those debaucheries which an infamous fashion has almost constituted as laws. Then, my dear hearer, if you wish to be of the small number of true Israelites, say, in the secrecy of your heart, It is thou alone, O my God! whom we ought to adore. I wish not to have connection with a people which know thee not; I will have no other law than thy holy law; the gods which this foolish multitude adores, are not gods: they are the work of the hands of men; they will perish with them: thou alone, O my God! art immortal; and thou alone deservest to be adored. The customs of Babylon have no connection with the holy laws of Jerusalem. I will continue to worship thee with that small number of the children of Abraham, which still, in the midst of an infidel nation, composes thy people; with them I will turn all my desires toward the holy Zion. The singularity of my manners will be regarded as a weakness; but blessed weakness, O my God! which will give me strength to resist the torrent of customs, and the seduction of example. Thou wilt be my God in the midst of Babylon, as thou wilt one day be in Jerusalem.

Ah! the time of the captivity will at last expire; thou wilt call to thy remembrance Abraham and David; thou wilt deliver thy people; thou wilt transport us to the holy city; then wilt thou alone reign over Israel, and over the nations which at present know thee not. All being destroyed; all the empires of the earth; all the monuments of human pride annihilated, and thou alone remaining eternal, we then shall know that thou art the Lord of hosts, and the only God to be adored.

Behold the fruit which you ought to reap from this discourse; live apart; think, without ceasing, that the great number work their own destruction; regard as nothing all customs of the earth, unless authorized by the law of God; and remember, that holy men have, in all ages, been looked upon as singular.

It is thus, that, after distinguishing yourselves from the sinful on earth, you will be gloriously separated from them in eternity.

ON CHARITY

"And Jesus took the loaves, and, when he had given thanks, he distributed to the disciples, and the disciples to them that were set down" (John 6:11).

IT IS NOT WITHOUT DESIGN that our Savior associates the disciples, in the prodigy of multiplying the loaves, and that he makes use of their ministry in distributing the miraculous food among a people pressed with hunger and want. He might again, no doubt, have made manna to rain upon the desert, and saved his disciples the trouble of so tedious a distribution.

But might he not, after raising up Larzarus from the dead, have dispensed with their assistance in unloosing him? Could his almighty voice, which had just broken asunder the chains of death, have found any resistance from the feeble bands which the hand of man had formed? It is because he wished to point out to them, beforehand, the

Reprinted from an old book without title page.

sacred exercise of their ministry; the part they were afterward to have in the spiritual resurrection of sinners; and that whatever they should unloose upon the earth should be unloosed in heaven.

Again, when there was question of paying tribute to Caesar, he needed not to have recourse to the expedient of Peter's casting his hook into the sea for the purpose of producing a piece of money out of the bowels of a fish: he who, even from stones, was able to raise up children to Abraham, might surely with greater ease have converted them into a precious metal, and thereby furnished the amount of the tribute due to Caesar. But, in the character of the Head of the Church, he meant to teach his ministers to respect those in authority; and, by rendering honor and tribute to the powers established by God, to set an example of submission to other believers.

Thus, in making use, upon this occasion, of the intervention of the apostles to distribute the loaves to the multitude, his design is, to accustom all his disciples to compassion and liberality toward the unfortunate: he establishes you the ministers of his providence, and multiplies the riches of the earth in your hands, for the sole purpose of being distributed from thence among that multitude of unfortunate fellow-creatures which surrounds you.

He, no doubt, might nourish them himself, as he formerly nourished Paul and Elijah in the desert; without your interference he might comfort those creatures which bear his image; he, whose invisible hand prepares food even for the young ravens which invoke him in their want; but he wishes to associate you in the merit of his liberality; he wishes you to be placed between himself and the poor, like refreshing clouds, always ready to shower upon them those fructifying streams which you have only received for their advantage.

Such is the order of his providence; it was necessary that means of salvation should be provided for all men: riches would corrupt the heart, if charity were not to expiate their abuse; indigence would fatigue and weary out virtue, if the succors of compassion were not to soften its bitterness; the poor facilitate to the rich the pardon of their pleasures; the rich animate the poor not to lose the merit of their sufferings.

Apply yourself, then, be whom you may, to all the consequence of this gospel. If you groan under the yoke of poverty, the tenderness and the care of Jesus Christ toward all the wants of a wandering and unprovided people will console you; if born to opulence, the example of the disciples will now instruct you. You will there see, first, the pretexts which they oppose to the duty of charity confuted: secondly, you will learn what ought to be its rules. That is to say, that in the first part of this Discourse we shall establish this duty against all the vain excuses of avarice; in the second, we shall instruct you in the manner of fulfilling it against even the defects of charity; it is the most natural instruction with which the history of the gospel presents us.

Part I. — It is scarcely a matter of controversy now in the world, whether the law of God makes a precept to us of charity. The gospel is so pointed on this duty; the spirit and the groundwork of religion lead us so naturally to it; the idea alone which we have of Providence, in the dispensation of temporal things, leaves so little room on that point to opinion or doubt, that, though many are ignorant of the extent of this obligation, yet there are almost none who do not admit of the foundation and principle.

Who, indeed, is ignorant that the Lord, whose providence hath regulated all things with an order so admirable and beautiful, and prepared food even for the beasts of the field, would never have left men, created after his own image, a prey to hunger and indigence, whilst he would liberally shower upon a small number of happy individuals the blessings of heaven and the fat of the earth, if he had not intended that the abundance of the one should supply the necessities of the other.

Who is ignorant, that originally every thing belonged in common to all men: that simple nature knew neither property nor portions; and that at first, she left each of us in possession of the universe: but that, in order to put bounds to avarice, and to avoid trouble and dissensions, the common consent of the people established that the wisest, the most humane, and the most upright, should likewise be the most opulent; that, besides the portion of wealth destined to them by nature, they should also be charged with that of the weakest, to be its depositaries, and to defend it against usurpation and violence: consequently, that they were established by nature itself as the guardians of the unfortunate, and that whatever surplus they had was only the patrimony of their brethren confided to their care and to their equity?

Who, lastly, is ignorant that the ties of religion have still more firmly cemented the first bonds of union which nature had formed among men; that the grace of Jesus Christ, which brought forth the first believers, made of them not only one heart and one soul, but also one family, where the idea of individual property was exploded; and that the gospel, making it a law to us to love our brethren as ourselves, no longer permits us to be ignorant of their wants, or to be insensible to their sorrows?

But it is with the duty of charity as with all the other duties of the law: in general the obligation is not, even in idea, denied; but does the circumstance of its fulfilment take place? A pretext is never wanting, either to dispense with it entirely, or at least to be quit for a moiety of the duty. Now, it would appear that the Spirit of God hath meant to point out to us all these pretexts, in the answers which the disciples made to Jesus Christ in order to excuse themselves from assisting the famished multitude which had followed him to the desert.

In the first place, they remind him that they had scarcely wherewithal to supply their own wants; and that only five loaves of barley and two fishes remained: behold the first pretext, made use of by covetousness, in opposition to the duty of compassion. Scarcely have they sufficient for themselves; they have a name and a rank to support in the world; children to establish; creditors to satisfy; public charges to support; a thousand expenses of pure benevolence, to which attention must be paid; now, what is any income, not entirely unlimited, to such endless demands? In this manner the world continually speaks; and a world the most brilliant, and the most sumptuous.

Now, I well know, that the limits of what is called a sufficiency are not the same for all stations; that they extend in proportion to rank and birth; that one star, says the apostle, must differ in lustre from another; that, even from the apostolic ages, men were seen in the assemblies of believers, clothed in robes of distinction, with rings of gold, while others, of a more obscure station, were forced to content themselves with the apparel necessary to cover their nakedness; that, consequently, religion does not confound stations; and that, if it forbid those who dwell in the palaces of kings to be effeminate in their manners, and indecently luxurious in their dress, it doth not at the same time prescribe to them the poverty and the simplicity of those who dwell in cottages, or of those who form the lower ranks of the people: I know it.

But, my brethren, it is an incontestable truth, that, whatever surplus you may have, belongs not to you; that it is the portion of the poor; and that you are entitled to consider as your own, only that proportion of your revenues which is necessary to support that station in which Providence hath placed you. I ask, then, is it the gospel or covetousness, which must regulate that sufficiency? Would you dare to pretend, that all those vanities of which custom has now made a law, are to be held, in the sight of God, as expenses inseparable from your condition? That every thing which flatters, and is agreeable to you, which nourishes your pride, gratifies your caprices, and corrupts your heart, is for that reason necessary to you? That all which you sacrifice to the fortune of a child, in order to raise him above his ancestors; all which you risk in gaming; that luxury, which either suits not your birth, or is an abuse of it: would you dare to pretend, that all these have incontestable claims on your revenues, which are to be preferred to those of charity? Lastly, would you dare to pretend, that, because your father, perhaps obscure, and of the lowest rank, may have left to you all his wealth, and perhaps his crimes, you are entitled to forget your family and the house of your father, in order to mingle with the highest ranks, and to support the same eclat, because you are enabled to support the same expense?

If this be the case, my brethren, if you consider as a surplus only that which may escape from your pleasures, from your extravagancies, and from your caprices, you have only to be voluptuous, capricious, dissolute and prodigal, in order to be wholly dispensed from the duty of charity. The more passions you shall have to satisfy, the more will your obligation to charity diminish! and your excesses, which the Lord hath commanded you to expiate by acts of compassion, will themselves become a privilege to dispense yourselves from them. There must necessarily, therefore, be some rule here to observe, and some limits to appoint ourselves, different from those of avarice; and behold it, my brethren—the rule of faith. Whatever tends to nourish only the life of the senses, to flatter the passions, to countenance the vain pomp and abuses of the world, is superfluous to a Christian: these are what you ought to retrench, and to set apart; these are the funds and the heritage of the poor; you are only their depositaries, and you cannot encroach upon them without usurpation and injustice. The gospel reduces to very little the sufficiency of a Christian, however exalted in the world; religion retrenches much from the expenses; and, did we live all according to the rules of faith, our wants, which would no longer be multiplied by our passions, would still be fewer; the greatest part of our wealth would be found entirely useless; and, as in the first age of faith, indigence would no longer grieve the church, nor be seen among believers. Our expenses continually increase, because our passions are every day multiplied; the opulence of our fathers is no longer to us but an uncomfortable poverty; and our great riches can no longer suffice, because nothing can satisfy those who refuse themselves nothing.

And, in order to give this truth all the extent which the subject in question demands, I ask you, secondly, do the elevation and abundance in which you are born dispense you from simplicity, frugality, modesty and holy restraint? By being born great, you are not the less Christians. In vain, like those Israelites in the desert, have you amassed more manna than your brethren; you cannot preserve for your use more than the measure prescribed by the law. Were it not so, our Savior would have forbidden pomp, luxury, and worldly pleasures but to the poor and unfortunate, those to whom the misery of their condition renders needless that defence.

Now, this grand truth admitted, if, according to the rule of faith, it be not permitted to you to employ your riches in the gratification of your appetites; if the rich be obliged to bear the cross, continually to renounce themselves, and to look for no consolation in this world, equally as the poor; what can the design of Providence have been in pouring upon you all the riches of the earth, and what advantage could even accrue to you from them? Could it be in order to administer to your irregular desires? But you are no longer bound to the flesh, to live according to the flesh. Could it be in order to support the pride of rank and birth? But whatever you give to vanity, you cut off from charity. Could it be for the purpose of hoarding up for your posterity? But your treasure should be only in heaven. Could it be in order that you might pass your life more agreeably? But if you weep not, if you suffer not, if you combat not, you are lost. Could it be in order to attach you more strongly to the world? But the Christian is not of this world; he is citizen of the age to come. Could it be for the purpose of aggrandizing your possessions and your inheritances? But you would never aggrandize but the place of your exile; and the gain of the whole world would be vain, if you thereby lost your soul. Could it be that your table might be loaded with the most exquisite dishes? But you well know, that the gospel forbids a life of sensuality and voluptuousness, equally to the rich as to the indigent. Review all the advantages, which, according to the world, you can reap from your prosperity, and you will find almost the whole of them forbidden by the law of God.

It has not, therefore, been his design, that they should be merely for your own purposes, when he multiplied in your hands the riches of the earth. It is not for yourself that you are born to grandeur; it is not for yourself, as Mordecai formerly said to the pious Esther, that the Lord hath exalted you to this point of prosperity and grandeur; it is for the sake of his afflicted people; it is to be the protector of the unfortunate. If you fulfil not the intentions of God, with regard to you, continued that wise Israelite, he will employ some other, who shall more faithfully serve him; he will transfer to them that crown which was intended for you; he will elsewhere provide the enlargement and deliverance of his afflicted people; for he will not permit them to perish; but you, and your father's house shall perish. In the designs of the Almighty, you therefore are but the ministers of his providence toward those who suffer; your great riches are only sacred deposits, which his goodness hath entrusted to your care, for security against usurpation and violence, and in order to be more safely preserved for the widow and the orphan; your abundance, in the order of his wisdom, is destined only to supply their necessities; your authority, only to protect them; your dignities only to avenge their interests; your rank only to console them by your good offices: whatsoever you be, you are it only for them; your elevation would no longer be the work of God, and he would have cursed you, in bestowing on you all the riches of the earth, had he given them to you for any other use.

Ah! allege, then, no more to us, as an excuse for your hardheartedness toward your brethren, wants which are condemned by the law of God; rather justify his providence toward all who suffer; by entering into his order, let them know, that there is a God for them as well as for you; and make them bless the adorable designs of his wisdom, in the dispensation of earthly things, which hath supplied them, through your abundance, with such resources of consolation.

But, besides, what can the small contributions required from you retrench from those wants, the urgency of which you tell us so much? The Lord exacteth not from you any part of your possessions and heritages, though they belong wholly to him, and he hath a right to despoil you of them. He leaveth you tranquil possessors of those lands, of those palaces, which distinguish you and your people, and with which the piety of your ancestors formerly enriched our temples. He doth not command you, like the young man in the gospel, to renounce all, to distribute your whole wealth among the poor, and to follow him: he maketh it not a law to you, as formerly to the first believers, to bring all your riches to the feet of your pastors: he doth not strike you with anathema, as formerly Annanias and Sapphira, for daring to retain only a portion of that wealth which they received from their ancestors — you, who only owe the aggrandizement of your fortunes perhaps to public calamities, or other shameful means of acquirement, he consenteth that, as the prophet saith, you shall call the land by your name, and that you transmit to your posterity those possessions which you have inherited from your ancestors — he wisheth that you lay apart only a portion for the unfortunate, whom he leaveth in indigence: he wisheth that, while in the luxury and splendor of your apparel you bear the nourishment of a whole people of unfortunate fellow-creatures, you spare wherewith to cover the nakedness of his servants who languish in poverty, and know not where to repose their head; he wisheth that, from those tables of voluptuousness, where your great riches are scarcely sufficient to supply your sensuality and the profusions of an extravagant delicacy, you drop at least a portion for the relief of the Lazaruses pressed with hunger and want: he wisheth that, while paintings of the most absurd and the most boundless price are seen to cover the walls of your palaces, your revenues may suffice to honor the living images of your God: he wisheth, in a word, that while nothing is spared toward the gratification of an inordinate passion for gaming, and every thing is on the verge of being for ever swallowed up in that gulf, you come not to calculate your expenses, to measure your ability, to allege to us the mediocrity of your fortune and the embarrassment of your affairs, when there is a question of consoling an afflicted Christian. He wisheth it; and with reason doth he wish it. What! shall you be rich for evil, and poor for good! — your revenues be amply sufficient to effect your destruction, and not suffice to save your soul, and to purchase heaven! — and, because you carry self-love to the extreme, that every barbarity of heart should be permitted you toward your unfortunate brethren?

But whence comes it that, in this single circumstance, you wish to lower the opinion that the world has of your riches? On every other occasion you wish to be thought powerful; you give yourselves out as such; you even frequently conceal, under appearances of the greatest splendor, affairs already ruined, merely to support the vain reputation of wealth. This vanity, then, does not abandon you but when you are put in remembrance of the duty of compassion. Not satisfied then with confessing the mediocrity of your fortune, you exaggerate it, and sordidness triumphs in your heart, not only over truth, but even over vanity. Ah! the Lord formerly reproached the angel of the church of Laodicea, "Because thou sayest, I am rich and increased with goods, and have need of nothing, and knowest not that in my sight thou art wretched, and miserable, and poor, and blind, and naked." But at present he ought, with regard to you, to change that reproach and to say, "O! you complain that you are poor and destitute of every thing, and you will not see that you are rich and loaded with wealth; and that in times when almost all around you suffer, you alone want for nothing in my sight."

This is the second pretext made use of in opposition to the duty of charity — the general poverty. Thus the disciples reply, in the second place, to our Savior, as an excuse for not assisting the famishing multitude — that the place is desert and barren, that it is now late, and that he ought to send away the people that they might go to the country round about, and into the villages, and buy themselves bread, for they had nothing to eat. A fresh pretext they make use of to dispense themselves from compassion — the misery of the times, the sterility and irregularity of the seasons.

But first, might not our Savior have answered to the disciples, as a holy father says, It is because the place is barren and desert, and that this people knows not where to find food to allay their hunger, that they should not be sent away fasting, lest their strength fail them by the way. And, behold, my brethren, what I might also reply to you — the times are bad, the seasons are unfavorable. Ah! for that very reason you ought to enter with a more feeling concern, with a more lively and tender anxiety, into the wants of your fellow creatures. If the place be desert and barren even for you, what must it be for so many unfortunate people! If you, with all your resources, feel so much the misery of the times, what must they not suffer, those who are destitute of every comfort! If the plagues of Egypt obtrude even into the palaces of the great, and of Pharaoh, what must be the desolation in the hut of the poor and of the laborer! If the princes of Israel, afflicted in Samaria, no longer find consolation in their palaces, to what dreadful extremities must the common people not be reduced! Reduced, alas! perhaps like that unfortunate mother, not to nourish herself with the blood of her child, but to make her innocence and her soul the melancholy price of her necessity.

But besides, these evils, with which we are afflicted and of which you so loudly complain, are the punishment of your hardness toward the poor: God avengeth upon your possessions the iniquitous use to which you apply them: it is the cries and the groanings of the unfortunate, whom you abandon, which draw down the vengeance of Heaven upon your lands and territories. It is in these times, then, of public calamity, that you ought to hasten to appease the anger of God by the abundance of your charities: it is then that, more than ever, you should interest the poor in your behalf. Alas! you bethink yourselves of addressing your general supplications to the Almighty, through these to obtain more favorable seasons, the cessation of public calamities, and the return of peace and abundance; but it is not there alone that your vows and your prayers ought to be carried. You can never expect that the Almighty will attend your distresses while you remain callous to those of your fellow creatures. You have here on the earth the masters of the winds and of the seasons: address yourselves to the poor and the afflicted; it is they who have, as I may say, the keys of heaven; it is their prayers which regulate the times and the seasons — which bring back to us days of peace or of misery — which arrest or attract the blessings of heaven: for abundance is given to the earth only for their consolation, and it is only on their account that the Almighty punisheth or is bountiful to you.

But, completely to confute you, my brethren, you who so strongly allege to us the evil of the times, does the pretended rigor of these times retrench any thing from your pleasures? What do your passions suffer from the public calamities? If the misfortune of the times oblige you to retrench from your expenses, begin with those of which religion condemns the use; regulate your tables, your apparel, your amusements, your followers, and your edifices, according to the gospel; let your retrenchings in charity at least only follow the others. Lessen your crimes before you begin to diminish from your duties. When the Almighty strikes with sterility the kingdoms of the earth, it is his intention to deprive the great and the powerful of all occasions of debauchery and excess: enter, then, into the order of his justice and his wisdom: consider yourselves as public criminals, whom the Lord chastiseth by public punishments. Say to him, like David, when he beheld the hand of the Lord weighing down his people, "Lo, I have sinned, and have done wickedly; but these sheep, what have they done? Let thine hand, I pray thee, be against me and against my father's house."

Behold your model. By terminating your disorders, terminate the cause of the public evils; in the persons of the poor, offer up to God the retrenchment of your pleasures and of your profusions, as the only righteous and acceptable sacrifice which is capable of disarming his anger; and seeing these scourges fall upon the earth only in punishment of the abuses which you have made of your abundance, bear you likewise, in lessening these abuses, their anguish and bitterness. But that the public misfortunes should be perceivable neither in the splendor and pride of your equipages, nor in the sensuality of your repasts, nor in the magnificence of your palaces, nor in your rage for gaming and every criminal pleasure, but solely in your inhumanity toward the poor; that every thing abroad, the theatres, the profane assemblies of every description, the public festivals, should continue with the same vigor and animation, while charity alone shall be chilled; that luxury should every day increase, while compassion alone shall diminish; that the world and Satan should lose nothing through the

misery of the times, while Jesus Christ alone shall suffer in his afflicted members; that the rich, sheltered in their opulence, should see
only from afar the anger of Heaven, while the poor and the innocent
shall become its melancholy victims: great God! thou wouldst then
overwhelm only the unfortunate in sending these scourges upon the
earth! Thy sole intention then should be to complete the destruction
of those miserable wretches, upon whom thy hand was already so
heavy in bringing them forth to penury and want! The powerful of
Egypt should alone be exempted by the exterminating angel, while
thy whole wrath would fall upon the afflicted Israelite, upon his poor
and unprovided roof, and even marked with the blood of the Lamb!
Yes, my brethren, the public calamities are destined to punish only
the rich and powerful, and the rich and the powerful are those who
alone suffer not: on the contrary, the public evils, in multiplying the
unfortunate, furnish an additional pretext toward dispensing themselves from the duty of compassion.

Last excuse of the disciples, founded on the great number of the
people who had followed our Savior into the desert: These people are
so numerous, said they, that two hundred pennyworth of bread is not
sufficient for them, that every one may take a little. Last pretext which
they oppose to the duty of charity – the multitude of the poor. Yes, my
brethren, that which ought to excite and to animate charity, extin-
guishes it; the multitude of the unfortunate hardens you to their
wants; the more the duty increases, the more do you think yourselves
dispensed from its practice, and you become cruel by having too many
occasions of being charitable.

But, in the first place, whence comes, I pray you, this multitude of
poor, of which you so loudly complain? I know that the misfortune of
the times may increase their number: but wars, pestilences, and irregularity of seasons, all of which we at present experience, have
happened in all ages; the calamities we behold are not unexampled;
our forefathers have witnessed them, and even much more melancholy and dreadful: civil dissensions, the father armed against the
child, the brother against brother, countries ravaged and laid waste
by their own inhabitants, the kingdom a prey to foreign enemies, no
person in safety under his own roof; we see not these miseries; but
have they seen what we witness – so many public and concealed
miseries, so many families worn out, so many citizens, formerly distinguished, now low in the dust, and confounded with the meanest
of the people? Arts become almost useless? The image of hunger and
death spread over the cities and over the fields? What shall I say? –
so many hidden iniquities brought every day to light, the dreadful
consequences of despair and horrible necessity? Whence comes this,
my brethren? Is it not from a luxury unknown to our fathers, and which
engluts every thing? From your expenses which know no bounds and
which necessarily drag along with them the extinction of charity?

Ah! was the primitive church not persecuted, desolated, and afflicted? Do the calamities of our age bear any comparison with the horrors of those times? Proscription of property, exilement and imprisonment were then daily; the most burdensome charges of the state fell upon those who were suspected of Christianity: in a word, so many calamities were never beheld; and, nevertheless, there was no poor among them, says St. Luke, nor any that lacked. Ah! it is, because riches of simplicity sprung up, even from their poverty itself, according to the expression of the apostle; it is, because they gave according to their means, and even beyond them; it is, because the most distant provinces, through the care of the apostolic ministers, flowed streams of charity, for the consolation of their afflicted brethren in Jerusalem, more exposed than the rest to the rage and hatred of the synagogue.

But more than all that; it is, because the most powerful of the primitive believers were adorned with modesty; and that our great riches are now scarcely sufficient to support that monstrous luxury, of which custom has made a law to us; it is, that their festivals were repasts of sobriety and charity; and that the holy abstinence itself, which we celebrated, cannot moderate among us the profusions and the excesses of the table, and of feasts; it is, that, having no fixed city here below, they did not exhaust themselves in forming brilliant establishments, in order to render their names illustrious, to exalt their posterity, and to ennoble their own obscurity and meanness; they thought only of securing to themselves a better establishment in the celestial country; and that at present no one is contented with his station; every one wishes to mount higher than his ancestors: and that their patrimony is only employed in buying titles and dignities, which may obliterate their name and the meanness of their origin: in a word, it is because the frugality of these first believers constituted the whole wealth of their afflicted brethren, and that at present our profusions occasion all their poverty and want. It is our excesses, then, my brethren, and our hardness of heart toward them, which multiply the number of the unfortunate: excuse no more then, on that head, the failing of your charities; that would be making your guilt itself your excuse. Ah! you complain that the poor overburden you; but they would have reason in retorting the charge one day against you: do not then accuse them for your insensibility: and reproach them not with that, which they undoubtedly shall one day reproach to you before the tribunal of Jesus Christ.

If each of you were, according to the advice of the apostle, to appropriate a certain portion of your wealth toward the subsistence of the poor; if, in the computation of your expenses and of your revenues, this article were to be always regarded as the most sacred and the most inviolable one, then should we quickly see the number of the afflicted to diminish: we should soon see renewed in the church that peace, that happiness, and that cheerful equality which reigned among the first Christians: we should no longer behold with sorrow that monstrous disproportion, which, elevating the one, places him on the pinnacle of prosperity and opulence, while the other crawls on the ground, and groans in the gulf of poverty and affliction: no longer should there be any unhappy except the impious among us; no secret miseries except those which sin operates in the soul; no tears except those of penitence; no sighs but for heaven; no poor, but those blessed disciples of the gospel, who renounce all to follow their master. Our cities would be the abode of innocence and compassion; religion, a commerce of charity; the earth the image of heaven, where, in different degrees of glory, each is equally happy; and the enemies of faith would again, as formerly, be forced to render glory to God, and to confess that there is something of divine in a religion which is capable of uniting men together in a manner so new.

But, in what the error here consists, is, that, in the practice, nobody considers charity as one of the most essential obligations of Christianity; consequently, they have no regulation on that point; if some bounty be bestowed, it is always arbitrary; and, however small it may be, they are equally satisfied with themselves, as if they had even gone beyond their duty.

Besides, when you pretend to excuse the scantiness of your charities, by saying that the number of the poor is endless; what do you believe to say? You say that your obligations, with respect to them, are become only more indispensable; that your compassion ought to increase in proportion as their wants increase; and that you contract new debts whenever any increase of the unfortunate takes place on the earth. It is then, my brethren, it is during these public calamities that you ought to retrench even from expenses which at any other period might be permitted, and which might even be proper; it is then that you ought to consider yourselves but as the principal poor, and to take as a charity whatever you take for yourselves; it is then that you are no longer either grandee, man in office, distinguished citizen, or woman of illustrious birth; you are simply believer, member of Jesus Christ, brother of every afflicted Christian.

And surely say—while that cities and provinces are struck with every calamity; that men, created after the image of God, and redeemed with his whole blood, browse like the animal, and through their necessity go to search in the fields a food which nature has not intended for man, and which to them becomes a food of death; would you have the resolution to be the only one exempted from the general evil? While the face of the whole kingdom is changed, and that cries and lamentations alone are heard around your superb dwelling; would you preserve, within, the same appearance of happiness, pomp, tranquillity, and opulence? And where, then, would be humanity, reason, religion? In a pagan republic, you would be held as a bad citizen; in a society of sages and worldly, as a soul, vile, sordid, without nobility, without generosity, and without elevation; and in the church of Jesus Christ, in what light, think you, can you be held? Oh! as a monster, unworthy of the name of Christian which you bear, of that faith in which you glorify yourself, of the sacrament which you approach, and even of entry into our temples where you come – seeing all these are the sacred symbols of that union which ought to exist among believers.

Nevertheless, the hand of the Lord is extended over our people in the cities and in the provinces; you know it, and you lament it: Heaven is deaf to the cries of this afflicted kingdom; wretchedness, poverty, desolation, and death, walk every where before us. Now, do any of those excesses of charity, become at present a law of prudence and justice, escape you? Do you take upon yourselves any part of the calamities of your brethren? What shall I say? Do you not perhaps take advantage of the public misery? Do you not perhaps turn the general poverty into a barbarous profit? Do you not perhaps complete the stripping of the unfortunate in affecting to hold out to them an assisting hand? And are you acquainted with the inhuman art of deriving individual profit even from the tears and the necessities of your brethren; Bowels of iron! when you shall be filled, you shall burst asunder; your felicity itself will constitute your punishment, and the Lord will shower down upon you his war and his wrath.

My brethren, how dreadful shall be the presence of the poor before the tribunal of Jesus Christ to the greatest part of the rich in this world! How powerful shall be these accusers! And how little shall remain for you to say, when they shall reproach to you the scantiness of the succor which was required to soften and to relieve their wants; that a single day cut off from your profusions, would have sufficed to remedy the indigence of one of their years; that it was their own property which you withheld, since whatever you had beyond a sufficiency belonged to them; that consequently you have not only been cruel, but also unjust in refusing it to them; but that, after all, your hard-heartedness has served only to exercise their patience and to render them more worthy of immortality, while you, for ever deprived of those riches which you were unwilling to lodge in safety in the bosom of the poor, shall receive for your portion only the curse prepared for those who shall have seen Jesus Christ suffering hunger, thirst, and nakedness in his members, and shall not have relieved him. Such is the illusion of the pretexts employed to dispense themselves from the duty of charity: let us now determine the rules to be observed in fulfilling it; and, after having defended this obligation against all the vain excuses of avarice, let us endeavor to save it from even the defects of charity.

Part II. – Not to sound the trumpet in order to attract the public attention in the compassionate offices which we render to our brethren;

to observe an order even of justice in charity, and not to prefer the wants of strangers to those with whom we are connected; to appear feeling for the unfortunate, and to know how to soothe the afflicted by our tenderness and affability, as well as by our bounty; in a word, to find out, by our vigilance and attention, the secret of their shame; behold the rules which the present example of our Savior prescribes to us in the practice of compassion.

First. He went up into a desert and hidden place, says the gospel; he ascended a mountain, where he seated himself with his disciples. His design, according to the holy interpreters, was to conceal from the eyes of the neighboring villages the miracle of multiplying the loaves, and to have no witnesses of his compassion except those who were to reap the fruits of it. First instruction, and first rule; the secrecy of charity.

Yes, my brethren, how many fruits of compassion are every day blasted in the sight of God, by the scorching wind of pride and of vain ostentation! How many charities lost for eternity! How many treasures, which were believed to have been safely lodged in the bosom of the poor, and which shall one day appear corrupted with vermin, and consumed with rust!

In truth, those gross and bare faced hypocrites are rare which openly vaunt to the world the merit of their pious exertions: pride is more cunning, and it never altogether unmasks itself: but, how diminutive is the number of those who, moved with the true zeal of charity, like our Savior, seek out solitary and private places to bestow, and, at the same time, to conceal their holy gifts! We now see only that ostentatious zeal, which nothing but necessities of eclat can interest, and which piously wishes to make the public acquainted with every gift: they will sometimes, it is true, adopt measures to conceal them, but they are not sorry when an indiscretion betrays them; they will not perhaps court public attention, but they are delighted when the public attention surprises them, and they almost consider as lost any liberality which remains concealed.

Alas! our temples and our altars, are they not every where marked with the gifts and with the names of their benefactors; that is to say, are they not the public monuments of our forefathers and of our own vanity? If the invisible eye of the heavenly Father alone was meant to have witnessed them, to what purpose all that vain ostentation? Are you afraid that the Lord forgets your offerings? If you wish only to please him, why expose your gifts to any other eye? Why these titles and these inscriptions which immortalize, on sacred walls, your gifts and your pride? Was it not sufficient that they were written, even by the hand of God, in the book of life? Why engrave on a perishable marble the merit of a deed which charity would have rendered immortal?

Solomon, after having completed the most superb and the most magnificent temple of which the earth could ever boast, engraved the awful name of the Lord alone upon it, without presuming to mingle any memorial of the grandeur of his race with those of the eternal majesty of the King of kings. We give an appellation of piety to this custom; it is thought that these public monuments excite the liberality of believers. But the Lord, hath he charged your vanity with the care of attracting gifts to his altars? And hath he permitted you to depart from modesty, in order to make your brethren more charitable? Alas! the most powerful among the primitive believers, carried humbly as the most obscure their patrimony to the feet of the apostles: they beheld with a holy joy their names and their wealth confounded among those of their brethren who had less than they to offer: they were not distinguished in the assembly of the faithful in proportion to their gifts: honors and precedency were not yet the price of gifts and offerings, and they knew better than to exchange the eternal recompense which they awaited from the Lord for any frivolous glory they could receive from men; and now the church has not privileges enough to satisfy the vanity of her benefactors: their places are marked out in the sanctuary; their tombs appear even under the altar, where only the ashes of martyrs should repose. Custom, it is true, authorizes this abuse; but custom does not always justify what it authorizes.

Charity, my brethren, is that sweet smelling savor of Jesus Christ, which vanishes and is extinguished from the moment that it is exposed. I mean not that public acts of compassion are to be refrained from: we owe the edification and example of them to our brethren: it is proper that they see our works; but we ought not ourselves to see them, and our left hand should be ignorant of what our right bestows: even those actions which duty renders the most shining, ought always to be hidden in the preparation of the heart: we ought to entertain a kind of jealousy of the public view on their account, and to believe their purity in safety only when they are exposed to the eyes of God alone. Yes, my brethren, those liberalities which have flowed mostly in secret, reach the bosom of God much more pure than others, which, even contrary to our wishes, having been exposed to the eyes of men, become troubled and defiled, as I may say, in their course by their inevitable flatteries of self-love, and by the applauses of the beholders: like those rivers which have flowed mostly under ground, and which pour their streams into the ocean pure and undefiled; while, on the contrary, those which have traversed plains and countries, exposed to the day, carry there, in general, only muddy waters, and drag along with them the wrecks, carcasses, and slime which they have amassed in their course. Behold, then, the first rule of charity which our Savior here lays down – to shun show and ostentation in all works of compassion – to be unwilling to have your name mentioned in them, either on account of the rank which you may here hold, or from the glory of having been the first promoter, or from the noise which they may make in the world, and not to lose upon the earth that which charity had amassed only for heaven.

The second circumstance which I remark in our gospel, is, that no one, of all the multitude who present themselves to Jesus Christ, is rejected: all are indiscriminately relieved; and we do not read that with regard to them our Savior hath used any distinction or preference. Second rule: charity is universal; it banishes those capricious liberalities which seem to open the heart to certain wants, only in order to shut it against all others. You find persons in the world, who, under the pretext of having stated charities and places destined to receive them, are callous to all other wants. In vain would you inform them that a family is on the brink of ruin, and that a very small assistance would extricate it; that a young person hangs over a precipice, and must necessarily perish, if some friendly and assisting hand be not held out; that a certain meritorious and useful establishment must fall, if not supported by a renewal of charity; these are not necessities after their taste; and, in placing elsewhere some trifling bounties, they imagine to have purchased the right of viewing with a dry eye and an indifferent heart every other description of misery.

I know that charity hath its order and its measure; that in its practice it ought to use a proper distinction; that justice requires a preference to certain wants: but I would not have that methodical charity (if I may thus speak) which to a point knows where to stop—which has its days, its places, its persons, and its limits—which, beyond these, is cruel, and can settle with itself to be affected only in certain times and by certain wants. Ah! are we thus masters of our hearts when we truly love our brethren? Can we at our will mark out to ourselves the moments of warmth and indifference? Charity, that holy love, is it so regular when it truly inflames the heart? Has it not, if I may so say, its transports and its excesses? And do not occasions sometimes occur so truly affecting, that, did but a single spark of charity exist in your heart, it would show itself, and in the instant would open your bowels of compassion and your riches to your brethren.

I would not have that rigidly circumspect charity which is never done with its scrutiny, and which always mistrusts the truth of the necessities laid open to it. See if, in that multitude which our Savior filleth, he apply himself to separate those whom idleness or the sole hope of corporeal nourishment had perhaps attracted to the desert, and who might still have sufficient strength left to go and search for food in the neighboring villages; no one is excepted from his divine bounty. Is the being reduced to feign wretchedness not a sufficient misery of itself? Is it not preferable to assist fictitious wants, rather than to run the risk of refusing aid to real and melancholy objects of compassion? When an imposter should even deceive your charity, where is the loss? Is it not always Jesus Christ who receives it from your hand? And is your recompense attached to the abuse which may be made of your bounty, or to the intention itself which bestows it?

From this rule there springs a third, laid down in the history of our gospel, at the same time with the other two: it is, that not only ought charity to be universal, but likewise mild, affable, and compassionate. Jesus Christ, beholding these people wandering and unprovided at the foot of the mountain, is touched with compassion; he is affected at the sight, and the wants of the multitude awaken his tenderness and pity. Third rule: the gentleness of charity.

We often accompany pity with so much asperity toward the unfortunate, while stretching out to them a helping hand – we look upon them with so sour and so severe a countenance, that a simple denial had been less galling to them than a charity so harshly and so unfeeling bestowed; for the pity which appears affected by our misfortunes, consoles them almost as much as the bounty which relieves them. We reproach to them their strength, their idleness, their wandering and vagabond manners; we accuse their own conduct for their indigence and wretchedness: and, in succoring, we purchase the right of insulting them. But, were the unhappy creature whom you outrage permitted to reply – if the abjectness of his situation had not put the check of shame and respect upon his tongue, what do you reproach to me? would he say. An idle life, and useless and vagabond manners. But what are the cares which in your opulence engross you? The cares of ambition, the anxieties of fortune, the impulses of the passions, the refinements of voluptuousness. I may be an unprofitable servant; but are you not yourself an unfaithful one? Ah! if the most culpable were always to be the poorest and the most unfortunate in this world, would your lot be superior to mine? You reproach me with a strength which I apply to no purpose; but to what use do you apply your own? Because I work not, I ought not to have food; but are you dispensed yourself from that law? Are you rich merely that you may pass your life in a shameful effeminacy and sloth? Ah! the Lord will judge between you and me, and, before his awful tribunal, it shall be seen whether your voluptuousness and profusion were more allowable in you than the innocent artifice which I employ to attract assistance to my sufferings.

Yes, my brethren, let us at least offer to the unfortunate, hearts feeling for their wants. If the mediocrity of our fortune permit us not altogether to relieve our indigent fellow-creatures, let us, by our humanity, at least soften the yoke of poverty. Alas! we give tears to the chimerical adventures of a theatrical personage – we honor fictitious misfortunes with real sensibility – we depart from a representation with hearts still moved from the disasters of a fabulous hero – and a member of Jesus Christ, an inheritor of heaven, and your brother, whom you encounter in your way from thence, perhaps sinking under disease and penury, and who wishes to inform you of the excess of his sufferings, finds you callous; and you turn your eyes with disgust from that spectacle, and deign not to listen to him? and you quit him even with a rudeness and brutality which tend to wring his heart with sorrow! Inhuman soul! have you, then, left all your sensibility on an infamous theatre? Doth the spectacle of Jesus Christ suffering in one of his members offer nothing worthy of your pity? And, that your heart may be touched, must the ambition, the revenge, the voluptuousness, and all the other horrors of the pagan ages be revived?

But, it is not enough that we offer hearts feeling for the distresses which present themselves to our view: charity goes farther: it does not indolently await those occasions which chance may throw in its way; it knows how to search them out, and even to anticipate them itself. Last rule: the vigilance of charity. Jesus Christ waits not till those poor people address themselves to him and lay open their wants: he is the first to discover them: scarcely has he found them out, when, with Philip, he searches the means of relieving them. That charity which is not vigilant, anxious after the calamities of which it is yet ignorant, ingenious in discovering those which endeavor to remain concealed, which require to be solicited, pressed, and even importuned, resembles not the charity of Jesus Christ. We must watch, and penetrate the obscurity which shame opposes to our bounties. This is not a simple advice: it is the consequence of the precept of charity. The pastors, who, according to faith, are the fathers of the people, are obliged to watch over their spiritual concerns; and that is one of the most essential functions of their ministry. The rich and the powerful are established by God the fathers and the pastors of the poor according to the body: they are bound, then, to watch continually over their necessities. If, through want of vigilance, they escape their attention, they are guilty before God, of all the consequences, which a small succor in time would have prevented.

It is not, that you are required to find out all the secret necessities of a city; but care and attention are exacted of you: it is required, that you, who, through your wealth or birth, hold the first rank in a department, shall not be surrounded, unknown to you, with thousands of unfortunate fellow-creatures, who pine in secret, and whose eyes are continually wounded with the pomp of your train, and who, besides their wretchedness, suffer again, as I may say, in your prosperity: it is required, that you, who, amid all the pleasures of the court, or of the city, see flowing into your hands the fruits of the sweat and of the labor of so many unfortunate people, who inhabit your lands and your fields; it is required that you be acquainted with those whom the toils of industry and of age have exhausted, and who, in their humble dwellings, drag on the wretched remains of dotage and poverty; those whom a languishing health renders incapable of labor, their only resource against indigence and want; those whom sex and age expose to seduction, and whose innocence you might have been enabled to preserve. Behold what is required, and what, with every right of justice, is exacted from you; behold the poor with whom the

Lord hath charged you, and for whom you shall answer to him; the poor, whom he leaveth on the earth only for your sake, and to whom his providence hath assigned no other resource than your wealth and your bounty.

Now, are they even known to you? Do you charge their pastors to make them known to you? Are these the cares which occupy you, when you show yourself in the midst of your lands and possessions? Ah! it is with cruelty to screw your claims from the hands of these unfortunate people; it is to tear from their bowels the innocent price of their toil, without regard to their want, to the misery of the times which you allege to us, to their tears, and often to their despair: — what shall I say? It is, perhaps, to crush down their weakness, to be their tyrant, and not their lord and their father. O God! cursest thou not these cruel generations, and these riches of iniquity? Dost thou not stamp upon them the marks of misfortune and desolation, and which shall soon blast the source of their families; which wither the root of a proud posterity; which produce domestic discord, public disgraces, the fall, and total extinction of houses? Alas! we are sometimes astonished to see fortunes apparently the best established, go to wreck in an instant; those ancient, and formerly so illustrious names fallen into obscurity, no longer to offer to our view but the melancholy wrecks of their ancient splendor; and their estates become the property of their rivals, or perhaps of their own servants. Ah! could we investigate the source of their misfortunes; if their ashes, and the pompous wrecks, which in the pride of their monuments remain to us of their glory, could speak — Do you see, they would say to us, these sad marks of our grandeur? It is the tears of the poor, whom we neglected, whom we oppressed, which have gradually sapped, and at last have totally overthrown them: their cries have drawn down the thunder of Heaven upon our palaces. The Lord hath blown upon our superb edifices, and upon our fortune, and hath dissipated them like dust. Let the name of the poor be honorable in your sight, if you wish that your names may never perish in the memory of men. Let compassion sustain your houses, if you wish that your posterity be not buried under their ruins. Become wise at our cost; and let our misfortunes, in teaching you our faults, teach you also to shun them.

And behold, my brethren (that I may say something respecting it before I conclude), the first advantage of Christian charity: blessings even in this world. The bread, blessed by our Savior, multiplies in the hands of the apostles who distribute it; five thousand are satisfied; and twelve baskets can hardly contain the remnants gathered up: that is to say, that the gifts of charity are riches of benediction, which multiply in proportion as they are distributed, and which bear along with them into our houses a source of happiness and abundance. Yes, my brethren, charity is a gain; it is a holy usury; it is a principle which returns, even here below, an hundred fold. You sometimes complain of a fatality in your affairs: nothing succeeds with you; men deceive you; rivals supplant you; masters neglect you; the elements conspire against you; the best concerted schemes are blasted:—associate with you the poor; divide with them the increase of your fortune; in proportion as your prosperity augments, do you augment your benefactions; flourish for them as well as for yourself; and God himself shall then be interested in your success; you shall have found out the secret of engaging him in your fortune, and he will preserve— what do I say?—he will bless, he will multiply riches, in which he sees blended the portion of his afflicted member.

This is a truth, confirmed by the experience of all ages: charitable families are continually seen to prosper; a watchful Providence presides over all their affairs; where others are ruined, they become rich: they are seen to flourish, but the secret canal is not perceived which pours in upon them their property: they are the fleeces of Gideon, covered with the dew of heaven, while all around is barren and dry.

Such is the first advantage of compassion, I say nothing even of the pleasure, which we ought to feel in the delightful task of soothing those who suffer, in making a fellow-creature happy, in reigning over hearts, and in attracting upon ourselves the innocent tribute of their acclamations and their thanks. O! were we to reap but the pleasure of bestowing, would it not be an ample recompense to a worthy heart? What has even the majesty of the throne more delicious than the power of dispensing favors? Would princes be much attached to their grandeur, and to their power, were they confined to a solitary enjoyment of them? No, my brethren, make your riches as subservient as you will, to your pleasures, to your profusions, and to your caprices; but never will you employ them in a way which shall leave a joy so pure, and so worthy of the heart, as in that of comforting the unfortunate.

What, indeed, can be more grateful to the heart, than the confidence that there is not a moment in the day in which some afflicted souls are not raising up their hands to heaven for us, and blessing the day which gave us birth? Hear that multitude whom Jesus Christ hath filled; the air resounds with their blessings and thanks: they say to themselves, This is a prophet; they wish to establish him their king. Ah! were men to choose their masters, it would neither be the most noble, nor the most valiant; it would be the most compassionate, the most humane, the most charitable, the most feeling: masters who, at the same time, would be their fathers.

Lastly, I need not add that Christian charity assists in expiating the crimes of abundance; and that it is almost the only mean of salvation which Providence hath provided for you, who are born to prosperity. Were charity insufficient to redeem our offences, we might certainly think ourselves entitled to complain, says a holy father; we might take it ill, that God had deprived men of so easy a mean of salvation; at least might we say that, could we but open the gates of heaven through the means of riches, and purchase with our whole wealth the glory of the holy, we then should be happy. Well, my brethren, continues the holy father, profit by this privilege, seeing it is granted to you; hasten, before your riches moulder away to deposit them in the bosom of the poor, as the price of the kingdom of heaven. The malice of men might perhaps have deprived you of them; your passions might have perhaps swallowcd them up; the turns of fortune might have transferred them to other hands; death, at last, would sooner or later have separated you from them: ah! charity alone deposits them beyond the reach of all these accidents; it renders you their everlasting possessor; it lodges them in safety in the eternal tabernacles, and gives you the right of for ever enjoying them in the bosom of God himself.

Are you not happy in being able to assure to yourself admittance into heaven by means so easy—in being able, by clothing the naked, to efface from the book of divine justice the obscenities, the luxury, and the irregularities of your younger years—in being able, by filling the hungry, to repair all the sensualities of your life—lastly, in being able, by sheltering innocence in the asylums of compassion, to blot out from the remembrance of God the ruin of so many souls, to whom you have been a stumbling-block? Great God! what goodness to man, to consider as meritorious a virtue which costs so little to the heart; to number in our favor feelings of humanity of which we could never divest ourselves, without being, at the same time divested of our nature; to be willing to accept, as the price of an eternal kingdom, frail riches, which we even enjoy only through thy bounty, which we could never continue to possess, and from which, after a momentary and fleeting enjoyment, we must at last be separated!

Nevertheless, mercy is promised to him who shall have shown it; a sinner, still feeling to the calamities of his brethren, will not continue long insensible to the inspirations of heaven; grace still reserves claims upon a heart in which charity has not altogether lost its influence; a good heart cannot long continue a hardened one; that principle of humanity alone, which operates in rendering the heart feeling for the wants of others, is a preparation, as it were, for penitence and salvation; and while charity still acts in the heart, a happy conversion is never to be despaired of. Love, then, the poor as your brethren; cherish them as your offspring; respect them as Jesus Christ himself, in order that he say to you on the great day, "Come, ye blessed of my Father, inherit the kingdom prepared for you from the foundation of the world. For I was an hungered, and ye gave me meat; I was thirsty, and ye gave me drink; I was a stranger, and ye took me in; I was naked, and ye clothed me; I was sick, and ye visited me: for, inasmuch as ye have done it unto one of the least of these my brethren, ye have done it unto me."

ON PRAYER

"Have mercy on me, O Lord, thou Son of David" (Matthew 15:22).

SUCH IS THE LAMENTATION of a soul touched with its wretchedness, and which addresses itself to the sovereign Physician, in whose compassion alone it hopes to find relief. This was formerly the prayer of a woman of Canaan, who wished to obtain from the Son of David the recovery of her daughter. Persuaded of his power, and expecting everything from his usual goodness to the unfortunate, she knew no surer way of rendering him propitious, than the cry of her affliction, and the simple tale of her misfortune. And this is the model which the church now proposes to us, in order to animate and to instruct us how to pray; that is to say, in order to render more pleasing, and more familiar to us, this most essential duty of Christian piety.

For, my brethren, to pray is the condition of man; it is the first duty of man; it is the sole resource of man; it is the whole consolation of man; and, to speak in the language of the Holy Spirit, it is the whole man.

Yes, if the entire world, in the midst of which we live, be but one continued temptation; if all the situations in which we may be, and all the objects which environ us, seem united with our corruption, for the purpose of either weakening or seducing us; if riches corrupt, and poverty exasperate; if prosperity exalt, and affliction depress; if business prey upon, and ease render effeminate; if the sciences inflate, and ignorance lead us into error; if mutual intercourse trivially engage us too much, and solitude leave us too much to ourselves; if pleasure seduce, and pious works excite our pride; if health arouse the passions, and sickness nourish either lukewarmness or murmurings: in a word, if, since the fall of nature, everything in, or around us, be a fresh danger to be dreaded; in a situation so deplorable, what hope of salvation, O, my God! could there be still remaining to man, if, from the bottom of his wretchedness, he had it not in his power to make his lamentations to be continually mounting toward the throne of thy mercy, in order to prevail that thou thyself may come to his aid; that thou may interfere to put a check upon his passions, to clear up his errors, to sustain his weakness, to lessen his temptations, to abridge his hours of trials, and to save him from his backslidings?

The Christian is therefore a man of prayer; his origin, his situation, his nature, his wants, his place of abode, all inform him that prayer is necessary. The church herself, in which he is incorporated through

---

Reprinted from an old book without title page.

the grace of regeneration, a stranger here below, is always plaintive and full of lamentation; she recognizes her children only through their sighs, which they direct toward their country; and the Christian who does not pray, cuts himself off from the assembly of the holy, and is worse than an unbeliever.

How comes it then, my brethren, that a duty not only so essential, but even so consoling for man, is at present so much neglected? How comes it that it is considered either as a gloomy and tiresome duty, or as appropriated solely for retired souls; inasmuch, that our instructions upon prayer scarcely interest those who listen to us, who seem as if persuaded that they are more adapted to the cloister than to the court?

Whence comes this abuse, and this universal neglect in the world of prayer? From two pretexts, which I now mean to overthrow. First, they do not pray, because they know not, say they, how to pray; and, consequently, that it is lost time. Secondly, they do not pray, because they complain that they find nothing in prayer but wanderings of the mind, which render it both insipid and disagreeable. First pretext, drawn from their ignorance of the manner in which they ought to pray. Second pretext, founded on the disgusts and difficulties of prayer. You must be taught, therefore, how to pray, since you know it not. And, secondly, the habit of prayer must be rendered easy to you, since you find it so troublesome and difficult.

Part I. — "The commandments which I command you," said formerly the Lord to his people, "are neither above your strength nor the reach of your mind; they are not hidden from you, nor far off, that you should say, who shall go up for us to heaven and bring them unto us, that we may hear them and do them? Nor are they beyond the sea, that you should say, who shall go over the sea for us and bring them unto us, that we may hear them and do them? But the word is very nigh unto you, in your mouth, and in your heart, that you may do it."

Now, what the Lord said in general of all the precepts of the law, that we have no occasion to seek beyond ourselves for the knowledge of them, but that they may be all accomplished in our heart and in our mouth, may more particularly be said of the precept of prayer, which is as if the first and the most essential of all.

Nevertheless, what they commonly oppose in the world against this duty is, that, when they come to prayer, they know not what to say to God, and that praying is a secret of which they have never as yet been able to comprehend any thing. I say, then, that the source of this pretext springs from three iniquitous dispositions: the first is, that they are mistaken in the idea which they form of prayer: the second is, that they are not sufficiently sensible of their own wretchedness and wants; and the third is, that they do not love their God.

First. I say that they are mistaken in the idea which they form of prayer. In effect, prayer is not an exertion of the mind, an arrangement of ideas, a profound knowledge of the mysteries and counsels of God; it is a simple emotion of the heart; it is a lamentation of the soul, deeply affected at the sight of its own wretchedness; it is a keen and inward feeling of our wants and of our weakness, and a humble confidence which it lays before its Lord, in order to obtain relief and deliverance from them. Prayer supposes, in the soul which prays, neither great lights, uncommon knowledge, nor a mind more cultivated and exalted than that of the rest of men; it supposes only more faith, more contrition, and a warmer desire of deliverance from its temptations and from its wretchedness. Prayer is neither a secret nor a science which we learn from men; nor is it an art, or private method, upon which it is necessary to consult skillful teachers, in order to be master of its rules and precepts. The methods and the maxims thereupon, pretended to be laid down to us in our days, are either singular ways which are not to be followed, or the vain speculations of an idle mind, or a fanaticism which may stop at nothing, and which, far from edifying the church, hath merited her censures, and hath furnished to the impious matter of derision against her, and to the world fresh pretexts of contempt for, and disgusts at, prayer. Prayer is a duty upon which we are all born instructed: the rules of this divine science are written solely in our hearts; and the Spirit of God is the sole master to teach it.

A holy and innocent soul, who is penetrated with the greatness of God, struck with the terror of his judgments, touched with his infinite mercies, who only knows to humble himself before him, to acknowledge, in the simplicity of his heart, his goodness and wonders, to adore the orders of his providence upon him, to accept before him of the crosses and afflictions imposed upon him by the wisdom of his councils; who knows no prayer more sublime than to be sensible before God of all the corruption of his heart; to groan over his own hardness of heart, and opposition to all good; to intreat of him, with fervent faith, to change him, to destroy in him the man of sin, which, in spite of his firmest resolves, continually forces him to make so many false steps in the ways of God: a soul of this description is a thousand times more instructed in the knowledge of prayer than all the teachers themselves, and may say, with the prophet, "I have more understanding than all my teachers." He speaks to his God as a friend to a friend; he is sorry for having offended him; he upbraids himself for not having, as yet, sufficient force to renounce all to please him; he takes no pride in the sublimity of his thoughts; he leaves his heart to speak, and gives way to all its tenderness before the only object of his love. Even when his mind wanders, his heart watches and speaks for him: his very disgusts become a prayer, through the feelings which are then excited in his heart: he is tenderly affected, he sighs, he is displeased with, and a burden to, himself: he feels the weight of his bonds, he exerts himself as if to break and throw them off; he a thousand times renews his protestations of fidelity; he blushes and is ashamed at always promising, and yet being continually faithless: such is the whole secret and the whole science of prayer. And what is there in all this beyond the reach of every believing soul?

Who had instructed the poor woman of Canaan in prayer? A stranger, and a daughter of Tyre and Sidon, who was unacquainted with the wonders of the law and the oracles of the prophets; who had not yet heard from the mouth of the Savior the words of eternal life; who was still under the shadows of ignorance and of death: she prays, however; her love, her confidence, the desire of being granted, teach her to pray; her heart being touched, constitutes the whole merit and the whole sublimity of her prayer.

And surely, if, in order to pray, it were requisite to rise to those sublime states of prayer to which God exalteth some holy souls; if it were necessary to be wrapped in ecstasy, and transported even up to heaven, like Paul, there to hear those ineffable secrets which God exposeth not to man, and which it is not permitted, even to man himself, to reveal; or, like Moses upon the holy mountain, to be placed upon a cloud of glory, and, face to face, to see God; that is to say, if it were necessary to have attained to that degree of intimate union with the Lord, in which the soul, as if already freed from its body, springs up even into the bosom of its God; contemplates at leisure his infinite perfections; forgets, as I may say, its members which are still upon the earth; is no longer disturbed, nor even diverted by the phantoms of the senses; is fixed, and as if absorbed in the contemplation of the wonders and the grandeur of God; and already participating in his eternity, could count a whole age passed in that blessed state, as only a short and rapid moment; if, I say, it were necessary, in order to pray, to be favored with these rare and excellent gifts of the Holy Spirit, you might tell us, like those new believers, of whom St. Paul makes mention, that you have not yet received them, and that you know not what is even that Spirit which communicates them.

But prayer is not a special gift set apart for privileged souls alone; it is a common duty imposed upon every believer; it is not solely a virtue of perfection, and reserved for certain purer and more holy souls; it is, like charity, an indispensable virtue, requisite to the perfect as to the imperfect, within the capacity of the illiterate equally as of the learned, commanded to the simple as to the most enlightened: it is the virtue of all men; it is the science of every believer; it is the perfection of every creature. Whoever has a heart, and is capable of loving the Author of his being—whoever has a reason capable of knowing the nothingness of the creature, and the greatness of God, must know how to adore, to return him thanks, and to have recourse to him, to appease him when offended, to call upon him when turned away, to thank him when favorable, to humble himself when he strikes, to lay his wants before him, or to intreat his countenance and protection.

Thus, when the disciples ask of Jesus Christ to teach them to pray, he doth not unfold to them the height, the sublimity, the depth of the mysteries of God; he solely informs them, that, in order to pray, it is necessary to consider God as a tender, bountiful, and careful father; to address themselves to him with a respectful familiarity, and with a confidence blended with fear and love; to speak to him the language of our weakness and of our wretchedness; to borrow no expressions but from our heart; to make no attempt of rising to him, but rather to draw him nearer to us: to lay our wants before him, and to implore his aid; to wish that all men bless and worship him; that his reign be established in all hearts; that his will be done, as in heaven, so on earth; that sinners return to the paths of righteousness; that believers attain to the knowledge of the truth; that he forgive us our sins; that he preserve us from temptation; that he assist our weakness; that he deliver us from our miseries. All is simple, but all is grand in this divine prayer; it recalls man to himself, and, in order to adopt it as a model, nothing more is required than to feel our wants, and to wish deliverance from them.

And behold, why I have said that the second iniquitous disposition, from whence the pretext, founded upon not knowing how to pray proceeded, is, that they do not sufficiently feel the infinite wants of their soul: for, I ask you, my brethren, is it necessary to teach a sick person to intreat relief? Is a man pressed with hunger difficulted how to solicit food? Is an unfortunate person, beaten with the tempest, and on the point of perishing, at a loss how to implore assistance? Alas! doth the urgent necessity alone not amply furnish expressions? In the sole sense of our evils, do we not find that animated eloquence, those persuasive emotions, those pressing remonstrances which solicit their cure? Has a suffering heart occasion for any master to teach it to complain? In it every thing speaks, every thing expresses its affliction, everything announces its sufferings, and everything solicits relief: even its silence is eloquent.

You yourself, who complain that you know not what method to take in praying, in your temporal afflictions, from the instant that a dangerous malady threatens your life, that an unlooked-for event endangers your property and fortune, that an approaching death is on the point of snatching from you a person either dear or necessary, then you raise your hands to heaven; then you send up your lamentations and prayers; you address yourself to the God who strikes and who relieves; you then know how to pray; you have no need of going beyond your own heart for lessons and rules to lay your afflictions before him, nor do you consult able teachers in order to know what is necessary to say to him; you have occasion for nothing but your grief, your evils alone have found out the method of instructing you.

Ah! my brethren, if we felt the wants of our soul as we feel those of our body – if our eternal salvation interested us as much as a fortune of dirt, or a weak and perishable health, we would soon be skillful in the divine art of prayer; we would not complain that we had nothing to say in the presence of a God of whom we have so much to ask; the mind would be little difficulted in finding wherewith to entertain him; our evils alone would speak; in spite of ourselves, our heart would burst forth in holy effusions, like that of Samuel's mother before the ark of the Lord; we would no longer be master of our sorrows and tears; and the most certain mark of our want of faith, and that we know ourselves not, is, that of not knowing what to say to the Lord in the space of a short prayer.

And after all, is it possible that, in the miserable condition of this human life, surrounded as we are with so many dangers; made up ourselves of so many weaknesses; on the point, every moment, of being led astray by the objects of vanity, corrupted by the illusions of the senses, and dragged away by the force of example; a continual prey to the tyranny of our inclinations, to the dominion of our flesh, to the inconstancy of our heart, to the inequalities of our reason, to the caprices of our imagination, to the eternal variations of our temper; depressed by loss of favor, elated by prosperity, enervated by abundance, soured by poverty, led away by custom, shaken by accidents, flattered with praise, irritated by contempt; continually wavering between our passions and our duties, between ourselves and the law of God; is it possible, I say, that, in a situation so deplorable, we can be difficulted what to ask of the Lord, or what to say to him, when we appear in his presence? O my God! why then is man not less miserable? Or why is he not better acquainted with his wants?

Ah! if you told us, my dear hearer, that you know not where to begin in prayer; that your wants are so infinite, your miseries and your passions so multiplied, that, were you to pretend to expose them all to the Lord, you would never have done: if you said to us, that the more you search into your heart, the more your wounds unfold, the more corruption and disorders do you discover in yourself, and that, despairing of being able to relate to the Lord the endless detail of your weaknesses, you present your heart wholly to him, you leave your evils to speak for you, you ground your whole art of prayer on your confusion, your humiliation, and your silence; and that, in consequence of having too much to say to him, you say nothing; if you spoke in this manner, you would speak the language of faith, and that of a penitent king, who, contemplating his repeated relapses, and no longer daring to speak to his God in prayer, said, "Lord, I am troubled, I am bowed down greatly; I go mourning all the day long; for mine iniquities are gone over my head; as a heavy burden they are too heavy for me. My heart panteth, my strength faileth me; for I will declare mine iniquity, I will be sorry for my sin. Forsake me not, O Lord: O my God! be not far from me. Make haste to help me, O Lord, my salvation." Such is the silence of compunction which forms before God the true prayer.

But to complain that you have no longer anything to say, when you wish to pray: alas! my dear hearer, when you present yourself before God, do your past crimes hold out nothing for you to dread from his judgments, or to ask from his mercy? What! your whole life has perhaps been only a sink of debaucheries; you have perverted everything, grace, your talents, your reason, your wealth, your dignities, all creatures; you have passed the best part of your days in the neglect of your God, and in all the delusions of the world and of the passions; you have vilified your heart by iniquitous attachments, defiled your body, disordered your imagination, weakened your lights, and even extinguished every happy disposition which nature had placed in your soul; and the recollection of all this furnishes you with nothing in the presence of God? And it inspires you with no idea of the method you ought to adopt, in having recourse to him, in order to obtain his forgiveness of such accumulated crimes? and you have nothing to say to a God whom you have so long offended? O man! thy salvation, then, must either be without resource, or thou must have other means of accomplishing it than those of the divine clemency and mercy.

But, my dear hearer, I go farther. If you lead a Christian life; if, returned from the world and from pleasures, you are at last entered into the ways of salvation, you are still more unjust in complaining that you find nothing to say to the Lord in your prayers. What! the singular grace of having opened your eyes, of undeceiving you with regard to the world, and withdrawing you from the bottom of the abyss; this blessing, so rare, and denied to so many sinners, doth it give rise to no grateful feeling in your heart, when at his feet? Can this recollection leave you cold and insensible? Is nothing tender awakened by the presence of your benefactor, you who pride yourself upon having never forgotten a benefit, and who so pompously display the feeling and the excess of your gratitude toward the creatures?

Besides, if you feel those endless tendencies, which, in spite of your change of life, still rise up within you against the law of God; that difficulty which you still have in doing well; that unfortunate inclination which you still find within you toward evil; those desires of a more perfect virtue, which always turn out vain; those resolutions to which you are always faithless; those opportunities in which you always find yourself the same; those duties which always meet the same repugnance in your heart; in a word, if you feel that inexhaustible fund of weakness and of corruption which remains with you after your conversion, and which alarms so much your virtue, you will not only have ample matter to address the Lord in prayer, but your whole life will be one continual prayer. All the dangers which shall threaten your weakness, all the accidents which shall shake your faith, all the objects which shall open afresh the former wounds of your heart, all the inward emotions which shall prove that the man of sin lives always within you, will lead you to look upwards to Him from whom alone you expect deliverance from them. As the apostle said, every place will be to you a place of prayer; everything will direct your attention to God, because everything will furnish you with Christian reflections upon yourself.

Besides, my dear hearer, even granting that your own necessities should not be sufficient to fill the void of your prayer, employ a portion of it with the evils of the church; with the dissensions of the pastors; with that spirit of schism and revolt which seems to be forming in the sanctuary; with the relaxation of believers; with the depravity of manners; with the sad progress of unbelief, and the diminution of faith among men. Lament over the scandals of which you are a continual witness; complain to the Lord, with the prophet, that all have forsaken him; that every one seeks his own interest; that even the salt of the earth hath become tasteless, and that piety is become a traffic. Entreat of the Lord the consummation of his elect, and the fulfilment of his designs upon the church; religious princes, faithful pastors, humble and enlightened teachers, knowing and disinterested guides; peace to the churches; the extinction of error, and the return of all who have gone astray.

What more shall I add? Entreat the conversion of your relations, friends, enemies, protectors, and masters; the conversion of those souls to whom you have been a stumbling-block; of those whom you have formerly estranged from piety through your derisions and censures; of those who perhaps owe their irreligion and free-thinking solely to the impiety of your past discourses; of those of whom your examples or solicitations have formerly either perverted the virtue or seduced the weakness. Is it possible that these great objects, at once so sad and so interesting, cannot furnish a moment's attention to your mind, or some feeling to your heart? Everything which surrounds you teaches you to pray; every object, every accident which you see around you, provides you with fresh opportunities of raising yourself to God; the world, retirement, the court, the righteous, the sinful, the public and domestic occurrences, the misfortunes of some, and the prosperity of others; everything, in a word, which meets your eyes, supplies you with the subject of lamentation, of prayer, of thanksgiving. Everything instructs your faith; everything excites your zeal; all grieves your piety, and calls forth your gratitude; and amid so many subjects of prayer, you cannot supply a single instant of prayer! Surrounded with so many opportunities of raising yourself to God, you have nothing to say to him when you come to appear in his presence? Ah! my brethren, how far removed must God be from a heart which finds it such a punishment to hold converse with him, and how little must that master and friend be loved, to whom they never wish to speak!

And behold the last and the principal cause of our incapacity in prayer. They know not how to pray and to speak to their God, because they do not love him. When the heart loves, it soon finds out how to communicate its feelings, and to affect the object of its love; it soon knows what it ought to say: alas! it cannot express all that it feels. Let us establish regularity once more in our hearts, my brethren; let us substitute God in place of the world; then shall our heart be no longer a stranger before God. It is the irregularity of our affections which is the sole cause of our incapacity in prayer; eternal riches can never be fervently asked when they are not loved; truths can never be well meditated upon when they are not relished; and little can be said to a God who is hardly known: favors which are not desired, and freedom from passions which are not hated, can never be very urgently solicited; in a word, prayer is the language of love; and we know not how to pray, because we know not how to love.

But, as you shall say, doth an inclination for prayer depend upon us? And how is it possible to pray, with disgusts and wanderings of the mind, which are not to be conquered, and which render it insupportable? Second pretext, drawn from the disgusts and the difficulties of prayer.

Part II. — One of the greatest excesses of sin is undoubtedly that backwardness, and, I may say, that natural dislike which we have to prayer. Man, innocent, would have founded his whole delight in holding converse with God. All creatures would have been as an open book, where he would have incessantly meditated upon his works and his wonders; the impressions of the senses, under the command of reason, would never have been able to turn him aside, in spite of himself, from the delight and the familiarity of his presence; his whole life would have been one continued contemplation of the truth, and his whole happiness in his innocence would have been founded on his continual communications with the Lord, and the certainty that he would never forsake him.

Man must therefore be highly corrupted, and sin must have made strange alterations in us, to turn into a punishment what ought to be our happiness. It is, however, only too true, that we almost all bear in our nature this backwardness and this dislike to prayer: and upon these is founded the most universal pretext which is opposed to the discharge of this duty, so essential to Christian piety. Even persons, to whom the habit of prayer ought to be rendered more pleasing and more familiar, by the practice of virtue, continually complain of the disgusts and of the constant wanderings which they experience in this holy exercise; insomuch, that, looking upon it either as a wearisome duty, or as a lost trouble, they abridge its length, and think themselves happily quit of a yoke and of a slavery, when this moment of weariness and restraint is over.

Now, I say, that nothing is more unrighteous than to estrange ourselves from prayer, on account of the disgusts and wandering of the mind, which render it painful and disagreeable to us; for these disgusts and wanderings originate – first, from our lukewarmness, and our infidelities – or, secondly, in our being little accustomed to prayer – or, thirdly, in the wisdom even of God, who tries us, and who wishes to purify our heart, by withholding for a time the sensible consolations of prayer.

Yes, my brethren, the first and the most common source of the disgusts and the dryness of our prayers, is the lukewarmness and the infidelity of our life. It is, in effect, an injustice to pretend that we can bring to prayer a serene and tranquil mind; a cool imagination, free from all the vain phantoms by which it is agitated; a heart affected with, and disposed to relish the presence of its God – while our whole life, though otherwise virtuous in the eyes of man, shall be one continual dissipation; while we shall continue to live among objects the most calculated to move the imagination, and to make those lively impressions on us which are never done away; in a word, while we shall preserve a thousand iniquitous attachments in our heart, which, though not absolutely criminal in our eyes, yet trouble, divide, and occupy us, and which weaken in us, or even totally deprive us of any relish for God and the things of heaven.

Alas! my brethren, if the most retired and the most holy souls; if the most recluse penitents, purified by long retreat, and by a life altogether devoted to Heaven, still found, in the sole remembrance of their past manners, disagreeable images, which force their way even into their solitude, to disturb the comfort and the tranquillity of their prayers; do we expect that in a life, regular I confess, but full of agitation, of occasion by which we are led away, of objects which unsettle us, of temptations which disquiet, of pleasures which enervate, of fears and hopes which agitate us, we shall find ourselves in prayer, all of a sudden new men, purified from all those images which sully our mind, freed from all those attachments which come to divide and perhaps corrupt our heart, in tranquillity from all those agitations which continually make such violent and such dangerous impressions upon our soul; and that, forgetting for a moment the entire world, and all those vain objects which we have so lately quitted, and which we still bear in our remembrance and in our heart, we shall, all of a sudden, find ourselves raised, before God, to the meditation of heavenly things, penetrated with love for eternal riches, filled with compunction for innumerable infidelities which we still love, and with a tranquillity of mind and of heart; which the profoundest retirement, and the most rigorous seclusion from the world frequently do not bestow? Ah! my brethren, how unjust we are, and into what terrible reproaches against ourselves shall the continual complaints made by us against the duties of piety one day be turned!

And, to go farther into this truth, and to enter into a detail which renders it more evident to you, you complain, in the first place, that your mind, incapable of a moment's attention in prayer, wanders from it, and flies off in spite of yourself. But how can it be otherwise; or how can you find it attentive and collected, if everything you do takes off its attention and unsettles it; if, in the detail of conduct, you never recollect yourself; if you never accustom yourself to that mental reflection, to that life of faith, which, even amid the dissipations of the world, find ample sources of holy reflection? To have a collected mind in prayer, you must bring it along with you; it is necessary that even your intercourse with sinners, when obliged to live among them, the sight of their passions, of their anxieties, fears, hopes, joys, chagrins, and wretchedness, supply your faith with reflections, and turn your views toward God who alone bestows collectedness of mind and the tranquillity of prayer. Then, even on quitting the world and those worldly conversations, where duty alone shall have engaged your presence, you will find no difficulty in going to recollect yourself before God, and in forgetting at his feet those vain agitations which you have so lately witnessed. On the contrary, the designs of faith which you shall there have preserved; the blindness of the worldly, which you shall there have inwardly deplored, – will cause you to find new comforts at the feet of Jesus Christ; you will there, with consolation, recreate yourself from the weariness of dissipation and of worldly nothings; you will lament, with increased satisfaction, over the folly of men who so madly pursue after a vapor, a chimerical happiness, which eludes their grasp, and which it is impossible ever to attain, for the world in which they seek it cannot bestow it; you will there more warmly thank the Lord for having, with so much goodness, and notwithstanding your crimes, enlightened and separated you from that multitude which must perish; you will there see, as in a new light, the happiness of those souls who serve him, and whose eyes, being opened upon vanity, no longer live but for the truth.

Secondly. You complain that your heart, insensible in prayer, feels nothing fervent for its God, but, on the contrary, a disgust which renders it insupportable. But how is it possible that your heart, wholly engrossed with the things of the earth, filled with iniquitous attachments, inclination for the world, love of yourself, schemes for exalting your station, and desires perhaps of pleasing; how is it possible, I say, that your heart, compounded with so many earthly affections, should still have any feeling for the things of heaven? It is wholly filled with the creatures; where then should God find his place in it? We cannot love both God and the world. Thus, when the Israelites had passed the Jordan, and had eaten of the fruits of the earth, "the manna ceased on the morrow after they had eaten of the old corn of the land, neither had the children of Israel manna any more"; as if to show, that they could not enjoy at the same time both the heavenly nourishment and that of the earth.

Love of the world, said St. Augustine, like a dangerous fever, sheds a universal bitterness through the heart, which renders the invisible and eternal riches insipid and disgusting to us. Thus, you never come to prayer but with an insurmountable disgust. Ah! it is a proof that your heart is diseased; that a secret fever, and perhaps unknown to yourself, causes it to languish, saps and disgusts it; that it is engrossed by a foreign love. Mount to the source of your disgusts toward God, and everything connected with him, and see if they shall not be found in the iniquitous attachments of your heart; see if you are not still a slave to yourself, to the vain cares of dress, to frivolous friendships, to dangerous animosities, to secret envies, to desires of rank, to everything around you. These are the source of the evil: apply the remedy to it; take something every day upon yourself; labor seriously toward purifying your heart; you will then taste the comforts and the consolations of prayer; then the world no longer engrossing your affections, you will find your God more worthy of being loved: we soon ardently love the only object of our love.

And, after all, render glory here to the truth. Is it not true, that the days in which you have been more guarded upon yourself – the days in which you have made some sacrifices, to the Lord, of your inclinations, of your indolence, of your temper, of your aversions; is it not true, that, in these days, you have addressed your prayers to the Lord with more peace, more consolation, and more delight? We encounter, with double pleasure, the eyes of a master to whom we have lately given some striking proof of fidelity; on the contrary, we are in pain before him when we feel that he has cause of a thousand just reproaches against us: we are then anxious and under restraint; we endeavor to hide ourselves from his view, like the first sinner: we no longer address him with that overflowing heart, and that confidence, which a conscience pure and void of offence inspires; and the moments when we are under the necessity of supporting his divine presence are anxiously counted.

Thus, when Jesus Christ commands us to pray, he begins with ordering us to watch. He thereby means us to understand that vigilance is the only preparation to prayer; that to love to pray, it is necessary to watch; and that fondness for, and consolation in prayer, are granted only to the recollection and to the sacrifices of vigilance. I know, that, if you do not pray, you can never watch over yourself and live holily; but I likewise know, that, if you exert not that vigilance which causes to live holily, you can never pray with comfort and with consolation. Prayer, it is true, obtains for us the grace of vigilance; but it is yet more true, that vigilance alone can draw down upon us the gift and the usage of the prayer.

And, from thence, it is easy to conclude, that a life of the world, even granting it to be the most innocent, that is to say, a life of pleasure, continual gaming, dissipation, and theatrical amusement, which you call so innocent, when attended with no other harm than that of disqualifying you for prayer; when this worldly life, which you so strongly justify, should contain nothing more criminal than that of disgusting you at prayer, of drying up your heart, of unsettling your imagination, of weakening your faith, and of filling your mind with anxiety and trouble; when we should judge of the security of this state merely from what you continually tell us, that you are incapable of arranging yourself for prayer, and that, on your part, it is always attended with an insupportable disgust and weariness; I say, that, for these reasons alone, the most innocent worldly life is a life of sin and reprobation; a life for which there is no salvation: for salvation is promised solely to prayer; salvation is not attainable but through the aid of prayer; salvation is granted only to perseverance in prayer; consequently, every life which places an invincible obstacle in the way of prayer, can have no pretensions to salvation. Now, you are fully sensible yourselves, my brethren, that a life of dissipation, of gaming, of pleasure, and of public places, puts an essential obstacle in the way of prayer; that it places in your heart, in your imagination, in your senses, an invincible disgust at prayer, an unsettledness incompatible with the spirit of prayer: you continually complain of this; you even make use of it as a pretext not to pray; and from thence be assured that there is no salvation for the worldly life, even the most innocent; for, wherever prayer is impossible, salvation must likewise be so. First reason of the disgusts and of the wanderings of our prayers – the lukewarmness and the infidelity of our life.

The second is our little usage of prayer. We pray with disgust, because we seldom pray. For, first, it is the practice alone of prayer which will gradually calm your mind, which will insensibly banish from it the images of the world and of vanity, which will disperse all those clouds which produce all the disgusts and the wanderings of your prayers. Secondly, you must ask for a long time before you can obtain; you must press, solicit, and even importune; the sweets and the consolations of prayer are the fruit and the reward of prayer itself. Thirdly, there must be familiarity in order to find pleasure in it. If you seldom pray, the Lord will be a strange and unknown God to you, as I may say, before whom you will feel yourself embarrassed, and under a kind of restraint; with whom you will never experience those overflowings of heart, that sweet confidence, that holy freedom, which familiarity alone bestows, and which constitute the whole pleasure of the divine intercourse. God requires to be known, in order to be loved. The world loses by being examined; the surface, and the first glance of it are alone smiling. Search deeper, and it is no longer but emptiness, vanity, anxious care, agitation, and misery. But the Lord must be tasted, says the prophet, in order to feel how good he is. The more you know, the more you love him: the more you unite yourself to him, the more do you feel that there is no true happiness on the earth but that of knowing and of loving him.

It is the use, therefore, of prayer, which alone can render prayer pleasing. Thus we see that the generality of persons who complain of the disgusts and of the wanderings of their prayers, seldom pray; think this important duty fulfilled when they have bestowed upon the Lord a few hasty moments of thoughtlessness and restraint; forsake it on the first symptom of disgust; make no exertion to reduce and familiarize their mind to it; and far from considering prayer as being rendered only more necessary to them, by their invincible repugnance to it, they regard that very repugnance as a legal excuse, which dispenses them altogether from it.

But how find time in the world, you will say, to make so long and so frequent a use of prayer? You, my dear hearer, not find time to pray? But wherefore is time given to you, but to intreat of God to forget your crimes, to look upon you with eyes of compassion, and to place you one day among the number of his holy? You have not time to pray? But you have not time, then, to be a Christian; for, a man who prays not, is a man who has no God, no worship, and no hope. You have not time to pray? But prayer is the beginning of all good; and if you do not pray, you have not yet performed a single work for eternal life. Ah! my brethren, is time for ever wanting to solicit the favors of the earth, to importune the master, to besiege those who are in place, to bestow upon pleasures, or upon idleness? What useless moments! What languid and tiresome days, through the mere gloom which ever accompanies idleness! What time lost in vain ceremonials, in idle conversations, in boundless gaming, in fruitless subjections, in grasping at chimeras which move farther and farther from us! Great God! and time is wanted to ask heaven of thee, to appease thy wrath, and to supplicate thine eternal mercies! How humbly, O my God, must salvation be estimated, when time is wanted to intreat of thy mercy to save us! And how much are we to be deplored, to find so many moments for the world, and to be unable to find a single one for eternity!

Second cause of the disgusts and of the wanderings of your prayers —
the little use of prayer itself.

It is true, my brethren, that this reason is not so general but that
souls, the most faithful to prayer, are often seen to experience all
those disgusts and those wanderings of which I speak! but, I say,
that these disgusts proceed from the wisdom of God, who means to
purify them, and who leads them by that path, only in order to fulfil
his eternal designs of mercy upon them. Last reason — that consequently, far from being repulsed by what they find gloomy and disagreeable in prayer, they ought to persevere in it with even more
fidelity than if the Lord had shed upon them the most abundant and
the most sensible consolations.

First. Because you ought to consider these disgusts as the just punishment of your past infidelities. Is it not reasonable that God make
you expiate the criminal voluptuousness of your worldly life by the
disgusts and the sorrows of piety? Weakness of temperament does not
perhaps permit you to punish, by corporeal sufferings, the licentiousness of your past manners: is it not just that God supply that, by the
punishment, and the inward afflictions of the mind? Would you pretend to pass in an instant from the pleasures of the world to those of
grace; from the viands of Egypt to the milk and honey of the land of
promise, without the Lord having first made you to undergo the barrenness and the fatigues of the desert; and, in a word, that he should
not chastise the delights, if I may venture to say so, of guilt, but by
those of virtue?

Secondly. You have so long refused yourself to God, in spite of the
most lively inspirations of his grace, which recalled you to the truth
and to the light; you have so long suffered him to knock at the gate of
your heart before you have opened it to him; you have disputed, struggled against, wavered, deferred so much, before you gave yourself to
him; is it not just that he leave you to solicit for some time before he
give himself to you with all the consolations of his grace? The delays and the tarryings of the Lord are the just punishment of your own.

But, even admitting these reasons to be less weighty, how do you
know if the Lord thereby mean not to render this exilement and this
separation in which we live from him, more hateful to you, and to
increase the fervency of your longings for that immortal country
where truth, seen in open day, will always appear lovely, because we
shall see it as it is? How do you know if he thereby mean not to inspire
you with new compunction for your past crimes, by making you sensible, at every moment, of the contrariety and disgust which they have
left in your heart to the truth and to righteousness? Lastly, how do
you know, if the Lord mean not, by these disgusts, to perfect the purification of what may as yet be too human in your piety — if he mean not
to establish your virtue upon that truth which is always the same, and

not upon inclination and fancy, which incessantly change; upon rules
which are eternal, and not upon consolations which are transitory;
upon faith which never fails to sacrifice the visible for the invisible
riches, and not upon feeling, which leaves to the world almost the
same empire that grace hath over your heart? A piety wholly of fancy
goes a short way, if not sustained and confirmed by the truth. It is
dangerous to let our fidelity depend upon the feeling dispositions of a
heart which is never an instant the same, and upon which every object
makes new impressions. The duties which only please when they console, do not please long; and that virtue which is solely founded on
fancy can never sustain itself, because it rests only upon ourselves.

For, after all, if you seek only the Lord in your prayers, provided that
the way by which he leads you conduct to him, it ought to matter little
to you whether it be by that of disgusts or of consolations, for, being
the surest, it ought always to appear preferable to all others. If you
pray only to attract more aids from heaven in relief of your wants, or
in support of your weakness, faith teaching you that prayer, even
when accompanied with those disgusts and those drynesses, obtains
the same favors, produces the same effects, and is equally acceptable
to God as that in which sensible consolations are found. What do I
say? – that it may become even more agreeable to the Lord, through
your acceptance of the difficulties which you there encounter; faith
teaching you this, you ought to be equally faithful to prayer as if it
held out the most sensible attractions, otherwise it would not be God
whom you sought, but yourselves; it would not be eternal riches, but
vain and fleeting consolations; it would not be the remedies of faith,
but the supports of your self-love.

Thus, be whom you may who now listen to me, imitate the woman of
Canaan; be faithful to prayer, and, in the fulfilment of this duty, you
will find all the rest sustained and rendered easy. If a sinner, pray: it
was through prayer alone that the publican and the sinful woman of
the gospel obtained feelings of compunction and the grace of a thorough penitence; and prayer is the only source and the only path of
righteousness. If righteous, still pray: perseverance in faith and in
piety is promised only to prayer; and by that it was that Job, that David,
that Tobias, persevered to the end. If you live amid sinners, and your
duty does not permit you to withdraw yourself from the sight of their
irregularities and examples, pray: the greater the dangers, the more
necessary does prayer become; and the three children in the flames,
and Jonah in the belly of a monster, found safety only through prayer.
If the engagements of your birth, or of your station, attach you to the
court of kings, pray: Esther, in the court of Ahasuerus, Daniel in that
of Darius, the prophets in the palaces of the kings of Israel, were solely
indebted to prayer for their life and salvation. If you live in retirement,
pray: solitude itself becomes a rock, if a continual intercourse with

God does not defend us against ourselves; and Judith, in the secrecy of her house, and the widow Anna in the temple, and the Anthonies in the desert, found the fruit and the security of their retreat in prayer alone. If established in the church for the instruction of the people, pray: all the power and all the success of your ministry must depend upon your prayers; and the apostles converted the universe solely because they had appropriated nothing to themselves but prayer and the preaching of the gospel. Lastly, be whom you may, I again repeat it, in prosperity or in indigence, in joy or in affliction, in trouble or in peace, in fervency or in despondency, in lust or in the ways of righteousness, advanced in virtue, or still in the first steps of penitence, pray. Prayer is the safety of all stations, the consolation of all sorrows, the duty of all conditions, the soul of piety, the support of faith, the grand foundation of religion, and all religion itself. O my God! shed, then, upon us that spirit of grace and of prayer which was to be the distinguishing mark of thy church, and the portion of a new people; and purify their hearts and our lips, that we may be enabled to offer up to thee pure homages, fervent sighs, and prayers worthy of the eternal riches which thou hast so often promised to those who shall have well intreated them.

FOR ADDITIONAL INFORMATION ABOUT JEAN BAPTISTE MASSILLON:

Blaikie, Prof. W. Garden. "Jean Baptiste Massillon, the Star of France." *The Homiletic Review* 37 (March, 1899): 195–201.
Janin, Jules G. *Biographie de Massillon*. Paris, 1861.
"Massillon as a Preacher." *The Homiletic Review* 13 (January, 1887): 86–87.
Massillon, Jean Baptiste. *The Charges of Jean Baptiste Massillon, Bishop of Clermont, Addressed to His Clergy; with Two Essays*. New York: D. and G. Bruce, 1806.
_____. *Massillon's Thoughts on Different Moral and Religious Subjects . . . Arranged Under Distinct Heads*. Translated by R. Morris. London: F. Westley, 1824.
_____. *Oeuvres*. 13 vols. Paris, 1810.

FOR OTHER SERMONS BY JEAN BAPTISTE MASSILLON:

Sermons of John Baptist Massillon and Lewis Bourdaloue. Translated by Flint Abel. Hartford: Lincoln & Gleason, 1805.

Willett, William, ed. *Sermons of John Baptist Massillon.* Boston: Waite, Peirce & Co., 1845.

Also: *Great French Sermons from Bossuet, Bourdaloue, and Massillon* (1917); *Selections from the Works of Jean Baptiste Massillon* (1826).